A History of Civilization

A History of

Crane Brinton

John B. Christopher

University of Rochester

Robert Lee Wolff

Archibald Cary Coolidge Professor of History, Harvard University

Civilization

1815 to the Present

Fourth Edition

Prentice-Hall, Inc., Englewood Cliffs, New Jersey

A History of Civilization

1815 to the Present, Fourth Edition

Brinton, Christopher, and Wolff.

Design by Mark A. Binn

Maps by Vincent Kotschar

PRENTICE-HALL INTERNATIONAL, INC., London
PRENTICE-HALL OF AUSTRALIA, PTY. LTD., Sydney
PRENTICE-HALL OF CANADA, LTD., Toronto
PRENTICE-HALL OF INDIA PRIVATE LTD., New Delhi
PRENTICE-HALL OF JAPAN, INC., Tokyo

Current printing:

2   3   4   5   6   7   8   9   10

0–13–389528–9

Preface

In preparing this fourth edition of *A History of Civilization* we have tried to incorporate the new discoveries that continue to add to our knowledge of the past, especially the remote past. Where new theories or approaches to a major subject have seemed to warrant change, we have made the change. We have recorded and sought to interpret the events of the years since 1967, when the third edition was published. Perhaps naturally, we regard this latest edition as a better book than its predecessors.

In particular, there is now a wholly new chapter on the ancient Near East, and there are wholly rewritten chapters on the Greeks and the Romans. The medieval chapters have also undergone substantial revision, especially in those sections that deal with letters and with art. Throughout the rest of the work, especially of course in Chapters 30 and 31, which deal with the quarter century since the end of World War II, we have recast and reinterpreted our materials. Extensive revisions have brought abreast of recent scholarship the chapters on the Reformation, the seventeenth century, and the economic and intellectual revolutions of the nineteenth century. We think the new illustrations are perhaps more successfully married to the text than ever before, and there are more of them in full color than there have been in earlier editions. Finally, our book is now available in three paperback volumes, with the chronological breaks coming at 1300 and 1815, as well as in two hardbound volumes dividing at 1715; the innovation, we hope, offers more flexibility for courses such as those scheduled on a quarter or trimester basis.

Our senior co-author, Crane Brinton, died on September 7, 1968, and we have had to try to carry on without him. His extraordinary gift for hitting off what he called the style—or essence—of a period, a nation, even a whole civilization, we shall always admire, and we have greatly missed. But the reader of this edition will find, we hope, that much of the substance and all of the spirit of his contributions to the earlier editions have been maintained.

We should like here to thank Elizabeth Genovese for her taste and resourcefulness in obtaining illustrative materials; Mark A. Binn and Helen Maertens of the Project Planning Department at Prentice-Hall, who have applied their skills and energies most generously and effectively; and Cecil Yarbrough, Project Planning editor, whose ingenuity, efficiency, wisdom, and tact have made the preparation of these volumes a pleasure.

v

A Note on the Reading Suggestions

A list of reading suggestions is appended to each chapter of this book. Almost all historical bibliographies nowadays begin with the statement that they are highly selective and do not, of course, aspire to be exhaustive. This apology is hardly necessary, for the fact is that in most fields of history we have outrun the possibility of bringing together in one list all the books and articles in all languages on a given topic. There are for the wide fields of this book, and in English alone, thousands of volumes and hundreds of thousands of articles in periodicals. The brief lists following each chapter are simply suggestions to the reader who wishes to explore a given topic further.

Each list attempts to give important and readable books, with special attention to paperbacks (noted in the list with an asterisk), which are often the editions most available in a college community. A useful guide is *Paperbound Books in Print,* a monthly review of new paperbacks, with encyclopedic cumulative issues published three or four times a year. In addition, good readings in original sources, the contemporary documents and writings of an age, are sometimes listed, though the reader can supplement these listings from the text itself and from the footnotes. In addition, there are many good collections of sources for European history, notably the *Introduction to Contemporary Civilization in the West* (3rd ed., 1960), prepared by faculty members at Columbia University; this begins with the Middle Ages and gives much longer selections from the sources than such compilations usually do. Other good collections are to be found in the Portable Readers (published by Viking). There are also many sourcebooks and pamphlets on central or controversial problems in European history. A good example is K. M. Setton and H. R. Winkler, eds., *Great Problems in European Civilization* (Prentice-Hall, 2nd ed., 1966). Another is the series of pamphlets edited by R. W. Greenlaw under the general title "Problems in European Civilization" (D. C. Heath).

Our lists also include historical novels and, occasionally, dramas. Professional historians are likely to be somewhat severe in their standards for a historical novel. They naturally want its history to be sound, and at bottom they are likely to be somewhat prejudiced against the form. The historical novels listed here are all readable and all reasonably good as history. But note that historical novels, like historical films, though accurate on such material matters as authentic settings and appropriate costumes, often fail to capture the immaterial aspects—the psychology, the spirit—of the age they are written about. Many such novels motivate their characters, especially in love, as if they were modern Europeans and Americans. Exceptions to this rule are noted in the lists.

It is easy to assemble more material on a given topic than is furnished by our reading lists. American libraries, large and small, have catalogs with subject and title listings, as well as a section of reference books with encyclopedias and bibliographies. Many libraries have open shelves where, once a single title is discovered, many others may be found in the immediate area. Perhaps the first printed list of books to be consulted is *A Guide to Historical Literature* (Macmillan, 1931) and its sequel, *The American Historical Association's Guide to Historical Literature* (Macmillan, 1961). For more recent books one can turn, for American history, to the *Harvard Guide to American History* (Belknap, 1954), edited by O. Handlin and others. And for the history of Europe and other areas there are many good bibliographies; see, for example, those in "The Rise of Modern Europe" series edited by W. L. Langer (Torchbooks); in the multivolumed *Oxford History of England;* and in R. R. Palmer and J. Colton, *A History of the Modern World* (Knopf, 1970). For historical fiction, one may consult two older specialized guides: E. A. Baker, *A Guide to Historical Fiction* (Macmillan, 1914) and J. Nield, *A Guide to the Best Historical Novels and Tales* (Elkins, Mathews, and Marrot, 1929). The more recent *Fiction Catalogue* (Wilson, 1951), while covering much besides historical fiction, does furnish keys to books that cover particular countries and particular historical eras.

What is much more difficult than assembling titles is securing an evaluation of individual books. For older books the *Guide to Historical Literature,* already mentioned, gives the most useful references to critical reviews of the titles it discusses. *The Book Review Digest* gives capsule reviews and references to longer ones. For current books the weekly book section of *The New York Times* and *The Times Literary Supplement* (published in London) usually provide informative reviews of historical works soon after they are published. Later—sometimes as much as three years later—full scholarly appraisals are published in the *American Historical Review,* its British equivalent, the *English Historical Review,* and in more specialized reviews, such as the *Journal of Modern History, Speculum* (for medieval studies), *The Middle East Journal,* and many others. An American scholarly journal, *History and Theory,* covers a field of great interest to historians today. By reading a few reviews of a book one can usually get a fair indication of its scope and quality. In our reading suggestions we have tried, within a very brief compass, to give comparable indications.

Contents

Maps

1815 to the Present

19

Revolution and Counterrevolution

1815–1850

I Introduction

While the half century after Napoleon recorded no crisis comparable to that of 1789 and produced no personality so dominant as Bonaparte, it was still crowded with major developments. Between 1815 and 1870 the Industrial Revolution came of age, modern doctrines of socialism were born, and Darwin's evolutionary hypothesis revolutionized the social sciences as well as biology. In politics, Great Britain and the United States moved steadily, and France more erratically, toward the practical establishment of democracy; Italy and Germany at last achieved national unification. All these developments, though they were well under way by 1850, reached a climax after the mid-century mark and will therefore be postponed to later chapters. The present chapter focuses on the interaction of cultural and political forces, particularly in continental Europe, during the post-Napoleonic generation from 1815 to 1850.

Above: Byron in Greek dress. Above right: Talleyrand: a drawing made in 1833. Right: Thomas Jefferson's Monticello, Charlottesville, Virginia.

706

The labels "reaction" and "counterrevolution" are often applied to this generation. By 1815, Europe was reacting strongly against the French Revolution, which had made Napoleon possible, and against the Enlightenment, which had made the Revolution possible. The reaction against the Enlightenment took the form of the Romantic movement. Romantic writers and artists protested against the rationalism and classicism of the eighteenth century and championed faith, emotion, tradition, and other values slighted by many philosophes. The political counterrevolution came of age at the Congress of Vienna in 1814–1815, where the leaders of the last coalition against Napoleon reestablished the European balance of power and repudiated the revolutionary principles, though not all the revolutionary achievements, that had shattered the eighteenth-century balance. Reason and natural law, in the judgment both of political leaders and of many Romantics, had led not only to progress but also to the Reign of Terror and Napoleonic imperialism.

Yet, despite the ascendancy of counterrevolutionary forces, the spirit of 1789 did not die in 1815. It inspired new and progressively more intense outbreaks of revolution in the 1820's, in 1830, and in 1848. The revolutions of 1848, though put down by the forces of order, marked a critical turning point in the form of the liberalism and nationalism bequeathed by the great French Revolution.

II   The Romantic Protest

It may seem paradoxical to bracket the Romantic movement together with counterrevolution. We tend to have the image of the Romantic as the rebel or the gallant defender of a cause—Shelley preaching anarchism, Byron dying in the Greek War of Independence, Victor Hugo forced into exile because he championed the cause of the short-lived Second French Republic against the dictatorship of a new Bonaparte. But the image is misleading. In a gallery of Romantic figures Shelley and Byron should stand alongside Wordsworth and Coleridge, whose youthful enthusiasm for the French Revolution soon evaporated, leaving them rather stodgy defenders of established political and ecclesiastical institutions. Hugo should be flanked by Chateaubriand, who published the *Genius of Christianity* during Napoleon's Consulate. While it is true that Romantic stress on the individual ultimately enriched the doctrines of liberalism and its emphasis on the historical evolution of communities strengthened nationalism, yet the immediate political influence of Romanticism was exerted in the main in support of God and king and in opposition to republicanism and anticlericalism.

On the other hand, the revolutionary qualities of the Romantics were always evident in literature and the arts, where they rebelled against the devotion of Jacobin and Napoleonic France to the cult of classical antiquity. Here we encounter another paradox: Revolutionary regimes tend to be quite unrevolutionary in aesthetic realms, clinging to traditional canons of expression, and cool or hostile toward innovation and experiment. This was to be true of the Communist revolutionaries in Russia and the Nazis in Germany; it had been true of revolutionary France with its attachment not only to Roman names, furniture, and fashions but also to neoclassical painting and architecture. The Romantics were truly revolutionary in their disdain for the literary and artistic canons of neoclassicism and their attraction to the medieval and the Gothic, to the colorful and the exotic, and to the undisciplined and the irrational.

The Revolt against Reason

The protest against reason reached full force during the first third of the nineteenth century—the Romantic decades of 1800 to 1830 or 1840—but it had been building up for a long time in the mounting challenges to the Enlightenment. Before 1750, Wesley in England and the Pietists in Germany were protesting against the deism of the philosophes and preaching a religion of the heart, not the head. Soon Rousseau proclaimed conscience, not reason, the "true guide of man";

Hume fastened on men's "sentiments and affections" as the mainsprings of their actions. Kant elevated intuition over the commonsense reason of the Enlightenment and restated, in very philosophical language, the Platonic belief in a noumenal realm of eternal verities beyond the world of transient phenomena.

In 1790 Edmund Burke's *Reflections on the Revolution in France* neatly turned against the philosophes their favorite appeal to the simple mathematical laws of Newtonian science. Natural rights, Burke argued,

entering into common life, like rays of light which pierce into a dense medium, are, by the laws of nature, refracted from their straight line. Indeed in the gross and complicated mass of human passions and concerns, the primitive rights of men undergo such a variety of refractions and reflections, that it becomes absurd to talk of them as if they continued in the simplicity of their original direction. The nature of man is intricate; the objects of society are of the greatest possible complexity. . . .*

The protest against the oversimplification of man and society, and the insistence on the intricacy and complexity of humanity, formed one common denominator of Romanticism. Other common denominators of this complicated and contradictory movement will emerge from a survey of the achievements of the Romantics, beginning with their most characteristic realm of activity—literature.

An Age of Feeling and of Poetry

Literary Romanticism may be traced back to the mid-eighteenth century—to novels like Richardson's *Clarissa* (1747) and Rousseau's *La Nouvelle Héloise* (1761) and to the French *comédies larmoyantes* ("tearful comedies"), sentimental plays addressed to a wide audience. Then a new intensity appeared in the very popular writings of the German *Sturm und Drang*—Goethe's novella, *Werther* (1774), and *The Robbers* (1781), a drama of social protest by Schiller that later won him the award of honorary French citizenship from the Convention. Schiller went

on to write a series of dramas with very unclassical heroes and heroines—William Tell, Wallenstein, Joan of Arc, Mary Stuart.

Goethe (1749-1832), whose career extended through the whole Romantic era, was himself no Romantic hero. In many respects he was a good eighteenth-century man of reason, interested in natural science, comfortably established at the enlightened court of a small German state at Weimar, and quite detached from the political passions sweeping Germany and Europe in the revolutionary and Napoleonic age. He wrote an epic in the neoclassical manner, *Herman and Dorothea* (1797). Yet Romantic values lie at the heart of his most famous writings—his short lyrics and, above all, *Faust*, which many have called the greatest work in the German language. Begun when he was in his twenties, and finished only when he was eighty, this long poetic drama was less a play in the conventional sense than a philosophical commentary on the main currents of European thought. According to the traditional legend, the aged Faust, weary of book learning and pining for eternal youth, sold his soul to the Devil, receiving back the enjoyment of his youth for an allotted time, and then, terror-stricken, went to the everlasting fires. Goethe partially transformed the legend. Faust makes his infernal compact with Mephistopheles, who points out how disillusioning and profitless intellectual pursuits are: "Grey, dear friend, is all theory, but the golden tree of life is green!" But Faust is ultimately saved through his realization that he must sacrifice selfish concerns to the welfare of others. A drama of man's sinning, striving, and redemption, Goethe's *Faust* is a reaffirmation of the Christian way that the Enlightenment had belittled.

The Enlightenment had also belittled any poetry except that following very strict forms, like the heroic couplets of Racine and Pope. The Romantics decried this neoclassicism as stilted and artificial and praised the vigor, color, and freedom of the Bible, Homer, and Shakespeare. The result was a great renaissance of poetry all over Europe, especially in England, which produced a galaxy of great poets—Byron, Shelley, Keats, Wordsworth, Coleridge, and others.

Of them all, Wordsworth (1770-1850) and Coleridge (1772-1834) pressed farthest in reaction against classicism and rationalism. In 1798, the two men published *Lyrical Ballads*, the first great landmark of English Romanticism.

---

* *Reflections on the Revolution in France*, Everyman ed. (New York, 1910), p. 59.

As Coleridge later explained, their purpose was explicitly anticlassical:

> In the present age the poet . . . seems to propose to himself as his main object . . . new and striking images; with incidents that interest the affections or excite the curiosity. Both his characters and his descriptions he renders, as much as possible, specific and individual, even to a degree of portraiture. In his diction and metre, on the other hand, he is comparatively careless.*

To *Lyrical Ballads* Coleridge contributed the *Rime of the Ancient Mariner*, a supernatural and very Romantic tale of the curse afflicting a sailor who slays an albatross. Later he created the very "striking images" of *Kubla Khan*, which has a surrealistic quality and has been likened to the experience of a man under drugs.

Among Wordsworth's contributions to *Lyrical Ballads* was an attack on conventional learning:

> *Come forth into the light of things,*
> *Let Nature be your teacher.*
>
> . . . . .
>
> *One impulse from a vernal wood*
> *May teach you more of man,*
> *Of moral evil and of good,*
> *Than all the sages can.*
>
> *Sweet is the lore which Nature brings;*
> *Our meddling intellect*
> *Mis-shapes the beauteous forms of things:—*
> *We murder to dissect.*
>
> *Enough of Science and of Art;*
> *Close up those barren leaves;*
> *Come forth, and bring with you a heart*
> *That watches and receives.*†

Wordsworth transformed the old concept of nature; nature was no longer something to be analyzed and reduced to laws but a mysterious, vitalizing force that had to be sensed and experienced. Here, from his long autobiographical *Prelude*, are two passages that express his beliefs more poetically:

> *Ye Presences of Nature in the sky*
> *And on the earth! Ye Visions of the hills!*

> *And Souls of lonely places! can I think*
> *A vulgar hope was yours when ye employed*
> *Such ministry, when ye, through many a year*
> *Haunting me thus among my boyish sports,*
> *On caves and trees, upon the woods and hills,*
> *Impressed, upon all forms, the characters*
> *Of danger or desire; and thus did make*
> *The surface of the universal earth,*
> *With triumph and delight, with hope and fear,*
> *Work like a sea?*
>
> . . . . .
>
> *Dust as we are, the immortal spirit grows*
> *Like harmony in music; there is a dark*
> *Inscrutable workmanship that reconciles*
> *Discordant elements, makes them cling together*
> *In one society.**

"Presences," "Visions," "Souls," "haunting"—this is truly Romantic language. In place of the light shed by Newton's laws, Wordsworth finds "a dark inscrutable workmanship," and in place of a mathematically ordered world-machine there is the Xanadu of Coleridge's *Kubla Khan*:

> *Where Alph, the sacred river, ran*
> *Through caverns measureless to man,*
> *Down to a sunless sea.*

To the Enlightenment all caverns could be measured and all seas were at least potentially sunny. Finally, Wordsworth abandoned the philosophes' belief in the perfectibility of man through reason and put his faith in the "immortal spirit" of the individual. He had lived in France during the early years of the Revolution and was disillusioned by the failures of rational reform.

The Return to the Past

It may seem a long leap from the almost pantheistic universe of Wordsworth to the Romantics' enthusiasm for the Middle Ages in general and for the earlier history of their own nations in particular. And yet nationalism is an irrational, almost mystical Wordsworthian force that—so its devotees believe—"reconciles discordant elements, makes them cling together in one society." The heightened sense of nationalism evident almost everywhere in Europe by 1815 was in part a matter of political self-preservation. In the crisis of the Napoleonic wars, for example, the Spaniards became more aware of their Spanish heritage and the Germans of their Germanic one. The Romantic return to the national past, however, though intensified by French imperialism, had begun before 1789 as part of the general retreat from the Enlightenment. The pioneers of Romanticism tended to cherish what the philosophes detested, notably the Middle Ages and the medieval preoccupation with religion.

The German writer Herder (1744–1803) provided intellectual justification for medieval studies with his theory of cultural nationalism. Each separate nation, he argued, like any organism, had its own distinct personality, its *Volksgeist* or "folk spirit," and its own pattern of growth. The surest measure of a nation's growth was its literature—poetry in youth, prose in maturity. Stimulated by Herder, students of medieval German literature collected popular ballads, and the brothers Grimm compiled their *Fairy Tales*. In 1782, the first complete text of the *Nibelungenlied* was published, a heroic saga of the nation's youth that had been much admired in the later Middle Ages only to be forgotten in succeeding centuries. By putting a new value on the German literature of the past, Herder helped to free the German literature of his own day from its bondage to French culture. Herder, however, was no narrow nationalist and asserted that the cultivated man should know cultures other than his own. So Herder also helped to loose the flood of translations that poured over Germany beginning about 1800—translations of Shakespeare, of *Don Quixote,* of Spanish and Portuguese poetry, even of works in Sanskrit.

Some German Romantics, stirred by the patriotic revival after the humiliations of Jena and Tilsit, carried national enthusiasm to an extreme that Herder would have deplored. Thus the Grimms claimed preeminence for the German language, and the dramatist Kleist (1777–1811) was sounding the trumpet for the defeat of the new Caesar in his *Battle of Arminius,* boasting of the prowess of the ancient Germans in defeating the legions of Augustus. For the Romantic extremists, the mere fact of being German appeared to be a cardinal virtue. Yet many German writers struck Herder's happy balance between national and cosmopolitan interests; Goethe, for example, prided himself on being a good European, not simply a German.

Other nations, too, demonstrated that the return to the past meant veneration of the Middle Ages rather than classical antiquity. In Britain, Sir Walter Scott (1771–1832) assisted in collecting the vigorous medieval folk ballads and went on to write more than thirty historical novels, of which *Ivanhoe,* set in the days of Richard the Lionhearted and the Crusades, is the best known. In Russia, the poet Pushkin (1799–1837) deserted the archaic Slavonic language of the Orthodox church to write the first major literary works in the national vernacular. He took subjects from Russia's past and introduced local color from its newly acquired provinces in the Crimea and the Caucasus. He also celebrated his own exotic grandfather, Hannibal, the African Negro slave of Peter the Great.

In France, the home of the "classical spirit," the Romantic reaction gathered slowly, beginning in the first years of the new century with Chateaubriand's *Genius of Christianity* and rather Rousseau-like tales *Atala* and *René.* In 1813 Madame de Staël, who was the daughter of the banker Necker, published *De l'Allemagne (Concerning Germany)*, a plea for the French to remember that they were the descendants not only of ancient Romans but also of Teutonic Franks, from whom they had inherited a very unclassical heritage. The great blow against classicism came early in 1830 at the first night of *Hernani,* by Victor Hugo (1802–1885), who deliberately flouted the classical rules of dramatic verse. When one of the characters uttered a line ending in the middle of a word, traditionalists in the audience set off a riot, and the issues were fought and refought at the theater and in the press for weeks to come, with the composer Berlioz and the painter Delacroix coming to Hugo's defense. In the next year Hugo published his great historical novel, *Notre Dame de Paris,* set in the dying days of Gothic France under Louis XI.

Music

Romantic musicians, like the poets, sought out the popular ballads and tales of the national past. They, too, were inventive and imaginative, seeking to make their compositions more dramatic and flexible, less constrained by classical rules. To achieve color and drama, composers of opera and song often turned for subjects to literature—Shakespeare's plays, Scott's novels, and the poems and tales of Goethe and Pushkin. Yet, although literature and music often took parallel paths during the Romantic era, the parallel was far from complete. Romantic musicians scarcely revolted against the great eighteenth-century composers in the way that Wordsworth and Coleridge revolted against their predecessors. Rather, Romantic music evolved peacefully out of the older classical school.

The composer who played the commanding part in this evolution was Beethoven (1770–1827), a Fleming by ancestry and a Viennese by adoption. Whereas Coleridge had said that the Romantic artist might be careless in matters of diction and meter, Beethoven showed a classical concern for the forms and techniques that were the musical counterparts of diction and meter.

Beethoven in 1820.

Yet his innovations also enriched the great tradition that he inherited from Bach, Haydn, and Mozart. For example, where Mozart and Haydn had used the courtly minuet for the third movement in a symphony, Beethoven introduced the more plebeian and rollicking scherzo. Where earlier composers had indicated the tempo with a simple "allegro" (fast) or "andante" (slow), Beethoven added such designations as "appassionato" and "Strife between Head and Heart." Part of the color and passion of Beethoven's works derived from his skill in exploiting the resources of the piano, which was perfected during his lifetime. He also scored his orchestral compositions for a greater number of instruments, especially winds, percussion, and double basses, than had been the practice of Mozart and Haydn.

After Beethoven, orchestral works took on increasingly heroic dimensions. The French composer Berlioz (1803–1869) projected an orchestra of 465 pieces, including 120 violins, 37 doublebasses, and 30 each of pianos and harps. While this utopian scheme remained on paper, Berlioz made some spectacular experiments with the theatrical potentialities of orchestral music, among them the *Fantastic Symphony* (based supposedly on Goethe's *Werther*), a symphonic interpretation of *Romeo and Juliet,* and a combination of symphony and opera, *The Damnation of Faust.* His *Requiem* called for a full orchestra, a great pipe organ, four brass choirs, and a chorus of two hundred. Incidentally, the Romantic propensity for bigness also affected the presentation of Bach's choral works like *The Passion According to St. Matthew,* originally composed for relatively few performers but revived with a full orchestra and a large chorus in a precedent-setting performance directed by Felix Mendelssohn in 1829.

Music for the human voice reflected both the increased enthusiasm for instruments, particularly the piano, and the general Romantic nostalgia for the past. In composing songs and arias, Romantic musicians devoted as much skill to the accompaniment as to the voice part itself. Franz Schubert (1797–1826), Beethoven's Viennese contemporary, made a fine art of blending voice and piano in more than six hundred sensitive Lieder (songs), seventy of them musical settings of poems by Goethe. Meantime, Weber (1786–1826) was striving to create a truly German opera, taking an old legend as the libretto for

Berlioz in 1845: a wood engraving from a French newspaper.

Der Freischütz (*The Freeshooter*, 1820). Its plot ran the good Romantic gamut of an enchanted forest, a magic bullet, and an innocent maiden outwitting the Devil, and its choruses and marches employed many folklike melodies. Weber was by no means the only serious composer to utilize national folk tunes. In Russia, Glinka (1804–1857) cast aside the Italian influences that had previously dominated the secular music of his country. He based his opera, *Russlan and Ludmilla* (1842), on a poem by Pushkin and embellished it with dances and choruses derived from the native music of Russia's Asian provinces.

The Arts

In the fine arts, the forces of Romanticism gained no such triumph as they won in literature and music. The virtual dictator of European painting during the first two decades of the nineteenth century was the French neoclassicist David (1748–1825). A deputy to the Convention, president of the Paris Jacobin club, and member of the Committee of General Security, David organized many of the great ceremonies of the Revolution, notably Robespierre's Festival of the Supreme Being (June 1794). He became Napoleon's court painter, then was sent into exile by the restored Bourbons. David's canvases formed a capsule history of the rise and decline of revolutionary fervor—before 1789, Roman republican heroes and victims of aristocratic persecution like Socrates; after 1789, dramatic moments like the Tennis Court Oath and the death of Marat; and, after Brumaire, Napoleon's crossing of the Alps and his coronation, both somewhat misrepresented, incidentally, to tally with the impression the publicity-conscious Bonaparte wanted to make. No matter how revolutionary the subject, David employed traditional neoclassical techniques, stressing form, line, and perspective.

The works of David's Spanish contemporary Goya (1746–1828) were much less conventional and much closer to the Romantic temper with their warmth and passion and sense of outraged patriotism. No one could have any illusions about Spanish royalty after looking at Goya's revealing portraits of the enlightened Charles III and his successors. After viewing Goya's etchings of French actions against the Madrid insurgents of May 1808, one can understand the story that Goya made his preliminary sketches in the very blood of the executed Spanish patriots whose agonies he was portraying.

Romantic painting did not acquire formal recognition until the official Paris exhibition of 1824. Although many of the pictures hung in the salon of 1824 came from the school of David, the two leaders of Romantic painting were also represented—the Englishman, Constable (1776–1837), and the Frenchman, Delacroix (1799–1863). Constable took painting out of doors, studied nature afresh, and produced a series of landscapes that stressed light and color more than classical purity of line, and paved the way for the impressionists of the later nineteenth century. Delacroix, too, championed color and light and urged young painters to study the flamboyant canvases of Rubens, whom David had banished from the ranks of orthodox artists. The purpose of art, Delacroix claimed in a good Romantic definition, was "not to imitate nature but to strike the imagination." His painting *The Massacre of Scio,* depicting a bloody episode in the Greek War of Independence, which seems conventional enough today, was denounced at the salon of 1824 as "barbarous, drunken, delirious"—the "massacre of painting." Delacroix's celebration of the French revolution of 1830, *Liberty Leading the People,* might almost be a campaign poster, but his paintings of Algerian women, a Moroccan Jewish wedding, and other subjects encountered on a trip to North Africa really do strike the imagination with their color and their emancipation from the artificial atmosphere of the classicist's studio. By the 1830's, French painters were divided into opposing schools: the still influential disciples of David, and the Romantic followers of Delacroix.

In architecture, also, two schools flourished during the first half of the nineteenth century— the neoclassical, looking to Greek and Roman antiquity, and the neo-Gothic, or Gothic revival, looking to the Middle Ages. Significantly, the label "Gothic" was no longer derogatory, as it had once been when employed by rationalist haters of things medieval. While there were obvious differences between the two schools, the contrast was not total. Many architects of the early 1800's mastered both styles; moreover, they did not so much copy ancient or medieval structures outright as adapt them to the needs and tastes of the day. Generally, the basic design was classical in its proportions, even if the external shell and decoration were medieval. The Houses of Parliament in London, rebuilt in the 1830's and '40's after a disastrous fire, seem very Gothic at first glance with their spires and towers. But a longer look shows that they also embody classical principles of balance and symmetry. Romantic architecture anticipated the eclecticism, the wide range of inspiration and style, characteristic of the later nineteenth century.

As the nineteenth century began, the Roman vogue, so firmly set by the French Revolution, reached a peak in Napoleonic Paris with triumphal arches patterned after those of Roman emperors, the Vendôme column modeled on Trajan's in Rome, and the Church of the Madeleine, which was an enlarged copy of an actual Roman temple surviving at Nîmes, in southern France, the Maison Carrée (square house). In America, the versatile Thomas Jefferson, who was a gifted designer, pronounced the Maison Carrée a perfect example of "cubical" architecture and adapted it to secular purposes for the

Virginia capitol building at Richmond. At Charlottesville, about 1820, Jefferson provided the University of Virginia with a most distinguished group of academic buildings focused on a circular library, derived from the Roman Pantheon (the perfect example of "spherical" architecture). From the library, somewhat in the manner of a large Roman villa, he extended two rows of smaller structures, each recalling a different Roman temple and interconnected by colonnades. By the second quarter of the nineteenth century, neo-Roman was yielding place to the "Greek revival," stirred in part by the wave of Philhellenic enthusiasm then sweeping the Western world in the wake of the Greek independence movement. London's British Museum and Philadelphia's Girard College are two of many splendid examples of the Greek revival.

Meantime, especially in Britain, the Gothic revival was gaining ground, stimulated by the wealth of medieval architectural lore in Scott's novels, by the revival of religion, and by buildings like Fonthill Abbey, which had been started in 1797 and boasted an immensely long and high hall. Though it cost its owner, an eccentric millionaire, £500,000, it was so shoddily built that the central tower collapsed twenty-five years later. Undeterred, British architects applied the Gothic manner to every kind of structure after 1820, to the embellishment of public buildings like the Houses of Parliament, to churches, to elaborate villas and modest cottages. Excessive "gloomth" often resulted, and the fad for "medieval" furniture, bristling with spikes, prompted one critic to warn that the occupant of a neo-Gothic room would be lucky to escape being "wounded by some of its minutiae." Though the Gothic revival prompted some monstrosities, it also fostered the preservation or restoration of medieval masterpieces half ruined by neglect or by anticlerical vandalism.

Religion and Philosophy

Neo-Gothic architecture was one sign of the Christian revival that formed part of the Romantic movement; another sign was the pope's reestablishment in 1814 of the Jesuit order, whose suppression in 1773 had been one of the great victories of the Enlightenment. Most of the Romantics were horrified by the religious skepticism of the philosophes: an outspoken atheist like Shelley was an isolated exception. In Germany, Catholicism gained many converts among Romantic writers; in England, Wordsworth wrote *Ecclesiastical Sonnets,* and Coleridge vigorously defended the established Church, declaring

that the scheme of Christianity, as taught in the liturgy and homilies of our Church, though not discoverable by human reason, is yet in accordance with it; that link follows link by necessary consequence; that Religion passes out of the ken of Reason only where the eye of Reason has reached its own horizon; and that Faith is then but its continuation. . . .*

Coleridge introduced his countrymen to the new Romantic philosophies of idealism being expounded in Germany. Chief among these German philosophers was Hegel (1770–1831), a follow of Kant and a professor at the University of Berlin. Like his master, Hegel attacked the tendency of the Enlightenment to see in human nature and human history only what first met the eye. The history of mankind, properly understood, was the history of human efforts to attain the good, and this in turn was the unfolding of God's plan for the world. For Hegel, history was a *dialectical* process—that is, a series of conflicts. The two elements in the conflict were the *thesis,* the established order of life, and the *antithesis,* the challenge to the old order. Out of the struggle of thesis and antithesis emerged the *synthesis,* no mere compromise between the two but a new and better way, another step in man's slow progression toward the best of all possible worlds. The synthesis, in turn, broke down; a new thesis and antithesis became locked in conflict; the dialectic produced another synthesis—and so on.

The death throes of the Roman Republic afforded Hegel an illustration of the dialectic at work. The thesis was represented by the decadent republic, the antithesis by oriental despotism, and the synthesis by the Caesarism of the early Roman Empire. Hegel explained that "This important change must not be regarded as a thing of chance; it was *necessary,*" a part of God's grand design. Julius Caesar himself Hegel called a "hero," one of the few "world-historical individuals" who "had an insight into the requirements of the time" and who knew

"what was ripe for development." This concept of the hero as the agent of a cosmic process is another characteristic of the Romantic temper.

The dialectical philosophy of history was the most original and influential element in Hegel's thought; it helped, for example, to shape the dialectical materialism of Karl Marx. It is perhaps difficult for citizens of a twentieth-century democracy to appreciate that Hegel was once even more famous as a liberal idealist. His emphasis on duty, his choice of Alexander the Great, Caesar, and Napoleon as "world-historical" heroes, his assertion that the state "existed for its own sake"—all suggest a link with authoritarianism. Yet Hegel himself seems to have foreseen the final synthesis of the dialectic not as a brutal police state but as a liberalized version of the Prussian monarchy.

The Romantic Style

Thus Hegel, like the philosophes, believed in progress and the perfectibility of man, though he also believed that the process would require far more time and struggle than a man like Condorcet had ever imagined. Indeed, the style of Romanticism by no means contrasted in every particular with that of the Enlightenment. Not only a modified doctrine of progress but also eighteenth-century cosmopolitanism lived on into the nineteenth. Homer, Cervantes, Shakespeare, and Scott won appreciative readers in many countries; the giants of the age, men like Beethoven and Goethe, were not merely Austrian or German citizens but citizens of the world.

These similarities and continuities notwithstanding, Romanticism did have a decided style of its own—imaginative, emotional, and haunted by the supernatural and by history. The Romantics could no longer view history in Gibbon's terms of a classical golden age followed by long centuries of benighted superstition. Rather history was, as Hegel and Herder had argued, an organic process of growth and development, which was indebted to the Middle Ages for magnificent Gothic buildings, religious enthusiasm, folk ballads, and heroic epics. Just as the Romantics rejected the Enlightened view of the past, so they found the Newtonian world-machine an entirely inadequate interpretation of the

* *Biographia Literaria,* Everyman ed., p. 334.

universe. It was too static, too drab and material-istic, and in its place they put the neo-Gothic world of religious mystery, the Hegelian world of dialectic and heroes, the poetic and artistic world of feeling, color, and "impulses from the vernal wood."

III The Reconstruction of Europe

Burke and De Maistre

The Romantic movement, by the very dif-fuseness of its nature, could scarcely have been expected to provide blueprints for the recon-struction of Europe after the defeat of Napoleon. The general guidelines, though not the specific details, for reconstruction lay at hand in the writings of Edmund Burke (1729–1797), not really one of the Romantics but a Whig politician and publicist, who set the tone of counterrevolu-tionary conservatism.

Unlike the champions of revolution, Burke could not accept simple black-and-white as-sumptions about the goodness of man and the unmitigated evil of the Old Regime. He revered the social and political institutions so painstak-ingly built up over the centuries. He, however, did not believe that these institutions were petri-fied; they had developed gradually in the past, they would develop gradually in the future. Political change was possible but difficult, he concluded. Reforms had to be introduced so that "the useful parts of the old establishment" might be preserved; they had to be managed slowly and "with circumspection and caution"—in a word, conservatively.

Burke approved of the American Revolution, for it was not so much a revolution as a reaffir-mation of the glorious tradition of 1688. The same reasoning drove Burke to violent condem-nation in his *Reflections on the Revolution in France* (1790). The men of 1789 destroyed everything, good, bad, and indifferent. Rage and frenzy, he observed, "pull down more in half an hour, than prudence, deliberation and foresight can build up in a hundred years";* thereby so-ciety itself is jeopardized. "Society is indeed a contract," Burke wrote, but he did not mean what Rousseau had meant:

The state ought not to be considered as noth-ing better than a partnership agreement in a trade of pepper and coffee, calico or tobacco, or some such other low concern, to be taken up for a little temporary interest, and to be dissolved by the fancy of the parties. It is to be looked on with other reverence, because it is not a partner-ship in things subservient only to the gross ani-mal existence of a temporary and perishable nature. It is a partnership in all science; a part-nership in all art; a partnership in every virtue, and in all perfection. As the ends of such a part-nership cannot be obtained in many generations, it becomes a partnership not only between those who are living, but between those who are living, those who are dead, and those who are to be born.*

Burke's doctrines were especially welcomed by the émigrés. Among them was Joseph de Maistre (1753–1821), a diplomat in the service of the king of Sardinia, who had been forced into exile when the French overran Savoy and Pied-mont. De Maistre combined Burke's conserva-tism with a Hobbesian view of the viciousness of the state of nature and a traditional Catholic view of man's depravity and need for discipline. The French Revolution, he believed, had been God's punishment of the philosophes' effrontery in believing that society could be remade with-out divine assistance. What men would need in the postrevolutionary world was firm control by an absolute monarch and inspired guidance from the Church. De Maistre carried the revival of Catholicism to an extreme of Ultramontanism, asserting for the papacy a universal authority the popes themselves had not claimed since the days of Innocent III and Boniface VIII.

Metternich and the Congress of Vienna

The force of tradition revered by Burke and De Maistre bore heavily upon the politics of post-Napoleonic Europe. Yet it was not so much

---

* *Reflections*, Everyman ed., p. 164.

* Ibid., p. 93.

ideological conviction as political pragmatism that accounted for the conservatism of the man who presided over the actual reconstruction of Europe. This was Metternich, Prince Clement Wenceslas Lothair Népomucène Metternich (1773-1859), Austrian foreign minister from 1809 to 1848 and the chief figure in European diplomacy during most of his long career. Handsome, dashing, an aristocrat through and through, Metternich retained some of the eighteenth century's belief in reform through enlightened despotism. But, he also believed, reform should proceed with Burkean caution, not at a revolutionary pace. His own family, living in the German Rhineland, had suffered directly from the French Revolution. Moreover, Metternich served a state that was particularly susceptible to injury by the liberal and nationalist energies released by the Revolution. Tradition, he knew, was the cement that held together the disparate parts of the Austrian Hapsburg realm; it should be fortified as much as possible.

In 1814 and 1815, Metternich was host to the Congress of Vienna, which approached its task of rebuilding Europe with truly conservative deliberateness. For the larger part of a year, the diplomats indulged to the full in balls and banquets, concerts and hunting parties. "Congress dances," remarked an observer, "but it does not march." Actually, the brilliant social life distracted the lesser fry while the important diplomats settled things in private conference.

Four men made most of the major decisions at Vienna—Metternich, Castlereagh, Talleyrand, and Czar Alexander I. Viscount Castlereagh, the

Statesmen at the Congress of Vienna.

British foreign minister, shared the conservative outlook of Metternich. He was less concerned with punishing the French for their past sins than with preventing the appearance of new Robespierres and Bonapartes. Castlereagh announced that he went to Vienna "not to collect trophies, but to bring the world back to peaceful habits." The best way to do this, he believed, was to restore the balance of power and keep any of the major states, including France, from becoming either too strong or too weak. "No arrangement could be wise that carried ruin to one of the countries between which it was concluded."

Talleyrand, the foreign minister of Louis XVIII of France, scored at Vienna the greatest success of his long career. Originally a worldly bishop of the Old Regime, he had in succession rallied to the Revolution in 1789, supported the Civil Constitution of the Clergy (one of the very few bishops to do so), served as Napoleon's foreign minister, and intrigued against him during the years after Tilsit. Now he was serving the restored Bourbon king, and in his old age he would take an important part in the Revolution of 1830. This supremely adaptable diplomat soon maneuvered himself into the inner circle at Vienna, and the representatives of the victorious powers accepted the emissary of defeated France as their equal. Talleyrand was particularly adept in exploiting his nuisance value—acting as the spokesman of lesser diplomats who resented being shoved aside, and making the most of the differences that divided the victors.

To these differences Alexander I contributed greatly. Metternich actually called the czar a Jacobin, although Alexander's reputation for enlightenment was only partially deserved, as we have already seen. By 1814, the czar had acquired a thoroughly Romantic enthusiasm for religion, spending hours on end praying and reading the Bible in the company of Madame de Krüdener. Under her influence he prepared a "Holy Alliance" whereby all states would regenerate their policies by following Christian teachings. In the first months at Vienna, it was not Alexander's Romantic scheme of a Holy Alliance but rather his Polish policy that nearly disrupted the Congress. He proposed a partial restoration of pre-partition Poland, with himself as its monarch. Austria and Prussia would lose the Polish lands they had grabbed late in the preceding century. Alexander won the support of Prussia by backing her demands for the annexation of Saxony, whose king had remained loyal to Napoleon. Metternich, however, did not want Austria's traditional Prussian rival to make such a substantial gain. Moreover, both Metternich and Castlereagh disliked the prospect of a large, Russian-dominated Poland.

The dispute over Saxony and Poland gave Talleyrand a magnificent chance to fish in troubled waters. Thus it was that in January 1815 the representative of defeated France joined Metternich and Castlereagh in threatening both Prussia and Russia with war unless they moderated their demands. The threat produced an immediate settlement. Alexander obtained Poland but agreed to reduce its size and allow Prussia and Austria to keep part of their loot from the partitions. Prussia took about half of Saxony; the king of Saxony retained the balance.

The Dynastic and Territorial Settlement

Once the Saxon-Polish question was out of the way, the Congress achieved a fairly amicable resolution of other important dynastic and territorial questions. According to the doctrine that Talleyrand christened "the sacred principle of legitimacy," thrones and frontiers were to be reestablished as they had existed in 1789. In practice, however, legitimacy was ignored almost as often as it was enforced, since the diplomats at Vienna realized that they could not undo all the changes worked by the Revolution and Napoleon. Although they restored Bourbon dynasties to the thrones of France, Spain, and Naples in the name of legitimacy, they did not attempt to resurrect the Republic of Venice or to revive all the hundreds of German states that had vanished since 1789.

In Germany, the Congress provided for thirty-nine states, loosely grouped together in a weak confederation. The German Confederation came close to reincarnating the impotent Holy Roman Empire; its chief organ, the diet, was to be a council of diplomats from sovereign states rather than a representative national assembly. Its most important members were Prussia and Austria, for the German-speaking provinces of the Hapsburgs were considered an integral part of Germany. Both states obtained important new territories at Vienna. Prussia, in addition to her Saxon annexation, expanded the old scattered Hohenzollern lands in western Germany into the imposing new Rhine Province. Austria lost Belgium, which was incorporated into the Kingdom of the Netherlands in order to strengthen the northern buffer against France. But she recovered the old Hapsburg territory of Lombardy in Italy, to which Venetia was now joined, and she also recovered the Illyrian Provinces along the eastern shore of the Adriatic.

In Italy, too, the Congress of Vienna confirmed the tradition of political disunity. It restored the Bourbon Kingdom of Naples in the south and the Papal States in the center. On the northern flanks of the States of the Church it also restored the Grand Duchy of Tuscany and the smaller duchies of Parma and Modena, all of them ruled by Hapsburg relatives (Napoleon's wife, Marie-Louise, was eventually installed in Parma). In the northwest the Kingdom of Piedmont-Sardinia acquired Genoa as a buttress against France. Austria was in a position to dominate Italy both by her possession of Lombardy-Venetia and by the close family ties between the Hapsburgs and the ruling dynasties in the other Italian states.

Elsewhere in Europe, the Congress of Vienna restored to independence the Republic of Switzerland and enlarged it somewhat as another buffer against France. It sanctioned the transfer of Norway from the rule of Denmark, which had generally been pro-French, to Sweden. And it confirmed the earlier transfer of Finland from Sweden to Russia.

Great Britain received the strategic little Mediterranean island of Malta and, outside Europe, the former Dutch colonies of Ceylon and the Cape of Good Hope plus a few insignificant French outposts.

France at first was given her boundaries of 1792, which included the minor territorial acquisitions made during the early days of the Revolution. Then came Napoleon's escape from Elba and the Hundred Days. The final settlement reached after Waterloo assigned France the frontiers of 1790, substantially those of the Old Regime plus Avignon. In addition, the French were to return Napoleon's art plunder to its rightful owners, pay the victorious allies an indemnity of 700,000,000 francs (roughly $140,-000,000), and finance allied military occupation of seventeen frontier fortresses on French soil for not more than five years.

Quadruple Alliance and Holy Alliance

The Vienna diplomats did not so much punish France as take measures to quarantine any possible new French aggression. Castlereagh conceived the policy of strengthening France's neighbors so that they would be able to restrain the troublemaker in the future. Thus to the north the French faced the Belgians and the Dutch combined in the single Kingdom of the Netherlands. On the northeast they encountered the Rhine Province of Prussia, and on the east the expanded states of Switzerland and Piedmont. The Quadruple Alliance, signed in November 1815, constituted the second great measure of quarantine. The four allies—Britain, Prussia, Austria, and Russia—agreed to use force, if necessary, to preserve the Vienna settlement. At Castlereagh's insistence, the allies further decided on periodic conferences to consider the measures "most salutary for the repose and prosperity of Nations, and the maintenance of the Peace of Europe." The Quadruple Alliance was to be both a watchdog against France and an experiment in settling disputes by international conference, a modest step along the road leading to the League of Nations and the United Nations of the twentieth century.

Public opinion, especially in the English-speaking countries, unfortunately confused the Quadruple Alliance with Alexander's Holy Alliance, which it identified with the blackest reaction. The Holy Alliance, signed in September 1815, was actually a fairly harmless document dedicated to the proposition that "the policy of the powers . . . ought to be guided by the sublime truths taught by the eternal religion of God our Saviour." Although most of the major European rulers signed the Holy Alliance, only Czar Alexander seems to have taken it seriously. Castle-reagh called it "a piece of sublime mysticism and nonsense," and Britain declined to participate—the first sign of the rift that was to open between her and the continental powers. The pope, refusing an invitation to join, remarked tartly that the Vatican needed no new interpretations of Christian doctrine by the laity. Both the Holy Alliance and the Quadruple Alliance failed to fulfill the expectations of their architects. At the first meeting of the Quadruple Alliance, at Aix-la-Chapelle in 1818, the allies agreed to withdraw their occupation forces from France, which had paid up the indemnity imposed upon her. Then Czar Alexander pressed the other allies to participate in a vague international union with the contradictory goals of promoting constitutional monarchy everywhere, repressing revolution, fostering disarmament, and supporting an international army to sustain governments and defend existing frontiers. Metternich and Castlereagh demurred, the latter deploring the czar's effort "to endow the transparent soul of the Holy Alliance with a body." At the next meeting of the allies, two years later, Metternich and Castlereagh would find themselves ranged on opposite sides on the issue of putting down revolutions under international auspices.

For these revolutions of 1820–1821 the Congress of Vienna was itself partly to blame, through its attempt to stifle both liberal and nationalist aspirations. Yet, as major international settlements go, that of Vienna was a good one, in many respects more successful than its two predecessors—Westphalia (1648) and Utrecht (1713) —and the Versailles settlement of 1919–1920. There was to be no war involving several powers until the rather second-rate Crimean conflict of the 1850's, and no major war embroiling the whole of Europe until a century after 1815. Seldom have victors treated a defeated aggressor with the wisdom and generosity displayed in 1815. Most of the leading diplomats at Vienna could have said with Castlereagh that they acted "to bring the world back to peaceful habits."

IV   The Persistence of Revolution, 1820-1829

The revolutionary leaders of the post-Napoleonic generation despised the traditions so revered by conservatives. Opposing the counter-revolutionary alliance of Throne and Altar, they stood for Liberty, Equality, and Fraternity. The first two words of the great revolutionary motto continued to signify the abolition of noble and clerical privileges in society and, with few exceptions, the application of laissez-faire to economics. They also involved the broadening of civil rights, the institution of representative assemblies, and the granting of constitutions, which would bring limited monarchy to most states but a republic to the truly advanced, like France. Almost every leader of revolution proclaimed himself a liberal, although, as we shall soon see, the kind of liberalism actually practiced varied from the narrow to the sweeping.

The third great revolutionary word now came to have a more precise meaning. Fraternity, intensified by the Romantic cult of the nation, continued to evolve into the formidable doctrine of nationalism. The nationalists of the post-1815 generation dreamed of a world in which each nation would be free of domination by any other, and all nations would live together harmoniously. In practical terms, this signified movements toward national unity and national independence. It meant growing pressure for the unification of Germany and Italy. And it inspired demands for freedom by peoples living under the control of a foreign power—by Belgians against their Dutch rulers, by Poles against Russians, by Greeks and Serbs against Turks, and by Italians, Hungarians, and Czechs against the Hapsburgs of Vienna.

The Iberian States and Naples, 1820

The first revolutionary outbreaks after 1815 took place in Spain, Portugal, and the Kingdom of the Two Sicilies. In all three states the return to legitimacy restored the Old Regime at its least enlightened. The great majority of the population responded to the restoration calmly, even enthusiastically. The aristocracy were delighted to recover their ancient privileges and the peasantry welcomed the return of familiar traditions; a small minority, drawn chiefly from the middle class, the intellectuals, and the army, dissented. In Spain and Italy, they greatly regretted the abrogation of the Code Napoléon, and of the antifeudal and anticlerical legislation introduced by the French. In all three states the discontent of the liberal minority produced the revolutionary movement of 1820.

The trouble began in Spain. During the war against Napoleon, representatives from the liberal middle class of Cadiz and other commercial towns had framed the Constitution of 1812. Based on the French revolutionary Constitution of 1791, this document limited greatly the power of the monarchy, gave wide authority to a Cortes elected on a broad suffrage, and deprived the Spanish church of some of its lands and privileges. This liberal constitution was doubtless too liberal to be very workable in traditionalist Spain, and the Bourbon Ferdinand VII soon suspended it after he assumed the Spanish crown in 1814. Ferdinand also restored the social inequalities of the Old Regime and reestablished not only the Jesuits but also the Inquisition. Army officers, alienated by his highhandedness and clericalism, and merchants, facing ruin because of the revolt of Spanish colonies in the New World, joined the political clubs and Masonic lodges that formed the liberal opposition.

It was Ferdinand's attempt to subdue the rebellious colonies that triggered revolution at home. The independence movement in Spanish America had been the outcome of the refusal of the colonial populations either to recognize Napoleon's brother Joseph as their king or to accept the closer ties between colonies and mother country proposed by patriots in Spain and implicit in the Constitution of 1812. Behind the Spanish-American independence movement lay several other factors: the powerful examples of the American and French revolutions; the sympathetic interest of Great Britain, anxious to release lucrative markets from Spanish mercantilist restrictions; and the accumulated resentment of colonial peoples at the centuries of indifferent rule by Spanish governors. The colonial rebels won their initial success at Buenos Aires in 1810, and their movement spread rapidly to Spain's other American possessions.

Ferdinand now determined to crush the rebels by force; to transport troops he augmented the small Spanish fleet with three leaky hulks purchased from Russia. At the end of 1819, this motley new armada, carrying 20,000 men, was about to sail from Cadiz. It never sailed, for on January 1, 1820, a mutiny broke out at Cadiz led by the liberal colonel Riego. Uprisings soon followed in Madrid, in Barcelona, and in other Spanish cities. The revolutionaries sang "Riego's Hymn," with the refrain "Swallow it, you dog" (the "it" referred to the Constitution of 1812). Ferdinand surrendered.

The liberal minorities in Portugal and Naples

followed the Spanish lead. An army faction seized control of the Portuguese government in 1820, abolished the Inquisition, and set up a constitution on the Spanish model of 1812. In Naples, the revolution was the work of General Pepe, backed by the Carbonari (charcoal burners). This secret society, with a membership exceeding 50,000, had been opposed to the French and their reforms in the days of Napoleon's hegemony but now sponsored a vaguely liberal program inspired by the French Revolution. King Ferdinand I of the Two Sicilies, who was the uncle of the Spanish Ferdinand VII, gave in at the first sign of opposition in 1820 and accepted a constitution of the Spanish type.

The strength of the revolutionary movement of 1820 ebbed as quickly as it had risen. The reforms introduced precipitately by the inexperienced liberal leaders in Spain and Naples alienated the bulk of the population at home and so alarmed the conservative leaders of the great powers that they sponsored counterrevolutionary intervention. The Spanish revolutionaries were further weakened by a split between *moderados,* who wanted to keep the Constitution of 1812, and *exaltados,* led by Colonel Riego, who wanted to go much farther and set up a violently anticlerical republic. Only in Portugal did the revolutionary regime survive, and only because it had British protection. Even so, there was enough confusion to enable the great Portuguese colony of Brazil to declare itself independent of the mother country (1822).

Counterrevolutionary
Intervention, 1821-1823

The revolutions of 1820 tested both the stability of the Vienna settlement and the solidarity of the Quadruple Alliance of Britain, Prussia, Austria, and Russia. Legitimacy was again restored in Spain and Italy, but in the process the Quadruple Alliance was split in two. While the continental allies increasingly favored armed intervention to suppress revolution, Britain inclined more and more toward the principle of nonintervention. The split became evident at the conference of the Quadruple Alliance meeting at Troppau in Silesia late in 1820. Castlereagh, the British foreign minister, knowing that the Neapolitan revolution threatened the Haps-

burg hegemony in Italy, was willing to see Austria intervene in Naples, but without the backing of the Alliance. The Alliance, Castlereagh declared, was never designed "for the superintendence of the internal affairs of other states," and Britain refused to participate formally in the Troppau meeting. Metternich, supported by Alexander, pressed for a blanket commitment from the Alliance, and the result was the Troppau Protocol (November 1820), signed by Austria, Prussia, and Russia. It declared that

States which have undergone a change of Government, due to revolution, the results of which threaten other states, *ipso facto* cease to be members of the European Alliance, and remain excluded from it until their situation gives guarantees for legal order and stability. If, owing to such alterations, immediate danger threatens other states, the Powers bind themselves, by peaceful means, or if need be by arms, to bring back the guilty state into the bosom of the Great Alliance.*

Under the terms of the Troppau Protocol, an Austrian army duly toppled the revolutionary government of Naples in 1821. In 1823, a French army crossed the Pyrenees and restored the absolute authority of Ferdinand VII, who proceeded to execute Colonel Riego and hundreds of his followers.

French intervention in Spain provoked the strong opposition of Great Britain and ended the Quadruple Alliance. Canning, who had succeeded Castlereagh as British Foreign Minister in 1822, suspected that the continental powers might now aid Spain to recover her former American colonies. So also did the United States, which had recognized the independence of the Latin-American republics. But America also feared both a possible Russian move southward from Alaska along the Pacific coast and an attempt by Britain to extend her sphere of control in the Caribbean. Therefore, when Canning proposed a joint Anglo-American statement to ward off any European interference in Latin America, the government of President Monroe refused the invitation.

In a message to the American Congress in December 1823, the President included the statement that is known to history as the Monroe Doctrine:

* Quoted in W. A. Phillips, *The Confederation of Europe* (New York, 1920), pp. 208-209.

Europe after 1815

—— Boundary of the German Confederation
■ Battle sites

FINLAND

L. Onega

L. Ladoga

Gulf of Finland

St. Petersburg

Volga R.

Moscow

W. Dvina R.

Oka R.

Ural R.

Königsberg

Niemen R.

R U S S I A

Volga R.

Warsaw

OLAND

EP. OF
ACOW

Kiev

Don R.

GALICIA

Dniester R.

Dnieper R.

Caspian Sea

OF

Pruth R.

Odessa

RIA

MOLDAVIA

*DANUBIAN
PROVINCES*

CRIMEA

WALLACHIA

Bucharest

Black Sea

ERBIA

Morava R.

Danube R.

MONTE-
NEGRO

O T T O M A N   E M P I R E

Vardar R.

Adrianople

Istanbul

Aegean Sea

Euphrates R.

Tigris R.

NIAN IS.

CHIOS

Athens

Navarino

CYPRUS

ARABIA

CRETE

In the wars of the European powers, in matters relating to themselves, we have never taken any part, nor does it comport with our policy so to do. It is only when our rights are invaded, or seriously menaced, that we resent injuries or make preparation for our defence. With the movements in this hemisphere, we are, of necessity, more immediately connected, and by causes which must be obvious to all enlightened and impartial observers. The political system of the allied powers is essentially different, in this respect, from that of America. . . . We owe it, therefore, to candor, and to the amicable relations existing between the United States and those powers, to declare, that we should consider any attempt on their part to extend their system to any portion of this hemisphere, as dangerous to our peace and safety. With the existing colonies or dependencies of any European power, we have not interfered, and shall not interfere. But with the governments who have declared their independence, and maintained it, and whose independence we have, on great consideration, and on just principles, acknowledged, we could not view any interposition for the purpose of oppressing them, or controlling, in any other manner, their destiny, by an European power, in any other light than as the manifestation of an unfriendly disposition towards the United States.

Although this document marked an important assertion of policy on the part of the youthful American republic, it had little immediate international significance. The European powers were not fully committed to the project of restoring Spain's American empire. And, so far as they were deterred from that venture, they were deterred not by President Monroe but by Canning and the possible actions of the British fleet.

Serbs and Greeks

The British fleet was soon to take an important role in the Greeks' bid for national independence. The Greek revolt was part of the general movement of the Balkan nations for emancipation from their Turkish overlords. During the last quarter of the eighteenth century, the Christian peoples of the Balkan peninsula began to awaken to their national identities under the impulse from French Revolutionary and Romantic ideas. They examined their na-

tional past with new interest and affection, and they put an especially high value on their native languages. The first outbreak against the Turkish authorities came in Serbia in 1804 and was led by a well-to-do pig raiser named Karageorge. From the first, the Serb nationalists knew they would need outside help; some turned to Russia, others to Austria, thereby fixing a pattern of conflicting interests that ultimately led to World War I. Napoleon's venture in the Illyrian provinces gave the Yugoslavs a taste of the Enlightenment and stimulated their desire for independence. After Karageorge's defection in 1813, leadership of Serb nationalism passed to his rival, Milosh Obrenovich, who won Russian support and succeeded by 1830 in becoming prince of an autonomous Serbia. Although he still paid tribute to the Ottoman emperor, and a Turkish garrison remained in the Serb capital of Belgrade, a major step toward eventual independence had been completed.

Meantime, the Greeks had launched a revolution. Leadership came from two groups—the Phanariot Greeks, named for the quarter where they lived in Istanbul, and the Island Greeks, merchants from the ports and islands of the Aegean. The Phanariots had long held positions of power and responsibility in governing the Orthodox subjects of the Ottoman Empire. The Island Greeks dominated the commerce of the Near East and had business outposts at Vienna, Marseilles, London, and Russia's Black Sea port of Odessa. The Island Greeks revived not only the old Greek mercantile tradition but also some of the old Greek zeal for self-government. From their home islands and from their merchant colonies abroad they poured forth a stream of patriotic exhortation. Greek nationalists sponsored a campaign to purge the modern Greek language of its Turkish and Slavic words and to return it to the classical tongue of the Age of Pericles. A revolutionary secret society was formed in Odessa, patterned after the Carbonari of Italy and headed by Ypsilanti, a Phanariot who was a general in the Russian army.

In 1821, Ypsilanti led an expedition into the Danubian provinces of the Ottoman Empire but failed in his aim to stir up a major revolt. The conspirators were more successful in the Morea (the ancient Peloponnesus) where they fomented an uprising among the peasants. The ensuing war for independence was a ferocious conflict:

the Morean peasants slaughtered every Turk they could lay their hands on; the Ottoman government retaliated by killing or selling into slavery thirty thousand Greeks from the prosperous Aegean island of Chios (Scio), an atrocity that inspired Delacroix's famous painting. In the work of repression, the Ottoman emperor supplemented his own inadequate forces by those of his vassal, the governor of Egypt, Mohammed Ali. By 1827, it appeared likely that the Egyptian expedition would recapture the last rebel strongholds. Then Britain, France, and Russia intervened to save the Greek independence movement at its darkest hour.

The three-power action resulted from the combined pressures of public opinion and strategic interests. In Britain and France, and also in Germany and the United States, the Philhellenic (pro-Greek) movement had won legions of supporters. Philhellenic committees sent supplies and money and demanded that civilized governments intervene directly. Intervention hinged on the action of Russia, for Greek patriots had formed their secret society at Odessa, on Russian soil and with Russian backing. For a time, Metternich was able to restrain Russia by pointing out the dangers to the European balance in supporting revolution in one country and

repressing it in others. Ultimately, however, Russia's Balkan aspirations won out over her concern for preserving the status quo, and she rallied openly to the Greek cause. Britain and France now felt obliged to take action because of Philhellenic pressure and, still more, because they feared to let Russia act alone lest she gain mastery over the whole Near East. A three-power intervention seemed the only course that would both rescue the Greeks and check the Russians.

Neither aim was fully achieved. In October 1827, Russian, British, and French squadrons sank the Turkish and Egyptian vessels anchored at Navarino, on the southwest corner of the Morea, and thus destroyed the chief Ottoman base. The subsequent Treaty of Adrianople, 1829, while allowing Russia to annex outright only a little Turkish territory, arranged that the Ottoman Danubian provinces of Moldavia and Wallachia (the heart of present-day Romania) should become a virtual Russian protectorate. After considerable wrangling, the European powers accorded formal recognition to an independent Greek kingdom of very modest size, which left many Greeks still within the Ottoman Empire. Neither nationalism nor liberalism had won a complete victory in the Greek war. Greek patriots now schemed for the day when they

Centers of Revolution

1820-1830   1848-1849

might enlarge the boundaries of their new kingdom. And Greek politicians were to threaten its stability and disillusion Philhellenists abroad by continuing the bitter feuds that had divided them even in the midst of their desperate struggle for independence.

The Decembrist Revolt in Russia

Russia, who did so much to determine the outcome of revolutions elsewhere, herself felt the revolutionary wave, but with diminished force. A brief uprising took place after the death of Czar Alexander I (December 1825), as the "Decembrists" vainly attempted to apply and extend the program of liberal reforms apparently promised by the czar but seldom implemented by him.

The last period of Alexander's reign, marked by the influence of the unpopular Arakcheev and by the establishment of the hated military colonies, had thoroughly disappointed Russian liberals. Liberal ideas, however, continued to penetrate the country. As in other European states, secret societies flourished in Russia after 1815. The introduction of Freemasonry during the eighteenth century, and the secret ritual connected with many of the lodges, had given jaded nobles a thrill and had also enabled them to meet on equal terms with men from other ranks of society. Masonry aroused humanitarian urges; it also afforded a cover of secrecy under which subversive ideas might be incubated. Moreover, the contrast between the relatively enlightened West and backward Russia made a deep impression on officers who had served in the campaigns against Napoleon. One of the future Decembrist leaders left this report of his reactions upon returning home:

From France we returned to Russia by sea. The First Division of the Guard landed at Oranienbaum and listened to the *Te Deum*. . . . During the prayer the police were mercilessly beating the people who attempted to draw nearer to the lined-up troops. . . . Finally the Emperor appeared, accompanied by the Guard, on a fine sorrel horse, with an unsheathed sword, which he was ready to lower before the Empress. But at that very moment, almost under his horse, a peasant crossed the street. The Emperor spurred his horse and rushed with the unsheathed sword toward the running peasant. The police attacked him with their clubs. We did not believe our own eyes and turned away, ashamed for our beloved Tsar.*

High-ranking officers at St. Petersburg secretly formed the Northern Society, which aimed to make Russia a limited, decentralized monarchy, with the various provinces enjoying rights somewhat like those of the states in the American republic. The serfs would receive their freedom but no land, and the whole series of reforms would be achieved by peaceful means. A second secret organization, the Southern Society, with headquarters at Kiev, included many relatively impoverished officers among its members; its leader was Colonel Pestel, a Jacobin in temperament and an admirer of Napoleon. On every main issue the program of the Southern Society went beyond that of the Petersburg group. It advocated a highly centralized republic, the granting of land to liberated serfs, and the use of violence—specifically, assassination of the czar—to gain its ends. Pestel himself planned to install a dictatorship, supported by secret police, as an interim government between the overthrow of the czardom and the advent of the republic.

Both the Northern Society and the Southern Society tried to profit by the political confusion following the death of Alexander I. Since Alexander left no son, the crown would normally have passed to his younger brother, Constantine, his viceroy in Poland. Constantine, however, had relinquished his rights to a still younger brother, Nicholas, but in a document so secret that Nicholas never saw it. On the death of Alexander, Constantine declared that Nicholas was the legal czar, and Nicholas declared that Constantine was. While the two brothers were clarifying their status, the Northern Society summoned the Petersburg garrison to revolt against Nicholas. Throughout the day of December 26, 1825, the rebels stood their ground in Russia's capital city until Nicholas subdued them. Two weeks later, the Southern Society launched a movement that was doomed from the start because its leader, Pestel, had already been placed under arrest.

The Decembrist revolt, for all its ineffectiveness, was an important episode. It thoroughly alarmed Czar Nicholas I (1825–1855), who now resolved to follow a severely autocratic policy. Although Nicholas dismissed the unpopular

* Quoted in Anatole G. Mazour, *The First Russian Revolution* (Berkeley, Calif., 1937), p. 55.

Arakcheev and put an end to the military colonies, he also had five of the Decembrists executed and exiled more than one hundred others to Siberia, where many of them contributed to the advance of local government and education. The Decembrists were the first in the long line

of modern Russia's political martyrs, and the program of Pestel's Southern Society may now be seen as a kind of early blueprint for the revolutionary dictatorship that was to come to Russia as a consequence of the Bolshevik uprising of 1917.

V The Revolutions of 1830

The Restoration in France

The next revolutionary wave—that of 1830—swept first over the traditional home of revolution, France. King Louis XVIII (1814–1824) had given the Bourbon restoration a rather ambiguous start. By personal inclination he would have preferred to be an absolute ruler, but he was sensible enough to know that a full return to the Old Regime was impractical, especially since he was declining in years and in health and suffered from the additional political handicap of having been imposed on the French by their enemies.

The ambiguities of Louis XVIII's policies were evident in the constitutional charter that he issued in 1814, before the Hundred Days. Some sections sounded like the unreconstructed absolute monarchy of Louis XIV. The Charter was "granted in the nineteenth year of our reign," and the preamble asserted the royal prerogative: "The authority in France resides in the person of the king." But the Charter then proceeded to grant a measure of constitutional monarchy. There was a legislature, composed of a Chamber of Peers appointed by the king, and a Chamber of Deputies elected on a very restricted suffrage that allowed fewer than 100,000 of France's thirty millions the right to vote. "In the king alone is vested the executive power," the Charter stated, and the Chambers had no formal right to confirm the king's choices as ministers. Yet since Louis tended to select ministers acceptable to majority opinion in the legislature, this was a kind of back-handed parliamentary government. The Charter confirmed many of the decisive changes instituted in France since 1789. It guaranteed religious toleration, a measure of freedom for the press, equality before the law, and equal eligibility to civil and military office; it likewise accepted the Code Napoléon and, still more important, the revolutionary property settlement.

The Charter, however, greatly irritated the ultraroyalist faction, drawn from the noble and clerical émigrés, who had returned to France after their revolutionary exile. These "Ultras," grouped around the king's brother and heir, the Count of Artois, were determined to recover both the privileges and the property they had lost during the Revolution. Louis XVIII held the Ultras at bay for five years. When the election of 1815 gave them control of the Chamber of Deputies, they proposed legislation to outlaw divorce and to institutionalize the "white terror" already launched by setting up special courts to deal with suspected revolutionaries. At the insistence of the allies, Louis XVIII dismissed the Chamber and held a new election, which returned a less fanatical majority. He chose moderate ministers who worked to pay off the indemnity to the victorious allies and, in general, to put French finances in good order.

Events, however, soon strengthened the Ultras' hand. Antirevolutionary fears swept France in the wake of the Spanish uprising of 1820 and of the assassination of the Duke of Berri, the king's nephew (February 1820), stabbed by a fanatic who hoped to extinguish the Bourbon line (the widowed duchess, however, gave birth to a son seven months later). The Ultras won control of the Chamber of Deputies, clamped controls on the press, and put through a law giving extra weight to the votes of the wealthiest twenty-five percent of the very restricted electorate. They also pressed Louis XVIII to appoint a reactionary ministry, which sent French troops to aid Ferdinand VII against the Spanish revolutionaries.

The tempo of the reaction quickened when Louis died and the Ultra leader, Artois, became King Charles X (1824–1830). A charming and graceful man, Charles had little sense of political realities. He tried to revive some of the medieval glamor of monarchy by staging an elaborate

Louis Philippe crying at the funeral of Lafayette: The monarch sheds crocodile tears in this lithograph by Daumier.

coronation ceremony—and arranged a nine-month prison term for the witty poet who called it "The Consecration of Charles the Simple." He greatly extended the influence of the Church by encouraging the activities of the Jesuits, who were still legally banned from France, and by appointing clerics as teachers and administrators in the state school system. He sponsored a law of indemnification granting state annuities to the émigrés as compensation for their confiscated property. It was widely, though not entirely correctly, believed that a concurrent reduction of the annual interest on government obligations from five percent to three was designed to help finance the annuities. The indemnification of the émigrés could be defended as a sensible political move that lifted the last threat of confiscation from those who had acquired property during the Revolution. But the reduction of interest on government obligations, together with Charles' clericalism, infuriated many influential Parisian bourgeois.

The Ultras, therefore, lost ground in the elections of 1827, and Charles for a time endeavored to put up with a moderate ministry. But in 1829 he appointed as his chief minister the Prince of Polignac, an Ultra of Ultras, who claimed to have had visions in which the Virgin Mary promised

him success. Polignac hoped to bolster the waning prestige of his monarch by scoring a resounding diplomatic victory. He therefore attacked the dey of Algiers (a largely independent vassal of the Ottoman emperor) who was notorious for his collusion with the hated Barbary pirates and who had insulted the French consul by striking him with a flywhisk. The capture of Algiers (June 1830) laid the foundation of the French empire in North Africa. Meanwhile, the liberal majority in the Chamber of Deputies had attacked Polignac's ministry as unconstitutional because it did not command the approval of the legislature. In the hope of securing a more tractable chamber, Charles X held a new election in May 1830, but the opposition won. On July 25, 1830, without securing the legislature's approval, Charles and Polignac issued ordinances muzzling the press, dissolving the newly elected Chamber, ordering a fresh election, and introducing new voting qualifications that would have disfranchised the bourgeois who were the mainstay of the opposition. The king and his chief minister believed that public opinion, mollified by the recent victory at Algiers, would accept these July Ordinances calmly. They miscalculated utterly.

The July Revolution

Aroused by the protests of liberal journalists, and encouraged by the fine summer weather, the Parisians staged a riot that became a revolution. During *les trois glorieuses* (the three glorious days of July 27, 28, and 29) they threw up barricades, captured the Paris city hall, and hoisted the tricolor atop Notre Dame. When Charles X saw the revolutionary flag through a spyglass from his suburban retreat, he arranged to abdicate on behalf of his grandson, the posthumous son of the Duke of Berri, and sailed to exile in England. Contrary to an impression often held, the July Revolution was not bloodless: some 1,800 insurgents and 200 soldiers were slain.

Contrary to another widespread impression, the revolutionaries were not the poor and the downtrodden. Although there was unemployment, as a result of bank failures, and although poor harvests created high food prices, suffering remained in the background. The revolutionary crowds in 1830 came mainly from the lower bourgeoisie and the skilled workers, whose numbers were increasing with the growth of industry in Paris. These were essentially the same social groups who had furnished the Vainqueurs de la Bastille in 1789. Leadership came from the parliamentary opponents of Charles X and from cautious young liberals like Adolphe Thiers (1797–1877) and François Guizot (1787–1874), both destined to play important political roles in the future. Thiers edited the paper *Le National*, which spearheaded the opposition; he had also written a history of the great revolution to show that it was not all bloodshed but had had a peaceful constructive side. Guizot, too, had written history, a survey of civilization focused on the rise of the bourgeoisie, and he had been active in an organization called *Aide-toi, le Ciel t'aidera!* (heaven helps those who help themselves) instrumental in getting out the vote to defeat the Ultras in the election of 1827.

The revolutionaries of 1830, like those of 1789, were not agreed on the kind of regime they wanted. Some wanted a democratic republic with universal suffrage and rallied around that aged symbol of revolution, Lafayette. Others wanted a safe and sane constitutional monarchy with a narrow suffrage; they wanted France's 1830 to be the counterpart of England's 1688. These moderates were headed by Thiers, by the

"Liberty Guiding the People (July 28, 1830)": A painting by Delacroix.

elderly but still astute Talleyrand, and by the banker Laffitte. They had the money, they had the brains, and they had the support not only of the parliamentary opponents of Charles X but also of veteran Napoleonic officials, who were weary of languishing in the political wasteland. And they had the perfect candidate for the throne—Louis Philippe, the duke of Orléans.

Louis Philippe's father had participated in the Paris demonstrations of 1789, had assumed the revolutionary name of Philippe Egalité, and voted for the execution of Louis XVI, only to be guillotined during the Terror. Louis Philippe himself had fought in the revolutionary army at Valmy in 1792, then had emigrated in 1793 before the worst of the Terror. He claimed to have little use for the pomp of royalty and dressed and acted like a sober and well-to-do businessman. Having deceived the gullible Lafayette into thinking he was a republican, he accepted the crown at the invitation of the Chamber that had been elected in May 1830, and that at last managed to meet.

The Chamber also revised the Charter of 1814, which now allowed the legislature more initiative, deleted references to royal absolutism, and implied that the Charter was not a grant by the monarch but a pact between him and the nation. Significantly, the revised Charter called Louis Philippe not king of France but, following the precedent of 1791, king of the French. It also substituted the revolutionary tricolor for the white flag of the Bourbons. The suffrage, though doubled in size, was still highly restricted; in 1831 only 166,000 Frenchmen had the right to vote. The July Monarchy, as the new regime was termed, left France far short of realizing the democratic potential of Liberty, Equality, and Fraternity. The 166,000 men who paid the minimum annual tax of 200 francs ($40) to qualify for the vote were divided between the business and professional men of the bourgeoisie and the large rural landowners. The France of Louis Philippe, rather like Whig Britain of the eighteenth century, functioned on the narrow social base of landed gentry and funded gentry.

Belgium

Within a month of the July uprising in Paris, a revolution began in Belgium. The union of Belgium and the Netherlands, decreed by the peace-makers of 1815, worked well only in economics. The commerce and colonies of Holland supplied raw materials and markets for the textile, glass, and other manufactures of Belgium, at that time the most advanced industrial area of the Continent. In the very sensitive areas of language, politics, and religion, however, King William I of the Netherlands exerted arbitrary power where he might better have made tactful concessions. He made Dutch the official language throughout his realm, including the French-speaking Walloon provinces. He denied the pleas of Belgians for more equitable representation in the States-General, where the Dutch provinces, with their two million inhabitants, and the Belgian, with their three and a half million, were given the same number of seats. He refused to grant special status to the Catholic church in Belgium and particularly offended the faithful by insisting that the education of priests be subject to state supervision. All these grievances tended to create a Belgian nationalism and to forge common bonds between the Catholic Dutch-speaking Flemings of the provinces north of Brussels and the Catholic French-speaking Walloons of the highly industrialized southern provinces. In later years, however, the Flemish-Walloon partnership was to be strained by differences in language and also by the divergence between the devout Flemings and the increasingly anticlerical Walloons, much influenced by the growing anticlericalism of France.

The revolution broke out in Brussels on August 25, 1830, at a performance of a Romantic opera which depicted a revolt in Naples. Headed by students, inspired by the example of Paris—and perhaps incited by French agents—the audience rioted against Dutch rule. By the end of September, Dutch troops had been driven out of Brussels, and Dutch rule was collapsing. The insurgents recruited their fighters chiefly from the industrial workers, many of whom complained of low pay and frequent unemployment. The better-organized middle-class leadership soon controlled the revolutionary movement and predominated in the national Belgian congress that convened in November 1830.

This congress proclaimed Belgium independent and made it a constitutional monarchy. The new constitution granted religious toleration, provided for wide local self-government, and put rigorous limits on the king's authority. Although it did not establish universal suffrage, the financial qualifications for voting were lower in Belgium than they were in Britain or France, and the electorate was proportionately larger. The congress first chose as king the duke of Nemours, a son of Louis Philippe. Britain protested violently, for this would have brought Belgium within the orbit of France. The congress then picked Leopold of Saxe-Coburg, a German princeling, the widowed son-in-law of George IV of Britain. Leopold was well fitted for the exacting role of a constitutional monarch in a brand-new kingdom. He had already shown his political shrewdness by refusing the shaky new throne of Greece; he now demonstrated it by marrying a daughter of Louis Philippe, thus mitigating French disappointment over the aborted candidacy of the duke of Nemours.

The Belgian revolution made the first permanent breach in the Vienna settlement. King William, stubborn as the proverbial Dutchman, tried to retake Belgium by force in 1831–1832. A French army and British fleet successfully defended the secessionists, and prolonged negotiations resulted in Dutch recognition of Belgium's new status in 1839. In 1839 also, representatives of Britain, France, Prussia, Austria, and Russia guaranteed both the independence and the neutrality of Belgium in a document that the German Empire was to term "a scrap of paper" when it invaded Belgium in 1914. In the 1830's Metternich and Czar Nicholas I of Russia were disturbed by Belgian independence but too distracted by revolutions on their own Italian and Polish doorsteps, respectively, to do very much about it.

Poland

The course of revolution in Poland contrasted tragically with that in Belgium. In 1815, the Kingdom of Poland possessed the most liberal constitution on the Continent; twenty years later, it had become a mere colony of the Russian Empire. The constitution given to the Poles by Czar Alexander I preserved the Code Napoléon and endowed the diet with limited legislative power. A hundred thousand Poles received the franchise, more than the total number of voters in the France of Louis XVIII, which had a population ten times greater. In practice, however, difficulties arose. Many of the men chosen for official posts in Poland were not acceptable to the Poles; indeed, one may doubt that any government imposed by Russia would have satisfied them. Censorship, unrest, and police intervention appeared during the last years of Alexander I.

The advent of the highly conservative Nicholas I in 1825 increased political friction, although the new czar at first abided by the Polish constitution. Meantime, Romantic doctrines of nationalism made many converts at the Universities of Warsaw and Vilna (in Lithuania). Polish nationalists demanded the transfer from Russia to Poland of provinces that had belonged to the prepartition Polish state—Lithuania, White Russia, and the Ukraine. Secret societies on the Carbonari model arose in these provinces and in the Kingdom of Poland.

A secret society of army cadets in Warsaw launched a revolution in November 1830. Seeking to widen their base of support, the rebels soon split into the two hostile camps of "Whites" and "Reds," the former allied with the highly conservative aristocrats, the latter with the somewhat less conservative gentry. Neither Whites nor Reds gained the support of the peasants, who had long been oppressed by both aristocrats and gentry. This was a revolution for national independence, not for rectification of the social imbalance of the Old Regime. The suffering of the Poles increased with a terrible epidemic of cholera, the first outbreak of that Asian disease in Europe. Russian forces, at first taken off guard, had mastered the situation by 1833. Nicholas I then scrapped the constitution, imposed a regime of permanent martial law, and closed the universities of Warsaw and Vilna, the chief centers of Polish nationalist propaganda. To escape the vengeance of Nicholas, Polish intellectuals fled the country by the tens of thousands, and Paris became a capital for Poles in exile.

Italy and Germany

In Italy and Germany the excitement of the July Revolution in Paris set off revolutionary fireworks that soon fizzled out. In 1831, Carbonari insurgents in north central Italy briefly controlled the little duchies of Parma and Modena and a sizable part of the Papal States, including the city of Bologna. Among the participants was the youthful Louis Napoleon Bonaparte, nephew of Napoleon I, who was later to become Emperor Napoleon III. The revolutionaries counted on French assistance, but the July Monarchy had no intention of risking war with Austria by poaching on the Hapsburg preserve. Again, as in 1821, Metternich sent troops to restore legitimacy in Italy.

Metternich did not require soldiers to preserve legitimacy in Germany; whenever a crisis arose, the Diet of the German Confederation obediently followed the Austrian lead. In Prussia, King Frederick William III (1797–1840) had never fulfilled his promise to grant a constitution, though he did set up provincial diets. Only Weimar and a few south German states enjoyed liberal constitutions, on the order of the French Charter of 1814. Political agitation came almost entirely from the small minority of intellectuals who had roused national resistance to Napoleon—journalists, Romantic writers, university professors, and students.

After 1815, German university students formed a new organization, the *Burschenschaft* (Students' Union). In October 1817 students of the University of Jena held a rally on the Wartburg, where Luther had worked on his German translation of the Bible, to celebrate both the tercentenary of the Ninety-Five Theses and the fourth anniversary of the battle of Leipzig. During the rally the Burschenschaft burned a diplomat's wig, a Prussian officer's corset, and books by reactionary writers. In March 1819 one of the writers, Kotzebue, who was also a Russian agent, was assassinated by a demented theological student. Metternich, already alarmed by the student prank of 1817, now got the Diet of the German Confederation to approve the Carlsbad Decrees (September 1819), which stiffened press censorship, dissolved the Burschenschaft, and curtailed academic freedom.

Despite the Carlsbad Decrees, mild political ferment continued in Germany, and the Burschenschaft reorganized underground. In 1830 and the years following, a few rulers in northern Germany, notably in Saxony and Hanover, were forced to grant constitutions. Excited by these minor successes, and by the appearance of Polish refugees, thirty thousand revolutionary sympathizers, including many students from Heidelberg and other universities in the region, gathered at Hambach in the Palatinate in May 1832. There they toasted Lafayette and demanded the union of the German states under a democratic republic. Effective action toward unification was another matter. In 1833 some fifty would-be republicans from the academic world tried to seize Frankfurt, the capital of the German confederation and seat of its Diet. The insurgents, together with hundreds of other students accused of Burschenschaft activities, were given harsh sentences by courts in Prussia and other German states.

The Lessons of 1830

The revolutionary wave of the 1830's revealed two great facts of political life. First, it widened the split between the West and the East already evident in the wake of the Revolutions of 1820. Britain and France were committed to support cautiously liberal constitutional monarchies both at home and in neighboring Belgium. On the other hand, Russia, Austria, and Prussia were more firmly committed than ever to the counter-revolutionary principles of the Troppau Protocol. In 1833, Czar Nicholas I, Metternich, and King Frederick William III formally pledged their joint assistance to any sovereign threatened by revolution, though they were unable to help King William of the Netherlands.

Second, revolution succeeded in 1830 only in France and Belgium, only where it enlisted the support of a substantial segment of the population, thanks in part to the dislocations caused by the Industrial Revolution. It failed in every country where the revolutionaries represented only a fraction of the people. In Poland, the peasantry viewed both Whites and Reds as oppressors. Italian revolutionaries still relied on their Romantic Carbonari tradition and on flimsy hopes of foreign aid. In Germany, revolution was a matter of student outbursts, toasts to Lafayette, and other gestures by a small minority. Conspirators and intellectuals needed to make their doctrines penetrate to the grass roots of society; they needed to develop able political leaders and to mature well-laid plans for political reform. These were the tasks which they undertook after 1830; their success was to be tested in the most formidable and the most extensive chain of political uprisings in the history of nineteenth-century Europe—the Revolutions of 1848.

VI The Revolutions of 1848

One of the common denominators of revolution in 1848 was nationalism. It prompted the disunited Germans and Italians to attempt political unification, and it inspired the subject peoples of the Hapsburg Empire to seek political and cultural autonomy. The Romantic movement had stimulated a nationalistic renaissance among most peoples in central and eastern Europe. For the national minorities within the Hapsburg Empire, as for the Christian nationalities within the Ottoman Empire, the new nationalism tended to be focused on language. The Czech language, for example, was on the verge of extinction in the later eighteenth century; the population of Bohemia increasingly used the German of their Austrian rulers. By 1848, however, a Czech linguistic and literary revival was in full swing. Patriotic histories of Bohemia and collections of Czech folk poetry kindled a lively interest in the national past and fostered dreams of a Pan-Slavic awakening in which the Czechs would lead their brother Slavs.

The nationalists of 1848 were not necessarily generous or liberal. While some of them preached with Mazzini, the democratic Italian patriot, that each nation's "special mission" fulfilled the "general mission of humanity," others held less generous views. John Stuart Mill, the English liberal observer, deplored those who ignored the welfare "of any portion of the human species, save that which is called by the same name and speaks the same language as themselves."* There were many self-styled Chosen People in the revolutions of 1848.

Liberalism, the second common denominator of the revolutions, also encompassed a wide range of programs. In central and eastern Europe,

* J. S. Mill, "The French Revolution and Its Assailants," *Westminster Review*, II (1849), 17.

where much of the Old Regime survived, liberals demanded constitutions to limit absolute monarchy and to liquidate feudal rights and manorial dues. In France, where constitutional monarchy had already been achieved, many liberals sought to replace the July Monarchy with a democratic republic. For many democracy meant that every man should have not only the right to vote but also the right to work, a formula that implied the need for government action to do something about unemployment and other social ills aggravated by the alternating prosperity and depression of this early period of industrial growth.

In the Europe of 1848, as in the France of 1789, an economic crisis helped to catalyze discontent into revolution. A blight ruined the Irish potato crop in 1845 and soon spread to the Continent; the grain harvest of 1846 also failed in western Europe. The consequences were a sharp rise in the price of bread and resulting bread riots; mass starvation occurred in Ireland, and widespread misery affected France, Germany, and Austria. The food crisis was compounded by an industrial depression, touched off in 1847 by the collapse of a boom in railroad construction. The number of unemployed mounted just as food prices were rising, thus intensifying popular suffering.

France

The economic crisis hit France with particular severity. Railroad construction almost ceased, throwing more than half a million out of work; coal mines and iron foundries, in turn, laid men off. Unemployment increased the discontent of French workers already embittered by their low wages and by the still lower esteem in which they were held by the government of Louis Philippe. Under the July Monarchy, French agriculture experienced a golden age, at the same time that industrialization was beginning to develop. The government, however, appeared to be indifferent to the social misery that accompanied the new prosperity. In eighteen years, it took only two steps to improve the welfare of the industrial working class: an extension of state aid to primary schools in 1833, and a laxly enforced law in 1841 limiting child labor. There was a great deal of truth in the famous judgment passed by Alexis de Tocqueville, himself a member of the

Chamber, that "Government in those days resembled an industrial company whose every operation is undertaken for the profits which the stockholders may gain thereby.

The "stockholders" of the July Monarchy were the Napoleonic veterans who emerged as prefects and diplomats after a wholesale overturn of official personnel, and the social and economic elite who had right to vote. Demands for liberalization of the suffrage were met with Guizot's curt injunction: *Enrichissez-vous!*—make yourself rich enough to meet the stiff fiscal qualifications for voting. The government banned labor organizations and repressed harshly the workmen of Paris and Lyons who demonstrated in the early 1830's to demand a republic and higher wages. The symbol of this repression was the massacre of the rue Transnonain (April 1834), when soldiers killed fourteen residents of a Paris house thought to be harboring a sniper. The press mercilessly caricatured the pear-shaped head, obese figure, and inevitable umbrella of Louis Philippe, until a censorship was imposed.

Opposition to the July Monarchy, though stifled in the 1830's, revived during the next decade. It was nourished in part by the humiliation suffered by France when international pressure forced her withdrawal of support from the empire-building of the ambitious Egyptian governor Mohammed Ali. The opposition, however, was far from united—a fact that goes far to explain the erratic course of the revolution it set off. Heading what might be termed the official or loyal opposition was Adolphe Thiers, identified with the July Monarchy from its beginning, but a victim of the collapse of France's Egyptian venture. Shelved by Louis Philippe in favor of Guizot, the chief minister from 1840 until 1848, Thiers continued to support the principle of constitutional monarchy. Cynics claim that the chief difference between him and Guizot was the fact that he was out of office while Guizot was in. The republicans formed a second opposition group, which increased in numbers with the growing political awareness and literacy of the working classes (in 1847 two out of three men mustered into the army could read). The third, and smallest, group took in various socialists, who were to gain recruits from the economic depression of the late 1840's. Potentially more formidable than any of these, but as yet representing only a vague, unorganized sentiment, were the Bonapartists. The return of the emperor's ashes from St. Helena to Paris in 1840 revived and renewed the legend of a glorious and warlike Napoleon, so different from the uninspiring Louis Philippe.

In the summer of 1847, constitutional monarchists of the Thiers faction joined with republicans to stage a series of political banquets throughout France calling for an extended suffrage and the resignation of Guizot. This campaign appeared comparatively harmless until a particularly huge banquet was announced for February 22, 1848, to be held in Paris. When the Guizot ministry forbade the banquet, the Parisians substituted a large demonstration. On February 23, Louis Philippe dismissed Guizot and prepared to summon Thiers to the ministry. But his concessions came too late. Supported by workers, students, and the more radical republican leaders, the demonstration of February 22 turned into a riot on the 23rd, in which more than fifty of the rioters were killed or wounded. The number of casualties intensified the revolutionary atmosphere, barricades were thrown up, and Thiers was so unnerved he made no attempt to form a ministry.

On the next day, February 24, 1848, Louis Philippe abdicated, and the Chamber set up a provisional government headed by an eloquent but cautious advocate of a republic, the Romantic poet Lamartine. Popular unrest, mounting along with unemployment (more than half the work force in some trades had been laid off), virtually obliged the provisional government to take in a few socialists. Notable among these was Louis Blanc (1811-1882), an advocate of "social workshops," which the workers themselves would own and run with the financial assistance of the state. As a gesture toward the "right to work," and also as a measure to restore calm in Paris, the provisional government authorized the establishment of "national workshops" in the capital. These national workshops, however, were not a genuine attempt to achieve the social workshops of Louis Blanc but simply a relief project organized along semimilitary lines, and enrolling more than 100,000 unemployed persons from Paris and the provinces. About 10,000 of the recruits received two francs (about 40 cents) a day for working on municipal improvements; the rest received a dole of one franc a day. Meantime, the provisional government was also trying to discount the international repercussions of flamboyant promises by left-wing politicians to

the effect that a democratic and republican France would help to liberate the other peoples of Europe. Lamartine was particularly concerned to reassure Britain that, while French words might be bellicose, French actions would not be.

The future shape of France now hinged on the outcome of the elections of April 23, 1848, when all adult males—nine millions as opposed to a quarter of a million in the last days of the July Monarchy—would be qualified to vote for the National Assembly, which would draw up a constitution for the Second French Republic. (The First Republic had lasted from September 1792 down to Napoleon's coronation in 1804; the second had existed in fact, if not formally, since Louis Philippe's abdication on February 24.) In this momentous election—the first in European history when there was real universal manhood suffrage—eight million Frenchmen went to the polls, 84 percent of the potential electorate. The conservative peasants, who still made up the bulk of the population, approved the fall of the July Monarchy but dreaded anything resembling an attack on private property. Of the almost 900 deputies elected, therefore, most were either monarchists or conservative republicans; only a hundred or so sympathized with the Paris radicals.

The latter, however, refused to accept the decision of the country. On May 15, a huge crowd of noisy but unarmed demonstrators invaded the National Assembly and proposed its dissolution and the formation of a new provisional government at the Paris City Hall. The moderates, now thoroughly alarmed, arrested radical leaders and decided that the national workshops threatened law and order because they concentrated so many economically desperate men in Paris. The Assembly decreed the orderly closing of the workshops, with their recruits given the alternative of enlistment in the army or accepting work in the provinces. From June 23 to June 26, 1848, the poor districts of the capital rose in insurrection until they were finally subdued by the troops brought in by General Cavaignac, the energetic minister of war.

These "June Days" were a landmark in modern history, the first large-scale outbreak with very strong overtones of class warfare. Most of the insurgents seem to have come not from members of the national workshops, who still received their dole, but from the unemployed who had tried vainly to enroll in the workshops and were now at the end of their tether, motivated more by desperation than by any hope of attaining a socialist millennium.

Among them were men of the new industrial age—mechanics, railroad men, stevedores—as well as winesellers, masons, locksmiths, cabinetmakers, and other artisans who had been prominent in the capture of the Bastille in 1789. The prospect of a social revolution, though it may have been remote as a practical matter, nevertheless terrified the propertied classes, and Tocqueville reported that "peasants, shopkeepers, landowners, and nobles" were all pouring into Paris by the new railroads to quell the uprising. The spirit of panic accounted for the severe repression: about ten thousand were killed or wounded, and about the same number were subsequently deported, chiefly to Algeria. All socialist clubs and newspapers were padlocked, and Louis Blanc fled to England. France became a virtual military dictatorship under General Cavaignac.

The fears of the moderates were evident in the formal constitution of the Second French Republic which the National Assembly completed in November 1848. The Assembly declared property inviolable and rejected a motion to list the right to work among the fundamental rights of French citizens. In other respects the constitution seemed to be a daring venture in representative democracy and in combining a strong president and a powerful legislature. It was, perhaps, not so daring as it appeared, since the elections of April 1848 had shown that universal suffrage could prove to be a conservative weapon against radicalism. The legislature was a single chamber, to be elected by universal male suffrage every three years. The president was to be chosen by popular election every four years. The French Constitution of November 1848 thus reflected the influence of both Montesquieu's doctrine of the separation of powers and the example of the United States.

Circumstances did not favor the success of the now formally constituted Second Republic. The military rule exercised by Cavaignac while the Assembly was drafting the constitution was one ominous sign. Another was the outcome of the presidential election in December 1848. Fewer than half a million votes were polled by the three genuinely republican candidates, a million and a half were cast for General Cavaignac, and some five and a half million votes and

the presidency of the republic went to Louis Napoleon Bonaparte (1808–1873). This nephew of the great Napoleon, the son of his troublesome brother Louis, was not a prepossessing figure, speaking haltingly in heavily accented French (the result of his boyhood exile in the Germanic part of Switzerland) and known for his association with disreputable people and ill-conceived projects. Yet he staged a clever campaign to identify himself with the cause of order and stability in 1848, including volunteering to serve as a constable when he was in London during the spring and a mass demonstration was anticipated. Above all, he had the enormous asset of bearing the Bonaparte name and drawing upon all the accumulated glamor of the Napoleonic legend. Politically, as a later chapter will show, he proved a true successor of his uncle, subverting the constitution of the Second Republic in a coup d'état late in 1851 and proclaiming himself Emperor Napoleon III a year later. The French Revolution of 1848, like that of 1789, had established a republic that ended in a Napoleonic empire.

Italy

In Italy, where the youthful Louis Napoleon had taken part in the miniscule revolution of 1831, the now discredited Carbonari tradition gave way to new movements of reform. Throughout the 1840's three schools of reformers were in competition for leadership of Italian nationalism; the competition and the fact that none of them yet commanded wide popular allegiance did not augur well for the success of an Italian revolution. Two of the reforming groups were moderate, agreeing that poltical power in an Italy emancipated from Hapsburg control should be limited to the nobility and the bourgeoisie, but at odds over the form that a united Italian nation should assume. One group, based in the north, favored the domination of Piedmont; the leader was the eventual unifier of Italy, Count Cavour, who was a great admirer of British and French liberal ways. Cavour was the editor of an influential newspaper in Turin, the capital of Piedmont—*Il Risorgimento* ("resurgence" or "regeneration"), which gave its name to the whole process of unification. The other moderate group called themselves Neo-Guelfs because, like the

Guelf political faction of the Middle Ages, they hoped to engage the pope in the task of freeing Italy from the control of a German emperor. The Neo-Guelf leader, the priest Gioberti, declared that the future depended on "the union of Rome and Turin." The pope would head, and the army of Piedmont would defend, a federation of Italian states, each with its monarch and its cautiously liberal constitution.

The third group of liberals, "Young Italy," so named because only those under the age of forty were eligible for membership, asserted that Italy should be unified as a democratic republic. Its founder, Mazzini (1805-1872), hoped to create an organization more effective than the Carbonari but was frustrated by his own prolonged exile and by the frequent ineptitude of his lieutenants. Nevertheless, Mazzini did win an enduring reputation as the great democratic idealist of modern Italian politics. Here is a statement of his political credo:

We believe, therefore, in the Holy Alliance of the Peoples as being the vastest formula of association possible in our epoch;—in the *liberty* and *equality* of the peoples, without which no true association can exist;—in *nationality,* which is the *conscience* of the peoples, and which, by assigning to them their part in the work of association, . . . constitutes their mission upon earth, that is to say, their *individuality,* without which neither liberty nor equality are possible;—in the sacred *Fatherland,* cradle of nationality; altar and workshop of the individuals of which each nation is composed.*

A good European as well as an ardent Italian nationalist, Mazzini inspired the formation of Young Germany, Young Poland, and similar movements, all joined together in a federation called Young Europe.

The prospects for reform in Italy brightened a little in the years immediately preceding 1848. In 1846, a new pope was elected, Pio Nono (Pius IX, 1846-1878), whose initial progressive actions, like the release of political prisoners and some rather haphazard steps to modernize the antiquated administrative machinery of the Papal States, aroused great expectations of a thorough liberalization of papal government. In the next year, King Charles Albert of Piedmont

relaxed the traditionally tight censorship of a very conservative monarchy sufficiently to permit Cavour to publicize in *Il Risorgimento* his own programs for economic and political improvements.

Actual revolution came to Italy before it occurred in Paris. In January 1848 an uprising in the Two Sicilies forced King Ferdinand II to grant a constitution on the pattern of the French Charter of 1814, as revised in 1830; in mid-February the Grand Duke of Tuscany was obliged to do likewise. News of the rising in Paris quickened the pace of the Italian revolutions, as Charles Albert in Piedmont and Pius IX became constitutional monarchs in the manner of the July Monarchy. Next came the turn of Lombardy and Venetia, where Hapsburg rule had been relatively mild but where the ideas of Young Italy had inspired a revolutionary movement. Ever since January 1, 1848, citizens of Milan, the capital of Lombardy, had been boycotting cigars as a protest against the Austrian tax on tobacco—a maneuver suggested by a professor's lecture on the Boston tea party; severe rioting resulted. News of a revolution in Vienna and the departure of Metternich (March 12-13) touched off five days of heavy fighting in Milan (March 18-22) which forced the Austrians to withdraw their forces. The Milanese improvised some extraordinary barricades, utilizing pianos, sentry boxes, and omnibuses in addition to the usual paving blocks. At the same time, Venice, the capital of Austria's other Italian province, proclaimed herself the independent Republic of St. Mark. The rapid collapse of Hapsburg rule in Lombardy-Venetia inspired a national crusade against the Austrians. Charles Albert of Piedmont assumed command of the Italian forces, which included contingents from Naples, Tuscany, and even the Papal States. Charles Albert refused an offer of help from the provisional government of the French republic with the famous, and inaccurate, prediction "Italia farà da se" ("Italy will do it alone"). For the moment it seemed possible that the Piedmontese and Neo-Guelf forces would unite to assure the victory of both nationalism and moderate liberalism in Italy.

But only for the moment. During the spring and early summer of 1848, Piedmont annexed Lombardy and the two small north Italian duchies of Parma and Modena. The other Italian states, jealous of their particularist traditions,

---

* "Faith and the Future," in *Life and Writings of Joseph Mazzini* (London, 1905), III, p. 129.

commenced to fear the imperialism of Piedmont more than they desired the unification of Italy. On April 29, 1848, Pius IX announced that his "equal affection" for all peoples obliged him to adopt a neutral position in the war with Austria and to recall his soldiers. The pope could not be both an Italian patriot and an international spiritual leader. Moreover, Pius was alarmed by the increasingly radical political temper of the Roman population and by the threats of German bishops to create an antipope. The Neo-Guelf cause had received a fatal blow. In May 1848 the king of Naples, who had scrapped his constitution, withdrew his contingents from the war. The Austrians, taking the offensive, reconquered Lombardy and crushed the forces of Charles Albert at Custozza (July 1848). Italy had not been able to do it alone.

A few months later, the revolutionary movement got a brief second wind. In Rome, adherents of Young Italy, dissatisfied with the constitution of March, rose up in November 1848. After Pius IX fled to Neapolitan territory early in the next year, they transformed the Papal States into a democratic Roman Republic, headed by Mazzini himself, who proved to be fairly authoritarian in a position of power. In March 1849 radicals in Piedmont forced the reluctant Charles Albert to renew the war with Austria, but within the month Austria again overwhelmed Piedmont, at the battle of Novara. In August 1849 the Austrians put an end to the Republic of St. Mark after a prolonged siege and bombardment of Venice, which suffered acutely from famine and cholera. Meanwhile (July 1849), Mazzini's Roman Republic had surrendered to French troops sent by President Bonaparte in a bid for Catholic gratitude.

Except for the French garrison stationed in Rome, Italy returned almost completely to its prerevolutionary status, again subdivided into many sovereign units, again dominated by the Hapsburgs. Both the Neo-Guelfs and Young Italy were discredited. The only bright spot in the picture was the emergence of Piedmont as the natural leader of Italian nationalism and liberalism. Despite the defeats at Custozza and Novara, despite the loss of the territories momentarily annexed in 1848, Piedmont enjoyed the prestige of having twice defied the hated Austrians. Moreover, it was also the only Italian state to retain the constitution granted in 1848. When Charles Albert, whose enthusiasm for

change was tepid, abdicated to retire to a monastery after the defeat of Novara, the crown passed to Victor Emmanuel II, who was to have the distinction of becoming the first king of modern Italy.

Germany

The course of the German revolutions in 1848 roughly paralleled that of the Italian. In Germany, too, liberalism and nationalism won initial victories and then collapsed in the face of internal dissension and Austrian resistance. The failure in Germany was the more surprising—and ominous—since the revolutionary movement had begun to recruit support among industrial workers, among craftsmen who feared industrial competition, and among peasants who wished to abolish the relics of manorialism. Liberal and nationalist agitation centered in the well-to-do business and professional classes, especially university professors, who enjoyed more influence and respect in Germany than anywhere else in Europe. Except for a few republicans and socialists, the German liberals were moderates. They wanted constitutional monarchies in the various German states, the strengthening of the German Confederation, and an end to the repressive hegemony of Metternich.

The hero of German liberals was King Frederick William IV of Prussia (1840–1861). Attractive and cultivated, but unstable and infatuated with Romantic concepts of divine-right kingship, Frederick William promised much and delivered little. He promised to carry out his father's unhonored pledge to give Prussia a constitution and an elected assembly; however, the meeting of representatives from the provincial diets he convoked at last in 1847 was a great disappointment.

Not this royal knight-errant, but the architects of the *Zollverein* (customs union) constituted Prussia's most solid contribution to German unification before 1848. In 1818, Prussia had abolished internal tariffs within its scattered territories and applied a uniform tariff schedule to imports. The first states to join the Zollverein were small neighbors of Prussia, already surrounded by her territories. Membership proved so profitable that by 1844 almost all the German

738

states, except Austria, had joined. The Zollverein liberated Germany from an oppressive burden of local tolls and taxes and cleared the way for her phenomenal economic development later in the century. Although it did not exercise a decisive influence on politics, it suggested that the state which had fostered German economic unification might naturally take the initiative in political unification.

Unification seemed almost a certainty in 1848. Stimulated by the example of Paris, the revolutionaries scored their first successes in the western German states at the end of February 1848. From there, the demands for constitutions, civil liberties, and a strengthened German Confederation fanned out rapidly. By mid-March, demonstrators were throwing up barricades in Berlin. Frederick William IV ac-

cepted some of the liberals' demands and appealed for calm among "ye inhabitants of my true and beautiful Berlin." Before his appeal could be publicized, rioting broke out with redoubled violence, and more than two hundred rioters, chiefly workingmen, were killed. The mob broke into the royal palace and forced the king to go through a grotesque ceremony of saluting the corpses of the victims. Overwrought by the humiliation to himself and by the death of his subjects, Frederick William accepted all the demands of liberals and nationalists. He summoned an assembly to draw up a constitution, declared Prussia "merged in Germany," and proclaimed himself "king of the free regenerated German nation."

Drastic reform of the German Confederation now began. In May 1848 a constitutional con-

"Storming the Arsenal": Wood engraving depicting the revolutionary outbreaks in Berlin in 1848, from an English newspaper.

vention held its first session in the Church of St. Paul at Frankfurt, the capital of the Confederation. Its 830 members, popularly elected throughout Germany, represented the flower of the German intelligentsia—18 doctors, 33 clergymen, 49 university professors, 57 schoolteachers, 223 lawyers and judges. While some 140 deputies were businessmen, there was only one dirt farmer, and not a single laboring man. The Frankfurt Assembly lacked a broad popular base, and, as events soon demonstrated, many of its members also lacked political experience and talent for practical statesmanship.

The Frankfurt Assembly had to decide the geographical limits of Germany. The Confederation included Austria proper but excluded most of the non-German Hapsburg territories. Neither did it include the eastern provinces of Prussia, notably those acquired in the partitions of Poland. The Austrian issue divided the Assembly into two camps: the "Big Germans" who favored the inclusion of Austria and of Bohemia, with its large Czech population, in the projected German state, and the "Little Germans," who opposed the idea. Austrian objections to a "Big Germany" insured the Assembly's adoption of the "Little Germany" proposal.

On the question of Prussian Poland, the nationalism of the Frankfurt Assembly overcame its liberalism. By a large majority it voted to include some Prussian areas in which the Poles formed the majority of the population. The arguments advanced against the Poles in the debates revealed German nationalism at its most superheated. One orator declared that the minority of Germans had a natural right to rule the Poles, who had "less cultural content":

It is high time for us . . . to wake to a wholesome national egotism, to say the word right out for once, which in every question places the welfare and honour of the fatherland uppermost. . . . Our right is none other than the right of the stronger, the right of conquest.*

In contrast, the national constitution promulgated by the Frankfurt Assembly in March 1849 was a decidedly liberal document, a combination of principles drawn from the American federal system and British parliamentary prac-

tice. The individual states were to surrender many of their powers to the German federal government. The federal legislature would consist of a lower house, elected by universal male suffrage, and an upper house, chosen by the governments and the legislatures of the constituent states. Ministers responsible to the legislature would form the federal executive. Over all would preside a constitutional monarch, the German emperor.

The Frankfurt constitution died aborning. The Assembly elected the king of Prussia to be emperor, but Frederick William, ignoring his fine promises of March 1848 and alarmed by Austrian opposition, rejected the offer. He called the Frankfurt constitution a "bastard" product:

The crown is no crown. The crown which a Hohenzollern could accept . . . is not one created by an Assembly born of revolutionary seed. . . . It must be a crown set with the seal of the Almighty. . . .*

Since the major candidate for the imperial office had balked, the Frankfurt Assembly soon came to an end. It had never secured recognition from foreign governments, had never raised a penny in taxes, and had never exerted real sovereignty over Germany. The couplet mocking the plethora of academic deputies, though it exaggerated their numbers, had been justified:

Hundert fünfzig Professoren!
Lieber Gott, wir sind verloren!
[*A hundred and fifty professors!*
Good God, we're sunk!]

German liberalism had suffered a major defeat. After the initial shock of the revolutions, the comfortably situated professional and business classes began to fear the radicalism of the workers and artisans. The German princes soon either revoked or abridged the constitutions that they had granted in 1848. In Prussia, Frederick William and his conservative advisers repeatedly doctored the work of the constitutional convention summoned in 1848. The end product, the Constitution of 1850, as a later chapter shows, made Prussia relatively safe for autocracy and aristocracy down to World War I.

---

* Quoted in J. G. Legge, *Rhyme and Revolution in Germany* (London, 1918), p. 397.

* Ibid., pp. 516–517.

The Hapsburg Domains

The fate of German and Italian nationalism in 1848 hinged partly on the outcome of the revolutions in the Hapsburg Empire. If these revolutions had immobilized the Hapsburg government for a long period, then Italian and German unification might have been realized. But Austria, though buffeted by wave after wave of revolution, rode out the storm. The success of the counterrevolution in the Hapsburg Empire assured its victory in Italy and Germany.

The nature and the outcome of the Hapsburg revolutions depended in turn on the complex structure of nationalities within the Austrian Empire. Here are the nationalities under Hapsburg rule in 1848:

Nationality	Percentage of Total Population
German	23
Magyar (Hungarian)	14
Czech and Slovak	19
South (Yugo-) Slav	
Slovene	4
Croat	4
Serb	5
Pole	7
Ruthenian (Little Russian)	8
Romanian	8
Italian	8

These national groups were not always neatly segregated geographically, each in its own compartment. For instance, in the Hungarian part of the empire, the dominant Magyars fell slightly short of a numerical majority. Hungary contained important minorities of Slovaks, Romanians, Croats, Serbs, and Germans. Moreover, while the bulk of the population was rural, the German element, chiefly bureaucrats and tradesmen, predominated in most of the towns and cities throughout the empire, even in the Czech capital of Prague and the Magyar capital of Budapest.

Among the component peoples of the Hapsburg realm in 1848 nationalism ran strongest among the Italians of Lombardy-Venetia, the Czechs of Bohemia, and the Magyars and Croats of Hungary. Language was an important issue with the Magyars as it was with Czechs; the replacement of Latin by Hungarian as the official tongue of the eastern part of the empire in 1844 marked a victory for Magyar nationalism. Since Hungary was overwhelmingly an agricultural land, nationalism, like all other aspects of political life, was dominated by nobles and country squires who monopolized the seats in the county assemblies and the central diet. One group of Magyar nationalists aimed at the gradual modernization of Hungary's culture and economy along moderate English lines. The more extreme nationalists, whose spokesman was the spellbinding orator Louis Kossuth (of Slovak rather than Magyar background), regarded the linguistic reform of 1844 as but the first in a series of revolutionary projects cutting all ties with the Vienna government. Magyar nationalists bitterly opposed the satisfaction of the growing national aspirations of their Slavic subjects. The most discontented were the Croats, whose national awakening had begun when their homeland became the Illyrian Province of Napoleon's empire.

The antagonism between Croats and Magyars revealed an all-important fact about the nationalistic movements within the Hapsburg Empire. Some groups—Italians, Magyars, Czechs, Poles—resented the German-dominated government in Vienna. Others, notably the Croats and Romanians, were not so much anti-German as anti-Magyar. Here was a situation where the central government in Vienna might apply the policy of "divide and conquer," pitting the anti-Magyar elements against the anti-German Magyars, and subduing both. This was substantially what happened in 1848. A similar policy had already been used in 1846 to suppress a revolt in Galicia, the province that Austria had acquired in the partitions of Poland. When the Polish landlords revolted, their exploited Ruthenian peasants rose against them and received the backing of Vienna.

Liberalism also played a significant part in the Hapsburg revolutions, especially in Austria proper. The expanding middle class desired civil liberties, a voice in government, and the lifting of mercantilist restrictions on business. In Vienna, as in Paris and Berlin, some workers went farther and demanded radical democratic reforms.

From 1815 to 1848, the Hapsburg government virtually ignored the grumblings and protests that arose in almost every quarter of the empire. If Prince Metternich had had his way, he would probably have made some concessions to liberal and nationalist aspirations. But Metternich, though he enjoyed a nearly free hand in foreign affairs, did not have his way in domestic policy. He was blocked by the emperors—the bureaucratic Francis I (1792–1835) and the feeble-minded Ferdinand I (1835–1848)—and by the vested interests of the aristocracy. The Hapsburg government, though buttressed by an army of censors and spies, was at best an inefficient autocracy; Austria, Metternich accurately stated, was "administered, but not ruled."

The news of the February revolution in Paris shook the empire to its foundations. Four separate revolutions broke out almost simultaneously in March 1848—in Milan and Venice, in Hungary, in Vienna itself, and in Bohemia. In Hungary, Kossuth and his ardent Magyar supporters forced Emperor Ferdinand to accept the March Laws, which gave Hungary political autonomy. The March Laws instituted parliamentary government and substituted an elected legislature for the feudal Hungarian diet. They abolished serfdom and ended the immunity of nobles and gentry from taxation. But they rode roughshod over the rights of non-Magyars by making the Hungarian language a requirement for election as a deputy to the legislature.

Aroused by the Hungarian revolt, university students, together with workingmen dismayed by growing unemployment, rose in Vienna on March 12. On the next day, Prince Metternich resigned from the post he had held for thirty-nine years and fled to Britain. Although the imperial government repeatedly promised reforms, the constitution it granted seemed a half-measure at best to the Viennese insurgents. Rioting continued in Vienna, and by May the political atmosphere was so charged that Emperor Ferdinand and his family left the capital for Innsbruck. Pending the meeting of a constituent assembly in July, a revolutionary council ran affairs in Vienna.

Meanwhile, in Prague, Czech nationalists were demanding rights similar to those granted the Magyars in the March Laws. Discontent mounted with the news that the "Big German" faction in the Frankfurt Assembly was contemplating the inclusion of Bohemia in a German federation. In June 1848 the Czechs organized a Pan-Slav Congress to promote the solidarity of Slavic peoples against "Big German" encroachments. The Pan-Slav Congress set off demonstrations, in the course of which the wife of Prince Windischgrätz, the commander of the Austrian garrison of Prague, was accidentally killed (June 12, 1848). Five days later, Windischgrätz, after bombarding Prague, dispersed the Czech revolutionaries and established a military regime in Bohemia. The counterrevolution was beginning.

A month later (July), the Austrian army in Italy defeated Piedmont at Custozza. In September 1848 the Vienna Constituent Assembly, which represented all the provinces of the empire except the Italian and Hungarian, passed a great reform measure that actually accelerated the counterrevolution. It emancipated the peasants from their last remaining servile obligations, notably the requirement to work for their landlords. The peasants, the core of the Hapsburg population, had achieved their main goal; they now tended to withhold support from further revolutionary activities.

The time was ripe for the policy of "divide and conquer." In Hungary, the Germans, Slovaks, Romanians, Serbs, and Croats, all outraged by the discrimination against them in the March Laws, had risen up against the Magyars. In September 1848 the imperial government authorized Jellachich, the governor of Croatia, to invade central Hungary. While the hardfighting Magyars held off the forces of Jellachich, the radicals of Vienna revolted again, proclaiming their support of the Magyars and declaring Austria a democratic republic. But the armies of Jellachich and Windischgrätz crushed the Vienna revolution (October 31, 1848) and executed the radical leaders.

The counterrevolution was hitting its full stride. In November 1848 the energetic and unscrupulous prince Felix Schwarzenberg, the brother-in-law of Windischgrätz, became chief minister of the Hapsburg government. Schwarzenberg arranged the abdication of the incapable Ferdinand I in December and the accession of Ferdinand's eighteen-year-old nephew, the emperor Francis Joseph (1848–1916). Schwarzenberg declared that the promises made by the old emperor could not legally bind his successor and therefore shelved the projects of the Austrian

Constitutent Assembly, though he honored the Assembly's emancipation of the peasantry. Schwarzenberg's high-handedness infuriated the Magyars, who fought on like tigers. In April 1849 the Parliament of Hungary declared the country an independent republic and named Kossuth its chief executive. Russia now offered Austria military assistance, for Czar Nicholas I feared that the revolutionary contagion might spread to Russian Poland unless it was checked. Schwarzenberg accepted the czar's offer, and in August 1849 Russian troops helped to subjugate the Hungarian republic.

"The Peoples' Springtime"?

The czar boasted in 1850 that Providence had assigned him "the mission of delivering Europe from constitutional governments." By 1850, almost the whole Continent was in the process of being delivered from the regimes of 1848. In France, the Second Republic faced a very uncertain future under an ambitious president and a conservative assembly, both very much concerned with preserving order against liberty. In Prussia, Frederick William IV, and in Austria and Italy, Prince Schwarzenberg, guided the triumphant course of the counterrevolution. Kossuth, Mazzini, and other revolutionaries went into exile. In the early months of 1848, enthusiastic liberals had hailed the arrival of "the peoples' springtime." It had been a false spring.

Mazzini undertook to explain why. In 1850, he wrote from London:

Why, then, has *reaction* triumphed?
Yes: the cause is in ourselves; in our want of organisation; . . . in our ceaseless distrust, in our miserable little vanities, in our absolute want of that spirit of discipline which alone can achieve great results; in the scattering and dispersing of our forces in a multitude of small centres and sects, powerful to dissolve, impotent to found.
The cause is in the gradual substitution of the worship of material interests . . . for the grand problem of education, which alone can legitimatise our efforts. . . . It is in the narrow spirit of *Nationalism* substituted for the spirit of Nationality; in the stupid presumption on the part of each people that they are capable of solving the political, social, and economical problem alone; in their forgetfulness of the great truths

that the cause of the peoples is one; that the cause of the Fatherland must lean upon Humanity. . . . The language of narrow nationalism held at Frankfurt destroyed the German Revolution; as the fatal idea of aggrandisement of the House of Savoy [Piedmont] destroyed the Italian Revolution.*

The revolutionaries of 1848 had not fully learned the lessons of 1830. They relied on moral exhortation and pinned their hopes on spontaneous uprisings when they would have done better to concentrate on discipline and organization. Many of them were either too doctrinaire or too idealistic to make practical politicians. The strength of the revolutionary forces was sapped by the tensions between artisans and industrial workers, between radicals and moderates, between the followers of Mazzini and those of Gioberti, between "Big" and "Little" Germans, and between Magyars and Slavs.

"The narrow spirit of nationalism" deplored by Mazzini was to grow ever more intense after 1848. It was to haunt the Hapsburg Empire for the rest of its days and eventually destroy it. The failure of the liberals to unify Italy and Germany in 1848 transferred the leadership of the nationalist movements from the amateur revolutionaries to the professional politicians of Piedmont and Prussia. In the case of Italy, the transfer augured well; Piedmont, alone among the Italian states, retained the moderate constitution it had secured in 1848; in the case of Germany, the antiliberal Bismarck was to achieve through "blood and iron" what the Frankfurt Assembly had not accomplished by peaceful means.

Equally prophetic were the first indications of political solidarity on the part of the working class—the campaign in France for the right to work, with its climax in the June Days and the long roster of casualties and exiles. Europe was experiencing the challenge of the forces released by the Industrial Revolution, and new demands for drastic social and economic improvement were arising alongside the older demands for political liberties and constitutions. The year 1848 was not only the year of abortive revolution but also the year when Marx and Engels published their guidelines for future revolutions in *The Communist Manifesto*. Stormy and oppressive though it often was, 1848 was a kind of peoples' springtime.

* *Life and Writings of Joseph Mazzini* (London, 1905), III, 76–77.

Reading Suggestions on Revolution and Counterrevolution, 1815-1850

GENERAL ACCOUNTS

F. B. Artz, *Reaction and Revolution, 1814-1832,* and W. L. Langer, *Political and Social Upheaval, 1832-1852* (*Torchbooks). Comprehensive volumes in the series "Rise of Modern Europe"; with very full bibliographies.

The New Cambridge Modern History, Vols. IX and X (Cambridge Univ. Press, 1965, 1960). Chapters by many scholars, uneven in quality, but providing information on topics and areas often neglected in general surveys.

Charles Breunig, *The Age of Revolution and Reaction, 1789-1850* (*Norton). Four of the seven chapters in this recent survey relate to the topics covered in our chapter.

Jacques Droz, *Europe between Revolutions, 1815-1848* (*Torchbooks). A survey by a French scholar stressing the working of economic and social forces and their political consequences.

THE ROMANTIC PROTEST

H. Hugo, ed., *The Romantic Reader* (*Viking). Imaginatively arranged anthology with an enlightening introduction. Another good anthology is J. B. Halsted, ed., *Romanticism* (*Torchbooks), a volume in "The Documentary History of Western Civilization." In addition, the full texts of almost all the landmarks in Romantic literature mentioned in this chapter are available in paperbound editions.

Lilian R. Furst, *Romanticism in Perspective* (St. Martin's, 1969). Helpful interpretation, with chapters on the historical perspective and on individualism, imagination, and feeling.

J. Bronowski and B. Mazlish, *The Western Intellectual Tradition from Leonardo to Hegel* (*Torchbooks); C. Brinton, *The Shaping of Modern Thought* (*Spectrum); W. H. Coates and H. V. White, *The Ordeal of Liberal Humanism* (*McGraw-Hill). Three lucid reviews of intellectual history.

G. Brandes, *Main Currents in Nineteenth Century Literature,* 6 vols. (Heinemann, 1901-1905). A celebrated detailed study.

I. Babbitt, *Rousseau and Romanticism* (*Meridian). A famous hostile evaluation by a champion of the classical proprieties. May be contrasted with the even more famous chapter in A. N. Whitehead, *Science and the Modern World* (*Free Press), defending the Romantic protest on behalf of value.

George Boas, *French Philosophies of the Romantic Period* (Johns Hopkins Univ. Press, 1934). Sympathetic and instructive study.

C. Brinton, *Political Ideas of the English Romanticists* (*Ann Arbor). A perceptive analysis.

Kuno Francke, *A History of German Literature as Determined by Social Forces,* 4th ed. (Holt, 1931). Old-fashioned but very informative.

M. Raynal, *The Nineteenth Century: Goya to Gauguin* (Skira, 1951). Handsomely illustrated survey of painting.

K. Clark, *The Gothic Revival* (*Penguin). Entertaining essay, focused on Britain.

H. R. Hitchcock, *Architecture: Nineteenth and Twentieth Centuries* (Pelican, 1958). Encyclopedic study, covering both Europe and America.

A. Einstein, *Music in the Romantic Era* (Norton, 1947). Very instructive account.

P. H. Láng, *Music in Western Civilization* (Norton, 1941). Massive volume, stressing relations between music and other aspects of civilization.

Jacques Barzun, *Berlioz and His Century,* rev. ed. (*Meridian). The career of the famous composer used to exemplify the quality of the age of romanticism.

CONSERVATISM AND
THE VIENNA SETTLEMENT

G. Bertier de Sauvigny, *Metternich and His Times* (Darton, Longman, and Todd, 1962). By a French expert on conservatism.

A. J. May, *The Age of Metternich,* rev. ed. (*Holt). Brief appraisal by an American expert on Hapsburg history.

H. F. Schwarz, ed., *Metternich, the Coachman of Europe: Statesman or Evil Genius?* (*Heath). Instructive cross section of contradictory interpretations.

Mack Walker, ed., *Metternich's Europe* (*Torchbooks). Useful collection of sources; a volume in "The Documentary History of Western Civilization."

E. L. Woodward, *Three Studies in European Conservatism* (Constable, 1929). Thoughtful essays on Metternich, Guizot, and the Catholic church in the nineteenth century.

P. Viereck, *Conservatism Revisited* (*Free Press). Sympathetic reappraisal.

H. Nicolson, *The Congress of Vienna* (*Compass); G. Ferrero, *The Reconstruction of Europe* (*Norton). Detailed studies of the settlement of 1814–1815.

H. A. Kissinger, *A World Restored* (*Universal). Efforts of the conservative forces to restore the European balance, 1812–1822.

THE MAJOR
CONTINENTAL STATES

G. Bertier de Sauvigny, *The Restoration* (Univ. of Pennsylvania Press, 1966). Sympathetic detailed interpretation of France under Louis XVIII and Charles X.

F. B. Artz, *France under the Bourbon Restoration, 1814–1830* (Harvard Univ. Press, 1931). Less friendly analysis from the liberal standpoint.

M. R. D. Leys, *Between Two Empires* (Longmans, 1955). Brief survey of French social and political history, 1814–1848.

T. E. B. Howarth, *Citizen-King* (Eyre and Spottiswoode, 1961). Biography of Louis Philippe.

D. Johnson, *Guizot: Aspects of French History, 1787–1874* (Routledge, 1963). Illuminating biography of the French conservative liberal.

R. Carr, *Spain, 1808–1939* (Clarendon, 1966). Scholarly account.

A. J. Whyte, *The Evolution of Modern Italy* (*Norton). Sound introduction.

D. Mack Smith, ed. *The Making of Italy, 1796–1870* (*Torchbooks). Excellent volume in "The Documentary History of Western Civilization"; compiled by a ranking expert on the subject.

G. Salvemini, *Mazzini* (*Collier). Sympathetic analysis. May be supplemented by the selections from Mazzini's writings in I. Silone, ed., *The Living Thoughts of Mazzini* (Longmans, 1939).

H. Treitschke, *History of Germany in the Nineteenth Century,* 7 vols. (McBride, Nast, 1915–1919). Very detailed and colorful, very Prussian and nationalistic in tone. A good brief antidote is A. J. P. Taylor, *The Course of German History* (*Capricorn).

T. S. Hamerow, *Restoration, Revolution, Reaction* (*Princeton Univ. Press). Scholarly reevaluation of German economics and politics, 1815–1871.

R. H. Thomas, *Liberalism, Nationalism, and the German Intellectuals* (Cambridge Univ. Press, 1952). Good study of the period 1822–1847.

W. O. Henderson, *The Zollverein* (Univ. of Chicago, 1959). The standard work on the subject.

J. C. Legge, ed., *Rhyme and Revolution in Germany* (Constable, 1918). Lively anthology of German history and literature, 1813–1850.

C. A. Macartney, *The Habsburg Empire, 1790–1918* (Macmillan, 1969). By a ranking expert in the field.

A. J. P. Taylor, *The Habsburg Monarchy, 1809–1918* (*Torchbooks). Spirited brief treatment.

A. G. Mazour, *The First Russian Revolution* (*Stanford Univ. Press), and Marc Raeff, *The Decembrist Movement* (Prentice-Hall, 1966). Valuable studies of the abortive coup of 1825 and its background.

C. M. Woodhouse, *The Greek War of Independence* (Hutchinson, 1952). Readable short account.

THE REVOLUTIONS OF 1848

G. Fasel, *Europe in Upheaval: the Revolutions of 1848* (*Rand McNally). Up-to-date concise account.

Priscilla Robertson, *Revolutions of 1848: A Social History* (*Torchbooks). Uneven narrative, valuable for stressing the role taken by women and by students.

R. Postgate, *Story of a Year: 1848* (Oxford Univ. Press, 1956). A lively and well-illustrated chronicle.

M. Kranzberg, ed., *1848: A Turning Point?* (*Heath). Diverse evaluations as to whether or not Europe failed to turn.

G. Rudé, *The Crowd in History, 1730–1848* (*Wiley). Includes a chapter on the socioeconomic background of the Parisian demonstrators of 1848.

G. Duveau, *1848: The Making of a Revolution* (*Vintage). By a leading French scholar.

L. B. Namier, *1848: The Revolution of the Intellectuals* (*Anchor). Trenchant essay castigating liberals, especially in Germany, for their illiberal attitudes.

P. H. Noyes, *Organization and Revolution* (Princeton Univ. Press, 1966). Enlightening study of working-class disunity in Germany.

R. J. Rath, *The Viennese Revolution of 1848* (Univ. of Texas Press, 1957). Detailed monograph.

20

The Industrial Revolution

I   The Stages of Economic Growth

The Most Important Event in World History?

On May 1, 1851, in London, Queen Victoria opened the Great Exhibition of the Works of Industry of All Nations. The first of many world's fairs, this international exposition displayed the latest mechanical marvels in a setting that was itself a marvel of engineering—the Crystal Palace, a structure of iron and glass stretching like a mammoth greenhouse for more than a third of a mile in Hyde Park. To the visitors who thronged the Crystal Palace it was evident that Britain was, as she claimed, the workshop of the world. Her exhibits featured mechanical wonders, while those of the continental states stressed traditional arts and crafts. To succeeding generations the London exhibition marked the heyday of British leadership in the Industrial Revolution. Machines

Above: Jeremy Bentham, 1823. Above right: Membership card of the International Workingmen's Association bearing the signature of Karl Marx in his capacity of corresponding secretary for Germany, 1869. Right: "Work," by Ford Madox Brown, 1852.

and factories had already begun to change the face of Britain in the late eighteenth century; since 1851 they have transformed not only Britain and other Western nations but also many other countries on the globe.

By the mid-nineteenth century revolutionary changes in technology and business organization were exerting a revolutionary impact on politics and society. Industrialism bound nations closer together by stimulating international trade and by lowering the barriers of distance through improved transport and communication. Yet it heightened international tensions by fortifying nationalism with economic appetite and by inspiring a bloodless war for markets and raw materials. Businessmen demanded that governments pursue policies that would augment profits, and they sought the political rights that would give them a voice in determining those policies. By making goods cheaper and more plentiful, industrialism raised standards of living and enabled increasing numbers of men to enjoy the decencies and comforts of existence. But it also created problems of unemployment, low wages, and bad living and working conditions. Laborers clamored for the right to work, the right to organize, to strike, and to vote.

The rise of industry and labor inspired divergent schools of economic and social thought. The classical economists advocated laissez-faire, preaching that the state should let the economy regulate itself, and that what was good for business was bound to be good for labor, too. If a worker wanted economic security and political status, he should win them through his own efforts, by getting rich, as Guizot had advised the citizens of the July Monarchy. Humanitarian liberals, exemplified by John Stuart Mill, on the other hand, believed that state intervention in economic life might sometimes be justified to protect or assist the working class. The prospect of moderate reform and of gradual advance toward democracy offered by these liberals satisfied some workers. Others, however, hoping for swifter achievement of their goals, favored the more drastic but still peaceful changes of the type recommended in Louis Blanc's "social workshops" and in the blueprints of his fellow utopian socialists. Still others embraced revolutionary socialism, the violent and inevitable class war predicted by Marx and Engels.

The Industrial Revolution thus brought to the fore economic and political issues still alive today. It created a new labor problem and intensified the older farm problem. It sharpened the differences between the champions of relatively free international trade and the economic nationalists who demanded protective tariffs. It divided liberals into the opponents and the defenders of the benevolent or welfare state. It created a radical wing of the working class, soon to be split between the rival schools of utopian and Marxian socialism. It altered the course of human history even more profoundly than did a great political upheaval like the French Revolution. The British economic historian E. J. Hobsbawm calls it "probably the most important event in world history, at least since the invention of agriculture and cities." *

Not all historians agree with Hobsbawm. 1776 and 1789 still have their champions, and others, including the present authors, suggest that the Industrial Revolution was only part of a great modern revolution also involving expansion overseas, the scientific leap forward during the "century of genius," the Enlightenment's faith in progress, and the attempts of Americans and Frenchmen to translate it into reality. In any case, it is hard to deny that the changes launching industry on its modern course produced a revolutionary impact on Western history.

Preparation and Take-off

What has made some historians shy away from the term "Industrial Revolution" is the fact that these economic changes occurred both too slowly and too peacefully to be called revolutionary. But the American economic historian W. W. Rostow, in his influential analysis *The Stages of Economic Growth*, has introduced the idea of an economic "take-off," when old inhibiting factors are overcome, production expands rapidly, and the economy moves into a long period of sustained growth. This crucial phase may be compressed into a relatively short period: In Britain, Rostow concludes, the economy "took off" in the two decades following 1783, a time span not greatly exceeding that of the American or French revolutions.

The relative abruptness of the "take-off" contrasted with the centuries of preparation that preceded it. The preparatory stage has been traced all the way back to the monasteries of the early Middle Ages, which, by their insistence on

* *The Age of Revolution, 1789–1848* (Mentor), p. 46.

discipline and on the performance of specified tasks at specified times, have been likened to a model for the organization of the labor force in a mine or mill. The factors that prepared Europe and America for industrialism included, obviously, the capitalism of medieval and Renaissance bankers and merchants, and the colonialism and mercantilism of the sixteenth and subsequent centuries. Less obviously, they also included most of the forces that shaped the early modern world. The rise of the competitive state system, the Protestant stress on hard work, the brushing aside of tradition by the scientists of the seventeenth century and by the philosophes of the eighteenth—all played their part in creating a society ready for sweeping economic changes.

Britain's Head Start

Why was Britain the first state to "take off"? Why not France, which was richer and much more populous, or the Dutch Republic, the "economic schoolmaster" of seventeenth-century Europe? Rostow summarizes the answers:

The Dutch became too committed to finance and trade, without an adequate manufacturing base. . . .
What about the French? They were too rough with their Protestants. They were politically and socially too inflexible. . . . The best minds and spirits of eighteenth-century France . . . had to think about political, social and religious revolution rather than economic revolution. Moreover, the French were committed heavily to ground warfare in Europe; and they cheated on shipping and naval strength at an historical moment when ships mattered greatly.
And so Britain, with more basic industrial resources than the Netherlands; more nonconformists, and more ships than France; with its political, social, and religious revolution fought out by 1688—Britain alone was in a position to weave together cotton manufacture, coal and iron technology, the steam-engine and ample foreign trade to pull it off.*

Rostow also suggests that English victories over a series of foreign enemies and competitors—over the Church of Rome and the Spain of Philip II in the sixteenth century, the Dutch in the

_____
* *The Stages of Economic Growth* (Cambridge, 1960), p. 33.

seventeenth, and the French in the eighteenth—gave English national self-confidence and drive a major boost.

More particular factors also accounted for Britain's head start in industrial development. She had ample supplies of capital from the profits of foreign and colonial trade. She possessed large and easily available deposits of coal and iron; the geographical compactness of the British Isles made shipments from mine to smelter and from mill to seaport short and cheap. Britain had a large reservoir of potential factory labor in the marginal farmers, driven off the land by the enclosure movement, and in the Irish, emigrating from their poverty-ridden and overcrowded island. The commercial and naval leadership gained by Britain in the eighteenth century and fortified by the French Revolutionary and Napoleonic Wars paved the way for her industrial leadership. It facilitated the search for raw materials and markets, and the profits from overseas trade and the empire swelled investment in industry. The wars themselves stimulated demand for metal goods and the invention of new machines. And the construction of great docks along the lower Thames during the wars entrenched London in its position as the greatest economic center in Europe.

Finally, it has also been argued, the fact that Britain did not have the rigid and elaborate centralized administrative structure found in France and other continental countries permitted more flexibility in accepting new enterprises. While this argument probably exaggerates the rigidity of the Old Regime on the Continent, the fact remains that the casual, almost slipshod, quality of British local government could be an asset. If, for example, a capitalist who wanted to set up a factory found himself blocked by vested interests in one locality, he simply went to another, where the local authorities were more agreeable. Thus it was that Manchester, which had the barest minimum of governmental apparatus in the eighteenth century, became the textile capital not only of Lancashire but also of the world.

Cotton Manufacture and the Steam Engine

The textile industry was the first to exploit the potentialities of power-driven machinery. Beginning with the spinning jenny of the 1760's the use of machinery gradually spread to other processes. In 1793, the American Eli Whitney devised the cotton gin, an engine that separated the fibers of the raw cotton from the seeds and enabled a single slave to do what had previously required the hand labor of fifty slaves. Meanwhile, British inventors perfected a power-driven loom for weaving cotton thread into cloth. By 1830, Britain operated more than 50,000 power looms, and cotton goods accounted for half of her exports. The British census of 1851 listed more than half a million workers employed in cotton manufacturing alone.

Advances in mechanical engineering made this rapid expansion possible. Earlier, for instance, the difficulty of securing exactly fitting parts had hampered the use of machines like Watt's steam engine. Then British engineers studied the precision techniques used by watchmakers. They devised a lathe that turned screws of almost perfect regularity, and they developed machines for sawing, boring, and turning the pulley blocks used by British vessels in the Napoleonic Wars. Eli Whitney, meantime, was undertaking important experiments at his arms factory in Connecticut. He explained that he

Mule spinning in a Lancashire mill, 1834.

planned to "make the same parts of different guns, as the locks, for example, as much like each other as the successive impressions of a copperplate engraving." In other words, Whitney was utilizing the concept of standardized parts, one of the basic principles of mass production.

It is important to realize that not all processes in an industry "took off" at the same time. The revolutionary implications of Whitney's experiments with standardization, for example, were long ignored by manufacturers; the survival of handicraft techniques also slowed down the process of mechanization. Even in cotton, weaving on the hand loom long continued in districts with a large reservoir of cheap labor, like Ireland and central Europe, where peasants could produce cloth in their cottages. In the woolen and clothing industries mechanization did not come until the 1850's, when Britain produced a machine for wool-combing and an American, Isaac Singer, popularized the sewing machine.

Coal and Iron

Coal ranked with cotton as an industry that pioneered in the solution of technical problems. Steam engines pumped water from the mines; ventilating shafts and power fans supplied them with fresh air; and safety lamps gave miners protection against dangerous underground gases. The coal output of Britain, then the world's leading producer, rose steadily from about 16,000,000 tons in 1816, to 30,000,000 in 1836, and 65,000,000 in 1856. The consumption of coal mounted because of its increased use as a household fuel in wood-short Britain, its importance in producing steam power, and its vital contribution to the expanding iron industry. Large quantities of coal were needed to make the coke used in smelting.

The efficiency of smelting advanced rapidly after the development of the blast furnace (1828), in which fans provided a blast of hot air to intensify the action of the hot coke on the iron. Thanks to the blast furnace, Britain produced iron strong enough for use in bridges and in factory buildings. Yet the best grade of iron lacked the tremendous strength of steel, which is iron purified of all but a minute fraction of carbon by a process of prolonged, intensive heating. Steel for industrial purposes could be made in

The Soho Engineering Works at Birmingham, England, where James Watt and Matthew Boulton manufactured steam engines, 1775–1800.

the early 1800's, but only by ruinously expensive methods. Then in 1856 Bessemer, an Englishman of French extraction, invented the converter, which accelerated the removal of impurities by shooting jets of compressed air into the molten metal. A decade later, Siemens, a German living in England, devised the "openhearth" process, which utilized scrap as well as new iron, and which handled larger amounts of metal than the converter could. The inventions of Bessemer and Siemens lowered the cost of making steel so substantially that the world output increased tenfold between 1865 and 1880.

Transport and Communication

The railroad consumed large amounts of iron and steel (on the average, 300 tons were required for a single mile of track). The revolution in transport began early in the nineteenth century with the growth of canals and hard-surfaced roads. During the century's first three decades many hundreds of miles of canals were dug in Europe and in North America, and highway construction was improved by a Scot, McAdam, who devised the durable road surface of broken stones that still bears his name. Shippers, how-

ever, also required a means to convey overland heavy items like coal and iron; the railroad furnished the solution. In the 1820's, methods of rolling rails and constructing solid roadbeds were already known, and only mechanization remained to be accomplished. Then George Stephenson and others put the steam engine on wheels and created the locomotive. In 1830, Stephenson's "Rocket" demonstrated its power by running twelve miles in fifty-three minutes on the new Liverpool and Manchester Railway, the first line to be operated entirely by steam. The railroad building boom was soon in full swing: Britain had 500 miles of track in 1838, 6,600 miles in 1850, and 15,500 in 1870.

Steam also revolutionized water transport, though more gradually. Fulton's steamboat, the *Clermont,* made a successful trip on the Hudson River in 1807, and soon paddle-wheel steamers plied the inland waterways of the United States and Europe. Ocean-going steamships, however, were uneconomical to operate because of the inefficiency of the marine engine. When the Scot Samuel Cunard inaugurated the first regular transatlantic steamer service (between Liverpool and Boston in 1840), the coal required for the voyage took up almost half of the space on his vessels. Consequently, only passengers and mails went by steamship; most freight was still handled in sailing ships, like the beautiful and efficient American clippers. Finally, in the 1860's, the development of improved marine engines and the substitution of the screw propeller for the cumbersome paddle wheel forecast the eventual doom of the commercial sailing vessel. All these improvements in transport by sea and land greatly aided industry by facilitating shipments of raw materials and finished products and by opening up almost the whole world as a potential market.

Meanwhile, communications were also experiencing radical improvements. A beginning was made in 1840, when Great Britain inaugurated the penny post: to send a letter from London to Edinburgh, for instance, now cost only a penny, less than a tenth the old rate. More dramatic was the utilization of electricity for instantaneous communication. An impressive series of "firsts" started with the first telegraph message, from Baltimore to Washington in 1844. Then came the first submarine cable, under the English Channel in 1851; the first transatlantic cable, 1866; and the first telephone, 1876.

Money, Banking,
and Limited Liability

The exploitation of all these new inventions and discoveries required a constant flow of fresh capital. From the first, the older commercial community supported the young industrial community. The slave traders of Liverpool financed the cotton mills of Manchester and other nearby towns in Lancashire, thereby increasing the demand for American raw cotton and for slaves to grow the cotton. Tobacco merchants of Glasgow provided the funds that made their city the foremost industrial center of Scotland, and tea merchants in London and Bristol aided the iron-masters of South Wales. Bankers played such an important role that Disraeli, the British politician, listed the Barings of London and the international house of Rothschild among the great powers of Europe. In the early nineteenth century each of the five Rothschild brothers, sons of a German Jewish banker, established himself in an important economic center—London, Paris, Frankfurt, Naples, and Vienna. The Rothschilds prospered because, in an age of frequent speculation, they avoided unduly risky undertakings, and because they facilitated investment by residents of one state in the projects of other states. The Paris Rothschild, for instance, negotiated the investment of British capital in the construction of French railroads during the 1840's.

Banks further assisted economic expansion by promoting the use of checks and banknotes in place of specie. During the Napoleonic Wars, when the shortage of coins forced some British millowners to pay their workers in goods, the British government empowered local banks to issue paper notes supplementing the meager supply of coins. But whenever financial crises occurred—and they came frequently before 1850 —dozens of local banks failed and their notes became valueless. Parliament therefore encouraged the absorption of small shaky banks by the larger and more solid institutions, and in 1844 it gave the Bank of England a virtual monopoly of the issuing of banknotes, thus providing a very reliable paper currency. It also applied, first to railroads and then to other companies, the principle of limited liability, indicated by the familiar "Ltd." after the name of British firms. Earlier, the shareholders in most British companies had incurred unlimited liability: they might find their personal fortunes appropriated to satisfy the creditors of an unsuccessful company. The practice of limiting each shareholder's liability to the value of his shares encouraged investment by diminishing its risks.

The End of Britain's
Head Start

In the mid-nineteenth century, the tangible signs of Britain's economic predominance were evident on every hand—in the teeming London docks, in the thriving financial houses of the City, in the exhibits at the Crystal Palace, in the mushrooming factory and mining towns of the Midlands, the North of England, and Scotland, and in other quarters of the globe as well. British

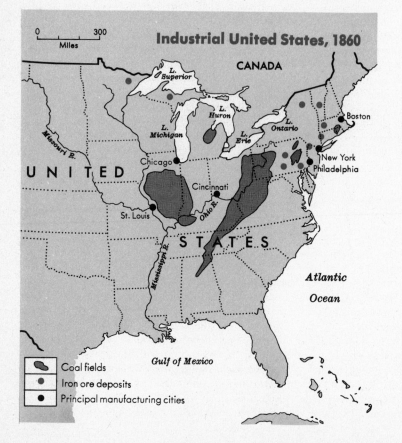

Industrial United States, 1860

0 — 300 Miles

CANADA

L. Superior

L. Huron

L. Michigan

L. Ontario

L. Erie

Boston

New York

Philadelphia

Chicago

Cincinnati

St. Louis

Missouri R.

Mississippi R.

Ohio R.

UNITED STATES

Atlantic Ocean

Gulf of Mexico

Coal fields

Iron ore deposits

Principal manufacturing cities

capital and thousands of skilled British workers participated in the construction of French railroads. American trains ran on rails rolled in British mills and on the capital from British investors. Cotton goods made in Lancashire clothed a sizable part of the world's population, and British entrepreneurs and inventors brought the Industrial Revolution to Belgium and parts of Germany.

Britain, even in the heyday of her leadership, did not monopolize inventive skill. Frenchmen, for example, devised the chlorine process of bleaching cloth and the Jacquard loom for weaving intricate patterns. German technicians led the world in agricultural chemistry and in the utilization of the valuable by-products of coal. And from the United States came Eli Whitney and the cotton gin, Morse and the telegraph, Singer and the sewing machine, and Cyrus McCormick, whose reaper (1831) was the first of many agricultural machines developed in America.

In a sense, the whole North Atlantic world, European and American, constituted an economic community. As one member of that community, Britain, matured, other members would be going through the stage of "take-off." After 1850, therefore, Britain began to lose the advantage of her head start and soon began to feel with increasing sharpness the pinch of competition. W. W. Rostow estimates that by 1850 three states were in the process of take-off—Belgium, France, and the United States, or more exactly the northeastern and midwestern states, which enjoyed an immense economic advantage over the South in the Civil War. Germany's take-off began about 1850 and was completed after the final lift provided by the country's triumphant unification as the German Empire in 1871. By the turn of the century the North Atlantic world was facing the prospect of losing the advantages of its head start as Japan and czarist Russia were engaged in "take-off."

The details of Rostow's timetable of industrialization do not satisfy all the experts, who suggest some shifts in dates and modifications that would underline the fact that "take-off" was often a rather lopsided and undramatic affair. This, of course, is the normal academic way of testing and refining a hypothesis. The figure of "take-off" remains a very useful one because it expresses so well the fact that economic growth proceeded erratically, with sudden bursts of activity. And in our own century the idea of "take-off" has fired the imagination of people in less developed countries all over the world, who yearn to share in the prosperity and status of becoming significant industrial states.

II The Economic and Social Impact of Industrialization

The Agricultural Revolution

The industrial and agricultural revolutions have always been interdependent. Industry relies on a more efficient agriculture for raw materials and for additions to its labor force, recruited from surplus workers no longer needed on mechanized farms; agriculture depends on industry for the tools and fertilizers that enable fewer and fewer men to produce more and more and transform farms into agrarian factories. In the nineteenth century, factory-made implements like the steel plow and the reaper improved the cultivation of old farmlands and permitted the opening of vast new areas, like the North American prairies, that could scarcely have been touched if the pioneers had had to rely on hand labor. The mechanical cream separator raised the dairy industry to a big business, and railroads and steamers sped the transport of produce from farm to market. The processes of canning, refrigeration, and freezing, all industrial in origin and all first applied on a wide scale during the last third of the century, permitted the preservation of many perishable commodities.

Farmers found a steadily growing market both in the industrial demand for raw materials and in the food needs of the mining and factory towns. International trade in farm products increased rapidly during the second half of the nineteenth century. The annual export of wheat from the United States and Canada rose from 22,000,000 bushels in the 1850's to 150,000,000 in 1880. Imported flour accounted for a quarter of the bread consumed in Britain during the 1850's and for half in the 1870's. Denmark and the Netherlands increasingly furnished the British table with bacon, butter, eggs, and cheese; Australia supplied its mutton and Argentina its beef.

Germany now partly assumed Britain's old role as the pioneer of scientific agriculture. German experimenters, shortly after 1800, extracted sugar from beets in commercially important quantities, thus ending Europe's dependence on the cane sugar of the West Indies. In the 1840's the German chemist Liebig published a series of influential works on the agricultural applications of organic chemistry. Plant growth, Liebig argued, depended on three basic elements— nitrogen, potassium, and phosphorus. But the production of crops and fodder leached these elements from the soil: unless they could be returned to it, fertile lands might go the way of "the once prolific soil of Virginia, now in many parts no longer able to grow its former staple productions—wheat and tobacco." Liebig's warnings promoted the wide use of fertilizers— guano from the nesting islands of sea birds off the west coast of South America, nitrate from Chile, and potash from European mines.

Farming progressed and prospered in the nineteenth century as never before. Yet the agricultural revolution exacted a price, sometimes a very high price. Faced with the competition of beet sugar, the sugar-cane islands of the West Indies went into a depression from which some of them have never fully recovered. In the highly industrialized countries the social and political importance of agricultural interests began to decline. Farming was no longer the principal occupation of Englishmen in the nineteenth century, and land was no longer the almost universal yardstick of wealth and power. The manufacturers and merchants of Britain scored a decisive victory over the landed gentry in the campaign to repeal the Corn Laws, the tariffs on the importation of the wheat and other cereals which the

English term collectively "corn." The powerful Anti-Corn Law League protested that the tariffs "artificially enhance the price of food," and "prevent the exchange of the products of industry for the food of other countries." Free trade was the remedy prescribed by the Anti-Corn Law League, and free trade came when Parliament repealed the Corn Laws in 1846. The decisive factor was the disastrous attack of black rot that ruined the Irish potato crop two years running and made the importation of cheap grain imperative to prevent the worsening of an already disastrous famine in Ireland.

The Population Explosion and the Standard of Living

When Britain thus abandoned any pretense of growing all the basic foods her people needed, her population was growing so rapidly that self-sufficiency was no longer possible. Despite substantial emigration, the number of inhabitants in England and Wales more than tripled during the course of the nineteenth century, from about 9,000,000 in 1800 to 32,500,000 in 1900. Scholars are still arguing about the reasons why and whether the Industrial Revolution was responsible. Some demographers have claimed that the British population explosion in the nineteenth century may be attributed not to a higher birth rate but to the lowered death rate resulting from the improved food and sanitation—especially cheap washable cotton materials—brought by industrialism. Others claim that neither diet nor sanitation improved until the second half of the century and that the population increase in the first half may be attributed to the rural areas and not to the cities, which had a much higher death rate. It is also pointed out that in Russia, still an agrarian country in the preparatory preindustrial state of growth, the population increased proportionately almost as fast as it did in Britain (36,000,000 in 1800, about 100,000,000 in 1900).

A similar controversy is focused on the extent to which the industrial revolution improved the standard of living, not just of the new capitalist and managerial classes but of the workers themselves. So far as the facts can be disengaged from the rather sketchy statistical data, they suggest that the overall standard of living in Britain did not begin a steady improvement until after the Napoleonic wars and the immediate postwar slump. From about 1820 on the purchasing power of the worker seems to have grown very slowly, as more goods and cheaper ones became available. At the same time, opportunities for steady regular employment also grew, as did the chances for the laborer to climb up the economic ladder a rung or two by mastering a skill enabling him to hold a better-paying job. But all these factors varied in their effect from industry to industry and from one locality to another; they also fluctuated with the ups and downs of the economic cycle. Many people appear to have felt that their standard of living was declining.

There is little debate about one most important social result of industrialism—the truly revolutionary changes it caused in the structure and balance of the population. Wherever mines and factories were opened, towns and cities appeared. Large areas of once-rural England became urban England, and a similar transformation was beginning in the lowlands of Scotland around Glasgow, in the northern French plain around Lille, in the German Rhineland, and along the rivers of the northeastern United States. The growth of an urban population caused a rise in the numbers and influence of the two social classes that form the backbone of an industrial society. These are the businessmen and the workingmen. Industrialists, bankers, investors, managers, and promoters of every sort joined the already established capitalists to form the modern middle class or bourgeoisie. Millhands, railwaymen, miners, clerks, and a host of other recruits swelled the ranks of wage-earning laborers.

The impact of capital and labor upon the life of industrial nations was becoming increasingly evident by the middle of the nineteenth century. Some of the signs pointed to steady material progress—the wonders of the Crystal Palace, or the conquest of space by the railroad, the steamship, and the telegraph. Other signs, however, portended serious dislocation and violent change. The repeal of the Corn Laws buried an old agrarian way of life in Britain. The collapse of the French railroad boom in the late 1840's suggested that in an industrial society economic slumps might have alarming consequences, for the hundreds of thousands thrown out of work aggravated the political unrest in Paris and, as we have seen, formed part of the background of the June Days of 1848.

Middle-Class Grievances and Aspirations

Both businessmen and workingmen nourished grievances—and aspirations. A revealing view of middle-class complaints and hopes is given in a famous parable published in 1819 by the French social planner, Saint-Simon. Saint-Simon supposed that France suddenly lost fifty of her best mechanical engineers, of her finest architects, doctors, bankers—and so on through a long list comprising the three thousand leading men in business, science, and the arts. These men, Saint-Simon stated, are "the most useful to their country"; "the nation would become a lifeless corpse as soon as it lost them."

Let us pass on to another assumption. Suppose that France preserves all the men of genius that she possesses in the sciences, fine arts and professions, but has the misfortune to lose in the same day Monsieur the King's brother [and many other members of the royal family]. Suppose that France loses at the same time all the great officers of the royal household, all the ministers (with or without portfolio), all the councillors of state, all the chief magistrates, marshals, cardinals, archbishops, bishops, vicars-general, judges, and, in addition, ten thousand of the richest proprietors who live in the style of nobles.

This mischance would certainly distress the French, because they are kind-hearted, and could not see with indifference the sudden disappearance of such a large number of their compatriots. But this loss of thirty thousand individuals, considered to be the most important in the State, would only grieve them for purely sentimental reasons and would result in no political evil for the State.

These suppositions underline the most important fact of present politics: . . . that our social organization is seriously defective. . . .

The scientists, artists, and artisans, the only men whose work is of positive utility to society, and cost it practically nothing, are kept down by the princes and other rulers who are simply more or less incapable bureaucrats. Those who control honours and other national awards owe, in general, the supremacy they enjoy, to the accident of birth, to flattery, intrigue and other dubious methods. . . .

These suppositions show that society is a world which is upside down.*

To the men of the middle class, society indeed seemed upside down. In the Britain of the 1820's the new industrialists had small opportunity to mold national policy. Booming industrial cities like Manchester and Birmingham sent not a single representative to the House of Commons. A high proportion of businessmen belonged not to the Church of England but to non-Anglican Protestant "chapels"; nonconformists, as these dissenters were now termed, still suffered discrimination when it came to holding public office or sending their sons to Oxford or Cambridge. Even in France, despite the gains made since 1789, the bourgeois often enjoyed only the second-class status sketched by Saint-Simon.

The middle classes very soon won the place in the sun which they felt they deserved. In Britain, the gradual process of reform gave them substantially all they wanted. The high spot, higher even than the repeal of the Corn Laws, was the Reform Bill of 1832, which extended the suffrage to the middle class, as the next chapter will show. In 1830, the French bourgeois got their citizen-king, and their Belgian counterparts scored a very great advance in political power. Elsewhere, both in 1830 and 1848, middle-class gains were less dramatic, but the class usually retrieved something after the dust of counter-revolution had settled—Piedmont, for example, kept its constitution granted in 1848.

Working-Class Grievances and Hopes

The grievances of workingmen were more numerous than those of their masters, and they were more difficult to satisfy. The difficulties may be illustrated by the protracted struggle of laborers to secure the vote and the right to organize and to carry on union activities. In Britain, substantial numbers of workers first secured the vote in 1867, a generation after the enfranchisement of the wealthier middle class. In France, universal male suffrage was tried for a

* Saint-Simon, *Selected Writings*, ed. F. M. H. Markham (New York, 1952), pp. 72–74.

brief period starting in 1848; it became permanent only with the establishment of the Third Republic after 1870. The unified German Empire had a democratic suffrage from its inception in 1871, but without some other institutions of democracy. Elsewhere, universal manhood suffrage came slowly—not until 1893 in Belgium, and not until the twentieth century in Italy, Austria, Russia, and even in Sweden, Denmark, and the Netherlands, which we are apt to assume have always been in the van of democratic progress.

During most of the nineteenth century, labor unions and strikes were regarded as improper restraints on the free operation of natural economic laws. Hence the specific ban on such combinations, as they were termed, imposed by the British Combination Acts at the close of the eighteenth century. Continental governments imposed similar restrictions: witness the Le Chapelier Law passed by the French National Assembly in 1791. It took labor a long time to win legal recognition of union activities—until 1890 in Germany, for instance, 1867 in Austria, and 1872 in the Netherlands. In France, the July Monarchy repressed strikes with great brutality; the Le Chapelier Law was finally relaxed in the 1860's and repealed outright in 1884. In Britain, Parliament modified the Combination Acts early, in the 1820's but did not repeal them until 1876.

Labor's drive for political and legal rights, however, was only a side issue during the early days of the Industrial Revolution. Many workmen faced more pressing problems: they had to find jobs and to make ends meet on inadequate wages. The modern Western world had long experienced the business cycle, with its alternations of full employment and substantial layoffs. The Industrial Revolution intensified the cycle. Boom periods became more hectic, and the general depressions, like that of the late 1840's, became more frequent and more severe. Factories at

"Hurrying Coal": A girl drawing a loaded wagon of coal weighing between 200 and 500 pounds underground in a Yorkshire mine, 1842.

first made little attempt to provide a fairly steady level of employment. When a batch of orders came in, machines and men were worked to capacity until the orders were filled; then the factory simply shut down to await the next batch.

A century and more ago labor sometimes got such low wages that a family man might have to put both his children and his wife to work as a matter of sheer economic necessity. Humanitarian tradition probably exaggerates the extent to which industry exploited and degraded women and children, probably tends to view the exceptional instance of extreme hardship as the average situation. Nevertheless, exploitation and degradation did occur. Here is the testimony of a factory worker. Samuel Coulson, before a British parliamentary committee in 1831–1832:

At what time in the morning, in the brisk time, did those girls go to the mills? *In the brisk time, for about six weeks, they have gone at 3 o'clock in the morning, and ended at 10, or nearly half-past, at night.*

What intervals were allowed for rest or refreshment during those nineteen hours of labour? *Breakfast a quarter of an hour, and dinner half an hour, and drinking a quarter of an hour.*

Was any of that time taken up in cleaning the machinery? *They generally had to do what they call dry down; sometimes this took the whole of the time at breakfast or drinking, and they were to get their dinner or breakfast as they could; if not, it was brought home.*

Had you not great difficulty in awakening your children to this excessive labour? *Yes, in the early time we had them to take up asleep and shake them when we got them on the floor to dress them, before we could get them off to their work; but not so in the common hours.*

What was the length of time they could be in bed during those long hours? *It was near 11 o'clock before we could get them into bed after getting a little victuals, and then at morning my mistress used to stop up all night, for fear that we could not get them ready for the time. . . .*

So that they had not above four hours' sleep at this time? *No, they had not.*

For how long together was it? *About six weeks it held; it was only done when the throng was very much on; it was not often that.*

The common hours of labour were from 6 in the morning till half-past eight at night? *Yes.*

With the same intervals for food? *Yes, just the same.*

Were the children excessively fatigued by this labour? *Many times; we have cried often when we have given them the little victualling we had to give them; we had to shake them, and they have fallen to sleep with the victuals in their mouths many a time.*

Did this excessive term of labour occasion much cruelty also? *Yes, with being so very much fatigued the strap was very frequently used.*

What was the wages in the short hours? *Three shillings a week each.*

When they wrought those very long hours what did they get? *Three shillings and sevenpence halfpenny.*

For all that additional labour they had only sevenpence halfpenny a week additional? *No more.* *

Excessively long hours, low pay, rigorous discipline, and subhuman working conditions were the most common grievances of early industrial workers. Many plants neglected hazards to their employees, few had safety devices to guard dangerous machinery, and cotton mills maintained both the heat and the humidity at an uncomfortable level because threads broke less often in a hot, damp atmosphere. Many workers could not afford decent housing, and if they could afford it, they could not always find it. Some of the new factory towns were reasonably well planned, with wide streets and space for yards and parks. Some even had a copious supply of good water and arrangements for disposing of sewage. But many had none of these necessities, and in rapidly growing London the Thames soon became an open sewer so foul that riverside dwellers were reluctant to open their windows. Fantastic numbers of human beings were jammed into the overcrowded slums of Lille in France and of Liverpool and Manchester in Lancashire.

Lord Shaftesbury, an English reformer of the 1840's, predicted that, unless conditions were improved, Lancashire would soon become a "province of pigmies." It was estimated that the life expectancy of a boy born to a working-class family in Manchester was only half that of one born to rural laborers. The industrial nations also threatened to remain nations of semiliterates. Until they made provisions for free public schools, during the last third of the nineteenth century, education facilities were grossly inadequate. In England, as often as not, only the Sunday school gave the millhand's child a chance to learn his ABC's. The millhand himself, if he had great ambition and fortitude, might attend one of the adult schools known as "mechanics' institutes." No wonder that in the 1840's a third of the men and half of the women married in England could not sign their names on the marriage register and simply made their mark. And no wonder that Disraeli, the Tory reformer, in his novel *Sybil* (1845), called Britain "two nations"—the rich and the poor.

III   The Responses of Liberalism

"The Dismal Science"

Faced with the widening cleavage between rich and poor, nineteenth-century liberals at first held to the doctrine of laissez-faire.

Suffering and evil are nature's admonitions; they cannot be got rid of; and the impatient attempts of benevolence to banish them from the world by legislation . . . have always been productive of more evil than good.†

Such was the argument advanced by liberals in the British Parliament against the first piece of legislation proposed to safeguard public health. The thinkers who advanced these ideas in the early nineteenth century are known to history as the classical economists; to their enemies they were the architects of "the dismal science." The most famous of them were two Englishmen, Thomas Malthus (1766-1834) and David Ricardo (1772-1823).

"Dismal science" is hardly too strong a term for the theories of Malthus. Educated for the ministry, Malthus became perhaps the very first professional economist in history; he was hired by the East India Company to teach its employees at a training school in England. In 1798 Malthus published the famous *Essay on the Principles of Population,* a dramatic warning that the human species would breed itself into starvation.

---

* Bland, Brown, and Tawney, *English Economic History: Select Documents* (London, 1915), pp. 510–513.

† *The Economist,* May 13, 1848.

In the *Essay*, Malthus formulated a series of natural laws:

The power of population is indefinitely greater than the power in earth to produce subsistence for man.

Population, when unchecked, increases in a geometrical ratio. Subsistence only increases in an arithmetical ratio. . . . Through the animal and vegetable kingdoms, nature has scattered the seeds of life abroad with the most profuse and liberal hands. She has been comparatively sparing in the room and the nourishment necessary to rear them. . . . Necessity, that imperious, all-pervading law of nature, restrains them within the prescribed bounds. Among plants and animals its effects are waste of seed, sickness, and premature death. Among mankind, misery and vice.*

Misery and vice would spread, Malthus believed, because the unchecked increase in human numbers would lower the demand for labor and therefore lower the wages of labor.

When the wages of labour are hardly sufficient to maintain two children, a man marries and has five or six. He of course finds himself miserably distressed. He accuses the insufficiency of the price of labour to maintain a family. . . . He accuses the partial and unjust institutions of society, which have awarded him an inadequate share of the produce of the earth. He accuses perhaps the dispensations of Providence, which have assigned to him a place in society so beset with unavoidable distress and dependence. In searching for objects of accusation, he never adverts to the quarter from which his misfortunes originate. The last person that he would think of accusing is himself, on whom in fact the whole of the blame lies. . . .†

The reduction of the human birth rate was the only hope that this prophet of gloom held out to suffering humanity. It was to be achieved by "moral restraint," that is, by late marriage and by "chasity till that period arrives."

Ricardo, too, was a prophet of gloom. He attributed economic activity to three main forces: there was rent, paid to the owners of great natural resources like farmland and mines; there was profit, accruing to the enterprising individuals who exploited these resources; and there were wages, paid to the workers who performed the actual labor of exploitation. Of the three, rent was in the long run the most important. Farms and mines would become depleted and exhausted, but their produce would continue in great demand. Rent, accordingly, would consume an ever larger share of the "economic pie," leaving smaller and smaller portions for profit-making capitalists and wage-earning workers.

Ricardo tempered his grim forecasts with qualifications and reservations. For instance, he did not believe that the size of the economic pie was necessarily fixed and thus did not subscribe entirely to the mercantilist idea that the total wealth of mankind was severely limited, so that more for one human unit meant less for another. And yet he did sketch a picture of eventual stagnation. While Adam Smith had cheerfully predicted an increasing division of labor, accompanied by steadily rising wages, Ricardo, in contrast, brought labor and wages under the Malthusian formula:

The market price of labour is the price which is really paid for it, from the natural operation of the proportion of the supply to the demand; labour is dear when it is scarce, and cheap when it is plentiful. . . It is when the market price of labour exceeds its natural price, that the condition of the labourer is flourishing and happy. . . . When, however, by the encouragement which high wages give to the increase of population, the number of labourers is increased, wages again fall to their natural price, and indeed . . . sometimes fall below it.*

Ricardo's disciples hardened this principle into the "Iron Law of Wages," which bound workmen to an everlasting cycle of high wages and large families, followed by an increase in the labor supply, a corresponding increase in the competition for jobs, and an inevitable slump in wages. Ricardo himself, however, regarded the cycle not as an Iron Law but simply as a probability. Unforeseen factors might in the future modify its course and might even permit a gradual improvement of the worker's lot.

What particularly separated the classical economists of the early nineteenth century from

---

* *Essay on the Principles of Population*, Book I, chap. 1.
† Ibid., Book IV, chap. 3.

* *On the Principles of Political Economy*, Chap. V in *The Works and Correspondence of David Ricardo*, ed. P. Sraffa (Cambridge, England, 1951), I, 94.

their eighteenth-century predecessors was their overall pessimism. Like the philosophes, they did not doubt that natural laws were superior to manmade laws and that laissez-faire was the best policy, but, unlike them, they no longer viewed nature as the creation of the beneficent God of the deists. To these adherents of the "dismal science" nature was at best a neutral force and at worst a sinister one. Man himself—wasteful, careless, improvident—seemed once more afflicted with a kind of original sin. The classical economists supplied a needed corrective to the naïve optimism of the philosophes.

Yet the classical economists, too, had their naïve faith. They viewed the economy as a world-machine governed by a few simple, almost unalterable laws—Malthusian laws of population, Ricardian laws of rent and wages. The history of the last hundred years has demonstrated the inadequacy of their view. The size of the economic pie has expanded far beyond the expectations of Ricardo, and so have the portions allotted to rent, to profit, and to wages. Malthus did not foresee that scientific advances would make the output of agriculture expand at a nearly geometrical ratio. He did not foresee that the perils of increasing birthrates would sometimes be averted by the use of contraceptives, first popularized during the nineteenth century, or by recourse to emigration. Many millions of people moved from crowded Europe to lightly populated America during the nineteenth century. The exodus from overcrowded Ireland, in particular, continued so briskly after the famine of the 1840's that by 1900 the Irish population was little more than half what it had been fifty years earlier.

Although the classical economists did not take sufficient account of the immense changes being worked by the agricultural and industrial revolutions, their laissez-faire liberalism won particular favor with the new industrial magnates. The captains of industry were perhaps disturbed by Ricardo's prediction that profits would inevitably shrink; but they could take comfort from the theory that "suffering and evil" were "nature's admonitions." It was consoling to the rich to be told, in effect, that the poor deserved to be poor because they had indulged their appetites to excess, that whatever was, was right, or at any rate ordained by nature. To the working class, the vaunted freedom of laissez-faire often meant freedom to be under-nourished, ill-housed, and alternately overworked and unemployed. The poor did not like to hear that they deserved to be poor, and they sometimes felt that whatever was, was wrong and needed to be remedied, if necessary by interference with natural laws, no matter how sacred.

To sum up: in the face of positive social evils, the classical economists offered only the essentially negative policy of laissez-faire. They were often very earnest men, honestly convinced that letting nature take her course was the only thing to do. Yet they were open to the accusation of acting without heart and without conscience, and of advancing economic theories that were only rationalizations of their economic interests. It is not surprising that, as a practical and social political philosophy, strict laissez-faire liberalism today is almost extinct.

Bentham and Utilitarianism

The retreat from laissez-faire originated with a man who was himself the friend and patron of the classical economists—Jeremy Bentham (1748–1832). Bentham behaved as popular opinion expects an eccentric philosopher to behave, astonishing his guests by trotting and bobbing about the garden before dinner, or, as he put it, performing his "anteprandial circumgyrations." He directed that at death his body be mummified and kept at the University College of London, which he had helped to found. In life, he projected dozens of schemes for the improvement of the human race, among them a model prison and reformatory which he called the "Panopticon," because guards stationed in a central block could survey the activities of all the inmates. He coined new words by the dozen, too; some of them have been happily forgotten but others have made valuable contributions to the language, like "minimize," "codify," and "international."

Bentham founded his social teachings on the concept of utility, a modern form of the Epicurean doctrines of antiquity:

Nature has placed mankind under the governance of two sovereign masters, *pain* and *pleasure*. It is for them alone to point out what we ought to do. . . . They govern us in all we can do, in all we say, in all we think: every effort we can make to throw off our subjection, will serve but to demonstrate and confirm it. . . . The *principle of utility* recognizes this subjection, and assumes it for the foundation of that system, the object of which is to rear the fabric of felicity by the hands of reason and of law. . . .

The interest of the community is one of the most general expressions that can occur in the phraseology of morals: no wonder that the meaning of it is often lost. . . . The community is a fictitious *body,* composed of the individual persons who are considered as constituting as it were its *members*. The interest of the community then is, what?—the sum of the interests of the several members who compose it.

It is in vain to talk of the interest of the community without understanding what is the interest of the individual. A thing is said to promote the interest, or to be *for* the interest of an individual, when it tends to add to the sum total of his pleasures: or, what comes to the same thing, to diminish the sum total of his pains.*

Bentham listed a dozen or so simple pleasures and pains—the pleasures of the senses and the pains of deprivation, the pleasure of wealth and the pain of impoverishment, the pleasure of skill and the pain of awkwardness, and so on. Each category was subdivided, the pleasures of the senses, for instance, into those of taste, intoxication, smelling, touching, hearing, seeing, sex, health, and novelty. And each pleasure or pain could be evaluated according to its intensity, its duration, its certainty or uncertainty, its propinquity or remoteness, its fecundity, and its purity. This "felicific calculus," as Bentham termed it, was a good example of the Enlightenment's attempts to measure the immeasurable and to apply the exact methods of natural science to the subtleties of human behavior.

Nevertheless, Bentham was no doctrinaire philosophe and had no patience with attempts to equate ethical principles with nature's laws. He made short work of the French revolutionaries' Declaration of the Rights of Man: "*Natural rights* is simple nonsense: natural and imprescriptible rights, rhetorical nonsense,—nonsense upon stilts." He dismissed the eighteenth-century theory of political contracts as a mere fiction. Ordinarily, he believed, governments could best safeguard the well-being of the community by following a hands-off policy. In social and eco-

nomic matters, they should act as "passive policemen," and give private initiative a generally free hand. Here a close and sympathetic relationship existed between Bentham and the classical economists. Yet Bentham realized that the state might become a more active policeman when the pursuit of self-interest by some individuals worked against the best interest of other individuals. If the pains endured by the many exceeded the pleasures enjoyed by the few, then the state should step in. In such a situation Bentham believed the state to be, in a word of his own devising, "omnicompetent," fit to undertake anything for the general welfare. Twentieth-century doctrines of the welfare state owe a considerable debt to his utilitarianism.

By the time of his death, Bentham was already gaining an international reputation. He had advised reformers in Portugal, Russia, Greece, and Egypt, and his writings were to exert a broad influence, particularly in France, Spain, and the Spanish-American republics. As late as 1920, his "Panopticon" provided the plan for an American prison (in Joliet, Illinois). Naturally, his most important disciples were English. The middle-class group called the Philosophic Radicals pressed for parliamentary legislation to reform and simplify court procedures and local government. Their aims, however, were sometimes so narrowly utilitarian that critics claimed they wanted to drain life of all its savor and variety.

Mill and Humanitarian Liberalism

Charles Dickens, an informed and compassionate observer of industrial England, stated most eloquently the case against the dehumanized sameness implicit in the teachings of the utilitarians and the laissez-faire liberals. Here from his novel *Hard Times* (1854), is his famous description of Coketown, which might have been any one of England's burgeoning industrial cities:

It contained several large streets all very like one another, and many small streets still more like one another, inhabited by people equally like one another, who all went in and out at the same hours, with the same sound upon the same pavements, to do the same work, and to whom every day was the same as yesterday and to-morrow,

* *An Introduction to the Principles of Morals and Legislation,* ed. Wilfrid Harrison (New York, 1948), pp. 125-127.

"Over London by Rail": An 1872 engraving after Gustave Doré showing the living conditions of the working class.

and every year the counterpart of the last and the next.

You saw nothing in Coketown but what was severely workful. If the members of a religious persuasion built a chapel there—as the members of eighteen religious persuasions had done—they made it a pious warehouse of red brick. . . . All the public inscriptions in the town were painted alike, in severe characters of black and white. The jail might have been the infirmary, the infirmary might have been the jail, the town-hall might have been either, or both, or anything else, for anything that appeared to the contrary in the graces of their construction. Fact, fact, fact, everywhere in the material aspect of the town; fact, fact, fact everywhere in the immaterial. The M'Choakumchild school was all fact, and the relations between master and man were all fact, and everything was fact between the lying-in hospital and the cemetery, and what you couldn't state in figures, or show to be purchaseable in the cheapest market and saleable in the dearest, was not, and never should be, world without end, Amen.*

Dickens saw what was wrong; John Stuart Mill (1806–1873) thought he knew what could be done to put it right.

Mill grew up in an atmosphere dense with the teachings of utilitarianism and classical economics. From his father, who worked closely with Bentham and was a good friend of Ricardo,

* Book I, chap. v.

762

he received an education almost without parallel for intensity and speed. He began the study of Greek at three, was writing history at twelve, and at sixteen organized an active "Utilitarian Society." At the age of twenty the overworked youth suffered a breakdown; as Mill relates in his *Autobiography,* he had become "a mere reasoning machine." So Mill turned for renewal to music and to the poetry of Wordsworth and Coleridge; presently he fell in love with Mrs. Taylor, a woman of warm personality, to whom he assigned the major credit for his later writings. They remained friends for twenty years until the death of Mr. Taylor at length enabled them to marry. Mill's personal history is important, for it goes far to explain why he endowed the liberal creed with the warmth and humanity it had lacked.

Mills' humane liberalism was expressed most clearly in his essay *On Liberty* (1859) and his *Autobiography* (1873). But it is evident, too, in his more technical works, notably *The Principles of Political Economy.* He first published this enormously successful textbook in 1848 and later revised it several times, each revision departing more and more from the "dismal science" of Ricardo and Malthus. The first edition of the *Principles* rejected the gloomy implications of the Iron Law of Wages:

By what means, then, is poverty to be contended against? How is the evil of low wages to be remedied? If the expedients usually recommended for the purpose are not adapted to it, can no others be thought of? Is the problem incapable of solution? Can political economy do nothing, but only object to everything, and demonstrate that nothing can be done?*

Of course something could be done, and Mill proceeded to outline schemes for curbing overpopulation by promoting emigration to the colonies and by "elevating the habits of the labouring people through education."

This one example is typical of the way in which Mill's quest for positive remedies led him to modify the laissez-faire attitude so long associated with liberalism. Although he did not accept the ultimate socialistic solution of abolishing private property, he sympathized with the French "National Workshops" of 1848 and with some of the socialistic blueprints that we shall examine shortly. He asserted that the workers should be allowed to organize trade unions, form cooperatives, obtain higher wages, and even receive a share of profits. These changes could best be secured within the framework of private enterprise, Mill believed, and not by public intervention. But he also believed that there were some matters so pressing that the state would have to step in. He read the reports of parliamentary investigating committees, like that on child labor cited earlier in this chapter, and he was shocked by their accounts of human degradation. So he recommended legislation to protect children and to improve intolerable living and working conditions.

Whereas Bentham had expected universal suffrage and universal education would be possible only in the distant future, Mill made them immediate objectives. All men, he believed, should have the right to vote; all should be prepared for it by receiving a basic minimum of schooling, if need be at state expense. Moreover, women should have the same rights—for Mill was a pioneer in the movement for feminine emancipation, thanks in part to his esteem for Mrs. Taylor. He also proposed the introduction of proportional representation in the House of Commons, so that political minorities might be sure of a voice and might not be overwhelmed by the tyranny of the majority. The proposal and the fears that actuated it are particularly characteristic of Mill. He made protection of the individual's rights the basis of his famous essay *On Liberty:*

A government cannot have too much of the kind of activity which does not impede, but aids and stimulates, individual exertion and development. The mischief begins when, instead of calling forth the activity and powers of individuals and bodies, it substitutes its own activity for theirs; when, instead of informing, advising, and, upon occasion, denouncing, it makes them work in fetters, or bids them stand aside and does their work instead of them. The worth of a State, in the long run, is the worh of the individuals composing it . . . a State which dwarfs its men, in order that they may be more docile instruments in its hands even for beneficial purposes—will find that with small men no great thing can really be accomplished. . . . *

---

* Book II, chap. xiii (Boston, 1848).

* *Utilitarianism, Liberty, and Representative Government,* Everyman ed. (New York, 1910), pp. 169–170.

Critics have claimed that Mill's eloquent defense of the dissenting individual had undemocratic implications, for he seemed to mistrust the opinions of the majority and to favor those of the intellectual elite. Yet Mill's fear of excessive state power and the hopes he placed in enlightened individuals kept him firmly in the liberal tradition. He did not so much reject laissez-faire liberalism as endow it with new sensitivity and flexibility. He had a more tender conscience than Adam Smith, Ricardo, or Bentham, and he lived at a later age, when the defects of industrialism were plainer. Therefore he found the exceptions to the rule of laissez-faire more numerous and urgent than had his predecessors. Liberalism, as we understand the term today, is the legacy not of the "dismal scientists" but of Mill and other political thinkers and of the enlightened politicians who have shaped modern Western democracies.

IV   The Socialist Responses

What Is Socialism?

In his later years, Mill referred to himself as a socialist; by his standard, however, most of us are socialists today. Universal suffrage for men and for women, universal free education, the curbing of laissez-faire in the interests of the general welfare, the use of the taxing power to limit the accumulation of masses of private property—all these major reforms foreseen by Mill are now widely accepted. But they are not authentically socialistic. The authentic socialist does not stop, as Mill did, with changes in the *distribution* of wealth; he goes on to propose a radical change in arrangements for the *production* of goods. The means of production are to be transferred from the control of individuals to the control of the community as a whole.

Socialism—like fascism, liberalism, democracy —is one of those words in the political vocabulary so laden with moral connotations and personal conviction that their real meaning is often obscured. Everyone uses the word, yet mostly to indicate emphatic approval or disapproval of a given policy. The historian attempts to use the word neutrally, for purposes of description and not of passing judgment. Historically, socialism denotes any philosophy that advocates the vesting of production in the hands of society and not those of private individuals. In practice, it usually means that the state, acting as the trustee of the community, owns major industries like coal, railroads, and steel. Socialism in its most complete form involves public ownership of almost all the instruments of production including the land itself, virtually eliminating private property.

Today we tend to call this complete form communism. In the mid-nineteenth century, however, the terms "socialism" and "communism" were used almost interchangeably. Over a hundred years of history have gone into making the distinction now usually drawn between the two, which is not simply a matter of more and less complete versions of the same thing. Especially since the Bolshevik Revolution in Russia in 1917, a communist has come to mean someone who believes that the collectivization of property can only be accomplished swiftly and violently, by revolution and outright seizure, while a socialist has come to mean someone who believes that it should be accomplished gradually and peacefully through normal political procedures and with at least some compensation for private owners. Though the ends have their similarities, the means are worlds apart. This highly significant difference started to appear long before 1917, with the development of two divergent schools of socialist thought in the mid-nineteenth century, the Utopian and the Marxian.

The Utopian socialists were essentially good sons of the Enlightenment. If only men would apply their reason to solving the problems of an industrial economy, if only they would wipe out manmade inequalities by letting the great natural law of brotherhood operate freely—then utopia would be within their grasp, and social and economic progress would come about almost automatically. This is the common belief linking together the four chief Utopians of the early nineteenth century—Saint-Simon, Fourier, Robert Owen, and Louis Blanc.

Saint-Simon

Henri, count of Saint-Simon (1760–1825), belonged to a French noble family so old and aristocratic that it claimed direct descent from Charlemagne. Educated by philosophes, Saint-Simon fought with the French army in the American War of Independence. During the French Revolution he won a large fortune by speculating in lands expropriated from the Church and the émigrés, then lost most of it through the trickery of an unscrupulous partner. Despite his own reverses, he never lost his enthusiasm for the industrial age.

In accordance with the parable quoted earlier in this chapter, Saint-Simon would have given supreme political authority to a Parliament of Improvements, composed of ten industrialists and five each of artists, philosophers, chemists, physiologists, physicists, astronomers, and mathematicians, and presided over by one of the mathematicians. He admonished the members of the new elite: "Christianity commands you to use all your powers to increase as rapidly as possible the social welfare of the poor!"* Reform should come peacefully, through "persuasion and demonstration," and it should affect particularly the rich drones of society, "parasites" who "prey" on the actual producers. Combining the Enlightenment's respect for science with Romanticism's zeal for the community, Saint-Simon proclaimed the one science transcending all others to be the application of the Golden Rule. Since even men of different nations were brothers, Saint-Simon envisaged a federation of European states. It would start with a union of the most advanced countries, France and Britain, under the "Council of Newton," and would culminate in the establishment of a European parliament when all states had been "organized" to the point where they could live together in "harmony."

"Organization," "harmony," and "industry" were three of Saint-Simon's catchwords. When all three elements were coordinated, he believed, mankind could achieve some of the major improvements he proposed, among them great net-

works of highways and waterways. After Saint-Simon's death, his followers focused on the strain of social Christianity in his teaching and formed a fantastic religious cult under the leadership of Prosper Enfantin. Saint-Simon's enthusiasm for public improvements proved more lasting, and Enfantin himself combined local railroads into the great trunk line, the Paris-Lyons-Mediterranean. Another Saint-Simonian was Ferdinand de Lesseps, who organized the digging of the Suez Canal and made an abortive start at digging across the Isthmus of Panama. The very vagueness of Saint-Simon's concepts, and his failure to define them precisely, permitted almost every kind of social thinker, from laissez-faire liberal to communist, to cite him with approval. Among his most enthusiastic disciples were Mazzini, Louis Blanc, the Russian revolutionary pioneer Herzen, and the French positivist philosopher Comte. What was socialistic about Saint-Simon was his goal of achieving the reorganization and harmony of society as a whole, rather than merely improving the well-being of some of its individual members.

Fourier

Saint-Simon's compatriot and contemporary, Fourier (1772–1837), also extolled harmony, and to achieve it drew up an elaborate blueprint. At the French textile center of Lyons, Fourier was shocked by the wealth of the silk manufacturers and the misery of their workmen. At Paris, he was shocked when he found that a single apple cost a sum that would have bought a hundred apples in the countryside. Clearly, he concluded, something was amiss in a society and economy that permitted such fantastic divergences. He compared the historical importance of his apple with that of Newton, and honestly believed himself to be the Newton of the social sciences. Just as Newton had found the force holding the heavenly bodies in a state of mutual attraction, so Fourier claimed discovery of the force holding the individuals of human society in a state of mutual attraction.

This force was *l'attraction passionnelle:* human beings are drawn to one another by their passions. Fourier drew up a list of passions, rather like the list of pleasures in Bentham's "felicific calculus"—sex, companionship, food, luxury,

---

* Saint-Simon, *Selected Writings*, ed. F. M. H. Markham (New York, 1952), p. 116.

variety, and so on, to a total of 810. Since existing society thwarted their satisfaction, Fourier proposed its remodeling into units that he called *phalanges*, "phalanxes," each containing 400 acres of land and accommodating 500 to 2,000 human beings. Volunteers would form a phalanx by setting up a community company, agreeing to split its profits three ways—five-twelfths to those who did the work, four-twelfths to those who undertook the management, and three-twelfths to those who supplied the capital.

Fourier's phalanx, with its relatively generous rewards to managers and capitalists, fell short of complete equality. Yet it did assign to labor the largest share of the profits, and it foreshadowed many other features of socialist planning. Each phalanx would be nearly self-sufficient, producing in its own orchards, fields, and workshops most of the things required by its inhabitants. Adult workers who performed the most dangerous or unpleasant tasks would receive the highest remuneration. The inhabitants of the phalanx were to live in one large building, a sort of apartment hotel, which Fourier called a *phalanstère*. The phalanstère would provide the maximum opportunity for the satisfaction of man's sociable passions, and it would also make the routine of daily living more efficient by substituting one central kitchen for hundreds of separate ones. The sordid features of housekeeping could be left to little boys, who loved dirt anyway and would cheerfully form squads to dispose of garbage and refuse.

Other details of the phalanx bore witness to Fourier's reaction against the kind of monotony pictured in Dickens' Coketown. Places of work would be made as pleasant as possible by frequent, colorful redecoration. Members of the phalanx would change their jobs eight times a day because of the human predisposition to the *passion papillonne* (butterfly passion)—"enthusiasm cannot be sustained for more than an hour and a half or two hours in the performance of one particular operation." They would work from four to five in the morning to eight or nine at night, enjoying five meals, plus snacks. They would need only five hours of sleep, since the delightful variety of work would not tire them and the days would not be long enough to permit them to taste all the pleasures of life. It would all be so healthy that physicians would be superfluous and everyone would live to the age of 140.

Fourier made substantial contributions to socialist theory and to social psychology. Some of his recommendations, like higher pay for dangerous jobs and devices for relieving the tedium of work, have become common practice in the modern business world. In the short run, however, he tended to make utopian socialism seem identical with "free love" and therefore, in the popular mind, with the grossest immorality. Both to eliminate the evil of prostitution and to allow human association the fullest possible scope, Fourier advocated complete sexual freedom in the phalanx; he recommended marriage only for the elderly, whose passions had begun to cool.

Owen

One of the greatest Utopians was a self-made British businessman, Robert Owen (1772–1858). When he was still in his twenties, Owen took over the large cotton mills at New Lanark in Scotland. Although the former owner of the mills had been accounted benevolent by the standards of the day, conditions there shook Owen to the core. A large part of the working force consisted of children who had been recruited from orphanages in Edinburgh when they were between six and eight years old. Although the youngsters did get a little schooling after hours, Owen found many of them "dwarfs in body and mind." Adult laborers at New Lanark fared little better.

Owen set out to show that he could increase his profits and increase the welfare of his laborers at the same time. He made New Lanark over into a model industrial village. For the adults he provided better working conditions, a ten-and-a-half-hour day, higher pay, and cleaner and roomier housing. He restrained the traditional Scottish Saturday night brawl by closing down the worst drinking places, making good liquor available at cheap prices, and punishing offenders who made themselves a public nuisance. As for the children, he raised the minimum age for employment to ten, hoping ultimately to put it at twelve, and he gave his child laborers time for some real schooling. His educational preferences followed Rousseau; advanced bookish subjects were avoided, while crafts, nature study, and other utilitarian subjects received much attention. A properly educated nation, Owen believed, would confute the gloomy predictions of Mal-

Factory in Tewkesbury, England, around 1860. Note the rules posted on the wall.

thus, who "has not told us how much more food an intelligent and industrious people will create from the same soil, than will be produced by one ignorant and ill-governed."*

Owen inherited much of the optimism of the philosophes; he also inherited some of their failures and disappointments. Despite his own success as a philanthropic capitalist, few businessmen followed his example. Disappointed but not disheartened, Owen drew up plans for an idealized version of New Lanark, very much like Fourier's phalanx. He called his utopia a parallelogram, for the buildings were to be arranged in that geometrical pattern. It was to be a voluntary organization, relatively small in size, neatly balanced between farming and industry, and decidedly advanced in Owen's recommendation for the partial abandonment of conventional ties of marriage and the family. In the 1820's, Owen visited America to finance an abortive effort to set up a parallelogram at New Harmony, Indiana. Undaunted by this failure, he spent the rest of his career publishing and supporting projects for social reform. He advocated the association of all

labor in one big union—an experiment that failed; and he sought to reduce the expenditures of workingmen by promoting the formation of consumers' cooperatives—an experiment that succeeded. He also offended many of his contemporaries by his advocacy of sexual freedom, by his Voltairean attacks on established religion, and by his enthusiasm for spiritualism.

Both Owen and Fourier attracted followers not only in their native lands but also in the United States, where religious sects were already launching ventures in communal living. The American Fourierists included many intellectuals, among them the crusading editor Horace Greeley and the poet John Greenleaf Whittier. They sponsored more than thirty attempts to set up phalanxes; two celebrated ones were Brook Farm, near Boston, and Phalanx, near Red Bank, New Jersey. America also witnessed more than half a dozen Owenite experiments in addition to New Harmony. Like it, however, most of these utopias did not prosper very long; and the few that were firmly established returned to conventional ways of individual profit-taking and family life.

Owen and Fourier relied on private initiative to build the model communities that they so

* Robert Owen, *A New View of Society* (Glencoe, Illinois, 1948), pp. 174–175.

New Harmony, Indiana, 1855. Robert Owen's model community ended up looking much like any other American town.

supervise the purchase of productive equipment and the formation of "social workshops"; it would withdraw its support and supervision once the workshops were on their feet. As the workshops gradually spread throughout France, socialistic enterprise would replace private enterprise, profits as such would vanish, and labor would be the only class in society.

Much of Louis Blanc's socialism is typically Utopian; he, too, relies on the workers to make their own arrangements for communal living. The real novelty of his plan lies in the role assigned to the state. With Blanc, socialism is beginning to move away from the realm of philanthropy and into the realm of politics. Ironically, politics were to prove his undoing. We have already seen that the "national workshops" of 1848 were a relief project wrongly identified by alarmed conservatives as an effort to implement his "social workshops." After the June Days in Paris, Louis Blanc was forced into exile.

Marx

With Karl Marx (1818–1883) socialism assumed its most intense form—revolutionary communism. Whereas the early socialists had anticipated a gradual and peaceful evolution toward utopia, Marx forecast a sudden and violent proletarian uprising, by which the workers would capture governments and make them the instruments for securing proletarian welfare. Dogmatic and cocksure, Marx was certain that he alone knew the answers and that the future of mankind would develop inevitably according to the pattern which he found in human history. His self-confidence, his truculence, and the fact that he was born at Trier, in the Prussian Rhineland, have earned him the label "the Red Prussian."

Marx found three laws in the pattern of history. First, *economic determinism:* he believed that economic conditions largely determined the character of all other human institutions—society and government, religion and art. Second, *the class struggle:* he believed that history was a dialectical process, a series of conflicts between antagonistic economic groups. In his own day the antagonists were the "haves" and the "have-nots"—the propertied bourgeois and the propertyless proletarians, who, possessing nothing but their working skills, had nothing to fall back on in

hopefully expected to become widely copied examples for the reconstruction of society. Expecting some millionaire to finance his phalanxes, Fourier vainly kept a daily office hour for ten years to receive him. Saint-Simon, with his stress on "organization," presumably meant to give government a larger role; his follower, Louis Blanc, explicitly advocated intervention by the state to achieve utopia.

Louis Blanc

Author of a pioneering history of the French Revolution from the socialist standpoint, and implacable critic of the bourgeois policies of the July Monarchy, Louis Blanc (1811–1882) projected a scheme for "social workshops." He outlined it first in a pamphlet, *The Organization of Labor* (1839). "What proletarians need," he wrote, "is the instruments of labor; it is the function of government to supply these. If we were to define our conception of the state, our answer would be that the state is the banker of the poor."* The government would finance and

---

* "L'Organisation du Travail," in *The French Revolution of 1848*, ed. J. A. R. Marriott (Oxford, 1913), I, 14. Our translation.

Karl Marx.

Hegelian dialectic into the language of economic determinism and the class struggle. In his own day he believed that capitalistic production and the bourgeoisie comprised the thesis; the antithesis was the proletariat; and the synthesis, issuing from the communist revolution, would be true socialism. In later years Marx summarized his relation to Hegel:

My dialectic method is not only different from the Hegelian but is its direct opposite. To Hegel, the life-process of the human brain, . . . which, under the name of "the Idea," he even transforms into an independent subject, is the demiurgos of the real world, and the real world is only the external, phenomenal form of "the Idea." With me, on the contrary, the ideal is nothing else than the material world reflected by the human mind, and translated into forms of thought. . . .

The mystification which dialectic suffers in Hegel's hands, by no means prevents him from being the first to present its general form of working in a comprehensive and conscious manner. *With him it is standing on its head. It must be turned right again,* if you would discover the rational kernel within the mystical shell.*

By the time Marx was thirty, he had completed the outlines of his theory of scientific, revolutionary socialism. He had also become a permanent exile from his native Germany. On leaving the University of Berlin, he worked for a newspaper at Cologne in the Prussian Rhineland, then moved to Paris in 1843 after his atheistic articles had aroused the authorities against him. Exiled again, because the government of Louis Philippe feared his antibourgeois propaganda, he went to Brussels in 1845. Wherever he happened to be, he read widely in the economists of the past and talked with the socialists and other radicals of his own generation.

Everything Marx read and everyone he met strengthened his conviction that the capitalistic order was unjust, rotten, doomed to fall. From Adam Smith's labor theory of value he concluded that only the worker should receive the profits from the sale of a commodity, since the value of the commodity should be determined by the labor of the man who produced it. The Iron Law of Wages, however, confirmed Marx's belief that

bad times and were thus at the mercy of their masters. Third, *the inevitability of communism:* he believed that the class struggle was bound to produce one final upheaval that would raise the victorious proletariat over the prostrate bourgeoisie in eternal triumph.

The Marxian philosophy of history derived from many older schools of thought. Although Marx himself was born and died in the nineteenth century, he belonged in spirit partly to the eighteenth. Both his grandfathers were rabbis, but his father was a deist and a skeptic who trained him in the rationalism of the Enlightenment. Marx early acquired the kind of faith in natural law that had characterized the philosophes. In his case it was faith in the natural laws of economic determinism and the class struggle, fortified by the materialistic teachings of the anti-Christian philosopher Feuerbach, who proclaimed that "Man ist was er isst" (One is what one eats). From all this followed the boast made by Marx and his disciples that their socialism alone was "scientific," as opposed to the Romantic doctrines of the Utopians.

The Romantic philosophy of Hegel, however, provided the intellectual scaffolding of Marxism. Although Hegel had died in 1831, his influence permeated the University of Berlin during Marx's student days (1836–1841). Marx translated the

* Preface to the second edition of *Capital,* Modern Library ed. (New York, n.d.), p. 25. Our italics.

capitalism would never permit the worker to receive this just reward. And from reading other economists and observing the depression of the late 1840's, he concluded that economic crises were bound to occur again and again under a system that allowed capital to produce too much and labor to consume too little.

Engels and "The Communist Manifesto"

Meanwhile, Marx began his long friendship and collaboration with Friedrich Engels (1820–1895). In many ways, the two men made a striking contrast. Marx was poor and quarrelsome, a man of few friends; except for his devotion to his wife and children, he was utterly preoccupied by his economic studies. Engels, on the other hand, was the son of a well-to-do German manufacturer and represented the family textile business in Liverpool and Manchester. He loved sports, women, and high living. But he also hated the iniquities of industrialism and, when he met Marx, had already written a bitter study, *The Condition of the Working Class in England,* based on his first-hand knowledge of affairs in Manchester.

Both Engels and Marx took an interest in the Communist League, a small international organization of radical workingmen. In 1847, the London office of the Communist League requested them to draw up a program. Engels wrote the first draft, which Marx revised from start to finish; the result, published in January, 1848, was *The Manifesto of the Communist Party*. Today, more than a century later, it remains the classic statement of Marxian socialism.

The *Manifesto* opens with the dramatic announcement that "A spectre is haunting Europe —the spectre of Communism." It closes with a stirring and confident appeal:

Let the ruling classes tremble at a Communist revolution. The proletarians have nothing to lose but their chains. They have a world to win.

Workingmen of all countries, unite!

In the few dozen pages of the *Manifesto*, Marx and Engels rapidly block in the main outlines of their theory. "The history of all hitherto existing society," they affirm, "is the history of class struggle." Changing economic conditions determined that the struggle should develop successively between "freeman and slave, patrician and plebeian, lord and serf, guildmaster and journeyman." The guild system gave way first to manufacture by large numbers of small capitalists and then to "the giant, modern industry."

Modern industry will inevitably destroy bourgeois society. It creates a mounting economic pressure by producing more goods than it can sell; it creates a mounting social pressure by narrowing the circle of capitalists to fewer and fewer individuals and depriving more and more people of their property and forcing them down to the proletariat. These pressures increase to the point where a revolutionary explosion occurs, a massive assault on private property. Landed property will be abolished outright; other forms of property are to be liquidated more gradually through the imposition of severe income taxes and the abolition of inherited wealth. Eventually, social classes and tensions will vanish, and "we shall have an association in which the free development of each is the condition for the free development of all."

"The free development of each is the condition for the free development of all"—the *Manifesto* provides only this vague description of the society that would exist after the revolution. Since Marx defined political authority as "the organized power of one class for oppressing another," he apparently expected that, in the famous phrase, "the state would wither away" once it had created a classless regime. He also apparently assumed that the great dialectical process of history, having achieved its final synthesis, would then cease to operate in its traditional form. But, readers of the *Manifesto* may inquire, how is this possible? Will not the dialectic continue forever creating economic and political theses and antitheses? Will not the state always be with us? To these questions Marx offered no satisfactory answer beyond the implication that somehow the liquidation of bourgeois capitalism would radically alter the course of history and transform humanity.

Marx oversimplified the complexities of human nature by trying to force it into the rigid mold of economic determinism and ignoring the nonmaterial motives and interests of men. Neither proletarians nor bourgeois have proved to be the simple economic stereotypes Marx supposed them to be. Labor has often behaved in scandalously un-Marxian fashion and assumed a markedly bourgeois outlook and mentality. Capital has put its own house in better order—and eliminated the worst injustices of the factory system. No more than Malthus did Marx foresee the notable rise in the standard of living that began in the mid-nineteenth century and has continued, with an occasional backward slip, down to our own day.

Marx never made a greater mistake than when he failed to observe the growing strength of nationalism. The *Manifesto* confidently expected the class struggle to transcend national boundaries. In social and economic warfare, nation would not be pitted against nation, nor state against state; the proletariat everywhere would fight the bourgeoisie. "Workingmen have no country" and "national differences and antagonisms are vanishing gradually from day to day." In Marx's own lifetime, however, national differences and antagonisms were increasing rapidly from day to day. Within a few months of the publication of the *Manifesto,* the revolutions of 1848 disclosed the antagonism between Italians and Austrians, Austrians and Hungarians, Hungarians and Slavs, Slavs and Germans.

The *Communist Manifesto* anticipated the strengths as well as the weaknesses of the communist movement. First, it foreshadowed the very important role to be played by propaganda, supplying the earliest of those effective catch phrases that have become the mark of Marxism—the constant sneering at bourgeois morality, bourgeois law, and bourgeois property, and the dramatic references to the "specter haunting Europe" and to the proletarians who "have nothing to lose but their chains." Second, the *Manifesto* anticipated the emphasis to be placed on the role of the party in forging the proletarian revolution. The communists, Marx declared in 1848, were a spearhead, "the most advanced section of the working class parties of every country." In matters of theory, "they have over the great mass of the proletariat the advantage of clearly understanding the line of march, the conditions, and the ultimate general results of the proletarian movement."

Third, the *Manifesto* assigned the state a great role in the revolution. Among the policies recommended by Marx were "centralization of credit in the hands of the state," and "extension of factories and instruments of production

owned by the state." Thus, despite the supposition that the state would wither away, the *Manifesto* faintly foreshadowed the totalitarian regime of the Soviet Union. And, finally, it clearly established the line dividing communism from the other forms of socialism. Marx's dogmatism, his philosophy of history, and his belief in the necessity for a "total" revolution made his brand of socialism a thing apart. Like a religious prophet granted a revelation, Marx expected his gospel to supplant all other. He scorned and pitied the Utopian socialists. They were about as futile, he wrote, as "organizers of charity, members of societies for the prevention of cruelty to animals, temperance fanatics, hole-and-corner reformers of every kind."

Marxism after 1848

Age neither mellowed Marx nor greatly altered his views. From 1849 until his death in 1883, he lived in London. There, partly because of his own financial mismanagement, the Marx family experienced at first hand the misery of a proletarian existence in the slums of Soho; poverty and near-starvation caused the death of three of the Marx children. Eventually, Marx obtained a modest income from the generosity of Engels and from his own writings.

Throughout the 1850's Marx contributed a weekly article on British politics or international affairs to Horace Greeley's radical paper, *The New York Tribune.* He produced a series of pamphlets, of which the most famous was *The Eighteenth Brumaire of Louis Napoleon,* a study of the fall of the short-lived Second French Republic. Meantime, he spent his days in the British Museum, reading the reports of parliamentary investigating committees and piling up evidence of the conditions of miners and factory hands. Thus Marx accumulated the material for his full-dress economic study, *Das Kapital.* The first volume of this massive analysis of capitalism appeared in 1867; two further volumes, pieced together from his notes, were published after his death.

In *Das Kapital,* Marx elaborated, but did not substantially revise, the doctrines of the *Communist Manifesto.* He spelled out his labor theory of value, according to which the worker created the total value of the commodity that he produced yet received in the form of wages only a part of the price for the item. The difference between the sale price and the worker's wages constituted *surplus value,* something actually created by labor but appropriated by capital as profit. *Das Kapital* goes on to relate surplus value to the ultimate doom of capitalism. It is the nature of capitalism, Marx insists, to diminish its own profits by replacing human labor with machines and thus gradually choking off the source of surplus value. Hence will arise the mounting crises of overproduction and underconsumption predicted by the *Manifesto*. In a famous passage toward the close of Volume I of *Das Kapital,* Marx compared capitalism to an integument, a skin or shell, increasingly stretched and strained from within. One day these internal pressures would prove irresistible: "This integument is burst asunder. The knell of capitalist private property sounds. The expropriators are expropriated." *

In 1864, three years before the first volume of *Das Kapital* was published, Marx joined in the formation of the First International Workingmen's Association. This was an ambitious attempt to organize workers of every country and of every variety of radical belief. A loose federation rather than a coherent political party, the First International soon began to disintegrate, and expired in 1876. Increasing persecution by hostile governments helped to bring on its end; but so, too, did the internal quarrels that repeatedly engaged both its leaders and the rank and file of its members. And Marx himself set the example, both by his intolerance of disagree-

ment and by his incapacity for practical politics.

In 1889, the Second International was organized; it lasted down to the time of World War I and the Bolshevik Revolution in Russia. The Second International was more coherently organized and more political in character than the First International had been. It represented the Marxian socialist or Social Democratic parties, which, as we shall see in later chapters, were becoming important forces in the major countries of continental Europe. Among its leaders were men more adept than Marx himself at the political game. Yet the old spirit of factionalism continued to weaken the International. Some of its leaders tenaciously defended laws handed down by the master and forbade any cooperation between socialists and the bourgeois political parties; these were the orthodox Marxists. Other leaders of the Second International, however, were from the orthodox standpoint heretics. They, too, called themselves disciples of Marx; yet they revised his doctrines in the direction of moderation and of harmonization with the views of the Utopians. These "revisionists" believed in cooperation between classes rather than in a struggle to the death, and they trusted that human decency and intelligence, working through the machinery of democratic government, could avert the horrors of outright class war. Though the precise connotations have varied with the shifts of the party line, "orthodox" and "heretical" communists have persisted. The factionalism that had split the First International lived on to plague the Second and its twentieth-century successors.

V   Other Responses

The various forms of liberalism and socialism by no means exhausted the range of responses to the economic and social problems created by the Industrial Revolution. As later chapters will show, nationalists were impelled to give new life to old mercantilist ideas, not only advocating tariffs to protect agriculture and industry but also demanding empires abroad to provide new markets for surplus products, new fields for the investment of surplus capital, and new settlements for surplus citizens. Here we shall ex-

amine the responses made by the apostles of violence and by the nonviolent preachers of mutualism and of Christian good will and good works.

The Apostles of Violence

Left-wing tradition assigns the honor of being the first modern socialists to Gracchus Babeuf and his fellow conspirators under the French Directory in 1796–1797. The equalitarianism of

* Modern Library ed., p. 837.

Babeuf, though fervent, was too loosely formulated to be called truly socialist; the only direct link between him and later socialist movements came through the book about his attempted coup, *The Conspiracy of the Equals* (1828). The author was Filippo Buonarroti (the nephew several generations removed of the great Michelangelo), who had been Babeuf's lieutenant. His book veiled the failure of the Equals in a romantic mist thirty years after the event. Buonarroti fired a new generation of would-be revolutionaries with the conviction that the only way to improve the human condition lay through immediate violent actions, in the manner of 1793–1794.

The leader of these new terrorists was Auguste Blanqui (1805–1881), a professional revolutionary who participated in the Paris revolts of 1830, 1848, and 1870–1871 (in the wake of France's defeat in the Franco-Prussian War and the collapse of the Second Empire). While Blanqui shared the socialists' sympathy with the exploited working class, he had none of their zeal for drawing up detailed blueprints and none of their patience in waiting until conditions for change were ripe. He was not an ideologist but an activist, believing that the imposition of a dictatorial regime by an elite vanguard of conspirators would be the only way to deal with a bourgeois capitalist society. An inveterate plotter of violence, he was put in jail by every regime in post-Napoleonic France, from the Bourbon restoration to the Third Republic, and spent forty years of his life span of seventy-six in prison. When his movement petered out in the 1870's, his followers tended to join the Marxian socialists. His dedication to activism made him a significant figure in left-wing history: it has been said that Lenin's formula for a successful Bolshevik revolution was Marxism plus Blanquism.

Other apostles of violence called themselves anarchists, believing that the best government is no government at all. Most of the recipes for socialism contained at least a dash of anarchism: witness the withering away of the state promised by the Marxists and the Utopians' mistrust of governments. For a few of Marx's contemporaries, however, it was not enough that the state should wither at some distant time; such an instrument of oppression should be annihilated at once. The means to this end was terrorism, especially assassination of heads of state. These terrorists provided the stereotype of the bearded, wild-eyed, bomb-carrying radical. At the turn of the century, their assassinations levied an impressive toll—the French president Carnot in 1894, King Humbert of Italy in 1900, and the American president McKinley in 1901. Otherwise the terrorists accomplished little except to drive the governments they hated to more vigorous measures of retaliation.

Though negative and destructive in practice, anarchism exerted an important doctrinal influence on the proletarian movement. The Russian scientist and thinker Prince Peter Kropotkin (1842–1921) made the most complete statement of its theory and ideals in his book *Mutual Aid: A Factor in Evolution* (1902). Kropotkin foresaw a revolution that would abolish the state as well as private property and that would lead to a new society of autonomous groups whereby the individual would achieve greater self-realization and would need to labor only four to five hours a day. The most famous anarchist was Kropotkin's countryman Bakunin (1814–1876), who helped to shape the Russian revolutionary movement and won the attention of workers from many countries by his participation in the First International. Although Bakunin drew only a vague sketch of his utopia, he made it clear that the millennium was to be achieved through an international rebellion set off by small groups of anarchist conspirators.

Bakunin contributed to the formation of the program known as anarcho-syndicalism (from the French word *syndicat*, which means an economic grouping, particularly a trade union). The anarcho-syndicalists disbelieved in political parties, even Marxist ones; they believed in direct action by the workers to culminate in a spontaneous general strike that would free labor from the capitalistic yoke. Meantime, workers could rehearse for the great day by forming unions and by engaging in acts of anticapitalist sabotage. These theories received forceful expression in *Reflections on Violence* published in 1908 by the French exponent of anarcho-syndicalism Georges Sorel.

Proudhon

The writer most frequently cited by the anarcho-syndicalists was the French publicist Proudhon (1809–1865). "What is property?"

Proudhon asked in a famous pamphlet of 1840; "property is theft." Marx praised the pamphlet for its "scientific" socialism and predicted it would rank in importance with Siéyès' *What Is the Third Estate?* Within a few years Marx's praise had turned to contempt, when he found that his own views no longer enlisted Proudhon's allegiance. A second pamphlet by Proudhon, *The Philosophy of Poverty*, elicited a Marxian rebuttal tartly entitled *The Poverty of Philosophy*. The property that Proudhon called "theft" was not all property but unearned income, the revenues that men gained from investing their wealth rather than from the sweat of their brows. Of all the forms of unearned income, the worst, in Proudhon's view, was the "leprosy of interest," and the most diabolical of capitalists was the moneylender. Under existing conditions, only those who were already rich could afford to borrow, but in the utopia envisaged by Proudhon all men would be able to secure credit. Instead of private banks and the Bank of France, there would be only a People's Bank, lending to all without interest and issuing notes that would soon replace ordinary money. The credit provided by the People's Bank would enable each man to become a producer on his own.

Thus, where Marx foresaw a revolution in ownership of the means of production, Proudhon foresaw a "revolution of credit," a revolution in financing production. Where Marx proposed to have the proletariat liquidate the bourgeoisie, Proudhon proposed to raise the proletarians to the level of the bourgeois by making every worker an owner. Proudhon's utopia was not collectivized or socialized; it was a loose association of middle-class individualists. Because Proudhon dreaded restraints upon the individual, he opposed the social workshops of Louis Blanc and the phalanxes of Fourier as too restrictive. He projected, instead, a society founded upon *mutualism*. Economically, mutualism would take the form of associations of producers in agriculture and industry, not unlike the producers' cooperatives found among farmers today. Politically, it would take the form of *federalism*—that is, a loose federation of associations would replace the centralized state rather on the model of the Swiss confederation of local cantons.

Proudhon's doctrines exerted a strong appeal in France, with its devotion to individualism and with the legacy of federalism bequeathed by the Girondins of the Revolution. Tens of thousands of small businessmen in France were often denied financial credit by the bankers denounced by Proudhon, and thus always stood on the edge of being displaced from the lower fringes of the middle class to the proletariat. Proudhon's attacks on the state naturally fed the anarchist strain in anarcho-syndicalism. Yet much of his teaching contradicted the syndicalist strain. Not only did he dislike trade unions as unnatural restrictions on individual liberty; he deplored all activities suggesting class strife, including the very strikes so beloved by the syndicalists. These views, together with his expressed hostility to Jewish moneylenders, have led some modern critics to call Proudhon an incipient fascist; other critics, however, have dismissed the charge as absurd because Proudhon seemed to reject entirely any kind of totalitarian state.

The Christian Socialists

Like Proudhon, the Christian socialists endeavored to mitigate class antagonisms. The name was first applied, in the mid-nineteenth century, to a small group of English reformers, drawn from the clergy of the established Church, who believed that the Church of England needed to put theological problems to one side and direct its efforts to ending social abuses. One of their best known leaders was Charles Kingsley (1819–1875), who wrote earnest social novels and a stream of pamphlets against the wickedness of laissez-faire. His didactic novel *Alton Locke* and his biting tract *Cheap Clothes and Nasty*, both published in 1850, exposed the sweating of labor in the "show shops" and "slop shops" which forced tailors and seamstresses to work long hours for meager pay, often in appallingly crowded and unsanitary surroundings.

The positive doctrine of the Christian socialists was notable for its attack on materialism and its stress on brotherly love as against unbrotherly strife, on association and cooperation as against exploitation and competition. It was notable also for its optimism: if men would only act as Christians, they might solve their social problems. The Christian socialists were far more Christian than socialist and relied more on private philanthropy than on state intervention. Kingsley himself set an example for concrete improvement when he helped to launch the Working Men's College in London and promoted other activities of the type that organizations like the YMCA have made familiar.

The Christian Democrats

Catholics, too, reacted against the evils of industrialism. Essentially, their program resembled that of the Anglican Christian socialists, but they called it by the more accurate name "Christian democracy" or "social Christianity." Christian democracy formed a central part of the Catholic response to the problems of the modern world. As we shall see in later chapters, these problems bore heavily upon the Church. Anticlerical legislation threatened its position in France, Germany, Italy, and elsewhere. The Papal States and then the city of Rome itself, after more than a thousand years of papal rule, passed to the control of the newly unified Kingdom of Italy. Science, nationalism, and the materialistic doctrines issuing from the industrial revolution were all competing for the loyalties of men. In Catholic countries the working classes especially were drifting away from the Church.

The Church first tried to take refuge in the past. Pope Pius IX (1846–1878), whose experience in the revolution of 1848 had ended his earlier flirtation with liberalism, issued in 1864 the *Syllabus of Errors,* condemning many social theories and institutions not consecrated by centuries of tradition. While Pius also condemned the materialism implicit in laissez-faire, socially minded Catholics were disturbed by his apparent hostility to trade unions and democracy and by his statement that it was an error to suppose that the pope "can and ought to reconcile and harmonize himself with progress, liberalism, and modern civilization."

The successor of Pius, Leo XIII (1878–1903), recognized that the Church could hardly continue to turn its back on progress, liberalism, and modernity without suffering serious losses. Pope Leo fully recognized the rapid changes being worked by science and technology; as a papal nuncio he had witnessed them at first hand in the industrial regions of Belgium, France, and Germany. He knew that Catholicism was flourishing in the supposedly hostile climate of the democratic and Protestant United States. Moreover, his studies of Saint Thomas Aquinas convinced him that the Church had much to gain and little to lose by following the middle-of-the-road social and economic policies recommended by that great medieval Schoolman. Accordingly, Leo XIII issued a series of famous documents, notably the encyclical letter *Rerum Novarum* (*Concerning New Things,* 1891).

In *Rerum Novarum,* the pope exposed the defects of capitalism with as much vigor as any socialist. Then he attacked with equal vigor the socialist view of property and the socialist doctrine of class war. He pronounced it a "great mistake" to believe

that class is naturally hostile to class, and that the wealthy and the workingmen are intended by nature to live in mutual conflict. . . . Each needs the other: Capital cannot do without Labor, nor Labor without Capital.

Leo therefore urged the economic man to act as a Christian man of good will:

Religion teaches the laboring man . . . to carry out honestly and fairly all equitable agreements freely entered into; never to injure the property, nor to outrage the person, of an employer; never to resort to violence . . . ; and to have nothing to do with men of evil principles, who work upon the people with artful promises, and excite foolish hopes which usually end in useless regrets, followed by insolvency. Religion teaches the wealthy owner and the employer that their workpeople are not to be accounted their bondsmen; that in every man they must respect his dignity and worth as a man and as a Christian; that labor is not a thing to be ashamed of, if we lend ear to right reason and to Christian philosophy, but is an honorable calling, enabling a man to sustain his life in a way upright and creditable; and that it is shameful and inhuman to treat men like chattels to make money by, or to look upon them merely as so much muscle or physical power.*

While Leo XIII believed that the state must always remain subordinate to the interests of the individuals composing it, he did not necessarily defend laissez-faire policies. On the contrary, he repeatedly cited Saint Thomas to prove that the state should take measures for the general wel-

---

* *The Great Encyclical Letters of Pope Leo XIII* (New York, 1903), pp. 218, 219.

fare. On behalf of capital, it should discourage agitators and protect property from violence. On behalf of labor, it should work to remove "the causes which lead to conflict between employer and employed." For example, it might regulate child labor, limit the hours of work, and insist that Sundays be free for religious activity and for rest. Leo also believed that the workers must help themselves, and *Rerum Novarum* concluded with a fervent appeal for the formation of Catholic trade unions.

These Catholic unions exist today, but they are only a minority in the realm of organized labor. Neither the Christian democracy of Leo XIII nor the Christian socialism of the Anglican reformers has achieved all that the founders hoped. Yet the Christian democrats eventually came to play a central part in the politics of Germany, Italy, and other European states, particularly after World War II. And in Britain both Marxism and the Christian socialist tradition helped to attract workingmen and middle-class intellectuals to the developing Labour party at the beginning of the twentieth century.

Reading Suggestions on the Industrial Revolution

THE INDUSTRIAL
REVOLUTION

H. J. Habakkuk and M. Postan, eds., *The Cambridge Economic History of Europe,* Vol. VI, parts i and ii (Cambridge Univ. Press, 1965). Essays on the Industrial Revolution by ranking scholars. The chapters by David Landes have been issued as *The Unbound Prometheus* (*Cambridge Univ. Press).

E. J. Hobsbawn, *The Age of Revolution, 1789–1848* (*Mentor). A provocative survey from the Marxian point of view.

A. Toynbee, *The Industrial Revolution* (*Beacon). Pioneering study, first published nearly a century ago, much under the influence of Christian socialist ideas.

S. Pollard and C. Holmes, eds., *The Process of Industrialization, 1750–1870* (St. Martin's, 1968). Useful compilation of documents.

W. W. Rostow, *Stages of Economic Growth: A Non-Communist Manifesto* (*Cambridge Univ. Press). Brief and stimulating essay on the timetable of industrialism.

P. M. Deane, *The First Industrial Revolution* (*Cambridge Univ. Press); P. Mantoux, *The Industrial Revolution in the Eighteenth Century* (*Torchbooks); T. S. Ashton, *The Industrial Revolution, 1760–1830* (*Galaxy); R. M. Hartwell, ed., *The Causes of the Industrial Revolution in England* (Methuen, 1967). Four useful works on the early history of modern industrialism.

L. Mumford, *Technics and Civilization* (*Harbinger). A sweeping survey, first published in the 1930's and still very suggestive.

J. Clapham, *An Economic History of Modern Britain,* rev. ed., 3 vols. (Cambridge Univ. Press, 1930–1938). Major scholarly study.

J. Clapham, *Economic Development of France and Germany, 1815–1914* (*Cambridge Univ. Press). Older study still worth reading.

W. O. Henderson, *The Industrial Revolution in Europe, 1815–1914* (*Quadrangle). Stresses Germany, France, and Russia.

M. C. Buer, *Health, Wealth, and Population in the Early Days of the Industrial Revolution* (Routledge, 1926). Balanced appraisal of the social consequences.

THE RESPONSES OF
LIBERALISM

C. Brinton, *English Political Thought in the Nineteenth Century* (*Torchbooks). Essays on Bentham, Mill, Owen, Kingsley, and other important figures.

W. H. Coates and H. V. White, *The Ordeal of Liberal Humanism* (*McGraw-Hill). Useful brief textbook account.

E. Halévy, *The Growth of Philosophic Radicalism* (*Beacon). Celebrated older study of Bentham and his Utilitarian followers.

M. Mack, *Jeremy Bentham* (Heinemann, 1962). More recent biography.

T. R. Malthus, *Population: The First Essay* (*Ann Arbor). The original essay of 1798, stating Malthusianism in its most undiluted form.

R. Heilbroner, *The Worldly Philosophers,* rev. ed. (*Clarion). A good introduction to the philosophy of laissez-faire.

M. S. Packe, *The Life of John Stuart Mill* (Macmillan, 1954). Sound biography.

J. S. Mill, *Autobiography* (*Signet) and *On Liberty* (*Appleton). Perhaps the most illuminating writings of the great Victorian liberal.

THE SOCIALIST RESPONSES   A. Fried and R. Sanders, *Socialist Thought* (*Anchor). Collection of documents.

H. W. Laidler, *A History of Socialism* (Crowell, 1968). Updated version of an older standard work.

J. C. Schumpeter, *Capitalism, Socialism, and Democracy* (*Torchbooks). Thoughtful survey, extending into the present century.

Edmund Wilson, *To the Finland Station* (*Anchor). A sympathetic and balanced history of socialism.

G. Lichtheim, *A Short History of Socialism* (*Praeger). Informative survey.

C. H. de Saint-Simon, *Social Organization, The Science of Man, and Other Writings* (*Torchbooks). The best introduction to this pioneer of "social engineering."

M. I. Cole, *Robert Owen of New Lanark* (Oxford Univ. Press, 1953). Standard study of the great British utopian socialist.

K. Marx and F. Engels, *Basic Writings on Politics and Philosophy* (*Anchor). Good selection.

I. Berlin, *Karl Marx: His Life and Environment* (*Galaxy). Brilliant study.

S. Avineri, *The Social and Political Thought of Karl Marx* (Cambridge Univ. Press, 1968), and G. Lichtheim, *Marxism: An Historical and Critical Study,* 2nd ed. (*Praeger). Thoughtful recent evaluations.

OTHER RESPONSES   A. B. Spitzer, *The Revolutionary Theories of Auguste Blanqui* (Columbia Univ. Press, 1957). Good study of the perennial French agitator and prisoner.

P. A. Kropotkin, *Selected Writings on Anarchism and Revolution* (*MIT Press). Useful introduction to his ideas.

G. Sorel, *Reflections on Violence* (*Collier). The famous defense of direct revolutionary action and the general strike.

Pope Leo XIII, *Seven Great Encyclicals* (*Paulist-Newman). Basic statements of the new position taken by the Vatican at the close of the nineteenth century.

R. Fülop-Miller, *Leo XIII and Our Times* (Longmans, 1937). Sympathetic study.

HISTORICAL FICTION   Charles Dickens, *Hard Times* (*several editions). The shortest of his great social novels, with memorable descriptions of Coketown and its citizens.

Mrs. Elizabeth Gaskell, *North and South* and *Mary Barton* (*Penguin). Instructive social novels by a close associate of Dickens.

Emile Zola, *Germinal* (*Signet). Famous French novel about a strike in a coal mine; less inhibited than its English counterparts.

E. Bellamy, *Looking Backward, 2000–1887* (*several editions). Sensitive adaptation of socialist views by a late nineteenth-century American.

21

The Western Democracies
in the Nineteenth Century

I Introduction:
Democracies Large and Small

This chapter follows down to 1914 the domestic history of the major self-governing Western nations—Great Britain, France, Italy, and the United States. They are all democracies today and, though they have all had their lapses from democratic standards, especially France and Italy, they are all relatively "old" democracies. But so are many of the smaller states of western and northern Europe. The Netherlands, Belgium, Switzerland, and the Scandinavian countries have all worked out their national variants of liberalism. In particular, Denmark, Norway, and Sweden, with their homogeneous populations, their common Lutheran religion, their common traditions, and their very high rate of literacy, have sometimes surpassed the larger states in making democracy function effectively. Visitors to Copenhagen or Stockholm are impressed not only by their tidiness but also by the absence

*Above: William Gladstone: An 1869 caricature
of the British prime minister.
Above right: Benjamin Disraeli, Lord Beaconsfield.
Right: The Crystal Palace, London, home of
the International Exhibition of 1851.*

778

of slums and other signs of poverty. And the cooperatives of Denmark and Sweden have received much praise as the "middle way" between welfare socialism and uncontrolled economic individualism.

The history of these smaller states is in no way insignificant or uninteresting, even though a book of this scope cannot treat it in any detail. They too underwent most of the stresses and strains of the rest of Europe. Belgium, notably, was divided—and still is—between French-speaking and Flemish-speaking areas, often in conflict. In 1847, Switzerland underwent a miniature civil war between the *Sonderbund*, a league of the more conservative and rural Catholic cantons, and the more liberal and urban Protestant cantons. The Sonderbund was dissolved, and the Swiss federal government strengthened on the model of the United States. Sweden and Norway, yoked together in 1815, parted company peacefully in 1907, after nearly a century of restive partnership.

These smaller states have also helped to maintain the balance of international politics and to shape European opinion, a role for which they are particularly well suited by their relative detachment from ambitious nationalist aspirations. They have collaborated effectively in many forms of international activity. The Hague was the meeting place of two pioneering conferences (1899 and 1907) called to formulate rules and machinery for the regulation of international disputes; after World War I Geneva became the capital of the League of Nations; and after World War II the

League's successor, the United Nations, chose a Norwegian and then a Swede as its secretary-general. Scandinavian contingents have been a mainstay of the peace-keeping forces stationed in trouble spots under United Nations auspices.

In many fields the citizens of the smaller European democracies have contributed proportionately more heavily to our modern Western culture than their numbers would suggest. To cite a few examples: Switzerland supplied the great historian of the Renaissance, Burckhardt, and Belgium the poet and playwright, Maeterlinck. From Finland came the composer Sibelius; from Norway, Ibsen and his modern social dramas; from Holland, the physicist Lorentz, winner of the Nobel Prize in 1902; and from Sweden, the novelist and playwright Strindberg as well as Nobel himself, the munitions king who endowed the prizes for peaceful achievement.

Spain, too, though not a democracy, had a varied and interesting history in the nineteenth century, swinging between conservative monarchy and radical republicanism after the revolution of 1820 had been suppressed. But Spain was now a minor power and, though especially in the novel, she had a distinguished cultural achievement, fuller consideration of Spanish history will be postponed until in the Civil War of the 1930's Spain once more enters the mainstream of events. We must now turn to the states that fate, or history, has assigned the major roles in our story. Of these in the nineteenth century, Britain was unquestionably the first, the leading power.

II   Britain, 1815-1914

The Process of Reform

In the years immediately after Waterloo, Britain went through a typical postwar economic crisis. Unsold goods accumulated, and the working classes experienced widespread unemployment and misery. Popular suffering increased as a result of the Corn Law of 1815, which was the most recent in a series of protective tariffs on grains and forbade the importation of cheap foreign grains until the price of the home-grown commodity reached a specified height. This assured the profits of the English grain farmer and

raised the cost of bread for the average English family. Although trade unions were outlawed by the Combination Acts, the workers none the less asserted themselves in strikes and in popular agitation that helped prepare the way for the parliamentary Reform Bill of 1832. But by the 1820's, economic conditions had improved, and Britain had embarked on the first stage of those political reforms that were to make of her a democratic state.

Into this process there went the economic and social drives noted in the last chapter, and the Britain of our own day was to be not only a very complete political democracy but also in part an economic and a social democracy. Yet the process of reform focused always on concrete political action. It is a process of which the British are very proud, for it was achieved without revolution and almost without violence or any serious civil disturbance. The fruits of discussion, education, and propaganda were consolidated in a specific "reform bill," followed by another stage of preparatory work and another reform bill.

The Beginning of Parliamentary Reform

The process is most clearly marked in the great milestones of parliamentary reform that transformed the government of Britain from an oligarchy into a political democracy. Britain emerged from the Napoleonic Wars with its executive, a cabinet of ministers presided over by a prime minister, wholly under the control of Parliament. The Crown was now, as the nineteenth-century political writer Bagehot was to put it, largely "decorative." On that decorative post, held for most of the century (1837–1901) by Queen Victoria, who has given her name to an age and a culture, were centered the patriotic emotions of loyal British subjects. Victoria never thought of herself as a mere figurehead; she was a determined, sensible, emotional, conventional, and intellectually unsophisticated Victorian lady.

Real power lay with Parliament, which, in the early nineteenth-century, was very far from being a broadly representative body. The House of Lords, which for all save money bills had equal power with the lower house, was composed of the small, privileged class of peers born to their seats in the Lords, with the addition of a relatively few new peers created by the Crown from time to time. The House of Commons, its members unpaid, was recruited wholly from the gentry, the professional classes, and very successful businessmen, with a sprinkling of sons of peers (who were for electoral purposes commoners). It was chosen by less than one-sixth of the adult male population. Both the working classes in town and country and the run of prosperous but not spectacularly successful middle-class people were generally excluded from the franchise, although, with characteristic British lack of uniformity, some boroughs had a much broader electorate. Moreover, the largely rural

south, once the most populous area of the kingdom, now had more representatives than it deserved, including a large contingent from the "rotten boroughs," towns of very small population, or, as in the notorious Old Sarum, once a lively medieval town, none at all. The teeming new industrial centers of the north, such as Manchester, Liverpool, and Sheffield, were grossly underrepresented.

Projects to begin modernizing the structure of representation came close to being adopted in the late eighteenth century. But the wars with Revolutionary and Napoleonic France made reform impossible; in wartime and in the immediate postwar years, even moderate reformers were denounced as Jacobins. In August 1819 a nervous Tory government permitted the soldiery to break up a large and peaceful mass meeting assembled at St. Peter's Field near Manchester to hear speeches on parliamentary reform. Eleven persons died and several hundred were wounded in what was called the "Peterloo" massacre, with its echo of Waterloo. In the aftermath of "Peterloo," postwar repression reached its height with Parliament's approval of the Six Acts (December 1819), curtailing freedom of speech and of assembly and abrogating other civil rights. Fortunately, moderation soon prevailed once more in Britain, together with economic prosperity, and the peaceful campaign of agitation which produced the parliamentary reform of 1832 was resumed.

In this campaign the middle class did not hesitate to appeal to the lower classes for aid by using freely the language of popular rights, and even of universal suffrage. Many popular leaders talked as if the Reform Bill would bring political democracy to England at once. Yet much of the preparation for reform was actually the work, not of liberal agitators, but of conservatives. Guided by enlightened individuals such as Canning and Robert Peel, the Tory governments of the 1820's lifted the restrictions on civil rights imposed during the long war with France and the postwar crisis. They weakened the Combination Acts to the extent of permitting laborers to organize into unions, though not to strike; they reformed the antiquated criminal code, so that, for example, the theft of a sheep no longer carried with it in theory a death penalty; and began the reduction in protective tariffs (though not as yet affecting the Corn Laws) that was to lead to free trade. The seventeenth-century Test

Europe in the
Mid - Nineteenth Century

— Boundary of the German Confederation

Miles
0 — 500

GREAT BRITAIN
SCOTLAND
Edinburgh
Glasgow
IRELAND
WALES
ENGLAND
Lancaster
Manchester
Liverpool
Oxford
Cambridge
London

NORWAY
Oslo
SWEDEN
Stockholm
FINLAND
St. Petersburg
Moscow

Atlantic Ocean
North Sea
Baltic Sea
DENMARK
Copenhagen
Kiel
SCHLESWIG
HOLSTEIN
Hamburg
HANOVER
NETH.
Brussels
BELG.
Lille
Amsterdam
LUX.
Metz
Frankfurt
RUHR
BADEN
WÜRTEM-BERG
BAVARIA
SAXONY
PRUSSIA
Berlin
Elbe R.
Oder R.
Memel
Königsberg
POLAND
Warsaw
Vistula R.

United with Prussia, 1824-1878

R U S S I A
Volga R.
Oka R.
Dvina R.
Don R.
Dnieper R.
Kiev
DONETS BASIN
Odessa
Dniester R.
Pruth R.

FRANCE
Paris
Seine R.
Loire R.
Bordeaux
Rhône R.
Marseilles
SWITZ.
Rhine R.
TYROL
VENETIA
Venice
LOMBARDY
PIEDMONT
GENOA
PARMA
MODENA
TUSCANY
PAPAL STATES
Rome
KINGDOM OF SARDINIA
SARDINIA
CORSICA
Naples
KINGDOM OF THE TWO SICILIES
SICILY
Str. of Messina
Tripoli

BOHEMIA
Prague
Olmütz
Vienna
AUSTRIAN EMPIRE
HUNGARY
Budapest
Zagreb
Belgrade
SERBIA
BOSNIA HERZEGOVINA
MONTENEGRO
Danube R.
Adriatic Sea

OTTOMAN EMPIRE
Constantinople
GREECE
Athens
Aegean Sea
CRETE
CYPRUS
SYRIA
Black Sea
Tigris R.
Euphrates R.
Suez
Cairo
EGYPT

Mediterranean Sea

SPAIN
Madrid
Ebro R.
Guadalquivir R.
PORTUGAL
Lisbon
BALEARIC IS.
MOROCCO
ALGERIA
TUNIS
TRIPOLI

Act, which, though not observed, legally excluded Nonconformists from public life, was repealed. Also repealed, under the banner of "Catholic emancipation," were the laws that really did exclude Catholics from public life. In international politics, as we have already seen, Canning lined Britain up against the conservative monarchies of central and eastern Europe and their principle of intervention to suppress revolutions.

The Reform Bill itself was enacted under the leadership of the Whig Lord Grey, backed by a full apparatus of agitation and pressure groups. Tory opponents of parliamentary reform were won over—even the very Tory Duke of Wellington was converted at the last moment—until only the Tory House of Lords blocked the measure. At this climax, Lord Grey persuaded King William IV (1830–1837) to threaten the creation by royal prerogative of enough new Whig peers to put the reform through the Lords. This threat, combined with the real, or perhaps merely widely feared, danger of popular violence, put the bill through on June 4, 1832.

The First Reform Bill is probably the most celebrated single act of legislation passed by Parliament. Yet, while it was a most important beginning, it by no means brought political democracy to Britain. It did diminish the great irregularities of electoral districts, wiping out more than fifty rotten boroughs and giving seats in the Commons to more than forty hitherto unrepresented industrial towns. The number of voters was increased by about 50 percent so that virtually all the middle class got the vote, but the property qualifications for voting excluded the great mass of workers. Ironically, the new, more uniform qualifications actually took the franchise away from some men who had enjoyed it in a few exceptionally liberal boroughs.

Chartism and Later Reform Bills

From the new ground of the partly reformed Parliament, the agitation for a still wider suffrage went on. The middle class had won its gains, not in the name of its own admission to an oligarchy, but in the name of the right of all competent men to have the vote. With the gradual spread of literacy to the lower classes, with

their gradual political awakening, the middle classes could not find very good arguments for refusing to extend the franchise; moreover, a good many of the British middle classes sincerely believed in a gradual widening of the franchise.

The more impatient workingmen were not content to wait for piecemeal reform; they wanted immediate direct representation in Parliament in order to press for legislation that would mitigate the hardships imposed upon them by the Industrial Revolution. These demands were formally drawn up in a "People's Charter," calling for universal manhood suffrage, the secret ballot, abolition of property requirements for members of Parliament, payment of members, equal electoral districts, and annually elected Parliaments. The Chartists, who greatly alarmed the conservative classes, were the closest English equivalent of the radical parties which on the Continent carried on the Jacobin tradition of the French Revolution, mingled with the elements of nascent socialism. Chartist strength lay in the urban industrial proletariat, particularly the union organizations, and was supported by many intellectuals of varied social and economic background. The movement presented to Parliament in 1839 a monster petition, with several hundred thousand signatures, urging adoption of the Charter. Parliament never considered the petition. Twice again the Chartists tried to petition Parliament (in 1842 and 1848), but the movement petered out in the mounting prosperity of the 1850's and '60's. Though Chartism seemed a failure, all of its major demands were destined to become law within the next two generations, except only for annually elected parliaments, which soon appeared pointless to even the most ardent reformers.

By the 1860's the groundswell of agitation for more parliamentary reform was so powerful that it moved even some members of the Conservative party (as the Tories now styled themselves). Disraeli (1804–1881), the Conservative leader in the Commons, almost certainly thought that if his party did not put through reform the Liberals (the former Whigs) would. With a politician's sense of reality, he decided that the Conservatives might as well get the credit. Disraeli also thought that the newly enfranchised urban working class, hostile to their middle-class employers, would vote for the Conservatives, who were country gentlemen, good responsible caretakers of the lower classes, not exploiters like the middle-class businessmen. He was proved wrong by the very first general election after the reform, for in 1868 his party was turned out of office.

The Second Reform Bill did not introduce full manhood suffrage. Like the first, it was a piecemeal change that brought the electoral districts into more uniformity and equality, but left them still divided into boroughs and shires as in the Middle Ages. It about doubled the number of voters in Britain by giving the vote to householders—that is, settled men owning or paying rent on their dwellings—in the boroughs. But the Reform Bill of 1867 did not give the vote in rural areas to men without the "stake" of property— that is, men who did not own a piece of real estate or even a bank account, men who were therefore felt by many upper-class Victorians to be irresponsible, willing to vote away other people's property.

The next reforms in the series were put through by the Liberal party, under the leadership of Gladstone (1809–1898). The bills of 1884 and 1885, while not yet introducing universal manhood suffrage, did double the size of the electorate, particularly by extending the franchise in rural areas. But migrant laborers, domestic servants, and bachelors living in parental households still did not have the vote. In addition, the medieval constituencies of borough and shire were modernized, and many smaller boroughs lumped together with surrounding county areas to form single constituencies. The political map of Britain was beginning to be redrawn so that all districts would have roughly the same population. And yet some striking inequalities continued. Workers could scarcely hope to become members of Parliament, for MP's served without pay; a few thousand voters with business property in one district and a home in another could vote twice; and graduates of Oxford and Cambridge could vote a second time for special university members; indeed, a university man with scattered property could, if he could get around to the polls fast enough, cast a dozen votes.

Still, by 1885 Britain was already a political democracy, in which the majority of the people, through their representatives in the House of Commons, were politically "sovereign." Perhaps not quite, for the hereditary House of Lords had still a veto power over legislation that did not specifically appropriate money. This last limitation was removed in 1911, when the Parliament Act of that year ended the real power of the Lords, leaving them with no more than a delaying or suspensive veto. Other codicils to the reforms of the nineteenth century were the institution of salaries for MP's (also in 1911) and a major act in 1918, which enfranchised all men over twenty-one, gave the vote to women over thirty and limited plural voting to two votes—a property vote and a university vote. After World War II the university votes were abolished, along with most of the few remaining powers of the Lords.

Liberals, Conservatives, and the Two-Party System

The dynamics of the process of democratizing British politics are in part explicable in terms of the class struggle, as the bourgeoisie and then the proletariat gained the vote. But the central human institution working this change, the political party, was something more than an instrument for advancing narrow class interests. When the Conservative Disraeli took the "leap in the dark" in 1867, he hoped that the newly enfranchised workers would vote for their "betters" in his own party. He was wrong in 1868, but in the longer run not wholly wrong, for after his death the Conservatives returned to power triumphantly under the still wider franchise of 1885 for a whole decade, 1895–1905.

Both the Conservative and Liberal parties were by now very different from their ancestors, the oligarchical eighteenth-century factions of Tories and Whigs. The Conservatives, first under Peel and then under Disraeli, kept their old electoral following among country gentlemen, army and navy officers, and Anglican clergymen, but they added many new supporters among agricultural laborers, tradesmen, and even some of the urban working and white-collar classes. The Liberals, who in the early and middle parts of the century were still led by men like Grey and Palmerston from the great aristocratic Whig families, found many new supporters among businessmen, large and small, the Nonconformists, white-collar radicals, and politically conscious workers. Both parties frankly appealed to the "people"; and the Conservatives, with their "Primrose League" in memory of Disraeli's favorite flower, their appeal to love of queen and country, their record of social legislation against the worst evils of the new factory system, did at least as good a job in building a party machine and getting out the vote as did the Liberals. In the Victorian heyday, the librettist Gilbert was quite justified in having his guardsmen sing in the operetta *Iolanthe*:

> *That every boy and every gal*
> *That's born into the world alive*
> *Is either a little Liberal*
> *Or else a little Conservative.*

The two-party system was almost wholly confined to the English-speaking lands—Britain, the United States, and the British dominions. On the Continent, not only in France, Italy, and pre-Hitler Germany, but also in the smaller democracies of Scandinavia, Switzerland, Holland, and Belgium, the multiparty system usually prevailed, and governments were generally coalitions of parties with separate organizations. While English-speaking opinion probably exaggerates the defects and dangers of multiparty democracy, a two-party democracy does have distinct advantages in the way of stability and continuity of policy, if only because a given group can enjoy a longer, more assured tenure of power.

In terms of political psychology, the two-party system means that the millions of individual voters who make up each party are in greater agreement than disagreement over what the party stands for; or at least that when they vote for a candidate they feel he stands more for what they want than for what they don't want. Each voter makes some kind of compromise within himself, takes something less in practice than he would ideally like. This sort of compromise the French voter of the 1880's, for instance, did not have to make, for he could choose, from among a dozen or more platforms and candidates, the one closest to his own convictions.

The reasons why Englishmen made these compromises must be sought in British history. One reason lies in the relative security of the islands from external foes, in the long years in which British political habits of moderation and compromise could mature without the constant pressure of foreign wars. All the continental states were repeatedly exposed to the dangers of war and the threat of invasion—an experience

that seemed to promote psychological tendencies to seek final and extreme solutions. This might have happened in Britain, too, had she undergone many repetitions of the kind of alarm raised over the possibilities of invasion by Napoleon and subversion by Jacobins.

Another reason may be found in the fact that continental states in the nineteenth century were still going through the popular revolutionary modification of royal absolutism. They were still torn by major class antagonisms between a noble privileged class, backed usually by orthodox religion, and a middle class. In England, the struggle against absolutism had occurred a full century and a half earlier and had never been quite so bitter as it was on the Continent. It had left England in charge of a ruling class that was itself the product of a compromise between the old landed gentry and the new commercial classes, a ruling class that would develop within itself habits of moderation and compromise. The deep abyss the French Revolution had dug on the Continent between royalists and republicans and between clericals and anticlericals did not exist in England.

Thus, even more important than the fact that the Liberals and Conservatives each held together as parties whose members could sink differences in a common party action is the fact that both parties had a wide area of mutual agreement above and beyond party. To put it quite baldly, there wasn't much difference between the Conservatives and the Liberals. When one went out of power and the other came in, the ship of state tacked a bit, but it did not change direction. The Conservative Disraeli and the Liberal Gladstone were perhaps not quite shadowboxing in their heated parliamentary exchanges, but they clearly were not fighting to kill, nor perhaps even for the knockout.

To sum up, government by discussion, Her Majesty's Government and Her Majesty's Opposition equally loyal to established ways, under the shelter of the English Channel and the British navy, in a prosperous land without deep-seated class antagonisms or insuperable class barriers and rigidities—all this had developed in the British people habits of compromise, of law-abidingness, a sort of political sportsmanship. And these habits survive vigorously today, when Victorian geographical security has gone with the airplane and Victorian economic preponderance has gone with the rise of competing indus-

Queen Victoria and some of her children grouped around a bust of "Dear Albert," 1867.

trial nations. The British, who once cut off a king's head and drove another king into exile, have for nearly two centuries enjoyed remarkable political stability.

Reforms of the Utilitarians

The Reform Bill of 1832 was soon followed by a series of major reforms that helped make over, not merely British political life, but British economic and social life as well. The inspiration of these reforms came in large part from a small but influential middle-class group of Utilitarians, the "Philosophic Radicals." These disciples of Bentham and of the Enlightenment believed that men are, if once properly educated, impelled by rational self-interest and thus automatically do what is best for themselves and all their fellows. Under the influence of the Philosophic Radicals, English local government and the English legal system were made simpler and were cleansed of some of the impediments to efficient government action left by the accumulated red tape of centuries. Legal procedures, for instance, which had

been so complicated that the Chancery Court was many years behind its backlog of cases, were gradually speeded up. The Municipal Corporations Act of 1835, though allowing medieval town and city offices to remain in name, vested basic authority in elective councillors, who supervised professional civil servants. Among the latter were the recently established professional policemen, who got their nickname "bobby" from Robert Peel.

The middle-class radicals, however, believed firmly that that government governs best which governs least, and they sought rather to expedite that minimum of government than to add to its tasks. They believed in education, but not in compulsory public education; private initiative would in their opinion do well what the government would do poorly and tyrannically. Large-scale government reform of British popular education had therefore to wait until 1870. Meanwhile, the private initiative preached by the Utilitarians sponsored mechanics' institutes and other means of adult and "practical" education. It also sponsored all sorts of private schools, and universities in London, Manchester, and some other British cities. These universities, resembling in many ways our American urban universities, first broke into the centuries-old monopoly of Oxford and Cambridge.

The typical Utilitarian reform, the one that stirred up public opinion most thoroughly, was the New Poor Law of 1834. This bill codified, centralized, and made more coherent a complicated system of public relief that had originated in the Elizabethan Poor Law of 1601 and earlier Tudor legislation. But it did more. It shifted the base of this relief. The old methods of home relief, "outdoor relief," had gradually come to permit supplementary payments from the parishes to able-bodied poor working on low wages, supplements for children, and in general relatively easygoing "doles" direct to families in their homes. The new system would have none of this laxness, this encouragement of men in what the Utilitarian, in spite of his belief in human rationality, rather feared was "natural" human laziness. Poor Law unions united parishes for greater efficiency, permitted greater supervision by the central government in London, and supplied—in formidable poorhouses in which the sexes were firmly separated—the "indoor relief" by which able-bodied paupers were made as uncomfortable as decency would allow.

These pains, it was held, would encourage them to try to become self-supporting outside. The New Poor Law offended humanitarians in the upper classes, but from the point of view of middle-class business interests it had the decided merit of making poor relief both more efficient and more economical. The poor at least managed to survive in the workhouses.

Free Trade

Greatest of these Utilitarian reforms in its long-run consequences was the repeal of the Corn Laws in 1846, after a long campaign headed by the Anti-Corn-Law League. This pressure group wanted Britain to exploit her head start in the Industrial Revolution by adopting free trade so that she might use exports of manufactured goods to pay for imports of raw materials and food. The victory of the free traders was achieved in 1846 when they persuaded the Conservative leader Peel to abandon traditional Tory protectionism in the face of the tragic potato famine in Ireland and the urgent need for massive importation of cheap grain. Britain was now a free-trade nation, the only major free-trade nation in a world that never quite lost its mercantilist preconceptions and habits. The repeal of the Corn Laws had, however, temporarily split the Conservative party into two groups, one the "Peelites," who accepted the repeal; the other, soon led by a brilliant young man named Disraeli, who continued to support high tariffs on wheat. Within a decade the Conservatives were once more united in a single party under Disraeli's leadership.

Labor, Education, and the Army

Still another series of reforms helped make the prosperous England of Gladstone and Disraeli. These were the Factory Acts, begun in 1802 and 1819 with bills sponsored by Peel's father. Addicts of the economic interpretation of history hold that middle-class people put through reforms like those of the Poor Law and the repeal of the Corn Laws, but that the landed gentry and upper-class intellectuals, jealous of

Disraeli Measuring the British Lion: Cartoon from "Punch," 1849, on the state of the nation three years after the repeal of the Corn Laws.

the new city wealth and outraged by the ugliness of the new industrial towns, put through reforms like those of the Factory Acts regulating hours and labor, sanitation, and the labor of women and children. It is true that many leaders of the movement for state regulation of economic life were either members of the Tory ruling class, like the Peels, or intellectuals, like Coleridge, Disraeli, Carlyle, Ruskin, and Matthew Arnold, who preached against the horrors of working-class life in prosperous Victorian England. And it is true that the formal philosophy of the British business class was laissez-faire.

But the practice was a different matter. None of the Factory Acts and similar reforms of the nineteenth century could have gone through Parliament successfully without some support from both political parties. Moreover, neither landed gentry nor industrialists and businessmen were mutually exclusive "classes" in a neat Marxist sense. Rather, they were thoroughly mingled in education, marriage, and even in economic interests, since the gentry invested in stocks and bonds and the industrialists invested in landed estates. The elder Peel, father of the Factory Acts, was a selfmade industrialist.

The Factory Acts followed a sequence not unlike the sequence of acts that reformed the suffrage. The first acts were very modest indeed; they underlined the frightful conditions they were designed to remedy. That of 1819, for instance, applying only to the cotton industry, forbade night work for children, and limited day work to twelve hours. Even so, it provided for no really effective inspection, and was violated with impunity by many employers. The Act of 1833, forbidding child labor entirely below the age of nine, and restricting it to nine hours for those below thirteen, and twelve for those below eighteen, marked an important stage by setting up salaried inspectors to enforce the law.

By the end of the nineteenth century, there was on the books a whole code of labor legislation, regulating hours of labor for everyone, giving special protection to women and children, and including provisions that made the employer responsible for workmen's compensation in industrial accidents. Then in 1911 came the great National Insurance Act, which provided through combined payments from the state, from employers, and from employees, compulsory health and unemployment insurance. The "welfare state" was firmly established in Britain well before the Labour party of our own day had come to power.

The same story of piecemeal but cumulative reforms holds true in education. The commonly held Victorian idea that education is not properly a function of the state postponed a general education act until 1870. The issue was complicated by the wrangling of Anglicans and Nonconformists, for many existing schools were controlled by a private society that made instruction in the doctrines of the Church of England compulsory. But even before 1870 a government committee had been aiding local education boards by grants from the national treasury (in 1860 they reached nearly a million pounds), by providing an inspection service, and by helping to organize teacher training. School attendance was not compulsory, however, and the average age for leaving school was eleven years. After many workers got the vote in 1867, worried Tories—and Liberals—began to urge the slogan "Educate your masters." The bill of 1870, put through under Gladstone's minister of educa-

tion, William Forster, did not quite set up compulsory national education at the elementary level. It did permit the local school boards to compel attendance, and it did extend national aid and supervision. Church schools continued to get aid from taxes levied by the central government, an offense to radicals who wanted complete separation of church and state.

Beginnings were made in publicly supported schools at the secondary level, though the British "public school," which in American terms is a private school, continued until our own day to maintain a privileged position in the British social system. In comparison with the public school systems in Germany, France, and the United States, British education on the eve of World War I was administratively complex and full of anomalies. On the whole, though, it got the job done, and the general level of popular education in the British Isles was at least as high as that of the other democracies at the time.

At the same time, Gladstone's ministry allowed the winds of modernization to enter other citadels of upper-class privilege. In 1871 the old requirement that students and staff of Oxford and Cambridge universities had to take religious tests to confirm their Anglicanism was at last abolished. And, in the same year, Cardwell, the secretary of war, put through a massive reorganization of the army, which had been discredited by its poor showing in the Crimean War of the 1850's. The ban on the sale of commissions weakened the virtual monopoly of the aristocracy and gentry over the higher grades of officers, and a reduction in the term of service made recruitment to the ranks more attractive.

Foreign and Imperial Policy

Nowhere does the basic unity that underlies the party strife of nineteenth-century Britain come out more clearly than in foreign relations. Almost everyone was agreed on the fundamental position of Britain: maintain the European state system in balance, preferably by diplomatic rather than military action; police the seas with the British navy; open world markets to British goods; maintain—and in Africa extend—the vast network of the British Empire. The Liberals were more likely to side with the democratic and nationalist movements in Europe than the Conservatives were. They sympathized with the struggling Italians, Greeks, and Poles, and disliked the old Metternichian powers, especially Russia. In mid-century the Liberal Palmerston pursued an active policy of near-intervention in behalf of oppressed nationalities, and British benevolence was a factor in the attainment of Italian unity.

Yet emotional and verbal partisanship had very little to do with Britain's entry into the only European war in which she was directly involved between 1815 and 1914. The Crimean War of 1854–1856 was fought to maintain the balance of power, as England joined France in opposing what they judged to be a Russian threat to their Near Eastern interests. They supported the Ottoman Empire, whose treatment of her own Christian minorities was a chronic source of Liberal indignation under other circumstances. While the war was mismanaged on both sides, it at least checked Russian advances for a time and made the ultimate disposition of the Balkan regions of the decaying Turkish Empire a matter for joint action by all the great powers.

On imperial policy, it seems at first glance as though British public opinion really was deeply divided. Disraeli and Gladstone were never so gladiatorially fierce as when the Conservative defended the greatness of the empire and the Liberal attacked imperialism at home and abroad as un-Christian, illiberal, and unprofitable. And it would be absurd to maintain that in action there was no real difference between the two. Disraeli bought up the financially embarrassed Egyptian khedive's shares in the French-built Suez Canal (1875), a step toward eventual British control of Egypt, and triumphantly made Queen Victoria empress of India (1876). Gladstone, in his succeeding ministry, withdrew British troops from Afghanistan in 1880, conceded virtual independence to the Boer Republics in South Africa by the Pretoria Convention of 1881, and in 1884–1885 neglected General Gordon surrounded by rebels in the Sudan. Yet Gladstone kept British armies on the northwest frontier of India, abutting Afghanistan. It was under his administration in 1882 that the British actually bombarded Alexandria and established a protectorate over Egypt. Gladstone did send troops to rescue Gordon, though they arrived too late, and even in South Africa the Boer Republics were freed only under the "suzerainty" of Britain. In short, Gladstone regretted and no doubt even neglected the Empire; but he kept it.

The Irish Problem

Much nearer home, a nationality problem grew more acute as the nineteenth century came to a close, and did draw something more than a verbal line between Conservatives and Liberals. This was the Irish problem, which had beset the English ever since the Norman-English conquest of Ireland in the twelfth century. The English, and the Scots who came to settle in the northern Irish province of Ulster in the sixteenth and seventeenth centuries, had remained as privileged Protestant landowners in the midst of a subject population of Catholic Irish peasants. While there were also native Irish among the ruling classes, many of them had been Anglicized and had turned Protestant.

For three centuries, religious, political, and economic problems in Ireland had remained unsolved. As the nineteenth century opened, the English attempted to solve the political problem by a formal union of the two kingdoms, with Irish members admitted to the British Parliament, in which they were of course a minority. On January 1, 1801, the United Kingdom of Great Britain and Ireland came into being. In the prevailing temper of nineteenth-century Britain, it was quite impossible to deny the Irish natives all political rights; and, beginning with the Catholic Emancipation Act of 1829, which allowed Irish voters to elect Catholics to office, most of the English reforms we have outlined above were extended to Ireland. The Irish, led by Daniel O'Connell, the "Great Emancipator," organized politically to press for more thoroughgoing changes and, eventually, for "home rule." They sought not only for self-government but also for land reforms to break the economic dominance of the Protestant minority and for disestablishment of the Anglican church in Ireland—that is, abolition of a state church supported by taxes levied on both members and nonmembers.

Irish hatred for the English was fanned by the disastrous potato famine of the 1840's, when blight ruined a crop essential to the food supply. The British government was not prepared for prompt and efficient relief measures, nor was the kind of international organization for such relief afforded nowadays by the Red Cross yet in existence. The result was a medieval famine in the heart of modern Western civilization, in which hundreds of thousands died of starvation or of typhus and cholera and other hundreds of thousands were forced to migrate, mostly to the United States. The immigrants added to British difficulties, for they carried their inevitable hatreds with them, and formed pressure groups like the Fenian Brotherhood, organized in New York in 1858 to raise funds to aid Irish resistance and to make trouble generally for the British wherever they could.

British governments made piecemeal reforms. The Anglican church in Ireland was disestablished in 1869, and in the next year an Irish Land Act began a series of agrarian measures that were designed to protect the tenant from "rack-renting"—the extraction by the landlord, often an absentee member of the British "garrison," of as high a rent as the tenants could pay. The reforms were neither far-reaching nor rapid enough to satisfy the Irish. Moreover, the emotional strength of Irish nationalism grew with the spread of elementary education and the usual literary and cultural forms of national self-consciousness. The Irish question was not just a matter of land, or of religion, but also of a peculiarly intense form of underdog awareness of cultural differences and of nationality. Then in the 1870's a brilliant Irish leader arose, Charles Parnell, himself a Protestant descendant of the "garrison," but a firm Irish patriot. Under the leadership of Parnell in the British Parliament, the Irish nationalists were welded into a firm, well-disciplined party which, though it held less than a hundred seats in the House of Commons of the United Kingdom, could often swing the balance between Liberals and Conservatives.

The critical step came when in 1885 Gladstone was converted to Home Rule, and introduced his first Home Rule Bill. This bill provided for a separate Irish parliament with some restrictions on its sovereignty, and of course under the Crown. Gladstone's decision split his own Liberal party in something like the way Peel's conversion to free trade had split the Conservatives in 1846. A group led by Joseph Chamberlain, who had begun political life as the reform leader of the great city of Birmingham, seceded under the name of Liberal Unionists. In effect, they joined the Conservative party, which was often known in the next few decades, so great were the passions aroused in Great Britain by this proposed cutting loose of Ireland, simply as the "Unionist" party. Gladstone lost the election brought on by the split, and Home Rule was dropped for the moment.

Agitation continued in Ireland. It became more bitter when Parnell, involved in a divorce scandal, was dropped by the virtuous Gladstone and by some of his own equally virtuous Irish followers. In 1892, however, Gladstone won a close election on the Irish issue—or, rather, he obtained enough English seats to get a Second Home Rule Bill through the Commons with the aid of eighty-one Irish nationalists. The bill was defeated, however, in the Conservative House of Lords, and was dropped once more. The Conservatives, when they came in for their ten-year reign in 1895, sought to "kill Home Rule by kindness," enacting several land reform bills that furthered the process of making Ireland a land of small peasant proprietors.

But Ireland was now beyond the reach of kindness, and Irish problems were no longer—if they ever had been—largely economic and administrative. Irish nationalism was now a full cult, nourished by a remarkable literary revival in English and in Gaelic which produced writers like W. B. Yeats, John Synge, and Lady Augusta Gregory. Irish men and women everywhere—including definitely the Irish-Americans—were keyed to a pitch of emotional excitement. They would be satisfied with nothing less than an independent Irish nation.

The Liberals, back in power after 1905, found they needed the votes of the Irish nationalists to carry through their proposal for ending the veto power of the Lords. After some soul-searching, the Liberals struck the bargain: Home Rule in return for the Parliament Act. They introduced in 1912 a Home Rule Bill which—the Parliament Act in 1911 having destroyed the veto power of the Lords—was placed on the books as a law. It never went into force, however, for as Home Rule seemed about to become a fact the predominantly Protestant north of Ireland, the province of Ulster, bitterly opposed to separation from Great Britain, was organized to resist by force of arms. The Home Rule Bill as passed carried the rider that it was not to go into effect until the Ulster question was settled. The outbreak of war in 1914 made such a settlement out of the question, and the stage was set for the Irish Revolution of the 1920's.

The Threat to Free Trade

As Great Britain approached the twentieth century, new problems arose to disturb the underlying serenity and assurance of the Victorian Age. Irish troubles, the Boer War in South Africa, the rising international tensions that were to lead to World War I, and the difficulties of raising the additional government income made necessary by the rise of the "welfare state" and by the naval armament race with Germany, confronted the British people all at once. Moreover, the long lead Britain had gained in the Industrial Revolution was being lost as other nations acquired the technical skills of large-scale production. Germany, the Low Countries, Switzerland, the United States, and in a measure all the West were competing with Britain on the World market.

Under such conditions, it was natural that some Britishers should come to doubt the wisdom of the free trade policies that had won the day in 1846. For the Germans and others were not only underselling the British abroad; they were actually invading the British home market. Why not protect that market by a tariff system? Few Britishers were foolish enough to believe that the home islands, already by the 1880's too densely populated to feed themselves and constitute a self-sufficient economy, could surround themselves with a simple tariff wall. But the empire was worldwide, with abundant resources in agricultural lands. Within it the classical mercantilist interchange of manufactures for raw materials could still in theory provide a balanced economic system. Britain could still be, if not the workshop of the world, at least the workshop of the quarter of the world that composed the British Commonwealth and Empire.

The same Joseph Chamberlain who led the secession from the Liberals on the question of Home Rule for Ireland also led a secession on an issue of even more fundamental importance. He became a protectionist and imperialist. He gave special importance to the establishment of a system of imperial preference through which the whole complex of lands under the Crown would be knit together in a tariff union. Many Conservatives, never wholly reconciled to free trade, welcomed the issue, and the new Unionist party made protection a major plank in its program. Liberal opposition, however, was still much too strong, and there was opposition also in Conservative ranks. Chamberlain, reversing the aims but imitating the methods of Cobden and the Anti-Corn Law League of the 1840's, organized a Tariff Reform League. In 1903, he made in the cabinet sweeping proposals that would have restored moderate duties on foodstuffs and raw materials (largely to give a basis for negotiating with the dominions, which already had tariff systems of their own) and on foreign manufactured goods. But the Conservative leader, Balfour, did not dare go so far, and Chamberlain resigned with his bill unpassed. Indeed, Chamberlain, who had already split the Liberal party on Home Rule, now split the Conservatives on tariff reform. Although the new Liberal government after 1905 continued free trade, the rift Chamberlain had made in the old Liberal party was never really repaired.

The Welfare State

The Liberals were, however, committed to another policy as contrary to the classical philosophy of laissez-faire as was protectionism. This was the welfare state—social security through compulsory insurance managed by the state and in part financed by the state, minimum-wage laws, compulsory free public education, public works and services of all kinds. The dramatic point in the working out of the program was the "People's Budget" of 1909, introduced by a new figure on the political stage, a Welshman, the Liberal chancellor of the exchequer, Lloyd George (1863-1945). This budget, which frankly proposed to make the rich finance the new welfare measures through progressive taxation on incomes and inheritances, was clearly no ordinary tax measure. It was a means of altering the social and economic structure of Britain; its opponents called it "not a budget, but a revolution." It passed the Commons, but was thrown out by the Lords, even though it was a "money bill." The Liberals went to the country for the second time in 1910 and after a close and exciting election were able to put through the Parliament Act of 1911, which took away from the Lords all power to alter a money bill, and left them with no

David Lloyd George, 1898.

themselves as Conservatives. For what happened in the generation after 1880 was a major change in the political orientation of British parties. The Liberals, who had believed that that government governs best which governs least, and least expensively, had come to believe that the state must interfere in economic life to help the underdog, and had adopted Lloyd George's plan for redistributing the national wealth by social insurance financed by taxation of the rich and well-to-do. And the Conservatives, who in the mid-nineteenth century had stood for factory acts and at least mild forms of the welfare state, were now in large part committed to a laissez-faire program against government "intervention," a program astonishingly like that of the Liberals of 1850.

The Labour Party

One factor in this change had been the growth of the British Labour party, which originated in a number of groups formed in the late nineteenth century. Labour, though not yet unified, had developed by 1905 into a party able to command fifty-three seats in the Commons. The political ideas that went into the making of the British Labour party antedate by a good deal its formal organization. They derive from the legacy of 1776 and 1789 as modified by the Marxists, by the Christian socialists, and by the rapidly growing trade unions. Labourites wanted the welfare state, and a great many of them also wanted a socialist state in which at least the major industries would be nationalized. Labour had the backing of many upper- and middle-class people who sympathized with the quest for social justice. From their ranks came intellectuals like G. B. Shaw, H. G. Wells, and Sidney and Beatrice Webb, who participated in the influential Fabian Society, formed in the 1880's, which preached the "inevitability of gradualness," the attainment of social democracy through the peaceful parliamentary adaptation of the strategy of advancing one step at a time used by the Roman republican general Fabius to wear down the Carthaginians.

Part of the motivation for the Liberal program of social legislation was a desire to forestall Labour. Just as in 1867 the Tories had caught the Whigs bathing and "walked away with the Whigs' clothes" by giving the workers the vote, so in 1909–1911 the Liberals stole Labour's

more than a delaying power of not more than two years over all other legislation. The Liberal program of social legislation was saved. It was saved under conditions strongly reminiscent of 1832, for the new king, George V (1910–1936), had promised Prime Minister Asquith that if necessary he would create enough new peerages—which might have meant several hundred—to put the Parliament Act through the House of Lords. As in 1832 the threat was enough, and the Peers yielded.

But was it a *Liberal* program? The dissenting Liberals who had followed Joseph Chamberlain out of the party in the 1880's thought not, and it was normal enough for Chamberlain's two sons, Austen and Neville, who played an important part in twentieth-century politics, to think of clothes and gave the workers social security. But these tactics worked no better in the twentieth century than they had in the nineteenth, and the workers on the whole stuck by the Labour party. The Liberal party was beginning a long decline, which would be hastened by the upsetting effects of World War I and would drive its right wing to Toryism and its left wing to Labour.

Not all the motivation of the Liberals in these early years of the twentieth century was, however, mere fear of Labour. In part, their conversion from laissez-faire to social security was a positive one, a sincere belief that the logic of their democratic assumptions must drive them to raise the general standard of living in Britain by state action. Something broadly analogous was happening throughout the democratic West—in France, in the smaller democracies, and, a few decades later, in the United States. An important part of the bourgeoisie in all these countries swung over, not to doctrinaire socialism, but to programs of social legislation put through by the usual machinery of change under a democratic franchise. The English Chartists back in the early nineteenth century had been justified in their apparently naïve belief that universal suffrage would eventually pave the way to greater social and economic equality.

III France: Second Empire and Third Republic

"The Eighteenth Brumaire of Louis Napoleon Bonaparte"

A century ago France seemed to many English-speaking critics, as she sometimes still appears, a rather uncertain member of the community of nations ruled by the democratic decencies—that is, government by discussion, peaceful alternation of "ins" and "outs" through the working of the party system, and the usual freedoms of civil rights. The democratic revolution, so optimistically begun in 1848, had by 1852 brought still another Bonaparte to the throne of France in the person of Napoleon III, nephew of the first Napoleon. ("Napoleon II," son of the first Napoleon by Marie Louise, never really ruled, any more than did the son of Louis XVI, the "Louis XVII" who died in prison during the great French Revolution.) As president of the Second Republic, Prince Louis Napoleon had soon quarreled with the new National Assembly elected in 1849, in which monarchist sentiment favoring a restoration of either the Bourbons or the house of Orléans greatly outweighed Bonapartism. The Assembly refused to amend the constitution of 1848 to allow him a second four-year term. Fearful of radicals and socialists, the Assembly also whittled down the universal male suffrage of 1848, depriving about 3,000,000 Frenchmen of the vote and enabling the prince president to denounce the move and act as the champion of persecuted popular democracy.

The coup d'état of December 2, 1851 was artfully timed for the sacred Bonapartist day of the coronation of Napoleon I (December 2, 1804) and the greatest Napoleonic victory, the battle of Austerlitz (December 2, 1805). Controlling the army and the police, Louis Napoleon and his fellow conspirators arrested seventy-eight noted anti-Bonapartists, thereby paving the way for the humiliation of the Assembly. Street fighting on the barricades of Paris, which broke out on December 3, proved to be no wholesale bloodletting. It left victims enough as martyrs, however, and, politically more important, it enabled the president to pose as the champion of order against a largely imaginary socialist plot. Napoleon strengthened his posture by massive arrests, which ultimately sent 20,000 Frenchmen to prison or into exile. What Karl Marx called "the eighteenth Brumaire of Louis Napoleon Bonaparte" was destroying the Second Republic.

Toward the end of December 1851 Napoleon restored universal male suffrage for a plebiscite which by 7,500,000 votes to 640,000 gave him the right to draw up a new constitution. The plebiscite was accompanied by skillful propaganda, but it was not crudely a work of force. Though many opponents of Napoleon simply did not vote, it seems that at least a very substantial majority of Frenchmen over twenty-one really were willing to try another dictator. There were many reasons why men voted yes. Almost all were weary of the struggles of the last three years. Many were frightened by the specter of socialism raised by the June days of 1848. For nearly three decades the full force of fashionable French literature had been at work making the Napoleonic legend and identifying the name of Napoleon with the "pooled self-esteem" of French patriotism. Many a man voted yes, not to Louis Napoleon, nor to any approval of dictatorship for itself, but to the music of the *Marseillaise,* the cannon of Austerlitz, to all the glories of France.

The Second Empire: Constitution and Economy

In 1852 yet another plebiscite authorized Louis Napoleon to assume the title of emperor and inauguarate the Second Empire, which he proceeded to do, inevitably, on December 2, 1852. The new constitution sponsored by the two plebiscites set up a lightly veiled dictatorship very much like that of Napoleon I. The emperor had full authority; he was responsible only to the nation. He governed through ministers, judges, and a whole bureaucracy, in the appointment of which he had the final voice. The popularly elected assembly, the Corps Législatif, was filled with "official" candidates whose succsss at the polls was assured by the pressure of the emperor's loyal prefects. It had no power to initiate or amend legislation; it had only a veto, which in the first few years it rarely used. Yet Napoleon III insisted that he was no mere tool of the possessing classes, no conservative, but an agent of real reform, an emperor of the masses, a "Saint-Simon on horseback" who would use strong government to realize the great public works and deeper international understanding dreamt of by the early utopian social engineer. Somewhat similar claims have been made by almost all the dictators of the twentieth century; communist, fascist, or merely nationalist, they all claim to be true democrats, protectors of ordinary men who in the classical Western democracies, they insist, are actually victims of capitalist exploitation. Napoleon III has sometimes been seen as the first of these modern dictators, as a protofascist; it must be said that both his methods and his ideology seem mild when put next to those of twentieth-century totalitarians.

Napoleon III did carry through a great program of public works, bringing to both the capital and many provincial cities great public markets known as Les Halles, new boulevards and promenades, and other manifestations of urban renewal. Urban France still bears the stamp of the Second Empire, especially in Paris, where the emperor's prefect, Haussmann, cut through the medieval maze of streets those broad straight avenues with their splendid vistas which all the world knows so well—and which could easily be swept by gunfire and made street fighting that much more difficult. The Second Empire also helped with housing and encouraged workers' mutual aid societies. Yet, by comparison with later social legislation in Germany, Britain, or Scandinavia, its concrete achievements directly benefiting the workers were meager. The legal code of labor in France in 1860 was less "modern" than that of England. The standard of living of French labor in the growing cities was well behind that of Britain, and behind that of Germany and the smaller democracies. French labor did indeed benefit from the general prosperity that came to France in the 1850's, but the gains in wages were at least partly counterbalanced by rising prices. France lagged as a welfare state.

It was the bourgeoisie that gained most from the Second Empire, greatly assisted by the capital supplied through the government-sponsored Crédit Foncier and Crédit Mobilier, set up to promote investment in real estate and movable property, respectively. Napoleon's government also encouraged improvement in banking facilities, helped the great growth of French railways by state guaranties, and in general furthered the rise of industry in the two decades after 1850. Paris grew into a major metropolitan area, and centers like Lyons and Rouen in textiles, Clermont-Ferrand and St. Etienne in metallurgy, and many other cities came to have genuine industrial economies, with all the accompanying problems. Yet both under the Second Empire and under its successor, the Third Republic, many Frenchmen remained loyal to older methods of doing business, to small firms under family control, to luxury trades in which handicraft skills remained important in spite of the machine. In consequence, the industrial growth of France was slower than that of leading economic powers, especially in heavy industry. In the Sixties France lost her continental leadership in iron and steel production to the new Germany, and was subsequently far outdistanced by the burgeoning economy of the United States.

The French rate of population growth also lagged, and the exodus to the cities from impoverished rural departments, especially in the mountainous southern half of the country, was beginning under the Second Empire. At the end of the nineteenth century, France was not much more than 50 percent more populous than at the beginning—and this with almost no emigration. Britain, in spite of a large emigration, had about tripled her population, and Germany, too, was growing rapidly. Even Italy, with slender natural resources and less industry than France, was growing in population faster than France despite heavy emigration, and was to outstrip her in our own times. Though the reasons for French demographic weakness are imperfectly understood, a major factor in this country of a great many small proprietors appears to have been a determination to avoid division of modest inheritances among many heirs.

Napoleon III's Foreign Policy

Nevertheless, the France of the Second Empire was still a very great power, and the extent of her comparative decline was by no means clear to contemporaries. Although the French gained little from the Crimean War, they did at least have the satisfaction of playing host to the post war congress at Paris in 1856. And the Paris Exposition of 1855, a counterpart of the famous London exhibition of 1851, was a great success that showed Napoleon III at the height of his power. He had pledged himself to use that power for peace; but he allowed himself, partly through a romantic interest in "oppressed nationalities," partly from age-old motives of prestige, to join Piedmont in a war against Austria for the liberation of Italy. In this war of 1859, French armies won victories at Magenta and Solferino—names which, incidentally, were soon exploited commercially, as in the new shade called magenta introduced by the fashion trade. Yet the defeated Austrians were not knocked out of the war. In the summer of 1859, sickened by the bloodshed on the battlefields and fearful that Prussia might come to Austria's assistance, Napoleon III suddenly made a separate peace with Austria, which agreed to relinquish Lombardy, but not Venetia, to Piedmont.

In 1860 the Italians took things into their own hands and set about organizing almost the whole peninsula, including papal Rome, into an Italian kingdom. Napoleon depended too much on Catholic support at home to be able to permit the extinction of papal territorial power; moreover, the too great success of Italian nationalism was threatening the European balance of power. He therefore temporized, permitting the union of most of Italy under the house of Savoy, but protecting the pope's temporal power with a French garrison in Rome and leaving Venetia still in Austrian hands. In 1860, as a reward for his services, he received from Piedmont the French-speaking part of Alpine Savoy plus the Mediterranean city of Nice and its hinterland. Napoleon III thus managed to offend most Italians, and liberals everywhere, as well as most of his own Catholic supporters at home.

To make matters worse, in 1861 he used the Mexican government's defaulting on payments of its foreign debt as the pretext for a wild imperialist venture. A French expedition installed the Austrian prince Maximilian as emperor of Mexico, and French arms and men continued to assist him. The europeanized Mexican upper classes were in part willing to support this venture, for like most Latin Americans of the nineteenth century, their cultural ideal was France. But from the start the Mexican people resented the foreign intruder, and Maximilian had to rely heavily on French support to penetrate to Mexico City, where he was proclaimed emperor in June 1863. The United States, engaged in the Civil War, could do nothing at the time against what Americans regarded as an infraction of the Monroe Doctrine. But after peace had been restored in the United States, the American government protested strongly. The rival of Maximilian, the republican leader Juárez, had no difficulty in defeating the Mexican supporters of Maximilian, once Napoleon under American pressure had abandoned them. The unfortunate Maximilian fell before a firing squad in 1867.

The Liberal Empire

Louis Napoleon had come to power in 1848 on a platform of order and national unity against the threat of socialist upheaval. But, in spite of his one-sided victories in the presidential election of 1848 and the plebiscites of 1851 and 1852, it became more and more clear that if France had a national unity, it was not of the monolithic, totalitarian sort, but a unity that had to be worked out in the open competition of modern Western political life with parties, parliamentary debate, newspapers—in short, with government by discussion. Napoleon could not in fact be a symbolic head of state, above the struggle, nor even a final umpire. He could not be a republican; he could not be a legitimate monarchist, though much of France, and particularly the conservative France which held authoritarian views, was loyal to the legitimacy of the Bourbons, or the somewhat dubious legitimacy of the Orléanists. He could not even be a good devout Catholic, in spite of the orthodoxy of his wife, the empress Eugénie, for his Bonapartist background was heavily tinged with the anticlericalism of the eighteenth century, and his bungling of the Italian problem had deeply offended clericals. He could only head an "official" party, relying on the manipulative skills of his bureaucrats to work the cumbersome machinery of a parliamentary system designed, like that of Napoleon I, as a disguise for dictatorship.

As the pressure of genuine party differences rose, in reflection of genuine moral, social, and economic group interests, Napoleon slowly abandoned the measures of repression he had begun with and sought to establish himself in something like the position of a constitutional monarch. An act of 1860 gave the Legislative Assembly power to discuss freely a reply to the address from the throne, and throughout the 1860's these powers were extended in the name of the Liberal Empire. Gradually, political life in France took on a pattern of parliamentary government, with a Right, Left, and Center. As a result of the general election of 1869, the government was faced with a strong legal opposition, thirty of whom were declared republicans. On July 12, 1869, Napoleon capitulated and granted the Legislative Assembly the right to propose laws, and to criticize and vote the budget. Partial ministerial responsibility to the legislature seemed just around the corner as Napoleon entrusted the government to the head of the moderates, Emile Ollivier. A plebiscite in May 1870 overwhelmingly ratified these changes.

It is possible that the Second Empire might thus have been converted into a constitutional monarchy with full parliamentary government. Yet the changes had been wrung from an ailing and vacillating emperor by popular agitation, which was not just political but also economic in the form of strikes, since the Liberal empire had relaxed the ban on unions and strikes imposed by the Le Chapelier Law of 1791. Thus, it is also possible that a radical republican groundswell would have submerged the empire in any case. But the Franco-Prussian War, into which Napoleon III was maneuvered by Bismarck in July 1870, put an abrupt end to the experiment of the Liberal empire. The sluggish mobilization and overconfidence of the French armies gave the Prussians a decisive head start. Within six weeks Napoleon III and a large French army capitulated at Sedan, September 2, 1870. Two days later, rioting Parisians forced the remnant of the Legislative Assembly to decree the fall of the empire, and at the classic center of French republicanism, the Paris City Hall, the Third Republic was proclaimed. Napoleon III went to captivity in Germany and eventually to exile in England, where he died in 1873.

The Birth of the Third Republic

The new republic was too good a child of 1792 to give up the war against the national enemy. A government of national defense tried to continue the struggle, but the miracle of Valmy was not to be repeated. In October, General Bazaine surrendered a large French force at Metz, and the disorganized elements of other French armies were helpless before the powerful German forces. An exhausted nation, sick of the war, chose in February a National Assembly that met at Bordeaux and sued for peace. The special circumstances of that election, however, placed on the new republic an additional handicap. For meanwhile Paris, besieged by the Germans, had resisted desperately until starvation forced its surrender in January 1871. Even under pressure of the siege, Parisian radicals tried to seize power and revive the old Paris Commune, or city government, of 1792. These radicals could not stomach the capitulation that the rest of the country seemed to be preparing. In the elections to the National Assembly, their intransigence helped to turn the provincial voters toward conservative candidates pledged to make peace—and to restore, not the republic, but the old monarchy.

This new Assembly, on March 1, 1871, voted to accept a peace ceding Alsace and a substantial part of Lorraine to Germany and paying an indemnity of five billion francs (about a billion dollars). Then the Paris National Guard, which had not been disarmed by the Germans, went over to the radicals because the National Assembly had suspended its pay. The Assembly and the provisional government it had set up under the veteran Orléanist politician Thiers sent troops into Paris in a vain attempt to seize National Guard artillery on the heights of Montmartre. Thiers and the Assembly established themselves in Versailles; in Paris the Commune was set up, March 18, 1871.

Marxist legend has consecrated the Parisian Commune of 1871 as the first major socialist government. Most of the Communards were in fact rather Jacobins, radical anticlericals and highly patriotic republicans who wanted a society of small independent shopkeepers and artisans, not the abolition of private property. While some Communards were affiliated with the First International, most of these were followers of Proudhon rather than of Marx; some other Communards were followers of Blanqui, the now aged champion of revolutionary violence who was arrested in the provinces before he could get to Paris. Neither Proudhonians nor Blanquists were socialists in any Marxian sense. In any event, the Communards had no chance to introduce sweeping social reforms. But their revolutionary aspect alarmed the rest of France, and their refusal to accept the peace was a challenge the National Assembly had to meet. To the horrors of the first siege by the Germans were added the horrors of a new siege by the government of the National Assembly, which gathered its troops at Versailles and in the "Bloody Week" of May 21-28 advanced through the barricades to clear the city. Twenty thousand Frenchmen died in the fighting, a total far exceeding that of the June Days of 1848.

The Third Republic, born in the trauma of defeat and civil war, at once came into a heritage of unresolved cleavages. More than half the members of the new National Assembly were monarchists, anxious to undo the formal declaration of a republic made in republican Paris right after Sedan. But now we encounter one of those concrete events that are the despair of those who seek the clue to history in vast impersonal forces beyond the play of human personality. About half the monarchist deputies were pledged to the elder "legitimate" Bourbon line represented by the count of Chambord, grandson of Charles X, and the other half to the younger Orléanist line that had come to the throne in 1830, represented by the count of Paris, grandson of Louis Philippe. Since Chambord was childless, he agreed to designate the count of Paris as the eventual heir to the throne. Chambord might have become in fact what he was to his supporters, King Henry V, had he also been willing to make the slightest concession to Orléanist sentiments and accept the revolutionary blue, white, and red tricolor flag that Louis Philippe had himself accepted as the flag of France. But he insisted on the white flag and gold lilies of Bourbon, which for millions of Frenchmen meant complete repudiation of all that had happened since 1789. Chambord did not, of course, act just for a white flag and against a tricolor one; behind these symbols lay real motives tied up with all French history. He meant to be not just a Victorian symbol, a purely "decorative" monarch, but a real king. No one, however, could be that sort of king in France at that moment.

In the resulting stalemate, the republican minority was able to maintain itself, and slowly gather strength. Thiers was recognized as "president of the Republic" and carried through the final settlement with Germany. Thiers, however, pushed a little too hard to convince the Orléanists that they should endorse the republic as "the regime that divides us least." In 1873 he lost what amounted to a vote of confidence in the Assembly, and he was succeeded by Marshal MacMahon (a descendant of a Catholic British Jacobite who had fled to France after the departure of James II), a soldier and a monarchist who was chosen to hold the government together until the monarchist majority of the Assembly worked out a compromise between its legitimist and Orléanist wings. The compromise was never achieved, as Chambord continued to insist on the white flag. Ultimately, Thiers's strategy worked, and in 1875 enough Orléanists joined the republicans for the Assembly to pass a series of constitutional measures formally establishing the Third Republic.

The Constitution of 1875

These laws, known collectively as the Constitution of 1875, provided for a president elected by an absolute majority of Senate and Chamber of Deputies sitting together as a National Assembly. The Chamber of Deputies was directly elected by universal male suffrage; the Senate was chosen, one-third at any given time, by elected members of local governmental bodies. All legislation had to pass both houses, though only the lower could initiate finance bills. The critical point was that of the responsibility of the ministers. Had the president been able to dismiss them, a new Napoleon III might easily have arisen to destroy the republic. MacMahon attempted to exercise this power when on May 16, 1877, he dismissed the anticlerical premier, Jules Simon, and got the conservative duke of Broglie to form a cabinet. But the Chamber was now really republican—or at least antimonarchist—and voted "no confidence" in Broglie by a big majority. MacMahon dissolved the Chamber and called for a new national election—which he could do constitutionally. In the new elections the republicans, though losing some seats, still retained a good majority in the Chamber, and could now force the president to name a republican premier. Disgruntled, MacMahon resigned in 1879 and was succeeded by a conservative republican, Jules Grévy. This crisis of the Seize Mai (May 16) set a precedent for the Third Republic. No president thereafter dared to dissolve the Chamber, and the presidency became a ceremonial office, made fun of in the press and on the stage. But at any rate, nine years after its establishment in name, the Third Republic had at last become a fact.

It was in form a kind of republican transposition of constitutional monarchy, with an ornamental president instead of an ornamental king. The real executive, as in England, was the ministry, in effect a committee responsible to the legislature—indeed to the Chamber of Deputies, which soon became the focus of political action, leaving the Senate little real power. The Chamber, reflecting the political habits of the ideologically divided country, was composed, not of two, but of a dozen or more parties, so that any ministry had to be supported by a coalition sub-ject to constant shifting in the play of personalities and principles. The result was a marked instability of ministries. The "life expectancy" of a ministry under the Third Republic was hardly a year.

Yet such a figure is misleading. A French ministry under the Third Republic did not usually resign and give way to a totally different ministry with totally different policies. Instead, its personnel was shifted a bit, a compromise or so was made with certain parliamentary groups, and the new ministry carried on much as did the old. For instance, Briand, the great champion of collective security (after the war of 1914-1918), headed ten different cabinets at various times between 1909 and 1926; Delcassé, the architect of France's entente with England, served as foreign minister continuously through several cabinets and seven years (1898-1905). Moreover, the day-to-day task of governing was carried on by a civil service, by experts in the law courts and in the educational system as well as in the executive department. This permanent personnel, or "bureaucracy," subject only to broad policy control from above, preserved a basic continuity in French political action, especially in foreign policy.

The system was highly democratic, for it could work only by means of constant and subtle compromises. These, the essence of democratic government, were made in France—and in most of the democratic world outside the English-speaking countries—by the several parties in open debate and voting in the legislature *after* an election. In the English-speaking countries, these compromises are made *before* an election, *within* each of the two major parties, often in the privacy of the famous smoke-filled room. Probably the English-speaking method both conceals antagonisms and encourages the habit of willing compromise more effectively than does the continental method. But neither method will work if the underlying antagonisms are really intense and beyond compromise. For example, the American two-party system obviously failed to avert the Civil War.

Boulanger and Panama

Bitter antagonisms did in fact threaten the Third French Republic between 1879 and 1914, but they did not destroy it. For one thing, the republic's opponents on the Right and on the Left could never get together. On the Right, although the legitimists eventually patched up their quarrels with the Orléanists, the monarchists could not recover the strength they had dissipated in the 1870's. Nor could the Bonapartists make serious gains in public opinion, though they survived as a political group into the twentieth century. After the accession of Pope Leo XIII in 1878 the Catholics were gradually encouraged to develop their way of life by frank acceptance of the freedom of worship that the Constitution of the Republic offered them. Many Catholics, however, feared the anticlericalism of many republicans, particularly after a law of 1882 making education free and compulsory for French children to the age of thirteen and forbidding religious instruction in public schools. Clerical and Rightist enemies of the republic often did violence to their own conservative principles by seeking some new man who would win over the malcontents, including those on the Left and among labor, and then set up a dictatorship.

In the 1880's, they hoped that they had found such a man in General Boulanger, an ambitious soldier who had as minister of war catered to French desire for revenge on Germany. But the Boulangist movement was founded on a man of straw. The general cut an impressive figure in public appearances, and in by-elections to fill vacancies caused by deaths or resignations in the Chamber he showed he could command a popular following. But from the point of view of many traditional conservatives he had compromising origins and radical friends, and, as it became clear that Boulanger in power might rush the country into war, his following threatened to desert him. In January 1889 he swept a by-election in Paris, but his nerve failed when he was faced with the need to resort to the classic technique of the coup d'état. Instead of seizing power by force of arms, he sought refuge with his mistress. The government now took courage and threatened to try him for treason; Boulanger fled to Brussels and committed suicide on the grave of his beloved in 1891. The republic had surmounted its first great crisis.

Boulanger's cause had gained strength from a scandal in republican ranks. Daniel Wilson, President Grévy's son-in-law, was implicated in the selling of posts in the Legion of Honor. The opposition press made out that the government was riddled with graft. More fuel went on the fire in the early 1890's, when there burst into publicity one of those crises of graft and racketeering that seem endemic in modern Western societies. This was the Panama scandal which was brought on by the failure of De Lesseps' attempt to duplicate in Panama his success in building the Suez Canal. It involved accusations of criminal corruption against ministers, deputies, financiers, and an unfortunate Jewish banker, Reinach, who either committed suicide or was murdered just before his trial. As in the somewhat comparable Crédit Mobilier scandal in the United States in 1873, it was established that ministers and deputies had accepted financial reward for backing the shaky Panama company. Bad as it was, the Panama scandal was to pale before the Dreyfus affair, in which the force of anti-Semitism first attained dramatic intensity and worldwide attention.

Boulanger as General Bonaparte: An English cartoon comment on Boulanger's return as deputy by a huge electoral majority in 1889.

The Dreyfus Case

Dreyfus, a Jew and a captain in the French army, was the almost accidental victim of an espionage intrigue and of the anti-Semitism then prevalent in France, especially in military and Catholic circles. Accused of selling military secrets to the Germans, he was railroaded into trial as a scapegoat and was convicted of treason in 1894. Colonel Picquart, an intelligence officer, became convinced that the document on which Dreyfus had been convicted was a forgery, and that the real traitor was a disreputable adventurer of Hungarian blood but of French birth, Major Esterhazy. Picquart was quietly shipped off to Africa by his superiors, who wished to let sleeping dogs lie. But the Dreyfus family, by independent investigation, arrived at the conclusion that Esterhazy was the traitor, and sought to reopen the case. Esterhazy was tried and acquitted, but the affair was now too public for such silencing. In 1898, the famous novelist Zola brought matters to a crisis by publishing his open letter, *J'Accuse*. Zola accused the military leaders, one by one, of sacrificing an innocent man deliberately in order to save the reputation of the army.

France was now divided into Dreyfusards and Anti-Dreyfusards; the former defended in Dreyfus the republic, the latter attacked it. Almost all the far Left, which had hitherto held aloof from the affair as just one more example of the rottenness of the bourgeois state, now rallied to the Third Republic. Dreyfus was brought back from his prison on Devil's Island in French Guiana and was retried in the midst of a frenzied campaign in the press and on the platform. The military court, faced with new evidence brought out by the suicide of Colonel Henry, the real forger of the most incriminating of the original documents used to convict Dreyfus, again found Dreyfus guilty of treason, but with the almost incredible qualifications—in a treason case—of "extenuating circumstances." This attempt at face-saving saved nothing. Dreyfus was pardoned by the president of the republic in 1899, and in 1906, after the tensions had abated, he was acquitted and restored to the army with the rank of major.

The Dreyfus affair presents a remarkably

An English cartoon of 1898 on Emile Zola's sentence of imprisonment and fine for libeling the court martial that tried and acquitted Major Esterhazy during the Dreyfus Affair.

well-documented case study in social psychology. The simple juridical issue—was this man guilty or not guilty of treason—never wholly disappeared in the mass hysteria. Many Frenchmen who did not like Dreyfus or Jews or who did revere the Church, army, and the whole apparatus of the Right, none the less sought to make up their minds solely on the basis of the facts. Yet many on both sides worked themselves up to a point where the question of Dreyfus' guilt was wholly submerged in this great confronting of the "two Frances"—the France of the republic, heir to the great revolution and the principles of 1789, on the one hand, and, on the other, the France of the monarchy, of throne and altar, and of the army, which had never really reconciled itself to the great revolution. For the ordinary person the open admission of forgery by Colonel Henry and his subsequent suicide were enough; he now thought Dreyfus innocent. But for the violent Anti-Dreyfusard, Henry's act made him a hero and a martyr; he had died for his country! A paper was circulated in Paris asking for a memorial to Henry:

Colonel Henry's Devotion to his Country.

Public subscription for a monument to be raised to him.

When an officer is reduced to committing a pretended forgery in order to restore peace to his country and rid it of a traitor, that soldier is to be mourned.

If he pays for his attempt with his life, he is a martyr.

If he voluntarily takes his life,
HE IS A HERO.*

A More Republican Republic

With the victory of the Dreyfusards, the republic moved to the Left and punished the Church for its support of the army and the Anti-Dreyfusards. The triumphant republicans in a series of measures between 1901 and 1905 destroyed the Concordat of 1801 between Napoleon I and the pope which had established the Roman Catholic church in a privileged position in the French state. The Catholic teaching orders were forced to dissolve, and some 12,000 Catholic schools, which had been formidable rivals of the state school system, had to close down. The state was no longer to pay the clergy, and private corporations organized by the faithful were to take over the expenses of worship and the ownership and maintenance of the churches. The Catholics refused to accept this settlement, and the churches remained technically government property.

But, though the separation had been carried out amid great bitterness, though the debates had revived the ferocious language of the 1790's, there was no recourse to the violence of the past. Catholicism was not proscribed, and somehow or other worship continued in churches that were not the full legal property of the faithful.

* F. C. Conybeare, *The Dreyfus Case* (London, 1898), p. 298.

Catholic education, while severely handicapped, was not formally persecuted. The separation did not really alter the fundamental social position of the Church in France. The upper classes, and the peasantry of the north, northeast, and west, remained for the most part loyal Catholics; many of the urban middle and working classes, and many peasants in parts of the south, southwest, and center remained what they had become over the last few centuries, indifferent Catholics or outright and determined secularists.

The indifferent Catholics and the anticlericals formed the backbone of the central supporting party of the republic, the Radical Socialists, who were not socialists at all but petty bourgeois. The French republic of the early twentieth century was a typically bourgeois state. It made certain concessions to demands from the workers for social security and better living conditions, but not nearly so many as the British constitutional monarchy was then making, nor indeed so many as the only partly constitutional German monarchy had made already. A measure initiating the progressive income tax, widely considered the most equitable way of raising revenue in a free-enterprise democracy, failed of passage on the eve of World War I. Trade unions in France were legal, but they had hard sledding against the reluctance of French workers to pay dues and accept union discipline. Moreover, good republicans like Clemenceau and Briand had no scruples about using force against strikers; when railroad workers went on strike, they were conscripted into the army so that trains could be kept running under military management, even though it was peacetime.

The Third Republic had become more republican without moving very noticeably toward the welfare state. This was hardly surprising in a country that remained what it had been since 1789, a land of small farm-owning peasants, very conservative in their agricultural methods, and of relatively small family-controlled industries, very conservative in their business methods. Although in the early 1900's, French steel production was actually growing faster than that of Britain, Germany, and the United States, this was a relatively isolated exception to the rule that France did not welcome large-scale industry. Yet it is worth noting that the French economy, while backward by the standards of ever-advancing industrialization, was well balanced by old-fashioned measures of self-sufficiency.

The Third Republic had weathered the storms of domestic differences because, though some Frenchmen disliked it intensely, and though many Frenchmen felt toward it that distrust of the "government" familiar to Americans, most Frenchmen felt it somehow to be the embodiment of *la patrie,* the fatherland. Differences did arise among them, notably on questions of colonial policy. The Third Republic's great territorial expansion in Africa, Indo-China, and Oceania, which made the world empire of France second only to Britain's, was the work of a determined minority. Many Frenchmen viewed their colonies with apathy or with antagonism as improper distractions from the main business of foreign policy.

That business was revenge for 1870 and the recovery of Alsace and Lorraine; disagreements over foreign policy concerned details of timing and tactics rather than major goals. Toward those goals the foreign ministry of the Third Republic worked systematically, despite shifts in personnel at the upper level occasioned by the operation of the multiparty system, until France gained enough strength and sufficient allies to make revenge a real possibility.

Democracies are sometimes held to be at a disadvantage in the conduct of foreign relations in comparison with states under strong monarchic or dictatorial control. After the war with Prussia, democratic France was isolated, and imperial Germany was the center of a marvelous system of alliances; yet by 1914 democratic France was firmly allied with a powerful Britain and a Russia powerful at least for the moment; and imperial Germany, save for a weak Austro-Hungarian ally and a dubiously loyal Italian one, was essentially isolated.

IV Italy, 1848-1914

Cavour and Garibaldi

Italian national unity, which seemed almost as remote as ever after Piedmont's two defeats by Austria in 1848–1849, was nevertheless accomplished between 1859 and 1870. The three men who led the *Risorgimento* in its years of triumph were the romantic nationalist adventurer, Garibaldi (1807–1882), Victor Emmanuel II of the house of Savoy, king of Piedmont-Sardinia (and a gradually united Italy) from 1849 to 1878, and, above all, Victor Emmanuel's chief minister, Cavour (1810–1861). Though of aristocratic origin himself, and trained for the highly conservative career of an army officer, Cavour enthusiastically supported the economic revolutions and the aspirations of the business classes. He visited France and England as a young man and was deeply influenced by their economic accomplishments and by their economic and political ideas and institutions. Back in Piedmont, he applied the newest agricultural methods to his family estates and promoted the introduction of steamboats, railroads, industries, and banks in order to prepare Piedmont for leadership in unified Italy. Cavour was a good, moderate, mid-nineteenth-century liberal.

Cavour was also a superlatively adept practitioner of the realistic diplomacy often called *Realpolitik.* As the chief minister of Piedmont, he set about cultivating French and English support, bringing Piedmont into the Crimean War on their side against Russia. He got no immediate award, for England was unwilling to take steps that would offend Austria, possessor of Lombardy and Venetia. But, though bitterly disappointed, he put a good face on his defeat and finally persuaded Napoleon III that the Austrian hold in northern Italy was an anachronism, a flying in the face of the principle of nationality. In 1859, France and Piedmont went to war with Austria, and won the not quite decisive battles of Magenta and Solferino in June. Meantime, sympathetic nationalistic risings in Tuscany and the Papal States seemed likely to bring their merger into an expanding Piedmont. Dismayed by this prospect and by that of Prussian intervention on Austria's behalf, Napoleon III backed out of the war. At a conference with Francis Joseph, the Austrian emperor, at Villafranca, July 1859, he arranged a compromise whereby Lombardy was to go to Piedmont, Venetia was to remain Austrian, and the old arrangements were to be restored in the other states. Cavour resigned in bitter protest.

He had, however, already won. The wave of popular agitation rose higher in northern and central Italy; in Parma, Modena, Tuscany, and the Romagna, the most northerly province of the Papal States, there were largely bloodless revolutions and plebiscites demanding annexation to Piedmont. Early in 1860, Cavour returned to office in order to manage the annexations and also to pay off Napoleon III by ceding to France the Piedmontese territories of Savoy and Nice. Next, he turned to the rapidly developing situation in the Papal States and the south. In May 1860 an expedition outfitted in ports under Piedmontese control, but not acknowledged by Cavour's government, set out for Naples and Sicily under the redshirted Garibaldi. A republican, nationalist agitator, romantic in temperament, Garibaldi had served his apprenticeship in Mazzini's Young Italy, then won a reputation as a formidable guerilla fighter in South America, and, in 1849, fought for a lost cause with distinction when he defended Mazzini's Roman

Unification of Italy, 1859-1870

republic against a French siege. Cavour deeply distrusted Garibaldi's radicalism, which he feared might make Italy a republic and might so alarm the powers that they would intervene to undo Cavour's own annexationist achievements. For these reasons, Cavour sought to control Garibaldi's expedition and exploit its success in the interests of his own policy. Garibaldi and his thousand "redshirts" had relatively little trouble in overcoming the feeble opposition of the Bourbon Francis II in Sicily. Recruits swarmed to his flag. Popular opinion throughout the West, even in cautious England, was overwhelmingly on the side of this romantic adventurer. Garibaldi, who had announced his loyalty to the king of Piedmont, Victor Emmanuel, now crossed the Straits of Messina to continue his victorious march on the mainland territories of Naples; he had the support of the British minister, Lord Palmerston, with the implication that British naval forces might act to block outside intervention against his movement. Cavour, alarmed lest Garibaldi bring on a new crisis by taking the city of Rome from the pope and offending France and other Catholic powers, sent Piedmontese troops to occupy all the remaining papal territories except the city of Rome and its environs. King Victor Emmanuel soon joined forces with Garibaldi near Naples and assured the triumph of Cavour's policy. In the autumn of 1860 Sicily, Naples, and the papal domains of Umbria and the Marches voted for union with Piedmont.

The upshot of all these rapidly unrolling developments was the proclamation of the Kingdom of Italy, essentially a much-enlarged Piedmont-Sardinia, with Florence as its capital and Victor Emmanuel as its monarch. This was in March 1861; in June, Cavour died, a grave loss for a struggling new kingdom with many problems. Territorially, however, the work of the Risorgimento was almost complete. Only two more major areas were needed—Austrian Venetia, and the remnant of the Papal states in Rome and its vicinity; both were soon acquired through the play of international politics. Venetia came as a reward for Italy's siding with Prussia in the brief war of 1866 that saw Prussia defeat Austria; Rome came when the war of 1870 with Prussia forced Napoleon III to withdraw from papal territory. On October 2, 1870, Rome was annexed to the Kingdom of Italy and became its capital. All the peninsula, save for Trieste and Trent in the North, was now under one rule. These two

Right Leg in the Boot at Last: English cartoon of 1860 commenting on Garibaldi's retirement after having given Italy to Victor Emmanuel.

small bits of Italia Irredenta (Italy unredeemed) were of no small importance, for Italian nationalists remained unreconciled to Austrian possession of them and went to war against Austria and her German ally in 1915 largely to obtain them.

Assets and Liabilities of United Italy

The new kingdom started out with the asset of favorable public opinion throughout the non-Catholic segments of the Western world. Italian national unity seemed a natural and desirable thing, and it had been achieved without very much bloodshed, with a mixture of Garibaldian romance and Cavourian realism. Within the kingdom the enthusiasm that had brought the Risorgimento to fruition was now in the service of united Italy. Italians were a frugal, hardworking people, and in the north they made promising beginnings in the new industry of the machine age.

Yet striking liabilities impeded the new Italy. Italians, too, were divided between Catholics and anticlericals, though perhaps not so sharply as the French were; more Italians were inclined to seek the middle of the road on clerical issues in practice. Nevertheless, ardent Italian Catholics were deeply embittered by the "Roman question," that is, by the circumstances of the final drive for union and the annexation of the Papal States without the pope's consent. Italy lacked coal and iron; in terms of modern economic competition, she was a "have-not" country, a shocking discovery that the Italians made in the years following unification. Much of mountainous central Italy and all southern Italy were really marginal to nineteenth-century Western civilization, with a poverty-stricken, illiterate peasantry rooted in age-old local ways utterly different from those of modern urban life, and with a small feudalistic aristocracy to whom a man like Cavour was really quite incomprehensible. Neapolitans and Sicilians resented the new political preponderance of north Italians in the unified kingdom, much as American southerners resented Yankee "carpetbaggers" after the Civil War. If one spoke of the "two Italies," the division would be that between the already somewhat industrialized north, especially the thoroughly "modern" Po Valley, and the rural, impoverished south, still "medieval."

Moreover, at least half of Italy lacked experience in self-government. It had no tradition of government by discussion, of law-abidingness, of comfortable middle-class compromise. Italy was not indeed the land of mixed stereotypes—sunny gaiety, dark passions, music, and *banditti*—which northern Europeans and Americans believed it to be. It was a land of deep-seated class antagonisms, regional variations, fervent localism, a whole inheritance from the past which made democratic government very difficult. Consequently, united Italy moved very cautiously toward more democracy. Its constitution remained that granted to Piedmont in 1848 by Charles Albert; it put effective checks on the power of the king by making the ministers responsible to the Chamber of Deputies, but it also put severe limitations on the suffrage. After 1881 the property qualifications was lowered to the payment of a direct tax of about four dollars a year, so that more than two million Italian men now had the franchise. It was only in 1912 that something close to universal male suffrage was introduced.

As time went on, the Roman question became a chronic rather than a critical one. The pope, who refused to accept the legality of the new kingdom, simply stayed in the Vatican Palace as a "prisoner." The Vatican remained the center of the worldwide organization of the Roman Catholic church, and in no important sense was the pope impeded in the exercise of his powers over the faithful throughout the world. Within Italy, the Church forbade Catholics to participate in politics and urged a Catholic boycott of the new state. Gradually, in fact, Catholics did take an increasing part in politics, but the Roman question itself remained unsettled until 1929, when Mussolini and Pope Pius XI agreed to set up the Vatican City as a sovereign state of 108 acres.

The new kingdom made appreciable economic progress. Railroads, built and managed by the state, were pushed rapidly into the backward south, where some of the seaboard area came by the twentieth century to look deceptively prosperous and modern; a brand-new merchant marine and an army and navy gave Italy some standing as a power. Even the national finances seemed for a time under conservative leadership to be sound. In the political field, the 1880's brought a letdown, the growth of parliamentary corruption, the beginning of a long era of unashamed political opportunism. Meantime, the industrial proletariat was small, labor inadequately organized, and the socialists were both too small and too rent by divisions to constitute a dynamic instrument of opposition and reform. Moreover, as recent economic historians insist, the very economic progress of the north, made in part at the expense of a south both exploited and neglected, increased regional differentiation and helped build up the social tensions that were to affect twentieth-century Italy very seriously.

Frustrated Empire-Building

Finally, in the 1880's and 1890's Italy launched herself on a career of imperial aspiration which seems a good example of the desire to keep up with the Joneses. Since France—the envied "Latin" sister—and Britain had empires, since a great power had to have an empire, and since Italy's leaders wanted her to be a great power, some way of territorial expansion had to be found. Economic explanations of the imperialist drive hardly make sense for Italy, a nation with no important exportable capital, with no need for colonial markets, and with plenty of domestic difficulties. True, Italy had a rapidly expanding population that found relatively few economic opportunities at home, especially in the south. But, since other countries had such a head start in empire-building, very little was left for the Italians, and the leftovers were not suitable for colonial settlement by Europeans. They were the poorer parts of Africa, hardly worth the difficulty of exploitation; Italy acquired two of them in the late nineteenth century—Eritrea, on the Red Sea, and Somaliland, on the "horn" of Africa where the Indian Ocean meets the Red Sea.

Next, Italy attempted to conquer the larger and more attractive neighbor of her new colonies, the independent highland empire of Ethiopia (then generally termed Abyssinia). The Abyssinian War drained the resources of the Italian government and was abruptly terminated by the disastrous defeat of the Italian expedition by a larger Ethiopian army at Adowa in 1896. This remote battle was a landmark in the history of European colonialism, much publicized by the press of the world; while the imperial powers had suffered temporary setbacks at the hands of native forces, Adowa was the first decisive native victory. It was not until 1935, under Mussolini, that the Italians took Ethiopia, which they then held for only a few years.

The disaster at Adowa cast a shadow over Italy that has been compared, with some exaggeration, to that cast over France by the Dreyfus case. The shadow was deepened by a bank scandal and by the general depression of the 1890's.

Grave bread riots broke out in Milan in May 1898, the *fatti di Maggio* (deeds of May), and in 1900 King Humbert (who had succeeded Victor Emmanuel II in 1878) was assassinated by an anarchist. The accession of a new king, Victor Emmanuel III, who was believed to have liberal leanings, gave new heart to many, and the years just before the outbreak of World War I were on the whole years of comparative quiet and prosperity, of partial reconciliation with the Church, and of the final establishment of universal suffrage. Parliamentary democracy seemed at last to be sending down solid roots. And in the years 1890—1914 the vast emigration to North and South America—the number of emigrants exceeded half a million in the peak year of 1913—almost canceled out the serious economic difficulties attendant on the high Italian birth rate and lack of new industrial employment.

Yet frustrated Italian imperialism was still seeking an outlet. Italy's leaders, and millions of their followers, could not content themselves with casting their country in the role, say, of a Mediterranean Sweden, quite outside the competition for empire with no pretensions toward the status of a great power. Denied Tunisia by the French occupation of 1881, then forced out of Ethiopia, Italy finally got from the great powers a free hand in poverty-stricken and parched Tripoli, a fragment of the old Ottoman Empire in North Africa, and now known as Libya. In 1911, Italy went to war with Turkey for Libya, thus initiating the cycle of Balkan wars that touched off the First World War, which in turn would bring Italian nationalism new expectations—and fresh frustrations.

V   The United States

World War I was also to mark the full participation in the international balance of another relative newcomer to the family of nations. The United States came to be a great power, despite words and even sentiments that placed her outside international competition, in "isolation." Two simple sets of statistics point up this fact. In 1790, the United States comprised 892,000 square miles, and in 1910 3,754,000 square miles;

even more important, the population of the United States was 3,929,000 in 1790, and 91,-972,000 in 1910, a total greater than that of either of the most powerful European states, Germany and Great Britain, and second only to that of Russia. And, still more important, the combined industrial and agricultural capacities of America were already greater than those of any other single country.

The Federal Union

The land that had become so powerful in a brief century was in the late 1700's almost empty beyond the Alleghenies, save for a few Indians of Stone Age culture; yet millions of acres were as suited to intensive human use as any in Europe. Most interested observers knew this at the end of the American Revolution, and they expected the central parts of the North American continent to fill up eventually with white men. But most of them, including Americans like Jefferson, did not believe that the process would be as rapid as it in fact was. Moreover, all but the most sanguine felt that the developed and fully peopled continent could not possibly come under one political rule. They felt that it must be divided—as indeed the South American continent came to be—into a number of independent nations on essentially the European model. Some unsympathetic observers did not believe that the thirteen Atlantic seaboard colonies gathered together to fight the British could possibly maintain their own union. Here is a sample prediction from the eighteenth century:

As to the future grandeur of America, and its being a rising empire under one head, whether republican or monarchical, it is one of the idlest and most visionary notions that ever was conceived even by writers of romance. The mutual antipathies and clashing interests of the Americans, their difference of governments, habitudes, and manners, indicate that they will have no centre of union and no common interest. They never can be united into one compact empire under any species of government whatever.*

Yet hold together the former colonies did. Though the union was often sorely tested, once in the bloodiest war Americans have yet fought, it is a central fact of history that the United States did not go the way of the Latin American states. Why the United States held together cannot be explained by any single factor. Geography was certainly kinder to her than to the Latin

Americans, for the Appalachians were no real barrier at all; the Rockies were not the barrier the Andes are; and the Mississippi Valley, unlike that of the Amazon, was a help rather than a hindrance to settlement and communications. The railroad and the telegraph arrived just in time to enable goods and ideas to move fast and far enough to hold Americans together. The communications and transportation network already developed by 1860 enabled the North to count on the West in the decisive struggle of the Civil War. The sheer size of the new republic after the acquisition of the Mississippi-Missouri Valley by purchase from Napoleon in 1803 seemed historically compatible with a loosely held empire of many tongues and peoples, like those of ancient Persia or Rome, but not with a unified nation-state. The achievements of modern technology in effect reduced sheer size to manageable proportions. After the first transcontinental railway was completed in 1869, Californians could get to the federal capital at Washington more quickly than New Yorkers could in 1801.

Moreover, the resistance to Britain had helped forge a genuine national patriotism. The colonists, in spite of contrasts between seventeenth-century "Puritan" New England and "Cavalier" tidewater South, in spite of Dutch and German elements in the middle colonies, recognized one language and one law, one basic culture. Almost all the colonies had "frontiers"—in the new American sense of the word, not a guarded line with custom houses as in Europe, but free areas on their western edges where a lively population was winning new lands from the wilderness. This frontier population was a powerful force for unity, for it had little attachment to the older centers of colonial (now state) group consciousness, and it had great confidence in its own "manifest destiny" to keep pushing westward with the blessing and patronage of, and without more than remote control by, the new federal government.

Americans gained their independence from Britain in a civil war and a social revolution that were rather mild compared with the French Reign of Terror. And, after the more committed Loyalists had left for Canada or Britain, Americans took up national life without any seriously alienated minorities. They achieved at the Philadelphia convention of 1787, and in the campaign for adoption during the next two years, a federal

---

* Josiah Tucker, Dean of Gloucester, quoted in John Fiske, *The Critical Period of American History, 1783-1789* (Boston, 1888), pp. 57-58.

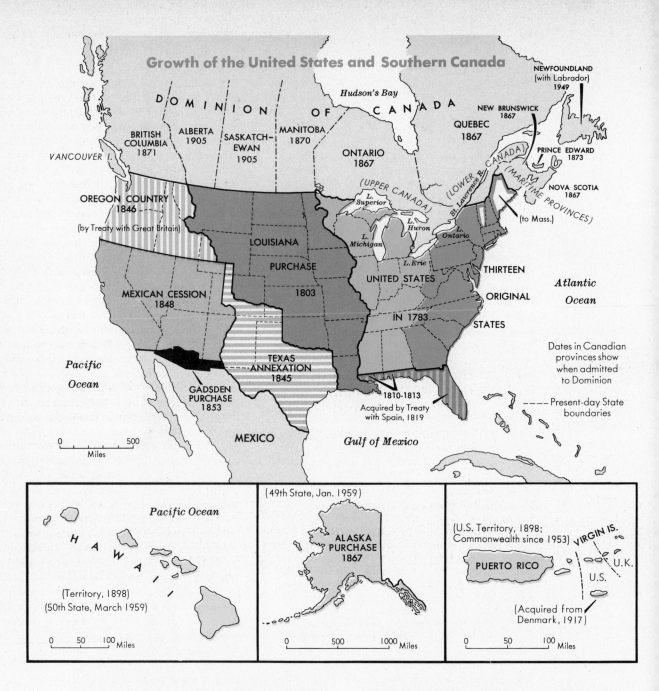

Growth of the United States and Southern Canada

NEWFOUNDLAND (with Labrador) 1949

DOMINION OF CANADA

Hudson's Bay

NEW BRUNSWICK 1867

QUEBEC 1867

PRINCE EDWARD 1873

BRITISH COLUMBIA 1871

ALBERTA 1905

SASKATCH-EWAN 1905

MANITOBA 1870

ONTARIO 1867

(UPPER CANADA)

NOVA SCOTIA 1867

VANCOUVER I.

(LOWER R. CANADA)

St. Lawrence R.

(MARITIME PROVINCES)

OREGON COUNTRY 1846

(by Treaty with Great Britain)

L. Superior

L. Huron

L. Michigan

L. Ontario

L. Erie

(to Mass.)

LOUISIANA

PURCHASE

1803

UNITED STATES

THIRTEEN

ORIGINAL

STATES

Atlantic Ocean

IN 1783

MEXICAN CESSION 1848

Pacific Ocean

Dates in Canadian provinces show when admitted to Dominion

- - - - Present-day State boundaries

TEXAS ANNEXATION 1845

GADSDEN PURCHASE 1853

1810-1813 Acquired by Treaty with Spain, 1819

MEXICO

Gulf of Mexico

0   500
Miles

Pacific Ocean

H A W A I I

(Territory, 1898)
(50th State, March 1959)

0   50   100 Miles

(49th State, Jan. 1959)

ALASKA PURCHASE 1867

0   500   1000 Miles

(U.S. Territory, 1898; Commonwealth since 1953)

VIRGIN IS.

PUERTO RICO

U.K.

U.S.

(Acquired from Denmark, 1917)

0   50   100 Miles

constitution that set up a central government with the essential attributes of all governments— the ability to tax individuals (not just to ask for monies as contributions from constituent states), to control armed forces, and to maintain a monopoly of foreign relations. The new constitution, in short, set up a sovereign federal state, not a mere league of sovereign states. On the whole, this result was achieved under conservative groups anxious to preserve their economic and social privileges, afraid that democracy in

separate, quasi-independent states would go too far. But this conclusion to the American Revolution gave the infant federal state a safer start. Finally, the threat that British control of Canada seemed to offer put a limit on domestic divisions. The United States grew up in its critical earliest years aware of the need for union against a possible foreign danger.

The new republic entered the world war of the Napoleonic period in 1812. Neither the French nor the British really tried to observe the freedom of commerce that the United States claimed as the right of a neutral, but the British, who were by 1812 masters of the sea, seemed to be infringing neutral rights more seriously than the French. Moreover, American expansionists, the "war hawks," saw a possible prize in Canada to be wrested from England, and no such prize to be got from France. The American attempt to invade Canada failed, not only from ineptness, but from the determined resistance of the Canadians. In isolated combats on the seas, the United States won victories that made up for her failures on land, and helped bolster national pride. The war on the whole was a stalemate, in which the United States experienced no important gains or losses. A generation later, she gained an enormous block of territory, from Texas to California, as a result of the Mexican War of 1846-1848, in which the United States was the aggressor, whatever justification it may have had from harassments by a Mexican government angry at the loss of Texas to rebellious Yankee settlers.

Civil War and Reconstruction

The great test of the Federal Union was the war which broke out in 1861 after long years of sectional strife within the union between North and South. The Civil War was really an abortive nationalist revolution, the attempt of the Confederate states to set up a separate sovereign nation. The South was predominantly agricultural, with a society based on plantation slavery and on cotton and tobacco, much of which was exported abroad. The North was increasingly industrial, with a society based on free labor and on independent farm owners.

To the conflict of economic interest was added a conflict of ideals, of ways of life. That conflict was not so deep-seated, so irreconcilable, as it seemed to be to the generation that went to war in 1861—or the South, like Ireland or Poland, would presumably have tried again to free itself, something it did not even really discuss seriously in the integration crisis of the 1950's and 1960's. The fires of conflict were fanned especially by the question of slavery, which seemed immoral to many in the North and which seemed the order of nature to many in the South. They were fanned also by writers and preachers

on both sides, the northerners thinking of themselves as heirs of the Puritans, the southerners as heirs of the Cavaliers. With the secession of South Carolina and its sister states, antagonism reached the point of open war.

In retrospect, the victory of the North has an air of inevitability, especially since by 1861 the middle and upper Mississippi Valley was bound firmly to the North by economic and cultural ties. In population—especially since the South did not dare use blacks as soldiers—and in industrial resources above all, the North was greatly superior. Yet, aided by a very able corps of officers, by the advantages in morale that accrue to determined underdogs, and by the disastrous early overconfidence of the North, the South won initial victories that gave its cause great momentum. But the North thwarted the efforts of Confederate diplomats to secure British intervention and was able to improvise a naval force that gradually established a blockade, shutting off the South from importation of necessary war materials. In the long run, northern strength in men and materials wore the southern armies down.

The striking thing about the Civil War is not that the North won it finally in the field, but that the South accepted the verdict of battle as final. The "Road to Reunion" after 1865 was not easy, and in the first years of the Reconstruction period after the war it appeared to many to be almost impossible. With the assassination of Lincoln by the fanatical Booth in 1865, the one great moderate who might have lessened the vengefulness of the northern radicals was lost. The South was occupied by northern soldiers, the illiterate blacks were enfranchised, and northern "carpetbaggers" and southern "scalawags"—and many sincere idealists who believed they could bring liberty and equality to a "misguided" South—combined to bring what seemed a reign of terror to old Confederates.

Yet even in these early days the Civil War did not end, as such wars have often ended, in wholesale reprisals, executions, and exile. Northerners had sung during the war, "We'll hang Jeff Davis to a sour apple tree"; but after the war Jefferson Davis, president of the Confederacy, was not hanged on a sour apple tree or anywhere else. He was imprisoned for two years, and then lived quietly for another thirty, of course writing a book to justify his career. The fate of Davis measures the miracle of reunion. There were extremely few political refugees of the kind that often attend defeated causes. The soldiers of the South returned, often to devastated homes and lost fortunes, but they returned home under amnesty. Gradually the crusading fervor of the North wore off, and the southerners, reinforced by new men, some of them immigrant northerners, took over control in their states. Slavery, abolished by Lincoln's proclamation in 1863, was never restored, but the blacks were in effect disenfranchised, "white supremacy" was restored, and the racial question in the New South took on forms familiar to us today.

The end of the attempt to make radical reforms in the South was clear when a disputed presidential election in 1876 saw the Republican Hayes win over the Democrat Tilden after political maneuvering which was contrary to the spirit of the Constitution. No doubt conservative, business-conscious northerners were anxious to get back to normal conditions, and quite willing to compromise with like-minded southerners at the expense of racial equality and other high ideals. Still, the final abandonment of idealistic reconstruction seems largely the inevitable letdown of the energies behind a great crusade. In a sense, the crusade was renewed in 1954 with the decision of the Supreme Court against segregated public schools.

The South of the later nineteenth century was in part a New South, which is one of the basic reasons why the region came to accept the Civil War as ended, with due sentimental compensations in wistful feeling for the past. Slowly in the late nineteenth century, more rapidly in the twentieth, it built up its own industries, took steps to free itself from cotton monoculture and to integrate its economy and its society with the rest of the country. The South remained throughout this period a relatively backward area, with its own special problems of poverty, illiteracy, and racial difficulties, but it was not an oppressed nationality eager to revolt.

The end of Reconstruction left the Democratic party in control of what came to be called the "solid South." This was a natural development, for it was the Republican party that had guided the North during the war, and that had tried to carry through Reconstruction. This fact worked to strengthen the American two-party system, since with so solid a block secure for the Democrats, the Republicans were forced either to make compromises among themselves to pre-

serve their own party unity, or to lose power; and the northern Democrats were forced to make compromises with their southern wing.

Free Enterprise and Government Regulation

In 1865, the American economy was still in some respects "colonial"—that is, it produced in the main foods and other raw materials to be exchanged abroad for manufactured goods—and, in financial terms, it was dependent on foreign money markets, chiefly London. But in the northern and midwestern states the Industrial Revolution had already entered the "take-off" stage. By 1914 the United States had been transformed into a great industrial nation, with its agriculture already to a high degree mechanized, and with financial resources so great that after World War I New York was to take over in part the place of London as a world financial center. This transformation could not have taken place, certainly not at the rate it did, without the existence of abundant manpower, of great and still almost untouched natural resources, and of the traditions of individual initiative and freedom of enterprise—which were in some degree a product of the "frontier." Europe played a significant role in American economic growth by furnishing investment capital and, above all, by sending forth a steady flow of emigrants.

This great expansion in national wealth was achieved in a climate of opinion that supported overwhelmingly the view that the federal government should not interfere directly with business enterprise beyond maintaining public order, enforcing contracts, exercising some control over the actual coinage of money—and maintaining a protective tariff. Nor, of course, were the state and local governments supposed to go beyond such appropriate limits. This view we have already met in the classical economists who followed Adam Smith in Britain and in some of the continental states. It is a view that in the West has generally accompanied the first stages of the Industrial Revolution. In the United States a belief in free enterprise and a minimum of government interference in economic activities maintained itself more firmly in the twentieth century than in the other parts of the Western world.

Accompanying the demands for economic reform early in the twentieth century was the woman suffrage movement. Here suffragettes march on Fifth Avenue in New York demanding participation in the nation's political life.

This belief was reinforced by the Fourteenth Amendment to the Constitution, passed in 1866 and aimed to protect the freed slaves in the South from state action to deprive them of civil rights. The Amendment contained the famous "due process" clause: "nor shall any state deprive any person of life, liberty, or property without due process of law." In the great era of free enterprise that followed the Civil War, the Supreme Court of the United States interpreted the celebrated clause to mean that state governments should not deprive businessmen—including corporations as "persons"—of property by regulating wages, prices, conditions of labor, and the like.

Immigration since the 1890's had brought in millions of aliens from eastern and southern Europe, men and women ignorant of American

ways, and readily exploited by unscrupulous or merely insensitive employers. These immigrants were hard to organize in labor unions; moreover, they and their children, uprooted, scorned, though they might be, readily absorbed the American belief that no man is a proletarian by nature, that there is always room at the top. Yet even at the height of this "Gilded Age" or "Age of the Robber Barons" there was a movement toward the welfare state.

Much the same forces that had produced the Factory Acts in Britain gradually brought to the United States minimum-wage acts, limitation of child labor and women's labor, sanitary regulation, control of hours of labor, and workmen's compensation. Characteristically, and in spite of the Fourteenth Amendment, these measures were taken at the state rather than at the national level, and they varied greatly in the different states. The state of Wisconsin early established a reputation for advanced social legislation, but many of the older northeastern states played an important part in the movement. By the early twentieth century, public opinion was ready for increased participation of the national government in the regulation of economic life.

Theodore Roosevelt, a Republican, president from 1901 to 1909, promised to give labor a "square deal" and to proceed vigorously with "trust-busting," attacks on the great trusts or combinations that had come to monopolize important sectors of the American economy. Although Roosevelt did not always fulfill his promises, his administration did assail the trusts in railroads and tobacco and did press the federal regulation of great corporations. A federal prosecution of the Standard Oil Company begun in 1906 resulted in 1911 in a Supreme Court decision dissolving the great holding company. Some of the separated parts familiar today, such as Esso (Standard of New Jersey), Mobil (Standard of New York), and Calso (Standard of California), are in fact "bigger" than was the dissolved par-

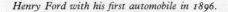

Henry Ford with his first automobile in 1896.

ent company of John D. Rockefeller. Yet the work of the radicals of 1900, particularly the "muckrakers" who wrote exposés of questionable business practices for popular magazines, was clearly not in vain. American "big business" was in the later twentieth century bigger than it had been in the days of Theodore Roosevelt. But, it was also aware of its responsibilities to the public —or at least afraid of what might happen if it followed the advice of one of the great nineteenth-century "robber barons," Cornelius Vanderbilt: "The public be damned!" In short, big business in the United States is ultimately, as in democratic theory it must be, under the control of public opinion.

During the first administration of Woodrow Wilson (1913–1917), a Democrat, the process of regulation gained momentum. The Federal Reserve Act of 1913, for example, gave federal officials more control over banking, credit, and currency. Approval of such measures was not, of course, unanimous, since Americans differed loudly and widely about almost everything from metaphysics to sports. To outsiders, and to many native critics, American life in the decades between the Civil War and 1917 often seemed one great brawl, a more-than-Darwinian struggle for wealth and power. Yet this apparently anarchistic society achieved extraordinary material which required the cooperation of millions of men and women disciplined to a common task. This paradox of the coexistence in the United States of "rugged individualism" and social cohesion still disturbs and puzzles many commentators on the American scene.

In spite of the substantial American distrust of "government," government in the United States came to play a larger and larger part in the lives of all. Although this was true of local and state governments too, it held more especially of the federal government. The gradually increasing importance of the federal government, and the gradually decreasing initiative of state governments, were as clear in the period 1789–1917 as was the material growth of the United States in population and wealth.

The Myth of Isolation

Quite as clear, though still the subject of infinite debate among Americans, was the emergence of the United States as a great international power. The United States was never literally "isolated." From the very beginning, this country had a Department of State, our senior department, and the proper apparatus of ministers, consuls, and, later, ambassadors. The United States was involved in the world war of the Napoleonic era, and by the Monroe Doctrine of the 1820's took the firm position that European powers were not to extend their existing territories in the Western hemisphere. This was no mere negation, but an active extension of American claims to a far wider sphere of influence than the continental United States. Although Americans took no direct part in the complex nineteenth-century balance-of-power politics in Europe, they showed an increasing concern with a balance of power in the Far East, where they had long traded. After the brief war of 1898 with Spain, a war that broke out in Cuba, always a close concern of the United States, Americans found themselves directly involved with the newly annexed territories of the Philippine Islands, Hawaii, Puerto Rico—in short, with what looked to outsiders, and to many Americans, like an American empire.

Theodore Roosevelt, who owed his rapid political rise partly to his military leadership of the "Rough Riders" in the Spanish War, was a vigorous imperialist. He pressed the building of the Panama Canal, upheld the Far Eastern interests of the United States, and advocated a larger navy. This new "navalism," which also had assertive spokesmen in Britain and Germany, derived many of its doctrines from the writings of an American officer, Captain Alfred T. Mahan. Mahan's book, *The Influence of Sea Power upon History* (1890), and his later works assigned navies a place of preeminent importance in determining power status and found an influential audience both at home and abroad. Furthermore, Americans as individuals had long been active in work for better international organization, and a world court.

Over these many decades of expanding wealth and trade, the United States had come to take full part in international commercial relations. In these relations she had, save when the federal government was blockading the Confederacy, stood out firmly for rights to trade even though there was a war on somewhere, stood out for the "rights of neutrals." This fact alone would probably have brought the United States into the world war of 1914–1918, as it had brought her previously into the world war of 1792–1815. But in 1917 America was, as she had not been in 1812, a great and active participant in the world state system, though she had followed the admonition of George Washington's "farewell address" and avoided "entangling alliances."

Reading Suggestions on the Western Democracies in the Nineteeth Century

GENERAL ACCOUNTS

F. B. Artz, *Reaction and Revolution, 1814–1832;* W. L. Langer, *Political and Social Upheaval, 1832–1851;* R. C. Binkley, *Realism and Nationalism, 1852–1871;* C. J. Hayes, *A Generation of Materialism, 1871–1900.* (*Torchbooks). These four volumes in the series "The Rise of Modern Europe" are particularly valuable for their full bibliographies.

R. R. Palmer and J. Colton, *A History of the Modern World,* 4th ed. (Knopf, 1970). A very successful textbook, with an exceptionally full bibliography.

C. Breunig, *The Age of Revolution and Reaction, 1789–1850;* Norman Rich, *The Age of Nationalism and Reform, 1850–1890;* Felix Gilbert, *The End of the European Era, 1890 to the Present* (*Norton). These three rapid survey volumes in "The Norton History of Modern Europe" have good bibliographies.

The New Cambridge Modern History, 14 vols. (Cambridge Univ. Press, 1957–1970). Volumes X, XI, and XII of this uneven collaborative work are a handy source of information on the smaller democracies.

GREAT BRITAIN

E. L. Woodward, *The Age of Reform,* new ed. (Clarendon, 1962), and R. C. K. Ensor, *England, 1870–1914* (Clarendon, 1936). Two very meaty volumes in "The Oxford History of England."

A. Briggs, *The Making of Modern England* (*Torchbooks). A more recent survey of the period 1783–1867; originally entitled *The Age of Improvement.*

E. Halévy, *A History of the English People in the Nineteenth Century,* 2nd rev. ed., 6 vols. (P. Smith, 1949–1951; vols. 1–3 also *Barnes & Noble). Though incomplete and often outdated, this study by a French scholar ranks as a classic. Halévy also wrote a standard work on the Utilitarians, *The Growth of Philosophic Radicalism* (*Beacon).

G. Kitson Clark, *The Making of Victorian England* (*Atheneum), and G. M. Young, *Victorian England: Portrait of an Age,* 2nd ed. (*Galaxy). Two very good introductions.

E. Longford, *Queen Victoria* (*Pyramid). Recent standard biography.

N. Gash, *Politics in the Age of Peel* (Longmans, 1953). Scholarly study of the 1830's and 1840's.

R. Blake, *Disraeli* (*Anchor); P. Magnus, *Gladstone* (*Dutton). Sound biographies of two famous Victorian statesmen.

M. Bruce, *The Coming of the Welfare State,* rev. ed. (Schocken, 1966). Good study of the post-Victorian reforms. May be supplemented by C. Cross, *The Liberals in Power, 1905–1914* (Barrie and Rockcliff, 1963), and by studies of two Liberal leaders: M. Gilbert, ed., *Lloyd George* (*Spectrum), and Roy Jenkins, *Asquith* (*Dutton).

FRANCE

Gordon Wright, *France in Modern Times* (Rand McNally, 1960); A. Cobban, *History of Modern France,* rev. ed., Vol. 2 (1799–1871) and Vol. 3 (1871–1962) (*Penguin). Enlightening surveys by an American and a British scholar, respectively.

D. W. Brogan, *The French Nation from Napoleon to Pétain* (*Colophon). Brilliant essay of interpretation by a British expert on democracy. Brogan has also written a detailed, allusive and perceptive study of the Third Republic, *France under the Republic* (Harper, 1940).

A. Guérard, *France: A Modern History,* rev. ed. (Univ. of Michigan Press, 1969). By an American scholar of French background and a defender of Caesarean democracy. Guérard also wrote sympathetic studies of Louis Napoleon: *Napoleon III* (Harvard Univ. Press, 1943) and a biography with the same title for the series "Great Lives in Brief" (Knopf, 1955).

J. M. Thompson, *Louis Napoleon and the Second Empire* (*Norton). The standard scholarly synthesis. Other useful up-to-date works on the Second Empire are T. Zeldin, *The Political System of Napoleon III* (St. Martin's, 1958); R. Williams, *The World of Napoleon III,* rev. ed. (*Free Press); and B. D. Gooch, *The Reign of Napoleon III* (*Rand McNally).

David Thomson, *Democracy in France since 1870,* 5th ed. (*Oxford Univ. Press). Brilliant essay of interpretation, particularly good on the period 1870–1914.

R. Soltau, *French Political Thought in the Nineteenth Century,* new ed. (Russell & Russell, 1959). An older and still useful work; rather harsh on conservative thinkers.

R. L. Williams, *The French Revolution of 1870–1871* (Norton, 1969). Sound study of the highly controversial period climaxed by the Commune.

G. Chapman, *The Dreyfus Case: A Re-assessment* (Viking, 1966). The most searching treatment available in English.

J. H. Jackson, *Clemenceau and the Third Republic* (*Collier), and G. Bruun, *Clemenceau* (Harvard Univ. Press, 1943). Succinct studies of a formidable politician.

H. Goldberg, *Life of Jean Jaurès* (Univ. of Wisconsin Press, 1962). Sympathetic study of the famous socialist leader.

ITALY

D. Mack Smith, *Italy: A Modern History* (Univ. of Michigan, 1959). Standard account by a ranking expert; he has also written other illuminating studies, including *Cavour and Garibaldi, 1860: A Study in Political Conflict* (Cambridge Univ. Press, 1954) and *Garibaldi* (Knopf, 1956).

C. Seton-Watson, *Italy from Liberalism to Fascism, 1870–1925* (Methuen, 1967). Detailed scholarly study.

A. W. Salomone, ed., *Italy from the Risorgimento to Fascism* (*Anchor). An informative survey of the background of totalitarianism.

B. Croce, *A History of Italy, 1871–1915* (Clarendon, 1929). A perceptive analysis by the famous philosopher-historian.

THE UNITED STATES

R. Hofstadter et al., *The American Republic*, 2 vols. (Prentice-Hall, 1970). A readable scholarly account.

R. B. Morris, ed., *Encyclopedia of American History* (Harper, 1961); O. Handlin et al., eds., *Harvard Guide to American History* (*Atheneum). Standard works of reference.

S. E. Morison, *The Oxford History of the American People*, new ed. (Oxford Univ. Press, 1965). Reworking of a popular earlier book, by a distinguished historian.

L. Hartz, *The Liberal Tradition in America* (*Harvest); R. Hofstadter, *The American Political Tradition* (*Vintage); C. Rossiter, *Conservatism in America* (*Vintage). Representative divergent interpretations of American political life.

Tocqueville, *Democracy in America* (*several editions). The famous pioneering study by the great French observer.

C. A. Beard and M. A. Beard, *The Rise of American Civilization* (Macmillan, 1936). An early and influential economic interpretation.

HISTORICAL FICTION

Disraeli, *Coningsby* (*Signet). A plea to democratize the program of the Tory party; written early in the career of the great Conservative.

Trollope, *The Prime Minister* (World's Classics; Oxford Univ. Press). Probably the best novel on Victorian politics; written by a Victorian.

Zola, *The Downfall* (Appleton, 1902). Very good novel of the Franco-Prussian War. Arnold Bennett's *Old Wives' Tale* (*Signet) has a superb account of life in Paris during the siege of 1870–1871.

Anatole France, *Penguin Island* (*Signet). French history satirized at the turn of the century.

R. Martin du Gard, *Jean Barois* (*Bobbs Merrill). Faithful fictional re-creation of the impact of the Dreyfus affair on French life.

William Dean Howells, *The Rise of Silas Lapham* (*several editions). The famous realistic social novel of late nineteenth-century Boston.

Upton Sinclair, *The Jungle* (*several editions). Celebrated exposé of the Chicago meat-packing industry around 1900.

Margaret Mitchell, *Gone with the Wind* (*Macmillan). The Civil War seen through a mist of Confederate nostalgia.

MacKinlay Kantor, *Andersonville* (*Signet). Grimly faithful account of military prison life in the Civil War.

22

Central and Eastern Europe

To the Outbreak of World War I

I   Introduction

In this chapter, we shall deal with Germany (1850–1914), the Hapsburg monarchy (1850–1914), and Russia (1825–1914). These three empires were partners in crime in the partitions of Poland of the late eighteenth century, and firm allies in the Metternich system of European balance after 1815. After 1850, they passed through periods of mutual affection and hatred. In 1914 all went to war, with Germany and Austria-Hungary as allies against Russia. Internally they had much in common, although each followed its own peculiar development. In contrast with the countries of western Europe, these were the lands of autocratic monarchy and relatively powerless parliaments appearing on the scene relatively late. In 1914, all were still "empires," a title that only the tottering Ottoman state also claimed in Europe.

Above: Francis Ferdinand, archduke of Austria, with his wife and children. Above right: A camp of the 5th Dragoon Guards during the Crimean War. Right: Police in St. Petersburg discovering a nihilist printing press, 1887.

II Germany, 1850–1914

In 1914, the militarist and nationalist German Empire was a powerful, unified industrial state with a highly educated, obedient, and competent population. By supporting the Balkan policies of its ally, Austria-Hungary, it helped to plunge the entire world into the first of the twentieth century's wars of mass slaughter. Germany had emerged as a great continental power only after 1850, although for more than 1,400 years millions of Germans had been living in the heart of Europe under a variety of political regimes. The militarism, the authoritarianism, the whole social and cultural tone of the Germany of 1914, were determined by the fact that it was the Kingdom of Prussia that had achieved German unification. Characteristic Prussian attitudes had overcome other German ways of looking at society and had imposed themselves on non-Prussians. The Prussian triumph was complete by 1871.

Between 1850 and 1871, and especially after 1862, Prussia moved with ever-accelerating speed from triumph to triumph. Doubters and protesters were silenced or dazzled by the glitter of each new achievement; moral objections were regarded as unpatriotic. Otto von Bismarck, who directed policy, spoke of respect for legality and decency as "humanitarian twaddle" and proclaimed an era when "blood and iron" alone would decide. The ends seemed so desirable and were being gained so rapidly that even stern moralists could tell themselves that this time they need not examine the means. They shook their heads and voted the government new subsidies.

The creation of imperial Germany was above all the work of Bismarck (1815–1898). Brilliant, unscrupulous, ruthless, a genius at maneuver and at concealing his real intentions, Bismarck was often bewilderingly inconsistent in his policies. Sometimes he pursued two apparently contradictory policies at the same time, until the moment came when he had to make a final decision on which policy to follow. His intense loyalty to the Prussian crown, however, did not falter during his long years in office, although after his dismissal by William II in 1890 he felt that his work was being undone, and he often tried to embarrass the emperor and his own successors in the government. He could not endure criticism of himself. At different periods, he loathed liberals, Catholics, and socialists. And he despised his intellectual inferiors even when they belonged to his own class, the Prussian landed nobility: the Junkers, who believed firmly in their own privileges, monopolized commissions in the Prussian army, and dominated the administrative services of the Prussian state. Whatever Bismarck's policy of the moment, force lay at its roots. Influential before 1862, he towered over Prussia from 1862 to 1871, and over the German Empire thereafter until 1890. Yet his efforts could not have succeeded had they not met with general approval from the German people, who had hungered for unity since before 1848.

Prussia and the German Confederation, 1850–1859

The first major question facing the statesmen of central Europe after the revolutions of 1848 was whether Prussia or Austria would dominate the German Confederation. A creation of the Congress of Vienna of 1814, it had been temporarily shaken and split by the developments of 1848, and now needed to be rebuilt. The "Big German" solution called for federation with Austria; the "Little German" solution called for separation from Austria or even from South Germany. The "Little German" program meant Prussian domination of the non-Austrian states, and therefore became Bismarck's goal.

The period after 1848 opened with a defeat for a Prussian "Little German" solution. King Frederick William IV, who had refused to accept the imperial crown "from the gutter" when it was offered by the Frankfurt Assembly, none the less cherished the hope that the German princes might offer it to him. Taking advantage of Austria's preoccupation with the remnants of the Revolution of 1848, and overriding his own Prussian conservatives, who wished simply to strengthen their own state, Frederick William IV formed the Erfurt Union of Princes, an agreement to pool military resources. This union was designed to lead to Prussian political as well as military dominance.

The Austrians managed to bring Russian pressure to bear on Prussia. The czar opposed the unification of the Germans no matter under whose auspices. At Olmütz, in November 1850, the Prussians renounced the Erfurt Union and reluctantly agreed to the revival of the Confederation. This episode is known as the "humiliation" of Olmütz, a term that shows how bitterly many Prussians resented it. Yet Bismarck himself defended the treaty, and as a result was sent as Prussian representative to the Diet of the Confederation.

At the Diet Bismarck took every occasion to work against Austria, and to thwart Austrian designs. As one facet of his policy, he favored Prussian neutrality in the Crimean War (1854–1856, in which England and France fought with Turkey against Russia, and Austria harassed rather than helped the Russians. Realizing that Austrian behavior was alienating Russia, and that Russian friendship would be valuable later when Prussia came to grips with Austria, Bismarck frustrated those Prussians who hoped that Prussia would enter the war against Russia and thus line up with the West. He was counting on a military showdown with Austria. With this purpose in mind, he also wooed the French emperor Napoleon III, despite the horror that many Prussians felt over dealings with a Bonaparte, whom they regarded as the heir of the French Revolution.

Both the constitutional and economic foundations of future Prussian development were laid during the 1850's. The Prussian Constitution of 1850, which lasted down to the end of World War I, provided for a bicameral legislature: a hereditary upper house including the nobles and royal appointees, and an elected lower house. But the method of electing this lower house made it certain that the popular will would be frustrated. Electors were divided into three classes, according to the amount of taxes they paid. The 4 percent of the electorate who paid high taxes selected one-third of the representatives. The 14 percent of middle taxpayers selected another third, and the remaining 82 percent of low taxpayers selected the last third. The preponderant power of the wealthy is clear.

Even so, the lower house had very little to do beyond approving the budget. Policy questions were decided in the upper house, or still more often by the king and his personal circle of military and political advisers. The king appointed his ministers, could veto any bill he disapproved, and had a fixed sum of money at his disposal for expenses. He had a special "military cabinet" for army affairs that reported neither to the ministers nor to the legislature. Practically speaking, the king and the Junkers ran Prussia.

With its possessions in western Germany, including the Ruhr, Prussia had the richest coal deposits in Europe. The iron and steel industry, without which her future political and military triumphs would have been impossible, now began its phenomenal growth. Alone among the continental nations, the Prussians turned over the planning of their new railway system to the army general staff, which laid out the lines with an eye to rapid and efficient mobilization and transportation of troops and military supplies in time of war.

Bismarck Comes to Power

Indeed, these military concerns led directly to the beginning of Bismarck's undisputed domination of Prussian policies. King William I, who succeeded Frederick William IV in 1861, was above all a soldier. His minister of war, Roon, a friend of Bismarck's, easily persuaded the king that an army reorganization was necessary. He wanted to increase the number of conscripts drafted each year from 40,000 to 63,000, and to lengthen the term of their service from two to three years. Roon hoped that a big conservative army might serve as counterweight to any liberal or revolutionary tendencies in the state. A prolonged political crisis arose over these aims in 1861 and 1862, when the Prussian parliament refused to vote the budget. At the very height of the crisis, the king, convinced that Bismarck could outwit the parliament, appointed him to the key posts of prime minister of Prussia and minister of foreign affairs.

On the fallacious principle that there was a "gap" in the constitution that permitted the government to collect taxes even when the budget had not been approved by parliament, Bismarck now collected and spent revenue quite illegally. Again and again he dissolved the parliament, called new elections, faced another hostile house, and then repeated the process. He suppressed opposition newspapers in defiance of a constitutional provision that the press should be free. He indicted an opposition deputy, himself a judge and a loyal Prussian, in spite of the constitutional provision that deputies could not be indicted for anything they said on the floor of the house. Yet after four years of this illegal behavior (1862–1866), he got away with everything in the end because of the glittering successes he scored by his unorthodox daring in foreign policy.

Since Bismarck intended to overthrow the German Confederation as it was then constituted, he opposed Austrian efforts to reform it. Austria wished to create an assembly of delegates chosen by the parliaments of the member states, in addition to those named by the princes, and a directorate of six monarchs. Bismarck prevented William I from attending a congress of princes called by Austria to discuss these proposals, and thus wrecked the congress (1862). In 1863, he kept Austria out of the Zollverein, the German customs union. He also consolidated his good relations with Russia during the Polish revolt by concluding the Alvensleben convention, which

Unification of Germany, 1866-1871

Prussia before 1866 — Annexed by Prussia, 1866
Other states that joined Prussia to form North German Confederation
·········· Boundary of North German Confederation, 1866
States joining Confederation to form German Empire
Territories annexed by Treaty of Frankfurt
—— Boundary of the German Empire, 1871   ■ Battle sites

allowed the Russians to pursue fleeing Poles onto Prussian territory and capture them there. Thus Bismarck wooed the Russians a second time, as he had during the Crimean War.

The Schleswig-Holstein Question, 1863-1865

When the king of Denmark died in late 1863, the celebrated Schleswig-Holstein question gave Bismarck further opportunities. The prime minister of England once remarked that only three men had ever understood this complex problem, and that one was dead and one insane, while he himself, the third, had forgotten all about it. In brief, the duchies of Schleswig and Holstein at the southern base of the Danish peninsula had been ruled by the king of Denmark, but not as part of Denmark. A fifteenth-century guarantee assured the duchies that they could never be separated from one another. Yet Holstein to the south was a member of the German Confederation; Schleswig to the north was not. Holstein was mostly German in population; Schleswig was mixed German and Danish. In 1852, Prussia had agreed in an international conference on an heir who would succeed both to the Danish throne and to the duchies. At the same time, Prussia had joined the other powers in recommending that Denmark and the duchies should be united by a constitution. But, when the constitutional union of Denmark and the duchies was attempted, the duchies resisted, and the Danes tried to incorporate Schleswig. German patriots objected. The Prussians and Austrians wanted the duchies to have special representation inside the Danish parliament and insisted that Schleswig should *not* be incorporated into Denmark. None the less, the king of Denmark in 1863 followed a policy that supported annexation.

Into this situation Bismarck now moved to win the duchies for Prussia. He wanted both the prestige that Prussia would gain and the valuable commercial port of Kiel in Holstein. First he maneuvered Prussia and Austria together into a victorious war against Denmark (1864), although Austria had no real interest in the duchies. Then he quarreled with the Austrians over the administration of the duchies. At the Convention of Gastein, 1865, it was decided that Prussia was to administer Schleswig and that Austria was to administer Holstein. But this arrangement provided only a temporary halt in Bismarck's drive against Austria.

War with Austria, 1866

Bismarck kept nagging Vienna about Austrian behavior in Holstein. He tried and failed to tempt France into an alliance. But he did succeed in signing a secret treaty with Italy, whereby the Italians obliged themselves to go to war on the side of Prussia if Prussia fought Austria within three months. This was contrary to the constitution of the German Confederation, which forbade members to ally themselves with a foreign power against other members. So distressed was William I at this illegality that he lied flatly when the Austrian emperor asked him if such a treaty existed. Finally, Bismarck suddenly proposed that the German Confederation be reformed, and that an all-German parliament be elected by universal suffrage, which everybody knew he hated.

Bismarck probably advanced this proposal for universal suffrage in order to make it appear that his quarrel with Austria rested on a less sordid ground than the mere Schleswig-Holstein question. Yet the proposal also reflected his calculation that enfranchisement of all Germans would weaken the Progressive party, heir to the liberalism of 1848, and would produce many conservative and royalist votes from the peasantry. He had seen how Napoleon III had risen to imperial power in France on the strength of universal suffrage. And he had been influenced by conversations with Ferdinand Lassalle, a German socialist, who argued that universal suffrage would weaken the middle classes. Bismarck had hoped that the Austrians might try to throw his plan out, but the other members of the Confederation asked Prussia to propose a full plan of reform. Austria now laid the Schleswig-Holstein question before the Diet of the Confederation. Bismarck ordered Prussian troops into Holstein and declared that Austrian motions in the Diet were unconstitutional. He succeeded in provoking war with Austria. It was an all-German civil war, since Bavaria, Württemberg, Saxony, Hanover (the four other German kingdoms), and most of the lesser German states sided with Austria.

The war lasted seven weeks and was virtually decided in less than three. The Austrians had to commit a substantial part of their forces against Italy. Skillfully using their railway network, the telegraph, and superior armaments, the Prussians quickly overran northern Germany, invaded Bohemia and defeated the Austrians at König-grätz (Sadowa), defeated the Bavarians, and entered Frankfurt, seat of the German Confederation. The states of Hanover, Hesse-Cassel, and Nassau were all annexed to Prussia and their dynasties expelled. Schleswig-Holstein and the free city of Frankfurt were also taken over.

Bismarck successfully opposed the generals, and even his king, who wished to punish Austria severely. Except for the cession of Venetia to Italy, Austria suffered no territorial losses as a result of the Peace of Prague (1866), but she did pay a small indemnity. Most important from Bismarck's point of view, Austria had to withdraw forever from the German Confederation, which now ceased to exist. Germany north of the Main River was to join a new North German Confederation to be organized by Prussia. However, it was stipulated that the German states south of the Main were to be free to form an independent union of their own. But Bismarck had previously concluded secret treaties of alliance with the most important south German states—Bavaria, Württemberg, and Baden—who promised to put their armies at the disposal of the king of Prussia in case of war. So the proposed South German union could never come into existence. Bismarck thus broke the Peace of Prague even before it had been concluded, a real piece of diplomatic skill. Bismarck's gentle treatment of Austria was not just a matter of generosity. He was convinced that Prussia would need Austrian help in the future. Now that he had expelled Austria from Germany, imposed a "Little German" solution, and elevated Prussia to the position of dominance, he had scored his point.

Now Bismarck was free to turn to the Prussian parliament, with which he had been feuding for four years. He asked for an "indemnity"—that is, a certification that all the revenue he had illegally collected and illegally spent, ever since the parliament had refused to pass the budget in 1861, had in fact been legally collected and legally spent. The deputies were so dazzled by the feats of arms against Denmark and Austria, and by the enormous new acquisitions of power and territory, that they voted the indemnity and awarded Bismarck personally a cash gift of roughly $300,000.

The North German Confederation

An assembly elected by universal manhood suffrage now debated and adopted a constitution for the new North German Confederation, of which the Prussian king was president. The draft that Bismarck submitted is eloquent testimony to his determination to "kill parliamentarism through parliament." The future parliament (Reichstag) was to have no power over the budget, and the ministers were not to be responsible to it. Instead, a Federal Council (Bundesrat), consisting of delegates from the member states and voting according to instructions from their sovereigns, would reach all key policy decisions in secret and would have veto power over any enactment of the Reichstag. A chancellor would preside over the Bundesrat, but would not have to explain or defend its decisions before the Reichstag. Since Prussia now had not only its own votes in the Bundesrat but also those of the newly annexed states, Bismarck's plan in effect made it possible for the king of Prussia to run Germany.

This plan was only slightly modified so that the future chancellor would have to sign every act undertaken by the king of Prussia as president of the Confederation. But the executive was in no way made "responsible" to the Reichstag. Bismarck's plan also specified that, beginning five years later in 1872, the size of the army would be fixed by law and that the Reichstag would have a vote on the budget. However, Bismarck, who became chancellor, saw to it that the debate on the military budget did not take place every year, but that sums were appropriated for long periods in advance.

Showdown with France

As long as Bismarck needed the benevolent neutrality of Napoleon III, he had hinted that he might not object if Napoleon took Belgium. Now the gullible Napoleon found that Bismarck no longer remembered the matter. Hoping to be compensated for his assistance in making peace between Prussia and Austria, Napoleon III tried to acquire Luxembourg by purchase from the king of Holland. Again he was frustrated by Bismarck. Suddenly confronted with the new Germany, many members of the French public and press hoped to get "revenge for Sadowa," and became strongly anti-German. The German press responded in kind. Napoleon III tried to obtain an alliance with Austria and Italy in order to thwart further Prussian expansion. But the Austrians shied away from a true commitment, and the Italians were unable to reach an agreement with the French because of the Roman question.

When the Spaniards ousted their queen in 1868, one of the candidates for the throne was a Hohenzollern prince, whom Bismarck secretly backed by discreetly bribing influential Spaniards. Because of family dynastic practice, it was necessary to secure the consent of the reluctant king William I of Prussia, and this Bismarck finally extracted without hinting that war with France might result. Napoleon III, also deep in Spanish intrigue, feared that a Hohenzollern on the Spanish throne would expose France to a two-front attack. French diplomatic pressure was exerted directly on King William, and the Hohenzollern candidate withdrew. At this moment, Bismarck seemed to be defeated.

But the French, overstimulated by their success, now demanded that William publicly endorse the withdrawal of the candidacy, and promise never to allow it to be renewed. William, who was at Ems, courteously refused, and sent a telegram to Bismarck describing his interchange with the French ambassador. Bismarck then abridged this famous Ems telegram, and released his doctored version to the press and all the European chanceries. He made it seem that William had thoroughly snubbed the French ambassador, and that the ambassador had been "provocative" to the king. Public opinion in Germany was now inflamed, and Bismarck set out to bait the French still further by unleashing a violent campaign against them in the German press, and boasting of his prowess in editing the Ems despatch. The French reacted as Bismarck had hoped. They declared war on July 19, 1870.

Within six weeks the Germans had advanced into France, bottled up one French army inside the fortress of Metz, defeated another at Sedan, and captured Napoleon III himself. The protracted siege of Paris followed, ending in surrender early in 1871. A new French government had to sign the treaty of Frankfurt. Bismarck forced the French to pay a billion-dollar indemnity, to cede the rich province of Alsace and about two-fifths of Lorraine (which the German military wanted as a defense against possible future French attack), and to support German occupying forces until the indemnity had been paid.

The German Empire

Even before this peace had been imposed, King William of Prussia was proclaimed emperor of Germany in the great Hall of Mirrors in Louis XIV's palace at Versailles. Bismarck had to make a few unimportant concessions to the rulers of the south German states to secure their entry into the new empire, but he never had to consult the Reichstag, which simply hastened to send its own deputation begging the king to accept the crown. The proclamation took place in a ceremony of princes and soldiers. When a constitution for the new empire was adopted, it was simply an extension of the constitution of the North German Confederation of 1867.

As chancellor of the German Empire from 1871 to 1890, Bismarck became the leading statesman in all Europe. He felt that Germany had no further need for territory or for war. As a nineteenth-century realist with no dream of world empire, he felt that his limited goals had been attained. As diplomat, he henceforth worked for the preservation of Germany's gains against threats from abroad, especially the threat that haunted him most: foreign coalition against Germany. As politician, he worked for the preservation of the Prussian system against all opposing currents.

Bismarck's chancellorship falls naturally into two periods: (1) a period of free trade, cooperation with the Liberals, and opposition to the Catholics (1871-1878); and (2) a period of protective tariffs, cooperation with the Catholics, and opposition to the socialists (1878-1890).

Domestic Developments, 1871-1878

At home, a multitude of economic and legal questions arose as a result of the creation of the new empire. Working with the moderate Liberal party in the Reichstag, Bismarck put through a common coinage and a central bank, coordinated and unified the railroads and postal systems, and regularized the legal and judicial systems. In 1871, the Reichstag voted to maintain one percent of the population under arms for three years. In 1874, Bismarck, simply by threatening to resign, forced the Reichstag to fix the size of the army at 401,000 for a seven-year period, until 1881. In 1880, a year before the period expired, he forced an increase to 427,000 for another seven years, to 1888. The privileged position of the army made a military career ever more attractive and served as a constant spur to German militarism.

But the great drama of the 1870's in Germany was furnished by Bismarck's attack on the Roman Catholic Church, the *Kulturkampf* ("battle for civilization"). The *Syllabus of Errors,* published by the Vatican in 1864 had denounced the toleration of other religions, secular education, and state participation in church affairs. Then in 1870 the Vatican Council, the first general council of the Church to meet since the Council of Trent in the Reformation period, adopted the dogma of papal infallibility. This dogma asserted that the judgments of the pope on faith and morals were infallible. To many non-Catholics, this seemed to say that no state could count on the absolute loyalty of its Catholic citizens.

In Germany, the Catholics were a large minority of the population. They had formed a political party, the Center, that quickly became the second strongest party in the empire. The Center defended papal infallibility, and wished to restore the pope's temporal power, which had been ended by the unification of Italy. The Center not only had many sympathizers in the Catholic Polish provinces of Germany but also sponsored a labor movement of its own, which seemed to pose a social threat. Catholic peasant and workman, priest and nobleman, all opposed the Protestant urban middle class and the Prussian military predominance in the state. Bis-

marck identified his clerical opponents with France and Austria, the two nations he had defeated in making the new Germany.

In collaboration with the Liberals, Bismarck put through laws expelling the Jesuits from Germany, forbidding the clergy to criticize the government, and closing the schools of religious orders. In Prussia, civil marriage was now required, appropriations for the Catholic church were stopped, and priests were forced to study at secular universities. The pope declared these laws null and void, and summoned all good Catholics to disobey them. Catholic services stopped in towns and villages, and many Catholics were deprived of their sacraments.

Bismarck never appreciated that the Church thrives on persecution. By declaring that he would not "go to Canossa," he summoned up for Protestant Germans the picture of the German emperor Henry IV humbling himself before the Pope in 1077. But Bismarck in the end had to go to Canossa, and repealed in the Eighties most of the anti-Catholic measures he had passed in the Seventies. By then he needed the support of the Center party against his former allies the Liberals, whose demands for power he found exorbitant, and against the growing menace of the Social Democrats. Moreover, the Protestant church itself and many of the conservative Prussian nobility had grown alarmed over the excesses of the anti-Catholic campaign.

Domestic Developments, 1878-1890

Indeed, in 1877 and 1878, Bismarck had begun a gradual shift in policy, dictated in the first place by the need for more revenue. The empire got its money in part from indirect taxes imposed by the Reichstag on tobacco, alcohol, sugar, and the like. The rest came from the individual states, which controlled all direct taxation and made contributions to the imperial budget. As military costs mounted, the government's income became insufficient, and Bismarck did not want to increase the empire's dependence on the states by repeatedly asking them to increase their contributions. He wanted the Reichstag to vote higher indirect taxes, but its Liberal members suspected that if they acceded he might do to them what he had formerly done to the

Prussian parliament: govern without them if a dispute arose, and depend on the money he would collect from the higher taxes they had granted him. Therefore they wanted some sort of guarantee before they united Bismarck's hands.

Basically, German tariff policy had been one of free trade, with little protection for German goods. But after a financial panic in 1873, the iron and textile industries put pressure on Bismarck to shift to a policy of protection that would help them compete with England. Moreover, an agricultural crisis led conservatives to abandon their previous support of free trade, and to demand protection against cheap grain from eastern Europe. In 1879, Bismarck put through a general protective tariff on all imports, a move on which his former allies, the Liberals, were split.

In order to avoid granting the constitutional guarantees demanded by the Liberals, Bismarck gradually abandoned the Kulturkampf. The Catholic Center favored his protectionist policy; moreover, the lessening of the clerical threat in France and the conclusion of a firm German alliance with Austria in 1879 removed the foreign causes for the attack on the Church. Bismarck therefore secured the support of the Center as well as that of the conservatives. Thus he was able to avoid making concessions to the Reichstag, and thus he launched Germany on an era of protection. The protectionist policy spurred still further the rapid and efficient growth of industry, especially heavy industry. Politically, the conservative Protestant agrarian forces now grew stronger, and gained many urban votes. But Bismarck never entirely trusted the Center, and strove successfully to remodel the Liberals into a staunchly conservative industrialist group.

While he was easing the Kulturkampf and swinging to protection in 1878–1879, Bismarck also began to proceed against the Social Democratic party. The Marxists Liebknecht and Bebel had founded this small party in 1869; in 1875, they enlarged it, much to Marx's own disgust, by accepting the followers of Lassalle, an apostle of nonviolence. The German Social Democrats were not nearly so revolutionary as their own Marxist phraseology suggested, and had no doubt inherited some of Lassalle's willingness to make a deal with the existing regime. They had many supporters among intellectuals and former liberals, and a substantial trade-union following, polling half a million votes in 1877, about ten percent of the total electorate. They were prepared to concentrate their efforts on improving working conditions rather than on revolution. But Bismarck always needed an enemy against whom he could unify his supporters; besides, he had been deeply impressed by the Paris Commune of 1871, and believed that something similar might occur in Germany.

Using as a pretext two attempts by alleged Social Democrats to assassinate William I, Bismarck called a general election in 1878, and rammed through the Reichstag a bill making the Social Democratic party illegal, forbidding its meetings, and supressing its newspapers. Individual socialists could even be expelled from their houses by the police. Abandoning their alleged principles, the Liberals supported this law, but they would not allow Bismarck to make it a permanent statute. He had to apply to the Reichstag for its renewal every two or three years; it was renewed each time, until just before Bismarck's own downfall in 1890. Interestingly enough, Social Democrats were still allowed to run for the Reichstag, and their votes increased during the years when they were suffering legal disabilities.

But Bismarck felt that "a remedy cannot be sought merely in repression of Socialist excesses— there must be simultaneously a positive advancement of the welfare of the working classes." As a result, all during the 1880's, the government put forward a series of bills in favor of the workers: in 1882 compulsory insurance against illness, and in 1884 against accidents. The sickness insurance funds were raised by contributions from both workers and employers; the accident insurance funds were contributed altogether by the employers. In 1889, old-age and invalidism insurance followed, with employers and employees contributing equally, and with an additional subsidy from the state. The German system of social security as developed initially under Bismarck did not reduce the Social Democratic vote, but it did provide much that the worker desired.

William II

Bismarck's faithful William I died at the age of ninety in 1888, and William's son, Frederick

III, already mortally ill, ruled for only about three months. The next emperor was Frederick's son, William II, a young man of twenty-nine whose advent his father had greatly feared because of his immaturity, impulsiveness, and conceit. William I had allowed Bismarck to act for him, but William II was determined to act for himself. This determination underlay the subsequent controversy between him and Bismarck.

On his accession, William loudly proclaimed his sympathy with the workingman. When the antisocialist law came up for renewal, the emperor supported a modified version that would have taken away the power of the police to expel Social Democrats from their residences. Bismarck opposed the measure, hoping that the Social Democrats would indulge in excesses which would give him the excuse to suppress them by armed force. As a result, there was no antisocialist law after 1890. Other differences arose between the chancellor and the emperor over relations with Russia, and over procedure in reaching policy decisions. Finally, in March 1890, William commanded Bismarck to resign.

Although four chancellors succeeded him during the years before the outbreak of war in 1914, none of them can be compared with Bismarck in ability and influence. The years 1890–1914 are truly the years of William II. Energetic but unsteady, pompous and menacing but without the intention or the courage to back up his threats, emotional and vacillating, William was ill-suited to govern any country, much less the militaristic, highly industrialized imperial Germany with its social tensions and its lack of political balance.

Domestic Tensions, 1890-1914

Party structure reflected the strains in German society. The Liberals, a party of big business, usually had little strength in the Reichstag, although many industrialists were on intimate terms with the emperor personally. The great landowners banded together in protest against a reduction in agricultural duties which was included in a series of trade treaties concluded between Germany and other continental European countries between 1892 and 1894. In 1894, they organized the Agrarian League, which spearheaded all conservative measures and became

"Dropping the Pilot": Cartoon by John Tenniel on Bismarck's resignation in 1890.

enormously powerful in German politics. In 1902, they forced a return to protection.

The electoral strength of the Social Democrats increased during William's reign from 1,500,000 to 4,250,000, and embraced a third of the voting population by 1914. Freed from interference by the removal of the antisocialist law, they organized trade unions, circulated newspapers, and successfully brought pressure on the regime for more social legislation. The party had no immediate plan for a revolution, although its radical wing expected, especially after the Russian Revolution of 1905, that a revolution would come. The moderate or "revisionist" wing, which expected no open conflict between capital and labor, hoped that, by allying themselves with the middle class to attain a majority in the Reichstag, the Social Democrats might eventually overthrow the militarist regime. This the radical wing scornfully dismissed a mere temporizing.

As the Social Democrats became more powerful, the government allied itself more closely with the Catholic Center. Between 1895 and 1906, and again between 1909 and 1914, a coalition of conservatives and the Center formed the majority group in the Reichstag. The coalition did not wish to see any increase in the powers of parliament. Yet left-wingers within the Center party occasionally called for a liberalization of the system, and for tactical purposes would even ally themselves with the Social Democrats.

Meanwhile, issues of military, colonial, and foreign policy began to complicate the internal politics of Germany. The size of the army rose from 479,000 in 1892 to 870,000 in 1913. And for the first time Germany sought a big navy, after Admiral Tirpitz became minister of the navy in 1897. The emperor issued a series of warlike and grandiose statements hailing Germany's "future on the waters," and he and Tirpitz planned a high-seas fleet to supersede the naval forces that had been designed for coastal defense and for the defense of commerce. The navy boom was at least partly intended to supply a market for the expanding steel industry. A Navy League, ostensibly a private organization but constantly hand in glove with the regime, spread propaganda on behalf of the new fleet. The first rather modest naval law of 1898 provided for a navy that was doubled by the second law of 1900.

But the army and navy were only the most obvious weapons of world power. Bismarck's satisfied country seemed satisfied no longer. The Colonial Society thrived, as Germany seized lands in the Far East and in Africa, despite the drain on the budget (for the colonies were never profitable), and despite scandal after scandal (for the Germans were often brutal colonial administrators). "Pan-Germans" planned the great Berlin-Baghdad railway to the Near East and cried shrilly for more and more adventure and conquest.

William's naval and colonial policies embittered Germany's relations with Great Britain. In 1896, the emperor himself sent the Boer president Kruger a telegram congratulating him on his having repelled the Jameson Raid and hinting that Germany would have been willing to intervene on the side of the Boers against Britain. Again in 1908, he gave an interview to a London

"Visiting Grandmamma": Cartoon by John Tenniel on Kaiser William's visit to England in 1889. "Now, Willie dear," says Queen Victoria to the emperor, "you've plenty of soldiers at home; look at these pretty ships, I'm sure you'll be pleased with them!"

newspaper, the *Daily Telegraph*, in which, with monumental indiscretion, he protested his friendship for Britain, yet at the same time declared that the English had been ungrateful to him in not acknowledging that his own military plans, sent to them in secrecy, had enabled them to win the Boer War. Of course there was nothing in his claim.

The *Daily Telegraph* affair aroused a storm of protest against William in Germany itself, and the emperor had to apologize and promise to do better in the future. This episode illustrates the dangerous instability of the man who was all-powerful in a mighty military state. Moreover, it also reveals the general uneasiness that underlay the apparently smooth and prosperous surface of William's Germany. The protest against the anachronistic system under which Germans lived and labored, and against the external bombast and internal insecurity of the regime, was expressed in the enormous vote of the Social Democrats in 1912.

In 1913–1914, a German army officer in the Alsatian town of Saverne (Zabern) wounded a lame shoemaker with his sword, and the commanding officer of the German garrison illegally arrested and jailed townspeople who protested. The bitter resentment of the Alsatians was echoed by many Germans who thoroughly disliked the outrageous and unrestrained behavior of their military. By a vote of 293 to 54, the Reichstag passed a resolution of censure against the government. Even more interesting is the sequel, for William decorated the guilty officer, who was acquitted by a court-martial. The Saverne affair proved that the German public was still capable of feeling discomfort over the excesses of their Prussian masters, but it also proved that even a public expression of disapproval had little effect on these masters—the emperor, the Junkers, and the military.

William II, center, observing army maneuvers just before the outbreak of World War I.

III   The Hapsburg Monarchy, 1850–1914

Character of the Empire

The extraordinary empire of the Hapsburgs has been called ramshackle, heterogeneous, and anachronistic. And much scorn has been poured upon it for its incompetence, its smugness, its stupidity, and its failure to keep up with modern times. No doubt these charges are largely justified. But during the past half-century voices have been raised mourning the empire's disappearance, and regretfully echoing a nineteenth-century Czech patriot's celebrated remark that if the empire did not exist it would be necessary to invent it. These expressions of longing came not only from monarchists and clericals lamenting a past hopelessly beyond recovery, but from many who experienced the far more oppressive nationalist or fascist regimes that governed much former Hapsburg territory in the 1920's and 1930's, or the communist regimes of the period since 1945. By contrast, even the Hapsburgs have seemed preferable.

For sixty-four mortal years, from 1850 to 1914, the emperor Francis Joseph sat on the Hapsburg throne. Simple in his personal life and immensely conscientious, he worked hard at his desk, reading and signing state papers for hours every day. But he was without fire or imagination, uninterested in books dealing with current problems, or even in newspapers, devoted to the rigid court etiquette prescribed for Hapsburgs, inflexibly old-fashioned and conservative. He was intensely pious. He loved to hunt. His mere longevity inspired loyalty, but it must be admitted that he was a dull fellow, in every sense of the term. His decisions usually came too late, and conceded too little. His responsibility for the course of events is large.

Political Experiments, 1850–1867

Hapsburg history between 1850 and 1914 divides naturally into unequal portions at the convenient date 1867, when the Empire became the dual monarchy of Austria-Hungary. After the suppression of the Revolution of 1848, there was a decade of repression usually called the Bach period, from the name of the minister of the interior, ending in 1859 with the war against Piedmont and France. Then came eight years of political experimentation, from 1859 to 1867, punctuated by the war of 1866 with Prussia.

In 1849, all parts of the empire were for the first time unified and directly ruled from Vienna by German-speaking officials. In 1855, the state signed a concordat with the Catholic church, giving clerics a greater influence in education and in other fields than they had enjoyed since the reforms of Joseph II. The repressive domestic policies of the Bach period required expensive armies and policemen. Instead of investing in railroads and industry, Austria went into debt by enforcing the Bach system. These expenditures left it at a disadvantage compared with Prussia. Then, during the Crimean War, instead of repaying Czar Nicholas I for Russia's aid in subduing the Hungarian Revolution, Austria "astonished the world by her ingratitude." Not only did Francis Joseph fail to assist the Russians; he actually kept them in fear of an attack by occupying the Danubian principalities (modern Romania), and so threatening the flank of the Russian armies. In 1857, Austria experienced a severe financial crisis partly as a result of this long mobilization.

The defeat of 1859 at the hands of the French and Italians, and the loss of Lombardy with its great city of Milan, brought about the end of the Bach system. War continued to threaten, and the nationalities inside the empire, especially the Magyars, could not be kept in a state of smoldering discontent which would render their troops unreliable. Several solutions were now tried in an effort to create a structure that would withstand the domestic and foreign strains, but that would not jeopardize the emperor's position. Francis Joseph made no effort to consult the people. Instead, he listened first to the nobles, who favored a loose federalism, and then to the bureaucrats, who favored a tight centralism.

The October Diploma (1860) set up a central legislature to deal with economic and military problems. To it the provincial assemblies (diets) throughout the empire would send delegates. All other problems were left to the provincial diets, elected by a system that worked to disfranchise the peasants and to benefit the rich and (in Bohemia) the German townspeople rather than the Czech farmers. But the October Diploma did not satisfy the most important non-German province: Hungary. The Magyars continued to press for autonomy, as they had in 1848. Francis Joseph, who really preferred the Bach system, opposed Magyar wishes for special treatment, and hoped that the nobles could stave off further liberalization.

On the other hand, the German liberals and bureaucrats of Austria felt that the October Diploma went too far and gave the Magyars too much. To them it seemed that the empire was being dismembered on behalf of the nobility, who dominated the provincial assemblies. The February Patent of 1861 was actually a new constitution in line with their views. It proclaimed a more centralized scheme. The imperial legislature took over most of the powers the October Diploma had reserved for the provincial assemblies or diets.

Naturally, the Magyars objected to this second solution even more than to the first, and flatly refused to participate. To the applause of the Germans in Vienna, including the liberals, Hungary was returned to authoritarian rule. Czechs and Poles also eventually withdrew from the central parliaments and left only a German rump. Disturbed, the emperor suspended the February Patent; he began to negotiate with the Magyars, who were represented by the intelligent and moderate Francis Deák, but the negotiations were interrupted by the war with Prussia in 1866. The Austrian defeat at Sadowa, the expulsion of Austria from Germany, and the loss of Venetia seemed to threaten the entire Hapsburg system. Francis Joseph resumed negotiations with the Magyars, with the help of the great Magyar noble Andrássy, and of Beust, who had become Austrian foreign minister. In 1867, a formula was found which was to govern and preserve the Hapsburg domains down to the World War of 1914–1918.

The Dual Monarchy, 1867

This formula was the famous *Ausgleich*, or compromise, which created the dual monarchy of Austria-Hungary. The Hungarian Constitution of 1848 was restored, and the entire empire was reorganized on a strict partnership basis. Austria and Hungary were united in the person of the emperor, who was always to be a Catholic legitimate Hapsburg, and who was to be crowned king of Hungary in a special ceremony in Budapest. For foreign policy, military affairs, and finance, the two states had joint ministers appointed by the emperor. A customs union subject to renewal every ten years also united them. Every ten years the quota of common expenditure to be borne by each partner was to be settled. A unique body, the "delegations," made up of sixty members from the Austrian parliament and sixty members from the Hungarian parliament, meeting alternately in Vienna and in Budapest, was to decide on the common budget. After the budget had been approved, it had to be ratified by the full parliaments of both countries, and signed by the emperor-king. The delegations also had supervisory authority over the three joint ministers, and might summon them to give an account of their activities. In practice, the delegations seldom met, and were almost never consulted on questions of policy. The system favored Hungary, which had forty percent of the population but never paid more than a third of the expenses. Every ten years, when the quota of expenses and the customs union needed joint consideration, a new crisis arose.

Otherwise, Hungary and Austria were separate states. As king of Hungary, Francis Joseph appointed cabinet ministers, professors, bishops, civil servants, and other officials. He was obliged at least once a year to summon the Hungarian legislature, which had an upper house of hereditary peers and a lower house elected by an elaborate system with more than fifty types of voters. However, qualifications regarding economic status and nationality made the Hungarian lower house entirely undemocratic; the voters never totaled more than six percent of the population. For its part, Austria retained the parliament and the seventeen provincial assemblies provided by the February Patent of 1861. According to the new Austrian Constitution of 1867, the authority of the emperor somewhat resembled that of other constitutional monarchs, with the fundamental exception that he could legislate by himself when parliament was not in session. Since he could dissolve parliament at will, he enjoyed a very large discretion, and was potentially a strong personal ruler.

The dual structure of Austria-Hungary was unique in Europe, and indeed in history. Because of it, many domestic developments in the two parts of the monarchy may be considered quite separately. Yet one overwhelmingly important and complicated problem remained

common to both halves of the monarchy: the problem of the national minorities that had not received their autonomy. Some of these minorities (Czechs, Poles, Ruthenes) were largely in Austria; others (Slovaks, Romanians) were largely in Hungary; the rest (Croats, Serbs, Slovenes, all of them south Slavs) were in both states. These nationalities were at different stages of development and of national self-consciousness. Some of them were subject to pressures from fellow nationals living in states outside the dual monarchy.

The Austrian Constitution of 1867 provided that all nationalities enjoy equal rights, and guaranteed that each might use its own language in education, administration, and public life. Even the Hungarians in 1868 abandoned on paper the fierce Magyar chauvinism of Kossuth and the superpatriots of 1848 and put on the statute books a law that allowed the minorities to conduct local government in their own language, to hold the chief posts in the counties where they predominated, and to have their own schools. But in practice, neither the Austrian nor the Hungarian statute was respected. The nationalities suffered varying degrees of discrimination and even persecution. Since the nationality problem was common to Austria and to Hungary, and since it ruined the entire dual monarchy in the end, after the disastrous defeats of World War I, we must examine it in some detail.

The Czechs

After 1867, many Czechs felt that they were entitled to an Ausgleich on the model which the Magyars had obtained. They argued that the lands of the Crown of Saint Wenceslaus (d. 929) —the provinces of Bohemia, Moravia, and Austrian Silesia—possessed rights comparable to those that the Magyars had successfully claimed for the lands of the Crown of Saint Stephen (975?-1038). But the Czechs never had the power or the opportunity that the Magyars had to bring pressure on the Austrians, although Czech deputies boycotted the Austrian parliament in the hope that Francis Joseph would consent to become king of Bohemia in Prague as he had become king of Hungary in Budapest.

In 1871, the emperor did indeed offer to be crowned as king of Bohemia. The Bohemian diet, from which all Germans had withdrawn in a fury, drew up proposals that would have produced a triple instead of a dual monarchy. The rage of Austrian and Bohemian Germans, the opposition of Magyar politicians, who predicted chaos, and a Slavic uprising in southern Austria forced Francis Joseph to change his mind. Deeply disappointed, the Czech nationalist leaders returned to passive resistance.

By 1879, when the Czech deputies returned to the Vienna parliament, they were divided into moderate "old Czechs" and radical and impetuous "young Czechs." In the 1880's and 1890's, each time the Czechs won cultural or political gains, the German extremists bitterly opposed them, strengthening the Czech extremists and weakening the moderates. A statute requiring all judges in Czech lands to conduct trials in the language of the petitioner led to the development of an experienced body of Czech civil servants, since many Czechs knew German already, while Germans usually had to learn Czech. In 1890, the government and the old Czechs had tentatively agreed on an administrative division of Bohemia between Germans and Czechs, but the young Czechs rioted in the Bohemian diet, and Prague was put under martial law, which lasted until 1897. When a new law was passed requiring that all civil servants would have to be bilingual after 1901, the Germans in the Vienna parliament threw inkwells, blew whistles, and forced out the ministry, while Czech extremists began to talk ominously about a future Russian-led Slavic showdown with the Germans. All moderation vanished in the waves of noise and hatred. No Austrian parliament could stay in session, and the government had to be conducted by decree.

Under the stress of prolonged agitation, and influenced by the apparent triumph of constitutionalism in Russia, Francis Joseph finally decided to reform the franchise. In 1907, all male citizens of the Austrian lands were enfranchised and could vote for deputies on their own nationality. Of the 516 deputies in the new parliament, 233 would be German and 107 Czech, a figure almost proportional to the census figures.

Yet in 1913 the Bohemian diet was dissolved by a coup, and in 1914 Czech deputies in the Austrian parliament refused to allow national business to proceed. Thus World War I began with both parliament and the Bohemian diet dissolved, and with the emperor and ministers ruling by themselves. Perhaps chief among the many causes for this general parliamentary breakdown was the failure to give the Czech provinces the self-government they had vainly sought since 1867. Most Czechs did not wish to cut loose from the empire and establish a separate state of their own. Amounting to about 23 percent of the Austrian population, the Czechs formed a hard core of discontent.

Yet, from the economic and cultural points of view, the Czechs were by far the most advanced of the Slavic peoples in the dual monarchy. By 1900, the famous Skoda armament works had become the largest in the empire, and the rival of Krupp in Germany. Porcelain and glassware, lace and beer, sugar and the tourist trade made the Czech middle class rich and Czech craftsmen famous. Laboring conditions were bad, however, and the Czech Social Democrats were weakened by their refusal to work with their German opposite numbers.

Czech nationalism was fostered by an active Czech-language press, by patriotic societies, by Czech schools, and by the famous *sokols* ("hawks"), a physical-training society with strong nationalist leanings. At the ancient Prague University, learned Czech scholars taught, of whom Thomas Masaryk, married to an American, became the most famous. Professor of philosophy and student of Slavic culture, but a lover of the West, Masaryk deeply influenced generations of students, and upheld democratic ideals in politics. Historians studied the heroic past of the Czechs, and poets, novelists, and musicians glorified it for the popular audience. Deprived of their national autonomy and exposed to German bias though the Czechs were, they can hardly be regarded as a persecuted minority. They had their language and their freedom to develop under Austrian domination.

Poles and Ruthenians

Of all the minorities in Austria, the Poles (18 percent of the population) were the most satisfied, the only contended Poles in Europe. Most of them lived in Galicia, where they formed the landlord class and generally oppressed their peasants, especially the backward Ruthenians (Ukrainians). Like the Czechs, the Galician Poles asked for provincial self-government on the Magyar model, and like the Czechs, they were denied. But they had their own schools, and Polish was the language of administration and the courts. The Poles enjoyed favorable financial arrangements, and after 1871 there was a special ministry for Galicia in Vienna. Since they hated Russia, pan-Slavism never tempted them as it did the Czechs; they were not even very much interested in a future independent Poland.

The contrast between this generous treatment and the brutality suffered by the Poles living in Prussian and Russian Poland led Poles everywhere to look to Austrian Galicia as the center of national life and culture. Polish refugees from tyranny elsewhere took refuge in the cities of Cracow and Lemberg. Here were splendid Polish universities, noble families living grandly as they always had in Poland, and opportunities to serve the Crown in the provincial administration. The universities trained generations of Poles who were available later for service in independent Poland. Polish literature and the study of Polish history flourished. Though slowly, industrialization began, and a promising petroleum industry was launched. Only the Ruthenians and the Jews suffered discrimination and hardship.

The Poles eliminated Ruthenians from the Galician diet, and until 1907 kept them from the imperial parliament. The Ruthenians themselves were divided into an older pro-Russian generation, and a younger generation of Ukrainian nationalists, often fanatical, who hated Poles and Russians alike, and who hoped for their own autonomous status within the monarchy. In 1908, a Ukrainian assassinated the Polish governor of Galicia after a horrible instance of Polish police brutality.

Other Minorities in Austria

The other minorities in Austria were far less numerous. Less than 3 percent of the population was Italian in 1910; about 4½ percent was Slovene; and less than 3 percent was Serb and Croat. The Italians of the south Tyrol and Istria, where their center was the seaport of Trieste, were far more important than their numbers warranted, however, because of the existence of the Kingdom of Italy across the monarchy's frontier. Almost all of them wanted to belong to Italy, and Italy regarded their lands as *Italia Irredenta*. Of all the Austrian minorities, the Italian steadily proved itself the most anxious to get out of the Hapsburg monarchy altogether.

Among the south Slavs in Austria proper, the Slovenes were the most contented. Scattered in six provinces, and often living at odds with their German or Italian neighbors, they usually made only local demands, like that for lecture courses in Slovene at Graz university. The Croats in Austria (mostly in Dalmatia) were fewer and less disaffected than those in Hungary, and the Serbs in Austria were far fewer and less disaffected than the Serbs in Hungary and in the separate province of Bosnia. Yet both Serbs and Croats in Austria were divided: some preferred autonomy within the empire and others hoped one day to join a still hypothetical south Slav state.

Minorities in Hungary: Slovaks, Romanians, South Slavs

In Hungary, minority problems were even more acute. Magyar behavior toward other national groups grew increasingly outrageous as moderate counsels vanished in the face of short-sighted demagoguery. The Slovaks, the Romanians, and the Serbs and Croats living in Hungary proper were the worst victims of a deliberate policy of magyarization, but even the Croatians of Croatia, whose province had its own constitutional special status, suffered. The Magyar aim was actually to destroy the national identity of the minorities, and to transform them into Magyars. The weapon used was language.

It is difficult to understand the passionate attachment felt by the backward peasant peoples of southeastern Europe for their own languages. Yet, deprived of economic opportunity and sometimes of complete religious freedom, these peoples in the nineteenth century found in the languages they talked a living proof of national identity. The Magyars too, who made up only 55 percent of the population of their own country exclusive of Croatia, had a fanatical devotion to their own language, an Asian tongue quite unrelated to the German, Slavic, or Romanian languages of the minorities. They tried to force it upon the subject peoples, particularly in education. All state-supported schools, from kindergartens to universities, had to give instruction in Magyar. The state postal, telegraph, and railroad services used only Magyar.

The Slovaks, numbering about 11 percent of the population of Hungary, were perhaps the most magyarized. Poor peasants for the most part, the more ambitious of them often became Magyars simply by adopting the Magyar language as their own. As time passed, a few Slovaks came to feel a sense of unity with the closely related but far more advanced Czechs across the border in Austria. The pro-Czechs among the Slovaks were usually liberals and Protestants. Catholic and conservative Slovaks toward the end of the century found their leader in a priest, Father Hlinka, who advocated Slovak autonomy. After Czechoslovakia had been formed in 1918, the Hlinka movement continued to be anti-Czech, and became pro-Hitler in the 1930's.

The Romanians, who lived in Transylvania, amounted in 1910 to 16½ percent of the population of Hungary, and possessed a majority in Transylvania itself. For centuries they had been downtrodden by the Magyars, and had had to fight to achieve recognition of their Orthodox religion. Indeed, largely in the hope of receiving better treatment, many of them had become Uniates, accepting the supremacy of Rome but otherwise preserving their own liturgy. Despite laws designed to eliminate the use of the Romanian language, and a great deal of petty persecution, the Romanians stoutly resisted assimilation. For redress of grievances, many looked to Vienna, which before the Ausgleich had often been a source of assistance against the Magyars, but which was now committed to give the Magyars a free hand. These Romanians hoped that Transylvania might again be made autonomous, as it had once been in the past. They pressed for the enforcement of the liberal Hungarian nationalities law of 1868. They wanted their language and their church to have equal standing with other languages and other churches.

But when in 1892 the Romanians petitioned Vienna on these points, their petition was returned unopened and unread. When they circulated the petition widely abroad, their leaders were tried and jailed. It was little wonder that many Transylvanian Romanians ceased to look west to Vienna for help that never came, and began to look south and east across the Carpathians to Romania, where their fellow nationals had a kingdom of their own and a strong wish to annex the whole of Transylvania.

Under Magyar rule, some Serbs and Croats lived in Hungary proper and others in Croatia. In 1910, those in Hungary totaled about 600,000, of whom two-thirds were Serbs. Living in a compact mass in the southern and western frontier regions, these were the inhabitants of the old Hapsburg "military frontier" against the Turks. They were transferred to Magyar rule in 1869, and they resented it. The Serbs especially disliked Hungarian administration and looked to the independent kingdom of Serbia to the south. But a far greater menace to Hungarian unity was provided by Croatia proper.

Croatia

The Croats, though connected since the eleventh century with the Crown of Hungary, had become strongly nationalistic under the impact of the Napoleonic occupation, and had fought on the side of the monarchy against the Magyar revolutionaries of 1848. None the less, Francis Joseph, as part of the Ausgleich settlement, handed them back to the Magyars. Croatian nationalists were deeply disappointed. Led by the Roman Catholic bishop Strossmayer, a man of deep intelligence, high culture, and liberal views, they had hoped for an autonomous Croatia and Dalmatia inside the empire, which would serve as a nucleus to attract all the other southern Slavs. But instead, the Magyar moderates, led by Deák, worked out in 1868 an Ausgleich of their own between Hungary and Croatia.

All military and economic affairs were to be handled in Budapest by a special cabinet minister for Croatian affairs. Representatives from the Croatian parliaments at the Croatian capital of Zagreb would sit in Budapest whenever Croatian affairs were under discussion. Croatian delegates would be part of the Hungarian "delegation" of the dual monarchy. The Croatian language could be spoken by Croat representatives at the sessions of any body they attended, and the language of command in the Croatian territorial army would be Croatian. The Croats would control their own educational system, their church, their courts and police, but all taxes would be voted by Budapest and collected by agents of Budapest. Although the Croats were far better off than any national minority in Hungary, this "compromise" did not satisfy them.

The "Party of the Right," the ancestor of Croat extremism in our own day, wanted a completely autonomous Croatia, and scorned as inferior the Serbs and other non-Catholic south Slavs, whom Strossmayer had hoped to attract. Further problems were created in Catholic Croatia by the existence of a Serb Orthodox minority (more than a quarter of the population), which spoke the same language as the Croats, and which was racially indistinguishable from them. But the Orthodox minority worshiped in different churches, and was therefore subject to religious discrimination.

For twenty years at the close of the nineteenth century, the Hungarian-appointed governor cleverly fostered this Serb-Croat antagonism by using the Serbs for local offices. He received the support only of those Croats who had become Magyar-speaking, usually great landowners or government officials.

By 1903, Serbs and Croats were beginning to cooperate against Hungarian rule, and to spread pro-Slav propaganda in Dalmatia. In 1905, Croats asked Vienna for Dalmatia and for electoral reforms, but professed that they wanted to observe faithfully the arrangement of 1868 with Hungary. Serbians endorsed these Croatian demands, though some Serbs hoped for union with independent Serbia, and some Croats still hoped for complete independence.

In spite of these hopeful signs, the hopes of the moderates were dashed by the fearfully unpopular Railway Servants Act (1907), which forced all railroad workers to speak Magyar. Croats began to boycott Hungarian-made goods; the Croatian diet refused to collaborate with the new governor, who in 1909 arrested fifty-odd Croats and Serbs and charged them with plotting to unite Croatia and Bosnia with Serbia. The evidence was ridiculously inadequate, and the defendants, though condemned, obtained a reversal of the sentences on appeal to a higher court. But these Zagreb trials gave the Slavic press a splendid opportunity to denounce the policy of the dual monarchy.

In the same year, 1909, a celebrated Austrian historian, Friedjung, charged in the Vienna press that the Croatian and Serbian politicians in Croatia were plotting with Serbians in Serbia. Friedjung was eventually forced to admit that his documentary sources, which in all probability had been fed to him by the Vienna foreign office, were forgeries. The Zagreb trials and the Friedjung case, coming only five years before the assassination of Francis Ferdinand by a Bosnian Serb and the outbreak of war, demonstrated the incompetence of the dual monarchy in dealing with its own loyal south Slav inhabitants. In 1912, 1913, and 1914, Bosnian students tried to assassinate the Hungarian governor of Croatia. These were omnious rehearsals for the crime of June 28, 1914, which led not merely to internal crisis but to world war.

Bosnia-Herzegovina

In the dual monarchy, the region of Bosnia-Herzegovina had a special status. By the 1870's, these two provinces had been part of the Ottoman Empire for about four centuries. Although solidly south Slavic by race, the population included in 1879 about half a million Muslims, half a million members of the Orthodox church, and perhaps 150,000 Catholics. Under Turkish rule, those who accepted Islam had enjoyed economic advantages. Most of the Orthodox Christian population consisted of peasants working on the estates of Muslim landlords, and looking across the frontiers to Serbia in hope of liberation. Some of the Catholics were educated in Strossmayer's seminary, and leaned toward eventual absorption in his south-Slav state, but almost nobody wanted to join the Hapsburg monarchy as it was then constituted.

The Herzegovinian uprising in 1875 against the Turks precipitated a general Balkan Slavic attack on the Turks. Russia too went to war against the Turks, but first the Austrian and Russian foreign ministers reached an agreement on the future status of the two provinces. But they later disagreed on what the agreement had been. At the Congress of Berlin in 1878, the Austrians obtained the right to occupy the provinces, but not to annex them.

From 1878 to 1908 then, the forces of the dual monarchy occupied Bosnia and Herzegovina. The sovereignty of the Turkish sultan was recognized throughout this period, but in fact the provinces were ruled from Vienna, though not as part of either Austria or Hungary. Instead, they were put under the common Austro-Hungarian minister of finance.

The discontent of the Orthodox Serbs of

Bosnia was fanned by propaganda from Serbia itself. Patriotic Serbs considered that the first logical step toward creating a greater Serbia would be to incorporate these provinces inside their own frontiers, and they resented the decision of the Congress of Berlin that had allowed Hapsburg occupation. However, so long as the occupation was not turned into annexation, the Serbs preserved the hope that the provinces might some day become theirs, and meanwhile flooded them with agents and plotters. The Muslims, though favored by the Hapsburg authorities, never reconciled themselves to the ending of Turkish rule, and the Catholics hoped to join Croatia.

Thus these provinces perpetually threatened to create an explosion. The more intelligent observers in Vienna pressed for some sort of an all-south-Slav solution, not unlike that of Strossmayer. This would have put Dalmatia, Croatia, and Bosnia-Herzegovina together into a south-Slav kingdom under Francis Joseph, with the same status as Hungary—a triple rather than a dual monarchy. The advocates of this solution, known as "trialists," met with violent Magyar opposition.

However, the Young Turk Revolution of 1908 caused the adventurous Austrian foreign minister Aehrenthal to fear that the status of the provinces might be changed. Fortified by a prior secret agreement with Russia, Aehrenthal simply annexed the two provinces in October 1908, and announced that they would be given a diet of their own. This move precipitated a major European crisis which threatened world war but which eventually subsided, leaving the Serbs bitterly resentful. Serbian ambition to acquire the provinces now seemed permanently checked. The humiliation of Serbia, the disappointment of Russia, the solidarity of Germany with Austria-Hungary as revealed by the crisis, helped set the stage for the catastrophe of 1914. The discontent of the population of Bosnia, when added to the discontent of the Czechs and Italians in Austria, and of the Slovaks, Romanians, Croats, and other south Slavs in Hungary, goes far to account for the wartime weaknesses and postwar disintegration of the dual monarchy.

Yet the minority question, critical though it was, does not provide the entire answer. We must now briefly consider the Austrian-German and Hungarian majorities, both in their separate development and in their critical relationship to each other. Only then can we see that even the two ruling groups were subject to divisive forces that crippled them individually and together.

Austrian Society and Politics, 1867-1914

From the earliest days of the Ausgleich, the Austrian liberals fought the clerical conservatives. They legalized civil marriages, secularized all but religious instruction, canceled the Concordat of 1855 after the proclamation of papal infallibility in 1870, and taxed church property (1873). These measures were the Austrian counterpart of the German Kulturkampf, but they were much milder, since Austria was 90 percent Catholic, and did not share the Protestant Prussian suspicion of the Vatican. The liberals were discredited by the financial crash of 1873, during which it was revealed that some of them had accepted bribes in return for voting in favor of charters for shady and unstable new companies. From this period dates the earliest political anti-Semitism in Austria, since some Jewish liberals were involved in the scandals and served as convenient scape-goats. Economic advance during the early years of the monarchy had brought the usual increase in the working class, which after the crash turned toward socialism in both its Marxist and its milder forms.

The Austrian nobles, who often owned great estates which they ruled almost like independent potentates, were on the whole frivolous in their tastes, and took little interest in the problems of the nineteenth and twentieth centuries. They squandered their incomes on high living and gambling. Yet they supplied almost all the political leadership that the nation got. The large size of their estates was one fundamental reason for the small size of the average peasant holding, and made it necessary even for landowning peasants to try to obtain part-time employment on a noble's property. The peasants' standard of living and level of literacy were extremely low, yet the influence of the clergy kept them subservient to their masters, loyal to the dynasty, and almost contented with their lot.

The middle class of town dwellers and men of business, so familiar in western Europe, came later and was smaller in number in Austria. The wealthier tried to imitate the aristocracy's mode of life and to buy their way into the charmed circle. Others joined the professions, which they found overcrowded and badly paid. The unemployment of intellectuals is an extremely dangerous matter politically.

Among the bourgeoisie there were many Jews. Numbering 5 percent of the total population of Austria, the Jews (except for very few) could not be nobles, peasants, members of the clergy, bureaucrats, or army officers. So they were forced to enter trade, the professions, and the arts, where they often prospered and distinguished themselves. What we mean when we refer loosely to prewar "Viennese" life, with its charm and gaiety, its cultivation, its music, its cafés, its high reputation in medicine and science, was the life of a society very largely Jewish or part-Jewish. Conversion, intermarriage, and assimilation were not uncommon among the upper-middle-class Jews.

Anti-Semitism, fanned by the continued migration of poorer Jews from regions of eastern Europe where oppression had rendered them squalid and uncouth, was general among the non-Jews of Austria. But we must distinguish between the social anti-Semitism of most aristocrats, which was often simply a form of snobbery, and the serious political anti-Semitism of the lower middle classes, often the unsuccessful competitors of the Jews in the world of small shopkeeping. Partly out of religious prejudice, partly out of distaste for the liberal politics usually preferred by the middle-class Jews, the clericals inveighed against them. One response among the Jews to the swelling chorus of anti-Semitism was Zionism (sponsorship of a future Jewish state in Palestine), which originated in the dual monarchy.

The stresses and strains inherent in this social structure, aggravated by the problems of the national minorities, produced in the late nineteenth century two important new political movements among the Germans of Austria: Pan-Germanism and Christian Socialism. In the early 1880's, even moderate Austrian Germans wanted to hand over the Slavic lands of Austria to the Hungarians to rule, and then, stripped to the German core, to unite economically with Germany. The Pan-Germans were more radical and more violent. They opposed the Hapsburg dynasty. They opposed the Catholic church and led a noisy movement called *Los von Rom* ("Away from Rome"). They demanded that Austria become Protestant, and unite politically with Germany. They were furiously anti-Slav and anti-Semitic. They adored Bismarck and Wotan, but Bismarck did not encourage them. Their leader, Schönerer, himself a convert to Protestantism, was elected to the Austrian parliament in 1873 from the same district that later gave birth to Adolf Hitler. But the Pan-Germans never managed to become more than an extreme vocal minority.

The Christian Socialists, on the other hand, became the most important Austrian political party. Strongly Catholic and loyal to the Hapsburgs, they appealed at the same time to the peasant and the small businessman by favoring social legislation and by opposing big business. They too were violently anti-Semitic. At first skeptical of the value of Christian Socialism, the clergy later made the movement its own, and especially in the country prevailed on the people to vote for its candidates. The most famous single Christian Socialist was the perennial mayor of Vienna after 1895, Karl Lueger, the idol of the lower middle classes of the capital. For years he sponsored public ownership of city utilities, parks, playgrounds, free milk for schoolchildren, and other welfare services. Lueger always catered to his followers' hatred of Jews, Marxian socialists, and Magyars. Hitler, who saw Lueger's funeral procession in 1910, hailed him in *Mein Kampf* as the greatest statesman of his times. It is impossible to understand the doctrines of German Nazism in this century without understanding the social and racial structure of the Hapsburg monarchy in which Hitler grew up, and especially the doctrines and the appeal of Pan-Germanism and Christian Socialism.

To the Pan-Germans and the Christian Socialists, the Austrian Social Democrats, founded in 1888, responded with a Marxist program calling for government ownership of the means of production and for political action organized by class rather than by nationality. But the Austrian Social Democrats were not revolutionaries, and set as their goals such political and social gains as universal suffrage, secular education, welfare legislation, and the eight-hour day. They were usually led by intellectuals, many of them Jewish, but they were followed by an ever-increasing number of workers.

On the nationality question, Social Democratic leaders strongly urged a reform in the direction of democratic federalism. Each nationality should have control of its own affairs in its

North Sea

NORWEGIANS

SWEDES

Baltic Sea

FINNS

SWEDES

ESTONIANS

GREAT RUSSIANS

DANES

GERMANS

LETTS

LITHUANIANS

WHITE RUSSIANS

DUTCH

GERMANS

FLEMINGS

POLES

WALLOONS

LUX.

ALSATIANS

CZECHS

RUTHENIANS

LITTLE RUSSIANS
(UKRAINIANS)

FRENCH

SLOVAKS

KALMUKS

SWISS

SLOVENES

MAGYARS

MAG.

CROATS

ROMANIANS

Black Sea

ITALIANS

Adriatic Sea

CROATS

GEORGIANS

SERBS

GREEKS

BULGARS

GREEKS

ALBANIANS

ARMENIANS

ARABS

Aegean
GREEKS
Sea

TURKS

KURDS

Mediterranean Sea

GREEKS

GREEKS

ARABS

Nationalities in
Central and Eastern
Europe

— About 1914 —

―――――― Political boundaries, 1914

– – – – – Boundary between Austria
and Hungary

own territory; in mixed territories, minorities should be protected; and a central parliament should decide matters of common interest. Cultural autonomy for the nationalities of a multinational state was by no means an impractical or doctrinaire Marxist idea. Its practicality was later attested by the Soviet Russians, faced as they were with a similar problem and much influenced by the thinking of Austrian Social Democrats on the question. Otto Bauer, a doctrinaire Marxist, tried to explain away national antagonisms in the empire as a manifestation of class warfare. But the program of another Social Democrat, Karl Renner, who lived to be chancellor of the Austrian Republic when it was founded in 1919 and again when it was recreated in 1945, might have averted the necessity for the foundation of any republic at all. A believer in the dual monarchy, Renner advocated treating the nationalities as if they were churches, and allowing each citizen to belong to whatever one he chose. Each of these "national associations" would have its own schools, and disagreements among them would be settled by a high court of arbitration. Who is to say that if these views had been adopted, the monarchy might not have been preserved?

Hungarian Society and Politics, 1867-1914

In Hungary, the social structure was somewhat different. The great landed nobility, owning half of Hungary in estates of hundreds of thousands of acres apiece, were a small class numerically. Loyal to the dynasty, sometimes kind to their tenants, and socially contemptuous of all beneath them, they were often intelligent and discriminating, yet more often just as frivolous and empty-headed as their Austrian counterparts. But Hungary had a much larger class of country gentlemen, the squirearchy or gentry, whose holdings were far smaller and whose social position was lower, but whose political influence as a group was even greater. After the emancipation of the serfs in 1848, and during later periods of uncertain agricultural conditions, many members of the gentry became civil servants or entered the professions. The peasantry suffered from small holdings, insufficient education, primitive methods of farming, and a low standard of living.

The Magyars were country folk, and the towns for centuries had been centers for Germans and Jews. But during the nineteenth century, the towns became steadily more Magyar, as members of the gentry and peasantry moved into them. The Jewish population grew enormously during the same period, mostly by immigration from the north and east. In Hungary, many Jews were converted and assimilated and became strongly Magyar in sentiment and behavior. When they grew rich enough, they bought land and titles, and became gentry. But here too they were greatly disliked, especially among the poorer city population, and in the countryside, where they were associated with moneylending and tavernkeeping, two professions that kept the peasant in their debt. Yet though anti-Semitism existed in Hungary, it never gained as many followers or became as important a political movement as in Austria.

At the bottom of the social pyramid was a small class (never more than 20 percent of the population) of industrial workers in the cities, mostly in the textile and flourmilling industries. Wages were low, and living and working conditions were abominable, like those in Russia rather than those in the West. Yet more and more welfare measures were passed toward the end of the century. Because of its feebleness and lack of self-consciousness, this class could not be organized into an effective socialist party.

The Catholic church was immensely powerful and rich in Hungary as in Austria, but in Hungary Catholicism was the faith only of about 60 percent instead of 90 percent of the population. Some Hungarian magnate families and many of the gentry had never returned to Catholicism after the Reformation. They remained Calvinists. Several hundred thousand Germans, chiefly in Transylvania, were Lutheran. And in Transylvania also there were Magyar Unitarians. Clericalism could never become in Hungary the dominant force it was in Austria.

Thus, because of its differing social and religious structure, Hungary could not produce strong parties like the Austrian Social Democrats and Christian Socialists. Austria had a relatively liberal franchise before 1907 and universal manhood suffrage thereafter. Hungary, in contrast, never really changed its law of 1874, by which only about 6 percent of the population could vote. Moreover, Magyars of all shades were pretty well united in their determination to subjugate the national minorities in Hungary. Internal political or social issues, therefore, did little to determine Hungarian political alignments. The only real issue, and the chief source of Magyar political differences, was the question of Hungary's position in the dual monarchy.

Hungarian opponents of the Ausgleich were in the early days organized into two groups. The Kossuthists favored complete independence; a slightly more moderate party called the Tigers wished to improve the position of Hungary inside the monarchy by securing for the Hungarians control over their own army, their own diplomatic service, and their own finances, and by limiting the tie with Austria to the person of the monarch. When the great Deák passed from public life, one of the Tigers, Coloman Tisza, abandoned his opposition to the Ausgleich, joined the pro-Ausgleich Deákists, and came to power in 1875, to govern as prime minister for the next fifteen years. Thereafter, this merger of the Tigers and Deákists dominated Hungary except for the period from 1905 to 1910, and stayed in power largely by electoral manipulation. Called the Liberals, this group resisted any reform of the franchise and agrarian conditions, or of the treatment of the minorities.

Kossuthists maintained their opposition to the Ausgleich. They wanted Magyar used as the language of command for all Hungarian troops in the army, and agitated against Austria. In 1902, when the government refused their demands, they began to filibuster, and effectively paralyzed the Hungarian parliament. The emperor refused to yield to pressure. Coloman Tisza's son, Stephen, became premier in 1903, and worked through the increasing storm to preserve the Ausgleich. When he tried to limit de-

bate in order to permit the accomplishment of official business, the Kossuthists wrecked the parliament chamber. In 1905, Tisza was defeated by an opposition coalition including the Kossuthists, who now won a majority. When Francis Joseph refused to meet the demands of the new majority and appointed a loyal general as premier, the Kossuthists screamed military dictatorship, and urged patriots not to pay taxes or perform military service.

This struggle between the partisans of dualism and those of independence moved only the ruling caste of Magyars and bore no relation to the sentiments and needs of the larger part of the population. To mitigate the struggle, Francis Joseph had only to threaten to decree universal suffrage for Hungary, as he intended to do in Austria. This would open the gates to the discontented minorities and would encourage social and economic change. Under this threat, the opposition coalition eventually yielded (1906) and voted the necessary economic and military laws. They obtained the right to revise the franchise themselves, a task they had every interest in putting off.

In 1910, the younger Tisza won a victory in the elections by the time-honored methods of corruption and intimidation. He dropped the separatists' demands, which had been convulsing the country for more than a decade. Hungary got no bank, no separate army, and no substantial franchise reform. Kossuthists had to be removed by force from parliament, and gag rule had to be imposed. Tisza was kept busy fighting saber duels with the Kossuthist leaders. It was in this deplorable atmosphere that Hungary received the news that Franz Ferdinand, heir to the throne, had been assassinated.

IV Russia, 1825-1914

Character of the Empire

The third and largest of the great eastern European empires, Russia, took far longer, as was its way, to catch up with the political and social developments elsewhere in Europe. Thus there was no parliament whatever in Russia until after the Revolution of 1905, and even then the czardom was able to weaken and eventually to

dominate the new representative body. Serfdom did not disappear until 1861, and agrarian problems were in some ways intensified by the liberation of the peasants. Each time reform came, in the 1860's and in 1905 and 1906, it came as a direct result of military defeat abroad, which rendered reform absolutely essential. Thus the reforms of Alexander II (1855-1881) were inspired by Russia's defeat in the Crimean War (1854-1856), and the revolution of 1905 was made possible by Russia's failure in the Russo-Japanese War (1904–1905). During most of the nineteenth and early twentieth centuries, even after the reforms, the Russian czars claimed for themselves the same autocratic rights that Peter the Great and his Muscovite predecessors had exercised. Thus the Russian people experienced long periods of reaction: the entire reign of Nicholas I (1825–1855), and a protracted period from 1866 through 1904, including the last fifteen years of Alexander II's reign (1866–1881), the whole of Alexander III's (1881–1894), and the first ten years of Nicholas II's (1894–1917), the last of the czars.

The failure to adjust willingly to the currents of the times and the attempt to preserve autocratic rule produced unparalleled discontent in Russia. Disillusioned and angry intellectuals in the 1830's and 1840's gave way to proponents of social change in the 1850's and early 1860's, and these in turn to determined revolutionaries and terrorists in the late 1860's and the years that followed. Although Marxist literature was known early in Russia, and Marxist political groupings existed after 1896, the Marxists were by no means either the most numerous or the most effective of Russian revolutionaries. Native non-Marxist revolutionary parties long performed the killings and other acts of violence that convulsed the regime and won the support of large groups of Russians. It was only Lenin's transformation of the Marxist doctrines and his adaptation of Marx to the Russian scene that made it possible for his Bolsheviks to emerge as an important threat. And it was only Lenin's supreme tactical skill and boldness that enabled him to bring his Bolsheviks, still a minority, to power during the Revolution of 1917, a movement that was itself made possible by Russian losses in still another war. There was nothing inevitable about the triumph of the Bolsheviks.

Amid the official attempt to preserve sixteenth-century patterns, Russia experienced the impact of nineteenth- and twentieth-century industrialization. New resources were developed, thousands of miles of railroads were built, and factories sprang up, engaged in both heavy and light industry. A new laboring class thronged the cities, as elsewhere in Europe, but it lived and worked under conditions far worse than those in any other country. The native Russian revolutionaries looked to the peasants, in traditional Russian fashion, to provide them with their base,

and they considered peasant problems paramount. The Marxists, on the other hand, true to the teachings of their master, recruited their following among this new proletariat and focused their attention on its problems. But they deliberately relied for their tightly organized leadership almost exclusively on a little body of intellectuals and theorists.

Despite censorship and an atmosphere of repression, Russia experienced during the nineteenth century an amazing literary flowering. Poets, novelists, and playwrights produced works that rank with the greatest of all time. Like a sudden blossoming of orchids on an iceberg, the Russian literary renaissance cannot easily be explained. The literary talents of the Russian people had long lain dormant, and now awoke in an expression of unparalleled vigor and beauty.

Nicholas I (1825-1855)

Coming to the throne amid the disorders of the Decembrist Revolution, Nicholas I (1825–1855) himself personally presided over the investigation of the revolutionaries and prescribed their punishment. He used their confessions as a source of information on the state of Russian opinion. Nicholas I has been more resoundingly damned by liberals, both Russian and foreign, than has any other czar. They have portrayed him as a kind of scarecrow of an autocrat. Reactionary and autocratic though he was, literal-minded and devoted to military pursuits, he was perhaps not such an inflexible tyrant as he has been made out.

Nicholas I worked hard at the business of the state, and firmly believed that the imperial word was sacred. Although he despised all constitutions, he honored the liberal constitution which his elder brother Alexander had granted to the Poles until the Poles themselves revolted. He believed that his own autocratic power had been ordained by God; the autocrat could not, even if he wished, limit his own authority. Naturally such a man loathed the thought of revolution anywhere, and was perfectly prepared to cooperate abroad with the Metternich system. At home, he was prepared to make changes and improvements, but not to touch the fundamental institution of the autocracy. Though he was uneasy over the dangers inherent in serfdom, he was afraid to reform it in any serious way, because he feared that concessions would stimulate revolution among the peasants. Nicholas leaned heavily on the nobility as a class, referring to its members as his "benevolent police chiefs."

So personal was Nicholas' rule that his own chancery or secretariat became the most important organ of Russian government. He enlarged it by creating several sections, including a notorious "third section" for political police activity, which spread rapidly and kept Russian political life under surveillance. This enormous expansion of the czar's own secretariat did not result in the abolition of any of the older organs of government. Consequently, bureaucratic confusion became very great, paperwork was multiplied, and much injustice was done through sheer incompetence. Although the Russian laws were collected under the direction of Speransky, for the first time since 1649, the collection was not a true codification or modernization.

In the field of education, Nicholas favored the improvement of technical schools, but was deeply worried about the possibility that subversive foreign ideas might penetrate into the universities. After the revolutions of 1848 in Europe, his reactionary minister of education, Uvarov, abolished the study of philosophy in the University of St. Petersburg, because, as he said, the usefulness of the subject had not been proved, and it might do harm. Uvarov formulated Nicholas' policies under the three heads of Autocracy, Orthodoxy, and Nationality: the unlimited power of the monarch, the sanctity of the Russian church, and the adoption of policies in accordance with the "Russian national character." The result was a police state, complete with censorship and terror, yet not nearly so efficient as a twentieth-century despotism.

We have already seen Nicholas putting down the Polish revolution of 1830 and intervening in 1849 to restore Hungary to the Hapsburgs. He believed in dynastic friendships, and counted on the alliance with Prussia and Austria without realizing that conflicting national interests were more important than friendships between monarchs. Thus he failed to see that Prussia would combat his own efforts to thwart the unification of Germany, and that Austria's interests conflicted with his own in southeastern Europe. It was partly Nicholas' failure to see the weaknesses of his own system of alliances that led him into the disastrous Crimean War.

The Crimean War

Like other Russian leaders before him, Nicholas confidently expected the collapse of the Ottoman Empire. Russia wished to protect the Orthodox subjects of the sultan, and also had important economic interests at stake. The great Russian wheat-producing areas in the south were being developed in earnest, and Odessa on the Black Sea had become a great commercial port for the grain trade. Nicholas hoped to establish a Russian sphere of influence in the Balkans, and even to take possession of Istanbul itself. We have already witnessed his intervention in the Greek War of the late 1820's. When the governor of Egypt, Mohammed Ali, revolted against the Ottoman sultan in 1832 and threatened Istanbul, Nicholas landed a Russian army and got credit for saving the sultan's capital.

In 1833, the Turks paid the bill for these services by signing the Treaty of Unkiar Skelessi with Russia. Nicholas took the Ottoman Empire under his protection, and the Turks agreed to close the Straits (the Bosporus and Dardanelles) to the warships of any nation. Alarmed at the preponderance that the treaty gave to Russia in an area of the world vital to British imperial and commercial interests, British diplomacy turned its efforts to undoing it. The next time Mohammed Ali revolted, in 1839, the British were able to put him down with their fleet before he came within distance of a Russian land force. In 1841, all the other important powers joined Russia in guaranteeing the integrity of Turkey, thus putting an end to the exclusive position obtained by Russia at Unkiar Skelessi.

During the next twelve years (1841–1853), Nicholas tried to reach an agreement with Britain on what should be done with Ottoman territory if Turkey collapsed. The British did not believe that such collapse was imminent, and they hoped to prevent Russia from doing anything to hasten it. The two parties misunderstood each other. By 1853, the czar mistakenly believed that Britain was not opposed to Russian domination of Turkey, and Britain mistakenly believed that the czar would not act in Turkey without consulting her.

Then a dispute arose over whether the Roman Catholics, backed by Napoleon III, or the

Orthodox clergy, backed by the czar, should have the right to perform certain functions in the Christian Holy Places in Palestine, which was still part of the Ottoman dominions. This trivial dispute was the immediate cause of the Crimean War. But the underlying cause was the czar's wish to reestablish the exclusive Russian position of the Treaty of Unkiar Skelessi, and the British unwillingness to permit him to do so. Nicholas coupled a demand for this exclusive position with the demand that the Turks settle the dispute over the Holy Places amicably. The latter demand was possible; the former was not. When Nicholas occupied the Danubian principalities to enforce his demands, the situation became even tenser. And so, after many months of elaborate diplomatic negotiations in which all the powers strove to work out a suitable formula to avoid war, the drift toward war proved too strong to be checked. England, France, and eventually the Italian kingdom of Sardinia fought the Russians to protect the Turks.

Famous as the occasion of the charge of the Light Brigade, and of Florence Nightingale's pioneer efforts to save the lives of sick and wounded soldiers, the Crimean War consisted mostly of the English and French siege of the great Russian naval base at Sebastopol in the Crimea. Military operations on both sides were inefficiently conducted, but eventually the Russians were compelled to surrender. In the Peace of Paris of 1856, Russia was forbidden to fortify the Black Sea coast or to maintain a fleet there. This made it impossible for the Russians to defend their own shores or to conduct their shipping in security. It now became the paramount

Cartoon by Gustave Doré showing Russian nobles betting their serfs in a card game.

object of Russian foreign policy to alter the Black Sea clauses of the treaty. Not only had Russia lost the war, but Prussia had not helped her, and Austria had been positively hostile. Nicholas did not live to see the total failure of his policy. He died during the war and was succeeded by his son Alexander II (1855–1881).

Alexander II and Reform

By this time a very substantial segment of Russian public opinion favored reforms, in reaction to the long period of repression at home and failure abroad. Moreover, the economic developments of the early nineteenth century had rendered the system of serfdom less and less profitable. In the south, where land was fertile and crops were produced for sale as well as for use, the serf tilled his master's land usually three days a week, but sometimes more. In the north, where the land was less fertile and could not produce a surplus, the serfs often had a special arrangement with their masters called quit-rent. This meant that the serf paid the master annually in cash instead of in work, and usually had to labor at home as a craftsman or go to a nearby town and work as a factory hand or small shopkeeper to raise the money. It is probable that about a quarter of the serfs of all Russia paid quit-rent by 1855. Neither in the south nor in the north was serfdom efficient in agriculture. As industries grew, it became clearer and clearer to factory owners who experimented with both serf and free labor that serf labor was not productive. Yet free labor was scarce, and the growing population needed to be fed. Many estates were mortgaged to state credit institutions, because of inefficient management and the extravagance of the landlords. Serfdom had become uneconomic.

But this fact was not widely realized among Russian landowners, who knew only that something had gone wrong somewhere. They wished to keep things as they were, and they did not as a class feel that emancipation was the answer. Yet the serfs showed increasing unrest, and cases of revolt rose in number. Abolitionist sentiment had now spread widely among intellectuals. Conscious of the unrest, Alexander II, though almost as conservative as his father, determined to embark on reforms, preferring, as he put it, that the abolition of serfdom come from above rather than from below. Through a cumbersome arrangement in which local commissions made studies and reported their findings to members of the government, an emancipation law was eventually formulated and proclaimed early in 1861.

A general statute declared that the serfs were now free, laid down the principles of the new administrative organization of the peasantry, and prescribed the rules for the purchase of land. A whole series of local statutes governed the particular procedure to be followed in the different provinces. All peasants, crown and private, were freed, and each peasant household received its homestead and a certain amount of land, usually the amount the peasant family had cultivated for its own use in the past. The land usually became the property of the village commune, which had the power to redistribute it periodically among the households. The government bought the land from the proprietors, but the peasants had to redeem it by payments extending over a period of 49 years. The proprietor retained only the portion of his estate that had been farmed for his own purposes.

This statute, liberating more than 40 million human beings, has been called the greatest single legislative act in history. There can be no doubt that it acted as an immense moral stimulus to peasant self-respect. Yet there were grave difficulties. The peasant had to accept the allotment, and since his household became collectively responsible for the taxes and redemption payments, his mobility was not greatly increased. The commune took the place of the proprietor, and differing local conditions caused great difficulty in administering the law. Moreover, the peasants in general got too little land, and had to

An English view of central Russia: A wood engraving from an English newspaper of 1864 showing a fair at Novgorod.

pay too much for it. They did not get important forest and pasture lands. The settlement, however, was on the whole surprisingly liberal, despite the problems it failed to solve and despite the agrarian crises that developed in part as a result of its inadequacies.

The end of the landlords' rights of justice and police on their estates made it necessary to reform the entire local administration. By statute, in 1864, provincial and district assemblies, or *zemstvos*, were created. Chosen by an elaborate electoral system that divided the voters into categories by class, the assemblies none the less gave substantial representation to the peasants. The assemblies dealt with local finances, education, medical care, scientific agriculture, maintenance of the roads, and similar economic and social questions. Starting from scratch in many cases, the zemstvos made great advances in the founding of primary schools and the improvement of public health. They brought together peasant and proprietor to work out local problems. They served as schools of citizenship for all classes, and led tens of thousands of Russians to hope that this progressive step would be crowned by the creation of a central parliament, or *duma*. Despite the pressure that such men tried to bring on the government, the duma was not granted, partly because after the first attempt on the life of the czar in 1866 the regime swung away from reform and toward reaction.

But before this happened, other advances had been made. The populations of the cities were given municipal assemblies, with duties much like those of the zemstvos in the countryside. The Russian judicial system and legal procedure, which were riddled with inequities, were reformed. For the first time, juries were introduced, cases were argued publicly and orally, all classes were made equal before the law, and the system of courts was completely overhauled. Censorship was relaxed, new schools were encouraged, the universities were freed from the restraints that Nicholas had imposed on them, and the antiquated and often brutal system of military service was modernized and rendered less severe.

Yet, despite all these remarkable advances accomplished in a relatively few years, Alexander II became the target for revolutionaries in 1866, and terrorist activity continued throughout the Seventies until the assassins finally killed the czar in 1881. It is impossible to understand these developments without taking a brief look at Russian intellectual life under Nicholas and Alexander.

Russian Intellectual Life

Early in Nicholas' reign, Russian professors and students, influenced by German philosophers, were devoting themselves to passionate discussions on art, philosophy, and religion. Many intellectuals outside the universities followed suit. These were the first groups known as the intelligentsia, a peculiarly Russian class. By the 1830's, they were beginning to discuss Russia's place in the world, and especially its true historical relationship to the West and the proper course for it to follow in the future. Out of their debates there arose two important opposing schools of thought: the "Westerners" and the "Slavophiles" (friends of the Slavs).

The Westerners stated their case in a famous document called the *Philosophical Letter,* published in 1836, though written earlier. Its author, Chaadaev, lamented the damaging effect of Byzantine Christianity and the Tatar invasions upon Russian development, and declared that Russia had made no contribution to the world. He hailed Peter the Great's efforts at westernizing Russia as a step in the right direction. He regarded the Roman church as the source of much that was fruitful in the West of which Russia had been deprived. Nicholas I had Chaadaev certified as insane, and commanded that he be put under house arrest with a physician visiting him every day. Yet, despite scorn and censorship, the Westerners could not be silenced. They continued to declare that Russia was a society fundamentally like the West, but that history had delayed its full development. Russia should now catch up. The implication was that the time had come for Russia to emerge from a period of absolutism, and to enter upon the paths of parliamentary government and constitutional monarchy already trodden by the West.

In response, the opponents of the Westerners, the Slavophiles, vigorously argued that Russia had its own national spirit, like the Volksgeist that Herder had discovered in the Germans. Russia was, they maintained, essentially different from the West. The Orthodox religion of the Slavs was not legalistic, rationalistic, and narrow like the Roman Catholicism of the West, but substantial, emotional, and broad. The Slavophiles violently attacked Peter the Great for embarking Russia on a false course. The West ought not to be imitated but opposed. The Russian upper classes should turn away from their europeanized manners, and look for inspiration to the simple Russian peasant who lived in the truly Russian institution of the village commune. Western Europe was urban and bourgeois; Russia was rural and agrarian. Western Europe was materialistic; Russia was deeply spiritual. Like the Westerners, the Slavophiles attached fundamental importance to the national religion, and made it the center of their arguments; but they praised where the Westerners damned. The Westerners' views had democratic and constitutional political implications; the Slavophiles' views had anticonstitutional and antidemocratic implications.

It is very important, however, to realize that this does not mean that the Slavophiles embraced the "nationality" doctrine of Nicholas I, or that they approved of his regime. These were not the chauvinist nationalists who appeared later. They opposed the tyranny and the bureaucratic machine of Nicholas I as bitterly as did the Westerners. But they wanted a patriarchal, benevolent monarchy of the kind they fancied had existed before Peter the Great, instead of a constitutional regime on the Western pattern. Instead of a central parliament, they looked back with longing to the feudal Muscovite assembly, the zemski sobor, and to other institutions of the czardom before Peter. Extremists among them went about the streets dressed in the old boyars' robes that Peter had made illegal. Many intellectuals shifted back and forth between the hotly debating camps, and few ever adopted in full the ideas of either side.

Alexander Herzen (1812–1870), for example, began his intellectual career as a Westerner and a devotee of French culture. The illegitimate son of a nobleman brought up in his father's house, he was charming, engaging, and highly intelligent. Like most Russians, he was not a reliable interpreter of Western society, however, and was deeply fascinated with the thought that its structure might be rotten and doomed. The failure of the Paris revolution of 1848, which he saw as an eyewitness, convinced him that this was true, and he now became a revolutionary socialist. At the same time, he became convinced

that the Westerners' thesis must be wrong. How could Russia in a short time pass through the stages of development which the West had taken centuries to experience but which Russia had missed? So Herzen became a Slavophile. As a revolutionary, he preached the destruction of existing institutions, and as a Slavophile he looked to Russia, with its peculiar institution of the peasant commune, the *mir*, to provide an inspiration for all Europe. Herzen became an influential publicist and issued a Russian-language paper in London which was widely read by Russian intellectuals. His memoirs provide perhaps the best picture preserved to us of the intellectual ferment of the age of Nicholas.

Michael Bakunin (1814–1876) reached roughly the same conclusions as Herzen at roughly the same time. But he was a practical anarchist tactician who loved violence, not a peaceful man of letters. He enjoyed participating in revolutions, and had a long career in and out of jail in most of the countries of Europe. He looked forward to a great revolution spreading perhaps from Prague to Moscow and thence to the rest of Europe, followed by a tight dictatorship; beyond this he was entirely vague about the future. Atheism was a fundamental part of his program—not a casual part, as it always was to the Marxists. In his long career, Bakunin was to exert from abroad a considerable influence on Russian radicals.

Nihilism, Populism, Terrorism

In the 1860's, and especially after the emancipation in Russia, the Russian intelligentsia, like intellectuals elsewhere in Europe, reacted against the romanticism of their predecessors. Suspecting idealism, religion, and metaphysics, they turned now to a narrowly utilitarian view of art and society. As one of these young men said, a pair of shoes to him was worth more than all the madonnas of a great Renaissance painter. All art must have a social purpose, and the bonds holding the individual tightly to society must be smashed. Away with parental authority, with the marriage tie, with the tyranny of custom. For these people the same "nihilist" (a man who believes in nothing) quickly became fashionable. The portrait of a nihilist was drawn by the great novelist Turgenev in Bazarov, the hero of his novel *Fathers and Sons*. Rude and scornful, obstinate and arrogant, Bazarov was actually accepted as a model by intellectual leaders of youth in revolt against established ways of behavior. Yet nihilism as such was not a political movement. The nihilists enjoyed shocking their parents by calling for an end to the old moral system, advocating, for instance, the extermination of everybody in Russia over the age of 25.

In the 1860's, many of these young Russian intellectuals went to Switzerland, where the proper Swiss bourgeoisie were scandalized at the men with their hair cut long and the girls with their hair cut short, at their loud voices and insolent behavior. The standard cartoonist's picture of a Russian revolutionary dates from the first startled glimpse which the Swiss had of the nihilists, who at the time had not even begun to be interested in political revolution. Herzen himself was shocked by their behavior. He died in 1870, his intellectual leadership forfeit. But Bakunin understood them, and influenced many of them during their stay in Switzerland. Bakunin urged them to go back to Russia and preach an immediate revolution to the peasants.

Also present in Switzerland were two other important Russian revolutionary thinkers: Lavrov and Tkachev. Lavrov (1823–1900) taught his followers that as intellectuals they owed a great debt to the Russian peasant, whose labor for many generations had enabled their ancestors to enjoy leisure, and had made their own education possible. More gradual in his approach and more realistic in his estimates of the Russian peasant than Bakunin, Lavrov advised the nihilist students first to complete their education and then to return to Russia and go among the peasants, educating them and spreading among them propaganda for an eventual, not an immediate, revolution of the masses. On the other hand, Tkachev (1844–1886) taught that no revolution could ever be expected from the peasant masses, but that it would have to come from a tightly controlled small revolutionary elite, a little knot of conspirators who would seize power. Though not very influential at the time, Tkachev was important in Lenin's later thinking.

Under the impact of these teachers, especially Bakunin and Lavrov, Russian nihilism turned to a new kind of movement, which is called populism. Young men and women, swept by idealistic fervor, decided to return to Russia and live among the peasants. When a government decree in 1872 actually summoned them back, they found that a parallel movement had already begun at home. About three thousand young people now took posts as teachers, innkeepers, or store managers in the villages. Some tried to spread revolutionary ideas, others simply to render social service. Their romantic views of the peasantry were soon dispelled. The young populists did not know how to dress like peasants or how to talk to peasants. Suspicious of their talk, the peasants often betrayed them. The populists became conspicuous, and were easily traced by the police, who arrested them in droves. Two famous mass trials were held in the 1870's, at which the general public for the first time learned about the populist movement. After the trials, the populists who remained at large decided that they needed a determined revolutionary organization. With the formation of the Land and Liberty Society in 1876, the childhood of the Russian revolutionary movement was over.

The revolutionaries had been stimulated by Alexander II's grant of reforms. So great had the discontent become that it is doubtful whether any Russian government could have proceeded fast enough to suit the radicals, who had come to believe in violent overturn of the regime, and were not satisfied with piecemeal and gradual reform. Stemming from John Stuart Mill and from Western Utopian socialists like Fourier and Robert Owen, Russian socialism was not yet greatly influenced by Marx. In some ways it was almost Slavophile, not urban but rural, not evolutionary but revolutionary, not a mass political party but a conspiracy. Its members lived underground, and developed a conspiratorial psychology. They proposed to overthrow a bourgeois society in Russia before one ever got started. The movement became more and more radical, and in 1879 those who believed in the use of terror as a weapon separated from the others and founded the group called the People's Will; the antiterrorists called themselves the Black Partition.

The members of the People's Will now went on a hunt for Czar Alexander II himself. They shot at him and missed. They mined the track on which his train was traveling, and blew up the wrong train. They put dynamite under the the dining room of the palace, and exploded it. But the czar was late for dinner that night, and eleven servants were killed instead. They rented

The assassination of Alexander II, March 13, 1881.

a cheese shop on one of the streets along which he drove, and tunneled under it. Finally they killed him (March 1881) with a crude handmade grenade, which blew up the assassin too. The supreme irony was that Alexander II had that day signed a document designed to summon a consultative assembly, which everybody expected to lead to further constitutional reform. His successor, the reactionary Alexander III (1881–1894), refused to confirm the document, and Russia was left to stagnate in a renewed repression. The terrorists were rounded up and punished, and their organization was smashed. Despite their occasional high-flown claims to enormous popular support, they had never numbered more than a mere handful of people, and their movement had been a failure.

Foreign Policy under Alexander II

In foreign policy, Alexander II made an uneven record. In Europe, the Russians successfully repressed the Polish uprising of 1863. They seized the opportunity provided by the Franco-Prussian War of 1870, and simply tore up the Black Sea provisions of the Treaty of Paris, declaring unilaterally that they would no longer be bound by them. This was an illegal act, to which the powers later reluctantly gave their assent. It was another illustration of the immorality in international affairs that Bismarck had made fashionable.

In 1877, the Russians went to war against Turkey on behalf of the rebellious Balkan Christians of Bosnia, Herzegovina, and Bulgaria. By the peace of San Stefano, dictated early in 1878 to the defeated Turks, Russia obtained, contrary to her previous agreements, a large independent Bulgarian state, which Russian policymakers hoped to turn into a useful Balkan satellite. But the powers at the Congress of Berlin later in the same year reversed the judgment of San Stefano. They permitted only about a third of the planned Bulgaria to come into existence as an autonomous state, while another third obtained autonomy separately, and the rest went back to Turkey. Russian public opinion resented the powers' depriving Russia of the gains scored in the Russo-Turkish War. Bitterness ran particularly high among those who hoped to unite all Slavs in a kind of federation, the Pan-Slavs (not to be confused with the Slavophiles).

Meanwhile, in Asia, encroachments begun under Nicholas I against the Chinese territory in the Amur River valley were regularized by treaty in 1860. Russian settlements in the "maritime province" on the Pacific Ocean continued to flourish. In central Asia, a series of campaigns conquered the native Turkish khanates and added much productive land to the Crown. Here, however, the advance toward the northwest frontier of India seemed to threaten British interests, and aroused public opinion in Britain against Russia.

The Reaction, 1881–1904

The reign of Alexander III and the first ten years of the reign of his son, Nicholas II, formed a quarter-century of consistent policies (1881–1904). Both czars loathed liberalism as expressed in the earlier reforms, and were determined that there would never be any more of it. Yet a peasant bank set up under Alexander III made the redemption payments easier for the peasants to pay. And a few pieces of labor legislation, enacted under the influence of Bismarck's example, made working conditions a bit more tolerable— for example, hours were shortened for women workers. Offsetting these measures were the establishment of a special bank that extended credit to the impoverished nobility, the reinstitution of rigorous censorship, and the institution in the countryside of so-called rural leaders or land captains in place of the elected justices of

the peace of Alexander II. Election procedure for the zemstvos and for the city assemblies was made far less democratic. Now there began a vigorous persecution of the minority nationalities, a policy called Russification, and quite in line with the "nationality" of Nicholas I's formula. The Finns, Poles, Ukrainians, Armenians, and Jews all suffered discrimination, varying from loss of their own institutions, which the Finns had enjoyed, to outright government-sponsored massacres in the case of the Jews. On his accession in 1894, Nicholas II referred to all hopes for a change as "senseless dreams."

These years were notable also for the steady growth of the Russian railroad network, largely built and owned by the state. The Donets coal basin was exploited for the first time; the Baku oilfields came into production; steel and cotton output soared. In 1892, there came to the Ministry of Finance a self-made railroad man, Witte, who for the next twelve years was personally responsible for the ever-mounting economic progress. Witte began the trans-Siberian railroad, put Russia on the gold standard, attracted much foreign capital, especially French, for investment, and balanced the budget, in part through the government monopoly of the sale of

Boys in a Russian shoe factory in 1888. Note the ubiquitous Singer sewing machine.

vodka. The railroad network doubled in length between 1894 and 1904, and the need for rails stimulated the steel industry. Correspondingly, the number of urban workers multiplied, and strikes called in protest against wretched working conditions mounted in number. In 1897, the working day was fixed by the state at eleven hours for adults, and other provisions were adopted to improve and regularize conditions. These laws, however, were difficult to enforce.

Under the circumstances, many of the young generation of revolutionaries now turned to Marxist "scientific" socialism, preaching the class struggle and predicting the inevitable downfall of capitalism. A small clandestine group of intelligentsia, formed in 1894–1895 at St. Petersburg, proposed to overthrow the regime, working with all opponents of the class system. The members of the group included Lenin, a vigorous young intellectual of upper-middle-class origin, whose brother had been executed for an attempt on the life of Alexander III. In 1898, this group and others formed the Social Democratic party, which in 1900 began to publish its own newspaper. Within party ranks, grave dissension sprang up over the question of organization. Should the party operate under a strongly centralized directorate, or should each local group of Social Democrats be free to agitate for its own ends? In the tradition of Bakunin and Tkachev, Lenin insisted on the tightly knit little group of directors at the center. At the party congress of Brussels and London in 1903, the majority voted with him. Lenin's faction thereafter was called by the name *Bolshevik,* meaning majority, as against the *Menshevik* (minority) group, which favored a loose democratic organization for the party. Both groups remained Social Democrats, or SD's, as they were often called.

Meanwhile, the non-Marxist revolutionaries, who were the direct heirs of the People's Will tradition, also organized a political party. They were the Social Revolutionaries, or SR's, with their own clandestine newspaper. Whereas the SD's as Marxists were interested almost exclusively in the urban workers, the SR's as populists were interested in the peasantry. Their chief aim was to redistribute the land, but they continued in their terrorist ways. They assassinated several cabinet ministers, using as their slogan the cry "We don't want reforms, we want reform."

A third political grouping was that of the moderates and liberals, not SD or SR in orientation, but mostly veterans of the zemstvos, and intellectuals indignant over the government's policies of repression, who favored nothing more radical than compulsory free private education and agrarian reform. The regime stupidly made no distinction between these men and the diehard terrorists or the rabid Marxists. Thus the moderates also gradually organized, and had their own clandestine paper favoring a constitution and a national parliament for Russia. In 1905, they took the name "Constitutional Democrats" and were thereafter usually referred to as Kadets, from the Russian initials KD. Faced by this political activity among its radical and moderate opponents, the government only tightened the reins and by 1904 had adopted the view that a short victorious war was all that would be necessary to unite the country.

The Russo-Japanese War

Trans-Siberian railway construction made it desirable for the Russians to obtain a right of way across Chinese territory in Manchuria. They took the initiative in preventing Japan from establishing herself on the Chinese mainland after her defeat of China in 1895, and then required the Chinese in exchange to allow the building of the new railroad. In 1897, they seized Port Arthur, the very port they had earlier kept out of Japanese hands. Further friction with the Japanese took place in Korea, where both powers had interests. Then, after the Boxer Rebellion of 1900 in China, the Russians kept their troops in Manchuria after the other nations had withdrawn theirs. Although the Russians promised to withdraw their forces by stages, they failed to do so, largely because Russian foreign policy fell into the hands of shady adventurers, some of whom had a lumber concession in Korea and wanted war with Japan. After it became apparent that the war party had got control in Russia, the Japanese without warning attacked units of the Russian fleet anchored at Port Arthur in February 1904. The Russo-Japanese War had begun.

Far from their bases and taken by surprise, the Russians none the less stabilized a front on land. But their fleet, which had steamed all the way around Europe and across the Indian Ocean into the Pacific, was decisively defeated by the Japanese in the battle of Tsushima (May 27, 1904). To the Russian people, the war was a mysterious, distant political adventure of which they wanted no part. Many intellectuals opposed it, and the SR's and SD's openly hoped for a Russian defeat, which they expected would shake the government's position. Alarmed at the growing unrest at home, the Russian government was persuaded by President Theodore Roosevelt to accept his mediation, which the Japanese also actively wished.

Witte, the go-getting businessman who had opposed the war from the first, was sent to Portsmouth, New Hampshire, as Russian representative. Here he not only secured excellent terms for Russia, but also won a favorable verdict from American public opinion, which had previously been strongly pro-Japanese, and had thought of Russians as either brutal aristocrats or bomb-throwing revolutionaries. By the Treaty of Portsmouth (1905), Russia recognized the Japanese protectorate over Korea, ceded Port Arthur and the southern half of Sakhalin Island, together with fishing rights in the North Pacific, and promised to evacuate Manchuria. Russian prestige as a Far Eastern power was not deeply wounded or permanently impaired by the defeat or by the treaty. Yet the effect of the defeat in Asia was to transfer Russian attention back to Europe, where a world crisis had already begun.

The Revolution of 1905

The most important immediate result of the Russo-Japanese War was its impact on Russian domestic developments. While it was still going on, Plehve, the reactionary minister of the interior, was assassinated by an SR bomb in July 1904. His successor was a moderate. The zemstvo liberals, the future Kadets, were encouraged, and held banquets throughout Russia to adopt a series of resolutions for presentation to a kind of national congress of zemstvo representatives. Although the congress was not allowed to meet publicly, its program—a constitution, basic civil liberties, class and minority equality, and extension of zemstvo responsibilities—became widely known and approved. The czar temporized, issued so vague a statement that all hope for change was dimmed, and took measures to limit free discussion.

Ironically, it was a police agent of the government itself who struck the fatal spark. He had been planted in the St. Petersburg factories to combat SD efforts to organize the workers, and to substitute his own union. He organized a parade of workers to demonstrate peacefully and to petition the czar directly for an eight-hour day, a national assembly, civil liberties, the right to strike, and a number of other moderate demands. When the workers tried to deliver the petition, Nicholas left town and ordered the troops to fire on the peaceful demonstrators, some of whom were carrying his portrait to demonstrate their loyalty. About a thousand workers were killed on "Bloody Sunday" (January 22, 1905). The massacre made revolutionaries out of the urban workers. Strikes multiplied, the moderate opposition joined with the radical opposition, and university students and professors demanded the same reforms as wild-eyed bomb hurlers.

Amid mounting excitement, the government at first seemed to favor the calling of a zemski sobor, consultative, not legislative, in the old Russian pattern rather than the Western parliamentary one, but still a national assembly of sorts. But then even this project was whittled away, as the timid, vacillating, and unintelligent Nicholas II listened to his reactionary advisers. Under the impact of delays and disappointments, demonstrations and outbreaks occurred during the summer of 1905. In October, the printers struck. No newspapers appeared, and the printers, with SD aid, formed the first *soviet* or workers' council. When the railroad workers joined the strike, communications were cut off between Moscow and St. Petersburg. Soviets now multiplied. Of the one formed in St. Petersburg, Lenin declared that it was "not a workers' parliament, nor an organization of proletarian autonomy, but a combat organization pursuing definite ends."

This reflects the Bolsheviks' view of the soviet as an instrument for the pursuit of their program of armed revolt, for the establishment of a provisional government, for the proclamation of a democratic republic, and for the summoning of a constituent assembly. This program, put forth by the most "extreme" of the revolutionaries of 1905, differed relatively little from the program of the most moderate liberals, who would, however, have kept the monarchy and striven to obtain their ends by persuasion and pressure rather than by violence. At the time, and for years to come, the Bolsheviks, like other Marxists, accepted the view that it was necessary for Russia to pass through a stage of bourgeois democracy before the time for the proletarian revolution could come. They were therefore eager to help along the bourgeois revolution.

Nicholas was faced, as Witte told him, with the alternatives of imposing a military dictatorship and putting down the opposition by force, or of summoning a truly legislative assembly with veto power over the laws. The czar finally chose the latter course, and in October 1905 issued a manifesto that promised full civil liberties at once, and a legislative assembly or duma to be elected by universal suffrage. In effect, this famous October Manifesto put an end to the autocracy, since the duma was to be superior to the czar in legislation.

Yet the issuance of the October Manifesto did not meet with universal approval or even end the revolution at once. On the Right, a government-sponsored party called the Union of the Russian People demonstrated against the manifesto, proclaimed its undying loyalty to the autocrat, and organized its own storm troops, or Black Hundreds, which killed more than 3,000 Jews in the first week after the issuance of the manifesto. The armies returned from the Far East, and proved to be still loyal to the government. Thus the soviets of 1905, unlike those of 1917, included only workers, and no soldiers. On the Left, the dissatisfied Bolsheviks and SR's made several attempts to launch their violent revolution, but failed, and the government was able to arrest their leaders and eventually to put them down after several days of street fighting in Moscow in December 1905. In the Center, one group of liberals, pleased with the manifesto, urged that it be used as a rallying point for a moderate program. These were the Octobrists, so called after the month in which the manifesto had been issued. The other group, the Kadets, wished to continue to agitate by legal means for further immediate reforms. But the real fires of revolution had burned out by the opening of the year 1906.

The Dumas, 1906–1914

Suffrage for the Duma was universal, but voters chose an electoral college which then selected the 412 deputies. Although SR's and SD's boycotted the elections out of discontent over the indirect election system, many of their number were elected. The Kadets were the strongest single party. Quite against the expectation of the government, the peasants' vote was not conservative, but highly liberal. But even before the first Duma had met, Witte was able to reduce its powers. He secured a large French loan, which made the government financially independent of the Duma, and issued a set of "fundamental laws," which the Duma was not to be competent to alter. The Crown was to continue to control war and foreign policy; the minister of finance was to control loans and currency. The czar's council of state was transformed by adding members from the clergy, nobility, the zemstvos, the universities, and chambers of commerce. It became a kind of upper house, which had equal legislative rights with the Duma, and could therefore submit a rival budget, for example, which the government could then adopt in preference to that of the Duma. Finally, the czar could dissolve the Duma at will, provided he set a date for new elections. When it was not in session he could legislate by himself, although his enactments had later to be approved by the Duma.

The first Duma, the "Duma of Popular Indignation," met between May and July 1906. It addressed a list of grievances to the czar, asking for a radical land reform that would give the peasants all state and church land, and part of the land still in private hands. The government flatly refused to accept this attack on property, and after some parliamentary skirmishing the Duma was dissolved. The Kadet membership, maintaining incorrectly that the dissolution was unconstitutional, crossed the frontier into Finland, and there issued a manifesto urging the Russian people not to pay taxes or report for military service unless the Duma was recalled. Its authors were soon tried and declared ineligible for office; so future Dumas were deprived of the services of this capable Kadet group of moderates.

With the dissolution of the first Duma there came to power as chief minister the highly intelligent and conservative Peter Stolypin, who stayed in office until 1911, when he was assassinated. Together with Witte, he was the leading statesman of the last period of czarist Russia. Stolypin put through a series of agricultural laws which enabled the peasants to free themselves from the commune. A peasant wishing to detach his property could demand that he be given a single tract, which meant that the scattered strips assigned to other families would also be consolidated so that each would obtain a single plot. This program Stolypin called the "wager on the strong and sober"; he was encouraging the initiative and enterprise of individual Russian peasants who had the will to operate on their own as successful small farmers. His program accomplished much of what he hoped for. It is estimated that about a quarter of the peasant households of European Russia (almost 9,000,-000) emancipated themselves from the communes during the years between 1906 and 1917. Only war and revolution kept the process from going still further. Lenin and others who hoped for revolution were deeply suspicious and afraid of Stolypin's agrarian reforms. They rightly feared that the peasant grievances would be removed, and understood that no revolution in Russia could succeed without the peasants.

Simultaneously with his agrarian program, Stolypin carried on unremitting war against terrorists and other revolutionaries. He showed no hesitation in acting in the most unconstitutional fashion when it suited him. He did everything he could to interfere with the elections to the second Duma, but the SR's and SD's were well represented, and the Duma itself (March-June 1907) would not work with the government. It was dissolved because it refused to suspend the parliamentary immunity of the SD deputies, whom Stolypin wanted to arrest.

After the dissolution of the second Duma, the government quite illegally altered the election laws, cutting the number of delegates from the peasants and national minorities, and increasing the number from the gentry. By this means the government got a majority, and the third Duma (1907-1912) and the fourth (1912-1917) lived out their constitutional lives of five years apiece. Unrepresentative and limited in their powers though they were, they were still national assemblies. In their sessions the left-wingers could be heard, and could question ministers like any other members. The Dumas improved the conditions of peasant and worker and helped strengthen national defense as the World War drew closer. Their commissions, working with individual ministers, proved extremely useful in increasing the efficiency of government departments. The period of the third Duma, however, was also notable for the continuation of russification, and the Finns in particular lost their remaining rights (1910).

Under the fourth Duma, the government, with Stolypin dead, tended more toward reaction. The Leftists organized busily for another revolution, working in unions, cooperatives, evening classes for workmen, and a whole network of other labor organizations. A vast web of police spies challenged them at every turn. Meanwhile, the imperial family drifted into a very dangerous situation, as the fanatically religious and autocratically minded empress fell more and more under the sway of a half-mad, wholly evil, dirty, ignorant, and power-hungry monk from Siberia. This man, Rasputin, had the mysterious ability, possibly hypnotic, to stop the bleeding of the young heir to the throne, who suffered from hemophilia. Since the empress had enormous influence on her beloved husband, Nicholas II, Rasputin became in a real sense the ruler of Russia, much to the horror of a great many loyal supporters of the imperial house, and greatly to the detriment of the rational conduct of affairs in an enormous twentieth-century state. At the moment when the World War began, Russia was in the throes of a major crisis precipitated by the government's reactionary policies, the scandal of Rasputin's influence, and the indignation of the loyal Duma. There was a threat of revolution, then, even before 1917.

V Conclusion

Parliamentary government was, as we have seen, a comparative stranger to the three eastern European empires. The king of Prussia, with Bismarck's help, used his extraordinary military system to conquer and unify Germany. He imposed on all non-Austrian Germans the Prussian system of autocracy almost undiluted by a weak and subservient parliament, and backed by the army and the Junkers. The Hapsburg emperor, though faced after 1907 with an Austrian parliament elected by universal suffrage, in 1914 still made virtually all policy decisions by himself. The Hungarian parliament was never genuinely representative, and the emperor, as king of

Hungary, successfully used universal suffrage as a threat to quell Magyar separatism. The czars, forced at last by defeat in wars to grant a modified constitution in 1905, were still able to hamstring their own central legislative body, and to wield a preponderant personal influence in politics.

In all three countries, none the less, for the first time in their history, modern political parties during this period coalesced around principles. As in the West, the governments collaborated with parties or coalitions of parties, but always faced an opposition. What a party stood for was determined largely by the peculiar circumstances of the country that gave it birth. Yet certain parallels reached across national boundaries. Although no group in Russia can be compared with the German Catholic Center, the Austrian Christian Socialists do resemble it in many ways. No group in either Germany or Austria is comparable with the Russian populists (Social Revolutionaries). Yet German Liberals, Austrian Liberals, and Russian Kadets or Octobrists can perhaps be roughly equated. So can the Pan-Germans with the Pan-Slavs. The Social Democrats were Marxist in all three countries, but increasingly less revolutionary in Germany and Austria-Hungary, and increasingly more so in Russia.

All three countries during this period experienced an economic boom and an occasional depression; the Industrial Revolution struck them late, but with terrific impact. By the turn of the twentieth century, Germany had made such advances that its steel production surpassed that of England, and was second in the world only to that of the United States. Though far behind Germany both in resources and in technology, Austria-Hungary too was becoming rapidly industrialized. In Russia, transport and industry boomed.

Yet in all three countries, the landed nobility continued to exercise political influence quite out of proportion to their numbers. Everywhere the existence of a new and underprivileged class of urban workers stimulated intellectual leaders to form Marxist political groups, to preach the class struggle, and, except in Russia, to strive for immediate improvements in conditions rather than for the violent overthrow of the regime. Last of all the European countries, Russia emancipated her serfs in 1861 and began a new era of agrarian experiment and unrest. In Germany, protection was the great agrarian issue after the late 1870's. In Austria-Hungary, the peasants suffered with docility.

All three countries had minority problems of varying seriousness. Germany persecuted the Poles and, after 1871 and less severely, she persecuted the Alsatians and Lorrainers. More and more, Russia persecuted the Finns, Poles, Ukrainians, and Armenians. In Austria-Hungary alone, however, the minority problem proved fatal. German anti-Slav sentiment in Austria, and Magyar mistreatment of all non-Magyars in Hungary, alienated potentially loyal subjects, and finally helped explode the state from inside. In all three countries, the Jews created a special problem and suffered different degrees of discrimination and persecution.

In Germany, a combination of circumstances led first to an assault by the government on the Catholic church, and then to an alliance between the government and the Catholic political party. In the Hapsburg monarchy, a milder anticlericalism had its day, but the Church retained its hold on the population, and continued to exercise enormous political influence. In Russia, the Orthodox church played almost no role in the cultural development of the people. But one group of influential intellectuals attacked it as the source of Russia's troubles, while another group hailed it as the true source of Russia's strength and the fountainhead of national virtue.

So it was that the main currents of the time flowed with uneven force over the Germans, Austrians, and Russians. Nationalism, materialism, militarism, imperialism, clericalism, constitutionalism, landlordism, and socialism were all experienced to a varying degree by all the countries. What determined each country's answer to social pressure, however, was its own peculiar past and its own peculiar character.

Reading Suggestions on Central and Eastern Europe

GENERAL ACCOUNTS   William L. Langer, *Political and Social Upheaval, 1832–1852* (Harper, 1969). Sensitive and brilliant synthetic treatment of a most difficult period.

R. C. Binkley, *Realism and Nationalism, 1852–1871* (Harper, 1935). Though this volume develops a somewhat implausible thesis about the possibilities of "federative polity," it provides an often illuminating discussion of the period.

C. J. H. Hayes, *A Generation of Materialism, 1871–1900* (Harper, 1941). Penetrating probing beneath the surface of an apparently successful era.

A. J. P. Taylor, *The Struggle for Mastery in Europe, 1848–1918* (Clarendon, 1954). A volume in "The Oxford History of Modern Europe"; crisp and provocative.

SPECIAL STUDIES: R. Flenley, *Modern German History* (Dutton, 1953), and K. S. Pinson, *Modern*
GERMANY   *Germany: Its History and Civilization* (Macmillan, 1954). Two textbooks, of which Pinson's is the longer and Flenley's perhaps the more useful.

A. J. P. Taylor, *The Course of German History* (Coward-McCann, 1946). A lively essay on the period since 1815, with strong anti-German overtones.

F. Meinecke, *The German Catastrophe* (Harvard Univ. Press, 1950). A useful antidote to Taylor, by a very great German historian.

T. Veblen, *Imperial Germany and the Industrial Revolution,* new ed. (Viking, 1954). An old, brilliant, and still very important analysis by a great American sociologist.

F. Darmstaedter, *Bismarck and the Creation of the Second Reich* (Methuen, 1948). A valuable study.

E. Eyck, *Bismarck and the German Empire* (Allen and Unwin, 1950). Translation and condensation of a large standard work in German.

A. J. P. Taylor, *Bismarck: The Man and the Statesman* (Knopf, 1955). A provocative and often hostile reevaluation.

H. von Treitschke, *History of Germany in the 19th Century,* 7 vols. (Humanities Press, 1915–1919), and *Origins of Prussianism,* ed. E. and C. Paul (Humanities Press, 1942). Emphasizing the period before 1870; strongly Prussian in tone.

SPECIAL STUDIES: A. J. May, *The Hapsburg Monarchy, 1867–1914* (Harvard Univ. Press, 1951). Con-
THE HAPSBURG   cise general account.
MONARCHY

A. J. P. Taylor, *The Habsburg Monarchy, 1809–1918,* 2nd ed. (Hamish Hamilton, 1948). A spirited brief treatment.

R. A. Kann, *The Multinational Empire,* 2 vols. (Columbia Univ. Press, 1950). A monograph, arranged nationality by nationality, and discussing national sentiments and the government's efforts to deal with them.

O. Jászi, *The Dissolution of the Habsburg Monarchy* (Univ. of Chicago Press, 1929). From a rare point of view, that of the liberal Magyar.

R. W. Seton-Watson, *German, Slav, and Magyar* (Williams and Norgate, 1916). By the greatest British authority on southeast Europe.

E. Wiskemann, *Czechs and Germans* (Oxford Univ. Press, 1938). A good case history of national antagonisms.

SPECIAL STUDIES: H. Seton-Watson, *The Decline of Imperial Russia, 1855–1914* (Praeger, 1952). The
RUSSIA   only sound work in English covering virtually all the period dealt with in this chapter.

G. T. Robinson, *Rural Russia under the Old Regime,* 2nd ed. (Macmillan, 1949). A splendid monograph on the peasant question.

A. Herzen, *My Past and Thoughts,* 6 vols. (Chatto and Windus, 1924–1927). The classic picture of nineteenth-century Russia, by its most distinguished rebel.

Martin Malia, *Alexander Herzen and the Birth of Russian Socialism* (*Grosset and Dunlap, Universal Library, 1965). Excellent monograph on Herzen's life and thought, considered in the framework of contemporary European ideas.

N. V. Riasanovsky, *Russia and the West in the Teaching of the Slavophiles* (Harvard Univ. Press, 1953). A useful study of one side of a major intellectual controversy.

Sidney Monas, *The Third Section: Police and Society in Russia Under Nicholas I* (Harvard Univ. Press, 1961). Pioneering study of the repressive machinery.

D. Footman, *Red Prelude* (Yale Univ. Press, 1945). A good biography of Zhelyabov, populist and terrorist.

Peter Kropotkin, *Memoirs of a Revolutionist,* ed. James A. Rogers (*Anchor, 1962). A delightful anarchist's story of his own life and times.

James Joll, *The Anarchists* (*Grosset and Dunlap, Universal Library, 1964). Excellent chapters on Bakunin and Kropotkin, and a fine study of the movement.

B. Pares, *The Fall of the Russian Monarchy* (Jonathan Cape, 1939). An excellent study of the period 1905–1917; by an authority who was frequently on the spot.

S. Witte, *Memoirs* (Doubleday, 1921). The somewhat apologetic memoirs of the man who did most to industrialize imperial Russia.

B. D. Wolfe, *Three Who Made a Revolution* (Dial Press, 1948; *Beacon). A fine triple study of Lenin, Trotsky, and Stalin; with emphasis on the period before 1914.

A. Lobanov-Rostovsky, *Russia and Asia,* rev. ed. (G. Wahr, 1951). A useful introductory survey.

B. H. Sumner, *Russia and the Balkans, 1870–1880* (Clarendon, 1937). A monograph including a helpful discussion of Panslavism.

HISTORICAL FICTION   T. Mann, *Buddenbrooks* (*Pocket Books). Novel of a family in imperial Germany.

G. Hauptmann, *The Weavers, Hannele, The Beaver Coat* (*Rinehart, 1951). Three plays that convey some of the flavor of nineteenth-century Germany.

R. Musil, *The Man without Qualities* (Coward-McCann, 1953). A novel steeped in the atmosphere of pre-1914 Vienna.

M. Jókai, *Eyes Like the Sea* (Putnam, 1901). Fictionalized autobiography of a romantic Hungarian novelist whose works give insights into Magyar nationalism.

N. Gogol, *The Inspector General* (many editions) and *Dead Souls,* trans. George Reavey (Oxford Univ. Press, 1957). Brilliant satirical play and novel.

I. Turgenev, *Fathers and Sons* (sometimes called *Fathers and Children*—many editions), and *Smoke* (Dutton, 1949; *Everyman). Superb contemporary realistic fiction reflecting Russian intellectual and political life.

F. Dostoevsky, *The Brothers Karamazov* and *Crime and Punishment* (*Modern Library). Famous novels depicting the turbulent life of Russian intellectuals in the mid-nineteenth century; more romantic in tone than Turgenev's works.

The Portable Chekhov (*Viking, 1947). A selection from the short stories and plays of A. Chekhov, a skillful portraitist of the upper classes in czarist Russia.

L. Tolstoy, *Anna Karenina* (*Modern Library). A celebrated novel set in late nineteenth-century St. Petersburg and the countryside.

23

The Intellectual Revolution of the Nineteenth Century

I An Age of Science

The nineteenth century could well be called an age of science. In the early years of the century, in the face of the Romantic revival of religion and philosophy, science lost some of the prestige and popularity it had enjoyed in the days of Newton and of the Enlightenment. But after 1840 it recovered rapidly, greatly helped by repeated demonstrations of its practical utility. The London exhibition of 1851, the Paris expositions of 1855 and 1867, and all their international successors in the last third of the century dramatized the great accomplishments of engineering. The telegraph, the submarine cable, the telephone, the great railroad bridges and tunnels, and the high-speed printing press all radically improved communications and stepped up the pace of life. University courses in science multiplied, partly eclipsing those in philosophy which had dominated the curriculum in the early 1800's.

Above: HMS "Beagle," on which Charles Darwin sailed as naturalist, off Rio de Janeiro in 1832. Above right: Dostoevsky: an oil painting of 1872. Right: "Invitation to the Sideshow," a pointillist painting by Seurat, in which tiny dots of color are applied to the canvas according to a rigidly systematic plan.

856

Most important of all, new scientific discoveries were made and fresh scientific theories advanced which not only had valuable practical applications but also deeply affected men's attitudes toward religion, politics, the arts, and other realms seemingly remote from science. The sum total of these changes constituted a new intellectual revolution, which in part confirmed, and in part challenged and modified the earlier intellectual revolution that had reached its culmination in the Enlightenment. In the seventeenth and eighteenth centuries mathematics and astronomy had been in the vanguard of progress. While they continued to advance in the nineteenth century, leadership passed to physics, chemistry, and, above all, biology, where Darwin's hypothesis about the evolution of species through natural selection sent a shock wave through the intellectual and ecclesiastical worlds.

The Conservation and Dissipation of Energy

Before turning to Darwinism, we may note other hypotheses which had significant implications for men's understanding of the universe. These were the laws of thermodynamics and the contrasting hypotheses of a universe of continuity, based on waves, and a universe of atomicity, subdivided into an infinitesimal quantity of particles. The study of thermodynamics was fostered by the steam engine, which used heat to create power and led physicists to the idea of the conservation of energy. According to this first law of thermodynamics, energy was in a sense immortal, transforming itself from heat into power and then back again into heat. Scientists from France, Britain, Germany, and Denmark all contributed to the formulation of the law in the mid-nineteenth century—one of many instances of fruitful international scientific collaboration. But it was also characteristic of nineteenth-century science that learned societies and their journals were slow to accept the new law and sponsor its publication.

Another law of thermodynamics, also the work of experts from many nations, soon modified the first. This was the law of the dissipation or degradation of energy: it stated that, though the total amount of energy in the universe remains constant, the amount of energy useful to human beings is being steadily dissipated. While scientists could contemplate with equanimity the possibility that the sun would gradually lose its heat and the earth would get colder and colder, many laymen could not. The pessimistic American intellectual Henry Adams (1838–1918), for instance, was obsessed with the likelihood that the universe was in the process of running down toward a kind of scientific final cataclysm or Day of Judgment.

Continuity and Atomicity

Meantime, a very different view of the universe was emerging from studies of electricity and magnetism made by the Dane Oersted, the Frenchman Ampère, the German Ohm, and the Britishers Faraday and Clerk-Maxwell. They noted so many similarities between the two sets of phenomena that they fused them into the single category of electromagnetism, which appeared to function in the manner of continuous waves. The idea of waves was also being applied to light. Since light waves must move through some medium, and not just empty space, it was supposed that space was filled with a conductor, a substance called the ether. Although the ether hypothesis created many difficulties, the wave theory of light convinced many physicists that they should abandon the Newtonian concept of light as made up of minute particles. To them mankind lived in a world of waves and therefore of continuity.

Yet to other physicists and also to chemists, biologists, and physicians, mankind continued to live in a world of particles, a world therefore of atomicity. Atoms of one chemical element combined with those of another to form molecules of some familiar substance, as in the case of hydrogen, oxygen, and water. But the process of combination raised some important questions. For example, the volume of hydrogen in water was twice that of oxygen, as indicated by the familiar formula H_2O; but experiments showed that the weight of the oxygen was eight times that of the hydrogen. It seemed evident, therefore, that an atom of oxygen must weigh sixteen times more than an atom of hydrogen. To establish a standard table of atomic weights an international congress of experts met in 1860 at Karlsruhe in Germany and devised a table based on the calculations of two Italians, Avogadro and Cannizzaro.

The biological counterpart of the atomic theory was the cell theory, the idea that all plant and animal structures were composed of living units known as cells. The medical counterpart was the theory of germs (today further refined into bacilli, viruses, and the like), a great advance over the older belief that disease was in effect a phenomenon of spontaneous corruption, as evidenced by the term "consumption" for tuberculosis. The German microbiologist Koch discovered the organisms causing tuberculosis and cholera; the American doctor Walter Reed found that the virus responsible for yellow fever was transmitted by a mosquito, with the result that careful mosquito control greatly reduced the incidence of disease among the force build-ing the Panama Canal. In Britain, the Quaker physician Lister studied the suppuration of wounds, demonstrated that germs caused the infections, and greatly reduced the mortality rate of surgical and battlefield patients by the application of rigorous antiseptic measures. In France, the chemist Pasteur became a veritable culture hero of science by developing a vaccine for inoculating victims of rabies, which was otherwise invariably fatal, and by devising the famous process of sterilizing milk. These great advances and dozens of others almost equally great brought Western medicine, surgery, and public health to the "take-off point" for impressive growth by 1900. In the twentieth century the average life expectancy in North American and many European countries was to increase by twenty to thirty years.

II Darwinism

"The Origin of Species"

In 1859 there was published in London a volume on natural history that began with the true scientist's caution:

When on board H.M.S. "Beagle," as naturalist, I was much struck with certain facts in the distribution of the organic beings inhabiting South America, and in the geological relations of the present to the past inhabitants of that continent. These facts . . . seemed to throw some light on the origin of species—that mystery of mysteries, as it has been called by one of our greatest philosophers. On my return home, it occurred to me, in 1837, that something might perhaps be made out on this question by patiently accumulating and reflecting on all sorts of facts which could possibly have any bearing on it. After five years' work I allowed myself to speculate on the subject, and drew up some short notes; these I enlarged in 1844 into a sketch of the conclusions, which then seemed to me probable: from that period to the present day I have steadily pursued the same object. I hope that I may be excused for entering on these personal details, as I give them to show that I have not been hasty in coming to a decision.*

* Charles Darwin, *The Origin of Species,* Introduction.

Darwin's *On the Origin of Species by Means of Natural Selection,* thus modestly introduced to the public, is one of the seminal books in intellectual history. Like all important revolutions, the Darwinian was no bolt from the blue. Into Darwin's work had gone long years of preparation, not merely his own extended field work in the 1830's as the *Beagle* made a leisurely voyage around South America, but those of his predecessors and colleagues in the study of what was then called natural history. Before him was the long record of the hundreds of thousands of years of organic life on earth. Already well established by geologists like Sir Charles Lyell and by paleontologists, this record told of the rise, the development, and sometimes the disappearance of thousands of different forms of plant and animal organisms, or *species*. The record contradicted an important part of the commonly accepted theory about the past of organic life. The Bible in the Book of Genesis described all forms of life as begun in the space of a single week by a Creator about 6,000 years ago. And it stated explicitly that all existing men and animals were descended from single pairs of each species preserved in Noah's ark during a great universal flood that took place some time thereafter.

Now Darwin was by no means the first to find a discrepancy between the historical and scientific record and the accepted biblical explanation. The men of the Enlightenment had already given up the biblical explanation as inadequate. Some of them had gone so far as to conceive of a very long evolutionary process in which no personal, Christian God had a hand, but only the impersonal forces of Nature or the deist's "watchmaker God." But they had arrived at no satisfactory explanation of how Nature or the watchmaker God had done the job; they had no satisfactory theory of how organisms had evolved. This Darwin gave the world.

Darwin found one clue in Malthus' *Essay on Population,* which maintained that organisms—including man—tended to multiply to a point where there simply was not food enough for them all. In the intense competition for food, some of these organisms did not get enough, and died. This was the germ of the conception Darwin phrased as the *struggle for existence.* He next asked himself what determined that certain individuals would survive and that others would die. Obviously the surviving ones got more food, better shelter, better living conditions of all sorts. If they were all identical organisms, the only explanation—apart from the intervention of a supernatural being or force—would have to be accidental variations in their environment. But it was clear from observation that individual organisms of a given species are not identical. Variations appear even at birth. Thus in a single litter of pigs there may be sturdy, aggressive piglets and a runt. The runt, even if a sentimental farmer tries to protect it, is likely to get shoved aside in suckling by his sturdier brothers, and starve. In the wild state, in free competition, the runt is almost certain to perish. In the struggle for existence, the runt is proved "unfit."

Here is the second of Darwin's key phrases, the *survival of the fittest.* The organism best endowed in its variations to get food and shelter lives to procreate young that will tend to inherit these favorable variations. The variations are slight indeed, but over generation after generation they are cumulative; finally an organism so different from the long-distant ancestor is produced that we can speak of a new species. This new species has *evolved.* It has evolved by the working of *natural selection.* Man as a plant and animal breeder has long made use of this process and has hastened and indeed guided it for his own purposes by *artificial selection,* by breeding only the best strains—"best," of course, from a human point of view. But man has been doing this with domesticated plants and animals for but a tiny period of geological time, and with but few species. Over the eons, natural selection has been the working force; and for man himself, according to the Darwinian system, natural selection alone has been at work, since man has yet to breed his own kind as he breeds his domestic plants and animals.

Darwin held that the variations in individuals of the same species at birth are accidental, and that they are generally transmitted through inheritance. Those biologists who developed his doctrine, notably the German Weismann, did not—and this is a very important point—believe that the evidence showed that variations produced in an individual organism in the course of its life could be transmitted to its offspring. Thus, orthodox Darwinism denies the inheritance of *acquired characteristics.* Obviously, a man with an amputated leg will not produce one-legged children. Experimenters have docked the tails of generations of laboratory rats, but their offspring are still born with long tails. The actual mechanism of heredity we know much better than Darwin did, thanks to the Austrian monk Gregor Mendel (1822–1884), whose experiments with crossbreeding garden peas laid the basis of modern genetics.

Darwin's theory has undergone later modification as scientists have found that variations of importance in the evolutionary process are probably not so much the numerous tiny ones Darwin emphasized, but rather bigger and much rarer ones now known as *mutations.* Scientists have begun to study the effect of various forms of radiation on such mutations. A still muchdisputed geological theory holds that catastrophic movements of the earth's crust in the past have so radically altered environment as to wipe out whole species and speed up the evolution of others. Emphasis on mutations or on extensive crustal movements tends also to be emphasis on the sudden and violent rather than on the gradual—an attitude perhaps typical of our own time, but decidedly out of tune with the nineteenth century.

"The Warfare of Science with Theology"

The first edition of *The Origin of Species* was sold out the day of its publication. What Darwin himself considered a book of interest only to students of natural history became a bestseller, reviewed in newspapers and magazines all over the world. The major reason for this attention was almost certainly the challenge that orthodox Christians found in the book. Darwinism was a phase of what President Andrew D. White of Cornell University called "the warfare of science with theology." Yet Darwin's book was no new denial of the fundamentalists' belief in the accuracy of the account of Creation in the Book of Genesis. Natural scientists had for over a century been publishing work that flatly denied the possibility that the earth could be only 6,000 years old. The doctrine of God's special creation of each species had also been challenged before Darwin.

Darwin got attention because he seemed to provide for the secularist a process (evolution) and a causal agent (natural selection) where before there had been only vague "materialistic" notions. He also seemed to have struck a final blow against the argument, still very popular in Victorian times, that the organic world was full of incontrovertible evidence of God the great designer. The human eye, for instance, the theologians said, was inconceivable except as the design of a God; and now Darwin said it is the result of millions of years of natural selection working on certain nerve ends "accidentally" more sensitive to light than others. Finally, Darwin gained notoriety because of the frequent, though unfair, accusation that he made the monkey man's brother. Later, in *The Descent of Man* (1871), Darwin carefully pointed out that *Homo sapiens* is descended not from any existing ape or monkey, but from a very remote common primate ancestor.

The Origin of Species stirred up a most heated theological controversy. Fundamentalists, both Protestant and Catholic, simply stuck by Genesis and damned Darwin and all his work. But the Catholic church and many Protestant bodies eventually took at least a neutral attitude toward Darwinism, which they viewed as a scientific biological hypothesis neither necessarily correct nor necessarily incorrect. The great majority of Christians tacitly or openly accepted sufficient modification of Genesis to accommodate themselves to the scientist's time scale, and adjusted the classic theological arguments from first cause, design, and the like to a God who worked his will in accordance with organic evolution. Moreover, it was quite clear to reflective men that

nothing Darwin or any other scientist or scholar could produce would give ultimate answers to the kind of problem set by the existence of God. It was quite clear to them that since God's eye is now on the sparrow, it must once have been on the dinosaur. Christians can be Darwinians: millions of them are. But Darwinism, if taken over completely into a philosophy of life, denies any supernatural intervention in the planning and running of the universe.

Social Darwinism

This theological conflict had pretty well run its course by the beginning of the twentieth century. More important in the long run was the use men made of some of Darwin's basic concepts—or at least of his more smoothly coined phrases—in debates on matters moral, economic, and political. The blanket term "Social Darwinism," which covers all these transfers of ideas from biology to the social sciences and human relations takes in a very wide range of persons and ideas. Darwin himself was a biologist, not a "Social Darwinist." He did not write as a social scientist. It must be noted, however, that in a free and literate society, ideas produced by scientists invariably spread to many people not trained in science, and that such ideas are modified in the process of spreading.

The central idea that social and political thinkers took over from Darwin was that of competition among individuals and groups of individuals. This was of course a conception already central in their thinking, but Darwin buttressed it with the prestige of the natural sciences. The majority of these late nineteenth-century thinkers interpreted the human struggle as a struggle for the means of livelihood. There is, they were sure, among men a human "struggle for life." The variations that counted here were the variations that brought success in economic competition—the variations that produced inventors, business organizers, even perhaps political, artistic, and professional leaders. Darwin's work in natural history came to confirm the economist's doctrine of laissez-faire and the nineteenth-century liberal's doctrine of individual freedom for a man to do what his capacities permitted.

Here was scientific confirmation of the middle-class conviction that the universe was designed to reward hard work, thrift, intelligence, and self-help and to punish laziness, waste, stupidity, and reliance on charity. Above all, Darwin seemed to confirm the notion that the poor were poor because they were unfit, badly designed for living, and the complementary notion that attempts by private charity or by state action to take from the well-to-do and give to the poor were useless and quite contrary to nature, shocking efforts to reverse the course of evolution. If a man cannot earn enough to feed himself, it was argued, he had better die; lowlier organisms too incompetent to feed themselves certainly die off, to the greater good of the species. Herbert Spencer (1820–1903), an ardent British evolutionist, summed it up neatly:

Of man, as of all inferior creatures, the law by conformity to which the species is preserved, is that among adults the individuals best adapted to the conditions of their existence shall prosper most, and the individuals least adapted to the conditions of their existence shall prosper least. . . . Pervading all Nature we may see at work a stern discipline which is often a little cruel that it may be very kind. . . . The ultimate result of shielding men from folly is to fill the world with fools.*

Spencer himself, if it came to that, could not have stood by while the unemployed and their families starved to death, for he was a kindly man. Yet he had an almost maniacal hatred of the state, of local government as well as national; he held out even against laws requiring houseowners to connect their houses with sewers in cities. Even Spencer could not transfer to the struggle for existence among human beings the ruthless freedom of the jungle, of what Tennyson called "Nature red in tooth and claw." He was against all forms of government provision for what we now call social security. But what government may not do he believed the ethically sound individual will do as charity. The well-to-do will take care of the poor voluntarily—not enough to spoil them, not enough to frustrate the designs of evolution by letting them prosper and propagate their kind, but enough to prevent their starving or freezing to death.

In his *Principles of Ethics,* Spencer discovered that the softer emotions promoted by Christianity

* Herbert Spencer, *Principles of Ethics* (London, 1879–1893), section 257; *Social Statics* (London, 1851), p. 149; *Autobiography* (London, 1904), II, 5.

and the other higher religions—kindness, dislike of cruelty, love—were also in accord with the intentions of the laws of the universe as summed up in evolution. Mutual extermination might be the law for tigers, but not for human beings. Indeed, Spencer and many other Social Darwinists held that the altruistic moral sentiments that impel us toward charity are the highest achievement of the evolutionary process, and that a society with many altruists is thereby shown to be the fittest for survival.

Eugenics

The Social Darwinists were, then, faced with this primary difficulty. Darwin seemed to have shown that the unmitigated struggle for life within a given species, and among rival species, was the law of the universe; but human history, and human feelings, showed that men could not in practice look on with indifference while their fellow men starved to death. One way out of the dilemma was that recommended by Spencer, a sort of humanized and mitigated struggle in which the incompetent were shelved but not destroyed. Many who held this view accompanied it with a faith in what came to be called eugenics.

Eugenicists sought to encourage child-bearing by the fit and to discourage it by the unfit. Darwin had begun his *Origin of Species* with a consideration of the extraordinary success men had had with artificial selection in the breeding of plants and animals. Why not do the same thing with human beings? Since, according to strict Darwinian theory, acquired characteristics were not transmitted by heredity, no amount of manipulation of the social environment, no amount of wise planning of institutions, would alter human beings. Therefore, the only way to secure permanent improvement of the race was by deliberate mating of the fit with the fit.

The eugenicists, however, ran at once against the fact that man, though he domesticates plants and animals, is still himself in this respect a "wild" animal. The individual human being in choosing a mate is no doubt influenced by a great variety of motives, but no master human breeder decides who shall mate with whom. So far, the eugenicists have had little success with the positive side of their program. On the negative side, they have urged that the obviously unfit, the idiots, the feeble-minded, the insane, be prevented, even if necessary by compulsory sterilization, from having children. Only a tiny handful of human beings, not enough to affect in the slightest the general course of human physical evolution, have undergone this treatment.

Racism

By far the commonest way out of the dilemma facing the Social Darwinists lay in the obvious notion that it is not so much among individual human beings that the struggle for existence really goes on, as it is among human beings organized in groups, as tribes, "races," or national states. The struggle that counts is not the struggle, say, among individual Englishmen to survive, but the struggle between Great Britain and its rivals. The struggle for existence among men is now lifted from the biology of the individual to the politics of the group. And for the nineteenth century the group had to be the nation-state, perhaps kindred nation-states that could be organized for the struggle as one bloc of states, such as the "Nordic" or the "Latin," or perhaps at the very widest the Caucasian or white peoples in competition with the colored peoples, yellow, brown, or black. This struggle had an ultimate form: war. The group that defeated another group in war had thereby shown itself to be fitter than the beaten group. It had a right—indeed, in evolutionary terms, which usually have moral overtones, a duty—to eliminate the beaten group, seize its lands, and people them with its own fitter human beings. The English imperialist Cecil Rhodes held that a world wholly and exclusively peopled with Anglo-Saxons would be the best possible world.

The idea of a Chosen People was not new in Darwin's time. But there is no doubt that Darwin's work, however little he may have meant it to be, became a most important element in the competition among organized states in the latter half of the nineteenth century, and right on to our own day. While Darwinism came too late to do more than prop up the philosophy of laissez-faire in economics it came at just the right time to intensify the international political struggle.

The particular groups or states that were to benefit as the elect of evolution in this special political sense varied with the aims, sympathies, and actual citizenship of the individual who was seeking to promote an ultimate evolutionary victory. Britain, Germany, the United States, the Latins, the Slavs, all were defended as the true elect of evolution. Most of the writers who preached this kind of political evolution proceeded from the assumption that at bottom the men of a given group had certain physical and therefore intellectual and spiritual traits in common, traits that gave them their superiority, and that could not possibly be transmitted to men of another group. Most of these writers, in short, were racists who believed that *Homo sapiens* had already evolved into what were really separate species. A black skin, for instance, was for them a sign of innate inferiority, and the blacks would simply have to go the way of the dinosaurs, into extinction. Evolution had spoken. Few of these writers quite dared to preach what has in our own day been christened genocide, the wholesale murder of those held to be of inferior race. Most of them were willing to see the inferiors duly subjected to the superiors, to have the less fit peoples serve as hewers of wood and drawers of water for their masters.

Some Social Darwinists applied their theories to a new form of caste organization, which came to be known as elitism. The fit were not limited to any one race, but they were still marked out by the rigid hand of biological inheritance. They were the master group, the elite, the "supermen"; and they should everywhere band together against the dull average men, and dutifully exploit them. The German Friedrich Nietzsche (1844–1900), who gave currency to the term "superman," was a subtle and difficult thinker, one who disliked Darwin as a grubbing Englishman and who was certaintly no racist, no Social Darwinian. Still Nietzsche's influence among the half-educated who admired him in the late nineteenth and early twentieth centuries was to further racist and elitist causes.

Theories of the evolution-guided superiority of certain groups were not limited to Europe. In the United States, the innate, unchangeable superiority of whites to blacks was an article of faith among many whites in the North and almost universally in the South. This faith was greatly bolstered by Darwinian anthropologists and biologists. The notion that the degree of blondness and other readily visible traits, such as longheadedness and tallness, measured suitableness for citizenship in a great democracy helped dictate the American immigration act of 1924, which encouraged immigrants from northwestern Europe and almost barred those from southern and eastern Europe. The American Madison Grant, in his *The Passing of the Great Race,* published in 1916, asserted that the Nordics were "a race of soldiers, sailors, adventurers and explorers, but above all, of rulers, organizers and aristocrats." Grant continued confidently and picturesquely:

Before leaving this interesting subject of the correlation of spiritual and moral traits with physical characters we may note that these influences are so deeply rooted in everyday consciousness that the modern novelist or playwright does not fail to make his hero a tall, blond, honest and somewhat stupid youth and his villain a small, dark and exceptionally intelligent individual of warped moral character.*

The title of Madison Grant's book betrays an anxiety that is never far from the surface even in the most confident of these Social Darwinists. Grant feared that his "great race," gifted summit of evolution though it was, was not going to survive. The lower races were breeding faster; democratic equalitarianism was lopping off the best and encouraging the worst. Somehow evolution was going wrong, producing degeneration, not progress. Like those other "scientific" determinists, the Marxists, the Social Darwinists believed that men of good will had to set to work with pen and tongue to help along the predetermined process and keep it on the right track.

A New Historical Determinism

Darwinian science no more than Newtonian science answered the great questions about good and evil, about the ends of human life, that men have been asking and trying to answer ever since we have had historical records. Darwinian science, and the physics, chemistry, and other sciences that flourished in the nineteenth century, recast for many the whole frame of reference in which these questions were asked. Traditional Christianity, as well as other transcen-

* Madison Grant, *The Passing of the Great Race,* 4th rev. ed. (New York, 1921), p. 229.

dental and supernatural faiths, survived Darwin as they had survived Newton. Many men continued to believe in a God or powers not bound by the laws men discovered in laboratory experiments, and, further, to believe that that God guided their steps and gave meaning to their lives in this world and in the other world after death. But with the spread of popular education, especially in the West, great numbers came to believe that no such God or powers existed, that the material universe of science and common sense went on its regular ways in accordance with laws which men might eventually understand completely, and which they were already beginning to understand quite well.

Darwin's work and that of many other scientists, in combination with the work of historians and philosophers and men of letters, worked a major change in the way men looked at their universe. It is a permissible oversimplification to say that the Newtonian universe was static, the Darwinian dynamic. The Enlightenment was certainly feeling its way toward a view of the universe as developing, progressing, evolving; but, as one can see from the work of a philosophe like Voltaire, the eighteenth century had no good explanation of the way change came about. This explanation Darwin provided for natural history, and the Romantic historians and their fellow workers in other fields provided it for human history.

Today many still believe in what has been labeled historicism—that is, in the doctrine that the course of history in the widest sense shows a regular, if bewildering, unfolding that has "determined" everything now existing and that will determine everything in the future. The wildest believer in this doctrine has had to admit that since he cannot in fact know the whole process in the past, he cannot wholly understand the present or predict the future. Nevertheless, the clue for him has lain in the past, out of which the present has developed.

The Christian and Hebraic calendar made the earth 6,000 years old, but the Darwinian calendar envisaged millions of years for organic life alone. It might seem, therefore, that historicism, especially when reinforced by the emphasis Darwin put on the immense reaches of time, would confirm conservative opposition to rapid change, or at least encourage in men a certain resignation in the face of the slow-moving process of evolution on this earth. And so it did

The Nineteenth Century Grows Into the Twentieth

The rebellion against academic painting, begun in the Romantic generation by Delacroix, continued in the mid-nineteenth century with the Frenchmen Daumier and Courbet. Courbet upset the academic painters by taking commonplace subjects and portraying them as they were, with no attempt to prettify them. Edouard Manet used real objects and events for his own artistic purposes, as occasions for effects of color and composition that he felt to be truer and more real than what the camera records.

The nature of light and color was of special interest to the Impressionists, who painted landscapes and seascapes for the most part, using thousands of little dabs of pure color for their trees, flowers, buildings, rocks, skies, and water. The result, when viewed from a proper distance, is magically transformed into a recognizable scene flooded with light. Claude Monet experimented with the depiction of light and mist by painting the same subject again and again—the cathedral at Rouen, the lily pond in his own garden—to show how greatly its appearance varied under changing conditions of light.

Two other qualities augmented the revolutionary impact of Impressionist painting. One was the abandonment of traditional conventions of symmetry in favor of an arrangement which put the principal figure well to one side, sometimes even partially cut off. The other was the concentration on subjects evoking everyday life rather than the artificial world of the studio. Milliners, prostitutes, cardplayers or solitary drinkers in a cafe, cabaret and circus performers populate the canvases of Degas, Toulouse-Lautrec, Renoir, Van Gogh, and Cézanne.

Most of these men are cataloged by historians of art as post-Impressionists, because they were going on from impressionism to further experiments. Cézanne, in particular, thought that impressionism was too obsessed with light at the expense of the geometrical and architectural qualities also to be found in the world of nature. He proposed to restore these qualities, not with the classic, flowing perspective inherited by the academics from the Italians, but with blocks or chunks of color. Much of twentieth-century painting stems from Cézanne. Cubism, which is the exaggeration of his insistence on three-dimensionality, is most in his debt, but so too are abstractionism and even surrealism.

Water-Lilies, by Claude Monet.
Formerly in The Museum of Modern Art, New York. Robert S. Crandall from The Granger Collection.

Woman with a Parrot, by Gustave Courbet.

The Metropolitan Museum of Art, bequest of Mrs. H. O. Havemeyer, 1929. The H. O. Havemeyer Collection.

Torero Saluting, by Edouard Manet.

The Metropolitan Museum of Art, bequest of Mrs. H. O. Havemeyer, 1929. The H. O. Havemeyer Collection.

Rouen Cathedral, by Claude Monet.

The Metropolitan Museum of Art, the Theodore M. Davis Collection, bequest of Theodore M. Davis, 1915.

In the Meadow, by Pierre Auguste Renoir.

The Metropolitan Museum of Art, bequest of Samuel A. Lewisohn, 1951.

The Gulf of Marseilles Seen from L'Estaque, by Paul Cézanne.

The Metropolitan Museum of Art, bequest of Mrs. H. O. Havemeyer, 1929. The H. O. Have-meyer Collection.

An Afternoon at La Grande Jatte, by Georges Seurat.

Sunflowers, by Vincent van Gogh.

The Metropolitan Museum of Art, Rogers Fund, 1949.

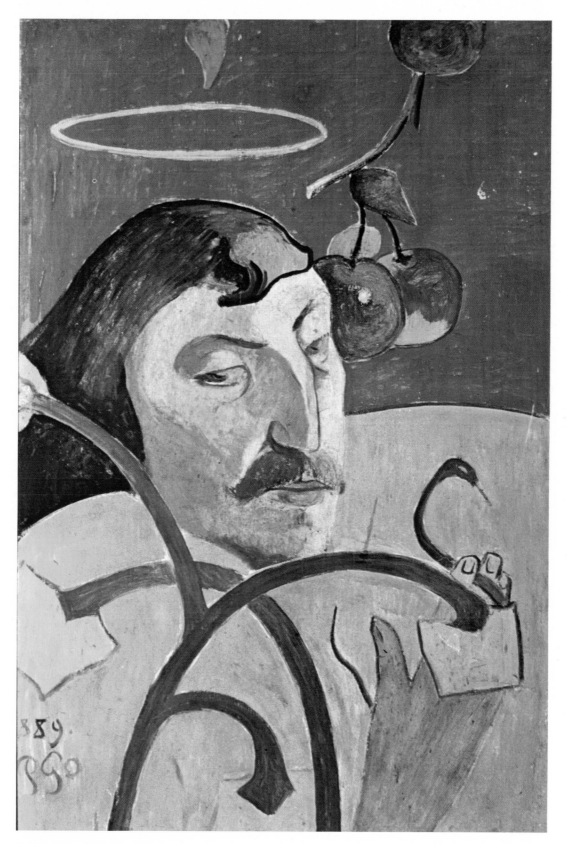

Self-Portrait, by Paul Gauguin.

The Granger Collection.

The Repast of the Lion, by Henri Rousseau.

The Metropolitan Museum of Art, bequest of Samuel A. Lewisohn, 1951.

Jane Avril, by Henri de Toulouse-Lautrec.

Lithograph, 1899. 22 x 14 inches. Collection The Museum of Modern Art, New York, gift of Abby Aldrich Rockefeller.

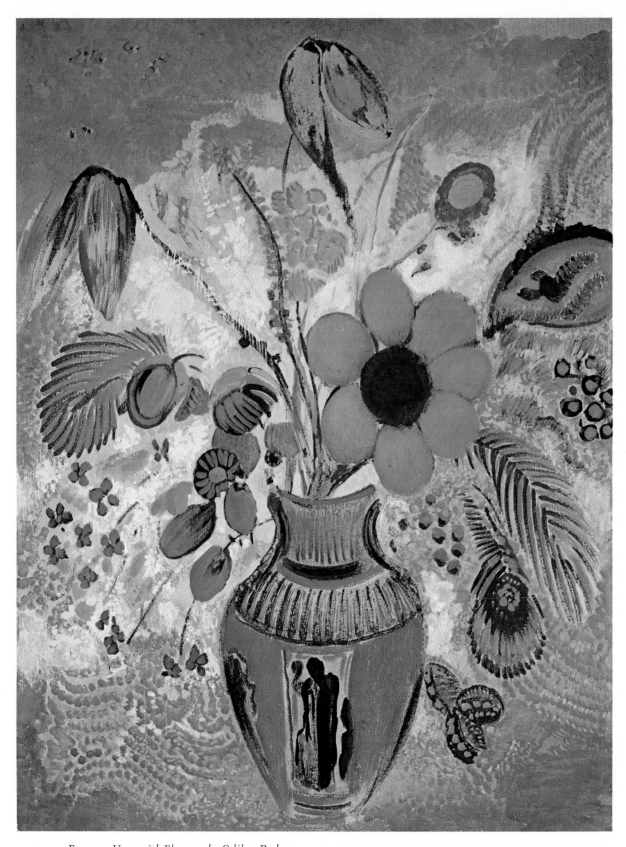

Etruscan Vase with Flowers, by Odilon Redon.

The Metropolitan Museum of Art, Maria DeWitt Jesup Fund, 1951; from The Museum of
Modern Art, Lizzie P. Bliss Collection.

L'Enfant Madeline, by Maurice de Vlaminck.

Robert S. Crandall from The Granger Collection.

The Voice, by Edvard Munch.

Museum of Fine Arts, Boston. Robert S. Crandall from The Granger Collection.

Blind Man's Meal, by Pablo Picasso.

Robert S. Crandall from The Granger Collection.

Yvonne Printemps and Sacha Guitry, by Jean Edouard Vuillard.

Robert S. Crandall from The Granger Collection.

for some men. Darwin's grandson, Sir Charles Galton Darwin, published in 1953 a book entitled *The Next Million Years*. He concluded that, since it is now held that it takes about a million years for a new species to evolve, it will be a million years before evolution produces a creature any better adapted than man; and that therefore for the next million years we shall have a history much like that of the last few thousand.

But historicism in the nineteenth and twentieth centuries has had for most others a quite different consequence. It has served to convince impatient and hopeful men that they have really mastered the secrets of the universe, that they have understood as their misguided predecessors

did not understand just where the forces of history are leading. They could, then, help the process instead of hindering it, perhaps even hasten it. Marxism is the classic example of this faith in historical determinism, but nationalism, racism, and a host of others all have drawn nourishment from it. The extraordinary speeding-up of technological improvements lent strength to this view that moral and political improvement could also be speeded up. The doctrine of evolution, then, though logically one can argue that it should have lessened the force of utopian faiths, did in fact increase it. People thought of the sureness of evolution and forgot its slowness.

III   Literature

The Victorian Age

In literature the later nineteenth century may well be called the Victorian Age. Because the label is applied here not only to Britain but also to the United States and to Germany, France, and other continental nations, we cannot expect the age to have the unified style to be found in Periclean Athens, for example, or Renaissance Italy or Elizabethan England. We can evoke a Victorian drawing room, where Maud or Mélanie in ringlets and crinolines, surrounded by whatnots, bric-a-brac, plush hangings, and Landseer engravings, reads Tennyson, Longfellow, or Heine, or plays Liszt on the pianoforte. But so much went on outside that drawing room!—not only in the lives of peasants, workers, country gentlemen, and businessmen, but even in art and letters. Maud or Mélanie might have been reading Dickens or Balzac, but these writers hardly fitted the drawing room. Nor would Thoreau and Melville, Zola and Dostoevsky. It is quite certain that the girls would not have been reading Marx.

The arts and letters of the second half of the nineteenth century were eclectic. In addition, much of the best work was now, more clearly than ever before in Western history, produced and cultivated by men and women in conscious revolt against the tastes of the politically and economically dominant class of their time—that is,

the middle class. Unless Maud and Mélanie were very advanced young women, they did not like much of what a hundred years later we single out as important in Victorian art and literature. If they were the usual middle-class young women, they read sentimental novels now forgotten save by the social historian, and they lived in a culture to which the derogatory overtones of the word "Victorian" may still be applied.

Their fathers and brothers were often so concerned with industry and trade that they had no time for literature and the arts, which they tended to leave to their womenfolk. Or if they did have wider concerns, these were with political and social problems, with the material betterment of their own class, and of the working class, too. But these middle-class men felt that the most that could be done for the workers was to raise their standard of living slowly under existing laissez-faire capitalism. They held that church and state should join to restrain by law and by religion of an essentially puritanical cast the lack of self-restraint these middle-class men found among their "inferiors." With these Victorians, laissez-faire liberalism was a strictly economic matter; in morals they believed firmly that organized institutions should interfere to restrain the populace from the drunkenness, idleness, and loose living they were supposedly inclined to. Libertarians in economics, the educated, middle-class Victorians were most certainly authoritarians in morals.

Realism and Naturalism in the Novel

In literature, the later nineteenth century was a great period for fiction, for the novel of realism in contrast with the romanticism of the earlier part of the century. Yet the Realists were children of the Romanticists. The Romantic of 1830, fleeing this ugly world for an idealized Middle Ages, when knighthood was in flower and there were no sooty factories, or writing of the idyllic Indian tribes of America, can look very different

Charles Dickens in 1855.

from the Realist of 1860, analyzing with fascination and disgust the men and women of the mill towns, the slums of the great cities, the unidyllic countryside of peasant labor. Yet both Romantic and Realist are individualists, and both are revolting against middle-class respectability. Both deny the older classical ideals of aristocratic measure, of a natural law of decency and decorum. Both are obsessed with the analysis of the individual human soul.

The Englishman Dickens (1812–1870), the Frenchman Balzac (1799–1850), and the Russian Dostoevsky (1821–1881) all have qualities that we label Romantic. They reveled in exaggerations, poured themselves out in undisciplined torrents of words, achieved an effect of unreal intensity. Yet they were thoroughly immersed in the world of their time, and were in many ways realists. Dostoevsky wrote about the Russia and the Russians he knew; but his was a dark Russia, and his Russians were tortured, possessed, unhappy seekers, no children of the Age of Reason. On the other hand, the leading French realist of the later nineteenth century, Flaubert (1821–1880), wrote one of his novels, *Salammbô,* about an ancient and, in spite of his great efforts at historical accuracy, not very real Carthage. And in his masterpiece, *Madame Bovary,* which analyzes the romantic longings of a small-town doctor's wife, Flaubert betrayed a most ambivalent feeling toward his heroine. He hated the bourgeois world he wrote about quite as much as the escapist writers of an earlier generation had hated theirs.

Some modern critics call these middle and late nineteenth-century writers "romantic realists," who eschewed the remote, the Gothic, the fantastic, and chose as a rule subjects close to their own time and place. But there were also more conventional—or at least more subdued—realists. Representative of these last were the Englishman Trollope, the Russian Turgenev, and the American Howells. Trollope (1815–1882) wrote dozens of novels about Victorian clergymen and politicians and country gentlemen, carefully observing the English decencies, never raising his voice or his style, but imparting understanding, sympathy, and a suitable, modest irony, not to mention specific information about the annual income that enabled his characters to live as they did, waited upon by many servants. Turgenev (1818–1883), who wrote about his fellows with classic restraint, skirting delicately the depths of the Slavic soul, also had a taste for irony. In *Fathers and Sons* he sketched a portrait of the nihilist Bazarov's old-fashioned mother—pious, superstitious, emotional, utterly devoted to her doctor husband and to her son—and then remarked: "Such women are not common nowadays. God knows whether we ought to rejoice!" William Dean Howells (1837–1920), editor of the *Atlantic Monthly* at the peak of its prestige, sought to apply realism to the American scene, notably in *The Rise of Silas Lapham,* chronicling the newly rich and socially ambitious in Boston's Back Bay. Howells was so restrained that today he is often pigeonholed as a follower of the "genteel tradition."

As the twentieth century drew near, the realists were confronted with a rebel generation that found them not "realistic" enough. This school rose first in France, where it took for itself the name naturalism, often defined as "realism with an ideology." The leader of the naturalists, Emile Zola (1840–1902), shows clearly the influence of the scientific revolution inspired by the work of Darwin. Zola was not content with the realist's aim to reflect the life around him with simple accuracy; he sought to arrive at laws of human development, much as the biologist seeks for laws of organic development. He would show what men are like, but he would also show how they came to be what they are, and even what they were going to be. He called his twenty volumes about a family under the Second Empire the "natural history" of a family. Each novel focused on some problem—*La Terre* (*The Earth*) about the land and the peasantry; *L'Assommoir* (*The Killer*) about alcoholism; and *Germinal* (named for the month of sprouting in the revolutionary calendar) about strikes in a coal mine and radical agitators.

The Literature of Pessimism and Protest

Zola's work points up one of the tendencies not only of the novel, in those days the spearhead of literature, but of other forms of writing in the late Victorian age as well. Literature was becoming what it was to be in the twentieth century, overwhelmingly a literature of discontent and protest. From the days of the ancient Greek philosophers and Hebrew prophets, many great thinkers have held that their own times were peculiarly out of joint. Yet there have been periods when intellectuals have been relatively well disposed to the existing government and society —the Augustan Age in Rome, the Elizabethan in England, the great century of Louis XIV. And there have also been periods when intellectuals, though bitterly opposed to the existing regime, have written with hope and confidence of what was to come—as in the Enlightenment. The succeeding Romantic generations exhibited a pessimistic strain, which deepened in the later nineteenth century and has continued ever since.

The pessimists reacted against the eighteenth-century doctrine of the natural goodness of man. Certainly "nature" and "natural" as they figure in the work of a Zola carry very different connotations from those they had had in the eighteenth century. By the close of the Victorian age nature apparently made most men greedy, selfish, combative, not very bright, and addicted to sexual irregularities which brought out to the full their other bad traits. Some writers, like the English novelist Thomas Hardy (1840–1928), built up this pessimism from a series of incidents in private lives into a grand cosmic irony not without its consoling side. But for the most part, these writers were concerned directly with the cruelties, stupidities, and aberrations of real people.

In France, Maupassant (1850–1893), a master of the short story, wrote sparely and simply, after the manner of his master Flaubert, about the tragedies and comedies of ordinary life; but the tragedies, or at least the ironies, prevail. In Russia, Chekhov (1860–1904), a medical man by training, used the prose drama and the short story to show how life harasses us all. Ibsen (1828–1906) in Norway, Brieux (1858–1932) in France, and George Bernard Shaw (1856–1950) in England all helped to develop the characteristically late-nineteenth-century form of the drama, the "problem play." The problem was sometimes one of wide moral and political concern, as in Ibsen's *Enemy of the People* or Shaw's *Man and Superman,* but it was very often concerned mainly with the stupid tangles of men's private lives. Ibsen shocked his contemporaries in *A Doll's House* by having his play begin at the point where the usual nineteenth-century drama ended and by permitting his heroine to rebel against the doll-house atmosphere her husband had created for her. Ibsen's *Ghosts* and Brieux's

Damaged Goods scandalized the public by bringing to the stage the problem of venereal disease.

The problem play, the problem novel, the problem short story spread throughout Western literature. In the United States, by the end of the nineteenth century the "genteel tradition" was already scorned by the bright young men, and the novelists Stephen Crane (1871–1900) and Theodore Dreiser (1871–1945) were bringing out the harsh realities of war, business, and love; but it was not until almost our own day, and then of all places in the South of magnolia and roses, that William Faulkner, Erskine Caldwell, and others really plumbed the depths of human perversities behind the four-letter words they used so freely.

Most of this realistic or naturalistic writing, even when it is by no means of Marxist inspiration, is hostile to the middle classes. The bourgeois is no longer just the Philistine whom the Romantic disliked, the puritanical conformist. He is still that, but he is also the rapacious titan of industry, the jingoistic nationalist, the authoritarian browbeater of his children, the tasteless addict of "conspicuous consumption" (a phrase of the American economist Thorstein Veblen), and the hypocritical practitioner of a "double standard" of sexual morality. In England, Samuel Butler (1835–1902) in *The Way of All Flesh* set the pattern for the kind of novel in which the writer-son blames all on the tyrannical male parent. Shaw found a simple phrase to sum up what was wrong—"middle-class morality." Ibsen's *Enemy of the People* is ironically named; the real enemy of the people is the people themselves, not the misunderstood leader who would bring them better things.

Even when writers are not embittered, the middle class does not often come out well. Bourgeois values are mocked or criticized by English novelists like H. G. Wells, Galsworthy, and Arnold Bennett, French novelists like Anatole France, and most writers of czarist Russia. An epitome of this attack is afforded by an American who wrote in the 1920's, chronologically rather later than the period with which we are here concerned but quite in its style. Sinclair Lewis' *Main Street* and *Babbitt* are realistic rather than naturalistic novels, and George Babbitt is almost a hero without ironic quotation marks. Still, Babbitt came to sum up for thousands of American intellectuals what was wrong with a naïve materialistic civilization. The novels of Sinclair Lewis sold by the hundreds of thousands, so that the George Babbitts of real life and their families must have read these satires on their way of life. Since most of these writers were able to sell their works in a mass market, one may conclude that a good portion of the middle classes in the West were in revolt against their own shortcomings.

Not all that was written between 1850 and the outbreak of war in 1914 was a literature of scorn or protest. The daughters of the Maud or Mélanie with whom we began could read the standard conventional fare, historical novels, novels of escape, and novels of true love. They could even find in writers like Kipling men who, if not exactly convinced that this was the best of possible worlds, were at least convinced that the English middle and upper classes were the least bad of the lot. They could, in short, read for pleasure and edification and go on with the serious business of life.

Poetry

In England Tennyson, in America Longfellow and his New England colleagues, in France Victor Hugo wrote the staple poetry the late nineteenth century liked and read a great deal. These poets deserve the tag "household words." In form, their work differs little from the norms set by the earlier Romantic movement, and their subjects are love, death, nature, patriotism, faith, doubt, and longing, the eternal lyric repertory. They sometimes came down into the arena to deal with politics, as in Whittier's antislavery poems and in James Russell Lowell's "Biglow Papers," poems in Yankee dialect on the crisis of the Civil War. The spiritual crisis brought on by loss of Christian faith in a scientific age is evident in many poems of Matthew Arnold and Arthur Hugh Clough, as well as Tennyson.

The horrors of the Industrial Revolution also caused poetic protests, the most famous of which was prompted by a London news report of the arrest of a seamstress for pawning articles belonging to her employer. Paid by the piece, she could earn at the maximum seven shillings ($1.75) a week, on which she was expected to support herself and two young children. Thomas Hood summed up the indignant public reaction in *The Song of the Shirt*, published in the Christmas number of *Punch* for 1843; the third, fourth, and final stanzas read:

> "Work—work—work
> Till the brain begins to swim;
> Work—work—work
> Till the eyes are heavy and dim!
> Seam, and gusset, and band,
>   Band, and gusset, and seam,
>   Till over the buttons I fall asleep,
> And sew them on in a dream!

> "O! Men, with Sisters dear!
> O! Men! with Mothers and Wives!
> It is not linen you're wearing out,
>   But human creatures' lives!
>   Stitch—stitch—stitch,
> In poverty, hunger, and dirt,
> Sewing at once, with a double thread
> A Shroud as well as a Shirt."

. . . . .

> With fingers weary and worn,
>   With eyelids heavy and red,
> A Woman sate in unwomanly rags,
>   Plying her needle and thread—
>   Stitch! stitch! stitch!
> In poverty, hunger, and dirt,
> And still with a voice of dolorous pitch,
> Would that its tone could reach the Rich!
> She sang this "Song of the Shirt"!

On a higher poetic level the American Walt Whitman exalted democracy and the common man, employing free verse (which has no regular patterns of rhyme and meter). Whitman was no radical innovator, however, and the common man he celebrated had no trouble understanding his poems.

Yet in these same years poetry was beginning to move along the road that brought it to our own times, when the serious poet usually writes difficult private verse not for a mass audience but for a handful of initiates. Romantic poetry reflected the poet's inner world, but the Romantic wanted to be read. In the second half of the nineteenth century, the French Parnassians deliberately sought the seclusion of perfect form, of polished verse fit for but few, or "art for art's sake." Symbolists like Mallarmé went on to very difficult verse, in which the meaning had to be wrung with effort from symbols nested one within another, in which the harmonies, like those of modern music, were by no means at once apparent to the untrained listener. Significantly, when twentieth-century poets went back for precedents to their literary teachers, they did not go to Tennyson, Hugo, Longfellow, or Kipling, but to late Victorian poets hardly known to their contemporaries, like the American Emily Dickinson and the English Catholic convert Gerard Manley Hopkins.

IV   The Arts

Painting, Academic and Realistic

In Victorian literature, there was a popular and conventional, but not vulgar, level of writing represented by men like Hugo and Tennyson. In painting, there was a similar level, represented by the Fontainebleau school in France; Watts, Burne-Jones, and Rossetti in England; George Inness, and later Winslow Homer and John Singer Sargent in the United States; animal painters like Rosa Bonheur (*The Horse Fair*) and Sir Edwin Landseer (*The Stag*); and many, many others throughout the West. The avant garde, the rebels and innovators in art, gave the paintings of these men the derogatory label "academic." Actually, the academic painters were technically very skillful, for they had the advantage of the long tradition of Western painting since the Renaissance. They could often mirror man and nature more faithfully then their great rival for the patronage of the many, the camera. They were sometimes realists, but they were not naturalists in Zola's sense. They rather avoided the shambles of the Industrial Revolution, and to their avant garde opponents they seemed too much concerned with the pretty in nature and with the aristocratic or striking in portraiture.

The rebellion against academic painting, begun in the Romantic generation by Delacroix, continued in the mid-nineteenth century with the Frenchmen Daumier (1808-1879) and Courbet (1819-1877), who also protested against the values of laissez-faire capitalism. Daumier exploited to the full the new technological develop-

Manet's "The Death of Maximilian."

ments that made it possible to mass-produce inexpensive copies of his lithographs. With a moral indignation and savage bite worthy of Voltaire or Hogarth, Daumier exposed the evils of French society, especially under the July Monarchy. He attacked its zeal for law and order in defense of class interests, and the selfishness and repressiveness of its judges and politicians, including Louis-Philippe himself, whose pear-shaped figure and inevitable umbrella afforded superb opportunities for caricature. Courbet upset the academic painters by taking commonplace subjects—wrestlers, stonecutters, nudes who bore no resemblance to classical nymphs—and portraying them as they were, with no attempt to prettify them. The hostility of the academics reached a peak in 1863 when canvases by followers of Courbet were refused showing in the annual Paris salon. The rejected artists countered by organizing their own "salon des réfusés," which gained the backing of Napoleon III.

Among the paintings by the "réfusés" was *Déjeuner sur l'Herbe* (*Picnic Lunch*) by Edouard Manet (1832–1883), depicting two fully-dressed young men with nude female companions. Manet defended himself against hostile comment by observing that a good realist simply painted what he saw. What Manet saw—or more exactly, the ways in which he saw things—did not necessarily correspond to the image recorded by the camera. His version of the execution of the hapless emperor in Mexico demonstrates the distortions so characteristic of modern art, and so disturbing to unprepared viewers. *The Death of Maximilian* destroys the Renaissance idea of perspective, placing the firing squad almost on top of its victim, and abandons factual accuracy by making the executioners French soldiers rather than the Mexicans they actually were. Manet used real objects and events for his own artistic purposes, as occasions for effects of color and composition that he felt to be truer and more real than what the camera records. This feeling that the artist sees more and sees it more profoundly than any mechanical device or any layman with conventional scientific training underlies the revolt of modern art against mere "representational" painting.

Impressionism and Post-Impressionism

That science might encourage, as well as impede, artistic revolution was evident in the case of the Impressionists, whose name was invented by hostile critics after viewing a painting entitled *Sunrise: Impression* by the leader of the school, Claude Monet (1840–1926). The Impressionists learned from physics that light was a complex phenomenon put together by the human eye from the prismatic reflections of nature. They proposed to break both light and shadow into

their component colors and then allow the viewer's eye to reassemble them. They painted landscapes and seascapes for the most part, using thousands of little dabs of pure color for their trees, flowers, buildings, rocks, skies, and water. The result, when seen from close on, is hardly more than a formless mesh of color, but when viewed from a proper distance is magically transformed into a recognizable scene flooded with light.

The nature of light and color had interested painters before the Impressionists, like the Romantic Constable, with his luminous landscapes, and his fellow Englishman Turner (1775–1851). Turner has been termed the great precursor of impressionism because his marine paintings led him to more and more daring experiments in the depiction of light and mist. Monet put experiment on a sustained scientific basis, painting the same subject again and again—the cathedral at Rouen, the lily pond in his own garden—to show

Cézanne's "The Card Players."

how greatly its appearance varied at differing times of day and under changing conditions of light.

Two other qualities augmented the revolutionary impact of Impressionist painting. One was the abandonment of traditional conventions of symmetry in favor of an arrangement which put the principal figure well to one side, sometimes even partially cut off. This technique, borrowed from the Japanese print, was employed with telling effect by the Frenchman Degas (1834–1917) and the American Whistler (1834–1903), who made misty London scenes look quite Japanese and who was, incidentally, quite ashamed of having been born in Lowell, Massachusetts. The other new departure was the concentration on subjects evoking everyday life rather than the artificial world of the studio. Milliners, prostitutes, cardplayers or solitary drinkers in a cafe, cabaret and circus performers, ballerinas in rehearsal populate the canvases of Degas, Toulouse-Lautrec, Renoir, Van Gogh, Cézanne, and other masters of the late nineteenth century.

Most of these men are cataloged by historians of art as post-Impressionists, because they were going on from impressionism to further experiments. Cézanne (1839–1906), in particular, thought that impressionism was too obsessed with light at the expense of the geometrical and architectural qualities also to be found in the world of nature. He proposed to restore these qualities, not with the classic, flowing perspective inherited by the academics from the Italians, but with blocks or chunks of color. Much of twentieth-century painting stems from Cézanne. Cubism, which is the exaggeration of his insistence on three-dimensionality, is most in his debt, but so too are abstractionism and even surrealism.

Self-portrait by Van Gogh, painted while the artist was recovering from a nervous breakdown in 1889.

The Other Arts

In contrast to painting, sculpture did not flourish exuberantly in the nineteenth century. An age that had mastered the industrial arts so well produced monumental statues aplenty, of which the most famous is Liberty in New York harbor, the work of the French sculptor Bartholdi, a gift from the Third French Republic to the American Republic. But the statues of statesmen and warriors that adorn public places everywhere in the West are so conventionally realistic that we hardly accept them as human beings. Sculpture would appear to be an aristocratic art, designed for the palace and the formal garden. Its nineteenth-century civic use seems at its best—or least bad—in Paris, in the decoration of the great Arc de Triomphe, a delayed memorial to the Grand Army of Napoleon I, and in the new Opéra and many other buildings. Toward the end of the century, the French sculptors Rodin and Maillot began to simplify, strengthen, and, to a degree, exaggerate the contours of their men and women, treating their subjects with less academic convention and more power. It should be noted that inexpensive, small-scale copies of the great sculpture of antiquity and the Renaissance now became common, and many a Victorian drawing room

Paul Gauguin, like Cézanne a post-Impressionist, set up a studio in Tahiti in 1890, where he painted "Two Tahitian Women."

boasted a plaster Venus or a bronze Mercury. Museums in various parts of the world could all afford large plaster casts of classical works, so some exposure to the great artistic achievements of the past was now possible for a very wide general public.

In consequence, the nineteenth century knew almost too much of the past of the arts and became too eclectic and derivative in its tastes. This eclecticism weighed heavily on architecture: banks, seeking an impression of appropriate dignity and permanence, favored Greek or Roman temples, at least for the façade; universities and churches, both with lofty aspirations, preferred the Gothic. The medieval predecessor of Gothic, the Romanesque, with its rounded arches and air of solidity, was revived by the talented American architect Richardson, and used for structures as diverse as Trinity Church on Boston's Copley Square, Sever Hall housing classrooms in Harvard Yard, and a series of stations along the Boston and Albany Railroad.

Two styles were particularly popular in the late nineteenth century. The architecture for public buildings was basically derived from the Renaissance, embellished with pediments and balconies and sometimes with domes or friezes, the particular adaptations varying somewhat from country to country. French public structures, much under the influence of the Ecole des Beaux Arts (the school of fine arts in Paris), looked vaguely like a château in Touraine; German buildings kept a touch of the huddled Middle Ages; and British buildings, much imitated in Boston, New York, and Philadelphia, were simpler, more in the manner of Palladio, the neoclassical master of the Renaissance. The other style, for private homes, was represented in Europe by the "villa," and in America by the "mansion" that the successful businessman built for himself on Elm Street. In the United States this style was at its most flaunting in the mansions of the 1870's, the "era of General Grant." These were big houses, for families were large, domestic servants were plentiful and cheap, and building costs were relatively low. They ran to high ceilings, for the bourgeois wanted nothing to remind him of the low rooms of his past. They looked too tall for their width, and their lines were broken by little towers, porches, scrollwork, and other sorts of decorative devices. But they had the latest comforts, if they were in a town large enough—gas light, bathrooms, and central heating, though western Europeans came rather slowly to this last innovation.

In architecture, as in painting and sculpture, true innovation began toward the end of the century. In structural steel, men now had a way of emancipating themselves from the limitations that had so taxed the Gothic builders; they could now go almost as high as they pleased. They began to do so in the United States, where the first "skyscrapers" were put up in Chicago in the 1880's. Although some later skyscrapers ended up in Gothic towers, abundantly decorated, the general tendency imposed by the materials was toward simplicity of line. This taste for simplicity began to spread, and with the twentieth century the way was open for modern "functional" architecture. Mention of structural steel may serve as a reminder that some of the

Fifth Avenue in New York, looking north from 65th Street, 1898.

finest examples of the late 1800's were designed by engineers. Great bridges, like the Brooklyn Bridge or the railroad span across the Firth of Forth in Scotland, are still handsome today as well as impressive and useful.

To sample the minor arts of furniture and household decoration, we return once more to the drawing room of Maud and Mélanie. It was incredibly heavy and incredibly dark. The height of the windows was canceled by the dark carpets, upholstery, hangings, and pillows, and by the mahogany or walnut furniture. Everywhere there was a clutter of objets d'art. The movement for simplification of decoration, however, began in Victorian England with William Morris (1834-1896), designer of the easy chair that bears his name, who wanted to go back to more austere medieval styles. And it was in full swing in the 1890's, particularly with art nouveau in France, which relied on botanical motifs and sought to give structures the look of living organisms.

Music

One great art remains to be discussed. Music recorded many great achievements in the Victorian decades—the symphonies of Brahms and Tchaikovsky, the hardy perennials of the opera repertoire like Bizet's *Carmen,* Gounod's *Faust,* and half a dozen works by Verdi—which did not differ greatly from the masterpieces of the Romantic generation. But the most ambitious composer of the age did attempt a greater break from the traditional. Richard Wagner (1813-1883) rechristened opera "music drama" and set out to make it the supreme synthesis of the arts, with drama, music, and scenery all fused in one great transcendence of the conventional world. Giving up the traditional alternation between aria and relatively undramatic passages of recitative,

Wagner sought to combine music and action in a realistic entity. His characteristic device was the *Leitmotiv,* a definite and recognizable melodic theme associated with a given character or symbolizing an element in the drama. He chose epic subjects: the four operas of the *Ring of the Nibelung,* in which he drew on the Teutonic myths, by no means without thought for Teutonic greatness; *Parsifal,* on the theme of the Holy Grail; *Tristan and Isolde,* a drama of fated love and death taken from the Arthurian legends. Wagner's reputation has also suffered because of his Victorian heaviness, the inordinate length and the great noise of his works. Nietzsche once remarked that Wagner's music "sweats."

In symphonic music, the Wagnerian desire to marry music to the rest of life continued in the vogue of program music, that is, music that suggests something definite—bird-calls, a thunderstorm, or a battle. It produced the "tone poems" of Richard Strauss (1864–1949), which develop themes orchestrally with little regard for the classic form of the symphony. Strauss wrote tone poems on Don Quixote, Nietzsche's *Zarathustra,* and even, in the *Domestic Symphony,* the cares and humors of family life. The Frenchman Debussy (1862–1918) reacted not only against the old norms of tonality, as had Wagner, but also against the grandiloquence of the tone poem and music drama. Influenced by Far Eastern music, he developed new harmonies and new rhythms and a new style often termed Impressionistic. The term is illuminating, for Debussy tried to preserve the sounds of a transitory moment as Monet had tried to paint its light and color.

V   Philosophy and Political Thought

Positivism

Even before Darwin published his *Origin of Species* a major attempt was undertaken to make the new discoveries of science the basis for a comprehensive program to secure the intellectual, political, and economic improvement of mankind. The program was called positivism, and it was put forward in the writings of the Frenchman, Auguste Comte (1798–1857). Comte had served his intellectual aprenticeship with Saint-Simon, the great champion of industry and spinner of projects for greater international harmony. Though Comte later broke with his mentor, his own recommendations for bettering the human condition retained some of the utopian and messianic qualities of Saint-Simonian teachings.

Comte applied the term "positivist" to the third stage of man's attitude toward the world around him. First, in the infant period of human history, man was in the theological age, when he stood in awe and fear of nature and sought to placate the gods that controlled it. Second, in the adolescence of human history, metaphysical concepts replaced divinities as the controlling forces of the world. Finally, science would enable man to understand nature without recourse to theological or metaphysical intermediaries so that he might take positive action to manipulate the world to his advantage. The epoch of maturity, the positivist age, was at hand.

Comte also ranked according to maturity the sciences that enabled humanity to emancipate itself from theological and metaphysical supports. He gave seniority to mathematics and astronomy, put chemistry and physics next, then biology and psychology, and last, and youngest, the science of society, or sociology. It was sociology, Comte believed, that would give man the key to the positive age.

In many ways, Comte was simply restating the Enlightenment's optimistic faith in the miracle-working potential of science; he was a belated philosophe, another would-be "Newton of the social sciences." Yet he also realized that the French revolutionary attempt to build a new society from the blueprints of eighteenth-century intellectuals had ended in terror and dictatorship. Accordingly, Comte concluded, utopia must be achieved peacefully through the teaching of dedicated men, who would enable the mass of their fellows to free themselves from their old dependency on theology and metaphysics. Comte envisaged these liberators as preachers of a new "religion of humanity," but his critics argued that they were a new set of priests, propagandists of a new positivist dogma that might be more intolerant than old religious

Wagner in 1868.

dogmas. The undemocratic implications of doctrines of leadership by a new elite continued to concern Western thinkers, we shall find, long after the transient popularity of Comte's teachings had passed. Comte's ultimate failure to base everything on science, his recourse to a "religion of humanity" to wean men away from traditional faiths, foreshadowed the uncertainties and perplexities that science engendered in the intellectual life of the Victorian age.

Idealism and Realism in Philosophy

The art and literature of the later nineteenth century furnish samples of almost the full range of human attitudes toward the world. The formal philosophy and the less formal view of life taken by educated people varied quite as widely, and we can find as many different schools in metaphysics and ethics as we can find in literature and art. The philosophical school of idealism was born in its modern form in the Germany of Kant and Hegel. In the later nineteenth century it continued to thrive in the land of its birth; it made converts in the Oxford School of T. H. Green, Bradley, and Bosanquet, and in the American philosopher Josiah Royce; and it even penetrated into the Latin countries. The philosophical opposite of idealism, now christened "realism," was at least as widespread. Modern realism as a philosophy attempted to answer questions the scientist does not try to answer in so far as he is a scientist. Yet it had its roots in the same soil as modern science and the scientific rationalism of the eighteenth-century philosophes, and was a product of the Enlightenment. Auguste Comte doubtless thought of himself as a realist.

The American philosopher William James (1842–1910) found two terms to sum up this polar antithesis of idealism and realism that runs through Western philosophical tradition. Men are, wrote James, by disposition either "tender-minded" or "tough-minded." They are either tough-mindedly convinced that the world of sense experience is the real world or tender-mindedly convinced that the world of sense-experience is somehow an illusion, or at any rate a flawed copy, if not a kind of caricature, of the real world which is in our minds imperfectly, and perfectly in God's mind.

One might conclude that, since the later nineteenth century was a period of great material progress, deeply concerned with this world of the senses, then the "tough-minded" would prevail over the "tender-minded." Yet this was by no means true in philosophy, where the tender-minded were quite numerous and articulate. Perhaps the unreflective man, at least in our Western civilization, leans toward the tough-minded side, if only because common sense urges upon him the presence of the world of matter. But there are no reliable statistics on this point, and to the extent that Christianity forms an inescapable underpinning for the world view of Western men, not even tough common sense can altogether dispose of the world of the tender-minded, of concepts like value judgments, soul, spirit, ideal, and otherworld.

Dynamism
and the Cult of the Will

Darwinism left its mark on the philosophy of the later nineteenth century. The thought of the period had a dynamic historical and evolutionary cast that not even the tender-minded could avoid. The idealist, following Hegel, believed that above the whirl and change of this world of the senses there was an unchanging, perfect world of the Absolute. But he also believed that this imperfect world was being slowly drawn toward that other world, developing by ways he could only incompletely understand, but growing, evolving. On the other hand, the nineteenth-century realist no longer held that his reason could give him a neat, static, mathematical formula for the good life; he too thought that everything grows, that even what is made according to human plans must take account of nature's mysterious ways of growth.

A second and related note in the thought of the period is an emphasis on will, often capitalized into Will, on doing, on the life force that makes the "struggle for existence." The word appears everywhere, even as a title—Schopenhauer's *World as Will and Idea,* Nietzsche's *Will to Power,* William James' *Will to Believe.* It appears but slightly disguised in the French philosopher Henri Bergson's "creative evolution" and *"élan vital"* and in Bernard Shaw's "life-force." It appears in the work of the Italian idealist philosopher Benedetto Croce, as an insistence that knowing is not a passive registering but a creative doing. It lies behind the use of the word "myth" by the French anarchosyndicalist Georges Sorel, and the German Hans Vaihinger's phrase "the philosophy of the as-if." For both these latter thinkers, the great ideas, the great abstractions of Right and Wrong, are not mere attempts of the mind to understand the world; indeed they are quite false if taken as analytically descriptive of this world. But they are, rather, the guides our desires, our wills, set up for our action. They are fictions, myths, "as-if," but all the more real for being such.

The pragmatism of William James, somewhat unfairly described by its critics as the philosophy that nothing succeeds like success, is one of these philosophies of the will. To James, himself "tough-minded," reality is no absolute as in the idealist tradition; indeed, reality is nothing fixed and certain. Reality is what works for us human beings; truth is what we want to believe. James thought he had saved himself from the obvious danger of this line of thought—that is, making reality and truth purely subjective, purely a matter of the individual's judgment or faith—by granting that not everything we want is practical, that not all our desires "work." If my will to believe tells me I can make a broad jump of three hundred feet, experience, the "pragmatic" test, will prove that I cannot. But to many of James' critics, he had by no means saved himself from subjectivism. Pragmatism remained to these critics a doctrine dangerously erosive of traditional values, leading either to an exaltation of mere vulgar success, or to "fideism," a silly belief in believing for the sake of believing.

The Revolt against Reason

The cult of the will brings us to a major current in the broad stream of later nineteenth-century thought, a current more evident among intellectuals and creative artists than among average educated men and women. This was an intensification of the revolt against reason already initiated by the Romantics earlier in the century; it may be called anti-intellectualism, irrationalism, or, more exactly, antirationalism. This antirationalism is one of the "roots" of twentieth-century totalitarianism, but it is by no means a simple synonym for totalitarianism or fascism. It is a much broader and more inclusive term. It is quite possible to have been influenced by antirational currents and remain a good, if not altogether orthodox, democrat and individualist. It is quite possible to be a Marxist totalitarian and reject a great deal, especially in its psychological core, of modern antirationalism. The conventional Marxist retains some of the naïve optimism of the eighteenth-century rationalist: Get the economy to work perfectly, he says, and men will behave themselves perfectly.

The basic position of antirationalism, and one for which it is heavily indebted to the Romantic movement, is a rejection of the Enlightenment's belief that the typical human being is naturally reasonable. To the extent that it rejects the Enlightenment, antirationalism is a negation, as the "anti" implies. But it has its positive side—the belief that if men can accept their true nature as human beings they can lead richer lives than any rationalist ever planned for them; what they must accept is the radical limitation of the potential of their thinking mind, or brain, to which so much of their experience never penetrates.

Broadly speaking, there are two kinds of antirationalism, which shade into one another: the moderate and the extreme. Moderate antirationalism at bottom is trying to salvage as much as possible of the eighteenth-century belief in human rationality. Such on the whole is the attitude of modern psychology, beginning with William James and Sigmund Freud. This psychology seeks to aid human reason by pointing out the difficulties under which it must work. Reason, these thinkers maintain, is limited by men's instincts or "drives," by their biological inheritance of animality, so much emphasized by the evolutionists, and by their sociological inheritance of custom and tradition so much emphasized by historians and by the school of Edmund Burke.

To use a metaphor from John Locke, (which he in turn derived from the slogan of the Cambridge Platonists, "the mind of man is the light of God"), moderate antirationalists regard human reason as a flickering candle, not as the great white universal light it appeared to be to philosophes like Condorcet. Far from wishing to extinguish this candle, they want to keep it alive, to nurse it along into greater and greater brightness. This process, in keeping again with the views of the evolutionist, they regard as inevitably long and slow, likely to be hindered rather than helped by ambitious plans to hasten it. These moderate thinkers are perhaps not so much antirationalists as they are chastened rationalists.

By contrast, the second kind of antirationalism would actually put out the candle of human reason. For the extreme antirationalists reason is not just feeble; it is bad. It is for them, so to speak, a mistake evolution has made—a wrong turning, from which the human race must somehow retrace its steps to a sounder life of pure unsullied instinct, emotion, and faith. Thomas Hardy, the English novelist, remarked, "Thought is a disease of the flesh." There was to be a strong dose of extreme antirationalism in the Nazi movement. Hitler himself distrusted reason, deeming it a degenerate French invention. Good Germans, he hoped, would come to think with their blood, with their German folk inheritance.

The Reaction against Democracy

Many of the extreme antirationalists turned violently against democracy, which seemed to them to rest on an altogether false estimate of what human beings were really like. The democrat believes at bottom that every man can be freed from the weight of erroneous traditions, habits, and prejudices. Once he has the real facts before him, he can attain by free discussion among his fellows a series of decisions that will be incorporated in acts and institutions under which all men can live more happily. But if you hold that most, or even many, men are by nature incapable of fair, dispassionate thinking and discussion, if you hold that men are by nature hopelessly irrational, you will at least have to revise drastically your notions of democracy, or reject them.

The German philosopher Nietzsche, who did most of his work in the 1880's, will serve as a sample of such political thinkers. Nietzsche wrote mostly in short aphoristic passages, which are hard to systematize and often quite contradictory. But the central line of his thinking led to the concept of a new aristocracy, to the "superman" (in German, *Ubermensch*). Nietzsche's followers, who were numerous throughout the West in the two decades before 1914, insisted that he meant a new *spiritual* aristocracy. The supermen would be above the petty materialism and national patriotism of the middle classes. Nietzsche's opponents, who were also many, held that he was just another preacher of Nordic superiority, that his supermen were, as he put it in one of his famous passage, "the blond beasts" who had so often terrorized Europe. Certainly some of his German followers held that he meant the real live Germans to be his supermen.

At any rate, Nietzsche was clearly an enemy of democracy, which he held to be second only to its child, socialism, as a society in which the weak unjustly and unnaturally ruled the strong. Here are some of his aphorisms, from which the reader can judge for himself:

Democracy represents the disbelief in all great men and in all élite societies: everybody is everybody else's equal. "At bottom we are all herd and mob."

Friedrich Nietzsche.

I am opposed to Socialism because it dreams ingenuously of "goodness, truth, beauty, and equal rights" (anarchy pursues the same ideal, but in a more brutal fashion).

I am opposed to parliamentary government and the power of the press, because they are the means whereby cattle become masters.*

Nietzsche may have hoped that the herd, the slaves, the masses would, in spite of their crass materialism, somehow recognize the true masters, the new enlightened despots; or he may have thought of himself as the prophet of a vast moral and religious revolution which would, in his own phrase, achieve a "transvaluation of all values," a new world for a new species of man. At any rate, it is—or should be—safe to say that he was no conventional democrat.

Even the defenders of the democratic values attacked by Nietzsche were also influenced by the doubts raised by the Romantics and the anti-rationalists. They were not at all sure about the

* Friedrich Nietzsche, *The Will to Power,* trans. A. M. Ludovici (London, 1910), II, 206.

reasonableness and the natural goodness of the average man and woman, about the beneficent workings of a free market and the "invisible hand" of laissez-faire economics, and about many other established doctrines of liberalism. John Stuart Mill in the mid-century had worried over the "tyranny of the majority." Walter Bagehot, a good English liberal much influenced by Darwin, pointed out in his *Physics and Politics* (1872) how strong was the accumulated force of habit and tradition, which he called the "cake of custom," how hard it was to persuade men to break the cake of custom and take rational action. By the end of the century, liberals throughout the West were facing the problem of revising their attitudes toward life to conform with the new emphasis on the tough network of habit, custom, and prejudice.

Elitism

Already by 1914 the broad lines of the social attitudes of our own time were being laid out. One line went toward some kind of revolutionary elitism, toward the seizure of power by a minority that believes itself to have the formula whereby the gifted few can put order into a society threatened with chaos because of attempts to make decisions democratically by counting heads, no matter what is inside them. The variety of these specific formulas was great. Some made race the mark of the elite, and went so far as to preach world rule for their chosen race. Others made class the mark of the elite, and sought to achieve the "dictatorship of the proletariat." Indeed, as Lenin developed Marxian socialism, its elitist implications came out in the doctrine often called the Leninist corollary—that the enlightened minority must seize power and rule dictatorially in the name of and in the "true" interest of the proletarian masses. Others dreamed of a brand-new elite, such as Nietzsche's supermen, to be created by a kind of new religion. Still others looked to eugenics to make possible the breeding of such a new elite.

A second line went toward a more flexible form of elitism, one that tried to conserve as much as possible of democratic values. On the whole, English Fabianism and continental revisionist socialism deserve this classification. The leaders of these movements wanted no violent overturns, no seizure of power. They believed in gradualness, even in the basic democratic counting of heads. But there was in all of them a strong touch of doubt as to the political capacity of the average man. They were not for the extension of New England town-meeting democracy to the millions of the modern state. They hoped they could persuade the millions to elect legislators who would listen to the wise planners who had studied the social sciences and could devise the wise new institutions that would make human life so much better. Above all, the planners themselves would by no means disdain what the antirationalists had taught them about human irrationality; they would use for good ends what they could learn from the politician, the advertising man, the skilled professional manipulator of human beings; they would be Machiavellians, but Machiavellians on the side of the angels.

A third line sought to preserve and protect an existing elite from democratic drives toward equality, especially in the form of state intervention in economic and social life to promote security for all. This was substantially the line followed by men like the American sociologist William Graham Sumner, by the English philosopher Herbert Spencer, and by many others throughout the West. They are not unfairly labeled conservatives, for they sought to preserve in its broad lines an established order. But they were not simply routine, unphilosophical conservatives who opposed any changes at all. They had a definite philosophy, strongly influenced by antirationalism. Their basic position was a distrust of the instrument of thought applied unsparingly to human society, and in this they go back to Burke and to philosophical conservatives throughout the western tradition.

They were clearly children of their age, above all in their concrete fears of "socialism." Most of them believed in progress, and most of them prized material plenty, peace, industrial society. They held, however, that the existing middle classes, the leaders of the business world, and the network of Victorian habits and morals were the best insurance that progress would continue. Above all, they feared planners and planning, at least in political positions. They distrusted the state, for they were good Darwinians, who believed that the evolutionary process depended on the struggle for life among competing individuals fettered as little as possible by attempts to "rig" the struggle. They believed that

social evolution could not be hastened, and that attempts to hasten it, no matter how well meant, would in fact retard it by limiting actual human variation and initiative. They are by no means altogether without sympathizers today, but it must be admitted that theirs has not, so far, been the "wave of the future." The Herbert Spencer who thought compulsory sewage disposal in cities was an interference with the "right" of the individual to conduct his own private struggle against typhoid fever would be even more uncomfortable in the late twentieth century than he was in the late nineteenth.

"The Century of Hope"

It would be a mistake to dismiss the whole nineteenth century as something altogether outlived. We are all still living with the achievements as well as the problems it bequeathed to us. The achievements are obvious, and we have noted them in the last few chapters. They add up to an impressive command over natural forces, attained by the collaboration, often the chance collaboration, of pure scientists, applied scientists and engineers, businessmen, bureaucrats, and politicians, and on down to clerks and laborers.

The problems are also evident. Above all, there was the widespread feeling, particularly among intellectuals, that "something was wrong," that the new and better world promised by 1776 and 1789 had proved illusory. It is easy to point out how many nineteenth-century writers—the youthful Marx, Flaubert, Nietzsche —were alienated from the ways of their world. It is even easier to find how many more can be labeled pessimistic, if not alienated—genteel Victorians like Matthew Arnold or John Ruskin, worried liberals like Mill and Tocqueville, deeply concerned critics of their national culture like the great Russian novelists. Even the Americans were not always optimistic children of the Enlightenment—think of James Fenimore Cooper, the bitter critic of American democracy, of Mark Twain despairing of the "damned human race," and of Thoreau who believed that even in gentle Concord men led lives of quiet desperation.

Yet, despite all this the nineteenth century has been entitled "the century of hope." The title can be reconciled with the record of the century's intellectual history in part by insisting that, while many thinkers inclined toward pessimism, the great majority of Europeans and Americans, especially the dominant middle class, were cheerful believers in progress. The bulk of newspaper and magazine writing, the testimony of informal letters, and much other evidence can support the social historian in contending that Victorian nonintellectuals, in contrast to intellectuals, were on the whole contented and hopeful, if a bit self-righteous. Even among the intellectuals there was an attitude, hard to pin down, that it was the century of hope. Few of them, no matter how bitter and indignant about their times or skeptical about human nature, displayed a cosmic despair. Almost all of them shared with their grandfathers of the eighteenth century a kind of energy and gusto, a conviction that what they wrote and said would have results, a belief in the future and in ultimate progress.

Reading Suggestions on the Intellectual Revolution of the Nineteenth Century

GENERAL ACCOUNTS   G. Mosse, *The Culture of Western Europe* (*Rand McNally). An informative textbook.

W. H. Coates and H. V. White, *The Ordeal of Liberal Humanism* (*McGraw-Hill). A very useful survey of intellectual history since 1789.

C. Brinton, *The Shaping of Modern Thought* (*Spectrum). A more rapid survey.

R. W. Stromberg, *European Intellectual History since 1789* (*Appleton). Another helpful textbook.

W. L. Langer, *Political and Social Upheaval, 1832–1852;* R. C. Binkley, *Realism and Nationalism, 1852–1871;* C. J. H. Hayes, *A Generation of Materialism, 1871–1900* (*Torchbooks). These three volumes in the series "The Rise of Modern Europe" have substantial sections on the topics covered in this chapter and full bibliographical listings.

F. S. Marvin, *The Century of Hope*, 2nd ed. (Oxford Univ. Press, 1927). A bird's-eye view of cultural history, rather old-fashioned in point of view. May be contrasted with Morse Peckham, *Beyond the Tragic Vision* (*Braziller), written from the standpoint of modern psychology.

SCIENCE   R. Taton, ed., *Science in the Nineteenth Century* (Thames and Hudson, 1965). An encyclopedic account by various French experts; Volume 3 of "A General History of Science."

W. P. D. Wightman, *The Growth of Scientific Ideas* (Yale Univ. Press, 1951). A most enlightening interpretation.

C. C. Gillispie, *The Edge of Objectivity* (*Princeton Univ. Press). Darwin and other nineteenth-century scientific innovators appraised.

L. Eisely, *Darwin's Century* (*Anchor). Instructive study of the doctrine of evolution and of the men who formulated it.

Charles Darwin, *Autobiography* (*Norton); *Voyage of the Beagle* (*Natural History Press; Doubleday); *On the Origin of Species* (*several editions). Three key works for understanding the development of Darwin's ideas. His writings may be sampled in two anthologies: *The Darwin Reader,* ed. M. Bates and P. S. Humphrey (*Scribner's), and *Darwin for Today,* ed. S. E. Hyman (*Compass).

Gertrude Himmelfarb, *Darwin and the Darwinian Revolution* (*Norton). Excellent introduction.

W. Irvine, *Apes, Angels and Victorians* (*World). A lively social study.

A. D. White, *A History of the Warfare of Science and Religion in Christendom* (*Free Press). By the first president of Cornell University and an American champion of Darwin's ideas.

Herbert Spencer, *Man versus the State* (*Penguin). Representative work by a wholehearted English Social Darwinist.

M. R. Davie, *William Graham Sumner* (*T. Y. Crowell). A good introduction to a leading American Social Darwinist. See also R. Hofstadter, *Social Darwinism in American Thought* (*Beacon), an admirable study by a highly respected historian.

Jacques Barzun, *Darwin, Marx and Wagner,* rev. ed. (*Anchor). Suggestive study stressing the common denominators among three contemporaneous innovators usually cataloged as very different from one another.

LITERATURE — Georg Brandes, *Main Currents in Nineteenth-Century Literature,* 6 vols. (Heinemann, 1901–1905). A valuable detailed study.

G. M. Young, *Victorian England: Portrait of an Age* (*Anchor), and W. E. Houghton, *The Victorian Frame of Mind, 1830–1870* (Yale Univ. Press, 1957). Informative introductions to the English literary scene.

E. Wilson, *Axel's Castle* (*Scribner's). A stimulating study of imaginative literature in the late nineteenth and early twentieth centuries.

F. Steegmuller, *Flaubert and Madame Bovary: A Double Portrait,* rev. ed. (*Noonday). Illuminating introduction to the great French realist and his celebrated heroine.

C. Graña, *Modernity and Its Discontents* (*Torchbooks). A suggestive study of French society and the man of letters in the nineteenth century; originally entitled *Bohemian versus Bourgeois.*

THE ARTS — F. Novotny, *Painting and Sculpture in Europe, 1780–1880* (Pelican, 1960). A most comprehensive study of these arts on the Continent.

J. C. Sloane, *French Painting between the Past and Present* (Princeton Univ. Press, 1951). A monograph on artists and critics during the crucial years of the Second Republic and Second Empire when "modern" painting was born.

M. Raynal, *The Nineteenth Century: Goya to Gauguin* (Skira, 1951). A handsomely illustrated survey. The same author has written a study of Cézanne (*Skira).

H. Read, *A Concise History of Modern Painting,* rev. ed. (*Praeger). By a ranking authority.

E. P. Richardson, *The Way of Western Art, 1776–1914* (Cooper Square, 1969). A useful general survey.

H. R. Hitchcock, *Architecture: Nineteenth and Twentieth Centuries* (Pelican, 1958). A massive detailed study.

J. E. Burchard and A. Bush-Brown, *Architecture of America,* abridged ed. (*Little, Brown). Emphasizing its relationship to society and culture.

H. R. Hitchcock, *Architecture of H. H. Richardson and His Times* (*MIT Press). An expert appraisal of the American leader of the Romanesque revival.

H. Morrison, *Louis Sullivan: Prophet of Modern Architecture* (*Norton). Study of a pioneer of skyscraper design.

R. Schmutzler, *Art Nouveau* (*Abrams). Study of the significant turn-of-the-century decorative style in Europe.

S. Giedion, *Mechanization Takes Command* (*Norton). Interesting analysis of the effects of industrialization on the arts.

D. J. Grout, *A History of Western Music* (Norton, 1960). A valuable survey.

PHILOSOPHY AND
POLITICAL THOUGHT

W. L. Burn, *The Age of Equipoise: A Study of the Mid-Victorian Generation* (*Norton). Stimulating study in British intellectual history.

F. E. Manuel, *Prophets of Paris* (*Torchbooks). The last of the five men treated is Comte, the prophet of positivism.

G. Masur, *Prophets of Yesterday: Studies in European Culture, 1890–1914* (*Colophon), and H. S. Hughes, *Consciousness and Society: The Reorientation of European Social Thought, 1890–1930* (*Vintage). Two very suggestive studies of the twilight of the nineteenth century.

K. Löwith, *From Hegel to Nietzsche* (Holt, 1964). Analysis of the revolution in nineteenth-century thought, especially in Germany.

W. Kaufmann, *Nietzsche: Philosopher, Psychologist, Antichrist* (*Vintage). Widely considered the best book on the controversial German.

G. D. Charlton, *Secular Religions in France, 1815–1870* (Oxford Univ. Press, 1963). Interesting and scholarly survey of surrogate religions.

H. D. Aiken, ed., *The Age of Ideology* (*Mentor). Selections from nineteenth-century philosophers, with helpful introductory comments.

NOVELS AND DRAMAS

Flaubert, *Madame Bovary* (*many editions). The classic novel of French realism.

Zola, *Germinal* and *L'Assommoir* (*Signet). Translations of two characteristic novels by the great French exponent of naturalism.

S. Butler, *The Way of All Flesh* (*many editions). A good example of gloomy naturalism in the novel, English-style.

S. Lewis, *Babbitt* and *Main Street* (*Signet). Novels that are important documents of American social history.

E. Bellamy, *Looking Backward, 2000–1887* (*several editions); H. G. Wells, *A Modern Utopia* (Scribner's, 1905); and W. Morris, *News from Nowhere* (Longmans, 1901). Three contrasting visions of utopia in the light of science and industrialism.

Ibsen, *Six Plays: A Doll's House, Ghosts, An Enemy of the People, Rosmersholm, Hedda Gabler, The Master Builder* (*Modern Library). Six pioneering dramas by a master.

E. Brieux, *Damaged Goods*, preface by G. B. Shaw (Fifield, 1914). Problem play treating venereal disease.

Shaw, *Man and Superman* and *Back to Methuselah* (*Penguin). Plays on aspects of the modern intellectual revolution.

24

Nineteenth-Century Imperialism

I The Movement in General

In the *Oxford English Dictionary*, which tries to find the earliest possible example of the use of a word, the editors can go no further back than 1881 for "imperialism: the principle of the spirit of empire; advocacy of what are held to be imperial interests." The word is new; what it stands for is in part very old indeed—as old as human war and conquest. Yet there were some important new elements in the imperialism of Western peoples in the nineteenth century. Nineteenth-century imperialism was in almost every country a major part of political life, with goals, methods, and advocates known to all who were concerned with politics. And since by 1900 almost all of western and central Europe, the United States, and indeed all the outposts of European culture enjoyed high literacy and widespread public discussion, imperialism took its place with liberalism, conservatism, national-

Above: The American Commodore Perry, who "opened" Japan: Japanese woodblock print, 1853. Above right: President Theodore Roosevelt on a steam shovel in Panama during the construction of the canal. Right: The opening of the Suez Canal in 1869.

ism, socialism, and a host of other isms as a subject of universal debate. Perhaps no important ism seems to us now, little more than a half-century after the heyday of this imperialism, to be quite so outdated. Even the term "imperialism" has been replaced by the still more pejorative "colonialism."

The Economic Aspect

Carefully defined, another element, the economic, may be said to distinguish nineteenth-century imperialism from early forms of imperialism. The material, acquisitive motive runs through all forms of territorial expansion from prehistoric times to the present. It is clear in the earliest days of Spanish and Portuguese expansion in the quest for gold, silver, and profits. But, as the nineteenth century wore on, imperialist nations were responding to economic pressures in a new form. Liberal, and especially Marxist, economists and sociologists no doubt exaggerated this new element, but there is a basis of truth in their arguments.

According to these economic critics of imperialism, capitalists and industrialists in the older countries began to discover in the nineteenth century that they were unable to market at home all they could produce. But, being capitalists, they could not bring themselves to solve their difficulties by paying proportionately *less* of the total product of society in interest, dividends, and other payments to their own kind of people, the upper classes, and paying *more* in wages, pensions, bonuses, and the like to their workmen. Instead of sharing the wealth and creating at home the mass purchasing power and the mass market they needed, they preferred to turn to the non-Western world, to markets abroad, to the exploitation of dependent peoples. This attempt to bolster the capitalist system meant competition among the great Western industrial powers for land and peoples to exploit. Lenin, in his *Imperialism as the Latest Stage of Capitalism* (1917), stressed the need to use the finance capital that was rapidly accumulating, rather than the need for markets. The great bankers, according to Lenin, drove the willing politicians into the search for dependencies in which this available capital could be profitably invested, a search that marked what he termed the inevitable "last stage of capitalism."

A non-Marxist would of course call attention to the fact that the "nineteenth-century colonial world" produced raw materials and little else; the exchange of these for European and American manufactured goods was easy, "natural," and not yet held to be wicked or unfair to the colonial areas. Furthermore, as we have already seen, leading industrial powers in both America and Europe were experiencing an increasing demand for higher tariffs by the late 1800's. In the United States and Germany, and even in free-trading Britain, industrialists wanted protection against foreign competitors. This was an era of neomercantilism, reviving and "streamlining" the older mercantilist doctrines of Colbert and others. Colonies as well as tariffs entered into the strategy of the neomercantilists, as they had done in the case of the old.

The Powers Involved

The year 1870 is a convenient dividing line between the more active age of imperialism that was to come and the less active age that had preceded. The period from 1815 to 1870 saw a partial decline in imperialist fortunes, as most of Spain's American colonies gained their independence, and as Britain took the first steps leading to the virtual independence of Canada. In this same period, however, the French established themselves in Algeria, and the British extended their rule in India. The dividing line of 1870 does not mark a sharp break in the history of imperialism, but rather the acceleration of a movement that had never ceased.

The successful competitors in nineteenth-century imperialism, those who brought new lands under their flags, were Great Britain, which already in 1815 had a great empire, France, Germany, Italy, and the United States. Even little Belgium, itself a "new" nation in 1830, acquired a tremendous piece of tropical Africa, the Congo, 900,000 square miles in area in comparison to the homeland's 11,775 square miles. Russia did not expand overseas, and indeed parted with her vast but thinly inhabited possession in North America when the czarist government sold Alaska to the United States in 1867. But she began the effective settlement of the great areas east of the Urals and began to push into the borderlands of the Middle and Far East, toward Persia, India, and China.

In the process of expansion, the expanding nations inevitably rubbed up against one another in all sorts of competition, from the economic to actual shooting war. Almost every great international conflict of the nineteenth century, save for the mid-century duels between Prussia and Austria and between Prussia and France, had a direct concern in imperialist rivalries outside Europe. Imperial competition is a complicated story, then, woven into the whole fabric of international relations in the nineteenth century. We shall note briefly the major areas of inter-European rivalries and then summarize the growth of the major empires over the century.

The Areas Involved

The Americas and the lands of the British Empire were, on the whole, outside the scramble. The Monroe Doctrine, toward which European nations were increasingly respectful as the strength of the United States increased, helped to keep both American continents free from further actual annexation by outside powers. So, too, did the British navy, for British policy was there to support the status quo. Toward the fateful year 1914, the competition between Britain and Germany for markets and for fields of investment in South America grew intense and was one of the many factors that brought these powers to war. Since no state was strong enough to take from Britain her older colonies, throughout the nineteenth century British problems in both colonies of settlement and colonies of exploitation were essentially internal problems of the British system itself.

A major field of imperialist rivalry and penetration was the Near or Middle East, essentially the widespread lands under varying degrees of Turkish control, and Persia. In earlier chapters we saw how the Balkans and the Straits became major issues in nineteenth-century diplomatic history. The whole "Eastern Question," as it used to be called, revolved around the problem of what was to be done with these old lands, which were peopled almost wholly by Muslims. They were backward lands by nineteenth-century Western standards, farmlands exhausted by centuries of primitive agriculture, mostly with poor rainfall, and with ancient irrigation systems often in disrepair. They were poor also in natural resources, for their great wealth in petroleum

was not really known or very important until the twentieth century. England, France, and Russia were in active competition over the Near East early in the nineteenth century, and they were later joined by Italy and Germany.

Africa was the scene of the most spectacular imperial rivalry. In 1815, except for the nominally Turkish lands of North Africa, the little Dutch settlement at the Cape of Good Hope (taken over by the British in 1815), and a string of Portuguese, Spanish, French, and British "factories" or trading posts along the old Portuguese exploration route that went back to the fifteenth century, Africa was untenanted by Europeans and, in the interior, almost unexplored. It was inhabited by black peoples, long subjected to the horrors of the slave trade and often living at the level of primitive tribesmen. The slave trade was almost abolished in many areas by mid-century, and exploration was well under way. Then in the latter half of the century the great powers—Britain, France, and Germany—with Portugal, Italy, and Belgium tagging along, succeeded in blocking out in territorial units under their respective flags almost the whole of the continent. The only exceptions were the small Republic of Liberia, which had been set up by American antislavery groups as a land for emancipated black American slaves (though very few of them went there), and the mountainous and backward inland state of Abyssinia (now known as Ethiopia). Abyssinia, coveted by Italy, had a very narrow escape. In 1896, the Abyssinians, under their emperor Menelek and with French help, defeated an Italian army at Adowa and secured a respite in independence until the Italians tried again under Mussolini in 1935.

The Far East, too, was a major scene of imperialist rivalries. European powers strengthened their hold on older colonies and acquired new ones in Southeast Asia—the mainland areas of Burma, Indo-China, and Malaya, and the island groups of Melanesia and Polynesia. But the ancient, thickly populated, highly civilized Chinese Empire was never subjected, as was Africa, to actual partition and direct annexation. China was, however, not well enough organized politically or industrially to stand up against European penetration and was by the end of the century subjected to a rough, de facto partitioning among Britain, France, Germany, and Russia. Each power, operating from certain "treaty ports" as centers, was able to exercise a degree

The city of Loango in the eighteenth century. A British engraving of an African city at the mouth of the Congo.

of control—basically economic—over considerable areas, typical "spheres of influence" as they were called. Rivalry among these European powers, and the rising power of the United States, which was exercised in favor of the "Open Door" policy of permitting as much free trade in China as was possible and of preserving Chinese sovereignty, served to counterbalance Chinese weakness and kept China throughout this period on the list of independent nations.

Finally, Japan kept herself isolated from the rest of the world for two centuries, from the mid-seventeenth to the mid-nineteenth. This compact island empire was closed to foreigners during the period when the European powers slowly strengthened their small holds in China. Then in 1853 the American naval officer Perry induced Japan to open her ports to outside trade. By adopting some Western ways, particularly economic ways, Japan was able not merely to preserve her real independence during the late nineteenth century but actually to begin her own imperial expansion on the mainland of Asia after winning a brief war with China in 1894–1895. Japan was thus the first modern nation-state in the Far East.

Africa and the Middle East, 1910

Legend:
- Belgian
- British
- French
- German
- Italian
- Portuguese
- Spanish
- British Occupation
- Independent

II   The British Empire

We may now move on through the imperial record, country by country. Nineteenth-century Britain retained and, with the help of emigrants from the mother country, developed the great areas that were suitable to white colonization—Canada, Australia and New Zealand, and South Africa. This section focuses on Britain's imperial possessions in Africa and Asia. The development of self-government in Canada, Australia, and New Zealand will come more appropriately at the close of this chapter, in our survey of the results of nineteenth-century imperialism.

South Africa

In 1815, Britain had just acquired Cape Colony at the southern tip of Africa from the Netherlands. Cape Colony was inhabited by a few Dutch and French Huguenot colonists and was suited, in spite of a relatively low rainfall, to European living. As Britishers moved in, the older colonists, known in their own Dutch vernacular as Boers, grew more and more discontented. The adoption of English as the sole official language, the abolition of slavery throughout the empire in 1834, the attempts of the government at London to protect the native blacks, and other measures of Victorian liberalism went against the grain of the patriarchal Boers, who were fundamentalist Christians for whom slavery was ordained of God and for whom liberalism was the work of the devil. Between 1835 and 1837, some ten thousand Boers moved north overland into country sparsely settled by primitive black tribes in the Great Trek, a heroic folk migration that bulks even larger in South African nationalist feeling than do the comparable sagas of covered-wagon days in American tradition. After some confused three-cornered fighting among Boers, British, and native Zulus, the Boers established two virtually independent states—the Transvaal and the Orange Free State. Well inland, on territory suitable for grazing but not for intensive agriculture, these thinly populated states lived on for a time hardly noticed by the outside world.

The British in South Africa noticed them, of course, and many of the British wished to add these lands directly to the empire. They settled from the sea another British province to the east, along the Indian Ocean side, known as Natal. In the course of the century, Cape Colony and Natal, which together had a black population heavily outnumbering the British and remaining Boers combined, acquired the self-governing rights that British colonies of settlement in Canada, Australia, and New Zealand were also acquiring. British South African leaders for the most part wanted to bring the Boer Republics under the British flag. But as the London home government swung between Tory and Liberal domination, it also swung between a policy of imperialist expansion and the "Little Englander" policy of leaving the Trekkers alone. In 1852, by the Sand River Convention, the British acknowledged the independence of Transvaal. But in 1877 they reversed themselves and annexed it as a step toward the federation of all South Africa under the British crown. The Boers revolted in 1880 and the Liberal Gladstone, then in power, lived up to his principles by making at Pretoria in 1881 a treaty with the Boers which reestablished Transvaal as independent, though under the "suzerainty" of Great Britain.

The British were already filtering up through the semidesert country to the west of the Boer Republics when the discovery of gold and the development of the diamond industry in these republics undid Gladstone's work. The Transvaal was no longer just a poor and isolated grazing country; it offered a great source of wealth that tempted quite different kinds of settlers. The region about Johannesburg, the famous Rand, filled up with adventurers and entrepreneurs of a dozen nations, all looking to Britain to protect them from the conservative Boers, to whom they were undesirable *Uitlanders* (outlanders, foreigners).

The Boer War and After

The inevitable conflict came to a head with the Jameson Raid of December 29, 1895—midsummer in South Africa. The British in South Africa were now under the leadership of Cecil Rhodes, prime minister of Cape Colony, a determined and articulate imperalist who had made a quick fortune consolidating the chaotic diamond industry. The raid itself, under a follower of Rhodes, Dr. Jameson, was an invasion of Transvaal from British territory to the west, and was planned to coincide with a rising of Uitlanders in Johannesburg. But the rising did not take place, and the president of Transvaal, Kruger, had no trouble in defeating Jameson's handful of invaders. The famous "Kruger telegram," in which the German kaiser congratulated the Boer president, was one of the critical steps in sharpening the Anglo-German rivalry that helped lead to world war in 1914. Its immediate effect in South Africa was to harden Boer resistance and bring about in 1899 open war between Britain and the two Boer Republics.

The war, following the pattern of British wars in modern times, went badly at first for the British. They did not have enough troops immediately available to put down determined men who had been brought up in outdoor life and who were fighting on their own ground. Western opinion, including opinion in the United States, generally sided with the underdog Boers, and in Britain itself many Liberals and Labourites strongly opposed the war as rank imperialism. But in the long run the overwhelming strength of the British prevailed. By the middle of 1900 the British had won in the field, but they needed another eighteen months to subdue the desperate

Cecil Rhodes.

composing their long quarrel and to be ready to collaborate in setting up a new outpost of the West. But there were ominous signs even then. The Boers had by no means been anglicized, and they were still fundamentally opposed to their partners in empire. And the two European elements together were in a minority of one to four as compared with the non-Europeans—the native blacks, the East Indians (who had come in numbers as immigrants, especially to Natal), and the "colored" peoples of mixed blood. The seeds of the later troubles in South Africa were clearly present even in the hopeful days immediately after the establishment of the Union.

Egypt

At the opposite end of Africa, Britain during the second half of the nineteenth century excluded the French from control of Egypt, nominally a vassal state of the crumbling Ottoman Empire. French influence had continued there, even after the collapse of Napoleon's venture and the setback suffered in 1840 by Mohammed Ali, the ambitious viceroy of Egypt and protégé of France. In the third quarter of the nineteenth century, French prospects in Egypt seemed particularly bright. Between 1859 and 1869 a private French company headed by Ferdinand de Lesseps built the Suez Canal, which united the Mediterranean with the Red Sea and shortened the sea trip from Europe to India and the Far East by thousands of miles. The British had bitterly opposed the building of this canal under French patronage; but now that it was finished, the canal came to be considered an essential part of the "lifeline" of the British Empire.

The British secured a partial hold over this lifeline in 1875, when Disraeli arranged the purchase of 176,000 shares of stock in the canal company from the financially desperate khedive Ismail (1863–1879). The shares gave Britain a very large minority interest in the company, though not a controlling one. Despite the sale of the stock, Ismail's fiscal difficulties soon increased, for he was a heavy spender, partly on useful public improvements and partly on vainglorious items like the new title of khedive (Persian for "prince"), which the Ottoman emperor granted for a stiff price. In 1876, with Ismail's bankruptcy threatening, the European

guerrilla bands into which Boer opposition dissolved. In 1902, by the Treaty of Vereeniging, the Boers accepted British rule, with the promise of ultimate self-government. This promise the British fulfilled speedily. In 1910 there came into being a Union of South Africa, linking Cape Colony, Transvaal, Orange Free State, and Natal. In the new state the central government was stronger than the provinces; English and Afrikaans, as the South African Dutch dialect had come to be called, were set up as equally official languages.

On the eve of World War I, South Africa was among the self-governing British dominions. British and Boer seemed to be well on the way to powers from whose private banks Ismail had borrowed large sums at high interest obliged Egypt to accept the financial guidance of a debt commission that they set up. Two years later, he had to sacrifice still more sovereignty when he was obliged to appoint an Englishman as his minister of finance and a Frenchman as minister of public works, and in 1879 Ismail himself was sacrificed when his European creditors prevailed on the Ottoman emperor to depose him. Egyptian nationalists, led by army officers whose pay had been drastically cut as an economy move, now revolted both against foreign control and against the khedivial government that had made this control possible. Both Britain and France threatened to intervene with force, but when an antiforeign riot in Alexandria claimed some European lives in the summer of 1882, the French held back because of a cabinet crisis at home and also because they were involved in establishing themselves in Tunisia, occupied the year before.

These events constituted one of those "fits of absence of mind" through which Britain enlarged her empire. By the eve of World War I she exercised virtual sovereignty over Egypt. Legally Egypt was still part of the Ottoman Empire, and the khedive and his government remained. But a British Resident was always at hand to exercise quiet but firm control, and each ministry was guided by a British expert. For a quarter of a century this British protectorate was in the hands of the famous imperial proconsul, Lord Cromer, Resident in Cairo from 1883 to 1907. Under Cromer and his successors the enormous government debt was systematically paid off and a beginning made at modernizing Egypt, symbolized by the completion of the first dam on the Nile at Aswan, which increased the amount of water for irrigation and thus the potential agricultural output. But nationalist critics complained that this was too small a beginning, that too little was being spent on education and public health, and that British policy was entirely aimed at keeping Egypt in a colonial economic status, exporting long-staple cotton and procuring manufactured goods not from home industries but from Britain. Egyptian nationalists were also offended by British tentativeness in permitting experiments in representative government and by British policy toward the Sudan.

This vast region, south of Egypt, today the largest of African states in area, had been par-

"Moses in Egypt": A Tenniel cartoon of 1875 commenting on Disraeli's purchase of Ismail's interest in the Suez Canal. The title is borrowed from that of Rossini's opera.

tially conquered by Mohammed Ali and Ismail, then lost in the 1880's as a result of a revolt by an Islamic leader who called himself the mahdi (messiah). Fears that some other power, especially France, might gain control over the Nile headwaters vital to Egypt decided Britain to reconquer the Sudan. The reconquest was completed in 1898, just in time for the British commander, Kitchener, to march south from Khartoum, the Sudanese capital, and confront a French expedition that had traveled from the Atlantic coast of Africa and reached Fashoda on the upper Nile. Again the French could not press their claim, this time because the uproar over Dreyfus was at its peak, and the British made the Sudan an Anglo-Egyptian condominium, an enterprise in which they clearly intended to function as the senior partner. Egyptian nationalists feared that Egypt had lost a province, while

Britain had gained one more possession and a vital link in their dream of an "all-red route" (see below) from Cairo to the Cape.

The Rest of British Africa

In between the Cape and Cairo the British pieced out their African possessions throughout the century. At its end, they had the lion's share of the continent. They had only 4,000,000 square miles out of over 11,000,000, but they controlled 61,000,000 people out of some 100,000,000. A mere listing of these holdings would be a dull and unenlightening catalog. They can be found, usually colored red, in any good atlas of the turn of the century and, also with British possessions colored in red, on a famous Canadian postage stamp of 1898. A good sample of these colonies is Nigeria, in which the great administrator Sir Frederick (later Lord) Lugard worked out the characteristic British method of colonial government in tropical Africa that was known as indirect rule.

The colony and protectorate of Nigeria, centering around the great river Niger, was formally put together from earlier west African colonies in 1914. Northern Nigeria was ruled by Muslim emirs of the Fulani people whose culture was superior to that of the subject and exploited blacks; southern Nigeria was inhabited by numerous heathen tribes that had long been harassed by slave raids. The British had first to subject the Fulani by force, a process that was completed late in the nineteenth century.

They then applied, as a French statesman put it, "with method but not with system," what came to be called indirect rule. Emirs and chieftains were confirmed in their separate rules, subject to the banning of internal warfare, the abolition of slavery, and similar measures imposed from above. A British Resident supervised the rule of the leading chiefs, with district Residents (later Commissioners) to supplement the work in the local subdivisions. But native law, native religion, and native traditions, in so far as they did not conflict violently with Western standards, were carefully maintained. The British staff was never large; Lugard complained that in 1903 he had only one British administrator on the average for every 400,000 natives. But somehow the handful of imperial officials were able to ensure the peace. Slowly, much too slowly for impatient idealists, railroads, roads, improved agriculture, commerce, and education—the externals at least of Western civilization—were extended to Nigeria. Early in this century the first black African students began to appear in British universities. By mid-century, there was already a small Western-educated group of native Nigerians who were using English as their chief language.

Other British Spheres

In the Americas, Britain maintained her colonial dependencies in the Caribbean, in Bermuda and the Bahamas, and, on the mainland, in British Honduras and British Guiana. Limited self-government of the seventeenth-century kind, which some of them had lost in the mid-nineteenth century, was only gradually granted them in the twentieth. These were all tropical or semitropical lands, with a relatively small planter class and with large black or mixed lower classes. These lands suffered gradual impoverishment as a result of economic developments, notably the great competition offered to the staple cane sugar of the region by the growth in temperate climates of the beet-sugar industry, together with an increase in population beyond the limited resources of the region. By 1914, the British West Indies had already become an impoverished "problem area."

In the Pacific and in Southeast Asia, Britain in the nineteenth century added some red dots on the map of her empire, and especially in Malaya she developed the great industries of rubber and tin that were to be major factors in her economy after World War I. She took an important part in the process of opening China to Western trade by means of treaty-port concessions and spheres of influence. Indeed, Britain took one of the great steps in breaking down Chinese attempts to keep off the foreigner, for in 1841 she waged what has come to be called invidiously but not unjustly the Opium War. This war was brought on by a Chinese attempt to control the opium trade in which British merchants had an important stake. By the Treaty of Nanking in 1842, Britain acquired Hong Kong and secured the opening of five ports, including Canton and Shanghai.

India

In China, however, Britain was but one, though the most important, of the great powers scrambling for empire in that densely peopled land. In India her victory over France in 1763, confirmed by her victory in 1815, left her in sole control over a subcontinent of Asia, for the remnants of French and Portuguese possessions there hardly counted. India was the richest of Britain's overseas possessions, the center and symbol of empire, as the imaginative Disraeli realized when in 1876 he had Queen Victoria proclaimed empress of India.

In 1763, India was already a great and well-peopled land, but not, in the Western sense, a single *nation*. It was a vast congeries of races and religions, ranging from the most cultivated and philosophic Brahmins to the most primitive tribesmen, still in the Stone Age. As the nineteenth century began, the two main methods of British control had already become clear. The richest and most densely populated regions, centering on the cities of Calcutta, Madras, Bombay, and on the Punjab, were maintained under direct British control. The British government did not originally annex these lands; they were first administered as the property, so to speak, of the English East India Company, a chartered enterprise surviving from the great days of mercantilism in the seventeenth and eighteenth centuries. The company in its heyday, led by empire makers like Clive and Warren Hastings, had taken on enormous territories and made treaties like a sovereign power. Hastings was prosecuted for "high crimes and misdemeanors" in a famous trial of the late eighteenth century. But what he acquired the British kept.

In the nineteenth century, the company was regarded by most economists and political thinkers as a shocking anomaly, and the India Office of the central government in London gradually took over the real control and administration of British India. The trading monopoly of the company had long since been undermined. In 1857, the company's native army of Sepoys rebelled. As usual in such major uprisings, the rebellion was brought on by a number of causes, fed by rumors that bullets issued to soldiers were coated with grease made from beef fat, repugnant to

Hindus, or from pork fat, repugnant to Muslims. But the basic cause was that all the soldiers had come to fear that British ways were being imposed on them to the destruction of their own ways. The Sepoy Rebellion was put down, but not before several massacres of Europeans had occurred, and not without a serious military effort by the British. The mutiny meant the end of the English East India Company. In 1858, the British crown took over the company's lands and obligations, announcing that no further annexations were sought in India.

The rest of India—roughly a third of its area and a fourth or a fifth of its population—came to be known as the "feudal" or "native" states. These were left nominally under the rule of their own princes, who might be the fabulously rich sultan of Hyderabad or the gaekwar of Baroda, or merely a kind of local chieftain. The "native" states were actually governed by a system of British Residents somewhat like the system we have just seen in Nigeria. The India Office never hesitated to interfere with the succession, or to disallow acts of princes, who were frequently irresponsible and extravagant, or even to assume direct rule for a time when it was thought necessary. The "native" states add many picturesque notes to a detailed history of India, but in the long run the distinction between direct and indirect rule in India did not mean very much in practice.

The years between 1763 and 1919 in India are a fascinating record of what Arnold Toynbee, the philosopher of history, calls "contacts between civilizations." Indeed, anyone who wants to understand the great contemporary problem of relations between the West and the rest of the world—to use clear terms, between white peoples and colored peoples—will do well to learn all he can of this great meeting of East and West in the subcontinent of India.

In material terms, many phases of the British rule in India are readily measurable. In 1864, the British *Statesman's Year Book* gave the population of India as about 136,000,000, and in 1904 close to 300,000,000. Although the latter figure includes additional territories, in Burma and elsewhere, it is clear that nineteenth-century India experienced a significant increase in total population. In 1901, one male out of ten could read and write, a low rate of literacy by Western standards, but already a high one by contemporary Asian standards. It is characteristic of In-

Asia and the Pacific, 1910

British territory
British protected States
Dutch territory
French territory
German territory
Japan and Japanese territories
United States and possessions

1 Port Arthur (Jap.)
2 Wei-hai-wei (Br.)
3 Kiaochow Bay (Ger.)

CANADA

UNITED STATES

MEXICO

San Francisco

ALASKA (U.S.)

ALEUTIAN IS. (U.S.)

60

30

Pacific Ocean

International Date Line

MIDWAY IS. (U.S.)

HAWAIIAN ISLANDS (U.S.)
Honolulu

JOHNSTON (U.S.)

KINGMAN REEF (U.S.)
PALMYRA

HOWLAND (U.S.)
BAKER (Br.)

PHOENIX IS. (Br.)

AMERICAN SAMOA (U.S.)
W. SAMOA (Ger.)

WAKE I. (U.S.)

MARSHALL IS. (Ger.)

Equator 0

GILBERT IS. (Br.)

ELLICE IS. (Br.)

FIJI IS. (Br.)

(Russia) (U.S.)

KAMCHATKA

KURILE IS.

SAKHALIN

JAPAN
Tokyo
Kyoto
Seoul
KOREA
Vladivostok

Port Arthur
OKINAWA

FOOCHOW
FORMOSA

MARIANAS IS. (Ger.)

GUAM (U.S.)

CAROLINE ISLANDS (Ger.)

BISMARCK ARCH. (Ger.)

NEW GUINEA (Ger.)
(Port.)

SOLOMON IS. (Br.)

NEW HEBRIDES (Br. and Fr.)

NEW CALEDONIA (Fr.)

Auckland

NEW ZEALAND

30

150

180

S I B E R I A

R U S S I A

Lena R.

L. Baikal
Chita

Krasnoyarsk

TRANS-SIBERIAN RAILROAD

Omsk
Irtysh R.

Yenisei R.

Ob R.

Aral Sea

AFGHANISTAN

PUNJAB
(Port.)
Diu
Daman
Bombay
Goa
Mahé (Fr.)

Chandanagar (Fr.)
Calcutta
Yanaon (Fr.)
Madras
Pondichéry (Fr.)
Karikal (Fr.)

INDIA

CEYLON

NEPAL
BHUTAN

TIBET

SINKIANG

TANNU TUVA

MONGOLIA

MANCHURIA
Amur R.

Peking
Tientsin
Yellow R.
Nanking
Shanghai
Wenchow
CHINA
Yangtze R.

YUNNAN
Canton
Hong Kong (Br.)
Macao (Port.)
Kwangchou (Fr.)

SIAM

BURMA

INDO-CHINA
Saigon
Mekong R.

FED. MALAY STATES (Br.)
Singapore

SUMATRA
Batavia
JAVA

DUTCH EAST INDIES
BORNEO
CELEBES
TIMOR (Port.)

Brisbane

QUEENSLAND

NORTHERN TERRITORY

WESTERN AUSTRALIA

SOUTH AUSTRALIA

AUSTRALIA

NEW SOUTH WALES
Sydney
Canberra
VICTORIA
Melbourne
Adelaide

Perth

TASMANIA

Indian Ocean

120

90

60

Philippine Islands inset

PHILIPPINE ISLANDS (U.S.)

Pacific Ocean

LUZON
Manila
MINDORO
PANAY
NEGROS
PALAWAN
SAMAR
LEYTE
MINDANAO

South China Sea

BORNEO

Miles
0   200

120

dian society that the comparable figures for women in the same census of 1901 show that only one out of one hundred and fifty could read and write.

Such statistics are plentiful, and what they show is an India on the eve of World War I with thousands of miles of railroads, telegraph lines, universities (teaching in English), hospitals, factories, and great and busy seaports. But, in proportion to the total population, India did not have these advantages to anything like the extent that even the poorest of European countries had them. Statistics show a native ruling class sometimes fantastically rich, and an immense peasant class for the most part living as their ancestors had lived, on the edge of starvation. A middle class was just beginning to form, and, like all the middle classes formed in non-European lands under European penetration, it had proportionately far more aspirants to genteel white-collar posts in the older "liberal" professions than to posts in commerce, engineering, and industry, to say nothing of scientific research.

The total wealth of India certainly increased under British rule in this century and a half, and in 1914 it was spread more widely among the Indian populations, save for the most primitive areas, than it had been in 1763. Proportionately less and less wealth went directly from an "exploited" India to an "exploiting" Britain. The familiar Englishman of the seventeenth and eighteenth centuries, the "nabob" who made a fortune in India and retired with it to comfort, and perhaps to a peerage, in England, almost ceased to exist as the nineteenth century wore on. Anglo-Indian economic relations took on more and more the form of trade between a developed industrial and financial society in Britain and a society geared to the production of raw materials—we should now call it an "underdeveloped" society—in India. In this trade, native Indians took an increasing part if only as middlemen, and toward the end of the century native industries, notably textile manufacturing, financed for the most part with British capital, began to arise in India.

Throughout the century, of course, a large number of British—small in proportion to the total population, but numbering in the thousands—were basically supported by the Indian economy; they "lived off India." Some of them were private businessmen, but the greater number were military and civilian workers, the latter the celebrated Indian civil service who "ran"

India. Yet natives were gradually working their way into positions of greater responsibility, into both private and public posts at the policy-making level.

Of this British ruling class in India one very important fact is now plain. It did not, like the English and Scots who went to Ireland in early modern times, really take root in India. Britain—one must be careful not to say "England," for the Scots played a conspicuous role in India as they did throughout the empire—was always "home," always the place where one hoped to end one's days. Though son not infrequently followed father in the Indian army or civil service, or even in business, these "sahibs" as a whole never became fully adjusted to life in India. The spiritual climate was perhaps an even greater barrier than the physical climate. Here is a letter from an Englishwoman in Madras in 1837:

It is wonderful how little interested most of the English ladies seem by all the strange habits and ways of the natives. . . .

I asked one lady what she had seen of the country and the natives since she had been in India. "Oh, nothing!" said she: "thank goodness, I know nothing at all about them, nor I don't wish to: really I think the less one sees and knows of them the better!"

The natives, too, often found the gap between East and West too great to be bridged. Another Englishwoman writes in 1913:

Coming home we saw a native cooking his dinner on a little charcoal fire, and as I passed he threw the contents of the pot away. Surprised, I asked why. "Because," I was told, "your shadow fell on it and defiled it!" *

Yet the work of raising the economic basis of Indian life was in large part the work of the British. They were often overbearing, insensitive, white men at their worst in their dealings with the natives. But they were, more often than the doctrinaire anti-imperialist will admit, men devoted to the task of bettering the lot of their charges, men who made a real effort to understand them. Some of them studied with Western scholarly methods the past and present of Indian culture and society, thus laying the foundations on which Indian scholars now build.

* Hilton Brown, ed., *The Sahibs* (London, 1948), pp. 225, 230.

III   The Other Empires

The French

The British victory in the "Second Hundred Year's War," capped by their defeat of Napoleon in 1815, had stripped France of all but insignificant remnants of her former empire. Yet during the nineteenth century France succeeded in building up a new colonial empire second in area only to that of the British. France, despite her frequent revolutionary changes in government, maintained an imperialist policy that added in the century before 1914 close to three and a half million square miles to the lands under the French flag, and some fifty million people, almost all non-European. The figures for area are somewhat misleading, for a million and a half square miles are included in the Sahara Desert, which is almost uninhabited.

Little of this second French colonial empire was suitable for settlement by Europeans. The great exception was French North Africa, including Tunisia, Algeria, and Morocco. As the provinces of Africa and Mauretania, these lands were once flourishing parts of the Roman Empire; after France took them over, they reached a greater degree of material prosperity than they had enjoyed for nearly eighteen centuries. These lands, which have a typically Mediterranean climate, were inhabited chiefly by Berber and Arab peoples of Muslim faith. Though the total native population increased greatly under French rule, something over a million European colonists moved in. In majority French, but with sizable groups of Italians and Spaniards, these colonists took some land from the natives, though they added to the total arable acreage by initiating irrigation projects and other improvements. They remained, however, an alien group.

The French got a toehold in North Africa in 1830 through an expedition against the Algerian pirates, with whose Tripolitan counterparts, incidentally, the United States had fought in 1801. The French stayed on, and it took them forty years to pacify the hinterland of Algiers in the face of stubborn native resistance. They added protectorates over Tunisia to the east (1881) and over Morocco to the west (1912). In 1904 Britain gave the French a free hand in Morocco as compensation for their exclusion from Egypt.

Especially in Algeria and Tunisia, the French promoted European settlement while trying what they thought was reasonably hard not to antagonize the natives. They called their policy one of "assimilation," in contrast with the British policy of hands off and indirect rule. They hoped, they explained, to assimilate Africans into French civilization, making them ultimately into good children of the eighteenth-century Enlightenment, good citizens of the republic founded on the principles of 1789. They hoped to create an empire of "100,000,000 Frenchmen," more than half of them overseas, and to draw on abundant native manpower to fill up the ranks of the republic's armies.

In the military sense, the policy of assimilation worked out somewhat as the French had hoped; in the main, however, assimilation was difficult and only partially successful. The French, always desirous of spreading their culture, did indeed assimilate part of the native ruling classes. Under the Third Republic they made Algeria politically a part of France itself, organizing it into three departments and giving them representatives to the Chamber of Deputies, with a franchise open to the relatively small group of europeanized natives as well as to colonists. In Morocco, the French took a somewhat different tack. They sought, in part successfully, to open this backward land to French business and to the international tourist trade. Their urban center of Casablanca became a great modern city. And, without quite admitting the fact, they really abandoned assimilation for something close to the British policy of indirect rule. In 1912, the very able colonial administrator Marshal Lyautey began to organize turbulent Morocco, applying the "splash of oil" policy—that is, he pacified certain key centers by establishing firm working relations with the natives and then let pacification spread over the surface of Morocco like a splash of oil on water. The sultan and his feudal subordinates were maintained in Morocco, relatively free to carry on many of their age-old ways but stripped of real power. Tunisia, like Morocco, was formally a protectorate (technically, a "regency"). Because it was small and easily pacified, assimilation worked more successfully in Tunisia than it did in other French possessions, thereby giving the Tunisians a head start in modernization when France relinquished her North African empire.

In 1815, the British had left France her small posts in West Africa at the mouth of the Senegal River, together with the slight foothold France had obtained in the seventeenth century on the great island of Madagascar off the East African coast. By 1914, the French had been very successful in the partition of Africa, perhaps at bottom because the British preferred French to German aggrandizement, especially after 1870. By 1914, at any rate, France numbered in Africa alone nearly as many inhabitants as in her home territories (about 39,000,000).

Except in North Africa, these people were almost all blacks of primitive material culture who were for the most part untouched by either Islam or Christianity. Except in certain coastal towns, where their administration and business were concentrated, the French had not by 1914 achieved very much toward assimilating or westernizing these vast districts. Most of their attempts to hasten the economic development of their African lands by organized joint-stock companies failed miserably.

It is quite possible that France spent more on these African colonies than she gained from them. Indeed, one of the stock arguments of nineteenth-century anti-imperialists was that colonies did not "pay" the mother country, and the French African colonies were one of their favorite exhibits. One economist—an Englishman, to be sure, and presumably unmoved by much that moves Frenchmen—concluded that in 1892 French gains from colonial trade were 16,000,000 francs, whereas net government expenditures for the colonies were 174,000,000 francs. For 1915, he made an even more discouraging estimate.* Such figures, however, seem not to have discouraged any of the great powers in their imperialist efforts. Obviously the simplest form of the economic interpretation of history, the notion that political entities are moved by simple bookkeeping concepts of governmental economic profit and loss, does not hold true for nineteenth-century imperialism. Furthermore, note that such statistics apply solely to government expenditures; many French private businessmen undoubtedly made money out of their colonial ventures.

Again, though French colonies in tropical Africa had by no means been modernized even in material conditions by 1914, everywhere a beginning had been made. Everywhere the tricolor went, there also went the beginnings of medicine and hygiene, modern methods of communication, industry, and agriculture, and formal education for at least a few natives. In justifying the policy of assimilation, the French claimed for themselves, in contrast with the British, a lack of race prejudice, a willingness to accept the blacks as equals. This contrast is underlined by the English author whose figures we have just quoted:

Of course, it is true that the French also attempt to understand the native and in the main to give him freedom to produce as he pleases. The Frenchman actually tends much more to be a "good fellow" with the natives than does the Briton, who is much more aloof. But this greater democracy does not seem to inspire a greater degree of confidence. Somehow, the Briton is more apt to succeed in instilling in the native confidence in the results of producing by the system that he recommends.*

Although there is some truth in the claim for greater French toleration, the deed is not quite up to the word. The French in Africa did not often marry blacks; but intermarriage is in this real world an unreal test of racial equality. Blacks very rarely commanded white Frenchmen in military or civilian activity. Both at home and in Africa, on the other hand, once the blacks seemed firmly under control, the French went a long way toward encouraging black arts and folkways, in keeping with a policy very close to the ideal delineated by Lugard for Nigeria. The British, however, especially in the twentieth century, edged toward some kind of assimilation; black African undergraduates in British universities took on a lot more of Britishness than just their fine standard English accent. The contrast between British and French African policies was far from complete—there were many similarities.

In Asia, the French took over in the nineteenth century lands that came to be called

* Constant Southworth, *The French Colonial Venture* (London, 1931), p. 122.

* Ibid., p. 193.

The French capture of Sontay (Indo-China) in 1883.

French Indo-China. These lands included two rich rice-growing deltas (around Hanoi in the north and Saigon in the south), inhabited by peoples culturally and in part racially related to the Chinese. They also included Cambodia, culturally related to India, and the primitive mountain peoples of Laos. French experience here on the whole ran parallel to imperialist experience elsewhere in Southeast Asia, though the Anglo-Saxon fondness for nagging the French has tended to create the impression that the French did far worse in Indo-China than did the Dutch in Java or the British in Malaya. Slow but real material progress was made, though the basic problem of poverty among the masses remained unsolved. Native nationalist movements, nourished by educated natives with jobs of less dignity and authority than they believed should be theirs, rose in strength as the years went on. France also took part, from her base in Indo-China, in the struggle for control of China proper. The French sphere of influence was southern China, in particular the province of Yunnan adjoining Indo-China, and in the year 1898 the French got a lease on a port in Kwang-chou Bay.

The Germans

We can be brief in listing the colonial acquisitions of the other powers. Germany and Italy came late to the imperial scramble, as they came late to national unity. Nevertheless, Germany was clearly a great power, and Italy aspired to be one; hence, both sought to acquire the token colonies, at least, that seemed necessary to that dignified status—the familiar policy of keeping up with the Joneses. Germany in 1914 had three really large pieces of tropical and subtropical Africa—the Kameruns (Cameroons), German Southwest Africa, and German East Africa—and the smaller Togoland, close to a million square miles in all, nearly four times the size of Texas. These were not rich or well-developed areas, and their total contribution to the German economy was almost negligible. The German achievement on the whole was not greatly different from that of other European powers in Africa; it was neither morally nor economically much better or much worse. In the Pacific, the Germans picked up some small islands, and a large, primitive territory on the island of New Guinea. Germany took part in the attempted partition of China; her ninety-nine-year lease was on Kiaochow Bay.

The German drive for colonies was quite self-conscious; it was well organized in a pressure group with all the fixings of modern propaganda. Bismarck himself, who cared little for the prestige of colonies, was obliged to give way and consent to African ventures. His successors went farther, and William II helped Germany to enter one of the most confused and dangerous fields of imperialist expansion, the Near East. On the eve of World War I, the German "Berlin to Baghdad" push was well under way, and the Germans had supplanted the British as patrons of the Turks.

The Italians and Belgians

Italy, condemned to the role of weakest of the great powers, got very little even out of the partition of Africa. Tunis, which she coveted, went instead to France. Italy's major effort centered on the African lands at the southern end of the Red Sea, but after her defeat by the Abyssinians under Menelek in 1896 she had to content herself with a few thousand square miles, most of it desert, in Eritrea and Somaliland. Italian efforts to add to this inadequate empire by taking Tripoli from its nominal Turkish suzerain succeeded in 1912, and they also secured the island of Rhodes and the smaller islands of the Dodecanese off the southwestern corner of Anatolia. But these same efforts caused the Italo-Turkish war of 1911–1912, which was in a sense the real beginning of World War I.

Little Belgium, largely through the enterprise of her king Leopold II (1865–1909), managed to acquire a large piece of equatorial Africa. This project began as the Congo Free State, with all sorts of noble ideals of cooperative European civilizing missions in Africa; but it ended up in 1908 as simply the Belgian Congo. Nineteenth-century scandal about forced labor and native exploitation in the Congo called Leopold's experiment to the attention of the world and provided anti-imperialists with fresh arguments. The Belgians soon moderated Leopold's policies and developed the Congo into one of the most profitable of colonies, thanks to its copper, rubber, and other riches. They made no move to groom the Congolese for eventual self-government, however.

The Americans

To the horror and indignation of many Americans, to the delight of others, the United States at the very end of the century joined the great powers and acquired overseas lands. In 1898, the United States waged a brief and successful war with Spain, for which the immediate cause was the still mysterious sinking of the American battleship *Maine* in the harbor of Havana, Cuba. The Spanish-American War left the United States in control of the remnants of the Spanish Empire in America (the Caribbean islands of Cuba and Puerto Rico) and the large archipelago of the Philippines (about the size of Montana) off the coast of Asia. Meantime, the United States also acquired Hawaii (1898) and part of the Samoan Islands in the Pacific (1899). In 1903 American support of a revolution in Panama, then a part of Colombia, assured the independence of a new republic and direct American control of the zone of the projected Panama Canal.

The Americans withdrew from Cuba, leaving her as an independent republic, though subject under the Platt Amendment of 1901 to what in foreign eyes always seemed American "protection." The Platt Amendment, named from its proposer, Senator Orville Platt of Connecticut, limited Cuban control of its foreign policy and its national debt and gave the United States the formal right to intervene to preserve Cuban independence. It was resented bitterly by Cuban patriots as an infringement of Cuban sovereignty and was given up by the United States in 1934. The rest of her acquisitions the United States kept for the time, though in the Philippines she had to put down an armed rising by Filipinos who wanted immediate independence. American anti-imperialists attempted to upset the somewhat anomalous arrangement under which their government kept lands without strict authorization from the American Constitution. But a Supreme Court decision in the so-called Insular Cases (1901) held that territory might be subject to American jurisdiction without being incorporated constitutionally in the United States of

Theodore Roosevelt: "The World's Constable." A cartoon by Dalrymple, 1905.

America. Under this decision, Americans began the process of training the Filipinos for eventual independence. Meanwhile, the United States, too, had an empire, which on the maps was duly colored as an American "possession."

The Japanese

One more empire was being formed during the decades before World War I, the only empire to be created by a people of non-European stock —the Japanese. Even during their long self-imposed isolation the Japanese had maintained an interest in Western developments through the trading station that the Dutch were allowed at Nagasaki. When Japan was opened to the world in 1853, its basic political and economic structure had long needed overhauling. An oligarchy of the feudal type ruled, but its ineffective government made it widely unpopular. Discontent was growing, especially among two important social classes. One was the urban middle class of merchants and craftsmen. Although the Industrial Revolution had not yet reached Japan,

the country already had populous cities, notably Tokyo (then called Yedo or Edo). The urban middle class, somewhat like the French bourgeoisie on the eve of 1789, wanted political rights to match their increasing economic power. The other discontented class may be compared roughly with the poorer gentry and lesser nobility of Europe under the Old Regime. These were the *samurai* or feudal retainers, a military caste now threatened with impoverishment and political eclipse. The samurai dreaded the growth of cities and the subsequent threat to the traditional domination of agriculture and the landlords; many of them also resented the fact that they were largely excluded from positions of power by the prevailing olgarchical regime. These social pressures, more than any outside Western influence, forced the moderization of Japan.

Economically, the transformation proceeded rapidly. By 1914, much of Japan resembled an advanced Western country. She, too, had railroads, fleets of merchant vessels, a large textile industry, big cities, and big business firms. The industrialization of Japan was the more remarkable in view of her meager supplies of many essential raw materials. But she had many impor-

Commodore Perry's landing in Japan.

tant assets. As a glance at the map will show, her geographical position with respect to Asia is very like that of the British Isles with respect to Europe. Japan, too, found markets for her exports on the continent nearby and used the income to pay for imports. The ambitious Japanese middle class, supplemented by recruits from the samurai, furnished aggressive business leadership. A great reservoir of cheap labor existed in the peasantry, a large and submissive class. The peasants, who needed to find jobs away from the overcrowded farms, were inured to a very low standard of living and were ready to work long and hard in factories for what seemed by Western standards indecently low wages.

Politically, Japan appeared to undergo a major revolution in the late nineteenth century and to remodel her government along Western lines.

Actually, however, the change was by no means so great as it seemed. A revolution did indeed occur, beginning in 1868 when the old feudal oligarchy crumbled under the pressure of the discontented elements. Authority and prestige were restored to the position of mikado (emperor), a largely forgotten office whose incumbents had for years had no real power. In 1889, the emperor bestowed a constitution on his subjects, with a bicameral diet composed of a noble House of Peers and an elected House of Representatives.

The architects of these changes, however, were not democrats. They were aristocrats, ambitious young samurai, supported by allies from the business world and determined to make Japan over from above as they wished. The result was to substitute a new oligarchy for the old; a small group of aristocrats dominated the emperor and the state. The Constitution of 1889, rather like that of the German Empire, provided only the outward appearances of liberal parliamentary government. The ministry was responsible not to the diet but to the emperor, and hence to the dominant ruling class. The diet itself was scarcely representative; the right to vote for members of its lower house was limited to a narrow electorate, including the middle class but excluding the peasants and industrial workers. As Sir George Sansom, a British expert on Japan, has observed, she had no trouble in accepting Western "things" but a great deal in handling Western "ideas."

Japan began her expansion by taking from China, after a brief war in 1894–1895, the island of Formosa, which she annexed, and the piece of Asiatic mainland closest to Japan, the peninsula of Korea, whose independence China was forced to recognize as a preliminary to eventual Japanese annexation. But Russia, too, had designs on Korea; the results of this rivalry were the Russo-Japanese War of 1904–1905 and a second great Japanese victory. Japan now secured unchallenged preponderance in Korea, which she annexed in 1910, special concessions in the Chinese province of Manchuria, and the cession by Russia of the southern half of the island of Sakhalin, to the north of the main Japanese islands. She had expanded in the classic European way by collecting an empire.

IV   The Debate Over Imperialism

In the nineteenth century all the Western countries, even monarchical states like Germany, had a wide range of free public opinion and some kind of government by discussion. The kind of expansion we call imperialism, therefore, had to be defended articulately, since it was attacked articulately. The defense and attack are both important parts of modern intellectual history.

The Argument from Social Darwinism

One central argument for the defense borrowed heavily from the Social Darwinists. Europeans both in Europe and in their "colonies of settlement," so ran the argument, were able to beat non-Europeans in war. By this very fact they had shown that they were in terms of evolution and progress more fit to survive than were the non-Europeans. Eternal competition is the price of survival and the best always survive—or *ought* to survive, for these theorists of imperialism had already begun to worry a bit. White men, this argument insisted, are simply better specimens of *Homo sapiens* than are colored men; Anglo-Saxons (or Germans, or Slavs, or Latins, depending on the writer's origins) are simply better specimens than other white men.

An imperialist like Cecil Rhodes, to judge from much that he wrote and said, very likely dreamed of a world which in the fullness of time and evolution would be peopled entirely by Anglo-Saxons. Their breed would actually be improved over their ancestors of 1900, after the inferior peoples had died out—or had been killed off. But these were very distant views indeed. The prospect of ruddy Kentish farmers actually established in freeholds along the Congo simply was unrealistic. More fashionable imperialistic doctrine held that throughout the tropical world, the superior white men would put order and prosperity into the lives of colored men, would as trustees of civilization give up the comforts of Europe to rule in discomfort in the hot countries. Some imperialists thought that this benevolent rule of white men in the tropics would last indefinitely, since in their opinion nonwhites were totally unable to undertake tasks of leadership and to assume moral responsibility.

The Argument of Duty

Other European imperialists, however, took the attitude that, though the nonwhites could not run their own affairs then, they could ultimately learn to do so. For the present and for a good many years to come, whites would have to educate them on the spot; someday—the length of time judged necessary varied with the temperament of the judge—these nonwhites would have matured sufficiently to take over responsibilities now confined to whites. These whites will not be owners, merely trustees. Kipling put the case comfortably enough—for white men—in his famous poem:

Take up the White Man's Burden—
 Send forth the best ye breed—
Go bind your sons to exile
 To serve your captives' need;
To wait in heavy harness,
 On fluttered folk and wild—
Your new-caught, sullen peoples,
 Half-devil and half-child.*

This argument of trusteeship was by all odds the most popular defense of imperialism, particularly among Anglo-Saxon peoples.

Yet the historian, aware of the complexities of human nature, will be wary of the notion that

* By permission of Mrs. George Bambridge and Macmillan & Co. Ltd.

A caricature of Rudyard Kipling, "with Britannia, 'is girl," by Max Beerbohm.

the ethical arguments of the imperialists were insincere. Many a European both in and out of the colonies of exploitation really believed in the trusteeship theory, and really did his best to live up to it. The Christian missionary was a major factor in the nineteenth-century expansion of the West. Kenneth Latourette's long and thorough history of the expansion of Christianity has a final volume entitled The Great Century for the nineteenth. More formal converts to Christianity were made all over the world in this century, so often labeled the century of materialism, than ever before.

The reality of the conversion of the colored peoples presents a difficult problem. In areas of primitive culture, whole tribes nominally accepted Christianity but continued many of the immemorial ways of their heathen past. In India, China, and Japan, old civilized countries with deep-rooted religious faiths of their own, Christianity did not win over anything like a majority of the people. Nevertheless, the missions did succeed in the course of the century in building up devoted native followers, of whom the most intelligent or most enterprising were often sent to Europe or the United States to complete their education.

The Defensive Argument

Finally, the imperialist philosophy of 1900 was by no means based on an unworried sense of white supremacy. Western civilization is one of the most worrying of all civilizations. Many publicists regarded imperialism as essentially defensive. The whites, outnumbered in a harsh world, had to organize themselves and hold the nonwhites off. There was talk of the "yellow peril" and of white "race suicide." The writings and speeches of such apparently confident imperialists as Rhodes, Kipling, the German emperor William II, and Theodore Roosevelt sounded this curious note of fear and uncertainty. We are the best, but really we are a little too good for this world; we cannot breed fast enough.

Another variant of the defensive argument hinged on the necessity of securing naval bases and coaling stations, the latter particularly important at a time when vessels had to refuel relatively frequently because of their dependence on coal. Here the British took the lead, with their enormous navy and merchant marine, and the sun never set on the bases strung along their imperial lifeline, from Gibraltar and Malta in the Mediterranean on east of Suez to Aden, at the southwestern tip of the Arabian peninsula, and to Singapore, off the southern end of Malaya. Other powers also raced to acquire bases and stations, notably along the Yellow Sea between China and Korea where Wei-hai-wei was British, Kiaochow Bay German, and Port Arthur first Russian and then, after 1905, Japanese.

Anti-Imperialist Arguments

Against imperialism, opponents marshaled a great many arguments. To the Social Darwinists the anti-imperialists replied by denying that the struggle for existence applied to human groups in the way it applied to plants and animals. It is precisely by sublimating the crude conflict of kill-or-be-killed into the higher rivalry for cultural excellence, they argued, that human societies transcend the struggle for life. Each group, each race, has something to contribute to the total of civilization, and the deliberate destruction or suppression of any group lames and lessens the others, prevents the true working out of evolution—that is, *cultural* evolution—among human beings as contrasted with mere animals. The anti-imperialists also brought forward very prominently the economic argument we have already noted. They worked hard to show that in fact, especially in Africa, colonies did not "pay," that the imperialist appeal to self-interest in the homeland was a delusion, the dishonest work of propagandists for the privileged minority in the homeland and in the colonies who *did* profit personally from imperialist ventures.

From this point the anti-imperialists went on to maintain that support at home for colonial expansion rested therefore on the ordinary man's vicarious satisfactions from national achievements. The ordinary man liked to see his country figure in the world atlas as an imperial power. He liked to think of Britain's empire on which the sun never set; or, if he was a Frenchman, of the tangible evidence that France was still a great power, still carrying on her *mission civilisatrice;* or, if he was an Italian, that at last Italy too was a nation, and behaving as nations should. The anti-imperialists were on the whole not very

successful in their attempts to use ridicule and irony against behavior that they found irrational. But their conviction that human action ought to be rational and devoted to the greatest good of the greatest number placed them firmly in the liberal tradition.

So strong was the anti-imperialists' belief that they were right—in spite of the growth of empires all about them—that in Britain the school of "Little Englanders," much influenced by laissez-faire economics, came to the comforting assurance that imperialism was impossible. The colonies, they held, must inevitably drop away from the mother country—to use their favorite stereotype—like ripe fruit from a tree. Why not then avoid getting into the futile process further by *not* taking any more of Africa or China? Why not hasten the inevitable by giving up the empire? In fairness, we must add that much liberal opposition to imperialism was motivated by humanitarian sympathy for the colored peoples under imperial rule.

Not all the anti-imperialists were liberals or idealists. Indeed in France some of the most vehement were the extreme nationalists who wanted *revanche* (revenge) on Prussia for the French defeat in the war of 1870. These *revanchards* were not sorry for the blacks; they opposed French colonialism because it distracted French energies from what they thought was the sole proper national business—getting ready to beat the Germans.

What sank into the mind and feelings of the ordinary Westerner as a result of the anti-imperialist arguments was an uneasy awareness that somehow the practice of imperial expansion did not square with the best avowed intentions of democracy. Particularly in the United States, the feeling grew that imperialism and colonialism were contrary to the ideas of liberty and equality, even if the imperialists honestly claimed to be following the "trusteeship" principle. America took over an empire in 1898, but not without vigorous protests from numerous groups of anti-imperialists, and not without specific promises from the government that it would "free" dependents the moment they were capable of self-rule. This opposition of Americans to colonialism, especially when practiced by themselves, is one of the important factors in the contemporary world situation. We shall return to it in later chapters, for it played a large part in American foreign policy.

V   The Colonies of White Settlement

Thus far our account of the nineteenth-century expansion of Europe has been limited largely to the "colonies of exploitation," the protectorates, and the spheres of influence held by Europeans. No such account is at all complete, for the most striking thing about this expansion was that it involved an actual transplantation of Europeans to "colonies of settlement" on a scale incomparably greater than in the previous three centuries since Henry the Navigator and Columbus.

The colonies of settlement were originally very thinly inhabited lands. Australia, indeed, was almost empty; and the whole native Red Indian population of America north of the Rio Grande was almost certainly in 1800 not over a million, perhaps less. The European settlers simply overwhelmed these primitive peoples. In Tasmania, a large island to the south of the Australian mainland, the natives were totally wiped out, and in Australia itself they were very nearly wiped out. In the United States the Red Indians were so far eliminated that many an American grew up in the later nineteenth century without ever so much as seeing a redman except perhaps in a Wild West show.

In most of Latin America, however, the native Indian stock, far from being wiped out, persisted; the upper class, politically and economically, was drawn from European "creole" stock; and a great many people of mixed European and Indian and Negro blood filled the lower social ranks. In the far south of the continent, in the Argentine, Uruguay, and Chile, conditions resembled more nearly those in the United States, and these twentieth-century nations are now almost wholly European in stock, largely from the Iberian peninsula and Italy.

The expansion of Europe into the Americas was also an expansion of Africa. By 1850 the leading European powers had pretty generally got the slave trade under control; but the nucleus of blacks brought into both North and South America by the trade in the earlier centuries continued to grow. Despite handicaps of race barriers, strongest in the United States, the blacks multiplied; by 1900, for example, there were some 9,000,000 of them in the United States.

Canada

Apart from the extraordinary growth of the United States, the most important phase of the nineteenth-century movement of Europeans overseas is the growth of what is now called the British Commonwealth of Nations, or, more correctly, simply the Commonwealth. Doubtless it is an oversimplification to claim that the British learned their lesson from the American Revolution, and that consequently in Canada, Australia, and South Africa they were wise enough to abandon the policies of George III and Lord North. But the formula is fundamentally sound. The first laboratory for this experiment in a new kind of "colonialism" was Canada.

The rebellious thirteen colonies of North America had wanted to add a fourteenth, and had tried hard to win Canada. But a complex of causes all contributed to leaving Canada in British hands at the peace in 1783. The Catholic French Canadians in Quebec distrusted the new Protestant power growing up to the south; the American rebels had grave difficulties keeping up an army to cope with the British in the United States itself; America's French ally did not wish the new country to be too strong. Later, the United States failed in the War of 1812 to reverse the verdict of 1783.

Upper Canada (Ontario), which was mainly British in stock, and Lower Canada (Quebec), which was mainly French, and the Maritime Provinces of Nova Scotia, New Brunswick, and Prince Edward Island were at first quite separate British "colonies," as the American thirteen had once been. Each had an apparatus quite like the old American one—a royal governor appointed by the Crown, a council appointed by the governor, and an elected assembly based on a more or less popular franchise. But just as in the thirteen colonies during the preceding century, the arrangement bred conflicts between

GREENLAND

0   500   1000
Miles

ALASKA

YUKON

NORTH WEST TERRITORIES

C A N A D A

Hudson's Bay

NEWFOUNDLAND

BRITISH COLUMBIA
1871

ALBERTA
1905

SASKATCH-EWAN
1905

MANITOBA
1870

ONTARIO
1867

QUEBEC
1867

ST. PIERRE AND MIQUELON (Fr.)

Vancouver

Winnipeg

1867 P.E.I.

1867 NOVA SCOTIA

NEW BRUNSWICK 1867

L. Superior

Quebec
Montreal
Ottawa

St. Lawrence R.

Pacific Ocean

L. Michigan

L. Huron

L. Ontario

L. Erie

Boston

New York
Philadelphia

Chicago

Detroit

Washington, D. C.

San Francisco

U N I T E D   S T A T E S

Missouri R.

St. Louis

Ohio R.

Atlantic Ocean

BERMUDA (Br.)

Los Angeles

Colorado R.

Mississippi R.

New Orleans

Platt Amendment, 1901

Rio Grande

MEXICO

Tampico

Mexico City

Vera Cruz

Gulf of Mexico

Havana

BAHAMAS (Br.)

CUBA

Santiago

JAMAICA (Br.)

HAITI

DOM. REP.

PUERTO RICO (U.S. 1898)

VIRGIN ISLANDS (Den.)

ST. KITTS (Br.)

BARBUDA (Br.)
ANTIGUA (Br.)
GUADELOUPE (Fr.)
DOMINICA (Br.)
MARTINIQUE (Fr.)
BARBADOS (Br.)
ST. VINCENT (Br.)
GRENADA (Br.)
TOBAGO (Br.)
TRINIDAD (Br.)

ST. LUCIA (Br.)

BR. HONDURAS

HONDURAS

GUATEMALA
Guatemala

EL SALVADOR

Managua

NICARAGUA

COSTA RICA
San Jose

PANAMA

Caribbean Sea

(Dutch) CURAÇAO
ARUBA   BONAIRE

VENEZUELA

COLOMBIA

GUIANAS

BR.   DU.   FR.

British
Danish
Dutch
French
Independent
United States and possessions

North America and the Caribbean, 1910

Dates indicate year of admittance into Dominion of Canada

the assemblies and the royal government. In 1837, revolts broke out in both Upper and Lower Canada, with popular leaders like Mackenzie and Papineau arrayed against the governor and his followers, and with essentially the same kind of constitutional and financial grievances that the thirteen colonies had had sixty years before.

The revolt of 1837 was a military fiasco, and it is probable that public opinion in both provinces was against the rebels; there was a fear that too close an imitation of the American Revolution would lead to absorption by the United States. But the British government was alarmed and sent out as governor-in-chief of all the British North American provinces the earl of Durham, a young lord of Whig antecedents and Utilitarian leanings. Durham, feeling that he was not properly supported from London, resigned after less than a year in Canada. But the famous report he made to the British Parliament on his return in 1839 became the cornerstone of the new British imperial structure of dominions, a constitutional document that Durham's admirers have sometimes ranked with Magna Carta.

The Durham Report proposed the union of Upper and Lower Canada and the establishment of responsible government—that is, a popularly elected legislature with ultimate authority—for both the union and each of the separate provinces. The report is still of great interest. Durham had all the average Englishman's insensitivity to things French, and it is an understatement to say that he never understood the Québecois of Lower Canada. But he was true to his principles—even these French Canadian Catholics must have their own responsible government. As he wrote, with prescience:

The maintenance of an absolute form of government on any part of the North American Continent can never continue for any long time, without exciting a general feeling in the United States against a power of which the existence is secured by means so odious to the people; and as I rate the preservation of the present general sympathy of the United States with the policy of our Government in Lower Canada as a matter of the greatest importance, I should be sorry that the feeling should be changed for one which, if prevalent among the people, must extend over the surrounding Provinces. The influence of such an opinion would not only act very strongly on the entire French population, and keep up among them a sense of injury and a determination of resistance to the Government, but would lead to just as great discontent among the English. . . .*

The actual realization of Durham's recommendations was achieved with due British slowness. The first step, passed by the British Parliament in 1840, the Union Act though uniting both Upper and Lower Canada, was at the very least unspecific on the critical point of responsibility—that is, on whether an administration defeated in the legislature had to resign or not. Nearly a decade later, under the governorship of Lord Elgin, the principle was quietly established in practice, never to be withdrawn. Nor was the next step unduly hurried. The British North America Act of 1867 achieved in principle the union of all the British provinces in North America, except Newfoundland, oldest of all,

* Sir Reginald Coupland, *The Durham Report* (Oxford, 1954), pp. 155-156.

whose separatist tendencies were so strong that it did not join Canada until 1949. The act of 1867, itself basically due to formal Canadian initiative at a meeting of the "Fathers of Confederation" at Charlottetown, set up the Dominion of Canada by the union of Ontario, Quebec, and the Maritime Provinces, with provision for the admission of territories in the west as provinces on something like the pattern for admission of the western states in the United States. There were still many survivals of the former "colonial" status of Canada, from the bestowal of titles, especially knighthood with its unrepublican and undemocratic "Sir," to the possibility of judicial appeal from Canadian courts to the Privy Council in Westminster. Above all, the relation of Canada to Britain in terms of international affairs, armed forces, right of secession, and much else was not yet spelled out, nor was it to be formally until the Statute of Westminster in 1931.

The Extension of Dominion Status

The individual provinces of Australia had common British origins and had relatively short lives as separate territorial units—the oldest, New South Wales, dates only from 1788. But, in spite of these facts, these provinces developed their local differences and separateness, symbolized by the fact that they used differing gauges for their railroads. They gained the essentials of self-government in the Australian Colonies Government Act of 1850, but federal union of New South Wales, Victoria, Queensland, and the others was not achieved until the Commonwealth of Australia was formed in 1901. The influence of the American example is clear in the constitution of the Commonwealth, which provides for a senate with equal membership for each of the six states, a house of representatives apportioned on the basis of population, and a supreme court with something close to the American power of judicial review. But in Australia as in the other British dominions, the parliamentary system of an executive (prime minister and cabinet) dismissible by vote of the legislative body was retained; the American "presidential" system was deliberately rejected.

Australia, like Canada, was essentially an empty country in 1800, and like Canada it filled gradually with immigrants, mostly from Britain.

Perhaps the head start of the United States, with its great attraction for British and European immigration, slowed down the growth of these British dominions. But the process, though slow, was steady, and by 1914 all the dominions, including the quiet islands of New Zealand, traditionally most "English" of them all, were prosperous, democratic societies just settling down from the last of the pioneer stage. Their narrative history is most interesting, but we cannot go into it here, nor into the fascinating and illuminating subject—insufficiently pursued—of the likenesses and unlikenesses of the corporate personalities of these new countries and the United States, all offsprings of the "frontier."

The Commonwealth in Review

In the nineteenth century, Americans pushing west and Russians pushing east added millions of square miles to their respective lands as colonies of settlement. Although in both, and especially in America, this process of the "frontier" had important effects on their national character, it did not create great immediate problems concerning the "independence" of the settlers. The British, however, went thousands of miles overseas for their colonies of settlement. They found very soon that these colonies could not be treated as the long tradition since Columbus prescribed— that is, as mere outposts of the mother land with no political self-rule, held in strict mercantilist economic leading strings. Nor could they be, if only because of the separating seas, simply added as a territorial continuation of the mother land as they filled up, as Siberia was added to Russia and the territories of the American West to the federal Union. By 1914, the British at home and the citizens of their overseas colonies of settle-

ment had worked out something new in political configurations, unprecedented in man's brief history.

Canada, Australia, New Zealand, and South Africa were by 1914 wholly self-governing. They could and did even levy customs dues on imports from Britain. They had the beginnings of military forces of their own, and of course complete control of that clear attribute of "sovereignty"— their own internal police. Men were even beginning to speculate about whether they were not in possession of that other clear attribute of sovereignty—the right to conduct foreign relations, both diplomatic and military. For example, could Canada be at peace with a country with which Great Britain was at war?

The first test came in 1914. All the dominions went to war against Germany and her allies. Even the dubiously loyal Union of South Africa went to war against the sender of the Kruger telegram; we are bound to record that the always land-hungry Boers had their eyes on the German colonies in Africa, and especially on the big empty colony of German Southwest Africa, directly adjacent to the Union. The government of each dominion, however, went through the formal process of declaring war, just as "sovereign" countries do. Yet the relation between Canada, for instance, and Great Britain was something different from the relation between two such sovereign countries as the Argentine and Spain. The dominions had not quite set up wholly for themselves, nor, to revert to the favorite cliché of the nineteenth-century Little Englander, had they dropped off like ripe fruit. The nature of the tie between the dominions and Britain was not clear then, and it must be admitted it is not fully clear even now. But it still exists, though greatly weakened, and to it also we shall return in a chapter on imperialism in our own day.

VI   The Results of Imperialism

The broad general results of this long phase of European expansion down to 1914 may now be summarized.

First and most obviously, in the nineteenth century almost the whole planet was affected by the process. The white man was almost every-

where by 1914, and white explorers not infrequently found that the tin can, that ubiquitous symbol of the West, had got there ahead of them.

Second, the expansion of Europe was accompanied by a numerical expansion of the whole human race. Between 1800 and 1900, the population of the world just about doubled, from some 800,000,000 in 1800 to some 1,600,000,000 in 1900. European white stock accounted for the most spectacular part of the rise, but nonwhites in Asia and elsewhere also increased. We do not sufficiently understand human population growth to say flatly that the expansion of Europe *caused* the growth of population among non-European peoples in the nineteenth century. But it did bring to many areas of the world some increase of law and order, some increase in material production and improvements in transportation and distribution, health and sanitation—factors that probably contribute to population growth. And, with such exceptions as the native Australian "Blackfellows" and some North American Indians, European expansion did not usually mean the physical extermination of non-European peoples.

Third, we may say with no reservations whatever that by 1914 it was quite clear that "natives" were beginning to reject the claims of white supremacy. Among the more civilized and long-established peoples in the Near East and Asia, the educated classes were already developing a sense of nationalism. They took over from the West that particular form of group consciousness that is attached to a territorial political unit and that is shared, in principle at least, by all who live within the unit. This nationalism was a new thing outside Europe, and a very important one for us today, for it has gone on increasing and developing. In the early twentieth century, it was most evident in Japan and, to some extent, China, and in advanced "colonial" nations like Egypt and India, though there were signs of it almost everywhere.

This new phenomenon was not the same thing as simple hostility to whites, or to particular nations among the whites. It was an organized political faith—in short, modern "patriotism." Naturally, Egyptian, Indian, and Chinese patriots were first of all concerned with getting rid of their European imperial masters; their attitudes were those of oppressed nationalistic groups everywhere, even in Europe itself. After all, the most striking and most successful rebellion of early twentieth-century nationalist movements against an imperial "master" was that of very European and very white Ireland against the British. These "colonial" peoples were touchy, addicted to nursing grievances imaginary as well as real, eager to seize on any national trait that

could be glorified, admiring, hating, and envying their masters. Above all, they were organized on a new principle taken from the West, a principle that is ultimately perhaps more destructive of their own traditional cultures than anything else that has come to them from the West. This is the equalitarian and leveling, if not democratic, spirit inherent in the secular religion of nationalism. In theory at least nationality transcends the dividing lines of profession, social class, and even caste. The fellah, the Egyptian peasant whose ancestry reaches back through the centuries, could claim to be as good an Egyptian as the aristocratic pasha—indeed a better one, since he was uncorrupted by European culture. People began to talk and write of "Arab" nationalism; yet the "Arabs" were not exactly a race, nor a people, nor any specific political-territorial entity —at most, "Arab" referred to a language, a culture, and to some of those who held the Muslim faith, and even then a significant minority of Arabs was Christian.

Fourth, and in spite of the gloomy economic conclusions of anti-imperialists, there seems no doubt that over the century the homelands of Europe gained in total wealth from their expansion overseas. Indeed, raw materials from overseas were necessary to maintain the standard of living in thickly populated countries like Britain, Germany, Belgium, and the Netherlands. Theoretically, these raw materials could have come into European lands in free trade with free countries overseas; actually they came in part from imperial expansion. In purely empirical terms, the imperialism of the nineteenth century does seem to confirm Professor Walter Webb's contention that the vast new lands of the frontier proved to be a decisive windfall to Western civilization.

Finally, imperialist rivalries, especially after 1870, exacerbated the normal rivalries among the European great powers and were thus a major factor in the complex of causes that brought on general war in 1914. This is particularly true of the Anglo-German rivalry, which, unlike that of France and England or of Austria and Russia, had no long historical background. This Anglo-German rivalry was everywhere by 1900—among commercial travelers of both nations, trying to sell machinery in Peru; among missionaries trying to convert the heathen in Africa; among army officers, naval officers, editors, organizers, all seeking to make German influence more important than British somewhere or to keep British influence more important than German. The rivalry extended even to the academic world and to that world in the United States. There were those who regarded the Rhodes Scholarships for study at Oxford (1904) as a British attempt to counterbalance the great prestige that the German universities, and especially their degree of Ph.D., had acquired in America during the latter nineteenth century.

Reading Suggestions on Nineteenth-Century Imperialism

IMPERIALISM IN GENERAL

W. L. Langer, *The Diplomacy of Imperialism, 1890–1902*, 2nd ed. (Knopf, 1951). Thorough and instructive study of the scramble for imperial prizes.

H. Gollwitzer, *Europe in the Age of Imperialism, 1880–1914* (*Harcourt). Useful general survey.

A. P. Thornton, *Doctrines of Imperialism* (*Wiley), and T. Kemp, *Theories of Imperialism* (Dobson, 1968). Illuminating analyses of the ideological background.

R. Koebner and H. D. Schmidt, *Imperialism: The Story and Significance of a Political Word, 1840–1960* (Cambridge Univ. Press, 1964). Lives up to its title.

J. A. Hobson, *Imperialism* (*Ann Arbor). Celebrated attack on imperialism.

Lenin, *Imperialism, The Highest Stage of Capitalism* (*China Books). The classic statement of the communist view.

B. Kidd, *The Control of the Tropics* (Macmillan, 1898). A defense of imperialism.

J. A. Schumpeter, *Imperialism and Social Classes* (*Meridian). A valuable essay on imperialism from the standpoint of the economist and sociologist.

D. K. Fieldhouse, *The Colonial Empires: A Comparative Survey from the Eighteenth Century* (Delacorte Press, 1967). Authoritative and complete.

K. S. Latourette, *A History of the Expansion of Christianity*, 7 vols. (Harper, 1937–1945). Volumes 5 and 6 concern its expansion into the non-European world.

T. Geiger, *The Conflicted Relationship* (*McGraw-Hill). Valuable study of the role of the West in the transformation of Asia, Africa, and Latin America.

Grover Clark, *A Place in the Sun* (Macmillan, 1936). Lucid discussion of the extent to which colonies were a paying proposition.

AFRICA

P. Duignan and L. H. Gann, *Colonialism in Africa*. Vol. I: *The History and Politics of Colonialism* (Cambridge Univ. Press, 1969). A comprehensive survey. The same authors have also published *Burden of Empire* (Praeger, 1967), a moderate defense of the contribution of the colonial powers to the development of sub-Saharan Africa.

R. Robinson and J. Gallagher, *Africa and the Victorians* (*Anchor). Excellent study of the climactic years of imperialism.

R. F. Betts, ed., *The Scramble for Africa* (*Heath). Excerpts from varying statements as to the causes and dimensions of the competition.

James Duffy, *Portugal in Africa* (*Penguin). The best study of an important and often neglected colonial enterprise.

C. Hollis, *Italy in Africa* (Hamish Hamilton, 1941). Valuable study of a late starter.

H. R. Rudin, *Germans in the Cameroons, 1884–1914* (Yale Univ. Press, 1938). Valuable case study of an imperialist venture.

F. D. Lugard, *The Dual Mandate in British Tropical Africa,* 3rd ed. (Blackwood, 1926). Significant detailed account of British policy in Nigeria.

D. S. Landes, *Bankers and Pashas* (*Torchbooks). Illuminating account of French economic imperialism in Egypt during the mid-nineteenth century.

R. L. Tignor, *Modernization and British Colonial Rule in Egypt, 1882–1914* (Princeton Univ. Press, 1966). Full and balanced appraisal of the British record.

L. de Lichtervelde, *Leopold of the Belgians* (Century, 1929), and L. Bauer, *Leopold the Unloved, King of the Belgians and of Wealth* (Little, Brown, 1935). Vindicating and denouncing, respectively, the great exploiter of the Congo.

C. W. de Kiewiet, *A History of South Africa, Social and Economic* (*Oxford Univ. Press), and E. A. Walker, *A History of South Africa,* 2nd ed. (Longmans, 1940). Two very good surveys by scholars who lived in South Africa.

B. Williams, *Cecil Rhodes* (Constable, 1921). Probably the best book on the great empire builder; for a different estimate see G. S. Millin, *Cecil Rhodes* (Harper, 1933).

W. K. Hancock, *Smuts: Study for a Portrait* (*Cambridge Univ. Press). Excellent sketch of the famous South African leader.

ASIA

K. S. Latourette, *China* (*Spectrum). Enlightening introduction by an expert.

J. K. Fairbank, *The United States and China,* rev. ed. (*Compass). By a leading scholar, with more stress on Chinese history and culture than the title might suggest.

J. T. Pratt, *The Expansion of Europe into the Far East* (Sylvan Press, 1947). Excellent introductory account.

G. Sansom, *The Western World and Japan, a Study in the Interaction of European and Asiatic Cultures* (Knopf, 1950). By a distinguished British scholar, the author of many other important works on Japan.

E. O. Reischauer, *Japan Past and Present,* 4th ed. (*Knopf). Admirable introduction by another distinguished scholar.

R. Coupland, *Britain and India, 1600–1941* (Longmans, 1941). Brief introduction by an authority on imperial questions. For fuller discussions consult M. Edwardes, *British India, 1772–1947* (Taplinger, 1968); H. Brown, ed., *The Sahibs: The Life and Ways of the British in India as Recorded by Themselves* (Hodge, 1948); and A. Seal, *The Emergence of Indian Nationalism* (Cambridge Univ. Press, 1968).

B. H. Sumner, *Tsardom and Imperialism in the Far East and Middle East, 1880–1914* (British Academy, 1944). Good short account.

J. F. Cady, *The Roots of French Imperialism in Eastern Asia,* rev. ed. (Cornell Univ. Press, 1967). Lucid scholarly study.

THE MIDDLE EAST

B. Lewis, *The Emergence of Modern Turkey,* rev. ed. (*Oxford Univ. Press). The best study of the Ottoman Empire in the nineteenth century.

R. H. Davison, *Turkey* (*Spectrum). Clear and concise introduction.

A. Hourani, *Arabic Thought in the Liberal Age, 1798–1939* (Oxford Univ. Press, 1962). Informative study, with considerable stress on Western influences.

THE BRITISH EMPIRE AND COMMONWEALTH

M. Beloff, *Imperial Sunset.* Vol. I: *Britain's Liberal Empire, 1897–1921* (Knopf, 1970). Recent study by a prolific scholar.

P. Knaplund, *The British Empire, 1815–1939* (Harper, 1941). An authoritative account.

C. E. Carrington, *The British Overseas: Exploits of a Nation of Shopkeepers,* rev. ed. (*Cambridge Univ. Press). Detailed study, very British in point of view.

The Cambridge History of the British Empire, 7 vols. (Macmillan, 1929–1940). With separate volumes on India, Canada, and Australia and New Zealand together.

G. M. Craig, *The United States and Canada* (Harvard Univ. Press, 1968). Sound scholarly study with more stress on Canadian developments than the title might suggest.

D. G. Creighton, *History of Canada: Dominion of the North* (Houghton, 1958); C. Glazebrook, *Canada: A Short History* (Oxford Univ. Press, 1950). Two good general accounts.

R. Coupland, ed., *The Durham Report* (Clarendon, 1946). The famous document that in a sense marks the beginning of the development of the British Commonwealth.

G. Greenwood, ed., *Australia: A Social and Political History* (Praeger, 1955). Good collaborative work, with bibliographies. A readable brief survey is in M. Barnard, *A History of Australia* (Praeger, 1963).

H. Belshaw, ed., *New Zealand* (Univ. of California Press, 1947). An informative volume.

J. B. Condliffe, *New Zealand in the Making* and *The Welfare State in New Zealand* (both Macmillan, 1959). These books provide a good economic history of 1792–1957.

OTHER EMPIRES   H. Brunschwig, *French Colonialism: Myths and Realties, 1871–1914* (Praeger, 1966). Perceptive study by a Frenchman.

S. H. Roberts, *History of French Colonial Policy* (Archon, 1963). Reissue of a valuable detailed older work by an Australian scholar.

M. E. Townsend, *The Rise and Fall of Germany's Colonial Empire, 1884–1918* (Macmillan, 1930). A useful account; may be supplemented by W. O. Henderson, *Studies in German Colonial History* (Quadrangle, 1963).

J. W. Pratt, *America's Colonial Experiment* (Prentice-Hall, 1950). Good survey.

D. Perkins, *A History of the Monroe Doctrine,* rev. ed. (*Little, Brown). A useful popular account by a leading specialist.

HISTORICAL FICTION   R. Kipling, *Kim* (*many editions) and *Soldiers Three* (many editions). Famous works by the even more famous champion of imperialism.

S. Cloete, *The Turning Wheels* (Houghton, 1937). A novel about nineteenth-century Boers.

A. Gide, *The Immoralist* (*Vintage). European hero corrupted by North Africa.

E. M. Forster, *A Passage to India* (*many editions). Classic novel on East and West.

L. Hémon, *Maria Chapdelaine* (Macmillan, 1940; *Image). The best-known novel about rural French Canada.

Hugh McLennan, *The Precipice* (Duell, Sloan, 1948). Instructive study of relations between English-speaking and French-speaking Canadians.

H. H. Richardson, *The Fortunes of Richard Mahony* (Readers Club, 1941). A series of novels about modern Australia by an Australian.

H. Rider Haggard, *King Solomon's Mines* (*Dell). A splendid example of the rousing novel of imperialist adventure.

25

The First World War

I Introduction

On June 28, 1914, the Hapsburg archduke
Francis Ferdinand, heir to the throne of Austria-
Hungary, and his wife were assassinated in the
streets of Sarajevo, capital of the recently annexed provinces of Bosnia and Herzegovina,
which had been occupied by Austria-Hungary
since 1878. The assassin, Princip, was a Serbian
nationalist, and Bosnia had long been coveted by
the Serbs. The Austro-Hungarian government,
alarmed by the ambitions of Serbian nationalists,
took the occasion of the assassination to send a
severe ultimatum to Serbia. The Serbian government's refusal to accept the ultimatum in its en-
tirety led to an Austrian declaration of war on
Serbia, on July 28. Within the week, the great
states of Europe were engaged in a general war—
the Central Powers (Austria-Hungary and Germany) against the Allies (Serbia, Russia, France,
and Britain). Princip's revolver shot was eventually to kill some ten million men.

Above: Aerial combat in World War I.
Above right: Gavrilo Princip, immediately after
his assassination of Archduke Ferdinand
at Sarajevo. Right: Marshal Foch's train, in
which the armistice was signed on November 11, 1918.

914

This was the first general war, the first war to involve most of the members of the world state system, since the wars of the French Revolution and Napoleon a century earlier. There had been wars enough, foreign and civil, in the century between. They had been, however, save for relatively minor wars like the Crimean War of 1853, wars between two parties, like the Franco-Prussian War of 1870, the American war between North and South in 1861–1865, and a whole series of colonial wars against rebellious natives.

In 1914 a great many people in Europe and America felt that this sort of general war was all but impossible. These people, predominantly liberal intellectuals, had been alarmed by the series of crises we shall shortly describe, crises that showed how close a general war might be. But they had followed hopefully the movements for international peace and cooperation—the Red Cross, the international labor movements, and the Hague conferences of 1899 and 1907, which, though they failed to achieve their avowed purpose of limiting armaments, did set up a tribunal for the arbitration of international disputes, the World Court. And many intellectuals simply refused to believe that a world war, should it break out, could last more than a few months. The cost of such a war, they maintained, would be so great that it would bankrupt any government. Such was the thesis of a bestseller, Norman Angell's *The Great Illusion* (1910).

World War I was long, bloody, and destructive. The shock of its outbreak, vastly increased by the strains of the war itself, and above all by the failure of the postwar peace settlement, brought on in the 1920's a most extraordinary discussion of the causes of the war. This discussion was by no means limited to professional historians. It was carried on in the press and on the platforms by all the agencies that touched public opinion. Most of it was designed to "revise" the verdict of the Versailles Treaty of 1919, in which the victorious Allies declared Germany and Austria-Hungary solely responsible for precipitating the war of 1914. The beaten Germans, penalized in the peace, had obvious reasons for trying to prove themselves innocent of war guilt. But important currents in public opinion in Great Britain, the United States, and even in France also flowed into this "revisionist" movement. So far did revisionism go in the 1920's that some American historians parceled out varying portions of the guilt among the victors and the vanquished alike, with the confidence of schoolmasters handing out merits and demerits.

We cannot be so confident today. From our further perspective, the question of war guilt in 1914 fades out into a question of historical causation, and into the fact of historical tragedy. We can say with the English writer George Meredith:

> *In tragic life, God wot,*
> *No villain need be! Passions spin the plot.*
> *We are betrayed by what is false within.**

No one power or group of powers "caused" the war of 1914. Its causes lie deep in the history of the state system of Western civilization, and, more particularly, in its history since 1870. They lie deep also in that fundamental form of group consciousness we call nationalism and in the very structure of the modern nation-state. The dramatic date of the assassination of Francis Ferdinand, June 28, 1914, serves as a dividing line between the ultimate, or long-term, factors and the proximate, or short-term, factors.

II Causes of the War

The Shift in the Balance of Power

In the long term, an obvious factor that made war more likely was the unification of Germany and Italy. The creation of these two new major states in the 1860's and 1870's altered the always delicate balance of power in the European state-system. The efforts of statesmen during the next forty years to adjust the system and to take account of the two new powers and their claims proved ultimately unsuccessful. The older established powers were by no means willing to give up their own claims. We have seen that ever since the modern European—or, better, the Western—state-system developed out of medieval fragmentation, the separate units, the states, have tried to grow. They have tried to grow in wealth,

* *Modern Love*, XLIII.

"Peace": Daumier's view of the European situation after 1871.

in prestige, and, most conspicuously of all, in territory. In the second half of the nineteenth century, with the principle of national sovereignty well established, and even the smaller states like Switzerland and Sweden generally accepted as not to be swallowed, there was little territory in Europe that could be easily disposed of for the purpose of making adjustments. Unification had closed off Germany and Italy, which as recently as 1815 had been classic areas for "compensation." Only southeastern Europe, the Balkan lands of the obviously weakening Turkish Empire, remained in the late nineteenth century as possible pickings for ambitious powers. Even there, the growth of national feeling in states like Romania, Serbia, Bulgaria, and Greece made sheer annexation difficult. Nevertheless, Russia and Austria-Hungary both had ambitions in the Balkans; behind them, aiming rather at domination of Turkey and the Near East, came Germany and Great Britain. Finally, as we have noted in the last chapter, much of Africa, Asia,

and Oceania had been partitioned among the great powers amid intense rivalry. It seemed always possible to redo this partitioning.

Meantime, influenced by their rivalries in Europe and abroad, the great powers were also choosing sides in a series of alliances and agreements. By the early years of the twentieth century two camps existed—the Triple Alliance of Germany, Austria-Hungary, and Italy, and the Triple Entente of France, Britain, and Russia. The system, as many people at the time saw clearly, had grown so tightly organized that there was almost no free play left, and with the wisdom of hindsight we can now see that after 1900 almost any crisis might have led to war. Sarajevo was the one that did.

This state of international politics was christened by an English liberal, Lowes Dickinson, "the international anarchy." It was, however, no chaos, but a highly organized rivalry, "anarchical" only in the sense that there was no higher authority to put a stop to the rivalry. In concrete instances, two or more powers wanted the same piece of land, as a territorial addition or as a sphere of influence. France and Great Britain both wanted Egypt; France and Germany both wanted Morocco; Russia and Austria-Hungary both wanted control over the Balkans; Russia and Japan both wanted Manchuria; and so on around the map. Compromises were made, lands and spheres of influence were shared, but in the long run there simply wasn't enough to go around.

The Role of Public Opinion

We have in this outline used the shorthand of names like Great Britain or Germany. But these are mere symbols, as colored blobs on a map are symbols, for millions of human beings whose desires somehow do add up into the actions of states, did add up to the war of 1914. In no state were the millions all in agreement. There were Germans who wanted no bit of Africa or any other piece of land. There were Englishmen who, far from being content with Britain's place in the world, wanted more, wanted Britain to be for the whole round world what Rome had been for the Mediterranean world in the first centuries of the Christian era, hoped eventually to eliminate all but Englishmen (and perhaps Scotsmen) in a fine

Darwinian struggle. There were everywhere in Europe at least a few absolute pacifists, men who were determined under any conditions to refuse to fight, men who once war broke out became "conscientious objectors." We must not think of the war and the events that led up to it as simply the work of a few men at the top in each nation, the professional soldiers, the villainous diplomats in frock coats and striped trousers. In all the countries, there was a spectrum that ran from militarist to pacifist, through all shades of opinion.

But the outbreak of the war saw in each belligerent nation a broad national public opinion in support of the government. In 1914, a good many men marched to war convinced that war was a beneficial thing; the bands played, the crowds shouted, and war, perhaps for the last time, seemed romantic as well as necessary. Here is the account of a young German on the last train out of Switzerland before the outbreak of war:

An elderly gentleman was sitting in our compartment. He began to talk to us at once, as if we were intimate acquaintances. On the back of his hotel bill he had added up the numerical strength of the European armies and balanced them against each other. He compared the two totals and assured my mother that the spiritual qualities of the German troops compensated for the numerical superiority of the Russians. For in this war spiritual qualities alone would decide the day, and Germany's spiritual qualities were the best in Europe. As a university professor he knew that our youth were ready for the fray, and full of ideals. At last the hour had come when our people could enter on its great world mission. . . .*

that toward the end he tried to avoid a general war. But he cannot be even partially absolved for the long-term, for the ultimate, causes of the war. In the decisive years between 1888 and 1914 he was the posturing, aggressive leader of patriotic expansion, the "White Knight" leading his people to glory. He was perhaps more of a figurehead, less of an actual maker of policy, than the world took him to be, but still a willing and effective figurehead for expansionists and violent nationalists.

German ambitions and German fears produced an intense hatred of Britain, a hatred mixed with envy and a sense of inferiority, a hatred that focused on the English upper classes, perfectly tailored, serene in effortless superiority, the favorite children of fortune. Many a German tourist, perhaps quite accidentally given an Italian hotel room inferior to that given a traveling Englishman, would come home burning with indignation at this personal evidence that Germany was being denied its place in the sun. In the German navy, in the years just before the war, there was a simple toast in the officers' mess: *Der Tag* (The Day). Everyone knew that this was the day of the declaration of war between Germany and Britain. These feelings are all condensed in the famous "Hymn of Hate" of the German poet Ernst Lissauer:

We will never forego our hate,
Hate by water and hate by land,
Hate of the head and hate of the hand,
Hate of the hammer and hate of the Crown.
Hate of the seventy millions choking down.
We love as one, we hate as one,
We have one foe and one alone:
                  England! ＊

German Aspirations

The Germans were led by their kaiser, William II, who had come to the throne in 1888. The "revisionist" historians have been able to show that in the hectic five weeks after the assassination at Sarajevo the kaiser, contrary to world opinion at the time, did not work steadily for war,

British Aspirations

Few Englishmen returned this hate; the English were still on top. Yet as the years wore on, the expensive race between Britain and Germany in naval armaments continued; in incident after incident German and British diplomats took opposite sides; and—this seemed especially impor-

* Ernst Glaeser, *Class of 1902*, trans. Willa and Edwin Muir (London, 1929), pp. 171–172.

* Ernst Lissauer, "A Chant of Hate Against England," trans. Barbara Henderson, in Burton E. Stevenson, comp., *The Home Book of Verse*, 3rd ed. (New York, 1918), II, 2549–2550.

tant to the hard-headed—German wares of all sorts undersold British wares in Europe, in North and South America, and in Asia. Englishmen began to think that someone ought to teach these ill-mannered Germans a lesson. Moreover, they had begun to worry about their own position of prosperity and leadership. In India, the greatest possession of the English, it was clear already that great concessions toward self-government would have to be made to the natives. Close at home the Irish crisis was in one of its most acute phases, with Protestant Ulster in arms against the proposed Home Rule. British officers there were guilty of planning actual mutiny, much as did French officers in 1961 during the Algerian crisis. Englishmen were worried about their obsolescent industrial plants, their apparent inability to produce goods as cheaply and as efficiently as the Germans; they were self-critical about their failures as salesmen abroad, their stodgy self-satisfaction.

A great many Britishers thought of themselves as good liberals and good internationalists, anxious to preserve the peace and the decencies of international life. Many were radicals and Labour party men committed to pacifism. The coming of war in 1914 was to show how thoroughly almost all these men identified Great Britain and righteousness. As for the bulk of the conservatives, they were as nationalist as in any other great country. In Britain, their nationalism attached itself to the empire, to the "White Man's Burden," to a whole set of symbols that the Germans found intolerable.

The Other Belligerents

In democratic France as in democratic England there was a wide spread of opinion on international politics. A numerous socialist Left was committed to pacifism and to the concept of an international general strike of workers at the threat of actual war. A more moderate group also opposed conventional patriotic aggressiveness toward the foreigner. Both among the men who conducted French foreign relations and among the general public, however, there remained right down to the eve of the Great War the embittered patriotism of the beaten. Frenchmen wanted *revanche*, revenge for the defeat of 1870. They wanted Alsace-Lorraine back. For all these years,

the statue representing Strasbourg among the cities of France in the Place de la Concorde in Paris was draped in black. With the warmest patriots, the organizers of patriotic societies, the editors of patriotic journals, this feeling for revenge was an obsession.

By the opening decade of the 1900's many observers thought that the new generation was losing its desire for revenge, that Frenchmen had at last decided to accept the verdict of 1870. But French diplomatists continued to preserve and strengthen the system of alliances against Germany, and in the excited weeks of July 1914 it was clear that Frenchmen were ready for war.

Among the other major belligerents, too, the ultimate decisions of governments won much popular support. Russians were filled with the "pooled self-esteem" of nationalism, were convinced that God and the right were on their side. Italians saw in war the chance to get Italia Irredenta (Trent, Trieste, and their surrounding lands) and still more territory from the Hapsburg monarchy. In the dual monarchy, as we have seen, the loyalty of subject nationalities could scarcely be counted on; but the dominant Germans of Austria and Magyars of Hungary welcomed the opportunity to put the troublesome Slavs in their place for good and all.

The Era of Bismarck, 1871-1890

The road to Sarajevo starts in 1871, at the Treaty of Frankfurt, where France was obliged to cede Alsace and Lorraine to the new German Empire. It was no straight road, but one of many twists and turnings, and few historians would now maintain that 1871 made 1914 inevitable. We cannot follow the road in detail, but we must map its main course.

For some twenty years Bismarck was its chief engineer. In fairness to the Iron Chancellor, it must be said that during his last twenty years in office he sought peace, and indeed obtained it. Powerful elements in the new empire made it impossible for him to grant to France the same kind of generous peace he had given Austria in 1866. Yet Bismarck did try to salve the wound he knew France had suffered; he encouraged her to expand her empire in North Africa by the acquisition of Tunisia in 1881, even though this offended the Italians, who also coveted Tunisia.

But he feared a French attempt at revenge and sought to isolate her diplomatically by building a series of alliances from which she was excluded. Germany, he insisted, was now a "saturated" power, and wanted nothing more in Europe; and in a famous phrase he insisted that all the Balkans were not worth "the bones of a single Pomeranian grenadier." Above all, he sought to keep on good terms with *both* Austria and Russia, and, what was much more difficult, to keep both these powers on good terms with each other. Since both wanted predominance in the Balkans, Bismarck's task was formidable.

He laid the cornerstone of his diplomatic system by a defensive alliance with Austria-Hungary in 1879, an alliance that held right down to 1918. And he was able to make a not-so-secret treaty, the so-called League of the Three Emperors, which bound Germany, Russia, and Austria together. The three powers agreed to act together in dealings with Turkey and to maintain friendly neutrality should any one of them be at war with a fourth power other than Turkey. Next, working skillfully on Italian annoyance over the French expansion in Tunis and on Italian fears that France might join an international effort to restore Rome to papal sovereignty, Bismarck secured an alliance among Germany, Austria-Hungary, and Italy, directed chiefly against France. This was the famous Triple Alliance of 1882, often renewed, which still existed on paper in 1914.

On this series of tightropes Bismarck maintained a precarious balance through the 1880's. Chief in his mind was the danger that the Russians, always fearful of Austrian schemes in the Balkans, would desert him and ally themselves with France, still a great power and anxious to escape from the isolation that Bismarck had designed for her. In 1887, Russia did refuse to renew the League of the Three Emperors, but Bismarck was able to repair the breach for the moment by a secret Russo-German agreement known as the Reinsurance Treaty. The two promised each other neutrality in case either was involved in a war against a third power; but this neutrality was not to hold if Germany made an "aggressive" war against France or if Russia made an "aggressive" war against Austria. Since Russian nationalist agitation continued against both Austria and Germany, Bismarck in 1888 made public as a warning to Russia the terms of the Austro-German alliance and allowed the main terms of the Triple Alliance to be known informally.

Formation of the Triple Entente, 1890–1907

Then in 1890 the young emperor William II dismissed Bismarck. The emperor's advisers, headed by Baron von Holstein, persuaded him not to renew the Reinsurance Treaty with Russia, in spite of Russian desire for such renewal. Shortly afterward, what Bismarck had worked so hard to prevent came about. After lengthy negotiations, Russia and France in 1894 came together in an alliance that ended French isolation. It was formally a defensive alliance, in which each was to come to the aid of the other if Germany or Austria made "aggressive" war against either, and it was accompanied by the necessary military agreements between the two general staffs. Against the Triple Alliance there now stood, quite openly, a Dual Alliance of republican France and absolutist Russia. Great Britain as yet remained technically uninvolved by any formal treaty with a European ally and indeed never did make a full legal commitment even with France.

The next great stage in the tightening network of alliances was to bring Great Britain in against the Triple Alliance, at least by informal agreement. In the two decades after the accession of William II, Britain made a formal alliance with Japan and informal "understandings" (*ententes*) with France and Russia. What chiefly drove Britain to these actions was the naval race with Germany and the rapid worsening of Anglo-German relations, a worsening even more evident perhaps at the level of public opinion than at the level of formal diplomacy.

A good concrete instance of this rising hostility is the Kruger telegram of 1896, in which the kaiser congratulated President Kruger of the Boer Republic of Transvaal on the defeat of the Jameson raid. It may be that the kaiser and his circle hoped at bottom that this gesture would be taken by the English government as a kind of polite and permissible diplomatic blackmail, an evidence of how great a nuisance the German government could be to the British if it were not on their side. But the British press took the telegram as an unbearable insult, and the German press replied angrily to British anger.

It was fear of Russia rather than fear of Germany, however, that inspired Britain to make the first break with formal isolationism, the alliance with Japan in 1902. The outbreak of war between Russia and Japan hastened negotiations between Britain and France. In the Anglo-French Entente of 1904, France gave England a free hand in Egypt, England gave France a free hand in Morocco, and various outstanding difficulties between the two in other parts of the world were ironed out. More important, the base was laid for general collaboration between the two in international affairs. Only six years previously, in 1898, there had been a grave flareup of the traditional colonial rivalry between France and England when a French column was met by a British column at Fashoda in the disputed Sudan territory of the upper Nile Valley. Fashoda caused quite as big an outbreak of fury in the French and the British press as the Kruger telegram only two years before had caused in the German and

"How can we shake hands?" A 1909 cartoon on the Anglo-German naval rivalry.

the British press. Yet Fashoda left wounds much less deep than the Kruger telegram; the contemporary press is not always a faithful guide to the climate of public opinion, let alone to that of professional diplomacy.

The final stage in aligning the two camps came in 1907 when Russia, chastened by her defeat at the hand of Japan and encouraged by the French, came to an understanding with Great Britain. Both countries made concessions in regions where they had been imperialist rivals—Persia, Afghanistan, Tibet—and the British at last made some concessions toward the Russian desire to open up the Straits. The agreement was scarcely based on any genuine sympathy between the two peoples, for the British, notably, had been Russophobic for well over a century. Nevertheless, it did round out the Triple Entente against the Triple Alliance.

A Decade of Crises, 1905-1914

The last decade before 1914 was a series of crises and local wars, any one of which might have spread into a world war. First came a deliberately theatrical gesture from the kaiser, when in 1905 he made a ceremonial visit to Tangier in Morocco as a way of telling the world that the Germans would not accept the Anglo-French assignment of Morocco to France. The net effect of this blustering was to tighten the entente between France and Britain, for the British indicated clearly to the French that they would support them. Indeed at this time there began the informal military and naval conferences between the British and the French that the French, at least, believed "committed" the British to armed support if the Germans attacked. Although the French foreign minister, Delcassé, a partisan of firm policy toward the Germans, was forced out of office, even this partial victory did the Germans no good. French public opinion was infuriated by this intervention in their domestic politics. In the end, a general international conference at Algeciras in Spain (1906) backed up the French, who went ahead with their plans for a protectorate in Morocco. At Algeciras American diplomatic influence was used on the side of France; the United States, too, was beginning to emerge from isolationism.

Diplomatic Alignments before 1914

Dates indicate Alliances

A second Moroccan crisis in 1911 heightened tensions and brought the possibility of a general war home to most Frenchmen. The kaiser sent a German gunboat, the *Panther,* to the Moroccan port of Agadir as a protest against French occupation of the old city of Fez. In ensuing negotiations, well publicized in the press, the Germans finally agreed to leave the French a free hand in Morocco, but only at a price the French considered blackmail: part of French Congo was ceded to Germany.

In the Balkans, a decisive turn of the road toward Sarajevo came in 1908. Austria formally proclaimed the annexation of the old Turkish provinces of Bosnia-Herzegovina, which she had occupied since 1878. Austria's decisive act infuriated the Serbs, who wanted to add Bosnia to their state. It also infuriated the Russians, all the more since few Russians knew that their diplomat Izvolski had in fact made an informal agreement with the Austrian minister Aehrenthal, in September 1908, to accept the annexation of Bosnia-Herzegovina in return for Austrian support of an agreement permitting Russian war-

ships to use the Straits. In the event, Austria did the annexing, but Russia did not get her use of the Straits. This wound to Russian pride was profound.

Meantime, a situation was developing that might give Russia a chance to salve her wounds. In the summer of 1908 nationalist revolutionaries called Young Turks, who were chiefly army officers, had risen successfully against the sultan. The Young Turks wanted the modern industrial achievements of the West, they wanted its political apparatus of representative government, and they wanted above all to have Turks respected, admired, and feared as members of a thoroughly modern nation. Some of their intellectuals followed the nineteenth-century Romantic pattern back into the past, where they found, not the nomad Turks of history, but fine sturdy "Turanians" from the inspiring steppes of central Asia. There was even a "Pan-Turanian" movement, strangest of the "Pan" movements, which sought to group Magyars, Turks, and the Turkish peoples of central Asia, who were all only distantly related to each other, as children of a comman destiny. No wonder the Hapsburgs were alarmed! It began to look as if those who hoped to divide up the Ottoman Empire had better hurry while the dividing was good.

In the hurry, the world was swept into World War I, the preliminary stages of which were the Italian war with Turkey for Tripoli, 1911–1912, and the Balkan Wars of 1912–1913. In the first Balkan War (1912), an alliance of Bulgaria, Serbia, and Greece, backed by Russia, beat the Turks and started the process of dividing up European Turkey. But here Austria imposed an absolute veto on granting Serbia territories that would give her access to the Adriatic Sea. Meanwhile, the victors quarreled among themselves, and in the Second Balkan War (1913) the Greeks and Serbs, joined by the Rumanians and the all-but-beaten Turks, readily defeated the Bulgarians. Turkey got back some of her territory in Europe. But the Balkans were in a state of uncertainty and bad blood when Francis Ferdinand was assassinated; and Bulgaria was ready to ally with Austria and Germany against her former allies.

The Final Crisis, July-August 1914

There are millions of words in print about the proximate causes of World War I in the six weeks between the assassination on June 28 and the general spread of war on August 4, when Britain came in against Germany. Thanks to the end of Hohenzollern, Hapsburg, and Romanov rule as a result of the war, the secret archives were thrown open much sooner than would be normal. And in the pressure of debate in the 1920's over the question of war guilt, even the victorious countries, Britain, France, and the United States, opened their archives to a surprising extent. These are weeks for which documents, often telegrams, can be dated by the hour and minute. These are weeks in which messages are constantly crossing each other, confusing things hopelessly. These are weeks in which professional diplomatists and statesmen, egged on by an excited—and it must be said often irresponsible—press, nevertheless tried for the most part to master the crisis without recourse to war. The diplomats and statesmen were drawn into war because almost all of them believed that

they faced an alternative worse than war, a defeat or loss of face for their nation. Austria believed correctly, though without positive proof, that the Serbian government had some foreknowledge or at least suspicion of Princip's plot and should therefore have given her warning. For this reason, and also because she wished to check the Serb agitation that had long been unsettling the Yugoslav peoples living in the dual monarchy, Austria-Hungary decided to make stiff demands on Serbia after the assassination of Francis Ferdinand. Before doing so, however, she consulted her German ally, who promised to support whatever policy Austria might adopt toward Serbia. This German response has become famous as a diplomatic "blank check," duly signed by Germany in advance with the precise amount to be filled in later by Austria.

Thus encouraged, the Austrian government, on July 23, sent Serbia an ultimatum to be answered within forty-eight hours. The ultimatum made many separate demands, which added up to an insistence that Serbia and Serb propagandists keep their hands off Hapsburg territories and populations, now and in the future. Most of the demands the Serbs accepted, at least in principle; but they refused to accept two of them, which would have permitted Austrian police or military men to take, on Serbian soil, an actual part in a Serbian investigation of Princip's plot. Probably Serbia had some assurance that Russia was willing to give her a kind of "blank check," and would assist her if the partial refusal of the ultimatum led to war. The Serbian reply, therefore, was a little less virtuously honest than it seemed to be to most of the world in July 1914. Still, the Austrian ultimatum appears to have been couched in terms deliberately unacceptable to the Serbs, and the Serb reply seems to have been a base for more consideration than it got from the Austrians. Because the Serbs had not accepted the whole of the ultimatum, Austria declared war on July 28, after turning down as inconsistent with national honor a European conference proposed by the British foreign minister, Sir Edward Grey, on July 26.

From this declaration of war on, the German diplomatists, backed by William II and actually resisting the German military men, tried to hold back their Austrian ally. It is impossible to clear William from responsibility for the German "blank check," which had emboldened Austria and had perhaps been designed by Germany to do just that. Now, however, the Germans certainly tried to revoke the check and made a last effort to stop the spread of the war. Since Russia was beginning the full mobilization of her armies, the kaiser, on July 29, told Czar Nicholas II in a personal telegram of the German attempt to get the Austrians to compromise. Apparently this telegram served to get full Russian mobilization modified into partial mobilization and to get direct Austro-Russian talks resumed on July 30. For a brief moment it looked as if the crisis might be overcome.

But mobilization was not easy in Russia, a country of long distances, poor communications, and bureaucratic red tape; and the Russian military feared that their enemies would get the jump on them. In perhaps the most crucial decision of this hectic last week, the Russian government, probably against the deeper inclinations of the czar himself, decided to renew general mobilization. Germany at once insisted that all Russian mobilization cease, and, when it continued, ordered her own at 4:00 P.M. on August 1, and declared war on Russia at 7:00 P.M. the same day. France, meantime, had determined to stand by her Russian ally, now evidently about to be attacked, and also mobilized at 3:55 P.M. on August 1. Germany declared war on France on August 3.

Britain was still wavering. Although her entente with France did not legally bind the two nations together, it had led to the very close coordination of defense plans by the French and British military and naval staffs. Perhaps, then, Britain would have come into the war anyway. What made her entry certain was the German violation of the neutrality of Belgium, which both Britain and Prussia (this was thirty years before German unification) had joined with other powers to guarantee in 1839. The German military were determined to take decisive action in the West and to knock France out of the war before the Russians could get their vast but slow-moving armies into action. Accordingly, German plans called for a sweep through a corner of Belgium to avoid the heavily fortified and hilly terrain in northeastern France. On August 2, the Germans had notified Belgium that they intended to march through her territory, though they promised to respect her territorial integrity in the peace to come.

Belgium rejected this demand and appealed to the other guaranteeing powers. Sir Edward Grey, though opposed in the British cabinet by the Liberals, Lord Morley and John Burns, who did not believe defense of the neutrality of Belgium worth a war, seized firmly on this ground of action. On August 4 Britain declared war on Germany. The German chancellor, Bethmann-Hollweg, informed of this action, let slip the phrase that Britain had gone to war just for a "scrap of paper"—the treaty of 1839 that established Belgium neutrality. This unhappy phrase, seized upon by the press of the world, not only solidified British opinion in favor of the war but was responsible more than any other single factor for the charge of war guilt that was laid against Germany.

The Entry of Other Powers

By August 6, when Austria declared war on Russia, all the members of the Triple Alliance and the Triple Entente had come to blows, with the exception of Italy, who, however, had never really been a good ally of Austria because of the Irredentist issue. Italy, refusing to consider herself bound by the Triple Alliance, declared her neutrality. The Central Powers of Germany and Austria-Hungary, then, stood against the Allies —Russia, France, Britain, and Serbia. Japan came in on the side of the Allies late in August, and Turkey came in on the Austro-German side in November 1914. After competing territorial offers from both Allies and Central Powers, Italy finally joined the Allies in May 1915. Bulgaria came in on the side of the Central Powers in 1915, Romania on the side of the Allies in 1916.

As the war turned into a stalemate, on both western and eastern fronts in the winter of 1916–1917, the Germans made the desperate decision to try to get at Great Britain by the only way that seemed available. They would use their submarines to cut off the food and raw materials that came to the British Isles from overseas, and without which their peoples would have starved. This unrestricted submarine warfare meant sinking American ships that Americans held were quite legally bringing such supplies, *not* contraband of war, to England and France. On April 6, 1917, the United States completed the roster of great powers involved in the conflict by declaring war on Germany. Lesser powers all over the world joined in, mostly against Germany, so that

U.S. Navy recruiting posters.

the United States as colonists or as an independent nation has sooner or later been drawn into every major general war in the Western state system. In purely empirical terms, it may be argued that the normal expectation is for the United States to enter into any world war. And in more disputable general terms, it may be argued that in the Western state system a general or world war never breaks out unless there is an aggressor nation whose activities appear to threaten the independent existence of all other nations. The United States, in this view, went to war in 1917 for a very deep-seated reason indeed. The possible victory of Germany threatened the very existence of the United States as an independent, but committed and cooperating, participant in an international order.

More specifically, in 1917 the United States insisted that the existing international order gave Americans the right to travel and to trade freely with neutrals and, in dealings with belligerents, to be limited only by well-known principles of international law forbidding actual transport of munitions, or other direct forms of aid to belligerents. This is the doctrine of "freedom of the seas," which would have allowed Germans to search American vessels, but which quite clearly did not permit German submarines to sink American vessels on sight and without notice. The German decision to undertake unrestricted submarine warfare was in Western historical precedent a completely adequate and normal justification of, and explanation for, the U.S. declaration of war. But, we must repeat, behind this reason lay a widespread though by no means universal feeling among many Americans, a feeling especially strong in those persons most concerned with foreign relations, that a German victory would mean a world order where the kind of America in which they wanted to live could not be secure.

Jefferson had delayed, but not prevented, American entry into the Napoleonic wars by abandoning the doctrine of freedom of the seas. The Embargo Act of 1807 had simply forbidden American vessels to trade either with the French or the British side. In 1917, the United States should have had to put an embargo on all American shipping to most foreign ports, or else put up with German torpedoing of American ships, and the drowning of American citizens. Neither course would seem to have been acceptable to a majority of Americans in 1917.

all told there were 53 declarations of war before the end of 1918.

Dissident Americans, then and since, have declared that the United States was enticed into the war by the wicked few—by sentimental lovers of England or France; by bankers who had lent money to the Allies and wanted to protect their investments; by silly idealists who agreed with President Wilson in wishing to "make the world safe for democracy"; and, of course, by scheming Allied diplomatists, corrupt Europeans who held a strange fascination over American "babes in the wood."

Deep-seated sentiments among many good Americans in 1916–1917 rebelled against jeopardizing American ideals by involving the country in the conventional—and wicked—European struggle for power. Even today, after a second general or world war in which American participation aroused much less opposition at home, it is difficult for the historian to discuss objectively the causes of U.S. entrance into this so-called First World War. The historian must indeed note that ever since what Americans call King William's War and Europeans usually call the War of the League of Augsburg (1688–1697),

III   The Course of the War

Resources of the Belligerents

As the opposing nations lined up in 1914, the Allies (British, French, Russians, and others) had an overwhelming superiority in total population and resources. The Central Powers (Germany, Austria-Hungary, and Turkey) had in their own continental lands not over 150,000,000 people; Britain, France, Russia, and Italy in their own continental lands had at least· 125,000,000 more people than their enemies. Moreover, in their overseas possessions, which included the 315,000,000 people of India, the Allies had many millions more. As for material resources, the Central Powers had, especially in Germany, admirably organized industries and enough coal and iron to fight a long war. But here too the statistics were overwhelmingly in favor of the Allies. Moreover, though German submarines and, in the early days, surface raiders were able to interrupt seriously Allied lines of communication overseas, on the whole the Allies were still able to get from these overseas sources indispensable food and other supplies. And when in 1917 a beaten Russia, in the throes of a revolution, ceased to be of aid, the Allies gained the great resources of the United States.

In the long run, much as in the American Civil War, the side with the most men and materials wore down its enemies and won the war. But it was by no means the uneven struggle that the statistics of total population and material resources would indicate. Again as in the Civil War, the weaker side had initially important advantages, won great victories, and seemed at critical moments on the point of final victory.

Geography gave Germany and Austria the advantages of being side by side, and of having interior lines of communication, which enabled them to make rapid transfers of troops from one threatened front to another. Though the Germans and Austrians did not always see eye to eye, they did speak the same language and had for long been firmly allied. Most important of all, Germany in particular was more ready for war than were her enemies. She had an efficiently organized military machine and a good stock of

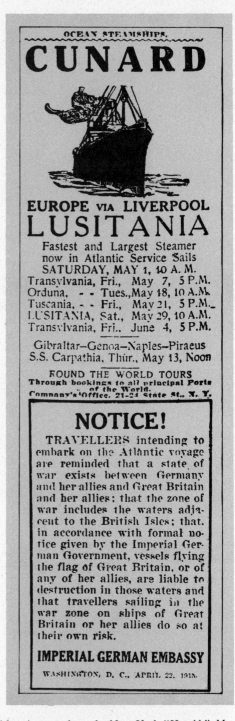

Advertisements from the New York "Herald," May 1, 1915. Six days later a German submarine torpedoed the "Lusitania" off the Irish coast.

munitions, her industry could be readily geared to war, her plans were complete, her people were united in support of the war, and they enjoyed the great psychological advantage of being on the offensive, of carrying the war to the enemy. Indeed, no important part of the war was ever fought on German soil; it ended, with important results for later history, with the German army still in being, with the German Fatherland still uninvaded.

By contrast, geography separated the Western Allies from Russia. German control of the Baltic and Turkish control of the Straits proved throughout the war a serious obstacle to communication between Russia and her allies, who had to take roundabout and difficult routes through Archangel in Arctic waters and even through Vladivostok on the Pacific at the end of the long, slow, single-track Trans-Siberian railway. For the Allies, transfer of troops between eastern and western fronts was militarily almost impossible, even had it been politically possible. It was not, however, politically possible, and here was one of the greatest weaknesses of the Allies.

Russia, Britain, and France had only recently come together, as "friendly" powers and not as close allies. Each of them was a strongly marked nationality, having many sources of conflict with the others. They had no long tradition of mutual cooperation, no common language. France and England were democracies, and though the peoples of both rallied firmly to the national cause in 1914, they were of recent years unused to the kind of firm, centralized political and military control that is necessary in war. As for unified military planning and administration, it was never achieved between Russia and the Western Allies. Even among Britain, France, and the United States on the western front, it was not achieved until the French general Foch was appointed commander-in-chief in 1918, and then only imperfectly, for full merging of staffs was not achieved.

Finally, of the three great Allied powers in 1914, only France was ready with a good big land force, and France, with only 39 millions of people against Germany's 65 millions, was the weakest of the Allies in manpower. Britain was well prepared on the sea, and her navy was an invaluable asset; but it could not be of direct use against the German army. Russia had universal military service and an army great in numbers. But she had vast distances to overcome, an inadequate railway system, a relatively undeveloped heavy industry, an army whose morale had been shaken by the recent defeat at the hands of the Japanese, a people whose morale had been shaken by the recent abortive revolution, and military and political organizations riddled with inefficiency and corruption.

The Western Front: German Offensive

The Germans had a plan, the so-called Schlieffen plan, which they immediately put into execution. It called for a holding operation on the left, with a strong right wing that was to advance swiftly through Belgium, take Paris, and then fall on the rear of the French armies. While this great enveloping movement in the West swiftly eliminated France, relatively weaker German forces, it was planned, would hold down the slow-moving Russians. With France beaten, the Germans could turn their full force against the Russians and beat them. Then there would be only the British left, and the future would take care of them.

The German plan almost succeeded. It failed for two reasons, to which a great number of separate tactical factors contributed. In the first place, the German chief of staff, Moltke, had seriously modified the Schlieffen plan by weakening the critical right wing, partly in order to send divisions to the East, which, ironically, arrived there too late to participate in the defeat of the Russians. By the time the German right wing neared Paris, it had too few divisions to take the capital and then roll up the French army to the eastward. In the second place, the French, though at first they rashly developed the offensive eastward, shifted their armies northward and westward to meet the invading Germans. With the help of the British they exploited a gap that developed between the German First and Second armies. The Germans lost this first great test, known as the Battle of the Marne (September 5-12, 1914).

The German advance, which had been almost continuous since August 2, had been stopped. In the next few weeks the opposing forces engaged in what came to be called the "race for the Channel," with the Germans trying to outflank the Allies and get the Channel ports, thus shutting the short sea passage to future British reinforcements. They failed here, too, and throughout the war the ports of Calais and Boulogne, and indeed a small southwestern corner of Belgium, were to remain in Allied hands—a valuable military advantage.

By the autumn of 1914 the western front was thus stabilized. For over three hundred airline miles between the Channel and the Swiss border of Alsace near Basel, hundreds of thousands of soldiers faced each other in a continuous line that was full of bends called "salients." Both sides "dug in" and formed a series of rough fortifications. The central feature of these fortifications was a series of parallel trenches deep enough to conceal a man standing upright. As time went on, these trenches were greatly improved; they were supplied with parapets, machine-gun nests, and an elaborate network of approach trenches and strong points, until the whole front became one immense fortification. Thousands of local actions in the four years of trench warfare shifted the lines here and there, and a series of partial breakthroughs occurred on both sides. But on the whole the lines held, and the actual fighting in the West was confined to an extraordinarily narrow, though very long, field.

On this western front the ultimate decision was reached; but there were many other fronts. Some of them were disparagingly called "the sideshows" by those who advocated concentrating in the West. Yet in perspective we can now see that they all played a part in determining the final result. Since, over the long pull, the Germans had fewer men and resources, the dispersal of energies that these "sideshows" called for, and the continuous need to bolster their Austrian, Turkish, and Bulgarian allies, were major factors in their defeat. For the sake of clarity, we shall here take up these other fronts separately and briefly, but the reader must never forget that for the belligerents the war was a whole; its wide-flung theaters were mutually dependent, with each one influencing the others.

The Eastern Front

The eastern front, where the Russians faced both the Germans and the Austrians, was certainly no mere sideshow. Millions of men were involved on both sides, and had the Russians not held out, as they did, until the end of 1917, the Allies in the West could hardly have withstood the reinforcements that the Germans and Austrians would have been able to send to France and Italy. The war in the East was more a war of movement than the war in the West. But even in the East there were long periods of stalemate, especially during the winters, periods when the opposing armies faced each other in long lines of improvised fortifications in trench warfare much like that in the West.

The Russians began well. Against the exposed Austrian salient of Galicia (Austria's share of the eighteenth-century partitions of Poland), the Russians threw in vast masses of men. They pushed the Austrians out of Lemberg (later the Polish Lwów, now the Soviet Lvov), and by the end of September 1914 they had reached the northern ends of some of the passes leading into Hungary through the Carpathian Mountains. Against the Germans, who also had to defend in East Prussia a salient surrounded on the east and south by Russian territory, the Russians won the Battle of Gumbinnen, in August 1914, and so alarmed the German general staff that the Germans felt obliged to reorganize their eastern command. General von Ludendorff, under the nominal command of his senior, Von Hindenburg, and aided by a brilliant junior, Von Hoffmann, turned successfully against the two Russian armies, which were attempting a pincers movement. Late in August, at Tannenberg, the Germans decisively defeated a Russian army under Samsonov, who committed suicide. And early in September they won another decisive victory against the Russians at the Masurian lakes, thus clearing East Prussia of Russians.

The Germans' hard-pressed Austrian allies to the south were by now clamoring for help, and the western front was still demanding men. Hindenburg and his aides had to do their best with what they had. In a series of hard-fought battles in Poland, they succeeded in relieving the pressure on the Austrians. The end of the year 1914 found the Austrians still hanging on in Galicia and found the Germans in a good position to push eastward from East Prussian and Polish bases. In two great joint offensives in May and July 1915 the Central Powers won substantial successes, inflicting on the Russians severe losses, from which they never really recovered. At the end of the year 1915 the battle line ran roughly from near Riga, deep in the Baltic provinces of Russia, to the eastern edge of Galicia at Tarnopol and Czernowitz.

In 1916, the Russians, with a new commander, General Brusilov, undertook a great new offensive against the Austrians in the south. The Russian need to bolster their failing morale would probably have made some action necessary, but the Russians were also being pressed by the Western Allies to do something to help the Italians, who were threatened by the Austrians in the region of Trent. It seems likely that the Brusilov offensive was begun too soon, without adequate preparation. It scored a striking success at first; in places, the Russians drove the Austrians back some eighty miles, and they took large numbers of prisoners. But once more the Germans came to the rescue; with fresh troops transferred from the West, they halted Brusilov before he had won a decisive success.

It was from the backwash of this defeat that the Russian Revolution, which began early in March 1917, was born. In the moderate phase of that uprising, before the Bolshevik revolution of

November 1917, Brusilov undertook one last desperate offensive. But he was soon checked, and the way was open for the Bolsheviks to carry out their promise to make peace. By the end of 1917, Russia was out of the war. She was forced by the Central Powers to sign the extraordinarily punitive Peace of Brest-Litovsk (March 1918), by which she lost her Polish territories, her Baltic provinces, the entire Ukraine, Finland, and some lands in the Caucasus. The Caucasian lands went to Turkey; most of the others came under what proved to be the temporary domination of Austria and Germany.

The Italian Front

In April 1915 Italy concluded with Britain, France, and Russia the secret Treaty of London, which promised the Italians their long-sought-for Trent and Trieste, and other lands at Austro-Hungarian and Turkish expense. In May, the Italians formally declared war on Austria-Hun-

Russian and German soldiers fraternizing after the December 5, 1917, armistice between Russia and the Central Powers.

gary (they did not declare war on Germany until August 1916), and a new front was added along the Austro-Italian frontier at the head of the Adriatic. Much of this front was too mountainous for effective action, and it was pretty much confined to some sixty miles along the Isonzo River. For two years there was a series of bloody but indecisive actions along this river that at least pinned down several hundred thousand Austrian troops. Then in the late autumn of 1917, with Russia already beaten, came the blow that very nearly knocked Italy out. Once again the Germans supplied the propulsive force. Ludendorff, now in supreme command, sent six German divisions to the Isonzo. The Germans and Austrians broke through at Caporetto and sent the Italians into a retreat across the Venetian plains, a retreat that was really a rout. French and British reinforcements were hastily rushed across the Alps, but what did most to stop the Austro-Germans was probably the grave difficulty, under modern conditions of warfare, of supplying mass armies of infantry in rapid advance. The Italians were finally able to hold along the line of the Piave River, almost at the Po.

The Dardanelles

One of the most important of the "sideshows," the Dardanelles campaign of 1915, not only proved in its failure to be a bad blow to the morale of the Allies, but was to have important repercussions in World War II. With the entry of Turkey into the war in November 1914, and with the western front capable for the moment of being held against the Germans by the French alone, a group of British military and political leaders advanced the idea that British strength should be put into amphibious operations somewhere in the Aegean area. A steady drive could also be made overland toward Vienna and Berlin through territory where the Central Powers were not expecting an attack in force. The great exponent of this "Eastern Plan" was Winston Churchill, first lord of the admiralty. The British decided to try the plan. The point of attack chosen was the Dardanelles, the more westerly of the two straits that separate the Black Sea from the Aegean. The campaign is sometimes known as the "Gallipoli campaign" from the long narrow peninsula on the European side of

the Straits which was one of the keys to the whole action. Here Allied victory would have had the additional advantage of opening communication with Russia via the Black Sea.

In March 1915 the British and French fleets tried to force the Straits, but they abandoned the attempt somewhat prematurely when several ships struck mines. Later landings of British, Australian, New Zealand, and French troops at various points on both Asian and European shores of the Dardanelles were poorly coordinated and badly backed up. They met with fierce and effective resistance from the Turks—a junior officer named Mustafa Kemal greatly distinguishing himself—and in the end they had to be abandoned. Russia remained sealed in by the Straits all during the war. But Churchill continued to believe that the Dardanelles plan had failed, not because it was a bad plan, but because it had not been carried out with determination. And in the Second World War he was to revive, against American military opinion, something of his old plan, which became known as the plan to strike at the "soft underbelly" of the Axis.

The Balkan Fronts

Serbia's part in the crisis that produced the war meant that from the start there would be a Balkan front. In the end there were several such fronts, and no Balkan state remained uninvolved. The Austrians failed here also, and although in December 1914 they did manage to take the Serbian capital, Belgrade, they were driven out again. Bulgaria, wooed by both sides, finally came in with the Central Powers in the autumn of 1915. The Germans sent troops and a general, von Mackensen, under whom the Serbs were finally beaten. The remnant of their armies was driven to take refuge on the island of Corfu in neutral Greece.

To counter this blow in the Balkans, the Allies had already landed a few divisions in the Greek city of Salonika and had established a front in Macedonia. The Greeks themselves were divided into two groups. One was headed by King Constantine, who at bottom was sympathetic with the Central Powers, but who for the moment was seeking only to maintain Greek neutrality. The other was a pro-Ally group headed by the able old politican Venizelos. Al-

Europe, 1914-1918

NORWAY
SWEDEN
St. Petersburg
Volga R.
IRELAND
GREAT BRITAIN
North Sea
Battle of Jutland
DENMARK
Baltic Sea
Riga
Königsberg
RUSSIA
Smolensk
Moscow
London
NETH.
Elbe R.
Berlin
GERMANY
Rhine R.
E. PRUSSIA
Masurian Lakes
Tannenburg
Niemen R.
Warsaw
POLAND
Oder R.
Brest-Litovsk
Vistula R.
Kiev
Dnieper R.
Ostend
BELG.
LUX.
Paris
Seine R.
Verdun
Loire R.
FRANCE
Danube R.
Prague
Cracow
Lemberg
GALICIA
Tarnopol
Czernowitz
Dniester R.
Belfort
SWITZ.
Vienna
Budapest
Locarno
Milan
Isonzo R.
AUSTRIA-HUNGARY
TRANSYL-VANIA
Bordeaux
Rhone R.
Piave R.
Caporetto
Genoa
Rapallo
Sava R.
BOSNIA
Sarajevo
Belgrade
ROMANIA
Bucharest
Black Sea
PORTUGAL
Ebro R.
Leghorn
CORSICA (Fr.)
ITALY
DALMATIA
SERBIA
MONTENEGRO
Danube R.
Tagus R.
Madrid
SPAIN
Rome
BULGARIA
Sofia
Constantinople
Bosporus
Gibraltar (Br.)
BALEARIC IS.
SARDINIA
ALBANIA
MACEDONIA
Salonika
GREECE
Gallipoli
The Straits
Dardanelles
SPANISH MOROCCO
CORFU
Athens
OTTOMAN EMPIRE
MOROCCO
ALGERIA
SICILY
DODECANESE (It.)
RHODES
CYPRUS (Br.)
TUNISIA
MALTA (Br.)
Mediterranean Sea
CRETE
Nile R.
LIBYA
Cairo
EGYPT
Suez Canal

Legend

- ☐ Allied and Associated Powers
- ☐ Central Powers and their Allies
- ☐ Neutrals
- —— Political boundaries, 1914
- —·—·— Boundary between Austria and Hungary
- — — — Greatest advance by Central Powers
- ·········· Greatest advance by Allies
- ■ Battle site

0 ____ 500
Miles

The Middle East, 1914-18

Black Sea
Trebizond
Caspian Sea
Tigris R.
Baghdad
Damascus
Euphrates R.
Basra
Mediterranean Sea
Nile R.
Jerusalem
Cairo
Persian Gulf

☐ Area of military action, 1914-18

Asia and the Pacific, 1914-15

Tsingtau
JAPAN
CHINA
Pacific Ocean
FORMOSA
INDIA
Madras
PHILIPPINE IS.
PENANG I.
YAP
CAROLINE IS.
Indian Ocean
Rabaul
AUSTRALIA

■ Battles and other military actions, 1914-15

though the Allies rode roughshod over formal notions of Greek neutrality, Venizelos did not get firmly into the saddle until June 1917, when Allied pressure compelled King Constantine to abdicate in favor of his second son, Alexander.

Meanwhile Romania, whom the Russians had been trying to lure into the war, finally yielded to promises of great territorial gains at the expense of Austria-Hungary and came in on the Allied side late in August 1916, at a time most inopportune for the Romanians. Stiffened by German help, the Austrians swept through Romania and by January 1917 held most of the country. When the Russians made the separate Peace of Brest-Litovsk with the Germans in March 1918, the Romanians were obliged to make cessions of territory to Bulgaria, and to grant a lease of oil lands to Germany.

T. E. Lawrence.

In spite of the formal accession of Greece to the Allied side in June 1917, the Macedonian front remained in a stalemate until the summer of 1918, when, with American troops pouring rapidly into France, the Allied military leaders decided they could afford to build up their forces in Salonika. The investment paid well, for under the leadership of the French general Franchet d'Esperey the Allied armies on this front were the first to break the enemy completely. The French, British, Serbs, and Greeks began a great advance on September 15, 1918, all along the line from the Adriatic to the Bulgarian frontier. They forced the Bulgarians to conclude an armistice on September 30, and by early November they had crossed the Danube in several places. The armistice in the West on November 11 found the tricolor of France, with the flags of many allies, well on its way to Vienna. This hark-back to Napoleon helped inspire in the French a somewhat unfounded confidence that they were once more the dominant nation on the continent of Europe.

The Near East and the Colonies

A whole series of fronts throughout the world was involved in what we may call the colonial "clean-up," the subduing of the German overseas empire and of the outlying parts of the Turkish Empire. The Turks, trained and in part officered by German experts, often resisted effectively. In Mesopotamia, in April 1916, in a blow to British prestige as bad as the Dardanelles defeat, they forced the surrender of the British general Townshend, who had landed at Basra from India in 1915 and had marched up the Tigris-Euphrates Valley. But the Turks were never able to take the Suez Canal, nor to advance far into Russian Armenia. Moreover, the British were able to play on the Arabs' dislike for their Turkish suzerains. The romantic Colonel T. E. Lawrence, an Englishman who knew the Arabs intimately, played a leading part in coordinating an Arab revolt with a British expedition from Egypt under Allenby. By the end of 1917, the British held Baghdad and Jerusalem. In September 1918, a great British offensive in Syria was so successful that on October 30 the Turks concluded an armistice which took them out of the war.

These campaigns, fought in the lands that had been the cradles of Western civilization, were of great importance in making the world we live in today. For from them came not only the independent Arab nations (Syria, Lebanon, Iraq, Jordan, Saudi Arabia, Egypt) but also the Jewish national state of Israel, to which these Arab states are so hostile. In November 1917, in the Balfour Declaration, the British promised "the establishment in Palestine of a national home for the Jewish people." This promise bore fruit in the mandate of 1922 from the League of Nations, by which such a home was set up under British protection.

In the overseas colonies the Germans, though cut off from the homeland by the British navy, fought well. In East Africa they actually managed to hold out to the bitter end in a series of skillful campaigns, so that they still had forces in the field on Armistice Day, November 11, 1918. But elsewhere they were fighting from inadequate bases and with inadequate forces, so that by the end of 1914 the British, Australians, South Africans, French, and Japanese had pretty well taken over the German overseas possessions. The Allies had won the "colonial war." Only years later, however, did the most important result of that war become clear. The subject races had learned that their rulers were by no means invulnerable.

The War at Sea

This brings us to a most important front—the war at sea. In the long pull, British sea power, reinforced by the French and later by the Italian and the American navies, once more proved decisive. The Allied command of the sea made it possible to draw on the resources of the rest of the world, and in particular to transfer with surprisingly few losses large numbers of British and American troops to the crucial western front. Quite as important, sea power enabled the Allies to shut Germany and her allies off from overseas resources. The Allied blockade slowly but surely constricted Germany, limiting not merely military supplies for her armies, but food supplies for her civilian population. At the end of 1918, many Germans were suffering from malnutrition, an important factor in the German willingness to surrender without fighting to the bitter end.

Yet the war at sea was not easy for the Allies. The submarine proved every bit as dangerous as British alarmists before the war had feared. When the Germans launched their unrestricted submarine warfare, they made dangerous inroads on the merchant ships that were essential to the very life of Britain. By the end of 1917, some 8,000,000 tons of shipping had been sunk by the Germans, most of it by submarines. And at one point in 1917, the British had barely enough food reserves to last a month. The submarine menace was eventually overcome by a series of measures co-ordinated between the Allies and the Americans—extensive use of the convoy system, attacks on submarines by depth bombs, constant anti-submarine patrols, and development of small, fast "subchasers." But we might wonder what would have happened in 1916-1917 (and again in 1942-1943) if the Germans had contented themselves with holding actions on land and had put all their productive and fighting energies into the submarine. This they did not do in either world war. Temptation for quick and obvious land success proved to be too great in both cases.

The navy of surface vessels that the Germans had built up since the 1890's—and that, as we have seen, was so important in the growth of Anglo-German hostility—never played a really decisive part in the war itself. German surface-raiders caused severe damage in the first year, but they were finally swept off the seas. Once, however, the main German fleet threw a very bad scare into the British. This was the famous Battle of Jutland, which has been refought over and over again by naval historians. This running battle, fought in the North Sea on May 31 and June 1, 1916, resulted in the sinking of twice as much British as German tonnage, and showed how good the German navy was. But the German admiral, Scheer, was forced to run into port before the British capital ships, for which he was no match. Although Jutland was a tactical victory for the Germans, the strategic victory remained with the British, for never again did the German surface navy seriously threaten British command of the sea in European waters. At the war's end the German high command attempted to get the fleet out in a heroic last stand. It was the German sailors' refusal to take the ships out— their mutiny, in fact—that gave a critical push to the German revolution which led to the Armistice of 1918.

The Western Front: Allied Victory

This war also saw the beginnings of air warfare. German lighter-than-air machines, the Zeppelins, raided London many times in 1916–1917, and both sides made airplane bombing raids on nearby towns. But the total damage was relatively light and had no decisive effect on the final result. The airplane was of more importance in scouting, and especially in spotting for artillery; in spite of its short range in those days, it also proved useful as a means of locating submarines. The fighter plane was greatly improved during the war, and the base was laid for the development of the air forces we now know. Indeed, the airplane made greater technical strides in these four years of war than it had made since the Wrights first flew at Kitty Hawk in 1903.

Although the great new invention of the airplane did not itself alter traditional warfare, a new type of warfare was indeed developed, especially on the great western front, the warfare of the trenches. The machine gun, the repeating rifle, and fast-firing artillery, with the guidance of spotter planes, could pour in such deadly fire that it was almost impossible for either side to break through the opposing trench systems on a wide front. Both sides tried to break through in the two years after the Marne, and both sides suffered losses of a magnitude that had never been suffered before.

Two new weapons almost broke the deadlock. The first was poison gas, which was first used by the Germans in shells in October 1914, with disappointing results. Then in April 1915 the Germans used chlorine gas discharged from cylinders. The overwhelmed French broke in a line five miles wide, leaving the line completely undefended. But the Germans had not prepared to follow through, and the gap was closed once the gas had dispersed. Meanwhile the experts developed a simple countermeasure, the gas mask, which became part of the equipment of every soldier on both sides. The age-old balance of attack and defense was once again reestablished.

The second new weapon came much nearer to producing decisive success. This was the tank, a sort of armored land battleship for which plans had been made back in the Renaissance by the fertile Leonardo da Vinci. But Leonardo's tank remained a mere sketch for lack of propulsive power. In the second decade of the twentieth century, however, the internal-combustion engine was ready to do what horses could not do. The tank was a British invention that had been nursed along in its infancy by the always adventurous Winston Churchill; it acquired its improbable name when early models were shipped under tarpaulins, which the curious were told simply covered water tanks. But the new weapon was used too soon, in inadequate numbers and before adequate mechanical tests had been made, in the British Somme offensive of 1916. Even so, nine tanks led or accompanied the infantry triumphantly through the German lines to the capture of Flers. Had the tanks been withheld for a few more months and been backed up with careful planning, they might have broken the German lines on a wide front. The Germans, however, were soon producing tanks of their own.

The Germans also developed a spectacular new weapon that struck the imagination of the world, though it had no effect on the outcome of the war. "Big Bertha" was a gun of incredibly long range, which began throwing occasional shells into Paris from the nearest point in the German lines, some seventy-five miles away. The Parisians were astounded, since no hostile planes had appeared. But "Big Bertha" could fire only a few shells before it needed repair and proved to be of no more than nuisance value.

Techniques of attack gradually developed over the years and in the end broke the defensive stalemate in the west. Long and massive discharge of artillery, known as a *barrage,* literally flattened out a section of the enemy defenses and the no-man's land in front of them and forced the enemy to retire to rear trenches. Then, accompanied or preceded by tanks, the infantry edged in while the artillery barrage was lifted and focused on the next enemy line. It was a slow and costly process which did not work on a wide scale until 1918. Then the Germans, with the Russians out of the fight, made a last and almost successful effort to break through, trying to separate the British from the French where their lines joined near Amiens. With the failure of this last German push in the summer, Foch ordered a general attack. French, British, and American armies had all broken the German lines by early autumn and were just gaining freedom of action in the open country when the Germans surren-

A tank supporting the Australian-American assault on the Hindenburg line.

dered. The Germans later maintained that they were not beaten decisively in the field. Most experts, however, now think that had the war gone on the Germans could not have stopped an Allied invasion of Germany in 1919.

Morale on the Fighting Fronts

The long, narrow battle lines of the four-year trench war were the scene of a concentrated destruction hardly equaled in the war of 1939–1945, except by the atomic bomb at Hiroshima; at some points in France the topsoil was blown completely away by shellfire, producing a desert that is still visible today. The war, however, was not unique, unprecedented, or unlike all other wars, as many an excited publicist at the time declared. It produced military heroes and military scapegoats, great generals and generals who failed. As with the Confederacy in the American Civil War, the defeated Germans seem to have had the most-praised generals, the Ludendorffs, the Mackensens, the Hoffmanns. The old traditional chivalrous warfare, the warfare of athletic heroes, was continued, and even heightened in the air, where the "aces" of the highly in-

dividualistic duels between planes were the Rolands of a machine age. And in many of the fronts on land, and in the war at sea, the age-old and for many males not altogether unhappy melodrama of war lost none of its reality. Lawrence in Arabia was no disgrace to the tradition of Sir Walter Scott or even, in the eyes of good patriotic Englishmen, to the tradition of Homer.

Yet especially on the western front, this war seemed to many of its participants an unheroic nightmare of blood and filth. Sensitive young intellectuals, who in earlier times would never have had to fight, survived to write bitterly about their experiences—in war novels like *Under Fire* by the Frenchman Barbusse, or *All Quiet on the Western Front* by the German Remarque, and in war poems like those of Siegfried Sassoon and Wilfred Owen. But this literature cannot be trusted fully as an accurate reflection of what the millions of common soldiers who were not intellectuals felt about the war. We know simply that for four years they bore up under it in stints in the front lines separated by rest leaves. For most of them the dullness, the discomforts, and the brief terror of battle must have tested their patriotism and worn out their sense of adventure.

Here is a passage, not by one of the most bitterly radical of the intellectuals, or about the western front. John Masefield, the British poet, is writing about Gallipoli, where he took part in the Dardanelles campaign:

Let the reader imagine himself to be facing three miles of any very rough broken sloping ground known to him. . . . Let him say to himself that he and an army of his friends are about to advance up the slope towards the top and that as they will be advancing in a line, along the whole length of the three miles, he will only see the advance of those comparatively near to him, since folds or dips in the ground will hide the others. Let him, before he advances, look earnestly along the line of the hill, as it shows up clear, in blazing sunlight only a mile from him, to see his tactical objective, one little clump of pines, three hundred yards away, across what seem to be fields. Let him see in the whole length of the hill no single human being, nothing but scrub, earth, a few scattered buildings. . . . Let him imagine himself to be more weary than he has ever been in his life before, and dirtier than he has ever believed it possible to be, and parched with thirst, nervous, wild-eyed and rather lousy. Let him think that he has not slept for more than a few minutes together for eleven days and nights, and that in all his waking hours he has been fighting for his life, often hand to hand in the dark with a fierce enemy, and that after each fight he has had to dig himself a hole in the ground, often with his hands, and then walk three or four roadless miles to bring up heavy boxes under fire. Let him think, too, that in all those eleven days he has never for an instant been out of the thunder of cannon, that waking or sleeping their devastating crash has been blasting the air across within a mile or two, and this from an artillery so terrible that each discharge beats as it were a wedge of shock between the skull-bone and the brain. Let him think too that never, for an instant, in all that time, has he been free or even partly free from the peril of death in its most sudden and savage forms, and that hourly in all that time he has seen his friends blown to pieces at his side, or dismembered, or drowned, or driven mad, or stabbed, or sniped by some unseen stalker, or bombed in the dark sap with a handful of dynamite in a beef-tin, till their blood is caked upon his clothes and thick upon his face, and that he knows, as he stares at the hill, that in a few moments, more of that dwindling band, already too few, God knows how many too few, for the task to be done, will be gone the same way, and that he himself may reckon that he has done with life, tasted and spoken and loved his last, and that in a few minutes more may be blasted dead, or lying bleeding in the scrub, with perhaps his face gone and a leg and an arm broken, unable to move but still alive, unable to drive away the flies or screen the ever-dropping rain, in a place where none will find him, or be able to help him, a place where he will die and rot and shrivel, till nothing is left of him but a few rags and a few remnants and a little identification-disc flapping on his bones in the wind.*

The Home Fronts

These soldiers and sailors were, for the most part, not professionals; they were civilians, "drafted," lifted from civilian families unused to the ways of the military. Behind the front, on the production lines, subject to the unheroic but harassing strains of rationing and all sorts of limitations in daily living, subject also to the constant prodding of war propaganda, the families too were part of this great "total war." They too bore up under it, though in France in 1917, after the bloody failure of a great offensive under General Nivelle, civilian and military discontent, fanned by politicians, came almost to the point of breaking French morale. And in Germany, the collapse that resulted in the armistice of November 11, 1918, though it obviously had many complex causes, looks like a general failure of morale, a psychological collapse under intolerable spiritual and material pressures.

For the Germans, still influenced by nineteenth-century ideas about the rights of the individual and laissez-faire economics, were slow to organize their society for total war. They failed notably to ensure the proper and equitable distribution of food supplies, so that as 1918 wore on whole sectors of the urban population began to suffer from malnutrition. Nor were finances and war production managed with that perfection of techniques that most of the world had already come to expect of the Germans. Rationing, strict control of production, price control, systematic use of the resources of conquered countries, these and many other measures were employed by the Germans, but not with the care, decisiveness, and long preparation that were to characterize them in the conflict of 1939–1945.

All countries engaged in the war, the democratic Western Allies as well as the autocratic

* John Masefield, *Gallipoli* (New York, 1916), pp. 96–99.

Central Powers, sooner or later felt obliged to introduce drastic wartime economic planning, which anticipated in some sense the more collectivistic economy of today. Everywhere there was compulsory military service. Even in Britain, proud of its long devotion to the rights of the individual, the famous Defense of the Realm Act—known with wry affection as DORA—clamped down severely on the Englishman's sacred right to say and do what he liked, even if he did not seem to be giving aid and comfort to the enemy. In the United States, all sorts of men, including the famous "dollar-a-year men," business executives who were working for the government for the first time, flocked to Washington and helped build up an enormous new central government, which regulated the economy as it had never been regulated before. And of course all the belligerents engaged in the war of propaganda, or, as it came to be called in the next great war, in psychological warfare.

The Allies won the battle of the production lines, in which the United States played a major if not a decisive part. We have already noted that in material resources the Allies had a marked potential superiority over the Central Powers; this superiority they were eventually able to realize to the full. Allied production was slow in getting started. There were mistakes, bottlenecks, and experiments like that of the tanks which failed at first because of undue haste. At the beginning the Allies were often at cross purposes in production as well as in actual military strategy. Nevertheless, by the end of 1917 the Allied military machine was adequately, indeed in some ways wastefully, supplied.

The Role of Propaganda

The Allies also won the most critical phase of the war of propaganda. They sought to convince the neutral world, especially the neutrals of Western civilization, the United States, Latin America, and the Swiss, Dutch, Scandinavians, and Spanish, that the Allies were fighting for the right and the Central Powers for the wrong. It was not a complete victory, for important groups in all these countries remained pro-German to

"France at Her Furnaces, 1917": A painting by James McBey pointing to the importance of factories in the war effort.

Women working in a U.S. factory to help the war effort.

the end, and Spain on the whole was probably throughout the war pro-German, or at least anti-French and anti-English. Still, it seems that a majority of the neutral West was early convinced that the cause of the Allies was just. This conviction was strengthened from the very start by the traditional liberalism of France and Britain in contrast with the traditional autocracy of the German and the Austrian empires, though the presence of the autocratic Russian Empire on the Allied side somewhat handicapped Allied propagandists. In the early days of the crisis of 1914, the intransigence of the Austrians toward the Serbs, and in particular the blundering phrase of Bethmann-Hollweg, that Britain had gone to war for a mere "scrap of paper," got the Central Powers off to a bad start in world opinion.

The sense of Allied rightness was strengthened by early Allied propaganda, which was often one-sided and unfair. Notably, it accused the Germans of frightful atrocities in Belgium. The Germans did indeed impose rigorous military controls on conquered populations, but little in their record was worse than is usual, and perhaps inevitable, in all warfare. Allied propaganda also simplified and falsified the complex chain of causation that produced the war, making it appear that the Germans and Austrians were wholly responsible for the outbreak of the war, that the "predatory Potsdam gang" had planned the whole thing from the beginning, and that Serbs, French, Russians, and British had been wholly innocent of deed or word that might have brought on the war. This propaganda backfired shortly after the war; revulsion against its unfairness had much to do with the widespread acceptance of the extreme—and false—revisionist thesis that on the whole Germany, in particular, had been quite guiltless of starting the war.

Political Repercussions

Except in Russia, the four years of war saw no major changes in political structure. The Central Powers retained until their collapse their incompletely responsible parliamentary governments, and the parliaments on the whole were reasonably submissive. And in spite of the inevitable strengthening of the executive in wartime, France, Britain, and the United States carried on their democratic institutions. In the United States the critical presidential election of 1916 came just before American entrance into the war, and resulted by a narrow margin in the return of the incumbent, Woodrow Wilson. In Britain and France the democratic process brought to power in the midst of wartime crisis two strong men—Lloyd George and Clemenceau—who carried through with great vigor the prosecution of the war, and who, though their fame was dimmed in the troubled years after the war, remain in historic memory as great national heroes of their respective countries.

In Britain the skillful but indecisive Liberal leader Asquith proved unable to master events, even though he widened his government into a coalition in May 1915. In December of that year he was succeeded by another Liberal, Lloyd George, the architect of Britain's social insurance system, who had also proven himself an admirable organizer of war production. Under Lloyd George the coalition really worked, and his position as war leader was to remain unchallenged. We shall meet him again at the peace negotiations, as we shall meet his French counterpart, Clemenceau. "The Tiger," as Clemenceau was known to his friends and enemies alike, came to power at the end of 1917, at a time when defeatism threatened both the military and the civilian strength of France. Clemenceau took firm command of the war effort and disposed summarily of the disaffected politicians with the decisiveness—and disregard for the peacetime "rights of man"—of an old Jacobin.

IV   The Peace Settlements

As in Westphalia in 1648, at Utrecht in 1713, and at Vienna in 1815, the warring powers gathered in a great meeting to make the peace settlement. This time they met at Paris—or, rather, in suburban Paris. They met at Versailles to settle with the Germans, and at other suburban chateaux to settle with the rest. Peace congresses almost never meet in a world that is really at peace. There are always aftermaths, local wars and disturbances. The aftermaths of 1918–1919 were particularly numerous and acute and conditioned the whole work of the peace congresses. To them we must turn briefly before we consider the actual settlements.

The Aftermath of World War

The sorest spot was Russia, then in 1919 in the throes of civil war and foreign invasion. No sooner had the Germans been forced to withdraw from the regions they had gained at Brest-Litovsk than the Allies sent detachments to various points along the rim of Russia—on the Black Sea, on the White Sea in the far north, and on the Pacific. The Allies still hoped to restore in Russia, if not the monarchy, at least a moderate democratic republic. Their dread of final Bolshevik success ("Bolshevism," not "communism," was the term almost universally used during this period) and of the possible spread of Bolshevism westward added to the tensions at Versailles and confirmed the conservative position that both Clemenceau and Lloyd George were taking.

Bolshevism was indeed spreading westward. The German revolution of November 1918 had been carried out under socialist auspices. But all through the winter of 1918–1919 there were communist riots and uprisings, and in Bavaria in April a soviet republic was proclaimed. The government of the new republic of Germany put these communist uprisings down, but only by an appeal to the remnants of the old army and to officers thoroughly hostile to any form of republic. In the break-up of the Austro-Hungarian monarchy in the autumn of 1918, the successor states—Czechoslovakia, Austria, Hungary, Yugoslavia, Romania—which had been formed in whole or in part out of the former Hapsburg lands, were disturbed by all sorts of social and economic troubles. In Hungary, Bela Kun, who had worked with Lenin in Moscow, won power by means of a socialist-communist coalition, and then elbowed out his socialist colleagues and set up a Bolshevik dictatorship. In August, a Romanian army that had invaded Hungary forced Bela Kun to flee. Finally, all through the Germanies groups of ex-soldiers, the Freikorps, were roving about, stirring up trouble and threatening the overthrow of the German Republic.

In the Near East the Allies had even worse troubles to face. Greece, which had been so hard to drag into the war, was now in full cry against the Turks. Her nationalists had revived the old hope of a restored Byzantine Empire, with the Greeks once more in command of the Straits. Her armies, not without Allied encouragement, landed at Smyrna in Asia Minor in the spring of 1919 and marched off in the track of Alexander the Great. The French and the British, to whom control over different parts of the former Turkish Empire had been assigned, began at once having trouble with their new Arab wards. The Jews were already pressing for the establishment of a national home in Palestine in accordance with the Balfour Declaration, and the Arabs were already opposing them.

In India the aftermath of war was particularly bad. The universal epidemic of influenza in 1918 (which most public-health experts believed killed more people than were killed in battle) had been especially disastrous in India. Indians had fought well as professional soldiers during the war on the Allied side; educated Indians thought their country was ripe for much more self-rule. The disorders of 1918–1919 culminated in the Amritsar massacre of April 1919, in which a British general, reverting to old-time methods, ordered his soldiers to fire on an unarmed crowd, killing or wounding some 1,600 people. Amritsar shocked world opinion, added to the odium the Allies were already acquiring among liberals everywhere, and knitted India more closely together in opposition to the British.

The situation in China was as shaky. The weakening of Russia had been taken by the Japanese as a signal to renew their ambitious plans in the north of China, and the American troops sent to Vladivostok in Siberia were there less to oppose the Bolsheviks than to oppose the Japanese.

So the world was in turmoil and disorder when the Allies, great, small, and middle-sized, assembled in and near Paris to make the peace. The problems that faced the peacemakers were worldwide, complex, and often insoluble—insoluble in the sense that no decision on a given problem, say the disposition of the Adriatic port of Fiume, which was claimed by Italians and Yugoslavs, could possibly satisfy all the major groups concerned, to say nothing of the minorities. Yet the world hoped, and indeed expected, from the peacemakers more than it had in any previous crisis. Public opinion in the eighteenth and nineteenth centuries had built up a tremendous faith in the possibility of a peaceful, just, and happy world. This war had been a war to "make the world safe for democracy," a "war to end war." It had produced in the American president Wilson a man who could phrase skillfully the hopes of men, and who as he journeyed to Paris after the Armistice appeared to be the heroic savior and hope of mankind.

All men were not Wilsonians. There were, inevitably, the selfish, the disillusioned, the narrow, the jingoists, and the professionals who had made promises to the Italians and the Romanians, who had planned all sorts of compensations and adjustments. There were the average men and women who wanted peace and security but who also wanted national glory and the punishment of the wicked Germans, who, they believed, had put them through those four years of hell. There were, in short, thousands of conflicting hopes and fears, all of them embodied in living human flesh, not just the abstractions they must seem to be on the printed page.

The Fourteen Points

The more generous of these hopes were in 1918 clearly embodied in one man and in one text. Woodrow Wilson, on January 8, 1918, in an address to the American Congress, had announced the famous Fourteen Points, which were widely accepted by people in Allied countries and even in Germany and Austria as a platform for the peace to come, but were also widely misunderstood and subject to the most divergent interpretations. Here is the whole of this most important document:

I. Open covenants of peace, openly arrived at, after which there shall be no private international understandings of any kind but diplomacy shall proceed always frankly and in the public view.
II. Absolute freedom of navigation upon the seas, outside territorial waters, alike in peace and in war, except as the seas may be closed in whole or in part by international action for the enforcement of international covenants.
III. The removal, so far as possible, of all economic barriers and the establishment of an equality of trade conditions among all the nations consenting to the peace and associating themselves for its maintenance.

The Big Four in Paris, December 1918. Seated, from left to right: Orlando, Lloyd George, Clemenceau, and Wilson.

IV. Adequate guarantees given and taken that national armaments will be reduced to the lowest point consistent with domestic safety.

V. A free, open-minded, and absolutely impartial adjustment of all colonial claims, based upon a strict observance of the principle that in determining all such questions of sovereignty the interests of the populations concerned must have equal weight with the equitable claims of the government whose title is to be determined.

VI. The evacuation of all Russian territory and such a settlement of all questions affecting Russia as will secure the best and freest co-operation of the other nations of the world in obtaining for her an unhampered and unembarrassed opportunity for the independent determination of her own political development and national policy and assure her of a sincere welcome into the society of free nations under institutions of her own choosing; and, more than a welcome,

assistance also of every kind that she may need and may herself desire. The treatment accorded Russia by her sister nations in the months to come will be the acid test of their good will, of their comprehension of her needs as distinguished from their own interests, and of their intelligent and unselfish sympathy.

VII. Belgium, the whole world will agree, must be evacuated and restored, without any attempt to limit the sovereignty which she enjoys in common with all other free nations. No other single act will serve as this will serve to restore confidence among the nations in the laws which they have themselves set and determined for the government of their relations with one another. Without this healing act the whole structure and validity of international law is forever impaired.

VIII. All French territory should be freed and the invaded portions restored, and the wrong done to France by Prussia in 1871 in the matter of Alsace-Lorraine, which has unsettled the peace of the world for nearly fifty years, should be righted, in order that peace may once more be made secure in the interest of all.

IX. A readjustment of the frontiers of Italy should be effected along clearly recognizable lines of nationality.

X. The peoples of Austria-Hungary, whose place among the nations we wish to see safeguarded and assured, should be accorded the freest opportunity of autonomous development.

XI. Rumania, Serbia, and Montenegro should be evacuated; occupied territories restored; Serbia accorded free and secure access to the sea; and the relations of the several Balkan states to one another determined by friendly counsel along historically established lines of allegiance and nationality; and international guarantees of the political and economic independence and territorial integrity of the several Balkan states should be entered into.

XII. The Turkish portions of the present Ottoman Empire should be assured a secure sovereignty, but the other nationalities which are now under Turkish rule should be assured an undoubted security of life and an absolutely unmolested opportunity of autonomous development, and the Dardanelles should be permanently opened as a free passage to the ships and commerce of all nations under international guarantees.

XIII. An independent Polish state should be erected which should include the territories inhabited by indisputably Polish populations, which should be assured a free and secure access to the sea, and whose political and economic independence and territorial integrity should be guaranteed by international covenant.

XIV. A general association of nations must be formed under specific covenants for the purpose of affording mutual guarantees of political independence and territorial integrity to great and small states alike.*

The fourteenth point, the germ of the League of Nations, was especially dear to Wilson.

Opposing Hopes and Promises

The hopes and promises that opposed and contradicted the Fourteen Points were not neatly embodied in a single document. We may classify

* Woodrow Wilson, *War and Peace: Presidential Messages, Addresses, and Public Papers,* (eds.) R. S. Baker and W. E. Dodd (New York, 1927), I, pp. 159-161.

them roughly in three categories: the previous diplomatic commitments made by the Allies; the immediate and widespread popular hopes fanned by Allied propaganda and confirmed at the last moment by some Allied statesmen; and—much more difficult to pin down—the long-established habits and traditions that had become part of the dominant policies and trends of each nation, big and little.

In the first category, the most difficult of the diplomatic commitments was the contradictory set of promises made to both Italy and Serbia by the original Entente, including Russia, about the disposal of Hapsburg lands. And there were other commitments, especially in the Balkans, that were very difficult to sort out. In the second category were the promises, widely believed by the British and French peoples, that Germany would be made to suffer to the full for her war guilt. She would have to pay the whole cost of the war in reparations, her war criminals would be punished, she would be rendered incapable ever again of assuming the role of the aggressor. In some vague way, everything would shortly be much better for everybody. Britain, for example, would be "a land fit for heroes."

Finally, in the third category were the deeply rooted drives of the various nations—French drives for revenge against Germany, for restoration of French hegemony in Europe, and, no doubt inconsistently but very humanly, for security; the Italian Irredentist drive; the British longing for a Victorian serenity and economic leadership well armored against German commercial competition; and the nationalist aspirations of the new states of central Europe, released at last from long frustration. And by no means the least important was the old and firmly held American tradition of "isolationism," the desire to be free from European alliances and entanglements.

The Process of Peacemaking

The Peace Conference first met formally on January 18, 1919. Nearly thirty nations involved in the war against the Central Powers sent delegates. Russia was not represented. None of the victorious great powers—Britain, France, the United States—was in a mood to invite the Bolsheviks, now in power in Moscow, to the peace table; and no Russian government-in-exile seemed to the Allies suitable for an invitation. The defeated nations took no part in the deliberations; they were simply notified of the final terms and asked to sign. The Germans, in particular, were given but the slightest chance to comment on or criticize the terms offered them. Very soon the German publicists coined a term for the treaty—"Diktat," the imposed, the dictated peace. The Germans' anger over this failure of the Allies to negotiate with their new and virtuous republic was to play a large part in the ultimate rise of Hitler.

Although a few Western liberals were from the first disillusioned by the exclusion of Communist Russia and the Central Powers from the Peace Conference, the conference did get off to a good start. Wilson's reception in Europe had been extremely enthusiastic. People everywhere were still rejoicing over the end of the nightmare. The Fourteen Points seemed already a realized peace; and for the future, it was held, the proposed association of nations, working together in the freedom of parliamentary discussion, would soon eliminate the costly burdens of armament. Wilson's hopeful phrases sounded in press and pulpit, and none more loudly than his "open covenants openly arrived at." To many a liberal these words meant that the peace would be made in a sort of big, idealized New England town meeting, in which the representatives of all the powers, big and little, would have their free say in public, in which decisions would ultimately be taken by majority vote, in which the caucus, the smoke-filled room, the back-stairs intrigues would all be missing.

These liberals were almost at once disillusioned, for the conference soon fell into the familiar pattern of centuries. The small nations were excluded from the real negotiations; the business of the conference was carried on in private among the political chiefs of the victorious great powers—the Big Four of Wilson, Lloyd George, Clemenceau, and Orlando (it was really a Big Three, for Italy was not strong enough to impose Orlando, who was a much less striking personality than his colleagues). Decisions were made in the traditional way of diplomacy, with all the pressures, chicanery, intrigues, compromises, and plain horse-trading that go on when leaders get together in private. Public opinion was consulted only indirectly, as each statesman sought to make sure that he had at least a ma-

jority of the politically important elements of his own nation behind him in his demands.

The hopeful members of the general public were by no means the only ones who grew disillusioned as the Paris Conference went the way of the Vienna Congress a hundred years before. The professional diplomatists of the little and middle-sized powers had probably never really expected that they would be treated on equal terms, but the completeness of their exclusion from the real work of the conference annoyed them, and angered their people back home. More important, all the major powers had brought with them large staffs of experts—economists, political scientists, historians, career men in many fields. These bright young men were sure they knew better than their elders how to solve the problems of human relations, were confident that they would do the real work and make the really important decisions. They drew up report after report, some of which went up through devious channels to Clemenceau or Lloyd George or Wilson. But they did not make policy. The disillusion of the young experts was great and long-lived, and since many of them were quite articulate they did much to discredit the work of the conference, especially among liberal intellectuals everywhere.

Wilson and his experts were gradually badgered into accepting harsher peace terms. The reparations bill against Germany was lengthened; Poland, Italy, and Japan made claims to lands that clearly could never be justified on the basis of self-determination by the peoples concerned; the victors more and more openly showed that they proposed to behave as victors in war habitually have behaved. Wilson gave way or compromised on a dozen points and then chose to stand fast against the weakest of the Allies. He would not let the Italians have the Adriatic seaport of Fiume, which had once been the sole seaport of Hungary. They might have neighboring Trieste and their coveted Trentino, where they could rule over German or Slavic-speaking minorities, indeed, in some areas, majorities; but Fiume they might not have. Fiume was indeed a difficult case. It was Italian-speaking and historically was linked with the great past of Venice; but it had never been part of modern Italy, and it had not been promised to Italy in the secret treaties of 1915. The Italian delegation left the conference in anger, but Wilson was immovable. The fate of Fiume was not

President Wilson.

permanent seats, and to which four other member states were chosen by the assembly for specific terms. A permanent secretariat, to be located at Geneva, was charged with administering the affairs of the League. In its working out, as we shall see, the League never fulfilled the hopes of the liberals. It did not achieve disarmament, nor did its machinery of peacemaking prove capable of preventing aggression. The great powers simply went on their usual ways, using the League only as their policymakers—their heads of state rather than their diplomatists— saw fit.

The Territorial Settlement

Central to all the work in Paris was the problem of territorial changes. Here, peacemakers were confronted not merely, as at most peace conferences in our Western society, with the claims of the victorious Allies but also with the claims of the new nations that had sprung up from the disintegrating Austrian, Russian, and Turkish empires. They had to try to satisfy the eternal land hunger of those who run nations, without violating too obviously the great Wilsonian principle of "self-determination of peoples." This principle was hard indeed to apply in much of central Europe, where peoples of different language and national self-consciousness were mixed together in an incredible mosaic of unassimilated minorities. The result was to multiply the number of "sovereign" nations in this world. Nationalism, which some hopeful people had thought was on the wane, was now fanned to intense new life in a dozen states.

France received Alsace-Lorraine back from Germany. Clemenceau also hoped both to annex the small but coal-rich Saar Basin of Germany as compensation for French coal mines destroyed by the Germans during the war, and to detach from Germany the territory on the left (or west) bank of the Rhine, thereby strengthening French security and setting up a Rhineland republic that might become a French satellite. Both French hopes, opposed by Wilson and Lloyd George, went unrealized. The Saar was to be separated from Germany for fifteen years as an international ward supervised by the League of Nations. At the end of the fifteen-year period a plebiscite would determine its future status; meanwhile,

settled at the conference; only in 1924, by treaty with Yugoslavia, did the city go to Italy in return for Susak, a port right next door that served the Yugoslavs quite adequately for the next two decades.

But Wilson did get his new international organization, the cornerstone of his plans for a better world. The covenant of the League of Nations was an integral part of the Treaty of Versailles. The League was no true supranational state, but a kind of permanent consultative system composed of the victors and a few neutrals. The way was left open for the Germans and the Russians to join the League, as they later did. But in 1919–1920, Wilson's League looked to many liberals a lot like Metternich's and Castlereagh's old Congress system of 1815, by no means worth the sacrifices Wilson had made to obtain it. The League had an assembly in which each member state had one vote, and a council in which the five great powers (Britain, France, Italy, the United States, and Japan) had

Areas lost:

by Germany
by Austria-Hungary
by Russia
by Bulgaria

········· Boundaries of 1914 ———— Boundaries of 1926

Demilitarized areas (Rhineland, "The Straits")
Allied Occupation Zone (Rhineland)

its coal output was to go to France. The Rhineland remained part of the German Republic, though it was to be demilitarized and occupied for a time by Allied soldiers.

Belgium was given some small towns on her German border. After a plebiscite provided for in the Treaty of Versailles, Denmark recovered the northern part of Schleswig, which the Danish crown had lost to Prussia in 1864. Italy redeemed her Irredenta of Trent and Trieste in generous measure, for thousands of German and Slavic-speaking peoples were included within her new boundaries. Poland, erased from the map as an independent state in 1795, was now restored and given lands that she had had before the partitions of the eighteenth century and that

contained important minorities of Germans and other non-Polish peoples. The old Hapsburg Empire was entirely dismembered. The heart of its German-speaking area was constituted as the truncated Republic of Austria, which was forbidden to join itself to Germany, and the heart of its Magyar-speaking area became a diminished Kingdom of Hungary. The Czech-inhabited lands of Bohemia and Moravia were joined with Slovakia and the Ruthenian lands of the Carpatho-Ukraine further east in the brand-new "succession state" of Czechoslovakia. This new state faced the problem of a large and discontented Sudeten German minority.

Another "succession state" was Yugoslavia, officially the Kingdom of Serbs, Croats, and

Slovenes, which, as its full name suggests, represented a great expansion of pre-war Serbia to include the south Slav territories of the Hapsburgs. Romania, too, profited by the break-up of the old dual monarchy by receiving the former Hungarian lands of Transylvania. Rewarded also with Bessarabia, a Russian province that the Bolsheviks could not defend, Romania emerged with doubled territory, and some restive non-Romanian minorities. In the southern Balkan Peninsula, Greece received all of Thrace, at the expense of Turkey and Bulgaria.

Out of the former czarist domains held at the end of the war by the Germans there were set up, in addition to Poland, the Baltic republics of Estonia, Latvia, and Lithuania. Once Europe had settled down, plebiscites were provided for to determine certain other territorial adjustments, notably whether certain parts of East Prussia and Silesia should go to Poland or remain German. The new Polish state had been granted access to the Baltic Sea through the so-called "Polish corridor," a narrow strip of land which had once been Polish, and which terminated in the almost wholly German city and port of Danzig. The Poles wanted Danzig, but the Allies compromised by setting up a Free City of Danzig and by giving the Poles free trade with the city. Even so, the Polish corridor now separated East Prussia from the rest of Germany, and Germans had to cross it in sealed trains.

Outside Europe, the Near East presented the most acute problems. By the Treaty of Sèvres the Turks were left in Europe with no more than Constantinople and a small strip of land around it, and in Asia with only their homeland of Anatolia. Mesopotamia and Palestine were given as mandates—a term we shall shortly explain—to Britain, while Syria and Lebanon were given as mandates to France. The Greeks were to hold Smyrna and nearby regions in Asia Minor for five years and then submit to a plebiscite. But the Treaty of Sèvres never went into effect, though it was duly signed by the sultan. In Anatolia a group of army officers headed by Mustafa Kemal led a popular revolt against the government at Constantinople and galvanized the Turkish people into a new national life. The Turks drove the Greek army out of their country and set up a Turkish republic with its capital not at Constantinople but at Ankara in the heart of Anatolia. With this new government the Allies were finally obliged to conclude the Treaty of

Lausanne in 1923. The new peace transferred the Smyrna area and eastern Thrace from Greek to Turkish control and was in general much more advantageous to the Turks than the Treaty of Sèvres had been.

The treaty of Lausanne embodied in dramatic form a principle new in part in the West—the formal transfer of populations. True, peoples had been evicted by conquerors before; witness among other instances the eviction of the French Acadians from Nova Scotia by the British in the eighteenth century, or the settling of our Indians in Indian Territory, now part of the state of Oklahoma. But here was an almost complete exchange: Greeks in Turkey were moved to Greece. Turks in Greece were moved to Turkey. No very significant discontented national minorities were left. Each government was to take care of the transferred populations, and though much hardship occurred, on the whole the plan worked. There was no such exchange of populations on Cyprus, the British-held island in the eastern Mediterranean destined to become a serious international trouble spot.

The Mandates

In the rest of the world the old straightforward policy of annexing overseas territories of defeated powers, as practiced in 1713, 1763, and 1815, seemed no longer possible in 1919. Liberal opinion both in Europe and in America had already been offended to the bursting point, and Wilson himself would never have permitted outright annexations. The consequence was the mandate system, whereby control over a given territory was assigned to a particular mandatory power by the League of Nations, which undertook periodic inspections to see that the terms of the mandate were being fulfilled. This system was designed by its proponents as a means of educating colonial peoples, leading them into the ways of democratic self-government, and preparing them for eventual independence. Under it the former German overseas territories and the non-Turkish parts of the Ottoman Empire were now distributed. Of Germany's African possessions East Africa (rechristened Tanganyika, and in 1964 merged with Zanzibar as independent Tanzania) went to Britain; Southwest Africa went to the Union of South Africa; and both the Cameroons and Togoland were divided between Britain and France. In the Pacific, the German portion of New Guinea was given to Australia, western Samoa to New Zealand, and the Caroline, Marshall, and Mariana island groups to Japan. In the Near East, as we have seen, France secured Syria and Lebanon, while Britain took Palestine, Transjordan, and Iraq (the new Arabic designation for Mesopotamia).

The mandate system may seem to have been a way of disguising annexation, the hypocritical tribute of reactionary vice to progressive virtue. And so to a man like Clemenceau it probably was. The Japanese quite openly annexed and fortified their new Pacific islands in defiance of the terms of their mandate. But to many of the men who put through the idea of mandates the system really was what it professed to be, a nursery for eventual nationhood. For the most part the mandatory powers did make some show at least of treating mandated territories in a way that would prepare them for eventual freedom. Most of them are now indeed "free," or at least independent, nations.

The Punishment of Germany

After land transfers, the most important business of the Peace Conference was reparations, which were imposed on Austria, Hungary, Bulgaria, and Turkey as well as on Germany. It was, however the German reparations that so long disturbed the peace and the economy of the world. The Germans were made to promise to pay for all the damage done to civilian property during the war, and to pay at the rate of five billion dollars a year until 1921, when the final bill would be presented to them. They would then be given thirty years in which to pay the full amount. The amount was left indefinite at Versailles, for the Allies could not agree on a figure. But the totals suggested were astronomical. It was clear from the first that the payments would ultimately have to be in goods—German goods in competition with the goods of the Allies. A Germany prosperous enough to pay reparations could not be the weak and divided nation that men like Clemenceau really wanted. Thus from the very start the "realists" at Versailles— Lloyd George and Clemenceau—cherished quite inconsistent hopes for the future.

The Versailles settlement also required Germany to hand over many of her merchant ships to the Allies and to make large deliveries of coal to France, Italy, and Belgium for a ten-year period. Furthermore, a whole miscellany of articles in the treaty was directed toward the disarmament of Germany on land, on sea, and in the air. The German army was to be limited in size to 100,000 men, and the western frontier zone, extending to a line 50 kilometers (about 30 miles) east of the Rhine, was to be completely "demilitarized"—that is, to contain neither fortifications nor soldiers. In addition, the Allies could maintain armies of occupation on the left bank of the Rhine for fifteen years, and perhaps longer. The treaty forbade Germany to have either submarines or military planes and severely limited the number and size of surface vessels in her navy.

Last, and by no means least important, Article 231 of the Treaty of Versailles obliged Germany to admit that the Central Powers bore sole responsibility for starting the war in 1914. Here is the article that was to cause so much history to be written—and made:

> The Allied and Associated Governments affirm, and Germany accepts, the responsibility of Germany and her allies for causing all the loss and damage to which the Allied and Associated Governments and their nationals have been subjected as a consequence of the war imposed upon them by the aggression of Germany and her allies.

The Settlement Evaluated

To the Germans, Versailles was of course a cruel and humiliating peace, the Diktat, the great national grievance on which Hitler was to play so skillfully. To liberals of the time and later it seemed an unsound, revengeful peace, above all disastrous in its unrealistic reparations policy. In our present world of cold and hot wars, Versailles almost arouses nostalgia. It was at least a settlement, and one that in the era of "fulfillment" in the later 1920's seemed a basis for slow improvement in international relations.

The League it set up was potentially a means by which a new generation of international administrators might mitigate the old rivalries of nations. The reparations could be, and indeed were, scaled down to something more reasonable. The new succession states were based on a modern popular national consciousness that had been developing for at least a hundred years. Though the theorist might protest at the "balkanization of Europe," the creation of more weak and discontented little states like those in the Balkans, the fact remains that it would have been hard to deny national independence, or at least autonomy, to the Czechs, the Poles, the Baltic peoples, and the south Slavs. Germany, though she certainly was not treated generously, was at least not wiped off the map, as Poland had been in the eighteenth century. She was not even actually demoted to a second-rate position in the world. She remained, as she was shortly to prove, a first-rate power. In the long series of settlements under our modern Western state system, which

goes back to the Italian wars of the fifteenth century, Versailles looks nowadays like neither the worst nor the best, but like a typical compromise peace.

It was, however, too much for the American people, who were not used to the harsh needs of international compromise. But it is an oversimplification to argue that this was solely a matter of American idealism turning away in disgust from a settlement that was all too spotted with unpleasant realities. The final American refusal to ratify the Treaty of Versailles, like all great collective decisions, was the result of many forces. Politics certainly played an important part, for the Republicans had won control of both the Senate and the House of Representatives in the congressional elections of November 1918. The president was still Wilson, a Democrat, and Wilson made no concessions to the Republicans

The Balkans and the Middle East 1921

either by taking a bipartisan delegation of Democrats and Republicans to Paris with him or by accepting modifications in the treaty which would have satisfied some of his Republican opponents. The Senate thereupon refused to ratify the treaty.

It is, however, extremely unlikely that even a much more pliable and diplomatic American president than Wilson could have secured from the Senate ratification of another important treaty involved in the proposed settlement. This was the project of a defensive alliance among France, Britain, and the United States into which Wilson had been pushed as part of the price of getting France to give up her proposals for a separate Rhineland republic and for annexation of the Saar. With the United States out, Britain refused a mere dual alliance with France against a German attack. France, still seeking to bolster her security, patched up a series of alliances with the new nations to the east and south of Germany—Poland, and the "Little Entente" of Yugoslavia, Czechoslovakia, and Romania, a rather unsatisfactory substitute for Britain and the United States as allies.

The peace thus left France with an uneasy hegemony in Europe, a hegemony dependent on the continued disarmament and economic weakening of Germany, on the continued isolation of Russia, and on the uncertain support of her new allies. Moreover, France had been disastrously weakened by the human and material losses of the war, and her position of leadership, though it alarmed the British with their long memories of French rivalry in the past, was an unreal thing. In reality, Germany was the strongest nation in Europe, and the Great War had checked, but not halted, her attempt to dominate the Continent and indeed the world. The next German attempt was to draw both Britain and America back from the isolation into which they attempted to withdraw after the collapse of the system planned at Paris in 1919.

A most important matter, however, was not directly touched by the Versailles settlement: Russia, or the Union of Soviet Socialist Republics (U.S.S.R.), the formal name of the new communist state, did not figure in the great treaties. Yet in many senses the most important result of World War I was the emergence of this new-old Russia, her strength and capabilities increased by the stimulus of successful revolution.

Reading Suggestions on the First World War

THE BACKGROUND

A. J. P. Taylor, *The Struggle for the Mastery of Europe, 1848–1914* (Clarendon, 1954). A crisp and suggestive survey.

O. J. Hale, *The Great Illusion, 1900–1914* (*Torchbooks). Stressing the economic and cultural background; with full bibliographies.

B. Schmitt, *The Coming of the War, 1914,* 2 vols. (Scribner's, 1930). Compare with the more revisionist S. B. Fay, *Origins of the World War,* 2 vols. (*Free Press).

L. Lafore, *The Long Fuse* (*Lippincott), and J. Remak, *Origins of World War I* (*Holt). Illuminating studies incorporating recent scholarship.

Barbara Tuchman, *The Proud Tower* (Macmillan, 1966). Instructive and very readable account of the European society that produced the great war.

W. L. Langer, *European Alliances and Alignments, 1871–1890,* 2nd ed. (*Vintage) and *The Diplomacy of Imperialism, 1890–1902,* 2nd ed. (Knopf, 1951). Detailed scholarly analyses, with valuable bibliographies.

R. J. Sontag, *Germany and England: Background of Conflict, 1848–1894* (*Norton); R. J. S. Hoffman, *Great Britain and the German Trade Rivalry, 1875–1914* (Univ. of Pennsylvania Press, 1933); E. L. Woodward, *Great Britain and the German Navy* (Clarendon, 1935). Excellent studies of Anglo-German tension.

C. Andrew, *Théophile Delcassé and the Making of the Entente Cordiale* (St. Martin's, 1938), and S. R. Williamson, *The Politics of Grand Strategy* (Harvard Univ. Press, 1969). Assessments of the Anglo-French rapprochement before 1914.

G. Monge, *The End of Isolation* (T. Nelson, 1963). British foreign policy reviewed. For Anglo-American relations, may be supplemented by Bradford Perkins, *The Great Rapprochement* (Atheneum, 1968).

W. Laqueur, *Russia and Germany: A Century of Conflict* (*Little, Brown). Yet another factor in the background scrutinized.

E. N. Anderson, *The First Moroccan Crisis, 1904–1906* (Univ. of Chicago Press, 1930), and Ima C. Barlow, *The Agadir Crisis* (Univ. of North Carolina Press, 1940). Two useful monographs on the Moroccan issue.

J. B. Wolf, *Diplomatic History of the Bagdad Railroad* (Univ. of Missouri Press, 1936). Review of another major issue in prewar diplomacy.

Outbreak of the World War: German Documents Collected by Karl Kautsky (Oxford Univ. Press, 1924) and *German Diplomatic Documents, 1871–1914* (Methuen, 1928–1931). English translations of some of the vast flood of documents released by the German republican government at the end of the war. May be compared with *British Documents on the Origins of the War, 1898–1914* (H. M. Stationery Office, 1926–1938).

THE WAR

A. J. P. Taylor, *History of the First World War* (*Medallion); B. H. Liddell Hart, *The Real War* (*Little, Brown). Lively and rather opinionated surveys.

C. R. M. Cruttwell, *History of the Great War,* 2nd ed. (Oxford Univ. Press, 1936); C. Falls, *The Great War* (*Capricorn); Hanson Baldwin, *World War One* (*Evergreen). Three sober and reliable accounts.

W. S. Churchill, *The World Crisis,* 6 vols. (Scribner's, 1923–1931). Detailed and often fascinating narrative; not always objective.

Barbara Tuchman, *The Guns of August* (*Dell). Well-written narrative of the first critical month of the war and the crisis preceding it.

G. Ritter, *The Schlieffen Plan* (Dufour, 1969). Scholarly reassessment.

Alan Moorehead, *Gallipoli* (Harper, 1956), and A. Horne, *The Price of Glory: Verdun, 1916* (*Colophon). Excellent accounts of particular campaigns.

R. M. Watt, *Dare Call It Treason* (*Simon and Schuster). The story of the most concerted French attempt to break the deadlock of trench warfare and of the mutiny that resulted in 1917.

E. R. May, *World War and American Isolation, 1914–1917* (*Quadrangle) and *The Coming of War, 1917* (Rand McNally). The most reliable and balanced treatment of the events that made the United States a belligerent.

T. E. Lawrence, *Seven Pillars of Wisdom* (*Dell). Colorful but untrustworthy account of the Arab revolt by a major participant.

F. P. Chambers, *The War behind the War* (Harcourt, 1939). On the "home front."

Economic and Social History of the World War: Outline of Plan, European Series (Carnegie Endowment for International Peace, 1924). Guide to an enormous series of monographs on home-front developments in all the major belligerent powers.

THE PEACE

P. Birdsall, *Versailles Twenty Years After* (Reynal and Hitchcock, 1941). Excellent appraisal by an American scholar.

H. Nicolson, *Peacemaking 1919* (*Universal Library). Informative study by a British expert on diplomacy.

T. A. Bailey, *Woodrow Wilson and the Lost Peace* and *Woodrow Wilson and the Great Betrayal* (*Quadrangle). Stressing the setbacks his program suffered in Paris and in Washington, respectively.

A. J. Mayer, *The Politics and Diplomacy of Peacemaking* (*Vintage), and John M. Thompson, *Russia, Bolshevism and the Versailles Peace* (Princeton Univ. Press, 1966). Playing up and playing down, respectively, the role of the fear of Bolshevism.

J. M. Keynes, *The Ecomomic Consequences of the Peace* (Harcourt, 1920), and E. Mantoux, *The Carthaginian Peace; or, the Economic Consequences of Mr. Keynes* (Scribner's, 1952). Respectively, the most famous attack on the Versailles settlement and a thoughtful study of the results of that attack.

HISTORICAL FICTION

J. Romains, *Verdun* (Knopf, 1939). Excellent and balanced novel about French troops on the western front, 1914–1916.

H. Barbusse, *Under Fire* (Dutton, 1917), and E. M. Remarque, *All Quiet on the Western Front* (*Crest). Two famous novels, by a Frenchman and a German respectively, reflect the horror aroused in intellectuals by trench warfare.

J. Dos Passos, *Three Soldiers* (*Sentry), and E. Hemingway, *A Farewell to Arms* (*Scribner's). Two American novels reflecting postwar disillusionment.

e. e. cummings, *The Enormous Room* (*Liveright), and A. Zweig, *The Case of Sergeant Grischa* (Viking). Respectively, on prisoners of war and the eastern front.

C. S. Forester, *The General* (Little, Brown, 1947). A careerist dissected.

John Buchan, *Greenmantle* (Nelson, n.d.), and W. Somerset Maugham, *Ashenden* (*Avon). Tales of espionage and high adventure.

26

Communist Russia, 1917–1941

I   Introduction

On June 22, 1941, Adolf Hitler's German armies poured over the frontier of his Russian ally and began a rapid advance toward Moscow, toward the major Russian industrial centers, and toward the most productive Russian agricultural regions. The Russia Hitler invaded was no longer the Russia into which Napoleon had sent the Grande Armée a hundred and twenty-nine years before, or the Russia whose millions of embattled soldiers had perished in the First World War against the Germany of William II and his Hapsburg allies. It was no longer the Russia of the czars. Since 1917 it had been the Russia of the Bolsheviks. Yet it was still Russia.

Along with the czars, the nobility and the bourgeoisie had gone down to ruin after the communist revolution of 1917, and the clergy as a class had suffered almost as much. A small, tightly knit, conspiratorial group of fanatical

Above: A postrevolutionary Soviet propaganda poster. Above right: Lenin and Stalin in 1923. Right: Pro-Bolshevik soldiers, red flags fixed to their bayonets, patrolling the streets of Petrograd in March 1917.

952

Marxist revolutionaries had seized power and for the next twenty-four years had striven to make Russia over. Drawn mostly from the peculiarly Russian class of the intelligentsia, and declaring themselves to be the representatives of the industrial proletariat, the Bolsheviks had worked gigantic changes, especially in the years after 1928. Industry, proceeding under forced draft, had expanded enormously, and the proportion of the population employed in industry had risen to almost 50 percent; the proportion engaged in agriculture had fallen correspondingly.

The peasant had been a victim of serfdom until 1861, had been subject to the initiative-destroying domination of the commune until 1906, and had then been encouraged by Stolypin to make himself a free farmer. Now, under the Bolsheviks, he found himself subjected to new and grievous pressure. Agriculture had been collectivized, and the age-old longing of the peasant for private property in land had been ruthlessly suppressed.

These staggering social and economic changes had not been accomplished without internal friction. Inside the government, personal rivalries, plots, counterplots, fake plots, and charges of plots had produced repeated purges extending down through the ranks of the population. The choking conspiratorial atmosphere which the Bolshevik rulers had breathed during their long years of underground preparation for a seizure of power now enveloped the citadels of power. Personal rivalries for domination of the machinery of the state were cloaked beneath the Byzantine theological language of doctrinal controversy over fine points in the sacred writings of Marx and Lenin. Yet the controversies had immediate significance in the formulation and choice of government policies. The Communist party, the secret police, and the army had become the interlocking agencies which ran the state at the bidding of the dictator. The dictator himself, Stalin, had made his own career possible chiefly through the ruthless use of his position as Secretary of the Communist party.

The foreign policy of the communist state had after 1917 passed through a brief period in which ideological considerations had seemed occasionally to outweigh national interest in the old sense. It had then returned to the pursuit of traditional Russian ends, coupled with the objective of promoting eventual world revolution. But in furthering Russian aims abroad, the Bol-

shevik leaders were now in possession of an instrument more flexible than any the czars had ever commanded. This was the Communist International, or Comintern, a federation of the Communist parties in the individual countries of the world. These parties could often be used as promoters of purely Russian ends rather than strictly communist ends. With the shifting stresses and strains of international politics during the late 1920's and 1930's, the "line" of the Comintern shifted often and bewilderingly, but always in accordance with the aims of the Soviet foreign office. Usually the majority of communists elsewhere in the world fell meekly into position and loudly proclaimed when necessary the opposite of what they had proclaimed the day before.

Yet the changes during the first twenty-four years of the Soviet period, vast though they were, could not conceal the continuities between the new Russian system and the old. The dictator of 1941, the revered leader of his people, for whom his followers made increasingly grandiose claims, was not unlike the czar of 1917 in his assumption of autocratic power. The individual Russian of 1941, despite his sufferings under the new system, had remained deeply patriotic, ready to sacrifice himself for his country, even under a government he hated. The peasant of 1941 still yearned hopelessly for his land; the worker struggled for economic advancement and social security. Bureaucrats, managers, intellectuals, and artists, all in the service of the state, formed in 1941 a new elite which replaced but did not differ greatly from the old privileged class. A police force superior in efficiency to those of Ivan the Terrible, Peter the Great, and Nicholas I, but not different in kind, in 1941 exercised thought control over all citizens and terrorized even prominent members of the system itself.

More and more, Stalinist communism had taken on the trappings of a religion, with its sacred books, its heresies, its places of pilgrimage, its doctrinal quarrels. Thus the old Russian orthodoxy had by 1941 not been replaced but rather modified. Russian nationalism, too, asserted itself ever more insistently and crudely, until finally, in the war that Hitler began, the government encouraged the cult of traditional heroes of earlier times, and even glorified Ivan the Terrible himself, a symbol no longer of "feudal" domination but of the Russian national spirit. The early revolutionary departures from accepted standards in Russian marriage, family life, and education, had by 1941 all been abandoned in favor of a return to conventional bourgeois behavior. This chapter will trace in some detail the series of vast changes here summarized and will attempt to demonstrate the continued survival of the old Russia beneath the veneer of the new.

II The Russian Revolution of 1917

The Immediate Background

Ridden by domestic crisis though Russia was in 1914, the country greeted the outbreak of World War I with demonstrations of national patriotism. The Duma supported the war and did yeoman service in organizing Red Cross activities. The left-wing parties—the radical agrarian SR's (Social Revolutionaries) and the Marxist SD's (Social Democrats)—abstained from voting war credits, but offered to assist the national defense. By 1917, more than 15,000,000 Russians had been drafted into the armies. Losses in battle were staggering from the first; the Russians suffered more than 3,800,000 casualties during the first year of war. On the home front, criticism was aroused by the inadequate handling of the supply of munitions, and by mid-1915 the Center and Left groups in the Duma were urging moderate reforms, such as the end of discrimination against minority nationalities and an increase in the powers of the zemstvos, the local assemblies. The empress Alexandra took the lead in opposing all such measures, and kept urging her weak husband, Czar Nicholas II, to act more autocratically. When Nicholas took personal command of the armies in the field and prorogued the Duma (autumn 1915), she became virtually supreme at home. The supremacy of the empress meant also the supremacy of her favorite, the unscrupulous adventurer Rasputin.

With the empress and Rasputin in control, a gang of shady adventurers, blackmailers, and profiteers bought and sold offices, speculated in military supplies, put in their own puppets as ministers, and created a series of shocking scandals. Confusion, strikes, and defeatism mounted at home during 1916, while the armies slowly bled to death at the front. Even the conservatives began to denounce Rasputin publicly, and in December 1916 he was poisoned, shot several times, and ultimately drowned, all in one nightmare evening, by a group of conspirators closely related to the imperial family. Despite repeated warnings from moderates in the Duma that the government itself was preparing a revolution by its failure to create a responsible ministry and to clean up the mess, the czar remained apathetic. Relatives of the imperial family and members of the Duma began independently to plot for his abdication. In the early months of 1917, all conditions favored a revolution, but the revolutionaries were not prepared.

The March Revolution

On March 8, strikes and bread riots broke out in the capital, and four days later Romanov rule, which had governed Russia since 1613, was doomed. Yet this revolution of March 1917 has

Rasputin.

A barricade in Petrograd, March 1917.

been well called leaderless, spontaneous, and anonymous. SR's and both Bolshevik and Menshevik factions of SD's were genuinely surprised at what happened. Indeed, the Bolshevik leaders were either abroad in exile, or under arrest in Siberia. The determining factor in the overthrow of the czar was the disloyalty of the garrison of Petrograd (the new Russian name given to St. Petersburg during the war). Inefficiency had led to a food shortage in the capital, though actual starvation had not set in. When the czar ordered troops to fire on striking workers, only a few obeyed, and on March 12, in revulsion against the order, the troops joined the strikers, broke into the arsenals, and began to hunt the police, who quickly disappeared from the scene. The Duma lagged behind the revolting troops and workers in estimating the situation, and the czar lagged behind the Duma. By March 14, when the czar had finally decided to appoint a responsible ministry, it was too late; the cabinet had vanished. Troops ordered to put down the revolt simply melted away and joined the rebels.

Leftists, released from prison by the mobs, formed a soviet of workers and soldiers, modeled on the 1905 soviet of workers, but now including soldiers as well. The Soviet proceeded to organize a workers' militia, to create a food-supply commission, and to issue newspapers. Its fifteen-man executive committee became the policy-makers of the revolution. The Soviet located its headquarters across the corridor in the same building as the Duma, which did not obey the czar's order to dissolve, but remained in session.

The Marxists among the Soviet leaders still believed in the necessity of a preliminary bourgeois revolution, and did not yet regard the Soviet itself as an organ of power. They favored the creation of a provisional government, in which they would not participate, but to which they would offer limited support. They put themselves at the disposition of the Duma, and asked that it temporarily run the country. Thus the Duma, a limited assembly elected by a restricted franchise, was literally forced by the Soviet into the position of leading the revolution.

Negotiations between the Soviet and a Duma committee brought a provisional government into existence. Despite the widely differing social and economic aims of Soviet and Duma, both agreed to grant political liberties immediately, and to summon a constituent assembly, which was to establish the future form of government by giving Russia a constitution. The provisional government was composed mainly of Kadets (Constitutional Democrats) and other moderates, and was headed by the liberal Prince Lvov, chairman of the union of zemstvos and of the Red Cross. It included also one radical member of the Soviet, Alexander Kerensky, minister of justice, a clever labor lawyer and member of the Duma also, who accepted office despite the understanding that members of the Soviet would not do so.

After some abortive efforts to save the dynasty in the person of the czar's brother, Nicholas finally abdicated, and his brother refused the throne because of the popular hatred of the family. Under pressure from the Soviet, the provisional government arrested Nicholas II and the empress on March 20. The Duma had thus accepted the mandate given it by the revolutionaries. Had it accepted instead its dismissal at the hands of the czar and gone home, it seems probable that the monarchy would have been preserved at the cost of some liberal concessions. But moderate reformers were now nominally in power, and Russia embarked on the troubled months between March and October 1917.

The Provisional Government

The provisional government is usually regarded as having been a total failure. Measured by the final results, such a view is perhaps justified. But the judgment of history must take into consideration the dreadful difficulties that faced the provisional government. These were not only immediate and specific but general and underlying. Russian moderates had had no experience of authority. They were separated by a great cultural gulf from the lower classes. Their opportunity to rule now came to them in the midst of a fearful war, which they felt they had to pursue while reconstructing and democratizing the enormous and unwieldy Russian Empire.

Moreover, the Soviet possessed many of the instruments of power, yet refused to accept any responsibility. Workers and soldiers in the capital supported the Soviet, while in the provinces the new governors appointed by the provisional government had no weapon except persuasion to employ against the local peasant-elected soviets,

which multiplied rapidly. Present-day critics of the provisional government often denounce its failure to suppress its revolutionary opponents, but they overlook the fact that the provisional government did not possess the tools of supression. The Petrograd garrison, for instance, by agreement with the Soviet, could not be removed or disarmed. The support given by the Soviet to the provisional government has been vividly compared to the kind of support that is given by a hangman's noose.

The two great specific issues facing the provisional government were agrarian discontent and the continuation of the war. The peasants wanted land, and they wanted it immediately. The provisional government, however, made up as it was of responsible liberals, believed in acting with deliberation and according to law. It refused to sanction peasant seizure of land, despite in-

The first session of the Duma of the provisional government, March 1917. The empty frame behind the speaker's platform formerly held the czar's portrait.

creasing disorder in the countryside. Instead, it appointed a commission to collect material on which future agrarian legislation was to be based —an act totally inadequate to the emergency.

As to the war, the members of the government felt in honor bound to their allies not to make a separate peace. Moreover, most of them still unrealistically hoped that Russia might win, and gain the territories which the Allies had promised. But the Soviet subverted discipline in the armies at the front by issuing a "declaration of the rights of soldiers," which virtually put an end to the authority of officers over enlisted men. Although the Soviet made it as hard as possible for the government to pursue the war, it did not sponsor a separate peace. Even the Bolshevik members of the Soviet, who now began to return from exile, demanded only that Russia participate in general peace negotiations, which, they urged, should begin at once.

Lenin and Bolshevism

The most important of the returning Bolshevik exiles was Lenin. His real name was Vladimir Ilyich Ulianov, but in his writings he used the pen name Lenin, to which he sometimes prefixed the initial N., a Russian abbreviation for "nobody," in order to tell his readers that he was using a pseudonym. This "N." has given rise to the mistaken but still widely held idea that Lenin's first name was Nikolai (Nicholas). Son of a provincial official and intellectual, Lenin became a revolutionary in the late 1880's and, as we have seen, took a chief role in the early years of the SD's as the leader of the party's Bolshevik wing. He had returned to Russia from abroad for the Revolution of 1905, but he left Russia once more in 1908, and stayed abroad until 1917.

When the news of the March Revolution reached Lenin in Switzerland, he made desperate efforts to get back home. Finally, through the Swiss Social Democrats, he made contact with the German general staff, which felt that it would be a good investment to see that Lenin reached Russia, where he might disrupt the Russian war effort against Germany. Thus it was that the German military transported Lenin across Germany from Switzerland to the Baltic in the famous sealed railroad car. He arrived at the Finland Station in Petrograd on April 16, 1917, a little more than a month after the March Revolution.

Most Russian Social Democrats had long regarded a bourgeois parliamentary republic as a necessary preliminary to an eventual socialist revolution and socialist society. For this reason, they were prepared to help in transforming Russia into a capitalist society, though not without grave doubts that the bourgeois capitalists might be as bad as the czar and the landlords, or that the masses might be "deluded" into accepting the new system. They favored the creation of a democratic republic, at the same time believing that complete political freedom was absolutely essential for their own future rise to power. Despite the Marxist emphasis upon the industrial laboring class as the only proper vehicle for revolution, Lenin early realized that in Russia, where the "proletariat" embraced only about 1 percent of the population, the SD's must seek other allies. At the time of the Revolution of 1905, he began to preach the need for limited alliances for tactical purposes between the Bolsheviks and the SR's, who commanded the support of the peasantry. When the alliance had served its purpose, the SD's were to turn on their allies and destroy them. Then would come the socialist triumph.

Instead of a preliminary bourgeois democratic republic, Lenin called in 1905 and later for an immediate "revolutionary-democratic dictatorship of the proletariat and the peasantry," a concept that seems to us self-contradictory and is surely vague. Lenin's view, however, was not adopted even by most Bolsheviks. Together with the Mensheviks, they continued to believe and urge that a bourgeois revolution and a parliamentary democracy were necessary first steps.

Because Lenin did not trust the masses to make a revolution (by themselves, he felt, they were capable only of "trade-union consciousness"), he favored a dictatorship of the Bolshevik party over the working class. Because he did not trust the rank and file of Bolshevik party workers, he favored a dictatorship of a small elite over the Bolshevik party. And in the end, because he really trusted nobody's views but his own, he favored, though never explicitly, his own dictatorship over this elite. Another future Russian leader, the brilliant intellectual Leon Trotsky, early warned that in Lenin's views one-man dictatorship was implicit.

Trotsky, for his part, voiced an opinion of his own, held by neither Mensheviks nor Bolsheviks. The bourgeoisie in Russia, he argued, was so weak that the working class could telescope the bourgeois and socialist revolutions into one continuous movement. After the proletariat had helped the bourgeoisie achieve its revolution, he believed that the workers could move immediately to power. They could nationalize industry and collectivize agriculture, and, although foreign intervention and civil war were doubtless to be expected, the Russian proletariat would soon be joined by the proletariats of other countries, which would make their own revolutions. Except for this last point, Trotsky's analysis accurately forecast the course of events. Between 1905 and 1917, Lenin himself accepted Trotsky's view from time to time, but warned that it endangered political democracy.

Lenin had been deeply depressed by the failure of 1905, and by the threat posed by Stolypin's agrarian reforms. He almost despaired when the socialist parties of Europe went along with their governments in 1914 and supported the war. To him this meant the end of the second socialist International, for the Social Democrats had failed to recognize the war as the "bourgeois-imperialist" venture that it appeared to Lenin to be. He preached defeatism as the only possible view for a Russian SD to follow.

Lenin's greatest talent was not as an original thinker but as a skillful tactician. He often seemed able to judge with accuracy just what was politically possible in a given situation, and he was not afraid to gamble. Thus, even before he returned to Russia in April 1917, he had assessed some of the difficulties facing the provisional government and decided that the masses could take over at once. Immediately upon his arrival, he hailed the worldwide revolution, proclaiming that the end of imperialism, "the last stage of capitalism," was at hand. Ignoring the positions previously taken by Bolsheviks and Mensheviks alike, he demanded now that all power immediately be given to the soviets. His speeches sounded even to his fellow SD's themselves like the ravings of a madman.

Almost nobody but Lenin felt that the loosely organized soviets could govern the country, or that the war would bring down the capitalist world in chaos. In April 1917 Lenin called not only for the abandonment of the provisional government and the establishment of a republic of soviets but for the confiscation of estates, the nationalization of land, and the abolition of the army, of government officials, and of the police. He was offering land at once to the impatient peasants, peace at once to the war-weary populace. This program fitted the mood of the people far better than the cautious and well-meant efforts of the provisional government to bring about reform by legal means. Dogmatic, furiously impatient of compromise, entirely convinced that he alone had the truth, Lenin galvanized the Bolsheviks into a truly revolutionary group waiting only the moment to seize power.

The Coming of the November Revolution

The months from March to November 1917, before the Bolsheviks came to power, can be divided into a period between March and July, during which revolution deepened, a feeble reaction from July to September, and a new quickening of the revolutionary current from September to the final uprising in November. In the first period, the government faced a crisis, because the Kadet ministers wished to maintain the Russian war aim of annexing the Straits, while the Soviet wanted a peace "without annexations or indemnities." Out of the crisis Kerensky, now war minister, emerged as the dominant leader. He failed to realize that it was no longer possible to restore the morale of the armies, which were dissolving under the impact of Bolshevik propaganda. A new offensive ordered on July 1 collapsed, as soldiers refused to obey orders, deserted their units, and rushed home to their native villages, eager to seize the land. Ukrainian separatism also plagued the officials of the government. The soviets became gradually more and more Bolshevik, as Lenin and Trotsky worked tirelessly at recruitment and organization. Although the June congress of soviets in Petrograd was less than 10 percent Bolshevik in make-up, the Bolshevik slogans of peace, bread, and freedom won overwhelming support.

Yet an armed outbreak by troops who had accepted the Bolshevik slogans found the Petrograd Soviet unwilling and unable to assume power. While the mob roared outside, the Soviet voted to discuss the matter two weeks later, and

A May Day parade in Petrograd, 1917. The banner reads "We repudiate the old world."

meanwhile to keep the provisional government in power. A regiment loyal to the Soviet protected it against the working class! The government declared that Lenin was a German agent, and, as his supporters wavered, raided the newspaper offices of *Pravda* (*Truth*, the Bolshevik paper); Lenin had to go into hiding to avoid arrest. This episode of mid-July is what is known among Bolsheviks as "playing at insurrection." Though shots had been exchanged and overt action had been embarked upon, there had been no revolutionary follow-through. Power had not been seized, probably because Lenin felt that the Bolsheviks did not have enough support in the provinces.

Now Kerensky became premier. The government hardened its attitude toward the Ukrainians, but could not come to a popular decision on either land or peace. General Kornilov, chosen by Kerensky as the new commander-in-chief of the armies, quickly became the hope of all conservative groups, and in August plotted a coup, intended to disperse the Soviet. His attitude toward the provisional government was uncertain, but, had he succeeded, he would probably have demanded a purge of its more radical elements. The plot, however, was a failure, because railroad and telegraph workers sabotaged Kornilov's movements, and because his troops simply would not obey him. The Bolsheviks, adopting the slogan "We will fight against Kornilov, but will not support Kerensky," threw themselves into preparations for the defense of Petrograd, which proved to be unnecessary. By September 14, Kornilov had been arrested, and the affair ended without bloodshed. The threat from the Right helped the Bolsheviks greatly, and sentiment in the Petrograd and Moscow soviets now for the first time became predominantly Bolshevik.

The Kornilov affair turned the army mutiny into a widespread revolt. Instances of violence multiplied. No longer satisfied with merely disobeying their officers, more and more soldiers murdered them instead. No longer satisfied with merely refusing to pay their rent or pasturing their animals on their landlords' land, more and more peasants burned the manor house and killed the owner. It was true that the nobility owned only a quarter as much land as the peasants, but the peasants no longer listened to statistics or to arguments that rash action retarded progress. As disorder mounted in the countryside, the Bolsheviks tightened their hold over the soviets in the cities.

Lenin returned to Petrograd on October 20. Soon thereafter the Bolsheviks got control over a Military Revolutionary Committee, originally chosen to help defend Petrograd against the advancing Germans, and now transformed, under the guidance of Trotsky, into a general staff for the revolution. Beginning on November 4, huge demonstrations and mass meetings were addressed by Trotsky, and on November 7 the insurrection broke out.

In Petrograd, the revolution had been well prepared, and proceeded with little bloodshed. Kerensky escaped in a car belonging to the American Embassy. The Military Revolutionary Committee, as an organ of the Petrograd soviet, simply took over. The Bolsheviks called a second congress of soviets, and when the Mensheviks and right-wing SR's walked out, Trotsky called them the refuse that would be swept into the garbage can of history. Cooperating with the left-wing SR's, and adopting their land program, Lenin abolished all property rights of landlords, and transferred the land thus affected to local land committees and soviets of peasant deputies. Though Lenin did not in the least approve of the system of individual small holdings which this decree put into effect, he recognized the psychological advantage which the adoption of the SR program would gain him. He also urged an immediate peace without annexations or indemnities, and appealed to the workers of Germany, France, and England to support him in this demand. Finally, a new cabinet, called a Council of People's Commissars, was chosen, with Lenin as president, and Trotsky as foreign commissar.

As commissar of nationalities the Bolsheviks installed a younger man, a Georgian, named Joseph Djugashvili, who had been a successful organizer of bank robberies in the days when the party treasury was filled in this way, but whose role had otherwise been relatively obscure. He had taken the name Stalin, which suggests a steel-like hardness. Under Lenin's coaching, Stalin had also become the party authority on questions of minority nationalities, and had published a pamphlet on the subject in 1913.

Outside Petrograd, the revolution moved more slowly. In Moscow there was a week of street-fighting between Bolshevik Reds and Whites, as anti-Bolshevik forces were already known. Elsewhere in factory towns, the Bolsheviks usually won speedily; in nonindustrial centers it took them longer. Most of Siberia and of central Asia came over, but Tiflis, the capital of Georgia, went Menshevik, and passed resolutions calling for a constituent assembly and the continuation of the war. The reason for the rapid and smooth success of the Bolsheviks was that the provincial garrisons opposed the war, and willingly allied themselves with the workers. Local military revolutionary committees were created in most places, and held elections for new local soviets. Naturally there was much confusion at first, but surprisingly little resistance to the consolidation of the authority of the new regime. Gradually the town of Rostov-on-Don, near the Sea of Azov, became the main center of resistance, as Kornilov and other generals, together with a number of the leading politicians of the Duma, made their way there.

This initial triumph of the revolution did not mean that the population of Russia had been converted to Bolshevism. By cleverly sensing the mood of the people, Lenin had opportunistically given the Bolsheviks a set of slogans around which the people could rally, although some of the slogans did not at all correspond with the true Bolshevik views. As we shall shortly see, the Russian people were in fact strongly anti-Bolshevik. But the Bolsheviks had triumphed, and the democratic hopes for freedom of the press and other freedoms were now doomed to disappointment.

Deprived of competent civil servants, the new regime worried along through an atmosphere of continued crisis. Late in November 1917, an agreement was reached with the Left-Wing SR's, three of whom entered the government, and peace negotiations were begun with the Germans. The revolution proper was over. Lenin was in power.

The Constituent Assembly

It is of great interest to record that the Bolsheviks now permitted elections for a constituent assembly. Lenin had no use for this sort of democratically chosen parliament, which he considered "inferior" to the soviet. Yet, probably because he had so long taunted the provisional government with delaying the elections, he seems to have felt compelled to hold them. The Russian people for the first and last time in their entire history had a completely free election, under universal suffrage. Lenin himself accepted as accurate figures showing that the Bolsheviks polled about a quarter of the vote. The other socialist parties, chiefly the SR's, polled 62 percent. As was to be expected, the Bolshevik vote was heaviest in the cities, especially Moscow and Petrograd, while the SR vote was largely rural.

Disregarding the majority cast for his opponents, Lenin maintained that "the most advanced" elements had voted for him. It was of course only his opinion that made those who had voted Bolshevik more "advanced" than those who had voted SR or Kadet. The constituent assembly met only once, on January 18, 1918. Lenin dissolved it the next day by decree, and sent guards with rifles to prevent its ever meet-

0   500

Miles

NORWAY

SWEDEN

FINLAND

Gulf of Bothnia

Helsinki

Kronstadt

L. Onega

L. Ladoga

Archangel

Petrograd
(Leningrad)

ESTONIA

Baltic Sea

LATVIA

LITHUANIA

Danzig

Vilna

GERMANY

*WHITE
RUSSIA*

Niemen R.

Warsaw

Brest-
Litovsk

POLAND

Bug R.

Vistula R.

Curzon Line

Kiev

UKRAINE

Vienna

AUSTRIA-

Budapest

HUNGARY

Dniester R.

Dnieper R.

Pruth R.

ROMANIA

BOSNIA

SERBIA

Danube R.

MONTE-
NEGRO

BULGARIA

ALBANIA

CRIMEA

Istanbul

GREECE

Black Sea

TURKEY

Volga R.

Kazan

Moscow

Samara

Don R.

Tsaritsyn
(Stalingrad
Volgograd)

Volga R.

Rostov-on-Don

Occupied by Germany, 1918

C A U C A S U S

GEORGIA

Tiflis

Kars

Caspian Sea

Baku

PERSIA

	Russian territorial losses, Brest-Litovsk, 1918
	Boundaries as of 1914
	Curzon Line
	Boundary between Poland and the U.S.S.R., 1920-1939

**Russia in Revolution,
1917-1921**

S I B E R I A

TRANS-SIBERIAN RAILROAD

Moscow

Omsk

Vladivostok

ing again. The anti-Bolshevik majority was
naturally deeply indignant at this pure act of
force against the popular will, but there was no
public outburst, and the delegates disbanded. In
part, this was because the Bolsheviks had already taken action on the things that interested

the people most—peace and land—and in part
because of the lack of a democratic parliamentary
tradition among the masses of the Russian
people.

In spite of the many years of agitation by intellectuals and liberals for just such a popular

962

assembly, Russia did not have the large middle class, the widespread literacy, the tradition of debate, and the respect for the rights of the individual which seem to be an essential part of constitutionalism. Yet it is surely hasty to decide that there was no chance for constitutional government in Russia in 1917–1918. Was the constituent assembly "an attempt to transplant an alien concept of government to a soil where it could never flourish"? Or was it "a noble experiment incorporating a sound principle but doomed by the crisis into which it was born"? The fact that Lenin had the rifles to prevent the constituent assembly from fulfilling the function which the popular will had assigned to it does not answer the question either way.

III   War Communism and NEP, 1917–1928

War Communism

The first period of Soviet history, which runs from the end of 1917 to the end of 1920, is usually called the period of war communism, or military communism. The term itself of course implies that the main features of the period were determined by military events. Civil war raged, and foreign powers intervened on Russian soil. But the term is also somewhat misleading. This was a period of militant as well as military communism, symbolized early in 1918 by the change of the party's name from Bolshevik to Communist. At the same time, the capital was shifted from Petrograd, with its exposed location on the western fringe of Russia, to the greater security of Moscow, in the heart of the country.

Flushed with victory in Russia, the Bolsheviks firmly believed that world revolution was about to begin, probably first in Germany, but surely spreading to Britain and even to the United States. This view led the Bolsheviks to hasten the construction of a socialist state in Russia and to take a casual attitude toward their international affairs, since they expected that relations with capitalist states would be very temporary. Although the actions of the Russian government during this period were later described almost apologetically as emergency measures, this is only partly true. Many of the decisions that were taken in part under the spur of military pressure were also regarded as leading to a new society.

A supreme economic council directed the gradual nationalization of industry. Sugar and petroleum came first, and then in June 1918 a large group including mines, metallurgy, and textiles. By 1920, the state had taken over all enterprises employing more than ten workers (more than five, if motor power was used). The state organized a system of barter, which replaced the free market. Internal trade was illegal; only the government food commissary could buy and sell; money disappeared, as the state took over distribution as well as production. It expropriated the banks, repudiated the czarist foreign debt, and in effect wiped out savings. Church and state were separated by decree, and judges were removed from office and replaced by appointees of the local soviets.

The government subjected the peasantry to ever more arbitrary and severe requisitioning. It mobilized the poorer peasants against those who were better off, called *kulaks* (from the word meaning "fist" and used to apply to usurers, as if to say "hardfisted"). By calling for a union of the hungry against the well-fed, the regime deliberately, and not for the last time, sowed class hatred in the villages, and stimulated civil war in the countryside. It should be remembered that by western European standards even a Russian kulak was often wretchedly poor. The decree forming the first secret police, the Cheka (from the initials of the words meaning "extraordinary commission"), was issued in December 1917, only a few weeks after the revolution and long before any intervention from abroad. Terror became a weapon in the civil war.

Before the communist government could function at all, peace was necessary, as the army had virtually ceased to exist. Negotiations between the Russians and the Germans and Austro-Hungarians at Brest-Litovsk dragged on into 1918, the Russians hoping that revolution would break out in Germany, and the Germans demanding enormous territorial cessions, stepping up their demands as the Russians delayed. Finally, on March 3, 1918, the Russians signed the Peace of Brest-Litovsk, which deprived them of

Russian soldiers returning from the front, 1917. Many men simply left the war and went home.

the entire Ukraine, the Baltic provinces, Finland, and some Caucasian lands. It cost Russia a third of its population, 80 percent of its iron, and 90 percent of its coal. Many communists resigned rather than accept the peace, and the Left SR's quit the government. The Germans overran the Ukraine and the Crimea and installed a highly authoritarian regime, against which the communists continued to agitate. The Whites, with German help, put down the Reds in Finland.

Civil War

During the months following Brest-Litovsk, disorder in the countryside as a result of requisitioning and class warfare was swelled by the outbreak of open civil strife. During the war, a brigade had been formed inside Russia of Czechs resident in the country and of deserters from the Hapsburg armies. When Russia withdrew from the war, it was decided to send the Czech brigade around the world: east across Siberia by rail, and next by ship across the Pacific, through the Panama Canal, and finally across the Atlantic to France, to fight the Germans there. On the rail trip across Siberia, the Czechs got into a brawl with a trainload of Hungarian prisoners, and one of the Hungarians was killed. This obscure quarrel on a Siberian railway siding between members of the unfriendly races of the Hapsburg Empire touched off civil war in Russia. When

the Soviet government tried to take reprisals against the Czechs, who numbered fewer than 35,000 men, the Czechs seized a number of towns in western Siberia. The local soviets were unprepared, and the SR's were sympathetic to the Czechs. Local anti-Bolshevik armies came into being. It was under threat from one of them, in July 1918, that a local soviet decided to execute the czar and his entire family rather than lose possession of them. All were murdered.

By late June 1918 the Allies had decided to intervene in Russia on behalf of the opponents of Bolshevism. The withdrawal of Russia from the war had been a heavy blow to them, and they now hoped to recreate a second front against the Germans in the East. The idea of a capitalist "crusade" against Bolshevism, later popularized by Soviet and pro-Soviet historians as the sole motive for the intervention, was in fact much less significant. Yet the Allies had been at war a long time, and their populations were war-weary. So it is true that they were apprehensive at the communist efforts to stimulate revolution in all the capitalist nations of the world.

Out at the eastern end of the Trans-Siberian Railroad in Vladivostok, the Czechs overthrew the local soviet in June 1918, and by early August British, French, Japanese, and American forces had landed. The assignment of the Americans was to occupy Vladivostok and to safeguard railroad communications in the rear of the Czechs. Of the Allies, only the Japanese had long-range territorial ambitions in the area. In effect, the Bolshevik regime had now been displaced in Siberia. The SR's disbanded the soviets and reestablished the zemstvos, calling for "all power to the constituent assembly." There were three anti-Red governments of varying complexions in three different Siberian centers. Elsewhere, in August 1918, a small British and American force landed at the White Sea port of Archangel. An SR assassin killed the chief of the Petrograd Cheka, and Lenin himself was wounded.

The regime now sped its military preparations. As minister of war, Trotsky imposed conscription, and, by a mixture of cajolery and threats of reprisals against their families, secured the services of about 50,000 czarist officers. The Red Army, which was Trotsky's creation, grew to over 3,000,000 strong by 1920. Its recapture of Kazan and Samara on the Volga in the autumn of 1918 temporarily turned the tide in the crisis that seemed about to engulf the Soviet state.

The German collapse on the western front in November 1918 permitted the Bolsheviks to repudiate the Treaty of Brest-Litovsk, and to move back into parts of the Ukraine, where they faced the opposition of a variety of local forces. Elsewhere, the opposition consisted of three main armies. General Denikin led an army of Whites, which moved from Rostov-on-Don south across the Caucasus, and received French and British aid. Admiral Kolchak's forces in western Siberia overthrew the SR regime in Omsk, and Kolchak became a virtual dictator. General Yudenich's army, including many former members of the German forces, oper-

ated in the Baltic region and threatened Petrograd from the west. Allied unwillingness to negotiate with the Bolsheviks was heightened by a successful Red coup of Bela Kun in Hungary, which seemed to foreshadow the further spread of revolution.

In the spring of 1919, the Reds defeated Kolchak, and by winter took Omsk. In 1920, the Admiral was arrested and executed. Though the Reds also reconquered the Ukraine, mutinies in their own forces prevented them from consolidating their victories and from moving, as they had hoped to do, across the Russian frontiers and linking up with Bela Kun in Hungary. In the summer of 1919, Denikin took Kiev and struck north, advancing to within two hundred

The first mobilization of Moscow workers in the spring of 1918.

and fifty miles of Moscow itself. But his position was weakened by the repressive character of the regime he brought with him and by his recognition of Kolchak as his superior officer, together with the poor discipline of his troops and his own rivalry with one of his generals, Baron Wrangel. Yudenich advanced to the suburbs of Petrograd, but the Reds by the end of 1919 were able to defeat the White threat everywhere, though Wrangel retained an army in the Crimea. Trotsky now called for the militarization of labor to reconstruct the ravaged country; labor battalions were formed, but recovery was long delayed.

Even after the defeat of the Whites, the Reds in 1920 had to face a new war with the Poles, who hoped to keep Russia weak, and to create an independent Ukraine. After an initial retreat, the Red armies nearly took Warsaw, failing only because the French chief of staff, General Weygand, assisted the Poles. The Reds, eager to finish off the Whites, and persuaded that there was after all no hope for the establishment of a communist regime in Poland, concluded peace in October 1920. The Poles obtained a large area of territory in White Russia and the western Ukraine. This area was not inhabited by Poles, but had been controlled by Poland down to the eighteenth-century partitions. It lay far to the east of the "Curzon line," the ethnic frontier earlier proposed by the British foreign minister, Lord Curzon. The Reds then turned on Wrangel, who had marched northward from the Crimea and had established a moderate regime in the territory he occupied. He was forced to evacuate, assisted by a French fleet, in November 1920. The White movement had virtually come to an end.

Why the Counterrevolution Failed

Many factors accounted for the Whites' failure and the Reds' victory. The Whites could not get together on any political program beyond the mere overthrow of the Reds. They adopted a policy of "nonanticipation," which meant that some future constituent assembly would settle the governmental structure of Russia. Their numbers included everybody from czarists to SR's, and they disagreed so violently on the proper course for Russia to follow that they could agree only to postpone discussion of these critical problems.

Moreover, their movement was located on the geographical periphery of Russia—in Siberia, in the Crimea, in the Ukraine, in the Caucasus, and in the Baltic. But the Whites never reached an understanding with the non-Russian minorities who lived in these regions. Thus they ignored the highly developed separatist sentiments of the Ukrainians and others, to which the Bolsheviks, by contrast, were temporarily willing to cater.

Furthermore, the Whites could not command the support of the peasantry. Instead of guaranteeing the results of the land division already carried out with Bolshevik sanction, the Whites often restored the landlords in areas they temporarily controlled, and undid the land division. During the civil war, the peasantry on the whole grew sick of both sides. This attitude explains the appearance of anarchist bands, especially in the south. Then too, the Whites simply did not command as much military strength as the Reds, who outnumbered them in manpower, and who had inherited much of the equipment manufactured for the czarist armies. Holding the central position, the Reds had a unified and skillful command, which could use the railroad network to shift troops rapidly. The Whites, moving in from the periphery, were divided into at least four main groups, and were denied effective use of the railroads.

Finally, the intervention of the Allies on the side of the Whites was ineffectual and amateurish. It may even have harmed the White cause, since the Reds could pose as the national defenders of the country, and could portray the Whites as the hirelings of foreigners. In the light of hindsight, it seems safe to say that either the Allies should have mounted a full-fledged military operation against the Reds, or, if this was impossible (as it probably was, in view of the condition of their own armies after the end of the First World War), they should have stayed out of Russia and allowed the civil war to burn itself out. It is still sometimes argued, however, that, although the Reds won the civil war, the Allied intervention helped keep them so heavily engaged inside Russia that they could not sponsor successful revolutions in other countries. This point of view may well have some justification.

NEP ("The New Economic Policy")

Since 1914, Russia had been deeply involved in fighting and turmoil. By early 1921, with the end of the civil war, famine was raging and sanitation had broken down. Family ties were disrupted, human beings brutalized, and class hatreds released on an unparalleled scale. Industry was producing at a level of about an eighth of its prewar output, and agricultural output had decreased by at least 30 percent. Distribution approached a breakdown. The communist regime appeared to be facing its most serious trial of all: the loss of support in Russia.

A large-scale anarchist peasant revolt broke out in early 1921 and lasted until mid-1922. Lenin remarked that this revolt frightened him more than all the Whites' resistance. But the decisive factor in bringing about a change in policy was the mutiny at the Kronstadt naval base near Petrograd in March 1921. Formerly a stronghold of Bolshevism, Kronstadt now produced a movement of rebellious anarchists who called for "soviets without communists" to be chosen by universal suffrage and secret ballot, for free speech and free assembly, for the liberation of political prisoners, and for the abolition of requisitioning. Except for the last item and for the phraseology of the first, the program was ironically similar to that of all liberals and socialists in czarist Russia. The Kronstadt movement seems to have expressed the sentiments of most Russian workers and peasants. Had the government been conciliatory, there might have been no bloodshed; but Trotsky went to war against the rebels, and defeated them after a bloody fight.

This episode led directly to the adoption of the New Economic Policy, always referred to by its initials as NEP. But the underlying reason for the shift was the need for reconstruction, which seemed attainable only if militant communism were at least temporarily abandoned. Lenin himself referred to "premature" attempts at socialization. It was also necessary to appease the peasants and to ward off any further major uprisings. Finally, the expected world revolution had not come off, and the resources of capitalist states were badly needed to assist Russian reconstruction. The adoption of NEP coincided with the conclusion of an Anglo-Russian trade treaty. Abroad, NEP was hailed as the beginning of a Russian "Thermidor," a return to normality like that following the end of the Terror in the French Revolution.

Under NEP the government stopped requisitioning the whole of the peasant's crop above a minimum necessary for subsistence. The peasant had still to pay a very heavy tax in kind, but he was allowed to sell the remainder of his crop and keep the money. The peasant could sell his surplus to the state if he wished, but he could also choose to sell it to a private purchaser. Peasant agriculture became in essence capitalist once more, and the profit motive had reappeared. Lenin imitated Stolypin by guaranteeing the peasant permanency of tenure. The whole system tended to help the kulak grow richer and to transform the poor peasant into a hired, landless laborer.

Elsewhere in the economy, under NEP the state retained what Lenin called "the commanding heights"—heavy industry, banking, transportation, and foreign trade. In domestic trade and in light industry, however, private enterprise was once more permitted. This was the so-called "private capital sector" of the economy, in which workers could be paid according to their output, and factory managers could swap some of their products in return for raw materials.

Lenin himself described NEP as a partial return to capitalism, and urged the communists to become good businessmen. Yet NEP was never intended as more than a temporary expedient. Lenin believed that it would take a couple of decades before the Russian peasant could be convinced that cooperative agriculture woud be the most efficient. He also argued that a temporary relaxation of government intervention would increase industrial production and give the Russians a useful lesson in entrepreneurship.

Economic recovery was indeed obtained. By 1926-1927, industrial production was back at prewar levels, although agriculture had not kept pace. But NEP was bitterly disliked by leading communists, who were shocked at the reversal of all the doctrines they believed in. By 1924, private business accounted for 40 percent of Russian domestic trade, but thereafter the figure fell off. Those who took advantage of the opportunities presented by the NEP were known as NEPmen. They were often persecuted in a petty way by hostile officials, who tried to limit their profits, tax them heavily, and drag them into court on charges of speculation. The kulak had essentially the same experience. Thus the government often seemed to be encouraging private enterprise for economic reasons and simultaneously to be discouraging it for political reasons.

Within the Communist party, one group favored the increase of the private sector and the extension of NEP, as a new road toward the socialist goal. These were the so-called Right deviationists. Their opponents favored the ending of concessions, the liquidation of NEPmen and kulaks, and a return to Marxist principles at home and the fostering of world revolution abroad—in short, the pressing of the "socialist offensive." These were the "Left deviationists," who included Trotsky. In the Center stood men who attacked both deviations, the Right as an abandonment of communism, the Left as likely to lead to a disruption of the worker-peasant alliance.

The Struggle for Power: Stalin against Trotsky

But the NEP question was not the only one to agitate the communist leaders in the early Twenties. Lenin suffered two strokes in 1922, and another in 1923, and finally died in January 1924. During the last two years of his life, he played an ever-lessening role. Involved in the controversy over NEP and the other controversies was the question of the successor to Lenin. Thus an individual communist's answer to the question of how to organize industry, what role to give organized labor, and what relations to maintain with the capitalist world depended not only upon his estimate of the actual situation but also upon his guess as to what answer was likely to be politically advantageous. From this maneuvering the secretary of the Communist party, Joseph Stalin, was to emerge victorious by 1928.

The years between 1922 and 1928, especially after Lenin's death, were years of a desperate struggle for power between Stalin and Trotsky. Lenin foresaw this struggle with great anxiety.

He felt that Trotsky was abler, but feared that he was overconfident, and inclined to make decisions on his own. He felt that Stalin had concentrated enormous power in his hands, in his role as party secretary, and feared that he did not know how to use it. When he learned that Stalin had gone counter to his orders in smashing the Menshevik Republic of Georgia instead of reaching an accommodation with its leaders, he wrote angrily in his testament that Stalin was too rude, and that his fellows should remove him from his post as general secretary. At the moment of his death, Lenin had published a scathing attack on Stalin, had broken off relations with him, and was about to try to relegate him to the scrapheap. Trotsky's suggestion that Stalin poisoned Lenin is not based on any evidence, but it is clear that Lenin's death rescued Stalin's career, and that, far from being the chosen heir, as he later claimed, he did not enjoy Lenin's confidence at the end.

During these years, Trotsky argued for a more highly trained managerial force in industry, and for economic planning as an instrument that the state could use to control and direct social change. He favored the mechanization of agriculture and the weakening of peasant individualism by encouraging rural cooperatives, with even a hint of the collective farms where groups of peasants, in theory, would own everything collectively, rather than individually. As Trotsky progressively lost power, he championed the right of individual communists to criticize the regime. He referred to the policies of Stalin and his other increasingly powerful enemies as "bureaucratic degeneration," and came to the conclusion that only through the outbreak of revolutions in other countries could the Russian socialist revolution be carried to its proper conclusion. Only if the industrial output and technical skills of the advanced Western countries could be put at the disposal of communism could Russia hope to achieve its own socialist revolution. This is the famous theory that socialism cannot succeed within the boundaries of one country. Either world revolution must break out, or Russian socialism is doomed to inevitable failure.

The opponents of Trotsky's "Left deviation" found their chief spokesman in Nikolai Bukharin. A man who never held such responsible administrative posts as Lenin or Trotsky or Stalin, and who had often shifted his position on major questions, Bukharin none the less took a consistent line during these years; as editor of *Pravda*, he was extremely influential. A strong defender of NEP, Bukharin softened the rigorous Marxist doctrine of the class struggle by arguing that, since the proletarian state controlled the commanding heights of big capital, socialism was sure of success. This view is not unlike the "gradualist" position taken by western European Social Democrats. Bukharin did not believe in an ambitious program of rapid industrialization; he favored cooperatives, but opposed collectives. In foreign affairs he was eager to cooperate abroad with noncommunist groups who might be useful to Russia. Thus he sponsored Soviet collaboration with Chiang Kai-shek in China and with the German Social Democrats.

In his rise to power, Stalin used Bukharin's arguments to discredit Trotsky and to eliminate him. Then, partly because Bukharin's policies were failing, Stalin adopted many of Trotsky's policies, and eliminated Bukharin. Original Stalinist ideas, however, developed during this process. Stalin was not basically an intellectual or a theoretician; he was a party organization stalwart. He adopted theoretical positions partly because they seemed to him the ones most likely to work, and partly because he was charting his own course to supreme power. He came to favor rapid industrialization, and to understand that this meant an unprecedentedly heavy capital investment. At the end of 1927, he suddenly shifted from his previous position on the peasantry, and openly sponsored collectivization. This shift arose because of his concern that agricultural production was not keeping pace with industry. He declared that the balance could be redressed only if agriculture, like industry, was transformed into a series of large-scale unified enterprises.

In answer to Trotsky's argument that socialism in one country was impossible, Stalin maintained that an independent socialist state could exist. This view did not at all imply the abandonment of the goal of world revolution, as has often been thought. Stalin always maintained that the socialist state (Russia) should be the center of inspiration and assistance to communist movements everywhere; Russia would help them and they would help Russia. But, in his view, during the interim period before the communists had won elsewhere, it was perfectly possible for Russia to exist as the only socialist state, and indeed to grow more socialist all the time. In international relations, this doctrine of Stalin made it possible for the Soviet Union to pursue either a policy of "peaceful coexistence" with capitalist states, when that seemed most profitable, or a policy of militant support of communist revolution everywhere, when that seemed most profitable. Stalin's "socialism in one country" also struck a responsive chord in the rank and file of Russian communists, who were disappointed in the failure of revolutions elsewhere. It also meant that Russia, not the West, was to be the center of the new society. Stalin's doctrine reflected his own Russian nationalism rather than the more cosmopolitan and more Western views of Trotsky.

The Struggle for Power: Stalin's Victory

Analysis of the rival theories competing for acceptance in Russia in the Twenties helps explain the alternatives before the communist leadership. It does not explain how Stalin won. To understand this, we must move from the realm of theory and political platforms to the realm of practice and political power. At the end of the civil war, Stalin was commissar of nationalities. In this post, he dealt with the affairs of 65,000,000 of the 140,000,000 inhabitants of the new Russian Soviet Republic. He managed the destiny of the Asians, whom he, as one of them, understood. Their local Bolshevik leaders became his men; where they did not, as in his native Georgia, he ruthlessly crushed them. Though a Georgian, he identified himself with Russian nationalism in the interests of a centralized Bolshevik state.

It was Stalin who took charge of creating the new Asian "republics," which enjoyed the appearance of local self-government, programs of economic and educational improvement, and a chance to use their local languages and develop their own cultural affairs, so long as these were entirely communist-managed. It was he who in 1922 proposed and guided the adoption of a new Union of Socialist Soviet Republics as a substitute for the existing federation of republics. In the U.S.S.R., Moscow would control war, foreign policy, trade, and transport, and would coordinate finance, economy, food, and labor.

And on paper it would leave to the republics home affairs justice, education, and agriculture. A Council of Nationalities, with an equal number of delegates from each ethnic group, would join the Supreme Soviet as a second chamber, thus forming the Central Executive Committee, which would appoint the Council of People's Commissars—the government. This reform was regarded by Stalin as an achievement equal to Trotsky's military organizational work during the civil war.

Stalin was also commissar of the Workers' and Peasants' Inspectorate. Here his duties were to eliminate inefficiency and corruption from every branch of the civil service, and to train a new corps of civil servants. His teams moved freely through all the offices of the government, observing and recommending changes, inspecting and criticizing. In creating this post, Lenin had hoped to clean house, but the ignorance and the lack of tradition that rendered the czarist and Bolshevik civil service incompetent and corrupt operated in Stalin's Inspectorate as well. Although the Inspectorate could not do what it was established to do, it did perform another role. It gave Stalin control over the machinery of government. Lenin attacked Stalin's work in the Inspectorate just before he died, but by then it was too late.

Stalin was also a member of the Politbureau, the tight little group of party bosses elected by the Central Committee, which included only five men throughout the civil war. Here his job was day-to-day management of the party. He was the only permanent liaison officer between the Politbureau and the Orgbureau, which allocated party personnel to their various duties, in factory, office, or army units. In addition to these posts, Stalin became general secretary of the party's Central Committee in 1922. Here he prepared the agenda for Politbureau meetings, supplied the documentation for points under debate, and passed the decisions down to the lower levels. He controlled party patronage—that is to say, all party appointments, promotions, and demotions. He saw to it that local trade unions, cooperatives, and army units were put under communist bosses responsible to him. He had files on the loyalty and achievement of all managers of industry and other party members. In 1921, a Central Control Commission, which could expel party members for unsatisfactory conduct, was created; Stalin, as liaison between this commis-

sion and the Central Committee, now virtually controlled the purges, which were designed to keep the party pure.

In a centralized one-party state, a man of Stalin's ambitions who held so many key positions had an enormous advantage in the struggle for power. Yet the state was so new, the positions were so much less conspicuous and so much more humdrum than the ministry of war, for instance, held by Trotsky, and Stalin's manner was so generally conciliatory, that the likelihood of Stalin's success did not become evident until it was too late to stop him. Inside the Politbureau he formed a three-man team with two other prominent Bolshevik leaders, the demagogue Zinoviev and the expert on doctrine Kamenev. Zinoviev was chairman of the Petrograd soviet and boss of the Communist International; Kamenev was Lenin's deputy and president of the Moscow soviet. All three were old Bolsheviks, in contrast to Trotsky, who had been a Menshevik and an independent member of the intelligentsia.

The combination of Stalin, Zinoviev, and Kamenev proved unbeatable. The three put down all real and imagined plots against them by the use of the secret police. They resisted Trotsky's demands for "reform," which would have democratized the party to some degree, and would have strengthened his position while weakening Stalin's. They initiated the cult of Lenin immediately before his death, and kept it burning fiercely thereafter, so that any suggestion for change coming from Trotsky seemed almost an act of impiety. They dispersed Trotsky's followers by sending them to posts abroad. They prevented the publication of Lenin's "testament," so that the rank and file of the party would not know about Lenin's doubts concerning Stalin. They publicized all Trotsky's earlier statements in opposition to Lenin, and did not hesitate to "revise" history in order to belittle Trotsky. They were confident, and rightly so, that Trotsky was too good a communist to rally around him such anti-Bolshevik groups as old Mensheviks, SR's, and NEPmen.

Early in 1925, Stalin and his allies were able to force the resignation of Trotsky as minister of war. Soon thereafter the three-man team dissolved; Stalin moved into alliance with Bukharin and other right-wing members of the Politbureau, to which he began to appoint some of his own followers. Using all his accumulated power, he beat his former allies on all questions of policy, and in 1926 they moved into a new but powerless alliance with Trotsky. Stalin now (1926) deposed Zinoviev from the Politbureau, charging him with intriguing in the army. Trotsky was the next one to be expelled from the Politbureau, and Zinoviev was ousted as president of the Comintern.

IV   Stalin's Supremacy: Russian Internal Affairs, 1928-1941

The Communist party congress that expelled Trotsky in December 1927 also brought NEP to an end, and proclaimed that the new "socialist offensive" would begin in 1928. The thirteen years between 1928 and 1941 were to see almost incredible changes in the domestic life of Russia—collectivized agriculture, speedy industrialization, forced labor, the great purges and the extermination of all political opposition, the building of an authoritarian state apparatus, and a "retreat" to bourgeois standards in almost every department of social and intellectual life.

Collectivized Agriculture

In 1928, the failure of the peasants to deliver to the cities as much grain as had been required seemed to underline the dangers inherent in the land divisions of 1917 and in the concessions of NEP. Farm productivity on the small individual holdings was not high enough to feed the city population. Food prices for the workers were high, yet the kulaks wanted further concessions. Grain was hoarded. Stalin had often inveighed

Russian peasants carrying banners bearing Stalin's 1929 slogan "Liquidation of the kulak as a class."

against "fanning the class struggle in the countryside," and had denied the intention of collectivizing agriculture rapidly or on a mass scale. The government economic plan issued during 1928 set a figure of 20 percent of Russian farms as the maximum to be collectivized by 1933. Yet during 1929, Stalin embarked on immediate full-scale collectivization, declared war on the kulaks, and virtually put an end to individual farming in Russia.

The government did not have the money or the credit to import food. Furthermore, no governmental machinery is adequate to force peasants to disgorge crops that they are hiding. Therefore, the government enlisted on its side the small peasants; in exchange for their assistance in locating and turning over the kulaks' crops, they promised them a place on a collective farm, to be made up of the kulaks' land and equipped with the kulaks' implements. Probably a good many of the subsistence farmers (about 20 percent of the number of private farms, possibly 5,000,000 households) more or less welcomed this opportunity. Initial encouraging reports led Stalin to go full speed ahead. The kulaks, he declared in late 1929, were to be liquidated as a class. There were about 2,000,000 households of them, perhaps as many as 10,000,000 people in all. They were now to be totally expropriated, and at the same time barred from the new collectives. Since no provision was made for them, this move turned collectivization into a nightmare.

Peasants now were machine-gunned into submission; kulaks were deported to forced labor camps or to desolate regions in Siberia. In desperate revolt against the command to join collectives, the peasants burned crops, broke plows, and killed their cattle rather than turn them over to the state. More than half the horses in all Russia, 45 percent of the cattle, and two-thirds of the sheep and goats were slaughtered. Russian livestock has never since caught up with the losses it suffered because of the excesses of collectivization. Land lay uncultivated, and over the next few years famine took a toll of millions of lives. As early as March 1930 Stalin showed that he was aware of the ghastly mistakes he had made. In a famous statement on "dizziness with success," he put the blame on local officials who had been too eager to rush through the program. By contradicting his own orders of a few months before, he managed to escape some of the hatred

that would otherwise have been directed at him. As usual, many Russian peasants disliked the man they could see, the local official, and were willing to exculpate the "little father" in the capital.

Fifty percent of Russian farms had been hastily thrown together into collectives during this frightful year. Only an additional 10 percent were added during the next three years, so that by 1933 60 percent in all had been collectivized. The number rose again later in the 1930's, until by 1939 more than 96 percent of Russian farms were collectivized. In 1941, there were 250,000 collectives, 900,000,000 acres in extent, supporting 19,000,000 families. Yet the excesses of the early "dizziness with success" were never repeated.

The 1930's also brought a modification of the original rules governing collectives. Originally, collectives had been of two main types: the *sovkhoz*, or soviet farm, not strictly a collective at all but a state-owned enterprise, operated by the government and worked by hired laborers who were government employees; and the *kolkhoz*, or collective farm proper. The sovkhozes were designed as centers of government research and development in agriculture, and were often very large in size. But they were mostly brought to an end by Stalin in the 1930's, when he ordered some forty million acres originally allotted to them to be distributed among the kolkhozes. As of 1941, the sovkhozes occupied no significant area of land.

The kolkhoz itself was also originally of two types: the commune, in which all the resources of the members without exception were owned together, and the *artel*, or cooperative, in which a certain amount of private property was permitted to the members. After Stalin's modifications of the system in the thirties, the artel became the overwhelmingly predominant form of form of collective farm. In an artel, each family owned its homestead, some livestock, and minor implements; these could be left by will to the owner's descendants. But most of the work was done on the collectively cultivated land. Each collective had its own managing board, responsible to the government, which supervised the work of the peasants, who were organized in brigades, each under a brigadier. Like factory laborers paid on a piece-work basis, peasants were remunerated according to their output, which was measured by the artificial unit of the labor-day. One day's

Tractor production in the Soviet Union, 1937. In the foreground is one of the first caterpillar tractors; previously the Russians had produced only the wheeled tractors shown in the background.

work in managing a farm might be, for example, assessed at three labor-days, while one day's work weeding a vegetable patch might be assessed at only half a labor-day.

Each kolkhoz turned over to the government a fixed amount of produce at fixed rates, and the total of all these amounts was designed to guarantee the feeding of the urban population, especially workers in heavy industry and members of the Red Army. In addition, the kolkhoz paid further taxes to cover government expenses for local construction and education. Any surplus might be sold by the peasant directly to the consumer, without the participation of any middleman. Private resale was regarded as speculation, and was subject to punishment. After 1934, the government obtained at least two-thirds of its reve-nue by the resale on the market at a large profit of farm produce bought at low fixed prices from the kolkhoz. This government profit was known as the turnover tax.

The government assisted and controlled the kolkhoz through the supply of mechanical equipment furnished by the Machine Tractor Stations. The collectives could not own their own tractors, but rented them from the stations, paying in exchange a fee ranging up to perhaps 20 percent of the crop. The stations became important centers for political surveillance. By the decision when and to whom to allot tractors, and how many tractors to allot, administrators of the Machine Tractor Stations could directly affect the success of a collective, so their good will was of utmost importance to the management.

Industrialization

Intimately related to the drive in agriculture was the drive in industry. Here, too, Stalin originally had viewed with scorn the grandiose plans of the "superindustrializers," and as late as 1927 had proposed an annual increase rate in industrial production of only 15 percent. But just as he shifted to the frantic pace of collectivizing agriculture, so he first gradually, then suddenly, shifted to forced draft in industry also.

In 1928 began the era of the five-year plans, each setting ambitious goals for production over the next five years. In 1929 and 1930, Stalin appropriated ever higher sums for capital investment, and in June 1930 he declared that industrial production must rise by 50 percent in the current year, a fantastic and impossible figure. Under the first five-year plan, adopted in 1928, annual pig-iron production was scheduled to rise from 3,500,000 tons to 10,000,000 tons by 1932, but in that year Stalin demanded 17,000,000 tons instead. It was not forthcoming, of course, but Stalin's demand for it was symptomatic of the pace at which he was striving to transform Russia from an agricultural to an industrial country.

Part of the reason for this rapid pace lay precisely in the collectivization drive itself. Large-scale farming, to which Stalin was committing Russia, must be mechanized farming. Yet there were only 7,000 tractors in all Russia at the end of 1928. Stalin secured 30,000 more during 1929, but this was nowhere near a beginning. Industry had to produce millions of machines, and the gasoline to run them. Since the countryside had to be electrified, power stations were needed by the thousands. And literally millions and millions of peasants had to be taught how to handle machinery. But there was nobody to teach them, and no factories to produce the machinery. The output of raw materials was inadequate, and the plants to process them were not there.

Another part of the reason for the drive to industrialize lay in the tenets of Marxism itself. Russia had defied all Marx's predictions by staging a proletarian revolution in a country almost without a proletariat. Yet despite the communists' initial political successes, Stalin felt that "capitalism had a firmer basis than communism in Russia, so long as it remained a country of small peasants." The communists felt that the world proletariat expected them to industrialize Russia, but even more they were determined to create as a support for themselves the massive Russian proletariat which as yet did not exist. Furthermore, Stalin was determined to make Russia as nearly self-sufficient as possible, in line with his theory of socialism in one country. Underlying this was a motive at least as intense as any dictated by Marxist doctrine—Russian nationalism.

The strength of this motive is revealed in a speech that Stalin made in 1931:

To slacken the pace means to lag behind, and those who lag behind are beaten. We do not want to be beaten. No, we don't want to. . . . Old Russia . . . was ceaselessly beaten for her backwardness. She was beaten by the Mongol Khans, she was beaten by Turkish Beys, she was beaten by Swedish feudal lords, she was beaten by Polish-Lithuanian gentry, she was beaten by Anglo-French capitalists, she was beaten by Japanese barons; she was beaten by all—for her backwardness. For military backwardness, for cultural backwardness, for political backwardness, for industrial backwardness, for agricultural backwardness. She was beaten because to beat her was profitable and went unpunished. . . . We are fifty or a hundred years behind the advanced countries. We must make good this lag in ten years. Either we do it or they crush us.*

Whatever one may think of this quotation as history (and it omits all Russia's *victorious* wars), it reveals that Russian national self-interest as interpreted by Stalin required the most rapid possible industrialization. And it is of interest that ten years afterward the Germans did attack, something Stalin could of course not have predicted so accurately, but something that he seems to have sensed.

Stalin seems also to have felt that he had only to keep a fierce pressure on the management of industry, and the desired commodities and finished goods would be forthcoming in the desired quantities. The goals of the first five-year plan were not attained, although fulfillment was announced in 1932. Immediately, the second plan, prepared by the state planning commission, went into effect, and ran until 1937; the third was in-

* Quoted in Isaac Deutscher, *Stalin* (New York, 1950), p. 328.

terrupted only by Hitler's invasion. Each time the emphasis was on the elements of heavy industry—steel, electric power, cement, coal, oil. Between 1928 and 1940, steel production was multiplied by four and one-half, electric power by eight, cement by more than two, coal by four, and oil by almost three. Similar developments took place in chemicals and in machine production. Railroad construction was greatly increased, and the volume of freight carried quadrupled with the production of new rolling stock.

By 1940, Russian output was approaching that of Germany, although Russian efficiency and the Russian standard of living were far lower. What the rest of Europe had done in about seventy-five years Russia had done in about twelve. Enthusiasm was artificially whipped up by wide publicizing of the high output of individual workers called Stakhanovites, after a coal miner who had set production records. "Stakhanovites" and "heroes of labor" were richly rewarded, and the others were urged to imitate them in "socialist competition."

All this was achieved at the expense of dreadful hardships, yet eyewitnesses report that many of the workers were as enthusiastic as if they had been soldiers in battle, as indeed in a sense they were. Valuable machinery was often damaged or destroyed by inexperienced workers right off the farm. The problems of repair, of replacement, of achieving balance between the output and consumption of raw materials, of housing workers in the new centers, of moving entire industries thousands of miles into the Ural region and Siberia, were unending and cost untold numbers of lives. An American eyewitness estimates that Russia's "battle of ferrous metallurgy alone involved more casualties than the battle of the Marne."

Administratively, the Russian economy was directly run by the state. The Gosplan, or state planning commission, drew up the five-year plans and supervised their fulfillment at the management level. The Gosbank, or state bank, regulated the investment of capital. An economic council administered the work of various agencies. Its major divisions were metallurgy and chemistry (iron and steel, nonferrous metals, chemicals, rubber, alcohol); defense (aviation, armaments, munitions, tanks, ships); machinery (heavy machines, medium machines, machine tools, electrical industry); fuel and power (coal, oil, electric power); agriculture and procure-

ment; and consumer's goods (grain, meat and dairy products, fisheries, textiles, light industry). Under iron and steel, for example, there functioned the production trusts controlling their own mines as well as blast furnaces and rolling mills. These were the so-called *combinats,* or great production complexes like that at Magnitogorsk in the Urals. In each plant, as in each collective, the manager was responsible for producing the quota set for him within the maximum cost allowed him. He was consulted on production targets, and had considerable leeway in selecting his staff and allocating labor and raw materials. He was bound to render a rigid accounting to the government, which of course fixed the price he must pay for his raw materials.

The Social Impact

The social effects of the economic program were dramatic. Urban population rose from about 18 percent in 1926 to about 33 percent in 1940. The number of cities with a population between 50,000 and 100,000 doubled, and the number of cities with a population exceeding 100,000 more than quadrupled. The largest cities, Moscow and Leningrad (the new name for Petersburg-Petrograd after the death of Lenin), almost doubled in size, and among smaller cities, to take just one example, Alma Ata in Siberia grew from 45,000 to 230,000 between 1928 and 1939. The entire social picture was radically altered.

The relative freedom to choose one's job which had characterized the NEP period disappeared. Individual industrial enterprises signed labor contracts with the kolkhozes by which the kolkhoz was obliged to send a given number of farm workers to the factories, often against their will. Peasants who had resisted collectivization were drafted into labor camps. In the factories, the trade unions became simply another organ of the state. The chief role of the unions was to achieve maximum production and efficiency, to discourage absenteeism and poor work. Trade unions might not strike, or engage in conflict with management. All they could do was administer the social insurance laws and seek improvements in workers' living conditions by negotiation.

Thus in the U.S.S.R. the old privileged

classes of noble landlords, already weak at the time of the revolution, ceased to exist. The industrial, commercial, and financial bourgeoisie, which was just coming into its own at the time of the revolution, was destroyed after 1928, despite the temporary reprieve it had experienced under NEP. Most of the old intelligentsia, who had favored a revolution, could not in the end stomach Stalin's dictatorship, and many of them emigrated. Of the million and a half émigrés from Russia after the revolution, only a very small number (contrary to the general view in the West) were cousins of the czar. Those of the old intelligentsia who remained were forced into line with the new Soviet intelligentsia, which Stalin felt to be a very important class. All were compelled to accept the new Stalinist dogma and to drop their interest in the outside world. The new intelligentsia was expected to concentrate on technical advance, and on new administrative devices for speeding up the transformation of the country.

Although the effect of these social changes would presumably have been to level all ranks, Stalin set himself against the old Bolshevik principles of equality. The Marxist slogan "From each according to his capacity, to each according to his needs" was shelved in favor of a new one, "From each according to his capacity, to each according to his work." Where Lenin had allowed none of the members of the government to earn more than a skilled laborer, Stalin set up a new system of incentives. A small minority of bureaucrats and skilled laborers, factory managers, and successful kolkhoz bosses earned vastly more than the great majority of unskilled laborers and peasants. Together with the writers, artists, musicians, and entertainers who were willing to lend their talents to the services of the regime, these men became a new elite, separated by a wide economic and social gulf from the toiling masses. They had a vested interest in furthering a regime to which they owed everything, and without which they would be nothing.

Soviet propagandists declared that this was a temporary situation. They described the present society in the Soviet Union as "socialist," while regarding "communism," not yet achieved, as the goal toward which the U.S.S.R. was still moving. Yet, just as the "withering away" of the state, which the Marxists predicted, was instead replaced under Stalin by the enormous swelling of state power and state machinery, so the equality predicted by the Marxists was replaced by a new caste system. The means of production were publicly owned in the Soviet Union, as the Marxists had urged. But the power of the state, the birth of a new elite, the brutalization of millions of human beings, and the ruthless use of force after the revolution had been achieved were all the contributions of Stalin.

The Purge Trials

Stalin's program was not achieved without opposition. The crisis of 1931 and 1932, when industrial goals were not being met, and starvation swept the countryside, created discontent inside the regime as well as outside. A small number of officials circulated memoranda advocating Stalin's deposition as general secretary, an act which the party had every right to perform. Stalin jailed them for conspiracy, and one leading Bolshevik committed suicide. It is widely believed that Stalin's own wife reproached him at this time with the ravages that the terror was working, and that she too committed suicide. At one moment, but only at one, we are told, Stalin's self-confidence wavered and he offered to resign, but nobody in the Politbureau dared accept the offer, and the moment quickly passed. His attack against those he believed to be his enemies took the form of the famous purges, which began in 1934 and continued at intervals until 1938.

These purges remain the most mysterious episode in Soviet history. They are often compared with the Jacobin Terror of the French Revolution, when the revolution "devoured its children." But, in contrast to the rapid appearance of the Terror in France, the purges did not begin for seventeen years after the Russian Revolution. Members of the opposition had been demoted, expelled from the party, and even exiled, as in the case of Trotsky, but nobody had been executed. There is an entirely credible story that the Bolshevik leaders had agreed among themselves early in their career never to start guillotining each other. Yet, when the terror began in Russia, it was even more drastic than it had been in France. Moreover, unlike Robespierre, Stalin managed to survive.

From exile, Trotsky continued to attack Stalin in a journal called *The Bulletin of the Opposition*. Clever as always, he scored telling points against Stalin, and his words were carefully read by Soviet officials. Yet the older generation of communists, though they may have hated Stalin, made no move against him. A younger group, however, seemingly more restless and convinced that Stalin had abandoned Lenin's program, found the model for conspiracy in the heroes of the terrorist movement who had assassinated Alexander II. They were apparently prepared to use terrorism against Stalin and his henchmen. Even within the Politbureau men loyal to Stalin grew restless at his ruthlessness, and urged him to relax the pressure; Sergei Kirov, boss of Leningrad, took the lead.

Stalin at times seemed to yield to this urging, as when he ordered more gentle treatment for rebellious kulaks in June 1932 and limited the powers of the political police. But at other times he seemed to be taking the opposite course, as when he issued a decree making an entire family responsible for the treason of any of its members. On the whole, however, tension relaxed during 1932–1934. Kirov proclaimed a new era of lenience at a party conference, and former leaders of the opposition, including Bukharin, were appointed to help draft a new and liberal constitution.

Then on December 1, 1934, Kirov was assassinated by a young terrorist communist in Leningrad. Although the story that Stalin himself had plotted the assassination cannot be confirmed, it is clear that Stalin now determined to strike at the opposition. The assassin was executed. Accused of complicity, Zinoviev and Kamenev were jailed, and forced to admit that they had plotted to restore capitalism. Yet the drafting of the new "democratic" constitution went on. Stalin became ever more withdrawn, ever more autocratic, even more resolved to destroy the old Bolsheviks, as Ivan the Terrible had destroyed the old nobility. After an interlude during 1935 and early 1936, during which Stalin said that "life had become more joyous," the purges proper began.

The official story was that Trotskyite agitation abroad was linked with the murder of Kirov, and with the alleged plans for the murder of Stalin. A series of public political trials took place. In the first (1936) Zinoviev, Kamenev,

and fourteen others admitted these charges and were executed. In the second (1937), seventeen other leading Bolsheviks declared that they had knowledge of a conspiracy between Trotsky and the German and Japanese intelligence services, by which Russian territory was to be transferred to Germany and Japan. All were executed. Then (June 1937) came the secret liquidation of the top commanders in the Red Army, who were accused of conspiring with "an unfriendly foreign power" (Germany) with a view to sabotage. All were executed after an announcement that they had confessed. The last of the public trials took place in March 1938, as twenty-one leading Bolsheviks, including Bukharin, confessed to similar charges and were executed.

But these public trials and the secret trial of the generals give only a faint idea of the extent of the purge. Every member of Lenin's Politbureau except Stalin and Trotsky was either killed or committed suicide to avoid execution. Two vice-commissars of foreign affairs and most of the ambassadors of the diplomatic corps, fifty of the seventy-one members of the Central Committee of the Communist party, almost all the military judges who had sat in judgment and had condemned the generals, two successive heads of the secret police, themselves the leaders in the previous purges, the prime ministers and chief officials of all the non-Russian Soviet Republics—all were killed or vanished. A list of those who disappeared reads like a "who's who" of high officialdom in state and party throughout the twenties and thirties. Literally thousands were executed or disappeared without a trace. The public trials probably included only those who were willing to confess, whether guilty or not. The rest were condemned privately and quite without due process of law.

Although it is clear that many of those who were executed opposed Stalin, the charges against them were certainly not true. Had they been true, the great conspiracy involving almost everybody but Stalin himself would surely have accomplished more than the assassination of Kirov. It is altogether unlikely that any of the top communists conspired with Hitler, little though they loved Stalin. Some who confessed may have felt so great a loyalty to the cause of communism, however perverted, that they sacrificed themselves for Stalin's soviet state. Some doubtless hoped to save their families, or even themselves, and a few leaders were spared the death penalty to encourage confessions from the others. Many may have hoped that the confessions were so ridiculous that nobody could believe them.

What Stalin apparently wanted was to destroy utterly all possibility of future conspiracies. So he trumped up charges against anybody who conceivably could become a member of a regime that might replace his own. Despite the enormous upheaval of the purges, no breakdown took place in the state. New bureaucrats were found to take the places of the old. The new Stalin-trained officials, uncultivated but competent, now manned all top-level positions.

The Authoritarian State

In the midst of the purges, in 1936, Stalin proclaimed the new constitution, the "most democratic in the world." By its provisions nobody was disfranchised, as priests and members of the former nobility and bourgeoisie had previously been. Civil liberties were extended, but even on paper these were never more than a sham, since the constitution provided that they could be modified in the "interest of the toilers." The fact that the U.S.S.R. was a one-party state prevented elections from being anything but an expression of unanimity. The right to nominate candidates for the Supreme Soviet belonged to Communist party organizations, trade unions, cooperatives, youth groups, and cultural societies; but all were completely dominated by the party. The party picked the candidates, and no more than one for each post was ever presented to the voters. The party controlled the soviets, and the party hierarchy and government hierarchy overlapped and interlocked.

Every citizen was eligible for membership in the party on application to a local branch, which voted on his application after a year of trial. Communist children's organizations fed the youth groups, which in turn fed the party. The party was organized both territorially and functionally in pyramidal form, with organizations at the bottom level in factory, farm, and government office. These were grouped together by rural or urban local units, and these in turn by regional and territorial conferences and congresses. The party organizations elected the All-Union party congress, which selected the Central Committee of the party, and which was in theory the highest policy-making organ, though actually no party congress was held between 1939 and 1954. The Central Committee selected the Politbureau. At each level of the party pyramid there were organizations for agitation and propaganda, for organization and instruction, for military and political training. The party exercised full control over the government, which simply enacted formally what the party had decided upon. The five-year plans, for example, were party programs that went into effect even before they were formally adopted by the government.

The highest organ of the government was the Supreme Soviet, made up of two houses—a Soviet of the Union, based on population, and a Soviet of Nationalities, elected according to national administrative divisions. In theory, the Supreme Soviet was elected for a term of four years. The Supreme Soviet itself did little; it appointed a presidium which issued the decrees and carried on the work of the Supreme Soviet between sessions. It also appointed the Council of Ministers (long called the Council of People's Commissars). This cabinet, rather than the Supreme Soviet or its presidium, enacted most of the legislation, and was thus the legislative as well as the executive organ of the Russian state. The chairmanship of the Council of People's Commissars, the chairmanship of the Politbureau, and the general secretariat of the Communist party were all posts held by Stalin, who in addition served as commissar of defense, chief of the State Defense Council, which ran the country during wartime, and generalissimo. Similar overlapping of party and government posts was the regular practice.

In 1924, Stalin's constitutional reform had created the new Union of Soviet Socialist Republics, including the enormously large Russian Federative Republic, the Ukraine, White Russia, Georgia, Armenia, and Azerbaidjan, and three central Asian Soviet Socialist republics: Uzbekistan, Turkmenistan, and Tadjikistan. In 1936, Kazakh and Kirghiz republics were added, making a total of eleven. As a result of the annexations of the Baltic states and of Finnish and Romanian territory in 1940, five more republics were created: Lithuania, Latvia, Estonia, Karelia, and Moldavia. These sixteen "Union" republics differed widely in population. Within the huge Russian republic were sixteen "autonomous" republics, and numerous other subdivisions, all called "autonomous." The larger SSR's had similar subdivisions.

Each of the Union republics and autonomous republics had a government patterned exactly on that of the Soviet Union, except that the supreme soviet of each republic was unicameral and not bicameral, since it lacked a chamber of nationalities. Many complaints have been heard in recent years about the way in which "Great-Russian chauvinism" has permeated official policy toward the individual minority republics. Although this soviet descendant of czarist russification policy has always been a menace, it is widely believed that in the years before World War II, the chief objective was not to try to russify the nationalities but to communize them. With this end in view, the party permitted and encouraged local nationalities to revive their culture, study their past traditions, and use their own language. Like every other cultural manifestation permitted in the U.S.S.R., these national cultural achievements were "managed." Not only was it impossible for anti-Soviet or anti-communist material to appear in print or in any of the plastic arts, but, as everywhere, all artistic effort was closely supervised and had to serve the regime positively. The value of "cultural autonomy" under these circumstances is of course highly debatable.

Although the Stalin constitution specifically gave each republic the right to secede, this provision was pure window-dressing. The central government was overpoweringly stronger than the government of any one republic, which in any case was often not even made up of natives. Although each of the sixteen republics was in 1944 given its own foreign office by an amendment to the constitution, this amendment was never intended to give them autonomy in this critically important field, Actually, it seems simply to have been a device for securing representation of the Ukraine and White Russia in the United Nations. The representatives of these two republics to the United Nations have never been anything but extra Soviet delegates; the first Ukrainian delegate to the UN was not even a Ukrainian, but a Russian who was once Soviet ambassador to the independent Ukraine of the revolutionary era.

The Russian Thermidor?

The period between 1934 and 1941, notable for the purges and for the constitutional development of Stalin's one-party state, is also called by many shrewd observers of revolutions the true Russian Thermidor, as distinct from NEP. The term "Thermidor" has come to mean a period in which a revolution has burnt itself out, and the prevailing mood shifts from messianic enthusiasm to one of desire for normality. In revolutionary France, the shift was signalized by the fall of Robespierre and the Jacobin regime, and the advent of the Directory, a different government with different objectives, policies, and personnel, which was in turn succeeded by Napoleon's dictatorship. In the U.S.S.R., the striking fact was that Stalin stayed in office throughout. He was in effect the Russian Robespierre, Directory, and Napoleon all rolled into one. If we accept the parallel, the Russian Thermidor was a managed and manipulated Thermidor, involving no real liberalization of the regime or relaxation of controls. Yet perhaps the parallel is not entirely valid, since Stalin resembled Napoleon far more than he did the weak Directory.

In any case, the period of the late 1930's saw a wholesale retreat from many ideas of the revolution. Simultaneously with the purges and the new constitution, the bread ration was raised; the kolkhoz was reformed to permit the individual farmer to own his homestead; new medals and titles were awarded to leading workers in plants, and to scientists, engineers, and military men. In the Red Army, the traditional czarist distinctions between officers and men were restored, and marshals were named for the first time. Thus, without relaxing political control, Stalin introduced an element of relaxation into the daily life of the rank and file, at the very height of his Terror. The standard of living went up, as the production of consumer's goods was encouraged, and as workers were invited to spend their earnings on little luxuries previously unavailable.

Simultaneously, the state rediscovered Russia's great past. The standard communist teaching had been that proletarians have no fatherland; the very name of Russia had almost been abandoned. Now, in contrast, officially controlled organs of opinion editorialized that one should love one's own country, and hailed the heroes of the czarist era. Alexander Nevsky, who had defeated the Teutonic Knights; Dmitri Donskoi, who had defeated the Tatars; Peter the Great; Kutuzov, who had defeated Napoleon; even Ivan the Terrible—all were praised to the skies. The reputations of the great literary figures of the nineteenth century underwent a similar rehabilitation. This retreat to Russian nationalism reached its climax during World War II, when the Marxist *Internationale* itself was dropped as the national anthem.

The old Bolsheviks had attacked the family as the backbone of the old order, had made marriage difficult and divorce easy, had drawn no distinction between legitimate and illegitimate children, and had encouraged promiscuity and abortions. Stalin's state now rehabilitated the sanctity of marriage, denounced the seducer, made divorces very hard to get, declared the family essential to the state, and encouraged children to obey their parents. Doubtless the shift came in part as a result of the falling birthrate and increasing juvenile delinquency, but it was none the less part of the abandonment of radicalism.

The early Bolsheviks had destroyed the old school system, abolished homework and examinations, and allowed children to administer the schools collectively with their teachers. Attendance fell off, the schools became revolutionary clubs of youngsters, and the training of teachers was neglected. The universities deteriorated, since anybody aged sixteen could enroll in them. Degrees were abolished, and technical training was stressed to the exclusion of other subjects. Under NEP, this chaotic situation was modified, and the basic problem of increasing literacy was seriously tackled. But the subjects of ordinary school curricula were replaced by the so-called "project" system with heavy emphasis

Early postrevolutionary education: A classroom in which adults were taught to read and write.

on labor problems and Marxist theory. The teachers had little to do except memorize texts, and quiz the children to test their mastery of them. The Communist party itself took over the universities, purged the faculties, and compelled the students to spend one week in three at work in factories—a system that helped neither the student nor the university, and cannot have increased industrial production by very much.

The thermidorean reaction, as might have been expected, changed this system drastically. Training of teachers improved, their salaries were raised, and regular ranks in the civil service were established for them. The old prerevolutionary system of admissions and degrees in the universities was restored, as was the prerevolutionary school curriculum. Examinations and homework reappeared; discipline was enforced on school children. The emphasis on political education was reduced, and coeducation was abandoned. Fees for tuition were restored for secondary schools, the Russian counterpart of the American high school or the French lycée. These tuition fees made higher education difficult to obtain except for children of the new elite or unusually talented students who were able to win state scholarships. Literacy rose to about 90 percent, if we may believe Soviet figures.

The educational reforms certainly made books, theaters, museums, and libraries available to many more Russians than ever before. Newspapers and periodicals multiplied, and the regime's respect for science and learning was genuine. But the regime's attitude was narrowly utilitarian and thoroughly intolerant. All cultural activities were measured by their positive contribution to the state. Education became indoctrination. Systems of ideas that might rival communism were not allowed to compete, since the government could always silence those who might be their spokesmen. In this respect the Soviet regime was even more authoritarian than that of a ruler like Czar Nicholas I.

Under Nicholas I, censorship prevented the writer from saying certain things, but it did not positively prescribe what he must say. It was a negative, not a positive censorship, and it left a margin of personal freedom that permitted some of the greatest works of all literature to be written in Russia. The Soviet censorship, on the other hand, was positive, and required of all artists that they constantly praise the new system and devote their talents to publicizing its merits. The party line extended into all cultural fields, even music, where talented composers had to apologize abjectly for failing to produce communist symphonies, whatever they may be. The creative artist, the scientist, the scholar did not know from day to day whether his efforts would win him a Stalin prize or a sentence to a Siberian labor camp.

The Russian Thermidor came last of all, and doubtless very reluctantly, to modify the traditional communist position on religion. Here militant atheism had been the policy of the early Bolsheviks. They jailed and sometimes executed bishops and priests; they sponsored an atheist society and a museum of antireligious propaganda. Behind this attitude lay more than the standard Marxist feeling that religion was the opium of the masses; in Russia, the Orthodox church had always been a pillar of czarism, and had held back the intellectual advance of the country. Many years of attacks on religion, however, failed to eradicate Orthodoxy from among the people. When in 1937 Hitler built a Russian church in Berlin, and took every occasion to speak kindly of the Orthodox church, Stalin moved in the religious field also. Declaring that Christianity had contributed to past Russian progress, the government called off its antireligious propaganda and enlisted its own atheist society to rehabilitate the Church. Church-going became respectable once more, although members of the party were not encouraged to profess religion. As a result, when war came, the leading church dignitaries supported the regime enthusiastically, although Hitler won a number of Ukrainian clerics to his side. In 1943, Stalin received high churchmen; the government lowered taxes on church property, lifted the curfew for Easter, and appointed a new patriarch, on whose subservience the regime could count.

Viewed together, the changes of the Thermidor period seem to have had a double purpose. They were designed in part to retain popular loyalty during a period when the party itself was being disrupted by the purges. But they were also designed in part to strengthen the country to meet an expected attack from Germany. However far the return to old and popular forms and ideas was carried, it was always the regime that took the lead. And never at any moment did Stalin relax his firm control over all departments of national life, both public and private.

V Soviet Foreign Policy, 1918-1941

Foreign Office
and Comintern, 1918-1928

During the period of "war communism," the Bolsheviks had a chance to reflect upon their previously firm conviction that the world revolution was to be expected in the immediate future. The communist states in Bavaria and in Hungary proved to be short-lived; everywhere the moderates triumphed. As the civil war drew to a close, Lenin and his followers realized that to rebuild a shattered Russia it would be necessary to deal with the capitalist world. In the Foreign Office they had two competent men: Chicherin, a learned aristocrat turned Bolshevik, and Litvinov, his shrewd and able chief assistant. These two and their staff now become diplomats in the service of the Soviet state, like diplomats in the service of other states.

But the idea of world revolution was of course not abandoned. Lenin in 1919 founded the Third International, known thereafter as the Comintern. It issued what amounted almost to a new Communist Manifesto, summoning communists all over the world to unite against the "bourgeois cannibals" of capitalism. Zinoviev was put in charge, and his chief assistants were also Russians. Labor, socialist, and anarchist parties in Bulgaria, Norway, Italy, and Spain began to adhere to the new organization, although many withdrew in disgust when it became clear that the Bolsheviks were establishing a dictatorship in Russia with secret police and an army. Yet the Comintern continued to operate side by side with the Foreign Office, and during the next few years often in seeming contradiction to it. This duality gave Russian foreign policy a unique aspect. The maintenance of the Comintern aroused suspicion abroad and made capitalist states reluctant even to recognize the new Russia.

The Foreign Office concluded a trade treaty with England in 1921, at the beginning of the NEP period, which bound Russia not to stir up the peoples of the British Empire by any means, and reopened trade between the two countries. Similar treaties were concluded between Russia and Poland, the Baltic states, Scandinavia, Germany, and Italy. A truce had been arranged between the communist and capitalist worlds. In 1922, the Russians were invited to an international economic conference at Genoa. The British and French were convinced that NEP meant a return to capitalism and had worked out a scheme for investment in Russia as part of a program for the postwar economic reconstruction of Europe. Not only did the Russians reject this plan, but they signed with defeated Germany the Treaty of Rapallo (April 1922), which provided for the renunciation of all claims for reparations, and implied a German willingness to recognize Bolshevik nationalizations. This recognition the other powers, especially France, were unwilling to grant because of the large amounts of capital they had invested in Russia before the revolution. Rapallo relieved Russian isolation, and brought German technical knowledge to the service of the Bolsheviks. They permitted the Germans to build and operate armament and aircraft factories on Russian soil in defiance of the Treaty of Versailles.

In 1923, at Lausanne, Russia lost a dispute with Britain over international regulation of the Straits, and further friction with Britain arose over Afghanistan. But Britain recognized the Soviet regime in 1924, despite Trotsky's description of the mild Labourite Ramsay MacDonald as a "Christian Menshevik" whose country was full of cockroaches—a comment whose characteristic vituperative tone illustrates some of Russia's difficulty in getting along with the rest of the world. Later in the same year, 1924, the so-called Zinoviev letter was published in England. It purported to instruct the British Communist party in the techniques of revolution, and it was almost certainly a forgery. But the "Zinoviev letter" influenced the British voters to elect a Conservative government, which denounced the treaties with Russia. In 1927, a raid on the offices of a Russian firm doing business in London produced further evidence of communist agitation in England, and the British government now broke relations with Russia altogether. The Anglo-Russian council of trade unions set up by the communists collapsed when the Russians criticized British moderation in the general strike of 1926. Meantime, the United States had no diplomatic relations with the Soviet regime, and did not recognize it until 1933.

During the years 1918–1927, the Comintern compiled a record of failure. First, the Russians failed to keep in line the leaders of the Italian Left in a conference at Leghorn in 1921, and thus contributed handsomely to the success of Mussolini in the next year. Next, they failed in Bulgaria to collaborate with a liberal agrarian regime, and allowed the triumph of a right-wing group in 1923. Most important, they failed in Germany, where a revolution actually threatened during 1923 as a result of French occupation of the Ruhr. After Lenin's death, the feud between Stalin and Trotsky was reflected in the Communist parties of other countries, and cost the Comintern heavily.

The Russians failed in Poland, where they helped Pilsudski to dictatorial power in 1926, after which he turned against them. They failed in the Muslim and colonial world. But their greatest failure came in China, where in 1923 the Chinese nationalist revolutionary leader, Sun Yat-sen, agreed to take communist advice and received one of the Comintern's best men, Borodin. Borodin helped Sun reorganize his political party, the Kuomintang, and admitted communists to it, although this alienated the right-wing supporters of the national party. In March 1926, Sun having died, his brother-in-law Chiang Kai-shek led a coup against the government, and began to arrest communists. It is often argued that, had Stalin at that moment broken with Chiang and proceeded to sponsor a Chinese communist revolution, he might well have won China. Indeed Trotsky analyzed the situation that way at the time. But Stalin in his own analysis fell back on a theory that the Bolsheviks had not espoused since Lenin's return to Russia in April 1917: the theory that a bourgeois revolution must precede a socialist revolution, and that all the communists could and should do in China was to help Chiang achieve this first revolution. The eventual result was a series of massacres of Chinese communists by Chiang, and a loss of prestige for Stalin and for Russia. It seems probable that neither then nor later did Stalin actually *want* the Chinese communists in power, in view of the enormous difficulty of maintaining Russian control there.

Indeed Stalin had apparently never really believed in the effectiveness of the Comintern as an instrument of world revolution. When he came to sole power, he could not abandon it, however, because of the criticism he would have aroused, and because he sought to dilute and eventually to eradicate the largely Trotskyite sentiments of communists in other countries. He therefore applied to the Comintern the same techniques he had used against the party at home, and established full control over it through use of the Russian delegation. This delegation was responsible to the Politbureau, and as the representative of the only successful revolutionary country it enjoyed great prestige. Successively, the Comintern was influenced to denounce the enemies of Stalin: Trotsky and the Left in 1924, Bukharin and the Right in 1928. Thereafter there was no divergence between the Comintern and the Foreign Office.

Stalin and the West, 1928-1939

Simultaneously with the adoption of the "new socialist offensive" at home, Stalin swung the Comintern leftward into a new period of militant revolutionary activity. The Social Democrats of Western countries were denounced now as "social fascists" and as the most dangerous enemies of communism. The communists were going to bring about revolutions by themselves. Yet Stalin's personal belief in the possibility of revolution elsewhere seems to have been small. "One Soviet tractor is worth more than ten good foreign communists" is a remark quoted as typical of the views of Stalin's entourage in the days of the first five-year plan; it reflects his real contempt for the rest of the world and his deep-rooted Russian nationalism.

This lack of real interest in the behavior of communists abroad and the failure to understand the true play of forces inside other countries led directly to the triumph of Hitler in Germany in 1933. The communists in Germany, who had been instructed by the Comintern that the Social Democrats and not the Nazis were their worst enemies, fought the Nazis in the streets, but allied themselves with them in the Reichstag. They believed that a Nazi triumph would very soon be followed by a communist revolution. Thus even after Hitler came to power, the Russians renewed their nonaggression pact with Germany.

Yet the shock of realization that Hitler had meant precisely what he said about liquidating communists, and the fear that the U.S.S.R. itself might be in danger, soon led Stalin to modify Russian policy in the direction of collective security. After Hitler had refused to guarantee the Baltic states jointly with Stalin, Russia entered the League of Nations in September 1934. The Soviet delegate, Litvinov, now became the most eloquent defender of universal disarmament and of punishment for aggressors. Soon afterward, the Russians began to negotiate for an "eastern Locarno" security pact to balance the agreement reached by the western European nations at Locarno in 1925. Although no such structure could be created because of Polish and German hostility to the U.S.S.R., Russia did sign pacts with France and Czechoslovakia in 1935 providing for consultation, under the terms of the League, in the event of aggression, and for mutual aid, if the League certified that aggression had occurred. Soviet aid to Czechoslovakia, if the Czechs became victims of aggression, was to be delivered only if the French, who were bound to the Czechs by a long-standing alliance, honored their obligations first.

In view of the shift in Soviet foreign policy, the Comintern also shifted its line. In 1935, their recent deadly enemies, the Social Democrats and bourgeois liberals of the West, were suddenly embraced as allies against the fascist menace. Communists were to take the lead in forming "popular fronts" against fascism, and might properly welcome anybody, no matter how conservative in other ways, who would stand together with them on this principle. Revolutionary propaganda and anticapitalist agitation were to be soft-pedaled. The communists in all the countries of the world led the fight for the defense budgets that they had previously sabotaged. Georgi Dimitrov, the Bulgarian communist, hero of the Reichstag fire trial (to be discussed) and a symbol of antifascist courage and wit, was made boss of the Comintern. Inside the Soviet Union, the adoption of the "popular front" strategy was probably not unrelated to the purges, since the "Right deviationists" were anxious to reach an accommodation with the fascist states, and the "Left deviationists" insisted on the steady pursuit of world revolution.

This was the period when popular front governments came to power in France and Spain, and when some people in the West naïvely ac-

cepted the communists as their true brothers in arms against the menace of Hitler. However effective the "popular front" may have been as a tactic with Western individuals, the purges inside Russia disillusioned Western governments. A state that had to exterminate its top civil and military personnel for the crime of collaborating with the enemy did not make an attractive ally. If one believed the purge charges, one regarded a Soviet alliance as of doubtful value; if one did not believe them, how could one trust Stalin? On Stalin's side, Western appeasement of Hitler and Mussolini doubtless increased his disillusionment with the West.

Russia and the western European bloc each assumed that the chief purpose of the other was to turn the full force of Hitler's forthcoming attack away from itself and in the opposite direction. That Hitler intended to attack nobody could doubt. On September 12, 1936, in a speech at Nuremberg, he specifically declared once more that

if I had the Ural mountains with their incalculable store of treasures in raw materials, Siberia with its vast forests, and the Ukraine with its tremendous wheatfields, Germany under National Socialist leadership would swim in plenty.*

There was, then, much reason for the West to hope that the attack would be directed against the U.S.S.R.; this Stalin was determined to avert.

Soviet intervention in the Spanish Civil War is an interesting demonstration of Stalin's real position. General Francisco Franco, who led an army revolt against the republican government of Spain in 1936, soon obtained aid from Mussolini and Hitler. The Russians, though reluctant to intervene in Spain at all because of their anxiety to prove their respectability to the Western powers, realized that a failure to help the Spanish republic would cost them support all over the world. But their aid was too little and came too late, and consisted largely of police agents who devoted themselves to fighting Spanish anarchists and Trotskyites. The Russians hoped that the Western powers would intervene also, feeling that if they did so they would be irrevocably committed to continue the fight against Hitler on other battlefields. But the fact of Western neutrality in Spain helped convince Stalin that a

* A. Hitler, *My New Order,* ed. R. de Sales (New York, 1941), p. 400.

Western alliance could not be counted upon.

A still more important factor here was the Western appeasement of Hitler, which reached its climax in the Munich agreement of Britain, France, Germany, and Italy in September, 1938. From the Russian point of view, the Munich cession of Czech lands to Hitler, and the French failure to support Czechoslovakia and thus make operative the Russo-Czech alliance, could have only one purpose—to drive Hitler east. Stalin was apparently ready to support the Czechs if the French did too; when they did not, he seems to have decided that he had better sound out Hitler for an understanding. Thus a truly operative alliance between Stalin and the West proved impossible between 1935 and 1939.

When the British and French realized that appeasement had failed to stop Hitler, they sought reluctantly for a firmer alliance with the U.S.S.R. From March to August 1939, Stalin kept open both his negotiations with the West and his slowly ripening negotiations with the Germans, which at first seemed to be concerned only with a trade agreement. The British and French mission, when it finally arrived in Moscow, was not composed of sufficiently high-ranking men to inspire Russian confidence. Moreover, the Western powers naturally refused to turn over to Stalin the territories that he wanted as a bulwark against Germany—Finland and the Baltic republics of Estonia, Latvia, and Lithuania.

The growing eagerness of the Germans to secure a nonaggression pact gave Stalin the opportunity he sought to divert the war from Russia. In May 1939 Litvinov was dismissed as foreign minister because he was Jewish and could therefore not negotiate with Germans; he was

"Rendezvous": Low cartoon comment on the Hitler-Stalin pact, August 1939.

replaced by Molotov. In the pact Molotov eventually reached with Hitler late in August 1939, each power undertook to remain neutral toward the other in the event of war. A secret additional protocol provided for a division between Germany and Russia of Poland, which Hitler was about to attack. At worst, this put Russia's frontier farther west in the event of a subsequent German attack. The Russians lived up to the economic clauses of the agreement to the letter, although the Germans did not. The publication of the Hitler-Stalin pact necessitated an abrupt shift in the world communist line, which had remained staunchly "popular front." Now it was once more necessary for puzzled communists to denounce liberals and Social Democrats as enemies. They had to call the war that Hitler launched against Poland within a few days an "imperialist war," in which there was no difference between the two sides and in which communists should not get involved.

Stalin and the Second World War

Stalin overrated the military power of the Poles to resist Hitler, and thus miscalculated the course of the first weeks of war. Faced with the complete collapse of Poland, he marched into the eastern portion. Disturbed by the lull ("the phony war") on the western fronts, he probably feared that Hitler would turn against him at once. This might well have happened had Hitler been able to secure peace with France and England, as he strove to do. During the lull, in December 1939, came Stalin's attack on Finland, which, unlike the Baltic states, had refused to grant him strategic bases. The attack on the Finns by Stalin aroused a storm of anti-Russian sentiment in the West. Both Britain and France supported the recruitment of armies of volunteers, and considered air raids against Russian targets in support of the Finns. The League of Nations expelled Russia. Despite severe setbacks to the Russian troops, the war against the Finns was won by the spring of 1940, before the Western allies had been able to give them effective aid.

And in the spring of 1940, Stalin's second major calculation went awry. Like many observers, he apparently expected France to hold out a long time, and believed that, even if Hitler eventually defeated the French, Germany would be greatly weakened. Now instead came the lightning German operations in the West, and the war on the Continent seemed to be over. Only the British held out. Preoccupied with the security of his western frontiers, Stalin simply seized the three Baltic republics, and staged rigged plebiscites in which the Latvians, Estonians, and Lithuanians asked to be included in the Soviet Union. He demanded of Romania in June 1940 the province of Bessarabia, whose loss after World War I the U.S.S.R. had never recognized, and also northern Bukovina, which had formerly been Austrian, not Russian, territory, but which had a large Ukrainian population and was strategically valuable. Parts of these territories were annexed to existing SSR's and parts were incorporated into the new Moldavian SSR. The Germans had expected Russian seizure of Bessarabia, but not of northern Bukovina; they permitted the seizure, however, telling the Romanians that they could expect no help from Hitler. But that was as far as Hitler's cooperation with Stalin in eastern Europe went. The reannexation of Bessarabia had given the U.S.S.R. the mouths of the Danube, controlling an important artery. The Russians seemed to be moving into southeast Europe, a region in which the Germans were not prepared to let them operate alone.

Only a few weeks after the Russian seizure of Romanian territory, Hitler asserted his own southeastern interests by forcing the Romanians to cede territory to Hungary (August 1940) and then guaranteeing the new Romanian frontiers, a guarantee that could apply only against the U.S.S.R. Soon afterward, German troops appeared in Finland, "to reinforce the German armies in Norway," Hitler explained. And in the autumn of 1940, German troops entered Romania proper, "to guard the Romanian oilfields against British sabotage." These maneuvers on his new frontiers deeply disquieted Stalin, as well they might have.

In October 1940 Italy attacked Greece, and open war had spread to the Balkans. In November, when Molotov went to Berlin, Hitler tried to dazzle him with grandiose offers of an enormous future Soviet sphere of influence extending through Persia to the Persian Gulf and Indian Ocean, and including India, after the British Empire was destroyed. Each time this luscious

bait was held out, Molotov tried to bring the discussion back to southeast Europe and Finland,
and to establish Russia's sole rights in this sphere.
This the Germans would not allow. After the
failure of the conversations, Hitler ordered preparations for an attack on the U.S.S.R.

In the spring of 1941, the Germans had to
rescue the Italians from the Greek campaign,
which had bogged down in Albania. This rescue
was preceded by the movement of German
troops into Bulgaria, which the U.S.S.R. regarded as essential to its own defense. Then
came an unsuccessful German effort to win
Yugoslavia without war, and swift victorious
German campaigns in Yugoslavia and Greece
(March–May, 1941). Germany alone ruled supreme in the Balkan region, and, though the
Yugoslav and Greek resistance had delayed the
German timetable, Hitler was able to launch the
invasion of the U.S.S.R. on June 22, 1941. Stalin
must have known it was coming; indeed the
Western powers had warned him. But he seems
to have hoped against hope to the end. A few
weeks before it came, Stalin, proudly calling
himself an Asiatic, had secured a neutrality pact
with Japan, Hitler's ally. The Japanese, deeply
engaged in China, and intending to go to war
with the United States, wished as much as did
the Russians for insurance against a war on two
fronts.

VI   Conclusion

Karl Marx, who scorned and disliked Russia,
would have been utterly dumbfounded had he
lived to see that backward agricultural land, almost without a proletariat, produce the only
successful European communist revolution. Although much ink has been spilled in an effort to
discover why a Marxist revolution took place in
the country where, in theory, the conditions were
least favorable, the problem is not really so difficult. Two possible general solutions suggest
themselves. Either Marx was wrong, or what
happened in Russia was not a Marxist revolution
at all. Or perhaps both these answers are partly
right. It seems clear that Marx did not correctly
estimate the revolutionary force latent in the
Russian peasantry; since Marx died in 1883, he
could not foresee the full inadequacy of the
czarist regime, the extent of the tensions created
by World War I, or the feebleness of the provisional government of 1917. But it also seems clear
that to bring the Bolsheviks to power it took
Lenin's appreciation of the importance of the
peasantry, his grasp of the immediate situation,
his willingness to risk everything, and his luck at
being in the right place at the right time with the
right weapons.

On the other hand, the revolution was not
wholly Marxist. Once the Bolsheviks were in
power, of course, it was inevitable that the succession of real situations they faced should
modify their Marxist-Leninist theories. Thus
civil war and foreign intervention brought chaos,
from which NEP provided a necessary respite.
And in Stalin there came to power an amalgam
of Marxist, Russian nationalist, and power-
hungry politician such as nobody could have
foreseen. Moved by a combination of motives,
Stalin proceeded hastily and brutally to make
over Russia in a decade. Although he fell short of
his goal, his program had created an industrial
state not totally unprepared for the blows that
Hitler was to deal it. Slaves of the state though
they were, collectivized by force, industrialized
by force, purged, terrorized, and struggling by
the million to exist in forced labor camps, the
Russians in World War II succeeded, with much
help from the United States, in defeating Hitler
and his allies.

How much the loyalty of Russians to Stalin
was due to the failure of the German invaders to
treat them well, and how far Hitler with a different policy might have won their support are
questions with which we cannot deal here. The
Russians were facing a coalition of fascist states—
Germany, Hungary, Romania, and others
grouped together in an alliance called "the Axis
powers" (from the German-Italian "Axis"), a
coalition pledged to the utter destruction of
communism. We turn now to the history of these
powers.

Reading Suggestions on Communist Russia, 1917-1941

GENERAL ACCOUNTS

E. H. Carr, *A History of Soviet Russia*. Ten volumes of this work, still in progress, have so far appeared (Macmillan, 1950–1969). The only attempt at a complete history of the Soviet Union from original sources; Carr is a somewhat uncritical admirer of Lenin, and his work must be used with care.

B. Moore, Jr., *Soviet Politics: The Dilemma of Power* (Harvard Univ. Press, 1950). An illuminating analysis of the relationship between the communist ideology and Soviet practice.

R. N. Carew Hunt, *The Theory and Practice of Communism* (Macmillan, 1951). An excellent introduction to the subject.

M. Fainsod, *How Russia Is Ruled*, 2nd ed. (Harvard Univ. Press, 1963). An analysis of the Soviet system in 1953, firmly rooted in the historical background. Second edition, up to date, 1963.

Robert V. Daniels, *The Nature of Communism* (*Vintage). A valuable study of totalitarianism.

SPECIAL STUDIES

W. H. Chamberlin, *The Russian Revolution, 1917-1921*, 2 vols. (*Grosset's Universal Library). Still the standard work on the subject.

L. Trotsky, *The History of the Russian Revolution*, 3 vols. (Simon and Schuster, 1932). A brilliant but biased study by one of the leading participants.

B. D. Wolfe, *Three Who Made a Revolution* (Dial, 1948; *Beacon). Excellent triple study of the careers of Lenin, Trotsky, and Stalin down to 1914.

D. Shub, *Lenin* (Doubleday, 1948; *Mentor abridgment). The best biography of Lenin in English.

I. Deutscher, *The Prophet Armed, The Prophet Unarmed, The Prophet Outcast* (Oxford Univ. Press, 1954, 1959, 1963; *Vintage). Biography of Trotsky, written by an admirer of the man.

I. Deutscher, *Stalin: A Political Biography* (Oxford Univ. Press, 1949). The most complete account in English.

J. Maynard, *Russia in Flux* (Macmillan, 1948). Enlightening though sometimes farfetched attempts to show basic continuities between the old and new regimes in Russia, written by a British civil servant stationed in India who made the study of Russia his avocation.

C. Brinton, *The Anatomy of Revolution*, 2nd ed. (Prentice-Hall, 1952; *Vintage). Comparison of the Russian Revolution with the French Revolution of 1789 and the English seventeenth-century Revolution.

M. Fainsod, *Smolensk Under Soviet Rule* (Harvard Univ. Press, 1959). A uniquely important study, based on a huge collection of captured documents, of the actual workings of the communist system in Smolensk in the 1930's.

R. C. Tucker and S. F. Cohen, eds. *The Great Purge Trial* (New York: *Grosset's Universal Library, rev. 1965). Manuscript of the 1938 purge trial with excellent notes.

H. Schwartz, *Russia's Soviet Economy,* 2nd ed. (Prentice-Hall, 1954). Good introduction to the subject.

N. Timasheff, *The Great Retreat* (Dutton, 1946). An account of the "Russian Thermidor."

R. Pipes, *The Formation of the Soviet Union,* 2nd ed. (Harvard Univ. Press, 1964). Excellent monograph on the question of national minorities in Russia, 1917–1923.

J. L. Wheeler-Bennett, *Brest-Litovsk, The Forgotten Peace* (Macmillan, 1938). Excellent monograph.

L. Fischer, *The Soviets in World Affairs,* 2nd ed. (Princeton Univ. Press, 1951). The only study of Soviet foreign policies up to 1929.

M. Beloff, *The Foreign Policy of Soviet Russia,* 2 vols. (Oxford Univ. Press, 1947, 1952). A solid study covering the years 1929–1941.

R. H. Crossman, ed., *The God That Failed* (Harper, 1959). Brief statements by Arthur Koestler, Stephen Spender, Ignazio Silone, and other intellectuals recording their disenchantment with communism.

Svetlana Alliluyeva, *Twenty Letters to a Friend,* trans. P. J. McMillan (Harper, 1967). Memoirs of Stalin's own daughter, perhaps the most prominent of the many Soviet citizens who have escaped to the West.

HISTORICAL FICTION   A. Koestler, *Darkness at Noon* (Modern Library, 1956; *New American Library). A famous novel, presenting in fictional form a keen analysis of the attitudes of the Old Bolsheviks whom Stalin purged.

V. Serge, *The Case of Comrade Tulayev* (Doubleday, 1950). Another excellent novel of the purges.

G. Blunden, *The Room on the Route* (Lippincott, 1947). Perhaps the most vivid fictional portrayal of the impact of terror on the ordinary person.

A. Tolstoy, *Road to Calvary* (Knopf, 1946). Translation of a Stalin Prize Novel about the revolution and civil war.

27

The Rise of Fascism

1918–1939

Mein Kampf

Eine Abrechnung
von
Adolf Hitler

1. Band

1 9 2 5

Verlag Franz Eher Nachfolger G. m. b. H.
München NO 2

I Introduction

In this chapter we shall deal with the rise of fascism in Europe in the period between the two great wars. By 1939, authoritarian governments of the Right had taken firm control of Italy, Germany, Spain, and all the countries of eastern and southeastern Europe except Russia. The process by which these regimes came to power differed widely from country to country, as did some of the external features of the regimes. At first glance, fascism is more complex and more difficult to understand than communism, whose development as a doctrine can be traced from Marx through Lenin before its followers were able to put it, or something like it, into practice in Russia. Unlike communism, fascism has no such line of theoretical development. Its proponents often seem to have acted first and worried about doctrine later, devising theories to meet the needs of the moment.

Above: The title page of the first edition of "Mein Kampf." The subtitle, "Eine Abrechnung," means "a settling of accounts." Above right: Berliners selling discarded tin cans to a sidewalk scrap merchant during the inflation of 1923. Right: Hitler and Mussolini in Venice, 1933.

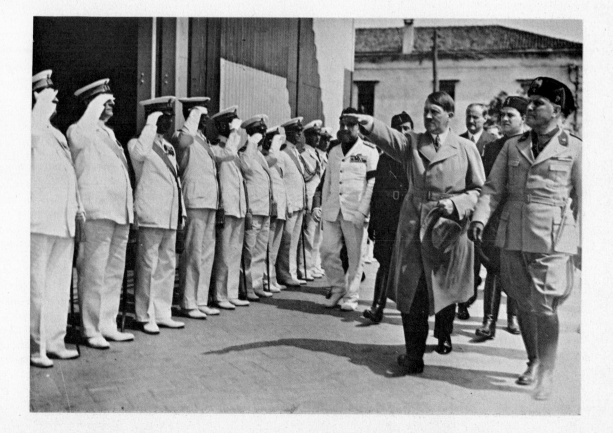

Fascism has been called the revolution of the classes of order. Political parties on the Continent have often represented the interests of the various social classes; when those interests have seemed to be about evenly balanced in a parliamentary state, a long and indecisive political tug-of-war has often ensued. For example, let us assume that a revolution from the Left threatens or can be made to seem to threaten. Then the middle classes, so the theory runs, seize power and take refuge in their own form of extremism—fascism, that is, nationalism tricked out with a few radical phrases to win mass support, and draped in mystical garments. This formula can be applied to Mussolini's rise to power in Italy in 1922, to Hitler's rise to power in Germany in 1933, to Franco's rise to power in Spain in 1936–1939, and to many of the eastern European dictators. Yet the formula takes us only so far. Only a study of the different circumstances in each of the countries can give it body and meaning.

Economic depressions played a role in the rise of almost every dictator—in Italy the postwar depression, and elsewhere the worldwide depression of 1929 and later. We notice, moreover, a certain similarity in the externals of fascism everywhere—colored shirts, private armies, mass hypnotism, special salutes, special war cries and ceremonies, mystical glorification of the nation, and a vast program of conquest. The dictator justifies his program by references to "have" and "have-not" nations; his own nation is always a "have-not," always oppressed.

Fascism is just as violent in its hatred of democracy, liberalism, and parliamentary institutions as in its professed dislike of communism. Indeed fascism shares communism's abhorrence of constitutional procedure, its disregard of the individual human being, and its insistence that the state is supreme. Fascism persecutes its enemies, both real and fancied, with the same ruthlessness we have observed in Stalin's Russia. Censorship, political police, concentration camps, the rule of the bludgeon, the end of legal protection—all these practices are common to both fascism and communism.

When Mussolini ruled in Rome, public buildings everywhere carried the admonition to loyal Italians "Credere, combattere, obbedire" ("Believe, fight, obey"). Presumably this was intended to be inspiring. Yet all it really means is: Believe (what Mussolini tells you), fight (for Mussolini and his backers), obey (Mussolini). When put this way, the formula is seen to subvert all religion and all human decency. Yet, under the stress of the unbearable pressures on individuals generated by the tension of the years between the wars many an idealist was taken in, surrendering his right to think and to make his own decisions.

II Italy and Fascism

The Setting

Although Italy was a member of the victorious Allied coalition, she finished the First World War with a sense of defeat. Six hundred and fifty thousand Italians had been killed and a million wounded. Industry slumped immediately after the war, and within a few months 10 percent of the industrial workers were unemployed. Prices rose rapidly, and wages failed to keep up. The promised pensions for wounded veterans and families of the killed were long delayed. Strikes and disorders became frequent. Many of the young men released from the armies with no trade but war and no job to go to drifted restlessly and discontentedly, fit prey for leaders with glittering promises.

Perhaps most important, the Italian government itself, hoping to influence the peace negotiations, began to spread propaganda among the Italian people to the effect that their wartime allies were robbing them of the Slavic lands in Dalmatia, across the Adriatic, promised to Italy by the secret Treaty of London (1915) in exchange for Italy's entrance into the war. This arrangement the United States had never agreed to, and now would not accept. Although the Allied leaders at the Paris Peace Conference remained unaffected by the storms of protest arising from Italy, the Italian people did come to believe that they had shed their blood in vain. Popular sentiment in Italy, especially in the army, swung toward extremists.

Some Italians hysterically supported Gabriele d'Annunzio, a short, bald nationalist poet and romantic novelist who formed a band of volunteers. They seized the city of Fiume, the Adriatic seaport over which Croatians and Hungarians had long disagreed. Referring to "the stench of peace," and denouncing Woodrow Wilson, d'Annunzio declared that the time for heroic individual action was at hand. Fiume had actually not been awarded to Italy even by the Treaty of London, but d'Annunzio felt that Italy must have it, and that was enough. He ran his own government in Fiume until the end of 1920.

D'Annunzio patterned his regime there upon that of an imaginary medieval commune in a poem by Italy's Romantic poet Carducci (1835–1907). Modeling himself consciously upon the governor of the commune in the poem, d'Annunzio would appear on the balcony of the city hall, address an inspirational harangue to the crowd, and ask for its unanimous consent for whatever he wished to do. This his listeners would grant, raising their right hands high, as the imaginary citizens of Carducci's commune had done. Some of d'Annunzio's followers wore black shirts. When d'Annunzio asked them to whom Fiume belonged they would shout "*a noi*" —"to us"—and when he asked them to whom Italy belonged, they would give the same answer. Indeed, he planned to lead his followers from Fiume to Rome, and thence out into the world to conquer it, presumably with daggers, which he preferred to mechanized weapons. He drafted the Statutes of Fiume, a constitution in which he made a conscious attempt to organize society along the lines he imagined to have existed in the guilds and artisans' corporations of the Middle Ages.

In November 1920 the Italian government signed the Treaty of Rapallo with Yugoslavia, by which Fiume was to become a free city. Italian forces drove d'Annunzio out, and into retirement in a villa on the Italian lakes. But the techniques of force, the haranguing of the mob from the balcony, the straight-arm salute, the black shirts, the rhythmic cries, the plans for conquest, and the "corporative" scheme of the Statutes of Fiume served as precedent and inspiration for Benito Mussolini, founder of Italian fascism.

In the first four years after the end of the war, Mussolini created and brought to power a new political force in Italy. In October 1922 he was summoned to office by King Victor Emmanuel III (1900–1947); from then on he gradually created a totalitarian state of which he was the sole,

undisputed ruler. Suppressing all opposition at home, and threatening the peace abroad, the fascist state in Italy served in some degree as model for the Nazis in Germany, for the Falangists in Spain, and for totalitarian regimes in virtually all the European successor states of the Hapsburg and Ottoman empires. Eventually, Mussolini was forced, largely by his own propaganda, into an alliance with Hitler. In 1940, this alliance took Italy into World War II, and in 1945 it brought Mussolini himself to an ignominious death, upside down on a communist partisan gallows, with his mistress beside him.

Mussolini's Early Career

Mussolini was born in 1883, in the Romagna, a province of central Italy famous for its political extremists, and for the violence with which they express themselves. His father was an ardent socialist who had begun his career as an anarchist under the influence of Bakunin. Trained as an elementary-school teacher, Mussolini was already a passionate socialist by the time he was eighteen. He spent some time as an agitator among Italian emigrant laborers in Switzerland (1902–1904) and in Austria (1909) but was expelled by the police. Back in Italy, he was imprisoned for opposing the war against Turkey over Tripoli (1911). In 1912, he became editor of the most important Italian socialist newspaper, *Avanti* (*Forward*).

When World War I began, Mussolini at first vigorously opposed Italy's entry. But then, during 1914, he changed his mind. First he favored "relative neutrality," meaning that socialists should leave themselves free to support Italian entry if such a course seemed likely to prove favorable to them. When the Italian Socialist party refused to follow this idea, he resigned as editor of *Avanti*. Soon afterward (November 1914), he founded his own newspaper, *Il Popolo d'Italia* (*The People of Italy*) in Milan, and began to advocate an immediate Italian declaration of war on the side of the Allies. For this the Socialist party expelled him.

But these bare bones of a biography reveal only the externals. As a socialist, Mussolini before 1914 was a passionate left-winger. He was an apostle of violent social revolution and a bitter opponent of milder evolutionary and reformist doctrine. He urged that a small, well-knit armed minority should seize power and establish a dictatorship. He loathed militarism, was himself a draft-dodger, and urged soldiers to desert the army. He hated monarchy, and savagely attacked in his writings all the crowned heads of Europe, especially the Italian House of Savoy. He was a vigorous atheist, urged workers to stay away from church, and scorned the teachings of Christ. As an international revolutionary, he opposed nationalism, and even referred to the Italian flag as "a rag to be planted on a dunghill."

Yet he was to repudiate almost all these positions, and as fascist chieftain to substitute almost the exact opposites. As a fascist, he attacked Bolshevism and all left-wing movements; he made his peace with the monarchy and the Church; he became a militant nationalist, a mystic patriot, and a rabid militarist. The repudiation of the views he had held so long and advocated so skillfully is not nearly so astonishing as it seems at first. Mussolini did not much care for programs; what he wanted was to rule.

A complete opportunist, he could shift his line on any question at a moment's notice if it seemed advantageous. For example, after the war, though he was now a fascist, he at first supported a radical program of social change, indistinguishable from the program he would have advocated had he still been a socialist. He favored the action of the Italian workers in the fall of 1920 when they occupied the factories in a kind of sit-down strike. Yet, within a year, he was using the fears which this strike had aroused in the middle classes to argue that he was the only possible bulwark against "Bolshevism." About certain matters, however, he was consistent. He always hated parliaments and loved violence.

Mussolini's switch from isolationism to interventionism in the war in 1914 was the first of his important shifts. After his expulsion from the Socialist party, he agitated furiously for war, speaking to groups of similarly minded young men called *fasci* (the image is of a bundle of rods, a symbol of office in the Roman Republic of antiquity). Soon after Italy did enter the war in 1915, Mussolini was conscripted and sent to the front. He was wounded in 1917 by an Italian mortar shell that exploded during practice. When he got out of the hospital, he continued to edit his newspaper, spewing forth a mixture of extreme revolutionary and extreme nationalist propaganda.

Mussolini's Rise to Power

In March 1919 Mussolini founded the first *fasci di combattimento* ("groups for combat"). There was no sign as yet to indicate that by October 1922 the leader of this small movement would become the most powerful man in Italy. In 1919, he called for every kind of revolutionary violence—seizure of the land, attacks on the factories, shooting of storekeepers who charged high prices, expropriation of mines and transports, and war by the vanquished "proletarian" nations against the victorious capitalists who had kept Italy from annexing Dalmatia. He now maintained that socialism was too conservative; his movement, far from setting itself against a revolution, was in the vanguard of those who were crying for one.

Yet in Italy a revolution along Bolshevik patterns was most unlikely, if not impossible. The peasants were not very revolutionary, for they already held much of the land except in the extreme south. And the industrial workers, though often discontented, knew that a revolution could be starved out because the country needed to import most of its raw materials. The Socialist party was overwhelmingly in the hands of moderates, and in 1919 Catholics founded the Popular party (*Partito Populare Italiano*), designed to compete with the Socialists for the votes of the lower classes, who now had universal suffrage.

In the postwar disorders the peasants seized without consent of the landowners less than a tenth of a percent of the arable land in Italy. The leaders of the Socialist party and the General Confederation of Labor voted down the proposals of anarchist and communist extremists to turn the workers' occupation of the factories into a revolution. The government waited for the workers to grow tired. This they did in less than a month (September 1920); then they left the occupied factories and went home.

Yet, although the danger of revolution was small, the fear of revolution was great. During 1920 and 1921, the industrialists and landowners, squeezed by taxation and inflation, became bitter. Shopkeepers and tradesmen wanted street disorders to end, food prices to be regulated, and the cooperative food stores of the Socialist and Catholic parties to be put out of business as competitors. Professional men and others with fixed incomes suffered as prices and wages went up and salaries lagged behind. The police grew tired of suppressing local disorders and of being repaid with insults. Ex-servicemen, insulted by anarchists and communists for their war records, naturally grew more patriotic.

All these groups identified the forces they did not like as Bolshevik, and accepted as an article of faith the myth of an impending Bolshevik revolution. After a series of fascist-socialists street fights and riots, these "anti-Bolsheviks" began to look to Mussolini's fascist bands as the defenders of their interests. D'Annunzio's defeat left Mussolini as his natural heir. The Left opposition to Mussolini was weakened when the communists split off from the Socialist party in 1921. The fasci grew enormously, from 30,000 in May 1920 to 100,000 in February 1921 to more than 300,000 at the time of the "March on Rome" in October 1922. No longer were they merely squads of discontented and idle youths with vaguely revolutionary and nationalist ideas. Now, says one fascist of the period, "the sons and hangers-on of the bigwigs" poured into the organization.

They had come into the Fascio for their own ends. . . . If they met men in working clothes, they fell on them and began beating them. Their mentality was on a par with that of the Communists, who had beaten and murdered anybody who was decently dressed. One saw . . . the well-known surly and rapacious faces of war profiteers . . . and we were obliged to accept their money because we needed it to stifle an evil worse than they.*

The liberal parliamentary leaders of Italy felt that the fascist bands were teaching the Left a useful lesson. They encouraged the commanding officers of the army to issue rifles and army trucks and gasoline to the fascists, and even assigned army officers to command their operations. The police were encouraged to look the other way during disorders started by the fascists, and local judges were urged to help by releasing arrested fascists. Mussolini's newspaper was circulated free to the soldiers in the army as a "patriotic" sheet.

---

* Umberto Banchelli, *Memorie di un Fascista*, quoted by G. Salvemini in *The Fascist Dictatorship* (New York, 1927), pp. 67–68.

A campaign of terror now began against the socialists and Christian Democrats, as the fascist squadrons cruised around Italy in trucks, burning down labor-union offices, newspaper offices, and local Socialist party headquarters, and beating up and sometimes murdering labor leaders or local antifascist politicians. The fasci forced duly elected officials to resign. The torch, the cudgel, and the famous castor-oil treatment were all characteristic weapons. It is estimated that 2,000 people, antifascist and fascist, policemen and innocent bystanders, died by violence between October 1920 and October 1922.

The "March" on Rome

In the elections of May 1921 Mussolini and thirty-four other fascists were elected to Parliament, along with ten Nationalists, their political allies. The momentum of the fascist movement was now too great to be slowed down. Mussolini abandoned his anti-monarchical views, and fascism became a political party (November 1921) as a necessary step in the drive for power. Too late, the government became alarmed, and tried to take measures against the fascists, but the squads were too strong, the police too accustomed to collaborating with them, and the politicians themselves as yet unaware that a tightly directed armed mob could really take over the state. Inside the royal family, the king's cousin, the duke of Aosta, had become a fascist sympathizer, as had many army generals, the entire Nationalist party, and the leading industrialists.

In the fall of 1922, it was clear that the army would not resist a fascist coup in Rome itself. When a decree of martial law was presented to the king, he refused to sign it, probably influenced by his knowledge that the army would not fight the fascists, and that the duke of Aosta would gladly take his crown. The refusal of the king to declare martial law greatly heartened the fascists. Now, as the fascists "marched" on Rome, mostly by storming railroad trains and stealing free rides, the king (October 29, 1922) telegraphed Mussolini in Milan to come to Rome and form a cabinet. Mussolini arrived by sleeping-car the next morning.

Fascism, which had begun as a patriotic anti-Bolshevik movement, and had then turned into

Mussolini (left center) and some of his followers at the time of the march on Rome.

an antilabor movement in the service of the industrialists and landowners, had finally come to power as a conspiracy against parliamentary government in the service of a military clique. Just before taking office, Mussolini announced:

Our program is simple: we wish to govern Italy. They ask us for programs, but there are already too many. It is not programs that are wanting for the salvation of Italy but men and will-power.*

The Fascist Dictatorship

Mussolini now moved gradually to turn his premiership into a dictatorship. A month after coming to office, he obtained dictatorial powers that were to last only until the end of 1923. Al-

* Quoted by H. Finer, Mussolini's Italy (New York, 1935), p. 152.

though the constitution theoretically remained in force, Mussolini proceeded to take over the administration. He created a fascist militia almost 200,000 strong, which owed complete allegiance to him. He enlarged the regular army, and required its members to take an oath of personal loyalty to him. Before his dictatorial powers expired, he secured from Parliament by pressure a new electoral law. This law provided that the political party which received the largest number of votes in a general election, if that number amounted to at least one-quarter of the vote, should automatically receive two-thirds of the seats in Parliament. The rest of the seats would be divided proportionately. This law made certain the fascists' domination of future parliaments. Indeed, in the election of April 1924, the fascists actually polled 65 percent of the vote cast; but this figure reflects a widespread use of intimidation and terrorism at the polls. The first all-fascist cabinet was now appointed. Meanwhile, local administration was made secure by the appointment of fascist prefects and subprefects in the provinces; these officials pursued the enemies of fascism with the same weapons of murder and mayhem that had been used before Mussolini's March on Rome.

Early in 1924, the leader of the opposition to Mussolini, the socialist Giacomo Matteotti, published a book called *The Fascists Exposed*, in which he detailed many of the outrages the fascists had committed on their way to power. It seemed probable that further revelations were in store, exposing some of Mussolini's cabinet members as corrupt. On June 10, 1924, Matteotti was "taken for a ride" in true gangster style and murdered. The crime was traced to members of Mussolini's immediate circle. This scandal rocked Italy, and for a moment it even seemed possible that Mussolini would fall. But he dismissed from office those who were involved, and pledged himself to restore law and order. Actually, he delayed trying the guilty men until March 1926, and even then they all got off lightly.

What really helped Mussolini over the crisis, ironically enough, was the departure of most of the opposition deputies from Parliament. They declared that they would not return until the Matteotti murder had been solved and the government had been shown to be innocent. Far from making things harder for Mussolini, as they had intended, their departure actually made things easier. Mussolini denied his own guilt, imposed a rigid press censorship, and forbade the opposition to meet. Most of the deputies never did return to Parliament, and in 1926 their seats were declared forfeit.

Next, a series of laws called the "most fascist laws" (*legge fascistissime*) tightened control over the press, abolished secret societies like the Freemasons, whom Mussolini had loathed ever since his socialist youth, and replaced all elected local officials by men appointed from Rome. Opponents of the regime were arrested and exiled to desolate islands off the Italian coast. Early in 1926, Mussolini was empowered to govern by decree. Three attempts on his life led to a new law providing the death penalty for action against the king, the queen, or Mussolini. All opposition political parties were abolished in the same year, and the Fascist party was left as the only legal political party in Italy.

More and more the Italian state and the Fascist party were brought into coordination.

Mussolini was both the *duce* (leader) of the fascists and the *capo di governo,* the chief of state. At one moment he also held eight cabinet posts simultaneously. The members of the Fascist Grand Council, a "politbureau" numbering roughly twenty of the highest party functionaries, all appointed by Mussolini, held all the important posts in the administration not held by Mussolini himself. In 1928, the Grand Council was given important constitutional duties: preparing the lists of candidates for election of the Chamber, advising Mussolini, and proposing changes in the constitution or the succession to the throne. The Grand Council thus became a kind of third house, above the other two houses of Parliament, the Senate and the Chamber.

The Corporative State

Mussolini believed that the interests of labor and capital could and must be made to harmonize with the overriding interests of the state. Instead of a political system as we understand it, he accepted the idea that representation should be based on economic interests organized in "syndicates." Such an idea was not new: the French syndicalist Georges Sorel had already argued in this vein. But Sorel believed in class warfare, and in government by syndicates of workers only. Mussolini, following the Italian nationalist syndicalist Rossoni, believed in capitalism, class collaboration, and producers' syndicates as well as workers' syndicates.

In 1925, fascist labor unions were recognized by employers as having the sole right to negotiate labor contracts. Then, in April 1926, the state officially recognized producers' and workers' syndicates in each of six areas—industry, agriculture, commerce, sea and air transport, land and inland waterway transport, and banking—plus a syndicate of intellectuals, making thirteen syndicates in all. Each syndicate could bargain and reach contracts and could assess dues upon everyone engaged in its own economic field, irrespective of membership in the syndicate. Strikes and lockouts were both forbidden. When labor conditions did not improve, a "charter of labor," promising insurance and other benefits, was issued in 1927. In 1926, the syndicates were put under the control of a special Ministry of Corporations; Mussolini was the minister.

In 1928, the system of parliamentary representation was changed in accordance with fascist syndicalism. A new electoral law provided for a new Chamber of Deputies (400 instead of 560 members). The national councils of the thirteen syndicates could nominate a total of 800 candidates. Each syndicate had a quota, half to be selected by the employers and half by the employees. Cultural and charitable foundations could nominate 200 more candidates. When the total list of 1,000 was completed, the Fascist Grand Council could either select 400 of them, or strike out names and add names of its own, or even substitute an entire new list. The voters would then vote in answer to the question: "Do you approve of the list of deputies selected by the Fascist Grand Council?" They could vote yes or no on the entire list, but they could not choose from among the candidates. If a majority voted yes, the list was elected; if not, the procedure was to be repeated. Despite the highly touted role of the syndicate, all the power obviously lay with the Fascist Grand Council. Universal suffrage was abolished even for this very limited form of election. Payment of a minimum tax or dues to a syndicate was required of each voter; women could not vote. In 1929, the elections under this system produced a yes vote of 8,519,559 and a no vote of 137,761.

Between 1930 and 1938, several constitutional steps were taken which seemed to move the syndicates into the center of the stage. Representatives from the syndicates and the government were now formed into a Council of Corporations, which was to act as a coordinating committee, settle disputes between syndicates, assist production, and establish the fascist corporations themselves, which had not yet been created. The Council was divided into seven sections corresponding to the seven syndicate areas, and in 1931 each of these sections of the Council was simply declared to be a corporation. In 1933, it was announced that the whole corporate system would be revised; and in 1934 the new elections (which of course returned the Fascist Grand Council's list of candidates) produced a "suicide" Chamber of Deputies, which was expected eventually to put an end to its own existence. Its replacement was to be a new "revolutionary assembly," which Mussolini called into existence in the fall of 1934. The assembly, also called the Central Committee of Corporations, contained 824 members, representing twenty-two newly created corporations. The Fascist party, as well as employers and employees, was represented on each corporation.

Finally, in 1938 the "suicide chamber" replaced itself with the Central Committee of Corporations, now called the Chamber of Fasces and Corporations. Nothing remained of the old parliamentary constitution that had been set up by Cavour except the Senate, nominally appointed by the king but actually subservient to Mussolini, who on one occasion had the king appoint forty fascist senators all at once. This new structure, the corporative state, was influenced by d'Annunzio's strange medieval ideas, and by Mussolini's own wish to produce new political and economic forms. But in spite of much oratory by fascist sympathizers about the corporative state and its virtues, it does not appear that the new bodies ever had very much to do with running the economic or political life of Italy, which remained firmly under the direction of the fascist bureaucracy.

Other Fascist Domestic Policies

During the Thirties, the fascist version of the planned economy made its appearance in Italy. The government issued or withheld permits for factory construction. In agriculture, a concerted effort was launched to make Italy more nearly self-sufficient. This effort was dramatized with the "Battle of Wheat," in which the Italians were treated to contests, prizes, and personal appearances by Mussolini. In 1932, official figures reported that wheat production had risen to a point where it could supply 92 percent of the nation's normal needs, and the drive was enlarged to include other cereal products. The government subsidized steamship and air lines, encouraged the tourist trade, and protected Italian industries by means of high tariffs on foreign products. Marshes were drained and land was reclaimed; the incidence of malaria was reduced. Enormous sums were spent on public works, and great strides were made in the development of hydroelectric power. The trains, at least so thousands of tourists reported, ran on time; many argued that "there must be something in this man Mussolini." Yet Italy's weakness in essential raw materials proved to be insuperable.

The state reached into the life of the individual at almost every point. Though Italy was overpopulated, and had for decades relieved the situation only by mass emigration, Mussolini made emigration a crime. He encouraged people to marry and have the largest possible families. He reduced their taxes, extended special loans, taxed bachelors, and extended legal equality to illegitimate children. He hoped in this way to swell the ranks of his armies, and to strengthen his claim that Italy must expand abroad. Children, the future party members, were enrolled in a series of youth movements, beginning at the age of six. The textbooks in the schools, the books in the libraries, the professors in the universities, the plays on the stage, and the movies on the screen were all made vehicles of fascist propaganda. The secret police, OVRA (from the initials of the Italian words for "Vigilance Organization against Anti-Fascist Crimes"), endeavored to discover and suppress all opposition movements.

In 1929, Mussolini settled the Roman question—that of the annexation of the Papal States without the pope's consent— by entering into the Lateran Treaty with the papacy. This treaty recognized the independent state of Vatican City, and thus restored the temporal power of the pope, though on a greatly reduced scale. Mussolini also recognized Catholicism as the state religion, and promised to halt antipapal propaganda. He gave up the right to tax contributions to the Church or the salaries of the clergy, and paid $105,000,000 to compensate the papacy for the Italian occupation of papal territories since 1870. A further concordat legalized religious marriages and extended religious instruction in the schools. The Church agreed not to engage in politics in its newspapers and periodicals.

Yet, despite the fact that many church officials viewed the fascist movement sympathetically, difficulties arose after these agreements had been concluded. In an encyclical, Pope Pius XI (1922–1939) indicated his disapproval of Mussolini's "relentless" economic policies and of the corporations as "serving special political aims rather than contributing to the initiation of a better social order." Mussolini now charged that the Church's "Catholic Action" clubs were engaged in politics, and dissolved them. The pope denied the charges and denounced the Fascist party's practice of monopolizing the time and education of the young. In 1931, however, a fur-

ther agreement was reached, and the clubs were reopened.

Fascist Foreign Policy and Its Consequences

Since Mussolini's foreign policies form an integral part of the international relations leading up to World War II, we shall discuss them more fully in a later chapter. Here we may simply point out that his extreme nationalism, his love of panoply and parades, and his militarism were the logical extensions of his domestic ideas and accomplishments. Mussolini's wish to recreate the glories of ancient Rome impelled him to undertake a policy of adventure in the Mediterranean, which he called *Mare Nostrum* (Latin for "our sea") as a sign that he was the heir to the Caesars. This policy began in 1923, when five Italians working for the League of Nations were assassinated as they marked out the new frontier between Albania and Greece. Mussolini bombarded and occupied the Greek island of Corfu and refused to recognize the League's right to intervene. Only British pressure led to a settlement of the matter.

Later, Mussolini's policy of adventure led him to military aggression in Ethiopia, in Spain, and in Albania (which he dominated during the 1920's and occupied in April 1939). It drove him into an alliance with his fellow fascist Hitler, and led him to voice loud claims against the French for Corsica, Tunisia, Nice, and Savoy. And it alienated Italy from her natural allies, France and Britain. Thus, Mussolini's grandiose fascist ideology first spurred Italy to win self-sufficiency, to rebuild her seaports, and to create a merchant fleet and navy. But the same ideology ultimately separated her from the only powers who might have saved her from the disaster toward which Mussolini was driving.

The German alliance was also responsible for a striking new departure in fascist domestic policy. This was the official adoption of anti-Semitism, which took place in 1938. With only 70,000 Jews, most of whom had long been resident, Italy had no "Jewish problem." Italian Jews were entirely Italian in their language and sentiments, and could be distinguished from other Italians only by their religion. Many of them were prominent in the fascist movement, and many were antifascist. There was no widespread sympathy in Italy for the government's adoption of Hitler's racial policies. Yet Hitler's dominating influence led Mussolini to expel Jews from the Fascist party, and to forbid them to teach or attend school, to intermarry with non-Jews, and to obtain new licenses to conduct businesses.

In summing up Mussolini's career, we may turn to a quotation from an article that he himself wrote in 1920 to denounce Lenin. In reading it, substitute Italy for Russia and Mussolini for Lenin, and you will have a clear idea of fascism:

Russia is a state . . . composed of men who exercise power, imposing an iron discipline upon individuals and groups and practicing "reaction" whenever necessary. . . . In the Russia of Lenin there is only one authority: his authority. There is only one liberty: his liberty. There is only one opinion: his opinion. There is only one law: his law. One might either submit or perish. . . . Russia . . . swallows up and crushes the individual and governs his entire life. . . . Whoever says state necessarily says the army, the police, the judiciary, and the bureaucracy. The Russian state is the state *par excellence.* . . . It has *statized* economic life . . . and formed a huge army of bureaucrats. At the base of the pyramid, . . . there is the proletariat which, as in the old bourgeois regimes, obeys, works, and eats little or allows itself to be massacred. . . .*

III   Germany and the Weimar Republic, 1918-1933

Whereas Mussolini took over in Italy less than four years after World War I ended, the Germans experimented with democracy for fifteen years before succumbing to Adolf Hitler. Two days before the armistice of November 11, 1918, the German Social Democrats proclaimed a republic. On July 31, 1919, this republic adopted a constitution drawn up by a national assembly at Weimar; it is therefore known as the Weimar Republic. The Weimar Constitution was never formally abandoned, but after Hitler became chancellor on January 30, 1933, Germany was in fact a dictatorship.

The history of the Weimar Republic divides itself naturally into three periods: a period of political threats from Left and Right and of mounting economic chaos, from 1918 to the end of 1923; a period of political stability, fulfillment of the Versailles Treaty requirements, and seeming economic prosperity, from 1924 to late 1929; and a period of economic depression and mounting right-wing power, from late 1929 to January 1933.

The Impact of Defeat

For the overwhelming majority of the German people, defeat in 1918 came as a great shock. The military authorities who ran the German Empire during the last years of the war had failed to report to the public German reverses on the battlefield. No fighting had ever taken place on German soil, and the Germans had got used to thinking of their armies as in firm possession of the foreign territories they had overrun. Now these armies came home. It is often argued that the Allies committed a grave blunder by their failure to march to Berlin and demonstrate to the German people that they had actually been defeated. Schooled in reverence for their military forces, the Germans could not grasp the fact that their armies had lost the war. Moreover, the Allies, under the leadership of Wilson, simply refused to deal with the Supreme Command of the German armies. Field Marshal von Hindenburg, as supreme commander, was never required to hand over his sword to Marshal Foch, or to sign the armistice. Rather, it was the civilian politicians who had to bear the odium. In this way, the Allies unintentionally did the German military caste a great favor.

Before the ink was dry on the armistice agreement, the generals, led by Hindenburg himself, were explaining that the German armies had never really been defeated. This was exactly what the public wanted to believe, and the harsh facts—that Ludendorff and Hindenburg had insisted on surrender because the armies could no longer fight—were never effectively publicized. So the legend that Germany had somehow been

* Mussolini on Lenin in 1920, quoted by G. Megaro, *Mussolini in the Making* (Boston, 1938), pp. 325-326.

"stabbed in the back" by civilians, by liberals, socialists, communists, and Jews, took deep root, and became almost an article of faith among many Germans. This legend was widely disseminated by politicians, especially by those who had a stake in the old Prussian system—the monarchists, agrarians, industrialists, and militarists. All through the period of the Weimar Republic, these groups remained hostile toward it; their hostility ranged from political opposition to conspiracies to overthrow the government.

The Allies added another error by including the celebrated "war-guilt" clause in the Treaty of Versailles. The German signatories were obliged to acknowledge what none of them believed, and what subsequent historians would disprove: that Germany alone had been responsible for the outbreak of the war. The war-guilt clause made it harder for the German public to acknowledge defeat and the evils of the past system, to sweep away the militarists, and to bend to the task of creating a virile republic. Instead, it led many Germans to dissipate their energies in denying war guilt, in hating the enemies who had saddled them with the charge, in bewailing the sellout of their generals, and in waiting for a chance to show by force that they had been right all the time.

Postwar Political Alignments and Activities

Threats to stability from the Left further strengthened the antirepublican forces of the Right. Responsibility for launching the republic and for preventing disorder fell upon the "majority socialists," made up of Social Democrats and right-wing Independent Socialists, and led by a Social Democrat, Ebert. The Social Democrats were a moderate group. They made no attack on agrarian property, and they allowed the Junkers to maintain intact their estates and the social and political position that went with them. True to their reformist tradition, the Social Democrats concluded with the industrialists collective bargaining agreements that guaranteed the eight-hour day, rather than trying to launch a serious movement for nationalizing German industry.

But to the left of the Social Democrats, the left wing of the Independent Socialists and the communist "Spartacists" (named for Spartacus, the leader of a slave revolt in ancient Rome) agitated for a proletarian revolution on the Russian pattern. Unable to operate effectively through soviets, the Left tried to stage a revolution in the winter of 1918–1919, but Ebert called in the army to stop it. The generals used not only regular units but also newly formed volunteer units, or "Free Corps," made up mostly of professional soldiers, who were embittered by Germany's recent military defeat and were violently opposed to democracy.

Now the right wing of the Independent Socialists withdrew from the government, and sole responsibility thenceforth rested with the Social Democrats, who put their man, Noske, into the war ministry. As the civil strife continued, the communists attempted a coup, which Ebert, Noske, and the troops put down. Cavalry officers murdered the two chief leaders of the communists after peace had been restored at the cost of more than a thousand casualties. Meanwhile, in Catholic Bavaria, disorders led to the brief emergence of a Soviet republic, which was liquidated in May, leaving Bavaria the home of a sort of permanent red-scare. The Bavarian local authorities, throughout the entire life of the Weimar Republic, encouraged the intrigues of monarchists, militarists, and nationalists. It was in Bavaria that Free Corps assassinations were planned, and it was there that Hitler got his start.

In these ways the forces of the German Right, ostensibly crushed by the war, were given a powerful new lease on life. Meantime, Germany still had an army, the Reichswehr, limited in size to 100,000 men, consisting chiefly of officer cadres, magnificently trained and able to take over the command of far larger numbers if and when troops became available.

The political constellation of the new Germany did not consist solely of Social Democrats and extremists of Right and Left. The old parties of imperial Germany reappeared, often with new labels. The right wing of the old Liberals now emerged as the People's party, including the more moderate industrialists, with a platform of private property and opposition to socialism. Its leader was Gustav Stresemann. Former progressives and left-wing Liberals now formed the new Democratic party, a genuine middle-class republican and democratic group, including many of Germany's most distinguished intellectuals. The Catholic Center party reemerged with its name and program unchanged. It accepted the republic, rejected socialism, and—under pressure from its left wing of trade-union members—favored social legislation, but—under pressure from its right wing of aristocrats and industrialists—opposed far-reaching reform. The Social Democrats, the Democrats, the Center, and the People's party represented those groups, which, though not all enthusiastic, were willing to try to make the new state work. On the Right, the former Conservatives reemerged as the National People's party or Nationalists, dominated by the Junkers as before. The Nationalists had the support of some great industrialists, of most of the bureaucrats, and of a substantial section of the lower middle class, which hoped to return to the good old days of the monarchy. The Nationalists did not accept the republic.

The Weimar Constitution, 1919

When the Germans voted for a national constituent assembly in January 1919, the parties supporting the republic won more than 75 percent of the seats (see table p. 1005), with the Social Democrats alone obtaining nearly 40 percent. The assembly met in Weimar, elected Ebert president of Germany, and formed a government that reluctantly signed the Treaty of Versailles after a delay of some months. The assembly then adopted the new constitution. The new Germany was still a federative state, but the central government had great authority to legislate for the entire country. The president might use armed force to coerce any of the states that failed to obey the constitution or national laws. The cabinet was responsible to the lower house, or Reichstag, which was to be chosen by universal suffrage of all citizens (including women) over twenty.

The president, who was to be elected every seven years by the entire people, was given considerable authority. He was empowered to make treaties, appoint and remove the cabinet, command the armed forces and appoint or remove all officers, dissolve the Reichstag, and call new elections. Furthermore, he could take any measure he deemed necessary to restore order when it was threatened, and might temporarily suspend the civil liberties that the constitution granted. Yet the Reichstag could order such measures

repealed. Inside the cabinet, the chancellor was a real prime minister, with responsibility for planning policy. The constitution also provided for popular initiative. One-tenth of the electorate could bring in a bill or propose an amendment to the constitution. On the economic side, the constitution provided that the government might socialize suitable enterprises, but it guaranteed both private property and the right of inheritance.

Several other contradictions reflected the conflict of interest between the Social Democrats and the middle-class parties. But the powers of the president and the introduction of proportional representation were perhaps the two chief weaknesses. The powers of the president made dictatorship a real possibility. Proportional representation required that votes be cast for entire party lists of candidates, and thus prevented independent voters from "splitting the ticket," and independent politicians from obtaining office. This system encouraged small splinter parties to multiply.

Right and Left Extremism, 1920-1922

In 1920, pressure from the Right loomed as the most serious threat to the Republic. In March 1920 a coup (in German, *putsch*) drove the government from Berlin for several days. The commander of the Berlin military districts, supported by Ludendorff and the Free Corps leaders, hoped to bring to power an East Prussian reactionary official named Kapp. Ebert managed to defeat this "Kapp putsch" by calling a general strike that paralyzed Germany. Because the prewar monarchical judicial system still existed, the men arrested and tried for the Kapp putsch all got off with extremely light sentences, whereas left-wingers brought before the courts were very harshly punished.

As an immediate outgrowth of the strike called by the government, a communist revolt took place in the Ruhr. In pursuit of the communists, German troops entered the area, which had been demilitarized by the Versailles Treaty; this action in turn led to French military intervention and a brief occupation of the Ruhr and Frankfurt (April-May 1920). In the elections of June 1920, the electorate began to support the extremists of

Right and Left. The Democrats and Social Democrats lost strength.

In April 1921, when the Allies presented the bill for reparations, which totaled 132 billion gold marks, the politicians of the Right favored simple rejection of the terms, while the Weimar parties realistically decided that the threat of invasion made this course impossible. Again, the moderates had to take responsibility for a necessary decision that was sure to prove unpopular, and that they themselves did not approve. The minister for reconstruction, Walter Rathenau, a Democrat and a successful industrialist, hoped that a policy of "fulfillment" might convince the Allies that Germany was acting in good faith, and might in the long run lead to concessions. An intensely patriotic German, Rathenau was also a Jew, and drew the particular venom of the anti-Semitic nationalist orators.

The secret terrorist groups of the Right began a campaign of assassination. They began (August 1921) by murdering Matthias Erzberger, the Catholic Center politician who had signed the armistice, and a leading moderate. His assassins escaped through Bavaria. When one of them was caught, the courts acquitted him. When the League of Nations awarded to Poland a substantial area of the rich province of Upper Silesia, containing many German inhabitants, the Right grew still angrier. Rathenau was killed in June 1922 by men who believed in the "stab-in-the-back" theory, and thought that by murdering a Jew they could avenge the "betrayal" of the German army.

Hitler's Early Career

During the months between the assassinations of Erzberger and Rathenau, a new and ominous element had emerged among the welter of right-wing organizations in Bavaria. This was the National Socialist Party of the German Workers

Nazi party membership card no. 1, held by Hitler.

(called "Nazi" as an abbreviation of the word *National*) led by Adolf Hitler, the son of an obscure, illegitimate Austrian customs official, whose real name had been Schicklgruber. Born in 1889, Hitler early quarreled with his father, and seems always to have felt bitter and frustrated. In 1907 he was rejected by the Vienna Academy of Fine Arts, where he wished to study painting. He became an odd-job man, selling an occasional watercolor, but always hovering on the edge of starvation. It was during these years that his hatred of the Jews began. Lower-middle-class Vienna at the time was deeply devoted to its anti-Semitic Mayor Lueger, whom Hitler admired. Because Karl Marx himself had been of Jewish origin and because many Viennese Jews were socialists, Hitler associated socialism with the Jews and lumped both together as somehow responsible for his own personal troubles and for the ills of the world.

Hitler drew support for his anti-Semitism from several nineteenth-century theorists. The French count Joseph Arthur de Gobineau (1816–1882) had laid the pseudoscientific foundation for modern theories of "Nordic" and "Aryan" supremacy. One of Gobineau's most influential readers was the great German composer Richard Wagner. Wagner's son-in-law, the Englishman Houston Stewart Chamberlain (1855–1927), wrote a long and turgid book called *The Foundations of the Nineteenth Century,* which glorified the Germans and assailed the Jews; one section was devoted to a "demonstration" that Christ had not been of Jewish origin. Chamberlain furiously opposed democratic government and, interestingly enough, capitalism. Thus he provided Hitler with a congenial mixture of racism, nationalism, antidemocratic thought, and radicalism.

Hitler came to hate Vienna as a cosmopolitan and Jewish community, and moved to Munich in 1913. In 1914, he enlisted in the German army, and fought through the war as a corporal. He won the iron cross for bravery, but was regarded by his commanding officer as too "hysterical" to deserve a commission. After the war, he went back to Munich, where, as might have been expected, he loathed the new republic and the "Bolsheviks," admired the Free Corps, and decided to become a politician.

Ludendorff had moved to Munich, and had become the center of the reaction. Hitler was employed as a political education officer for the troops. While engaged in this work, he discovered a small political group that called itself the German Workers' party. This group combined nationalism and militarism with a generous amount of radicalism. Hitler joined the party in 1919 and soon proved himself to be a far abler politician than any of his colleagues. He urged intensive propaganda for the union of all Germans in a greater Germany, the elimination of all Jews from political life, a state guarantee of full employment, the confiscation of war profits, the nationalization of trusts, the encouragement of small business, and a land grant to the peasantry. The seemingly radical character of his program caused many Germans otherwise sympathetic to hesitate before giving Hitler money. As early as 1920, he began to reassure them by saying he opposed not "industrial capital" but only "Jewish international loan capital."

Hitler was an extremely successful orator, with almost hypnotic gifts of capturing a crowd. By 1921 he had made himself the absolute leader, the *Führer* (compare with *duce*), of the Nazi party, and in the same year he strengthened himself by founding the SA (*Sturmabteilung,* or storm troops), brown-shirted units largely recruited from the Free Corps. The storm troopers wore arm bands with the swastika emblem, patrolled mass party meetings, and performed other services for the leader. Their commander was a notorious pervert, Captain Roehm, who was also political adviser to the commander of the infantry stationed in Bavaria. So the Nazis, like the Italian fascists, could use their sympathizers in the army to obtain illegal access to government supplies of arms.

Besides Roehm, Hitler's closest collaborators included Hermann Goering, a wartime aviator who had shot down twenty Allied planes, but who found himself restless in peacetime and took on the job of giving the SA a military polish; Rudolf Hess, his Egyptian-born lieutenant and private secretary; and Alfred Rosenberg, a Baltic German distinguished for fanatical hatred of Jews and Bolsheviks, and first editor of the party newspaper.

Hitler and his Nazis were still a very minor political force in 1922 when the middle-of-the-road parties attempted to strengthen the republic. After the assassination of Rathenau, Stresemann's People's party moved away from the Nationalists, who were now tainted by murder, and entered into a collaboration with Center and Democrats. So tense was the political situation that the scheduled presidential elections were postponed to 1925.

The Inflation, 1922-1923

Political maneuvers to meet the increasing threat from the Right, however, were largely nullified by the increasing economic problem posed by steadily growing inflation, which in 1922 and 1923 reached unheard-of extremes. Inflation is a complicated economic phenomenon, and no mere list or description of its causes can really tell the full story. But the single chief cause for the runaway inflation in Germany after 1921 was probably the failure of the German government to levy taxes with which to pay the expenses of the war. The imperial regime had expected to win, and to make the losers pay Germany's expenses by imposing huge indemnities. So it paid for only about 4 percent of the war costs by means of taxation. As defeat neared, the government borrowed more and more money from the banks. When the loans came due, the government repaid them with paper money that was not backed by gold. Each time this happened, more paper money was put into circulation, and prices rose; each rise in prices naturally led to a demand for a rise in wages, which had to be paid with more paper money. The inflationary spiral was under way. Instead of cutting purchasing power by imposing heavy taxes, the government permitted buyers to compete with each other for goods in short supply, thus causing prices to shoot up and speeding up the whole process of inflation.

Many other forces helped inflation along. For several reasons, Germany lacked gold to back its currency. Germany had to pay in gold for goods bought abroad during the war; the rich sent great sums out of Germany for fear that the government would attach them to pay reparations. Raw materials were in short supply; industry was disorganized; and credit was curtailed. The armies of occupation had to be maintained at German expense, and reparation payments had to be made. Nationalist Germans maintained that these expenses, especially reparations, were the cause of inflation; but, though reparations certainly helped the process, they were by no means solely responsible for it. The total sums involved in reparations were never great enough to affect the German currency until long after the inflation was under way. Indeed, the inflation was partly due to the industrialists' wish to avoid paying reparations, and to clear their own indebtedness by letting the currency become worthless.

The following timetable shows how bad the situation had become by the end of 1922. When the war was over, the mark, normally valued at 4.2 to a dollar, had fallen to 8.4. In January 1921 it was 45; by December, 160. By September 1922 it was 1,303, and at the end of the year it was 7,000. In these months, the government begged for a moratorium on reparations payments and for a foreign loan. But the French were unwilling. They had already paid billions for the re-

German Elections to the Weimar Assembly and Reichstag, 1919-1933
(Number of seats obtained by the major parties, arranged with the Left at the top, the Right at the bottom.)

	Jan. 1919	June 1920	May 1924	Dec. 1924	May 1928	Sept. 1930	July 1932	Nov. 1932	Mar. 1933
Communists	—[a]	2	62	45	54	77	89	100	81
Independent Socialists	22	81	—[b]						
Social Democrats	163	112	100	131	152	143	133	121	125
Democrats	74	45	28	32	25	14	4	2	5
Center	71	68	65	69	61	68	75	70	74
People's party	22	62	44	51	45	30	7	11	2
Nationalists	42	66	96	103	78	41	40	51	52
Nazis			38	20	12	107	230	196	288

[a]The Communist party boycotted the elections to the Weimar constituent assembly.
[b]In these and succeeding elections the Independent Socialists had merged with the Social Democrats.

Officials of the Berlin Reichsbank carrying baskets of devalued currency during the severe inflation of 1923.

building of those parts of France that the Germans had devastated during the war, and they wanted the Germans to pay the bill. As a guarantee, the French demanded the vitally important German industrial region of the Ruhr. Despite British opposition, the French occupied the Ruhr in January 1923, after the Germans had defaulted on their reparations payments. The French intended to run the mines and factories for their own benefit, and thus make up for the German failure to pay reparations.

The Germans could not resist with force, but they declared the occupation of the Ruhr illegal, and ordered the inhabitants to embark on passive resistance—to refuse to work the mines and factories or to deliver goods to the French. This order the people of the Ruhr obeyed. Local tension in the occupied area became serious when the French took measures against German police and workers, and when German Free Corps members undertook guerrilla operations against the French.

But the most striking result of the French occupation of the Ruhr was its effect upon the already desperate German economy. Not only was the rest of Germany cut off from badly needed goods from the occupied area, but the Ruhr inhabitants were idle at the order of the German government, and had to be supported at government expense. The printing press struck off ever-increasing amounts of ever-more-worthless marks. Now the exchange rate went from thousands of marks to the dollar to millions, to billions, and, by December 1923, well up into the trillions.

The Consequences of Inflation

Such astronomical figures are meaningless except in terms of the personal and social consequences. A student set off one afternoon for the university with his father's check in his pocket to cover a year's tuition, room, board, and entertainment. When he arrived the next morning after an overnight journey, he discovered that the money he got for the check would pay for one short streetcar ride! Lifetime savings were rendered valueless; people trundled wheelbarrows full of marks through the street in an effort to buy a loaf of bread. Those who lived on fixed incomes were utterly ruined, and the savings of the investing middle classes were wiped out. Real property took on fantastic value. The story is told of two brothers, one frugal and the other spendthrift, who had shared equally in a fortune inherited from their father. The frugal one had invested his money; the spendthrift had bought a fine wine cellar, which he had proceeded to drink up. When inflation came, all the frugal brother's investments would not buy him a haircut, but the spendthrift found that the empty bottles in his cellar were worth billions on billions of marks apiece, and that he was rich again. Under such circumstances, speculation in real estate flourished and speculators made fortunes.

For the German worker, inflation did not mean the liquidation of his savings, because he usually had none. It did mean a great drop in the purchasing power of his wages, so great that he could no longer afford the necessities of life. His family suffered from hunger and cold. Since the financial position of the labor unions was destroyed, they were no longer able to help the workers, who gave up their membership in droves. The great industrialists, however, gained from the inflation, in part just because it did cripple the labor unions, but still more because it wiped out their own indebtedness, and enabled them to absorb small competitors and build giant business combines.

Politically, inflation greatly strengthened the extremists of both Right and Left. The middle classes, although pushed down to the economic level of the proletariat, still possessed the middle-class psychology. In status-conscious Germany, they would not adhere to the working-class parties of Social Democrats or Communists. Disillusioned, they would not adhere to the moderate parties that supported the Republic—the People's party, the Center, and the Democrats. So the Nationalists, and Hitler's Nazis above all, reaped a rich harvest. The hardships of the working class led many workers to turn away from the Social Democrats to the Communists. But Soviet Russian restraint on the leaders of the German Communist party prevented any concerted revolutionary drive until the fall of 1923, by which time poor organization and strong governmental repressive measures had doomed their efforts.

With the country seething in crisis, Stresemann as chancellor in the fall of 1923 proclaimed that because of the economic dislocation Germany could not keep up passive resistance in Ruhr. He ordered work to be resumed and reparations to be delivered once again. Political troubles multiplied when the Right refused to accept the new policy. At the height of the agitation in Bavaria, Hitler in early November 1923 broke into a right-wing political meeting in a Munich beer hall and announced that the "national revolution" had begun. At gun point he tried to get other local leaders to support him in a march on Berlin. They agreed, but let him down when they learned that the national government was prepared to put down the Nazis. Although Ludendorff himself joined the Nazi demonstration in Munich, as he had joined the Kapp putsch of 1920, troops broke up the demonstration with only a few casualties.

The trials of Ludendorff and Hitler have become famous as the most striking example of the Weimar judicial system's partiality for men of the Right. Ludendorff was respectfully acquitted. Hitler was allowed to use the dock as a propaganda platform for his ideas and was sentenced to the minimum term for high treason: five years. He actually spent eight months in comfortable confinement, during which time he wrote large portions of *Mein Kampf* (*My Battle*), the famous bible of the Nazis.

The End of Inflation, 1923-1924

Communist disorders and the Nazi beerhall putsch marked the last phase of the inflation period. A couple of weeks before Hitler's effort, the government had given extraordinary financial powers to Hans Luther, minister of finance, and Hjalmar Schacht, banker and fiscal expert. All printing of the old currency was stopped. A new bank was opened to issue new marks, which were simply assigned the value of the prewar mark (4.2 to the dollar). The new currency was backed not by gold but by an imaginary "mortgage" on all Germany's agricultural and industrial wealth, a psychological gesture that won public confidence. It took one trillion of the old marks to equal one of the new. Simultaneously, rigorous economy was put into effect in every branch of the government, and taxes were increased. The public protested loudly, but the measures remained in force until they had accomplished the intended effect. The cure for inflation produced serious hardships too. Prices fell, and over-expanded businesses collapsed. Unemployment rose sharply, wages stayed low, and workers labored long hours.

During 1924, the Allies contributed to the ending of the crisis in Germany by formulating the Dawes Plan, named for Charles G. Dawes, the American financier and later vice-president under Calvin Coolidge. The plan recommended the evacuation of the Ruhr by the French, the establishment of a special bank to receive reparations payments, gradually rising annual payments for the first five years, and an international loan to finance the German deliveries in the first year. The Nationalists violently attacked the proposals as a sinister scheme to enslave Germany to foreign masters. In the Reichstag elections of May 1924 the Nationalists scored impressive gains, as did the Nazis and the Communists, while the moderate parties all suffered. But a coalition managed to win acceptance of the Dawes Plan in August 1924 by the device of promising the Nationalists representation in the cabinet. When new elections were held in December, the Nazis and Communists suffered losses, and the Social Democrats and moderates gained. Early in 1925 a Center-People's party–Nationalist coalition took office and governed Germany. One wing of the Nationalists, however, led by the enormously rich industrial press and film magnate, Alfred Hugenberg, who had made a fortune during the inflation, opposed all cooperation with the republic. Though Germany had moved appreciably to the Right, foreign policy remained in the conciliatory hands of Stresemann, who remained foreign minister through all governments between November 1923 and his death in October 1929.

Recovery at Home, 1924-1929

During these less-troubled middle years of the Weimar Republic, economic recovery proceeded steadily, until, in 1929, German industrial output exceeded that of 1913. First-rate German equipment, coupled with superb technical skill and a systematic adoption of American methods of mass production, created a highly efficient industrial machine. This "rationalization" of industry increased production, but brought with it overborrowing and some unemployment. "Vertical trusts," which brought together in one great corporation all the parts of an industrial process from coal- and iron-mining to the output of the finished product; and cartels, associations of independent enterprises that controlled sales and prices for their own benefit, were characteristic of the German system. The emphasis was always on heavy industry, which meant that continued prosperity would depend upon a big armaments program.

All through this period, reparations were paid faithfully, with no damage to the German economy. Indeed, more money flowed into Germany from foreign, especially American, investment than flowed out from reparations. Dependence on foreign capital, however, which would cease to flow in time of depression, made German prosperity artificial.

In 1925, after President Ebert died, a presidential election was held in which three candidates competed. The Catholic Center, the Democrats, and the Social Democrats supported the Center leader, Wilhelm Marx. The Nationalists, People's party, and other right-wingers joined in support of Field Marshal Hindenburg, then seventy-seven years old. The Communists ran their own candidate, and thus contributed to the election of Hindenburg, who won by a small plurality. Abroad, the choice of a man so intimately connected with imperial militarist Germany created dismay; but until 1930 Hindenburg acted entirely in accordance with the constitution, to the distress of most of the nationalist groups. The domestic issues of this period all aroused great heat, but were settled by democratic process. In the elections of 1928, the Social Democrats were returned to power, and the Nationalists and Nazis were hard hit. All in all, prosperity encouraged moderation and a return to support of the republic.

"Fulfillment" Abroad, 1925-1930

In foreign affairs, this middle period of the Weimar Republic was one of gradually increasing German participation in the system of collective security. Thus in 1925 Germany signed the Locarno treaties, which took the French armies out of the Rhineland, substituted a neutral zone and a frontier guaranteed by Britain and Italy, and set up machinery for the arbitration of disputes between Germany and her neighbors. These treaties did not, however, guarantee to Poland and Czechoslovakia the eastern frontiers of Germany. In 1926, Germany was admitted to the League of Nations, with a permanent seat on the League's Council. In 1929, Germany accepted the Kellogg-Briand Pact, which outlawed aggressive war.

In 1929, a new reparations plan named after the American Owen D. Young, chairman of the committee that drew it up, substantially reduced the total originally demanded by the Allies. The Young Plan also established lower rates of payments than those under the Dawes Plan, and allowed the Germans a greater part in their collection. Before June 1930 the Rhineland was evacuated by the Allies, four years ahead of the date set by the Treaty of Versailles. Many of these gains for Germany were accomplished only with so much preliminary difficulty that they were robbed of their sweetness, and the German Nationalists, Nazis, and Communists thoroughly opposed them all. Yet German foreign policy was generally calculated to reassure the rest of the world.

The Impact of the Depression, 1929-1931

But even before the last achievements of this "period of fulfillment," the depression had begun to knock the foundations out from under prosperity and moderation. Unemployment rose during 1929. After the American stock-market crash in October, foreign credits, on which prosperity had so largely depended, were no longer available to Germany. Short-term loans were not renewed, or else were recalled. Tariff barriers were hurting foreign trade. Hunger reappeared.

Although unemployment insurance cushioned the first shock for the workers, the lower middle classes, painfully recovering from the inflation, had no such barrier between them and destitution. Their desperation helped Hitler, whose fortunes during the years of fulfillment had fallen very low, although he had attracted a number of new followers who were later to be important in his movement.

Paul Joseph Goebbels, publicist and journalist, proved to be a master of mob psychology and an effective orator. Heinrich Himmler, a mild-mannered but ruthless chicken farmer, took charge of the elite black-shirted SS (*Schutzstaffel,* or defense corps), which was formed as a special guard of honor. The SS, with a higher standing than the SA, and with special membership requirements of "racial purity," was later to become the nucleus for the Gestapo, or secret police. Hitler also recruited Joachim von Ribbentrop, champagne salesman and Nazi party ambassador to the German upper classes.

The government fell in 1930 over a disagreement on a question of unemployment insurance benefits. Hindenburg appointed to the chancellorship Heinrich Bruening, a member of the Catholic Center party. Bruening would have liked to support parliamentary institutions and to continue Stresemann's policies of fulfillment, but he was to find it impossible to do either. President Hindenburg, now eighty-two, had fallen more and more under the influence of General Kurt von Schleicher, an ambitious political soldier who had intrigued himself into the president's favor.

Hindenburg was now itching to rule by decree, as the constitution authorized him to do in an emergency. By failing to pass Bruening's economic program, the Reichstag gave Hindenburg the opportunity he wanted. Bruening agreed, partly because he felt that a genuine emergency existed, but partly because he was determined to keep his bitter political rivals, the Social Democrats, from replacing him in office.

A presidential decree proclaimed the new budget. When the Reichstag protested, Hindenburg dissolved it and called new elections (September 1930). Nazis and Communists fought in the streets, but both gained greatly at the expense of the moderates. The Nazis' Reichstag representation rose from 12 to 107, and the Communists' from 54 to 77. Bruening had to carry on against the wishes of the electorate; supported only by Hindenburg, he too now turned authoritarian.

In order to avoid a new government in which Nazis would participate, the Social Democrats decided to support Bruening. When the Reichstag met, Nazis and Communists created disorder on the floor, but voted together in opposition to government measures. These measures passed only because the Social Democrats voted for them. In 1931, Bruening made an effort to arrange an Austro-German customs union which would coordinate the tariff policies of the two countries, and help them both fight the depression without affecting their political sovereignty. Whether such an arrangement between two countries that were both suffering from unemployment would actually have succeeded cannot be decided; nor can we be sure whether the impulse for Germany and Austria to unite politically might not have proved overpoweringly strong. At any rate, the whole project raised in the minds of the Allies, especially the French, the specter of a "greater Germany," and the scheme was vetoed by the World Court.

The collapse of the great Austrian bank, the Kredit-Anstalt, further deepened the depression, despite a British loan to Austria in 1931, and despite the one-year moratorium on reparations payments procured for Germany by the American president Herbert Hoover.

The Republic in Danger, 1931-1932

Now Nazis, Nationalists, the veterans organization of the Steel Helmets (*Stahlhelm*), the Junkers' Agrarian League, industrialists, and representatives of the former princely houses formed a coalition against Bruening. This coalition had great financial resources and a mass backing, chiefly Nazi. It had its private armies in the SA, in the Stahlhelm, and in other semimilitary organizations. Because the Left was split, and the Communists in effect acted as political allies of the Right, nothing stood between this new right-wing coalition and a political victory except the person of Hindenburg, who controlled the army, and by virtue of the Weimar Constitution was able to keep Bruening in office. Early in 1932, the great industrialist Fritz Thyssen invited Hitler to address a meeting of coal and steel magnates. Hitler won their financial support by convincing them that if he came to power he would be their man. Though some of Hitler's followers were now impatient for a new putsch, he curbed them, believing that the Nazis could come to power legally.

In the presidential elections of March 1932 Hitler ran as the candidate of the Nazis, and Hindenburg as the candidate of the Center, Social Democrats, and other moderate parties. The Nationalists nominated a Stahlhelm man, and the Communists of course ran their own candidate. Hitler polled 11,338,571 votes, and Hindenburg polled 18,661,736, only four-tenths of a percent short of the required majority. In the run-off election, the Nationalists backed Hitler, whose total rose to 13,400,000 as against Hindenburg's 19,360,000. The eighty-four-year-old marshal reelected as the candidate of the moderates, was, however, no longer a moderate himself, but the tool of the Junkers and the military.

Although the government now ordered the Nazi SA and SS disbanded, the decree was not enforced. In April 1932 the Nazis scored impressive victories in local elections, especially in all-important Prussia. Bruening was unable to procure in time either an Allied promise to extend the moratorium on reparations payments or permission for Germany to have equality in armaments with France. Schleicher, who was now deeply involved in intrigue against Bruening, worked on Hindenburg to demand Bruening's resignation. This Hindenburg did on May 29, 1932, the first time a president had dismissed a chancellor simply because he had lost personal confidence in him. Bruening's successor was Franz von Papen, a rich Catholic nobleman and a member of the extreme right wing of the Center, who installed a cabinet composed of nobles. Papen was Schleicher's man—or so Schleicher thought.

The Center disavowed Papen, who had the real support of no political party or group, but whom the Nazis temporarily tolerated because he agreed to remove the ban on the SA and SS. In foreign policy, Papen succeeded where Bruening had failed, for the Allies scrapped the Young Plan and required Germany to pay only three billion gold marks into a fund earmarked for general European reconstruction. Instead of being bound for many decades to pay reparations, Germany was now freed from all such obligations.

On July 31, 1932, new elections for the Reichstag took place, called by Papen on the theory that the Nazis had passed their peak, that their vote would decrease, and that they would then be chastened and would cooperate in the government. But the Nazis won 230 seats and became the biggest single party in the Reichstag; the Communists gained also, chiefly at the expense of the Social Democrats. The Democrats and the People's party almost disappeared, while the Nationalists suffered, and the Center scored a slight gain. Papen had failed. He now wanted to take some Nazis into the government, but the Nazis demanded the chancellorship, which Hindenburg was determined not to hand over to Hitler. Papen now planned to dissolve the Reichstag and to call new elections. By repeating this process, he hoped to wear down Hitler's strength each time, until he brought Hitler to support him and accept a subordinate place. As Papen put pressure on the industrialists who had been supporting Hitler, the Nazi funds began to dry up, leaving Hitler seriously embarrassed. The elections of November 6, 1932, bore out Papen's expectations. The Nazis fell off from 230 seats to 196; and, although the Communists gained substantially and ominously, Papen too won some support. Now the Nazis were really desperate. Goebbels wrote in his diary:

Received a report on the financial situation of the Berlin organization. It is hopeless. Nothing but debts and obligations, together with the complete impossibility of obtaining any reasonable sum of money after this defeat.*

Hitler's Rise to Power, 1932-1933

Had Papen been permitted to continue his tactics, it is possible that Hitler might have been kept from power. But Papen resigned as a matter of form because he could not count on majority support in the Reichstag. Angry with Schleicher and sorry to lose Papen, Hindenburg forced Schleicher himself to take the office on December 3, 1932. Now the backstairs general was chancellor, but he had no political support whatever, and had alienated even Hindenburg. He lasted in office only about eight weeks before Hitler was appointed chancellor.

Schleicher did score a great diplomatic success by winning a five-power declaration that recognized in principle Germany's right to parity in armaments. At home, he made every effort to appeal to all shades of opinion except the extreme Left. But this attempt in itself alienated the implacably antilabor industrialists and the Junkers. The tortuous Papen, eager for revenge, intrigued with these enemies of Schleicher. Early in January 1933 Papen met Hitler at the house of the Cologne banker Baron Kurt von Schroeder. The industrialists, who had temporarily abandoned Hitler, now agreed to pay the Nazis' debts. Hitler, in turn, no longer insisted on the chancellorship. He thus led Papen to hope that he would come back into office with Hitler's backing. Hindenburg, too, was enlisted. When the president refused to give Schleicher the authority to dissolve the Reichstag at its first new session, which would surely have voted him down, Schleicher had no choice; he was forced to resign (January 28, 1933).

But Hitler had now raised the ante, and demanded the chancellorship for himself. Papen consented, provided Hitler undertook to govern in strict accordance with parliamentary procedure. Papen was to be vice-chancellor, and still thought he could dominate the government, since only three of its eleven ministers would be Nazis. He therefore persuaded Hindenburg to accept Hitler as chancellor. But Papen underestimated Hitler. Though Hitler swore to Hindenburg that he would maintain the constitution, he had no intention of keeping his oath. The Weimar Republic was doomed from the moment Hitler came to the chancellor's office on January 30, 1933.

IV   Germany under Hitler, 1933-1939

The Nazi Dictatorship

Hitler's first weeks in power were devoted to transforming his chancellorship into a dictatorship. He dissolved the Reichstag and called for new elections. During the campaign, opponents

* Quoted by S. William Halperin, *Germany Tried Democracy* (New York, 1946), pp. 511-512.

of the Nazis were intimidated by violence and threats, and were denied radio time and free use of the press. Yet a Nazi victory in the election still did not seem sure. On February 27, 1933, fire opportunely broke out in the Reichstag building. Hitler pointed to it as a sample of the disorders that the Communists were likely to instigate. Hindenburg issued emergency decrees suspending free speech and the free press, and thus made it even easier for the storm troops to use terror against their political opponents. It is now generally supposed that the Nazis themselves set the Reichstag fire, but they convicted and condemned to death a Dutch communist named Vanderlubbe, who apparently was mentally deficient.

Despite their campaign, the Nazis won only 44 percent of the votes, which gave them 288 seats in the Reichstag. Using the SA as a constant threat, Hitler bullied the Reichstag. Except for 94 Social Democrats (the Communists were denied their seats), all members voted for the famous Enabling Act (March 23, 1933). This act conferred dictatorial powers upon the government, and suspended the constitution. The act was renewed in 1937 by a subservient Reichstag, and again in 1943.

Now Hitler could act as he chose, unimpeded by the laws. He instituted a ministry of propaganda under Goebbels. He stripped the state governments of the powers they had had under Weimar, and made Germany a strongly centralized state (April 1933) by appointing governors from Berlin who had the power to override the state legislatures. When President Hindenburg died in August 1934, at the age of eighty-seven, Hitler assumed the office of president as well as that of chancellor, but he preferred to use the title *Der Führer* (the leader) to describe himself. This new move was approved by a plebiscite, in which Hitler obtained 88 percent of the votes cast.

Political parties which opposed Hitler were forced to dissolve. The government banned Communists and Socialists (May 1933); the Nationalists dissolved themselves (June 1933); the government put an end to the Catholic parties (July 1933) and all monarchist groups (February 1934). The Stahlhelm was incorporated into the Nazi party (June 1933) and was deprived of its identity (November 1935). As early as July 1933 the Nazis were declared to be the only legal political party in Germany.

The appeal of the Nazis to the German people lay in part in their denunciation and repudiation of the "disorderly" parliamentary system. A strong man who got things done struck a responsive chord in the public. In the last elections, November 1933, there were no opposition candidates, 92 percent of the electorate voted Nazi, and there were only two non-Nazi deputies in the chamber of 661. As in fascist Italy and com-munist Russia, youth groups fed the party, which soon had a powerful regional organization all over Germany and among Germans abroad.

Within the Nazi party itself, however, a difficult situation was created by those who had believed Hitler's more radical pronouncements on social and economic questions. Many of these Nazis were concentrated in the SA, whose members, most of them from the lower classes, were also distressed by the way in which Hitler had treated their organization. The SA had made possible his rise to power, but now it was rather an embarrassment to him, no longer quite respectable, and certainly not in favor, as were the SS and especially the army.

On June 30, 1934, Hitler ordered and personally participated in the celebrated "blood purge," or, as he himself called it, "the night of the long knives." Roehm himself, founder and leader of the SA, was shot, and so were, by Hitler's own admission, seventy-three others, including Schleicher and his wife. Other estimates of the casualties run as high as 1,000. In any case, after June 1934 there was no further opposition to Hitler.

Racism and Political Theory

Within a few days after the passage of the enabling law, Hitler struck the first of his many blows against the Jews, whom he had so long denounced. In a country of approximately 60,000,000 people, the Jews counted less than 1 percent of the population (something under 600,000), not including part-Jewish Germans. The Jews had become leading members of the professions and the arts, and had made outstanding contributions to German culture. Since most Jews were assimilated and patriotic Germans, many of them would probably have become Nazis if they had been permitted. They would have supported Hitler in everything but anti-Semitism. Instead, anti-Semitic doctrines required their ruthless elimination.

The businesses and professions of the Jews were boycotted; they were forbidden to hold office (April 1933), although a temporary exception was made for veterans of World War I. In the "Nuremberg laws" of September 15, 1935, a Jew was defined as any person with one Jewish grandparent. All such persons were deprived of

German citizenship. Intermarriage between Jews and non-Jews was forbidden as "racial pollution." Jews might not fly the national flag, write or publish, act on stage or screen, teach in any educational institution, work in a bank, exhibit paintings or give concerts, work in a hospital, enter any of the government's labor or professional bodies, or sell books or antiques. They were not eligible for unemployment insurance or charity; and the names of Jews who had died for Germany in World War I were erased from war memorials. Many towns and villages, under the spur of government-sponsored propaganda, refused to permit Jews to live inside their precincts.

In November 1938 a Jewish boy of seventeen, driven to desperation by the persecution of his parents, shot and killed a secretary of the German embassy in Paris. Two days later, organized German mobs looted and pillaged Jewish shops all over Germany, burned and dynamited synagogues, and invaded Jewish homes to beat up the occupants and steal their possessions. The state then compelled the Jews to restore the damaged properties and to pay an enormous fine. Jews were forced to take special names, to wear yellow stars of David, and to belong to a Reich "Union of Jews." Although some Jews managed to leave Germany, it was usually at the cost of abandoning all their possessions; yet they were the lucky ones. All these measures and many others (for example, "cows purchased from Jews may not be serviced by the communal bull") designed to drive the Jews into ghettos and starvation were but the prelude to the physical extermination in gas ovens to which they were to be subjected by the Nazis during World War II. What distressed many horrified Western observers almost more than the actions themselves was the failure of any substantial number of highly educated and "civilized" non-Jewish Germans to register any form of protest.

Enthusiasm for "racial purity" had its positive as well as its negative side. The blond, blue-eyed ideal "Nordic types" were urged to mate with each other early and to have many children. German motherhood was made the object of paeans of praise. And, to keep the race pure, sterilization was introduced, supposedly for the prevention of the inheritance of disease. The functioning of such a law depended upon the condition of the medical and legal professions, which soon fell into the hands of charlatans. Medical experimentation of horrifying cruelty and of no conceivable scientific value was practiced during the war on human beings of "inferior" races—Jews, Poles and other Slavs, and gypsies. These practices were the direct outcome of Nazi pseudoscientific "eugenic" legislation.

The Bases of Foreign Policy

In the field of foreign affairs, German racism justified the incorporation of all territory inhabited by Germans, including Austria, the western borderlands (Sudetenland) of Czechoslovakia, Danzig, the Polish corridor, and other less important places. And the doctrine of *Lebensraum* ("living space") justified the incorporation of non-German areas—the rest of Czechoslovakia, Poland, and all southeastern Europe, as well as large areas of Russia. Hitler felt that what the Germans needed, they were entitled to take, since they were a superior people.

Some German intellectuals looked back with longing upon the Holy Roman Empire of the Middle Ages, the first Reich. Now that the war had ended the second Reich of William II, they hoped to behold a third one, incorporating the old territories, no matter who now lived in them. This is the meaning of Hitler's use of the term "Third Reich" to describe the Nazi state, which he proclaimed would last a thousand years. A "scientific" basis for the Lebensraum theory was supplied by the teachers of "geopolitics," chief among whom was Karl Haushofer, professor of geography, retired major-general and teacher of Hitler's close friend Rudolf Hess. Haushofer declared that Britain and France were decadent, that small powers must disappear (except for Switzerland and the Vatican City), that Germany, preserving its master race pure, must possess the will to power, and expand ruthlessly, occupying the "heartland" of Eurasia, from which the world could be dominated.

Another school of thought in Germany argued that Germany's future lay in an alliance with Russia in which Russia's inexhaustible manpower would be joined with Germany's industrial output and military techniques for purposes of conquest. This notion had been strong in German army circles in czarist days and continued to exist after the Bolshevik Revolution, especially after the Treaty of Rapallo concluded between Germany and the Soviet Union in 1922.

Chancellor Adolf Hitler.

Outside the army, other German nationalists, who were just as antiliberal and antiparliamentarian as Stalin, retained the Bismarckian attitudes of hostility to the West and to Poland and of friendship toward Russia, whatever the color of her regime. Moreover, many German Marxists were highly nationalistic. Indeed, Hitler's "national socialism" succeeded in part because he knew how to use old Marxist clichés in presenting an essentially nationalist program.

Legal and Economic Policies

Hitler entirely revamped the judicial system of Germany, abandoning traditional legal principles and substituting "folk" justice, which, Hitler said, subordinated the individual totally to the people (*volk*). So mystic a doctrine meant in practice that whatever Hitler wanted was German law. People's Courts were established (May 1934) to try all cases of treason, a crime that was now extended to include a wide variety of lesser offenses, such as circulating banned newspapers. Hitler appointed all the judges of the People's Courts. Concentration camps were established for enemies of the regime, who could be immured or executed by the headsman's axe without appeal. In fact, they could not even have defense counsel of their choice, but had to accept counsel approved by the courts. The Gestapo (*Geheime Staatspolizei*, Secret State Police) was established in April 1933 in Prussia, and a year later was extended to all of Germany. It had a free hand in opening private correspondence, tapping wires, and spying on individual citizens.

All economic life was brought under the regime. In agriculture, the Nazis aimed at the largest possible measure of self-sufficiency, and, of course, at political control over the peasantry. The Junkers were protected, and no effort was made to divide their vast estates. In 1933, a special law protected farms of less than 312 acres against forced sale and attachment for debt, an act that won the small farmer to Hitler. But the government determined the production required of farms, and fixed farm prices and wages, and fees for distributing farm products. Unused land was put under cultivation, and private citizens were required to grow vegetables in greenhouses. This was part of Hitler's preparation for war. By 1937, Germany was 83 percent self-sufficient in agriculture, a rise of 8 percent since the Nazis had come to power. Fats and coffee were perhaps the two most important deficiencies remaining.

In industry, taking a leaf out of Stalin's book, Hitler proclaimed a Four-Year Plan in 1933 and a second one in 1936. The first was aimed chiefly at economic recovery and at ending unemployment. Labor camps for men and women helped decrease unemployment, as did rearmament and a program of public works. By 1936, unemployment had dropped from about 7,000,000 to less than 1,500,000. The second plan was designed to prepare for war, and especially to make Germany blockade-proof. Output of raw materials was increased and the materials were distributed first and foremost to armament and other war industries; labor was allocated with similar ends

1014

in view; and prices and foreign exchange were controlled. Goering was made boss of the plan.

Under his direction fell the new Goering Iron Works, designed to make up for the loss of the rich iron resources of Alsace-Lorraine, which had yielded three quarters of Germany's supply. To this end, low-content ores were worked, and the government absorbed the higher costs. Output went up in two years more than 50 percent. Germany's gifted scientists were enlisted to make up for other deficiencies by devising successful but expensive synthetic products. Important in this field were the distillation of motor fuel from coal, and the production of synthetic rubber. The state also built strategic highways, the Autobahnen, excellent modern expressways.

The Nazis abolished all labor unions in 1933, and employers' associations in 1934. To replace them, a "Labor Front" was established under Dr. Robert Ley, including all wage earners, salaried persons, professionals, and employers. Strikes and lockouts had been forbidden. Workers were assured of jobs so long as they quietly accepted the entire system. The Labor Front in one of its aspects was a huge spy organization constantly on the alert for anti-Nazis in the factories; it could reduce their pay, fire them, or put them in jail. An adjunct to the Labor Front was the "Strength through Joy" organization, which provided paid vacation trips for German workers to resorts or tourist centers, and which sponsored concerts and other entertainments.

As the second Four-Year Plan went into effect, the worker found himself increasingly immobile. He had a work book detailing his past training and positions held, and he could not get a new job unless the state decided it would be more suitable for him. All graduates of secondary schools had to register with the employment authorities. Men and women of working age were liable to conscription for labor. Just before the war, all agricultural and mining and certain industrial workers were frozen in their jobs. On the side of capital, the big cartel became the all-pervasive feature of German industrial organization—a system of profitable monopoly under state control. The interlocking directorate made the system even tighter than it looked. Six industrialists, for example, held among them one hundred and twenty-seven directorates in the largest corporations, were presidents of thirty-two, and all held government posts besides. The minister of economics sat at the top of the economic pyramid, authorizing plant expansion, controlling imports and exports, fixing prices and establishing costs, and allocating raw materials.

Religion and Culture

The Christian churches, both Protestant and Catholic, posed a problem for the Nazis. Extremists among Hitler's followers had always been in favor of a return to paganism and the old German gods celebrated by Wagner's operas. Hitler himself, born a Catholic, had once declared that Germany was his only god. Yet office brought sobering second thoughts, since Germany was after all nominally a Christian country. In the hope of avoiding state domination, the Lutheran ministry in 1933 organized a national synod, which the Nazis almost immediately took over by appointing their own bishop. The efforts of extreme Nazis to purge the Bible and to abandon the crucifix led to discontent. The dissidents, led by pastor Martin Niemoeller, objected to Nazi theology and efforts at control. But Niemoeller also pledged his loyalty to Hitler, made no objections to Nazi racism, and went to a concentration camp solely out of determination to resist dictation over the Lutheran Church. The "confessional" movement he led probably did not extend beyond about 15 percent of the Protestant clergy.

In July 1933 Hitler and the German Catholics reached a concordat guaranteeing freedom of worship and permitting religious instruction in the schools. Catholics were to be allowed to form youth groups and to appoint professors of theology. But the Nazis did not live up to these terms. They interfered with the circulation of Catholic magazines, persecuted the youth groups, and insulted Catholic priests in their press as members of the "black international." On the other hand, the Catholic church found much to oppose in the teachings to which Catholic children were exposed in the Hitler youth groups. Cardinal Faulhaber of Munich denounced the Nazi violation of the concordat in 1933, but his action only intensified the struggle. Not that millions of Catholics, both clerical and lay, did not support the regime wholeheartedly, persecutions of the Jews and all. They did; and no voice was raised from among the clergy of either major

Christian sect to protest against Nazi racism or militarism.

The Nazi process of Gleichschaltung (co-ordination) was applied in every area of the national life, including education and the arts. One of the leading Nazi officials once remarked, "When I hear the word culture, I reach for my revolver," a revealing and not untypical reflection of the extreme Nazi attitude. Hitler's own artistic views were simple in the extreme. He preferred nudes, the more luscious and Germanic the better, and this taste he strove to impose on the nation, denouncing most modern and experimental trends in art as non-Aryan. The school curriculum, especially history, could no longer be taught with that "objectivity" which was a "fallacy of liberalism," but had to be presented to the student in accordance with the Nazi doctrine of "blood and soil." Nazi racial doctrines, the great past achievements of Germany, the military spirit, and physical culture—these were the cornerstones of the new education.

Hitler and the Nazi high command at the opera.

V   The Failure of Parliamentarism in Spain and Eastern Europe, 1918-1939

In the troubled years between the wars, non-democratic authoritarian governments emerged not only in Italy and Germany but also in Spain, in the successor states to the Hapsburg Empire (except Czechoslovakia), and in the other states of eastern and southeastern Europe.

Spain: The Background

Spain differs widely from the other European countries, and one can understand Franco's triumph only in terms of the special Spanish social, economic, cultural, and political conditions. In Spain, local affection—for the language and traditions of a single province—has usually moved most men more than love of the country as a whole. Catalonians and Basques often have striven to create separate states of their own. Although Spain approaches economic self-sufficiency in both agriculture and industrial raw materials, the soil is poor, the system of farming is backward, and the rural areas are heavily over-populated. Poverty is endemic; discontent is everywhere.

Religion united Spaniards against the Muslims in the Middle Ages, and against the Protestants in the sixteenth and seventeenth centuries. But early in the nineteenth century, the Catholic church in Spain decided to lead against liberalism the same kind of struggle it had led against its earlier enemies. So in most parts of Spain the Church became identified with the landowners. Loss of faith became very widespread. Catholic sources report that by the 1930's only minute fractions of the population attended Mass. With the same devotion and passion they had once shown for the Church, the lower classes in Spain adopted one or another of the modern revolutionary doctrines.

When the Spaniards turned to revolutionary doctrine, it was chiefly in Bakunin's anarchist beliefs and later in Sorel's syndicalism that they found ideas they could cling to. Anarchism (and anarchosyndicalism) really took hold in Spain,

and in Spain alone. The industrial workers of Catalonia and the miserable peasants of Andalusia were anarchist; they wanted to destroy the state utterly rather than conquer and use it. Despite a long history in Spain, anarchism, which at its peak numbered a million to a million and a half adherents, could only harass governments but could not overthrow them, and its positive achievements were limited to securing by means of strikes an occasional increase in wages. It was deeply puritanical in tone, and fanatically anti-Catholic. Shrewd observers have likened it to a Christian heresy that took all too literally the social teachings of the New Testament. Its adherents turned against the Church with all the fanaticism with which they had once supported it, because they felt that the Church had let them down. The burning of churches and the killing of priests, by which Spanish revolutions have always been marked, have been the work chiefly of anarchists.

But in the 1930's Spain also had an increasingly substantial Marxist Socialist party, with its own federation of trade unions parallel to that of the anarchists. The socialists drew their first strength from the urban workers of Castile and from the mining and steel-producing centers of the north. When Spain became a republic in 1931 (see below), the socialists added many rural supporters, and the party numbered a million and a quarter in 1934. The socialists were moderates, who had refused to adhere to the Comintern in 1920, but who had joined the revived Second International a few years later. Dissidents founded a small Communist party, from which there were soon Trotskyite deviations. Catalonians had their own socialist formation, and the Church itself supported labor unions of its own in the north, where it had not become identified with the landlords. The socialist doctrine that each should be rewarded according to his needs sustained the traditional Spanish contempt for success and property. In fact, Spain had never accepted the capitalist system or the industrial revolution any more than it had accepted the Protestant Reformation.

Carlism, the doctrine of the extreme Right, is another vivid illustration of Spanish maladjustment to the outside contemporary world. Founded in the nineteenth century as a movement supporting Don Carlos, a pretender to the throne, Carlism called for the restoration of the Inquisition, regarded the railroad and the telegraph literally as inventions of the devil, and rejected the Copernican theory of the universe. Carlism had its lower-class devotees, too, especially among the rebellious farmers of Navarre in the north.

Birth of the Spanish Republic

King Alfonso XIII, a constitutional monarch strongly ambitious for absolute power, ruled over Spain until 1923. In his governments—based on electoral corruption and intimidation—"liberals" and "conservatives" took orderly turns at office, and the real power rested with the local political bosses. Not having participated in World War I, Spain was spared much of the ensuing anguish. Yet wartime trade with the combatants had built up Spanish industry and by making war profiteers had increased the tension between rich and poor.

In 1923, General Primo de Rivera, acting with the approval of Alfonso, proclaimed martial law, imposed censorship, and persecuted political opponents. His dictatorship lasted until 1930, but lost its popularity after 1926. He spent too much on public works, and was caught in the depression. Moreover, he did not fulfill the promises for a constituent assembly and political reform. He got the socialists to participate in his regime, and put through appropriate labor legislation in the hope of weakening the anarchists. But, since he depended on the army and the landowners, he could not institute agrarian reform. He also alienated the Catalonians, and his repressive measures deprived him of middle-class support.

After Primo de Rivera's resignation and death in 1930, King Alfonso soon restored the constitution. Municipal elections (April 1931) resulted in a victory for the republicans, representing the lower middle classes of the towns, small tradesmen, intellectuals, teachers, and journalists. The king left the country without abdicating. Elections to a constituent assembly in June 1931 brought in a republican-socialist majority, and in November the assembly forbade the king's return and confiscated his property. Spain was a republic. The monarchy, having stood only for clergy, army, and aristocracy, had failed.

The assembly went ahead to adopt a new constitution in December. This provided for a responsible ministry, a single-chamber parliament, and a president to be chosen by an electoral college consisting of parliament and an equal number of electors chosen by popular vote. It was clear that the army would rise against the republic whenever the opportunity was presented, and that the army would have the support of the Church and the large landowners. Moreover, although the republic temporarily had socialist support, it did not have the support of the anarchists. Danger threatened from both the Right and the Left.

Crisis of the Spanish Republic, 1933-1936

The first crisis arose over a new constitutional statute defining the position of the Church. The assembly rejected a moderate proposal which would have preserved the Church as a special corporation with its own schools, and which might have proved acceptable to most Catholics, even though the cardinal-primate of Spain had already denounced the republic. Instead, the assembly's law was far more extreme: it closed church schools and ended state grants to the Church after two years. This hurt education badly, and lost the republicans many supporters, especially among the lower clergy itself. Although the Republic secured much Catalan support by a grant of autonomy, it failed to act decisively on agrarian reform.

The anarchists expressed their dissatisfaction by major risings (1933), which the government put down by force. The jails were full, and unemployment was as high as ever. Repression of the anarchists lost the republic much Left support, but failed to gain it that of the Right, which came back strongly in the elections of November 1933 as the largest party in parliament. Now the government helplessly swung to the Right, and much of its previous legislation, especially laws affecting the Church and the working classes, remained a dead letter. The Church and monarchists put forward a young man named Gil Robles, a staunch fascist and admirer of the Austrian chancellor Dolfuss (see below).

On the Left, the socialists no longer collaborated with the government. Grown more revolutionary, they now engaged in strenuous competition with the anarchists for the loyalty of the Spanish workers. Strikes and disorders multiplied. In October 1934 the socialists called a general strike in protest against the inclusion of three of Robles' followers in the government. Catalonia declared itself an independent republic and was deprived of its autonomy. The coal miners of the Asturias in the north staged a revolt, joined in by both anarchists and socialists, which was put down with the loss of more than 3,000 lives. The government's use of Moors (Muslims from North Africa) against Spaniards was deeply resented; the Moors had been dispatched by the new minister of war, Francisco Franco.

Thus the Right in turn lost its public support; and now the Left, under the impact of the Asturias uprising, and influenced by the line of the Comintern, united in a "Popular Front" for the elections of February 1936. For the first time, anarchosyndicalists went to the polls and voted for a common list with republicans, socialists, and communists. The Left won a considerable victory, perhaps largely because it promised an amnesty for men involved in past outbreaks. Catalan autonomy, land reform, and anticlerical measures were of course the first order of business. The moderate Republican Azaña was elected president.

But moderation had gone out of fashion on the Left. The Popular Front was a coalition for election purposes only. Instead of entering Azaña's cabinet, Largo Caballero, leader of the left wing of the socialists, now "played at revolution." He acted as if he intended to seize power. *Pravda* hailed him as a new Lenin. Yet he had no forces of his own. The route to power for left-wing revolutionaries could open up only if the Right attempted a military coup, if the government then armed the workers to fight it, and if the workers then won.

On the Left also, and for the first time, the Spanish Communist party in 1936 emerged as a considerable element. Under Primo de Rivera's dictatorship, the communists had been so insignificant that he had not even taken the trouble to suppress their newspaper. But their participation in the Asturian uprising and the Popular Front

gained them political strength despite their numerical weakness (3,000 members). Oddly enough, they were more moderate in their immediate aims than the socialists, because they felt the need for a long preliminary period of Popular Front cooperation to increase their own power, and because this was Stalin's "respectable" period.

Simultaneously in 1936, on the Right, there emerged, also for the first time, the *Falange* (phalanx), a party founded in 1932 by the son of Primo de Rivera, a fascist on the Italian pattern ("harmony of all classes and professions in one destiny") who did not oppose agrarian reform or other socialist programs. The Falange had its symbol, a bunch of arrows and a yoke, and its slogan, "Arriba España" ("Upward, Spain"); its program called for national expansion in Africa, the annexation of Portugal, the building of an empire in South America; it established youth groups and a private army. Although the Falange polled relatively few votes in the election of 1936, most of Gil Robles' right-wing support went over to it after the Popular Front victory. Through the spring of 1936, the Falange worked with army, monarchist, clerical, and Carlist groups for a counterrevolution. Everybody knew a military coup against the government was in the offing. In July it came, under the military leadership of General Franco.

The Spanish Civil War, 1936-1939

The Spanish Civil War (1936–1939) was the first act in the conflict that was to ripen into World War II. Decisively aided by Germany and Italy, Franco's forces pushed on to eventual victory, with the capture of the republican strongholds of Madrid and Barcelona in 1939. During the war, the functions of the weak republican government were usurped by a series of workers' committees, and then a Popular Front regime under Largo Caballero came to office in September 1936. In government territory terror reigned, at first the work of anarchists, and, after their suppression, of the communists, who, with Russia behind them, ruthlessly worked against their rival leftist parties in the regime. The rebels made Franco chief of staff in November 1936. In their territory terror also took its toll, as men of all sorts connected with the Republic were killed.

Prisoners captured by the Spanish government forces along the Ebro River, in 1938.

After the Franco triumph, the prisons were filled and the executioner was kept busy.

With all its fascist trappings, the Franco regime, the only fascist regime to survive World War II, still depended after the war upon the same classes that had supported the Spanish monarchy—the landowners, the army, and the Church. It was presumably opposed by the poor in city and country alike. But the fear of a new civil war, which lay heavily on all classes, prevented open opposition.

Eastern Europe

The triumph of the Right in one form or another in eastern Europe is explained partly by the lack of a firm parliamentary tradition; partly by the failure to solve grievous economic problems, especially after the great worldwide depression of 1929; and partly by a popular fear of Bolshevism, sometimes quite out of proportion to any serious threat, but skillfully played upon by unscrupulous leaders. Perhaps as important as all the other factors put together was the initial impression created by the successes of Mussolini

and Hitler. The way to get ahead in the world, at least after 1935, seemed to be to put on a uniform, proclaim a doctrine of extreme nationalism, and launch a war of nerves against your neighbors by loudly voicing your claims, and by threatening to make them good by violence.

After the depression, the economic pressures exerted by Germany, whose industrial economy complemented the agrarian economy of these states, enabled her to dominate their foreign trade, especially in the Balkan area. To examine these factors, let us look at three case histories—Austria, Hungary, and Yugoslavia.

Austria

The Austria that was left at the end of World War I had an almost purely German population of about 8,000,000, about 2,000,000 of whom lived in the former imperial capital of Vienna. Long the great market for an enormous hinterland and the supplier of industrial finished goods to the agricultural provinces, Vienna was now cut off from its former territories by political boundaries and tariff walls. Between 1922 and

1925, Austrian finances were under direct League of Nations supervision; a League loan and reconstruction policies brought a measure of recovery. But what might have represented one road to economic salvation—union of Austria with Germany—though voted by the assembly of the new Austrian republic in March 1919, was forbidden on political grounds by the Allies in the Treaty of St. Germain (September 1919). These two problems, economic survival and union with Germany, were complicated by the continuation in even more violent form of the basic political struggle of imperial Austria: Social Democrats against Christian Socialists. The Social Democrats were a gradual-reformist, but Marxist, party with strong urban support, especially in Vienna itself. The Christian Socialists were a conservative clerical party with a mass following in the countryside and among the urban lower middle classes, and counted many priests among their leaders.

In the mid-Twenties, the two hostile parties, usually almost evenly balanced in the Parliament, organized private armies: the Christian Socialists, the Heimwehr (home guard), and the Social Democrats, the Schutzbund (defense league). The Social Democrats governed Vienna, introducing measures for relief and for workers' housing, paid for by taxes on the rich: a program the Christian Socialists opposed. After 1930, when a treaty was signed with Italy, Mussolini more or less overtly supported the Christian Socialists, who grew more and more fascistic in their outlook. The failure of Bruening's plan for a customs union with Germany and the related collapse of the Vienna Kredit-Anstalt bank increased tension in 1931, and in September, 1931, the Heimwehr tried its first fascist *coup,* which failed. Efforts in 1932 to organize a Danubian economic cooperation scheme—an alternative to Austrian union with Germany, and favored by France—were rendered futile by Italian and Ger-

Franco's troops enter Barcelona.

man opposition. After Hitler came to power in early 1933, many Christian Socialists became openly Nazi.

The Christian Socialist chancellor, Engelbert Dollfuss, however, strove to curb the Nazis. To this end he suspended parliamentary government in March 1933, and in effect ended parliamentary democracy. He forbade the wearing of uniforms by political groups, and tried to expel Nazi agitators. In retaliation, Hitler made it prohibitively expensive for German tourists to visit Austria, and thus destroyed one of the most lucrative sources of Austrian income. In the face of Nazi-inspired disorder, Dollfuss banned the Nazi party (June 1933). But, instead of burying the hatchet and uniting with the Social Democrats against Hitler, Dollfuss pursued them too. He banned all parties except his own "Fatherland Front," a union of all right-wing groups except the Nazis, and raided Social Democratic headquarters, precipitating a workers' riot. The government then bombarded with artillery the workers' new apartment houses, in which the Social Democratic leaders had taken refuge (February 1934), breaking the Social Democratic Party, but alienating the workmen of Vienna, and uniting them in opposition to the regime. Dollfuss had to depend more and more upon Italy to support him against the threat from Hitler. He established himself as a fascist dictator (April 30, 1934), but the Nazis assassinated him in July. Only Italian troop concentrations on the frontier prevented Hitler from taking Austria.

Dollfuss' successor, Schuschnigg, was committed to the same policies. But Mussolini now needed Hitler's support for Italian aggression in the Mediterranean. Schuschnigg made plans looking toward a Hapsburg restoration, tried to concentrate armed power in his own hands rather than those of the Heimwehr, and strove to come to an understanding with France and her allies to replace the one with Italy. But he failed in the face of German aggression. In February and March 1938 Hitler increased the pressure on Schuschnigg, who was subjected to the first of the famous series of grim interviews between Hitler and statesmen of smaller countries. The Führer demanded and obtained privileges for the Nazis in Austria. When Nazi disorders broke out, Schuschnigg desperately tried to win working-class support, but it was too late.

When Schuschnigg announced that he intended to hold a plebiscite on the question of Austrian independence, Hitler marched in, installed a Nazi chancellor, put Schuschnigg in jail, and began the extension of the Nazi system to Austria. In April 1938 he held a plebiscite on the question of Austrian union with Germany and obtained a 99.75 percent yes vote. Mussolini had to bow in 1938 to what he had prevented in 1934, and Austria, increasingly fascist since 1930, became a mere province of Nazi Germany.

Hungary

On October 31, 1918, eleven days before the armistice, Count Michael Karolyi became prime minister of Hungary, after the country had already severed its ties with Austria. One of the richest of the great magnates, Karolyi was also a democrat, and imbued with Wilsonian ideas. He proved his own sincerity as a social reformer by handing over the 50,000 acres of his own estate to be divided among the peasants, and by preparing a land-reform law. He made every effort to reach a compromise with the national minorities, but understandably enough they would no longer trust any Magyar. The French commander of the Allied armies did not assist Karolyi, and demanded that the Hungarians withdraw from Slovakia. In March 1919 Karolyi resigned, in protest over the loss of Transylvania.

Thwarted nationalism now combined with a growing radicalism, stimulated by the news of Bolshevik activities in Russia brought by returning Hungarian prisoners of war. A left-wing government took over, more and more dominated by Bela Kun, Lenin's agent, a Hungarian-born Jew. He put through revolutionary nationalization decrees, and installed a soviet political system by bloody-handed terrorist methods, especially in the countryside, where the peasants resented the delay in giving them the land. The Allies could not tolerate a Bolshevik regime in Hungary. The Romanians invaded and drove Kun out; during 1919 and part of 1920 they occupied the country, and stripped it of everything they could move. Meanwhile, under French protection, a counterrevolutionary government was formed, and returned to Budapest, where Admiral Horthy, a member of the gentry, became regent and chief of state (March 1, 1920). Hungary was now a kingdom without a king, Horthy an admiral without a fleet. Twice the Hapsburg king Charles tried to regain the throne, but was frustrated largely because Hungary's neighbors objected. The new counterrevolution gave free rein to a "White Terror" directed largely against the Jews but also against Magyar workers and peasants.

The Treaty of Trianon (June 1920) confirmed Hungary's losses: a small strip of land to Austria, Transylvania to Romania, Slovakia to Czechoslovakia, and Croatia and other Serb and Croat territories to Yugoslavia. Thereafter in Hungary the most important political issue for the ruling groups was "revisionism," the effort to revise the treaty and get these lands back. No tourist who visited Budapest could escape the huge statue of Hungary mourning the lost provinces, north, east, south, and west, or the great map laid out in flowerbeds in the public park showing in different-colored blossoms the far-flung territories relinquished but still claimed by the Magyars. The national motto was now "Nem, nem, soha" ("No, no, never").

The rank and file of Hungarians, however, who had never cared much about the nationalist questions that had agitated the upper classes, cared relatively little about revisionism. Hungary had no land reform; the great estates remained intact; and magnates and gentry retained their dominant position. Behind a thin screen of parliamentary government, an authoritarian dictatorship governed the country on behalf of the old ruling groups. It was helped by a swollen bureaucracy, and it became more and more fascist in character as the years went by.

For ten years (1921-1931), Count Bethlen as prime minister ran the country as if nothing had changed since 1914. The peasants were effectively disfranchised as they had always been; the Social Democrats were tolerated as a trade-union party; and the upper house of magnates was reestablished. The League of Nations helped economic recovery by a loan and a reconstruction plan (1923-1926), and in 1927 a treaty with Italy began an intimate relationship between Hungary and Mussolini. The depression and the financial crisis of 1931 drove Bethlen from office. His successor, the strongly nationalist and fascist-minded Gömbös, was pro-German as well as pro-Italian, and permitted the first Nazilike organizations to form. Of these the Arrow Cross was the strongest, but it remained on the fringes of power until almost the end of World War II,

largely because Hitler got what he wanted in Hungary without it.

After Gömbös died in 1936, his successors were all men of the same stripe. The Italians supplied arms to the Hungarians; Hitler favored their revisionism along with his own. After Austria had fallen to Hitler, he had Hungary in his pocket, and, when he broke up Czechoslovakia in March 1939, the Hungarians seized the extreme eastern portion, Ruthenia, and a small part of Slovakia. To pursue revisionism, the Hungarians had to follow Hitler, since he alone offered the opportunity to redraw the map as they felt it should be drawn. So, before war broke out, they had withdrawn from the League, and had enacted anti-Semitic laws in the Nazi pattern. But because Hitler needed Romania too, he would not give the Magyars all of Transylvania. Ironically enough, the price they paid for espousal of revisionism between the wars was the Soviet-dominated regime installed in Hungary after World War II.

Yugoslavia

In the new "Kingdom of the Serbs, Croats, and Slovenes," proclaimed in December 1918, there came together for the first time in one state the former south-Slav subjects of Austria and Hungary and those of the former independent Kingdom of Serbia. This was in most respects a satisfied state from the territorial point of view; revisionism therefore was not an issue. But, as the name of the new state shows, it faced the serious problem of creating a governmental system that would satisfy the aspirations of each of its nationality groups. Over this problem democracy broke down and a dictatorship was established. The dictatorship was not of the fascist type, although, as German power waxed, important politicians in the country became convinced that the future lay in Hitler's hands, and responded accordingly. The rank and file of the population, by and large, were peasants deeply devoted to freedom, although unskilled in Western forms of parliamentarism. They opposed fascism, and, when they got the chance, ousted the politicians who sought to align them with it.

Serbian political ambitions had helped to start the war. The Serbs were more numerous than Croats and Slovenes together (approximately six million to three and a quarter million Croats and a few over one million Slovenes in 1931). Many Serbs felt that the new kingdom, which their Serbian king ruled from his Serbian capital of Belgrade, should be that "greater Serbia" of which they had so long dreamed. Orthodox in religion, using the Cyrillic alphabet, and having experienced and overthrown Ottoman domination, many Serbs tended to look upon the Croats as effete subjects of the Hapsburgs who were lucky to get the chance to live in the same state with them. Roman Catholic in religion, using the Latin alphabet, and having opposed Germans and Magyars for centuries, many Croats felt that the Serbs were crude Easterners who ought to give them a full measure of autonomy within the new state. Thus the issue was posed; Serb-sponsored centralism against Croat-sponsored federalism. The Slovenes, more conciliatory and less numerous, sometimes acted as a balance wheel to keep the political machinery moving. But the Serbs forced the acceptance of their answer to the constitutional question. This brought about dictatorship, alienated large numbers of Croats, bred extremism among them, and contributed greatly to the benefit of the country's enemies and to its own sufferings during the second war.

The Croats, under their peasant leader Radich, boycotted the constituent assembly of 1920, and the Serbs put through a constitution providing for a strongly centralized state. In the 1920's, both sides generally refused to compromise, although occasionally temporary understandings were reached. When a Serb deputy shot Radich dead on the floor of parliament in June 1928, a crisis arose that terminated only when King Alexander proclaimed a dictatorship in January 1929. Alexander made every effort to settle the problem by wiping out all vestiges of old provincial loyalties. There was to be no more Serbia or Croatia, but new artificially created administrative units named after the chief rivers that ran through them. The whole country was renamed Yugoslavia, as a sign that there were to be no more Serbs and Croats. But it was still a Serbian government, and the Croats could not be made to forget it. Elections were rigged by the government, and all political parties were dissolved. Croat leaders spent much time in jails, which, like most Balkan jails, were highly uncomfortable. This dictatorship of King Alexander passed no racial laws, elevated no one political party to

exclusive power, and had no colored shirts, special songs, or other fascist paraphernalia. But it was unmistakably authoritarian and antidemocratic.

One result was the strengthening of Croat extremists, who had wanted an independent Croatia in the days of the Hapsburgs, and who now combined this program with terrorism, supported from abroad by the enemies of Yugoslavia —Italy and Hungary. The Croat extremists were called *Ustashi* (rebels), and their leader, Ante Pavelich, was subsidized by Mussolini. He was deeply involved in the assassination of Alexander at Marseilles in October 1934. Under the regency of Prince Paul (Alexander's cousin) the dictatorship continued. As German economic power in the Balkans grew, leading politicians grew enamored of Germany, and some efforts were made to bring Yugoslav policies into line with those of the Axis. But these policies met with such unconcealed popular opposition that they were never pursued very far. In the summer of 1939, on the very eve of war in Europe, an agreement was finally reached with the Croats that established an autonomous Croatia. But by then it was too late, since the Croats were not satisfied with the boundaries of their new province.

Though the Yugoslavs in 1941 bravely resisted German invasion, they did not have the military power to hold Hitler's armies back. When the conquering Germans and Italians split the country up, they turned Croatia over to the extremist Croat Pavelich, head of the Ustashi, who carried out horrifying massacres of Serbs and Jews. The innocent men, women, and children suffering death and torture at the hands of Pavelich's forces owed some of their anguish to the shortsightedness of Serbian politicians who had failed to solve the problem of Croat autonomy within a peaceful Yugoslavia, and who had thus stimulated the extremists.

Other Authoritarian Regimes

The case histories we have been considering are unique in detail, yet they furnish interesting parallels to developments elsewhere in eastern Europe. Thus in Poland, Pilsudski led a military coup against the democratic government in 1926, and exercised a military dictatorship that became

The assassination of King Alexander I of Yugoslavia at Marseilles, October 9, 1934.

ever more authoritarian, especially after the depression. This coup was made possible largely because of the government's failure to grant concessions to Lithuanians and other national minorities, and to deal with the economic problems left by the years of war and occupation. Tension was heightened when Germany denounced a trade treaty and precipitated a crisis in the Polish coal industry. The violent hatreds that divided the political parties made it even easier. Once he had won power, Pilsudski turned to the great landowners and big industrialists and built his government on their support and on that of his military clique.

In Romania, it was the deep entrenchment of corruption in political life that initially jeopardized the parliamentary system, as the party in power usually rigged elections without shame. In addition, there was widespread anti-Semitism, which was adopted as the chief program of the "Iron Guard," a Romanian Nazi party. Greenshirted and wearing bags of Romanian soil around their necks, the Guard began a program of assassinating moderate politicians early in the 1930's. Economic dislocation and peasant misery brought about by the worldwide agricultural depression strengthened the Guard and other fascist groups. To head off a Guardist coup, King

Carol of Romania installed his own fascist dictatorship in 1938. Although the Guardist leaders were "shot while trying to escape," Romania could not avoid German pressure. After Hitler had acceded to Russian seizure of Bessarabia and Northern Bukovina, and had given Hungary northern Transylvania (August 1940), Carol had to leave the country, and Hitler's man, Marshal Antonescu, took over with Iron Guard support.

In Bulgaria, always a strongly pro-Russian country, the genuine threat of communism was a serious problem. Moreover, Bulgaria, like Hungary, was revisionist because of her failure to gain the Macedonian territory given by the peace treaties to Yugoslavia and Greece. The issue was exacerbated by the presence in the country of thousands of Macedonian refugees, who tended to join revolutionary terrorist societies. Bulgaria, an egalitarian country with no minorities problem, no rich landowners, no aristocracy, and no great industries, none the less produced political hostilities even more violent than those in countries where economic inequality prevailed. Unparalleled ferocity has marked its political life. In the early twenties, a peasant politician, Stambolisky, gave the country a period (1920–1923) of reasonably popular government. But even he curbed the press as he fought both Macedonian terrorists and communists. His imposition of high income taxes alienated the bourgeoisie, and his conciliatory policies toward Yugoslavia infuriated the army. In 1923, right-wingers murdered him, and installed a strongly authoritarian regime. From then on, communist plots and bomb outrages and Macedonian terrorist strife racked the country. After 1930, the Italian marriage of King Boris led to a rapprochement with Mussolini. In 1934, a military coup brought a group of army officers to power; they dissolved the political parties and tried their hands at a dictatorship of their own. But this development was successfully countered in 1936 by King Boris himself, who, like Alexander of Yugoslavia and Carol of Romania, imposed a royal dictatorship, which lasted from then until his mysterious death during World War II.

In Greece between the wars, the main issues were whether the country should be a monarchy or a republic, and how to overcome the economic difficulties consequent on the transfer of 1,250,-000 Greeks from Turkey. On the constitutional question, the population wavered, voting for a monarchy in 1920, for a republic in 1924, and for a monarchy again in 1935, always by enormous majorities. Economic dislocation brought strength to communism among the refugees and in labor groups. The political exuberance for which Greece is celebrated made the regular conduct of parliamentary government impossible. The interwar period was punctuated by a whole series of coups by generals, some republican, some monarchist, all more or less authoritarian, but most of them ineffective and none especially bloodthirsty. The last of these was the most fascist, General John Metaxas, who became dictator in August 1936. Metaxas abolished political parties, instituted censorship and political persecution of his opponents, launched a program of public works, and imitated the Nazis in other ways. But when the Italian invasion came from Albania in October 1940, Metaxas ordered resistance, which was the beginning of Greece's heroic showing in World War II.

Fascism in Review

None of these regimes in eastern Europe was fascist in the full sense of the term. In Italy and Germany the regimes rested, at least initially, upon the popular support of a substantial proportion of the people, even though that support was kept alive by the technique of artificial stimulation. In eastern Europe, on the other hand, the dictatorships rested on the police, the bureaucracy, and the army, and not on the support of the peasant masses. To an eastern European politician of almost any complexion, an election was an occasion for bribery, intimidation, and making promises that he had no intention of trying to fulfill. The hope placed by some Western liberals in peasant parties proved in the end illusory.

Thus the growth of antidemocratic governments of the Right in Europe during the period between the wars strikingly reveals the difficulties in the way of moderate parliamentary regimes in countries without parliamentary traditions. This does not mean that the Western liberal tradition cannot be exported. But a liberal constitution on paper and a liberal franchise are in themselves no guarantee that a regime on Western models can become stabilized. The postwar economic agony had scarcely disappeared before the depression of the late Twenties and early Thirties struck. Under these circumstances, men turned to extremists of the Left and Right. But the fear of communism, combined with the seductive nationalist propaganda of the Right, brought about fascist victories in Italy and Germany. Mussolini's and Hitler's successes helped to tip the scale: the triumph of the Right elsewere was assured, and a new world war was inevitable.

Reading Suggestions on the Rise of Fascism

THE ROOTS OF FASCISM

A. Cobban, *Dictatorship: Its History and Theory* (Scribner's, 1939). Highly suggestive survey, reaching well back into history.

P. Viereck, *Metapolitics: From the Romantics to Hitler* (Knopf, 1941). A survey of the background in German political thought.

C. J. Hayes, *A Generation of Materialism, 1871-1900* (Harper, 1941). Contains a concise and corrosive section on the seedtime of fascism.

Note: The titles listed above present differing views on the origins of fascism, a subject still much debated by historians. Further titles bearing on the subject may be found in the reading suggestions for the chapter "The Intellectual Revolution."

ITALY

G. Magaro, *Mussolini in the Making* (Houghton, 1938). An unequaled study of Mussolini's early career.

H. Finer, *Mussolini's Italy* (Holt, 1935), and H. A. Steiner, *Government in Fascist Italy* (McGraw-Hill, 1938). Two very solid studies by expert political scientists.

G. A. Borgese, *Goliath: The March of Fascism* (Viking, 1938), and G. Salvemini, *Under the Axe of Fascism* (Viking, 1936). Lively works by important antifascist Italians.

G. Salvemini, *Prelude to World War II* (Doubleday, 1954). A survey of Mussolini's foreign policy, by one of his most implacable enemies.

GERMANY

A. Hitler, *Mein Kampf* (Reynal and Hitchcock, 1939). A complete English translation of the Nazi bible, the basic work to be read for an understanding of the movement.

A. Hitler, *My New Order,* ed. R. de Sales (Reynal and Hitchcock, 1941). Speeches after the Führer's coming to power.

A. L. C. Bullock, *Hitler: A Study in Tyranny* (Oxham's, 1952; *Bantam abridgment). The best biography.

S. W. Halperin, *Germany Tried Democracy* (Crowell, 1946). A reliable history of the Weimar Republic, 1918-1933.

R. G. L. Waite, *Vanguard of Nazism* (Harvard Univ. Press, 1952). A good study of the "Free Corps" movement.

J. W. Wheeler-Bennett, *Wooden Titan* (Morrow, 1936) and *Nemesis of Power* (St. Martin's Press, 1954). Two first-rate studies, the first dealing with Hindenburg, the second with the role of the German army in politics from 1918 to 1945.

F. L. Neumann, *Behemoth: The Structure and Practice of National Socialism* (Oxford Univ. Press, 1944). The best work on the subject.

F. von Papen, *Memoirs* (Dutton, 1953). An apologetic autobiography by the scheming right-wing politician.

Albert Speer, *Inside the Third Reich: Memoirs,* trans. Richard and Clara Winston (Macmillan, 1970). Memoirs of Hitler's own city planner and architect: an invaluable picture of life among the Nazis.

E. Wiskemann, *The Rome-Berlin Axis* (Oxford Univ. Press, 1949). A study of the formation and history of the Hitler-Mussolini partnership.

R. Fischer, *Stalin and German Communism* (Harvard Univ. Press, 1948). A study of the role played by the communist movement in the history of Germany between the wars.

Note: Some of the titles listed under the reading suggestions for the chapter that follows deal with international relations during the interwar period and will illuminate Nazi foreign policy.

OTHER COUNTRIES
G. Brenan, *The Spanish Labyrinth* (Macmillan, 1943). A useful study of the Spanish Civil War against its historical and economic background.

C. Bowers, *My Mission to Spain* (Simon & Schuster, 1954); C. J. Hayes, *Wartime Mission to Spain, 1942–1945* (Macmillan, 1945); and Lord Templewood (Sir Samuel Hoare), *Complacent Dictator* (Knopf, 1947). Three differing views of Franco and the Spanish problem, by three ambassadors, the first two American, the last British.

Hugh Thomas, *The Spanish Civil War* (Harper, 1961; rev. ed., *Penguin). The best single work on the subject.

G. E. R. Gedye, *Betrayal in Central Europe* (Harper, 1939). A careful journalist's account of Austria and Czechoslovakia.

H. Seton-Watson, *Eastern Europe between the Wars, 1918–1941* (Cambridge Univ. Press, 1946). A useful account dealing with all the eastern European countries except Greece and Albania.

R. L. Buell, *Poland: Key to Europe* (Knopf, 1939). A helpful survey.

R. West, *Black Lamb and Grey Falcon* (Viking, 1941). A highly subjective account of Yugoslavia, loaded with political bias, but fascinating and informative reading.

HISTORICAL FICTION
I. Silone, *Bread and Wine* (*Penguin, *New American Library) and *Fontamara* (Smith and Haas, 1934). Two good novels on rural Italy under fascism; by a distinguished antifascist writer.

C. Levi, *Christ Stopped at Eboli* (Farrar, Straus, 1947; *Universal Library). An antifascist Italian doctor and painter writes movingly of his exile in a remote and poverty-striken southern Italian village.

H. Fallada, *Little Man What Now?* (Simon & Schuster, 1933; *Ungar), and E. Remarque, *Three Comrades* (Little, Brown, 1937; *Popular Library). Two touching novels of depression-ridden Germany.

E. von Salomon, *"Der Fragebogen"* (*The Questionnaire*) (Doubleday, 1955). One of the plotters against Rathenau, a strong sympathizer with authoritarian movements, tells his life story satirically, against the background of American military government in post-1945 Germany.

E. Hemingway, *For Whom the Bell Tolls* (Scribner's, 1940). A characteristic Hemingway novel, set in the Spain of the Civil War.

28

The Democracies
and the
Non-Western World

Domestic and Imperial
Problems, 1919-1939

I Introduction: A World Unsafe
for Democracy

The central fact—and irony—of politics between the two world wars is that the war "to make the world safe for democracy" seemed to make it a difficult and dangerous place for democracy. Idealists like President Wilson had expected that the collapse of the old Romanov, Hapsburg, and Hohenzollern empires would automatically ensure an increase in the number of democratic states. But instead, much of Europe came under regimes that were hostile to liberal democracy. Even Italy, which had appeared to be evolving toward a democratic constitutional monarchy, turned fascist. In the 1920's and 1930's the core of democracy remained in the great North Atlantic powers—Britain, France, and the United States—and in the smaller states of Scandinavia, the Low Countries, and Switzerland.

Above: The young Mao Tse-Tung: a picture taken during the days of his early revolutionary actvities in China. Right: A Sunday afternoon in St. Louis, Missouri, in the 1920's.

The upsurge of communism and fascism created grave problems in international relations for the three great democracies. At times in the 1920's it looked as if they might successfully overcome these problems and bring the world back to peaceful habits. But in the 1930's the great worldwide depression, the advent of Hitler, and the aggressions of fascist states in the West and of an expansionist Japan in the Far East rapidly darkened the international scene. With the outbreak of another general war in 1939, it was clear that the two decades since 1919 had been at best a twenty years' truce, a truce broken with increasing frequency by international troublemakers.

Certainly the totalitarian aggressors bore the major responsibility for the unleashing of a second world war. Yet a far from minor factor in the deterioration of the twenty years' truce was the failure of the peaceful democracies to present a unified front against those who threatened world peace. In the 1920's Britain, France, and the United States became preoccupied with their own domestic problems. In the early 1930's their preoccupation increased as a result of the urgent crisis of the depression. But this was the very time when international problems demanded equally urgent attention. International trade was steadily shrinking in the face of the great depression and of mounting tariff barriers; the prospects for peace were steadily fading before the saber-rattling and actual saber-wielding of the enemies of democracy. Faced with two sets of problems, the democracies turned first to the domestic ones, only to discover that the international situation was rapidly moving toward war.

Nor was this all. During the twenty years' truce, the democracies faced a third set of problems, not as yet so urgent as the other two, but of very great potential importance. This third set involved imperial issues—the relationship between the great democracies and the non-Western peoples, many of whom were still under colonial rule or some other form of control by democratic mother countries. Particularly in Asia and the Middle East, the non-Western peoples were beginning to assert their nationalism and to demand the loosening of old imperial ties. This formidable political movement did not reach full intensity until the years following World War II when a long procession of former colonies, protectorates, and mandates began to join the ranks of independent states. But the nationalist movements that were to bring these newcomers into the family of nations after 1945 grew steadily in the 1920's and 1930's.

The three sets of problems—domestic, foreign, and imperial—faced by the democracies during the twenty years' truce were interconnected and interrelated in countless ways. We shall underline some of these interrelations, as we have shown the links between the internal and external policies of the communist and fascist states. But, in order to point up the main issues, we shall also separate national, international, and colonial problems in a way that must oversimplify the complexities of real life. The present chapter emphasizes first the chief domestic problems of the democracies in the interwar years and then considers the growing conflict between their colonialism and the nationalism of the non-Western world. The following chapter examines their foreign policies, as distinguished from their imperial policies. We begin here with an examination of the crisis confronting Britain on the home front after November 1918.

II   Great Britain

The Postwar Economic Crisis

Save for trifling losses from German Zeppelin raids and coastal bombardments, the British Isles suffered no direct material damage in World War I. But the British armed forces lost about seven hundred and fifty thousand men killed in action, and about a million and a half wounded. The casualties of the empire and the common-wealth as a whole came to nearly a million killed and over two million wounded. The economic losses of the mother country had been grave indeed—the almost incalculable difference between the actual cost of destructive war and what might otherwise have been productive effort.

The national debt after the war was ten times that of 1914. Many British investments abroad, returns on which had been a major factor in Victorian prosperity, had had to be liquidated to get purchasing power abroad for food and war materials. Forty percent of the great British merchant fleet, the income from which had helped to balance Britain's international accounts and pay for her imports, had been destroyed by enemy action. The whole fabric of international trade on which Britain depended was torn in a thousand places in 1918 and could not be rapidly restored in the unsettled conditions that prevailed in the postwar world. And, finally, to supplement the war production of Britain and France, the industrial plants of the United States, of Canada, and even of India had been called on, and had received a stimulus that made them in peacetime more effective competitors of the British. In the 1920's, the industrial plant of the Germans, nourished in part by loans from America, once more took up the rivalry that had so alarmed the British before the war.

In short, victorious Britain faced in an aggravated form the basic economic difficulty analyzed in an earlier chapter. The country that had been in Victorian days the "workshop of the world" had now lost its head start and could no longer give full employment to its millions of workers. Those workers were in no mood to accept a lower standard of living for they had made great gains in social security before the war, and they had fought the war in the hope of still better things to come. They had been promised that the defeated enemy would through reparations pay the costs of the war and thereby give Britain a new start.

This hope was very early disappointed. No substantial reparations came through; the return to peace caused a sudden boom in production to meet the postwar demand for goods, accompanied by a sharp rise in prices, and quickly followed by the collapse of the boom, leaving Britain in a severe postwar depression. By the summer of 1921 there were over two million people out of work, more than one-fifth of the labor force. In that same year the British government, faced with the rising cost of living, increased the very meager unemployment payments. These payments, soon given the derogatory name of the dole, were strictly speaking not old-fashioned poor relief, but payments on unemployment insurance policies that had been part of Lloyd George's social legislation of prewar days. However, large-scale unemployment continued—it did not drop below one million until World War II—and some young workers never acquired employment status. Unemployment insurance could not be maintained on a sound actuarial basis, and the payments became in fact a form of poor relief.

While the Great Britain of the 1920's experienced no equivalent of the "Coolidge prosperity" that the United States was to enjoy, we must not exaggerate: The British economic decline was not catastrophic. London, Manchester, and Liverpool did not become ghost cities, though some of the gravely depressed areas, like the coalmining regions of South Wales, did begin to show real signs of permanent decay. What happened was rather a relative decline, the slowing down of an economy geared to dynamic growth, with a working population conditioned psychologically to a gradually rising standard of living and a middle class similarly conditioned to traditional comforts. Moreover, this was the twentieth century, the century of the tabloid newspaper (first developed in Britain), the movie, and the radio. The British were well aware, for instance, that Americans had automobiles, radios, and a lot else that they, too, craved.

Britain was suffering from ills characteristic of economic old age, well illustrated in the coal industry. There was still a lot of coal in Britain; but much of it was costly to mine, since the most easily and cheaply worked seams were being exhausted. The industry was badly organized, with many small and inefficient mines running at a loss, and with machinery and methods that were antiquated in comparison with American and the best continental standards. Productivity per man-hour over the whole industry was low. Worst of all, perhaps, the 1920's saw the rapid rise all over the industrialized world of major competitors of coal—oil, and electricity based on water power—and the consequent decline of British coal exports. Since the British Isles had no petroleum, and no very great potential in hydroelectric power, coal, the historic basis of British industrial power, simply had to be mined. The workers were unionized and were in no mood to accept cuts in wages; the owners did not want to run their business at a loss. A strike in March 1921, after the government had rejected Labour party proposals for making permanent the wartime nationalization of the industry, focused national attention on this critical problem. The strike was settled in July, but only by the government's consenting to pay subsidies to cover increased wages.

The Conservative
and Labour Programs

Against the background of economic depression, British domestic politics during the twenty years' truce displayed a fairly clear class basis. The Conservatives, still often called Tories, tended to get the support of aristocrats and of middle-class people who wanted to attack new problems with traditional methods and with a minimum of government intervention. The Labour party tended to get the support of trade unionists and of intellectuals from all classes who demanded that the government intervene more vigorously in the economic field. While not every worker or reformer necessarily voted Labour nor every stand-patter Tory, economic issues did sharpen the differences between the two major British parties.

The first casualty in the struggle between Labour and the Conservatives was the old Liberal party, which was ground to a mere husk between the two contending groups. The Conservatives, who had won the lion's share of seats in the "khaki election" of 1918, held immediately after the armistice, decided in 1922 to withdraw their support from the coalition government headed by the immensely popular Liberal Lloyd George. In the ensuing elections the Conservatives won, and the Liberals lost heavily, split as they were between the followers of Lloyd George and those of the more cautious and less theatrical Asquith. Labour won 142 seats—more than the Liberals did—and became for the first time His Majesty's Opposition.

Both Conservatives and Labour realized the underlying difficulties of Britain's position. Both were fully aware that twentieth-century Britain had to sell enough goods and services abroad— enough manufactured goods and shipping, insurance, banking, and tourist services—so that the income from them would buy food for her people and much of the raw materials for her factories. But the parties were not agreed on how to achieve this necessary task. Broadly speaking, the Conservatives wanted to retain private industry, with government and other technical experts helping to make it efficient. But they were thwarted by high tariffs in the United States and elsewhere, by the drive to economic self-suf-ficiency all over the world, and by the difficulties of trade with communist Russia.

The state of world trade drove the Conservatives more and more to the solution the maverick Liberal Joseph Chamberlain had advocated at the turn of the century—protective tariffs against competing foreign goods, and the knitting of the empire and commonwealth, with their vast variety of resources, into a largely self-sufficient trade area by "imperial preference" agreements. Such agreements would give raw materials from the colonies and dominions preferred treatment in the British market in return for preferred treatment of British manufactures in the colonial and dominion markets. In theory, at least, the scheme could have worked, for the commonwealth and empire of the nineteen-twenties—one-quarter of the world's land and people—had the requisite natural resources and offered a potential market capable of supporting the British Isles in the style to which they were accustomed. In practice the great snag was the evident unwillingness of the constituent parts of the empire and commonwealth to accept for themselves the role of producers of raw materials in exchange for British manufactured goods and British services. The self-governing dominions, loyal though they had been during the war, were in no mood to assume a role essentially like that of colonies in the old mercantilistic days. They were looking toward independent nationhood, and they wanted what seems to go with nationhood in our world—their own industries. This was also true of what was potentially the richest unit in the empire, India.

The Labour solution was nationalization—that is, government purchase and operation of key industries with just compensation to their private owners, rather than seizure without compensation as in Soviet Russia. The key industries were transportation, utilities, coal, steel, perhaps even textiles, cutlery, pottery, machine tools— all the industries that seem to thrive best on large-scale organization. A good many Labourites wanted nationalization simply because, as socialists, they believed that profits, rent, and interest paid to private owners were forms of "capitalist" exploitation of the workers, which would cease under nationalization. But many of their leaders knew that even nationalized industries would still face the fundamental problem of selling enough goods abroad to keep the economy going. They argued, therefore, that nationalization would enable British industries to produce more cheaply and efficiently. It would do away with wasteful competition and with the inefficient firms so conspicuous in the coal industry, for instance. It would, they romantically believed, force into productive work both unnecessary managerial and selling staffs, and stockholders and other investors who lived without working.

Moreover, Labour supporters believed that, once nationalization had been achieved, the British workmen would take a new attitude toward their work. Knowing that they were now the *real* owners of their own industries, they would put their hearts into their work, abstain from featherbedding, absenteeism, and similar practices, and raise production to a point where the goods of Britain could undersell those of her capitalist rivals in world markets. This belief was reinforced by the somewhat paradoxical faith in free trade that the Labour party had inherited from the Liberals, and by its high hopes for improved international relations. Consequently, Labour was hostile to the Conservative policies of protective tariffs and imperial preference.

Politics between the Wars

During the twenty years' truce, neither the Conservatives nor the Labourites were able to carry out their full platforms. The Conservatives, by no means unanimous on the degree of economic self-sufficiency they wanted for the empire, were decisively held up by the refusal of the commonwealth countries to go much further than to accept certain limited imperial preferences. Labour itself came to power for two brief spans—with Ramsay MacDonald, an intellectual and not a worker, as prime minister—for ten months in 1924 and again from 1929 to 1931. In both instances, while Labour won more seats in the Commons than did any other party, it did not have an absolute majority. The Labour governments, obliged to rely on the Liberals for parliamentary support, were too shaky to introduce measures as controversial as the nationalization of any industry.

Despite the wider cleavage between the two parties, British politics still retained many of the amenities of Victorian parliamentary life. The House of Commons, even though it now included workingmen and others who by no means spoke with an upperclass "Oxford accent," was still one of the best clubs in the world. For a few weeks in 1926 some 2,500,000 trade-union members attempted a general strike in support of the coalminers, who were striking in protest against a cut in their wages. The general strike failed, but during its brief course fundamental British attitudes were revealed. Thousands of men from the middle and upper classes volunteered to keep essential services operating, and in Plymouth a soccer team of strikers played a team of police. Britain, despite mounting tensions, remained a land of general law-abidingness, where the class struggle that the Marxists talked so much about seemed to have come thoroughly under the control of the parliamentary decencies.

In 1928, almost unnoticed, the last step was taken in the political democratization of Britain that had begun in 1832. In 1918, in preparation for the "khaki election," the government had put through a reform bill which eliminated all the old exceptions to universal male suffrage and gave the vote to all men over twenty-one. Culminating a long and spectacular campaign in which suffragettes had demonstrated, marched, orated, and even chained themselves to lampposts, destroyed property, and gone to jail in behalf of women's rights, the bill also gave the vote to women. But, with almost a caricature of British caution, it set the voting age for women at thirty years, thus insuring that there would always be more male than female voters. The distinction was too irrational to stand up, especially after experience had demonstrated—as it also did in the United States—that women divide politically about the way men do. In 1928, a measure known as the "bill for flapper suffrage" gave women the vote at twenty-one.

Although the dole, depressed industries, and other signs of economic ill health persisted, Britain did experience a measure of recovery in the late 1920's. But then the great depression, the signal for which was given by the New York stock-market crash in October 1929, began its spread around the world. Britain, already weakened, was one of the first to be engulfed; in eighteen months the number of unemployed jumped from a little over one million to two and half million. Faced by a serious government deficit and unwilling to try to meet it by cutting the dole and other social services, the second

Suffragettes arrested outside Buckingham Palace in 1914.

Labour government of Ramsay MacDonald resigned in August 1931.

It gave way to a coalition of Conservatives, Liberals, and right-wing Labourites headed by the same MacDonald. Many Labourites, both in the leadership and in the rank and file, were dismayed by what seemed to them MacDonald's traitorous surrender to the forces of capitalism, and the deep split within the party crippled its effectiveness throughout the 1930's. The "national government," as the coalition cabinet was called, put through reductions in the dole and the social services. Late in 1931, it took the decisive step, a hard one in view of Britain's traditional financial leadership and devotion to the gold standard, of going off the gold standard and letting the pound fall in value. In 1932, it made the first move away from free trade by enacting protective tariffs, and in the same year Britain

ceased payment on her war debts to the United States, except for a few token payments. These measures did little to help the unemployed or to get at the roots of British economic troubles. Nevertheless, because of Labour's disarray, two general elections, in October 1931 and in 1935, returned a majority supporting the national government.

The coalition government was in fact dominated by Conservatives, and after the 1935 election the Conservative leader, Stanley Baldwin, took over the post of prime minister. Gradually the British economy pulled out of the worst of the depression, although—some economic theorists might say *because*—Baldwin did nothing beyond keeping the budget in balance. By 1936, however, Mussolini's and Hitler's aggressions were beginning to demand British attention. The economic question and the social question, by no means solved, faded before the threat of another war.

For a few months in 1936 the great issue confronting Baldwin's cabinet appeared to be not social or diplomatic but constitutional, as the cabinet forced the abdication of King Edward VIII in the year of his accession to the throne. Edward had had a long and successful career as prince of Wales, appearing indefatigably and effectively in public all over the world. He fell in love with an American divorcee, Mrs. Wallis Simpson, and wanted to marry her. His own family, the cabinet, and most of the British people opposed him, and he quietly abdicated (with the title of duke of Windsor), allowing his brother to become King George VI. Some of the opposition to Edward's marriage stemmed from dislike for America, but much more of it came from a strong feeling against having a divorcee on the throne and a vaguer feeling that Mrs. Simpson's background as a member of what was then called "café society" made her unfit for ceremonial functions. The episode—for it deserves no stronger name—attracted worldwide attention at the time but left little mark on British history.

The Irish Question

The years between the wars were of great importance for Ireland. Although the outbreak of war in 1914 put off the threatened revolt against Home Rule in Protestant Ulster, the Irish were hardly reliable partners in the war. In 1916, the faction furthest removed from the Ulster rebels, the Irish nationalists, got some German help in guns and ammunition and staged an armed rising in Dublin. The British put down this "Easter rebellion," but not before they had created a fresh and effective set of Irish political martyrs. The British government did not dare extend conscription to Ireland until April 1918, and the attempt made then led the Irish nationalists to boycott the British Parliament and to cease attending its sessions.

By 1919, Home Rule as decreed in 1914 was not enough for the nationalists of Ireland. The Home Rulers of prewar days had yielded to more extreme rebels, the Sinn Fein (meaning, in Gaelic, "ourselves alone"), who wanted complete independence. The years 1919–1921 were filled with violence, ambushes, arson, and guerrilla warfare, as the Irish, who now had their own illegal parliament, the Dail Eireann, moved into full revolution. The British, tired from four years of world war, were not in a state of mind to use force effectively; the Irish, on the other hand, were admirably organized and full of fight.

Yet the immediate upshot of the violent phase of the revolution was a compromise, for the Sinn Fein split in two. A moderate wing, led by Arthur Griffith and Michael Collins, was willing to accept a compromise in which Protestant Ulster would remain under direct British rule and the Catholic counties would be given dominion status. A radical wing, led by Eamon De Valera —exceedingly Irish in spite of his Spanish surname—insisted that the whole island achieve complete independence as a unified republic. The moderates negotiated with the British, and in 1921 obtained for the twenty-six counties of southern Ireland dominion status under the name of the Irish Free State. The Free State had its own parliament, the Dail, and was completely self-governing with its own army and its own diplomatic services; it merely accepted the British crown as symbolic head. The six Protestant counties of Ulster maintained their old relationship with Britain, including the right to send members to the Parliament at Westminster, but they also acquired their own parliament at Belfast and considerable local autonomy. Henceforth Britain was officially styled the United Kingdom of Great Britain and Northern Ireland.

This settlement was unacceptable to De Valera and the more extreme revolutionaries, and the Irish revolution now became a civil war between partisans of the Free State and partisans of a republic, with the old round of burning, ambush, and murder. But the Irish, too, were beginning to tire of violence. When the moderate leader Michael Collins, a man much closer to earth than De Valera, was assassinated by a republican, public opinion turned away from the extremists. Meantime the Free State was gradually settling down. De Valera, after refusing to sit in the Dail because he would have had to take an oath of loyalty to the king, changed his mind and decided to bring his fellow republicans into the national parliament in 1927.

From then on, almost in the manner of illogical and compromise-loving England, the Irish Free State gradually and peacefully got what the extremists had been killing and burning for. De Valera's party won a plurality in the Dail in 1932, and a majority in 1933; thereupon it proceeded to abolish the oath of loyalty to the Crown and to cut most of the slender threads that still tied the Free State to England. In 1939, Catholic Ireland was so free from British domination that she could declare and maintain her neutrality throughout World War II. In 1949, the final step was taken when Britain recognized her as the fully independent Republic of Eire (Gaelic for "Ireland").

The Commonwealth

No such secession took place elsewhere among the British possessions in the years between the two world wars. On the contrary, definite constitutional recognition of the essential independence of the dominions seemed to make them more loyal, though at the cost of any central British authority over their economic policies, and, at least in law, over their foreign policies. The capstone of a long process that had begun with the Durham Report nearly a century before was the Statute of Westminster of 1931. This spelled out the new relations between the dominions and the mother country that had been negotiated in an imperial conference five years earlier. The preparatory report of 1926 anticipated the gist of the Statute of Westminster by declaring that Britain and the dominions

are autonomous communities within the British Empire, equal in status, in no way subordinate one to another in any aspect of their domestic or external affairs, though united by a common allegiance to the crown and freely associated as members of the British Commonwealth of Nations.

That phrase "freely associated" means also "able freely to choose to be dis-associated." In other words, the right of a state to secede (which Americans fought a great civil war to decide is not a part of the United States Constitution) *is* a part of the constitution of the commonwealth. And the twenty-six counties of Southern Ireland in effect took advantage of this right to set up their republic quite outside the commonwealth. South Africa dis-associated itself in 1961 and became an independent republic, and in 1965 the Rhodesian government made a unilateral declaration of independence.

The new status acquired by the dominions in 1931 was symbolized by a change in terminology. Henceforward they were no longer to be considered parts of the British Empire but free members of the British Commonwealth of Nations (a title abbreviated to plain Commonwealth after World War II in deference to the many new non-Western members, who did not have the emotional ties binding some of the dominions to the Crown). In this new relationship, Britain would have to negotiate with Canada or Australia about tariffs, trade conditions, immigration, and the like, just as if they were foreign countries. Although Britain was unable to build a self-sufficient economic unity out of her dominions, still in 1939, as in 1914, the dominions all came into the war on Britain's side. They made this decision even though they had the legal right to follow the example of Ireland and remain neutral.

III France

The Impact of the War

In France, both World War I and the postwar difficulties caused more serious dislocation than they did in Britain. In the war itself, France lost proportionately more in human lives and in material damage than did any other major belligerent. Two million Frenchmen in the prime of life were either killed or so seriously mutilated as to be incapable of normal living. In a land of only 39,000,000, and with an already low birth rate, it is likely that this human loss impaired the French potentiality for achievement in all phases of civilization. Many of the men who would have been statesmen, industrialists, scientists, and artists in the 1930's were killed off in 1914–1918. Three hundred thousand houses and twenty thousand factories or shops were destroyed. In a land of conservative economic organization, where work was done slowly and for the most part without large-scale automatic machinery, this material setback would be long felt. Psychologically, the feeling of victory by no means compensated for the traumatic losses of the four years of struggle.

France set as her goal the laming of her recent enemy, Germany, in every possible way. She tried to extract reparations to the last possible sum, undeterred by the arguments of economic theorists that Germany could not pay. But she insisted even more on keeping Germany down, isolated in international relations, and without the physical means of fighting. In a pinch, most Frenchmen would probably have been willing to forego reparations in order to deprive Germany of the economic plant necessary for modern war. They would have preferred this to collecting reparations from a rich and productive Germany.

In the postwar years, French statesmen attempted to follow both policies simultaneously and of course failed. The culmination came in January 1923, under the premiership of the conservative Raymond Poincaré, when French and Belgian troops occupied the great German industrial region of the Ruhr in an effort to make Germany pay full reparations. The Germans replied by passive resistance, as we have already seen. The occupation of the Ruhr brought France no gains, only the censure of international opinion. The elections of 1924 resulted in a victory for the Cartel des Gauches, a coalition of mildly left-wing parties headed by the Radical-Socialists. The Poincaré ministry and the new government withdrew the last French troops from the Ruhr in 1925.

Meanwhile, the French were undergoing inflation. The inflation resulted in part from the cost of rebuilding the devastated areas—a cost that drained government finances and that was only partly covered by German payments. It resulted also from the high cost of maintaining armed forces (for the French dared not disarm), from the general disorder of international trade, and from the staggering debts piled up during the war by the French government, which, like the imperial German government, had preferred loans to taxes. By the mid-1920's, the franc had slipped from its prewar value of 20 cents to a dangerous low of about 2 cents. In the crisis, Poincaré was recalled to power to "save the franc." In 1926, he initiated new taxes and stern measures of economy which, together with the gradual restoration of normal international trade

after the French withdrawal from the Ruhr, stemmed the decline of the franc. In 1928, it was officially revalued at 3.92 cents.

The French inflation, though mild compared with the German, nevertheless caused economic and social dislocation. Frenchmen who had lent their government francs worth 20 cents now found themselves deprived of four-fifths of their loans. This very considerable repudiation fell with particular severity on the middle class, especially the lower middle class, the petite bourgeoisie. The greatest sufferers were those living on their savings or on relatively fixed incomes—on pensions, for example, or on the return from bonds, or even on the contents of the wool sock in which the suspicious French peasant traditionally hoarded his cash. Bourgeois people naturally fear pauperization, fear being pushed down into the ranks of the proletariat, and the French were no exceptions. Inflation thus weakened a social class that had long been a mainstay of republicanism in France and added to the social tensions that form the central theme of French domestic history in the period between the two world wars.

Social and Political Tensions

During World War I, the French had temporarily put aside the great political and social conflict they had inherited from 1789. After the war, the "sacred union" of political parties that had carried France through the struggle soon dissolved, and the traditional conflict was resumed. This is sometimes termed the conflict between the "two Frances"—the republican France of the Left, and the royalist or authoritarian France of the Right. The conflict was not quite a simple Marxian class struggle between rich and poor, capitalist and proletarian, though it was certainly in part such a struggle. On the Right were the wealthier classes, many of them openly hostile to the very existence of the parliamentary state. They were reinforced by conservative peasants and by small businessmen and investors, many of them petit bourgeois, who were not hostile to the Third Republic as such but who were determined to resist any attempt to extend the social services of the "welfare state." As a result of this right-wing resistance, France lagged behind Britain, Germany, Sweden, and other European states in providing measures of social security.

On the Left were the champions of the welfare state, the Socialists and the Communists, backed by the more radical workers, by many white-collar people, especially in the government service, and by some intellectuals. The effectiveness of the Left was hampered by the postwar split between the Communists, who followed the Moscow line, and the Socialists, who did not, and by a comparable schism within the major trade-union organization, the C.G.T. (Confédération Générale du Travail—General Confederation of Labor). Still nominally part of the Left, but actually in the political middle and not anxious to go far toward the welfare state, was the misleadingly named Radical-Socialist Party, long the political bulwark of the Third Republic. The Radicals were strong among the peasants of southern France, and among white-collar workers and smaller professional men.

Religious difficulties further embittered French politics. The widely held but unproven assumption that women would vote as the priests told them to delayed women's suffrage until after World War II. The traditional anticlericals in France were the Leftists, including the Radicals. After World War I they rashly attempted to introduce anticlerical measures into strongly Catholic Alsace, where the separation of church and state carried through in France after the Dreyfus crisis had not been applied because Alsace was at the time part of the German Empire. In the long run, the government was obliged to make compromises on the Alsatian question and on other clerical issues. After bitter public debate, it finally decided in the mid-1920's to resume diplomatic relations with the Vatican—relations which had been broken off at the time of the separation.

In the late 1920's, the years of increased prosperity that coincided with the revaluation of the franc, the Third Republic seemed to be getting the better of its internal difficulties. Indeed, the world economic crisis that began in 1929 was late in striking France, and for a while in 1930 it looked as though the French economy, less devoted to large-scale industry than that of the United States, Britain, or Germany, might weather the crisis much more easily. But France, too, depended on international trade, particularly on the export of perfumes, wines and brandies, Paris gowns, and other luxuries. By 1932,

the depression had struck, and the government was in serious economic and political difficulties.

The Stavisky Case and the Popular Front

The political crisis came to a head in February 1934 as a result of the Stavisky case, a financial scandal reminiscent of the Panama scandal of the 1890's. The full story of Stavisky's career has never emerged, but it is clear that he was a shady promoter and swindler who long managed to stay clear of the law because of his influential connections, particularly in Radical-Socialist circles. He was caught at last in a fraudulent bond issue of the municipal pawnshop of Bayonne in December 1933, and committed suicide—or, as many Frenchmen believed, was "suicided" by the police. France was rocked by the event, and also by the mysterious death of a judge who had been investigating the case. On the extreme Right, royalists, enjoying the freedom of a democratic society, had long been organized, notably in a pressure group known as the Action Française, and were gaining recruits among upper-class youth. The Camelots du Roi ("The King's Henchmen"), strong-armed squads of the Action Française, went about beating up Communists, who in turn responded with violence. Less fascist in character, yet also supporting the Right, was a veterans' organization, the Croix de Feu ("Cross of Fire"—the reference is to war), organized by Colonel de la Rocque. During the agitation following the Stavisky case, the Camelots du Roi and the Croix de Feu took part in riots against the government that broke out in Paris in February 1934. The Left countered with a brief general strike; France seemed to be on the eve of revolution.

Once more, however, as in the time of Dreyfus, the republican forces rallied to meet the threat, and once more after the crisis had been surmounted France moved to the Left. The February crisis itself was overcome by a coalition of all parties save royalists, Socialists, and Communists, and the formation of a national government including all living former premiers. But the franc was again falling in value. The conservative premier, Flandin, attempted to cut back government expenditures by measures similar to those that had worked a decade earlier under Poincaré;

this time they did not work. The forces of the Left responded by forming the Popular Front, which for the first time linked together the Radical-Socialist, Socialist, and Communist parties. It also had the backing of the C.G.T., which had temporarily healed the schism between Communist and non-Communist unions. In the elections of 1936 the Popular Front won a great victory, with the Socialists at the top. The premiership was accordingly offered for the first time to a socialist, the highly cultivated Jewish intellectual Léon Blum, who had been roughed up by the Camelots du Roi in the backwash of the Stavisky affair.

The Popular Front came to power with a mandate from voters who wanted a kind of French equivalent of the American New Deal. They were convinced that the classical formulas of economic retrenchment were not the remedy for the ills of France. They wanted a direct attack on the stronghold of retrenchment, the Bank of France, still a private institution dominated by the "two hundred families" alleged to control the French economy. They wanted more equal distribution of wealth by government action; in short, they wanted the "welfare state."

Other factors entered into the victory of the Popular Front. Mussolini had begun his Ethiopian adventure, and Hitler his rearmament; many a Frenchman in 1936 voted Left as a protest against the compromises that French politicians had been making with the dictators. Finally, these were the years when Russia, just admitted to the League of Nations, seemed to be pursuing a course of collaboration with the West against the threat of Nazi Germany. Moscow therefore urged the French Communists to give up their old policy of constant opposition and to cooperate with their hated enemies, the Socialists.

On taking office in June 1936, the Blum government rapidly introduced an ambitious program of reform. Labor gained a ceiling of 40 hours on the work week, higher wages, vacations with pay, and provision for compulsory arbitration of labor disputes. The Bank of France, the railroads, and the munitions industry were all subjected to partial nationalization. Strong-armed fascistic groups like the Camelots du Roi and Croix de Feu were ordered to disband.

Impressive as this program was on paper, everything conspired to block its successful implementation. The Communists did not really cooperate, for they refused to participate in the Blum cabinet and sniped at it from the sidelines in the Chamber and in the press. Businessmen took fright at the mushrooming membership of the C.G.T. and at the effectiveness of the "sit-down" or "stay-in" strikes of French industrial workers in June 1936—the first widespread use of this formidable economic weapon. The nation was soon bitterly divided between partisans and enemies of the Popular Front; business and farming classes were traditionally reluctant to pay income taxes, which would have to be raised to meet the costs of social services; the economy was not geared to labor-saving devices. It was in almost every way a bad time for a French New Deal. As the antidemocratic regimes in Germany, Italy, and Spain went on to new victories, France was driven to expensive rearmament. Capital, however, was rapidly leaving the country to be invested or deposited abroad, and the monied class would not subscribe to the huge defense loans that were essential if the French armed forces were to be put in shape to face the war that began to seem inevitable. Faced by mounting opposition from economically conservative Radicals in the cabinet and in the Chamber, Blum was obliged to call a halt in March 1937, and later in the year stepped down as premier in favor of a Radical. With the Socialists joining the Communists in opposition, the Popular Front now disintegrated, and the C.G.T. lost millions of its newly recruited members and suffered a new schism between Communists and anti-Communists.

Divided France

The morale of the French sagged badly after the collapse of the Popular Front. Under the mounting tensions of 1938 and 1939, the Radical-Socialist premier, Daladier, kept France on the side of Britain in opposition to the Rome-Berlin axis, and various measures of retrenchment—including virtual abandonment of the 40-hour week—kept the French economy from collapse. But the workers took very badly the failure of the Popular Front, and as late as November 1938 a general strike almost came off, and was combated by putting the railway workers under military orders. The "have" classes, on the other hand, were outraged by the fact that

Blum's experiment had been made at all; many of them were convinced that their salvation lay in a French totalitarian state—"better Hitler than Blum," as their despairing slogan went, with its anti-Semitic echo from the days of the Dreyfus affair. The France that was confronted with war in 1939 was not only inadequately prepared in terms of materials; it was psychologically and spiritually divided, uncertain of what it was fighting for.

Many Frenchmen before 1940 relied on their great empire to restore the flagging morale and material capabilities of the mother country. Colonial troops, particularly from Senegal and North Africa, had helped to replenish the diminished ranks of the army during World War I. Enthusiasts spoke of France as a nation not of just the 40,000,000 at home but of 100,000,000 Frenchmen, including the population of the colonial territories. But this was stretching the facts too far. Economically, the empire as a whole did advance in the 1920's and 1930's, yet only small native elite groups—only a relative handful of Indo-Chinese or Senegalese or Alger-

ian Arabs, for instance—were assimilated as Frenchmen or desired such assimilation. What the colonial populations were beginning to desire was some sort of home rule or independence. Although some leaders of the French Left urged concessions to native aspirations, little was in fact conceded, except in a half-hearted fashion to the new mandates of Syria and Lebanon. The Cartel des Gauches government in the mid-1920's did give the Syrians and Lebanese constitutions, which were subsequently often suspended in practice because of nationalist unrest. In 1936 the Popular Front government did negotiate treaties with Syria and Lebanon granting them independence, with many strings attached to safeguard the primacy of French interests. But even this moderate compromise was too much for the Chamber of Deputies, which refused to approve the treaties. Perhaps no policy pursued in the interwar years could have averted the disintegration of the French Empire that occurred after World War II, but the old-fashioned policy that prevailed did nothing to reconcile native nationalists to their French overlords.

IV   The United States

Neither the human nor the material losses of the United States in World War I were at all comparable with those of Britain and France. American casualties were 115,000 dead and 206,000 wounded; the comparable French figures were 1,385,000 dead and 3,044,000 wounded *in a population one-third as large.* Moreover, in purely material terms, the United States probably gained from the war. Heavy industries were greatly stimulated by Allied war orders; the war put the growing financial center of New York at least on equal terms with that of London; the dollar had begun to dethrone the monarch of the nineteenth century, the pound sterling. The Allies had borrowed from the American government, but until 1933 some interest came in on these loans. In addition, the stimulation of American industry resulting from these loans exceeded the loss from the final repudiation of war debts in the early 1930's. The United States came out of the war almost unscathed, victorious, and prosperous.

Yet in some ways the American revulsion

against the war in 1919 and the years following was as marked as that of Britain, France, and defeated Germany. On the level of party politics, it helped to unseat the Democrats, who, under President Wilson, had controlled the federal government since 1913. The Republicans won the presidential elections of 1920, 1924, and 1928, and three successive Republicans occupied the White House—Harding (1921-1923), Coolidge (1923-1929), and Herbert Hoover (1929-1933). While the elections were not very close, the campaign of 1928 was, however, notable for the bitterness aroused in many quarters by the unsuccessful candidacy of the Democrat Alfred E. Smith. Smith, who had a progressive record as governor of New York, was a Roman Catholic, with an accent clearly indicating that he had been born in the tenements of the lower East Side of New York City. Many informed observers felt that Al Smith's religion had been largely instrumental in his defeat, and they concluded that the American people simply would not elect a Roman Catholic or any non-Protestant to the highest office of state. Smith was also a "wet," committed to repeal of the Eighteenth Amendment (1919) outlawing, at least on paper, the sale of alcoholic beverages, while "dry" sentiment was still strong in the Protestant "bible belt" of the South and Midwest. No such controversy, incidentally, was engendered by the Nineteenth Amendment (1920), granting women the vote.

Isolationism

On the level of policy and public attitudes, American revulsion against war took the form of isolationism, the desire to withdraw from international politics. This isolationism was by no means universal among Americans. Some historians feel that the drives and attitudes of millions of men had already made isolationism certain in 1919. Others feel that a slight shift in the words and deeds of men in high places could have changed the final decision and could at least have brought America into the League of Nations. If, as we have already seen, the Democratic president Wilson had been willing to meet Republican opposition in the Senate by a few concessions, then perhaps the Treaty of Versailles, League of Nations and all, might have achieved the two-thirds majority in the Senate the Constitution requires for treaties. Or if someone on the Republican side, with skill and prestige, had been able to put through the notion of a bipartisan foreign policy, then with patience and good will the United States might have been brought into the League. Public opinion, say those who take this view, was not against our carrying on the task we had begun in 1917; only a noisy minority in the country as a whole, and the little group of obstinate senators at the top, wanted us to withdraw.

Yet those who remember the years right after 1918 find it hard to deny that the country was swept by a wave of desire to get back to "normalcy," as President Harding later incorrectly termed it. A great many Americans felt that they had done all they needed to do in beating the Germans and that further direct participation in the complexities of European politics would simply involve American innocence and virtue that much more disastrously in European sophistication and vice. The not uncommon American reaction against its "strong" presidents took the

form of repudiating all of Wilson's work at Paris as un-American. Furthermore, as the months of negotiation went on with no final decisions reached, Americans, always an impatient people, began to feel that sheer withdrawal was about the only effective action they could take.

The Treaty of Versailles, containing at Wilson's insistence the League of Nations, was finally rejected in the Senate on March 19, 1920. The United States remained technically at war with Germany until July 1921, when a resolution making a separate peace was passed by Congress and signed under the presidency of Harding. American isolationism was expressed in these years in other concrete measures. The Fordney-McCumber Tariff of 1922 and the Smoot-Hawley Tariff of 1930 set successively higher duties on foreign goods and emphasized America's belief that her high wage scales needed to be protected from cheap foreign labor.

Yet the United States continued all through the 1920's to insist that the debts owed to her by the Allied powers be repaid. It is true that these were refunded in a series of agreements, and that in the closely related problem of German reparations Americans on the whole cast their weight on the side of a general scaling-down of German obligations. But Congress paid little heed to the argument, so convincing to most economists, that European nations could not repay save through dollars gained by sales of their goods in the American market, and that American tariffs continued to make such repayment impossible. Congressmen tended to reduce the complexities of international debts to President Coolidge's simple dictum: "They hired the money, didn't they?"

The spirit of isolationism also lay behind the immigration restrictions of the 1920's, which reversed the former American policy of almost free immigration. The reversal was motivated also by the widespread prejudice against the recent and largely Catholic and Jewish immigrants from Mediterranean and Slavic Europe. The act of 1924 set an annual quota limit for each country of two percent of the number of nationals from that country resident in the United States in 1890. Since the heavy immigration from eastern and southern Europe had come after 1890, the choice of that date reduced the flow from these areas to a mere trickle. Northern countries like Britain, Germany, and the Scandinavian states, on the other hand, did not use up their quotas.

The Road to Internationalism

Yet during this era of partial isolationism the United States by no means withdrew entirely from international politics. Rather, as an independent without formal alliances, it continued to pursue policies that seemed to most Americans traditional, but that in their totality gradually lined them up against the chief international troublemakers. Even before the drift of her commitments against Germany, Italy, and Japan became clear in the 1930's, Americans had in fact engaged themselves. In 1928, the Republican secretary of state Kellogg submitted to the great European powers a proposal for a renunciation of war as an instrument of national policy. Incorporated with similar proposals from the French Foreign Minister Briand, it was formally adopted in August of that year as the Pact of Paris, commonly known as the Kellogg-Briand Pact. It was eventually signed by twenty-three nations, including the United States. It is now the fashion to decry the pact as futile, and it is certainly true that it did not prevent World War II. Yet by this action the United States expressed a concrete concern over the peace of the world.

In a hundred ways the United States was at work laying the foundations for the position of world leadership it reached after World War II. American businessmen were everywhere; American loans were making possible the revival of German industrial greatness; American motors, refrigerators, typewriters, telephones, and other products of the assembly line were being sold the world over. In the Far East, the United States as early as 1922 took the lead in the Nine-Power Treaty that committed her and the other great powers, including Japan, to respect the sovereignty and integrity of China. If President Roosevelt in 1941 resisted the Japanese attempt to swallow China and other Far Eastern territory, he was simply following a line laid down under President Harding.

Boom—and Bust

In domestic affairs, the Coolidge era (1923–1929) has now become legendary. These were years of frantic prosperity; nearly everybody played the stock market, and the market value of stocks rose to fantastic heights. They were the years of "prohibition," the ban on the manufacture and sale of alcoholic beverages, enforced, in theory, by the Volstead Act of 1919 under the Eighteenth Amendment to the Constitution. And so they were also the years of the speakeasy and the bootlegger. They were the years of the short skirt (it was not nearly so short as the "mini" of the 1960's), of sex appeal (also known as "it"), of the Charleston and other forms of "sin." They were years which, like the "naughty nineties" of the nineteenth century, we look back on with a sort of reproving envy, years that now look colorful and romantic.

But the Coolidge era was by no means completely summed up in novels of the jazz age, like *The Great Gatsby* of F. Scott Fitzgerald, or even in Sinclair Lewis' half-satirical *Babbitt* and *Main Street,* with their sallies against the materialism and narrowness of provincial America. It was an era of marked industrial progress, of solid advancement of the national plant and productive capabilities. It was an era of the steady spreading in the United States of standards of living heretofore limited to the relatively few, standards of living that seemed to intellectuals vulgar and inadequate, but that were nevertheless a new thing in the world. These were the years when, if you had a servant, you could no longer take her for granted, but had to take some pains to keep her satisfied. They were years for which, at their best, the right symbol is no Hollywood character, no intellectual, no great pioneer of industry, nor even a gangster, but rather President Coolidge himself, sober, plodding, insensitive, who said that "the business of America is business."

At its most glamorous, the era ended with the onset of the great depression in the autumn of 1929. During the preceding year, Wall Street had enjoyed an unprecedented boom. Speculators by the millions were playing the market in the hope of quick resale of stocks at huge profits; they bought shares on margin, paying only a fraction of their cost in cash, and often borrowing the money to pay that small fraction. Not only stocks but many other purchases were financed on borrowed money. Credit had swollen to the point where it was no longer on a sound basis in a largely unregulated economy. Eventually, shrewd investors began to sell their holdings in the belief that the bubble soon would burst. The result was a disastrous drop in stock values, beginning in October 1929 and continuing almost without let-up to 1933. Both the speculators and the lenders from whom they had borrowed money were ruined.

The immediate cause of the depression, then, was the stock-market crash. About the more deep-seated causes the economic physicians are not wholly agreed. Yet this much seems certain: Coolidge prosperity was very unevenly distributed among the various sectors of the American economy and American society. Agriculture, notably, suffered a kind of permanent depression throughout the 1920's. At the close of World War I, farmers commanded very high prices for their produce and enjoyed an apparently insatiable market at home and abroad. They expanded their production—and borrowed to finance the expansion—often at a reckless rate. Then, as "normalcy" returned in the early 1920's, the foreign market dried up, the home market shrank, farm prices fell rapidly, and the inevitable foreclosure of farm mortgages began. Wage-earning workers, though not hard hit like the farmers,

gained comparatively little increase in their purchasing power during the 1920's. The worker did often raise his standard of living, by purchasing a house or a car, but he did it on credit, by assuming the burden of a heavy mortgage or by financing a purchase on installments to be paid over a long period. The "big money" of the Coolidge era went chiefly to business, above all to big business.

The great depression was very severe in many countries throughout the world, but nowhere was it worse than in the United States. Its effects may be measured by the round figure of 16,000,-000 Americans unemployed at the low point in the early 1930's—something like one-third of the national labor force. In terms of gross national product (GNP), the United States Department of Commerce sets for 1929 the figure of $103,828,000,000; for 1933, $55,760,000,000.

The most remarkable thing about this grave crisis in the American economy is that it produced almost no organized movements of revolt, no threat of revolution. The intellectuals of the 1930's did indeed turn to "social consciousness,"

A soup kitchen in New York City, 1931.

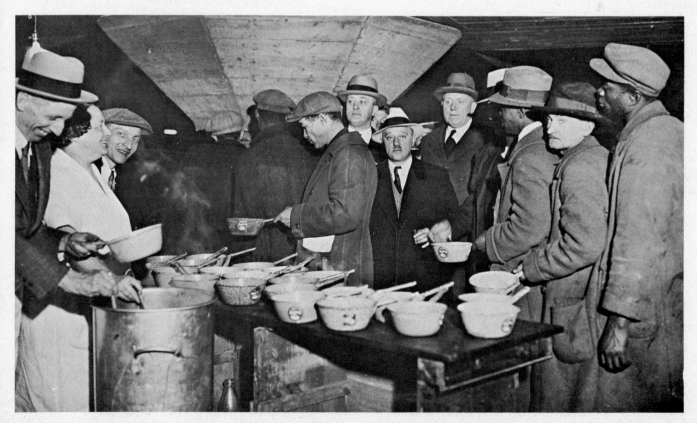

and Marxism made some converts among writers and artists. But the bulk of the population showed no serious signs of abandoning their fundamental belief that the way out lay through the legal means provided by existing American institutions. Even before the election of Franklin D. Roosevelt in 1932, local authorities and private charities did a good deal to soften the worst sufferings of the unemployed. They were helped by the establishment early in 1932 of the federal Reconstruction Finance Corporation (R.F.C.), which advanced government credits to release the frozen assets of financial institutions severely affected by a wave of bankruptcies and bank failures. The Republican administration of President Hoover, however, was generally committed to the philosophy of laissez-faire; aside from the RFC, it did little to cushion the effects of the depression. People who wanted a more vigorous attack on economic problems voted for the Democrats in 1932; most significantly, they did not vote in very important numbers for the socialist or communist presidential candidates. In the crisis of a great depression, the American two-party system continued to meet basic political needs.

The New Deal

The victory of the Democrats in 1932 seemed to give them a clear mandate to marshal all the resources of the federal government against the depression. The Democratic president, Franklin Roosevelt (1933–1945), who had succeeded Al Smith as governor of New York, took office on March 4, 1933, in the midst of a financial crisis that had closed the banks all over the country. He at once summoned Congress to an emergency session and declared a bank holiday. Gradually the sound banks reopened, and the New Deal began. Subsequently, under improving economic conditions, the American business community mostly turned with great bitterness against Roosevelt and all his works. But in those early months of 1933 the mere fact that a national administration was trying to do something about the situation was a powerful restorative to national morale. The nation emerged from the bank holiday with a new confidence, echoing the phrase from Roosevelt's inaugural address that there was nothing to fear "but fear itself."

The New Deal was in part a series of measures aimed at immediate difficulties and in part a series of measures aimed at permanent changes in the structure of American society. The distinction between its short-term and its long-term measures is in a sense arbitrary, for the men who carried both through were never quite clear in their own minds exactly what they were trying to do. What must chiefly interest us is the implications of their work. In the perspective of Western history, the New Deal was the coming to the United States, under the special pressures of the great depression, of those measures—"socialist" to some of their opponents—that we have already seen in European countries like Great Britain and imperial Germany. They are best summed up in that value-charged term the "welfare state."

The short-term measures of the New Deal aimed by releasing the dollar from its tie with gold to lower the price of American goods in a world that was abandoning the gold standard. They aimed to thaw out credit by extending the activities of the RFC and by creating such new governmental lending agencies as the Home Owners' Loan Corporation. They aimed to relieve unemployment by public works on a large scale, to safeguard bank deposits by the Federal Deposit Insurance Corporation, and to regulate speculation and other stock-market activities by the Securities and Exchange Commission. The National Recovery Act (NRA) of 1933 set up production codes in industry to regulate competition and insure labor's right to organize and to carry on collective bargaining. The historical significance of many of these innovations rested in the fact that they were undertaken not by private business or by state or local authorities but by the federal government. There was one exception to the rule of widening federal activity. The Twenty-first Amendment to the Constitution (ratified in December 1933) repealed the Eighteenth and abandoned the increasingly unsuccessful federal efforts to enforce prohibition.

The long-term measures of the New Deal were, of course, more important. The Social Security Act of 1935 introduced to the United States on a national scale the unemployment insurance, old-age pensions, and other benefits of the kind that Lloyd George had brought to Britain. Somewhat more equal distribution of the national wealth resulted from increased

F.D.R. speaking at Chicago Stadium, 1936.

federal taxation, especially taxes on individual and corporate incomes. Congress passed a whole series of acts on labor relations, the net effect of which has been to strengthen and extend the role of organized labor in American economic life. A series of acts on agriculture, though leaving the business of farming still in the hands of several million individual farmers producing for sale in a cash market, nevertheless regulated crops and prices and provided subsidies, all on a scale that would have been incomprehensible to a nineteenth-century farmer. And finally—the showpiece of the New Deal—a great regional planning board, the Tennessee Valley Authority, used government power to make over the economic life of a relatively backward area by checking the erosion of farmlands, by instituting flood control, and by providing cheap electric power generated at government-built dams.

The presidential election of 1936 gave Franklin Roosevelt an emphatic popular endorsement: Maine and Vermont were the only states he failed to carry. Yet the New Deal never regained the momentum it had had in his first term. Piqued by the Supreme Court's decisions that the NRA and some other New Deal measures were unconstitutional, Roosevelt in 1937 put before Congress legislative proposals that would have enabled the President to appoint additional justices to federal courts "where there are incumbent judges of retirement age who do not choose to resign." Supporters of the plan hailed it as a justified measure to emancipate the Supreme Court from "nine old men" who were blocking progress; opponents, including many Democrats in Congress, denounced it as "court-packing," striking at the roots of the separation of powers. Congress rejected the proposal. Meanwhile, aided by the protection of other New Deal legislation, organized labor was making great gains. The drive was spearheaded by the new CIO (Congress of Industrial Organizations), which was committed to organize all workers in an industry into one union and not into a series of craft unions, as was the traditional procedure of the older AFL (American Federation of Labor). Employing the French-devised "sit-down" strike, the CIO won recognition for its unions from the steel and automotive industries after a hard and not entirely peaceful fight. By 1938 further major advances on the domestic scene seemed unlikely in the face of a sharp recession at home and the gathering of war clouds abroad.

Confident America

In retrospect, although the New Deal is still a subject of much controversy, it seems evident that the measures taken by the Roosevelt administration, combined with the resilience of American institutions and culture, pulled the United States at least part way out of the depression. Full recovery, however, did not come until the end of the recession of 1938 and the boom set off by the outbreak of World War II. It seems evident, too, that the New Deal measures also restored a high degree of confidence to Americans. The intellectuals, whose role in modern America has generally been in opposition to the men of business, in the 1920's had found the United States a hopelessly crass and vulgar society. But in the 1930's, though some intellectuals flirted with Marxism, many of them turned to support the new American way marked out by the New Deal.

The onset of war in Europe found Americans, as we shall see in the next chapter, anxious not to jeopardize in war their still precarious prosperity, anxious to remain neutral if Europe should persist in going to war. Roosevelt and his Republican opponents had been for some time exchanging insults: the "economic royalists" fought back at "that man in the White House." Yet in the pinch of the international crisis of 1939–1941 it became clear that, although the nation was not completely united, at any rate it was not pathologically divided. As so often in American history, the violence of verbal politics masked a very basic unity. When the war came to the United States in 1941, Americans were largely ready for it psychologically and—what is really remarkable in a Western democracy—not too unready for it militarily.

When the war came, moreover, the United States had already made many efforts to enlist the support of the Latin-American states. In 1930, before the so-called "Roosevelt Revolution" in American diplomacy, President Hoover's State Department issued the Clark Memorandum, specifically stating that the Monroe Doctrine does not concern itself with inter-American relations but is directed against outside intervention in the affairs of the Western hemisphere. The United States was no longer to land the Marines in some Central American republic at the drop of a hat but was trying to strengthen hemispheric solidarity. And so, on the foundations of the Clark Memorandum, President Roosevelt built his celebrated "Good Neighbor" policy toward the other American nations.

Meantime, what may be called American imperial policy was likewise undergoing some liberalization, notably with respect to the Philippines. When the United States had annexed the islands at the close of the Spanish-American War, a stubborn Filipino insurrection broke out in protest, and it took American forces three years (1899–1902) to subdue the rebels. Filipino nationalists, though partially disarmed by the conciliatory measures taken by the United States after the suppression of the rebellion, none the less continued to advocate eventual freedom. In 1934, Congress passed an act promising the Philippines formal independence, with some strings attached, after 12 years, and bestowing a dilute kind of dominion status on the islands during the interim.

V The Loosening of Imperial Ties

The Filipino insurrection of 1899 was a portent. Even before 1914, there were signs that many of the more advanced "colonial" peoples were already chafing under imperialism. Native nationalist movements were creating trouble for the British in Egypt and India, for the French in Morocco and Algeria, and for all the imperial powers in China. The First World War itself speeded up the process of rousing national consciousness among the "natives" of the various empires, and at its end there was no doubt that the hold of the West had been loosened. Psychologically, the experience of the war gave a lift to non-Western peoples; they had often rendered important services to their white masters, and their leaders had widened their knowledge of the West. The Arab peoples of the old Ottoman Empire had raised armies of their own and had fought with European aid for their own freedom from Turkish rule. French colonial troops and British Indian troops had taken part in the conflict, sometimes in Europe itself.

The very spectacle of the masters quarreling among themselves did something to lower the prestige of the West among subject peoples. Moreover, the Allies had fought the war in the name of democratic ideals of self-determination for all peoples, and in their propaganda against the Central Powers they had stressed their opposition to imperialism. The fifth of Wilson's Fourteen Points asserted that in disputed claims to colonial territories "the interests of the populations concerned must have equal weight" with the interests of the colonial powers. It is true that the Allies did not give up any of their territories in 1919 but actually added to them under the mandate system. To many of the subject peoples, as to liberals in the West itself, the mandate was simply a disguise for the old imperialism; yet it is surely significant that a disguise seemed necessary to the imperialist powers. The West now appeared to be committed to a process of at least gradual emancipation of the colonial dependencies.

Japan

Alone among non-Western peoples, the Japanese were able to maintain themselves as a fully independent major political entity during the golden age of imperialism. More than that, as the twentieth century opened, Japan was experiencing the Industrial Revolution and advancing to the status of a great power, a full but somewhat unwelcome participant in the struggle for imperial position. As we have seen, the Japanese made these impressive accomplishments without radically altering their traditional oligarchical and absolutist political structure.

In the decade after World War I, it looked as though Japan might achieve a gradual liberaliza-

tion of her political institutions. The cabinets of the 1920's included many men from the business class who favored vigorous expansion abroad but who also granted some measures of cautious liberalism at home, The suffrage was gradually extended, and in 1925 all men received the right to vote. For the first time, political parties, Western-style, began to put down roots, especially in the urban population, and seemed likely to give new vitality to the Diet, the not very powerful central representative assembly of Japan. Trade unions also took shape and began to win a following.

Japan, however, did not evolve into a parliamentary democracy on the Western model during the twenty years' truce. By the early 1930's, political power was falling more and more into the hands of army and navy officers, many of whom were descended from the feudal samurai class. This officer clique hated the prospect of liberal civilian government and envied and mistrusted the business class. They found a potent political weapon in the institution of the emperor, who was supposed to possess the kind of political infallibility that Westerners associate with a divine-right monarch. Putting their own words into the emperor's mouth, the admirals and generals used his pronouncements to further their own ends. And, to make doubly sure, they assassinated or terrorized the chief spokesmen of nascent Japanese liberalism.

The consequence was the progressive clamping of a military dictatorship on Japan during the 1930's. Although popular elections continued to be held, their results were disregarded, and the Diet lost its recently acquired vitality. Businessmen supported the new regime out of fear or in anticipation of the huge profits to be secured from its adventures abroad. A cult of emperor worship, known as state Shinto, was concocted out of a rather innocuous traditional Japanese religion to focus popular loyalties on the divine mission of the emperor and to insure popular submission to the will of the men who ruled in his name. A corps of ruthless agents, picturesquely named "thought police," hounded anyone suspected of harboring "dangerous thoughts." In short, Japan now had a government that exploited many uniquely Japanese traditions but in its operations also bore a striking resemblance to the totalitarian governments of Europe.

Nowhere was the parallel with European

totalitarianism more marked than in the foreign policy of Japan between the two world wars. Like Hitler's Germans or Mussolini's Italians, the Japanese claimed to be a "have-not" nation. They, too, pointed to their steadily growing population—and did all they could to encourage its further growth. They, too, harped on the overcrowding of the homeland, its inadequate resources, and its restricted markets. Behind these arguments lay real economic problems of sustaining the Japanese economy in the face of the depression and the worldwide disruption of international trade, problems of providing food and work for the 60,000,000 Japanese in 1930. In seeking to solve these problems by imperial expansion, the militarists of the 1930's were following a pattern that had already been set by the West. And they were also following the path marked out by the Japanese officers and politicians who had secured Formosa in 1895 and annexed Korea in 1910. During World War I, Japan had tried in vain to subjugate China; by World War II, she had apparently almost succeeded in doing so. To follow the course of this Japanese imperialism we must turn to the history of its chief victim, China.

China

China, meantime, was engaged in a great struggle to free herself from the tutelage of the Western colonial powers. The conflict in China, however, was much more than a simple conflict between oriental nationalists and occidental imperialists. It was complicated by two additional elements—the increasing threat to Chinese independence from an expansionist Japan, and increasing communist intervention in Chinese politics. It is scarcely an exaggeration to say that China faced the prospect of simply exchanging one set of imperial overlords for another.

By 1900, the Chinese Empire was far gone in political decay. Nominally independent under the rule of its Manchu dynasty, it had lost much of its effective sovereignty through concessions of naval bases and economic and political privileges to the European powers and Japan. Following China's defeat by Japan in 1895, European imperialists engaged in a hectic scramble for further concessions. The Germans leased Kiaochow, the French Kwangchou Bay, the

Russians Port Arthur, and the British Wei-hai-wei. In 1899, the American secretary of state, John Hay, sought to end the scramble by getting the powers to accept the principle of the "Open Door," whereby all foreign goods could be marketed in China on equal terms, with no special favors to any one power. Although the interested states subscribed to Hay's policy in principle, the Open Door meant little in practice.

Meantime, a formidable reaction to the outburst of imperialist activity was gathering within China itself. The hard-pressed Manchu government encouraged the formation of an antiforeign nationalist secret society called the Boxers. The result was the Boxer Rebellion of 1900, in which more than 200 foreigners, mainly missionaries, were slain. The foreign powers, including the United States, used troops to protect their nationals and property against the Boxers. In 1901, they obliged the Manchu government to pay an enormous indemnity and to grant them further rights that, of course, further impaired Chinese sovereignty.

The Chinese Revolution of 1911-1912

The next Chinese rebellion, the revolution of 1911, was directed against the Manchu regime that had proved so incapable of resisting the encroachments of imperialism. In this revolution, a factor operated that may often be found in the whole process of national self-assertion by non-Western peoples. The movement was directed against the West—against Westerners themselves or against native governors who seemed to be the agents of the West. But it was a movement inspired at least in part by Western ideas and examples, led by often thoroughly "westernized" natives, a movement that could scarcely have come into being without the influence of the West.

The Chinese revolution of 1911 was comparatively bloodless in its early stages. It was sealed by the abdication on February 12, 1912 of the six-year-old Manchu emperor, Pu-yi. From the start, the two chief revolutionary groups displayed conflicting ideas about the nature of the new society that would replace the discarded Manchu regime. One group soon formed the Nationalist party, the Kuomintang, led by Sun

Yat-sen and many young intellectuals who had studied and traveled in the West. Its leaders wanted a democratic parliamentary republic of China modeled on the Western political system, though preserving as far as possible the basic Chinese family and village structure, on which Western industrial society was to be grafted. The other group, whose leader was Yuan Shih-k'ai, wanted a strong central government basically authoritarian in structure, with authority not in the hands of an emperor and the traditional and highly conservative mandarin bureaucracy, but in the hands of strongmen capable of achieving the modernization of China from above.

A struggle for power broke out between the assembly elected after 1911 and Yuan Shih-k'-ai. The party of Sun Yat-sen was defeated, and by 1914, after a purge of the Kuomintang members of the assembly, Yuan Shih-k'-ai issued a constitutional compact that put him in the presidential office for ten years. Sun Yat-sen and his followers had failed to turn China into a Western parliamentary democracy. Sun was, however, a gifted leader, and the ideas for which he stood, though they never were firmly rooted in China, have never quite disappeared. Sun remains somewhat paradoxically the great hero of the Chinese revolution of 1911.

Yuan's subsequent career bears some resemblance to that of another military reformer, Oliver Cromwell. Faced with continuing opposition, not only from the republicans of the Kuomintang but also from the monarchists, Yuan decided to follow the age-old Chinese pattern and set himself up as the first of a new dynasty of emperors to follow the Manchus. A revolt caused him to revoke his plans, and early in 1916 he reorganized the republic with a military cabinet. He died on June 6, 1916, leaving the new republic enmeshed in another age-old Chinese political pattern—the dissolution of all but the shadow of central control and the assumption of real power by regional strongmen. A new era of provincial warlords had begun.

In the years of crisis following 1911, China also faced the aggressive attempts of Japan to take over the Far Eastern imperial interests of European powers now at war among themselves. Early in 1915, the Japanese presented in secrecy to the Chinese government the "Twenty-One Demands," which amounted to a demand for something close to a protectorate over China and for all sorts of concrete concessions. The Chinese republic, now at the nadir of its strength, countered by declaring war against the Central Powers, thus securing at least the nominal protection of two of the Allies, Britain and France. The Japanese did not feel able to defy Western objections, and so contented themselves with taking over Kiaochow and other German concessions in the Shantung peninsula. At the end of the war, the victorious Allies, with the United States in the lead, acted to check the ambitions of their recent military partner, Japan. At the Washington Conference of 1922, Japan was forced to sign the Nine-Power Treaty guaranteeing the independence of China. This rebuff to Japan was one of the first events in the long chain that aggravated the hostility of Japan toward the United States, and ended, two decades later, in the attack on Pearl Harbor.

China in the 1920's

The details of Chinese history between the two world wars are extraordinarily complex. The main elements during this twenty-year period were the Kuomintang, the Communists, and the Japanese invaders. The Kuomintang, after the death of Sun Yat-sen in 1925, came under the leadership of Chiang Kai-shek, an army officer trained in Japan and the brother-in-law of Sun Yat-sen. The Nationalists of the Kuomintang were engaged in a constant and often very unsuccessful struggle to set up an effective central government against the power of provincial warlords. They were also often locked in battle with the Communists and the Japanese.

The Chinese Communist movement began in the early 1920's. It was inspired by direct contacts with the Comintern in Moscow, guided by Soviet agents, and encouraged at first by leaders of the Kuomintang. Sun Yat-sen hoped that the example and advice of the successful Russian party might help to strengthen his own faltering party organization. For a time, the Chinese Communists were no more than the left wing of the Kuomintang. Soon, however, the inevitable breach occurred between them and the more conservative elements among the Nationalists, led by Chiang Kai-shek.

The Communists lost out badly in this early struggle for power. In 1926, Chiang's forces began a campaign of persecution and assassination against them; in 1927, they were expelled from the Kuomintang. An important reason for this setback was the failure of the Chinese Communists to get effective support or help from Moscow. The years 1926 and 1927 were the years of the Trotsky-Stalin feud in Russia, and the conflict between these two titans was intensified by their differences over the "correct" Chinese policy for the Soviet Union to follow. Stalin, who was rapidly gaining the ascendancy, believed that China was not ripe for a proletarian revolution; therefore, he did nothing to succor his Chinese comrades.

All three of the main forces fought in word and deed for the allegiance—or at any rate for the passive acceptance—of nearly five hundred million Chinese, for the most part peasants, and for the most part illiterate. For the most part, too, the masses of China were so far from sharing Western attitudes toward the state that it is hardly an exaggeration to say that they felt toward politics as we Westerners feel toward the weather—that it is something beyond human control. In transforming the Chinese into a nation in the Western sense, the indispensable step was something more than building railroads and factories or promoting the study of modern science instead of the Chinese classics. It was getting the Chinese peasant to regard himself as an individual Chinese citizen.

This indispensable process was beginning in the 1920's and 1930's. It goes far to explain why the Japanese, when they renewed their aggression in 1931, were virtually beaten from the start in the attempt to become the true masters of

An American newspaper cartoon of 1931 on the Japanese seizure of Manchuria.

China. In an earlier age one can readily imagine the Japanese as military conquerors in China setting up a new dynasty, foreign in origin, but very soon thoroughly absorbed by the Chinese. That this age-old pattern was not followed in the 1930's shows that China herself was beginning to change.

The Japanese Invasion

The Japanese attack came in September 1931, on Manchuria, an outlying northern province of China that was a particularly tempting target for Japanese aggression. Manchuria had good resources of coal and iron; it adjoined Korea, already a Japanese possession; and it had never been fully integrated into the structure of Chinese government and looked, therefore, as though it could easily be pried loose. Moreover, the Japanese regarded themselves as the natural successors of the Russians, whom they had driven from Manchuria in the Russo-Japanese War of 1904–1905. By 1932, the Japanese were strong enough in Manchuria to proclaim it an "independent" state, which they called Manchukuo, under a puppet ruler, Pu-yi, who as a boy had been the last emperor of old China.

The Chinese responded to Japan's aggression in Manchuria by a very effective boycott of Japanese goods; the Japanese countered by carrying the war to the great Chinese port of Shanghai. Given the weakness of the Kuomintang government, effective Chinese resistance would have required full support from stronger outside powers. Neither the Western powers nor the League of Nations gave China more than verbal support; the Chinese had to give up their boycott of Japanese goods, and the Japanese remained in Manchuria. Tension between China and Japan persisted and the Japanese soon decided to attempt the absorption of all the rest of China. Their invasion came in July 1937, without a formal declaration of war.

In a purely military way the Japanese did very well. By October, when the key southern Chinese city of Canton fell, they had taken the strategic points of the coastal area and the thickly peopled lower river valleys. Chiang Kai-shek took refuge with his army and his fellow politicians of the Kuomintang in the interior province of Szechwan. There he set up his capital at Chungking; and there, protected by distance and a ring of mountains, receiving Western aid through India by the Burma Road and, when that was closed, by air, the Nationalist government held out until the end of World War II and the collapse of Japanese imperialism.

Yet the Japanese, even at the height of their success, had achieved no more than the stretching across China of a string of garrisons, and the control of great cities like Shanghai and Peiping. They held the railroads, subject to guerrilla attack, but away from the relatively sparse lines of modern communication they were helpless. Many a Chinese village in the area nominally Japanese never changed its ways during the occupation. Nowhere did the Japanese win over the acquiescence, to say nothing of the loyalty, of the Chinese people.

Nationalists and Communists in China

The Nationalists of the Kuomintang led the resistance to the Japanese from the beginning, yet they, too, ultimately failed to win the full loyalty of the Chinese people. This was partly a military matter. Chiang's armies were never able to stand on equal terms with the Japanese. They lacked a good modern industrial base, and, as the Japanese early seized the few industrial cities of China, Chiang was always relatively badly off in terms of logistics. In the long exile in Szechwan, moreover, the morale of the Nationalists decayed. The ordeal, far from purifying and strengthening them, emphasized their alienation from the masses of the Chinese, their corruption and intrigue, their inability to live up to the early promise of Sun Yat-sen and the Kuomintang. For it was not the Nationalists, but the Communists, who succeeded in capturing and harnessing the human emotions and aspirations, the binding power that will hold men together in society with the tightness modern material culture demands. It was the Communists, not the Nationalists, who apparently came to embody Chinese nationalism.

During the 1930's and the early 1940's the relative strength of Communists and Nationalists underwent a gradual and decisive shift. Both parties, it should be noted, were in a sense totalitarian. Both were organized on the one-party pattern, which left no place for an opposition; neither of them was geared to the give-and-take of Western party politics. The Communists, driven about over much of China during the 1930's, ended up with a base in the region of Yenan in the north; their strategic position somewhat resembled that of Chiang in his southern base of Szechwan. But there was an important difference. In the long years of Japanese occupation, Chiang remained in Chungking with his army and his bureaucracy. The Communists, on the other hand, managed to string their network of organized armies and local councils in and around the Japanese in the north; they extended their apparatus right down to the sea and up through Manchuria. By 1945, the Communists were ready for a successful conflict with the Kuomintang.

Southeast Asia

The turning point in the recent history of the Far East was World War II, with its aftermath of Communist victory in China, of French withdrawal from Indo-China, British from Burma and Malaya, Dutch from the East Indies, American from the Philippines. Before World War II there were few clear signs of the spectacular changes to come in Southeast Asia, that part of the Far East stretching east from India and south from China through the islands of Indonesia. But informed observers during the twenty years' truce noted the initial American steps toward granting the Filipinos independence, and they were also aware of the slow growth of nationalist opposition to imperial rule, particularly in Indo-China and the Netherlands East Indies. They saw that the British-controlled Malay peninsula, with its characteristic colonial economy of rubber and tin production, was peculiarly dependent on the economic health of the West and peculiarly vulnerable in a major depression.

India

In India, by contrast, it was the first World War that marked a crucial turning point. India made important contributions to the British armies, particularly to their victory over the Turks. Indians, growing in numbers and educated in the Western tradition, received the full impact of Allied propaganda in favor of the war to save the world for democracy. Monetary inflation and other war dislocations favored the growing agitation for self-government. Already in the war period the British viceroy and his experts, both British and Indian, were working toward a plan of reform. Public opinion not only in India but throughout the world was sharpened in favor of the Indians by what seemed to be a throwback to the crude days of imperial force when, in April 1919, British troops fired on demonstrators at Amritsar.

The Amritsar massacre, however, was an exception. One basic fact about India after World War I was the still relatively serene British rule with its slow but steady acclimatization of Indians to Western material things like railroads and hospitals and to Western ideas like equality and freedom. A second basic fact, growing out of the first, was the growing Indian demand for the termination of British colonial rule. A third basic fact, conditioning the second, was the existence of tension between Hindus and Muslims, which we must now examine in some detail.

A large Muslim minority, about a quarter of the total population, had grown up in the seven hundred years since the first invasion of India by Muslim peoples. In the Indus Basin and part of the Punjab in the northwest, and in part of Bengal in the east, the Muslims were actually a majority; elsewhere they lived scattered among the Hindus and other non-Muslims. Though some of the Muslims belonged to the aristocratic classes, the bulk were peasants, and on the whole the Muslim community was outstripped financially, industrially, and culturally by the Hindu community. Although some Muslims, especially in the upper classes, were proud descendants of foreign military conquerors, for the most part the Muslims and the Hindus were roughly of the same racial mixtures, both really native Indians.

Yet Muslims and Hindus felt—and feel—toward each other (we are talking in terms of average members of the two communities) in a way exceedingly difficult for most Westerners to understand. A friendly British observer has summed it up in this manner:

What are the things which keep Muslims and Hindus apart, which make them feel that they are different races and nations, which keep them permanently potentially on edge with each other? The first perhaps is the doctrinal issue of idolatry. The Muslim has borrowed from the Semitic races both his passionate rejection of polytheism and his passionate hatred of idolatry. . . . The worship of many gods, the portrayal of the divine in human form, is something to him which is less than human, the mark of the beast. It has, I think, no counterpart in the West; for it is far stronger than our ideas of good form or fair play or the behaviour of a gentleman. . . . The ramifications of these emotions are widespread through the whole realm of Hindu-Muslim relations because of the ubiquitous working of the Hindu doctrine of incarnation. So much in Hinduism is divine. The Muslim does not mind a Hindu not eating beef, for example, but he does object to his worshipping the cow. In

times of irritation there is consequently a strong urge to kill a cow out of sheer bravado. . . .

But the mental anguish of mutual relations is not all on the Muslim side. Hindus suffer acutely in the ceremonial sphere. Hindu feelings about the cow are as untranslatable into Western terms as are Muslim feelings about idolatry, and they are no less strong. A Hindu may literally turn sick at the sight or smell of beef. Muslim practice in the matter of food seems to the typical Hindu to be impure, dirty, and degraded, something beneath the level of man. He cannot understand, on the other hand, what he calls Muslim fanaticism on the subject of idolatry. Orthodox Hindu and Muslim individuals can be, and often are, very good friends, but they usually take good care that their intercourse avoids these danger areas.*

It is not surprising, therefore, that after serious attempts to bring Hindu and Muslim into a unified resistance movement against the British, two separate bodies grew up in the twentieth century—the Indian National Congress and the All-India Muslim League. Immediately after World War I, the two bodies did often succeed in presenting a common front against the British, but as time went on their mutual opposition, indeed their irreconcilability, tended to increase rather than diminish.

In spite of these difficulties, the Indian drive for self-government and independence went on steadily from the end of World War I. For the Hindus, the Congress party was held together effectively and given extraordinary influence over the masses by one of the great leaders of the twentieth century, Mahatma Gandhi (1869–1948). Gandhi was not a Brahmin (a member of the highest Hindu caste) but a member of the *bania* or shopkeeping caste. Educated as a lawyer at Oxford and therefore familiar with the West, trained in the harshness of practical politics as a young lawyer serving the Indian minority in South Africa, Gandhi was admirably equipped to deal with both British and Hindus. Among his own people he appealed by his simple and austere personal life, his fasts, and his exiguous native costume. He worked out the technique of insurrection called "nonviolent noncooperation," which appealed to the fundamental Hindu belief that force is illusory and therefore ineffective. Characteristic measures sponsored by Gandhi

The young Gandhi.

* Percival Spear, *India, Pakistan, and the West* (London, 1949), pp. 89–91.

were the organized Indian boycott of British goods, backed by his own recourse to the spinning wheel to publicize the resources of native cottage industries and by his march to the sea to make salt from it illegally in defiance of British regulations. The Mahatma also defied Hindu prejudice, directing some of his hunger strikes not against the British but against the continued position of the untouchables as pariahs outside the caste system.

Other Congress leaders, especially at the local level, were willing to use more clearly Western methods of agitation, propaganda, and, it must be admitted, rather violent nonviolence. Concession after concession was wrung from the British, and as the Indians gained political experience in provincial self-government and in the civil service, dominion status appeared to be just around the corner. This was the situation at the outbreak of World War II. By the time the war was over, however, it was evident that the mutual antagonism of Hindus and Muslims might well require the formation not of a single unified India but of two separate states.

The Middle East

The European powers had a long history of attempts to secure an imperial stake in the Near East—or Middle East, to use the term that gained currency in World War II. At the opening of the twentieth century the Middle East—Persia and the Asian and African lands that were still nominally part of the decaying Ottoman Empire—was still a poverty-stricken region. But by 1914 the first discoveries of petroleum had been made, discoveries that have gone on and on until today the Middle East contains the largest proved reserves of oil in the world. The whole of the area was not to share in this new wealth. The major fields were found in southwestern Persia, in the river valleys of Iraq (ancient Mesopotamia), and along the Persian Gulf.

The new-found riches of the Middle East did not lessen the interest of the European powers in the region during the twenty years' truce. And in the 1930's, as American experts began to worry about the depletion of oil reserves in the Western hemisphere, the United States entered the Middle East in something more than its older roles of Protestant missionary and benevo-

lent educator at the American colleges in Beirut (Lebanon) and Istanbul. American oil companies joined with British, Dutch, and French companies in developing and marketing Middle Eastern petroleum.

In the interwar years the Middle East was an area of increased economic imperialism. It was not, however, an area of the cruder sort of political imperialism, although the Western powers tried to maintain sufficient control to insure the orderly exploitation of oil resources. At the close of World War I the Arab territories of the old Ottoman Empire were administered as Western mandates, not annexed as Western colonies. The French got the mandates for Syria and for Syria's half-Christian neighbor, Lebanon. The British, who already held a protectorate over Egypt, got the mandates for Palestine and Iraq. The only Arab state of significance enjoying anything like full independence was Saudi Arabia, which occupied the bulk of the desert Arabian peninsula. It was an essentially medieval state, the personal creation of a remarkable tribal chieftain, a latter-day feudal warrior, Ibn Saud (1880–1953).

The postwar arrangements, which brought so much of the Arab world under a dilute form of imperial control, did not satisfy the aspirations of Arab nationalists. In these nationalist movements the usual ingredients—Western education, hatred of Westerners, desire to emulate them—were mixed with a common adherence to Islam, and a vague but real feeling of belonging to some kind of common Arab "nation." Arab nationalism was already being focused on the special problem of Palestine, for by the Balfour Declaration of 1917 the British had promised to open this largely Arab-populated territory as a "national home for the Jewish people." The immigration of Jews into Palestine, especially after the Nazis took power in Germany, raised their proportion of the population from about 10 percent to about 30 and caused repeated clashes between Arabs and Jews. Caught between the irresistible force of Jewish nationalism or Zionism and the immovable object of Arab nationalist intransigence, the British mandatory regime in Palestine tried in vain to please both sides. On the eve of World War II, mindful of Nazi attempts to woo the Arabs, the British restricted Jewish immigration into Palestine and Jewish purchases of Arab lands in the mandate. The seeds were being sown for the acute Palestine problem of the postwar period.

The French made few concessions to Arab nationalism; in fact, they infuriated the Syrians by bombarding their capital of Damascus in the course of quelling an insurrection in 1925 and 1926. A decade later, the expectations aroused by the Popular Front's willingness to grant at least a degree of independence to Syria and Lebanon were nullified when the French Chamber of Deputies rejected the draft treaties.

The British attempted a more conciliatory policy by granting some of their wards nominal independence and substituting the ties of alliance for the older imperial ties. In 1922, Egypt was proclaimed an independent state under King Fuad, though the British retained the right to station troops in the country and insisted that Westerners resident there continue to enjoy the special privilege of being under the jurisdiction not of regular Egyptian courts but of the "mixed courts," on which the Western judges (including one American as well as Europeans) outnumbered the Egyptians. In 1936 an Anglo-Egyptian agreement provided for the eventual termination of the mixed courts and the eventual withdrawal of British troops from the country, except along the Suez Canal. The controversial question of the future of the Anglo-Egyptian Sudan, which some Egyptians hoped eventually to annex, was left unsettled. Meanwhile, Egypt continued to be closely allied with Britain.

The British followed rather similar policies in Transjordan, the half-desert area east of Palestine, and in Iraq, nominally an independent kingdom but actually much influenced by British advisers and the presence of British air bases. Until World War II, it looked as though Britain might have found a way of leading the Arabs gradually to independence and retaining their friendship. But the exacerbation of the Palestine problem after the war and the rapid intensification of Arab nationalism were to blast any hope that the Arabs would remain grateful and loyal "old boys" of the British imperial school.

In the meantime, Turkey was undergoing a political renaissance. The losses suffered by Turkey as a result of World War I reduced her territory for the first time to a cohesive national unit, the largely Turkish-populated lands of Anatolia (or Asia Minor). To defend this Anatolian core against threatened additional losses to the Greeks and to the victorious Allies, the Turks launched an ardent nationalist revival extending considerably the reforms begun by the Young Turks before 1914. The leader of this new political revolution was a highly gifted army officer, Mustafa Kemal (1881-1938), who forced the expulsion of the Greek forces from Anatolia and negotiated more favorable terms with the Allies at Lausanne in 1923. Under his guidance, the old Ottoman Empire was abolished in 1922, and in its stead the Republic of Turkey was proclaimed, with a constitution modeled on Western parliamentary lines, though operated under a one-party system. To point up the new nationalistic focus of the republic, Kemal moved its capital from cosmopolitan Istanbul, on the western edge of Turkish territory, to Ankara in the heart of Anatolia.

Kemal also imposed rapid, wholesale, and sometimes ruthless measures of westernization. Women received the vote, began to serve as deputies in Parliament, and were, at least in theory, emancipated from Muslim restraints, though even Kemal did not dare to sponsor legislation actually banning the wearing of the veil in public. He did, however, require men to give up their traditional baggy trousers and substitute a hat or cap for the fez (a symbol of modernity when it was introduced into Turkey a century earlier but now a symbol of reaction). The whole fabric of social and political life was removed from the highly conservative influence of Islam, again in principle at least. The office of caliph, with its vague memories of medieval Muslim grandeur, was abolished along with that of Ottoman emperor. The sacred law of Islam was abandoned in favor of an advanced European law code; Sunday, not the Muslim Friday, was made the weekly day of rest; even the Turkish language was drastically reformed by the requirement that it employ a Western alphabet—a move of major importance, for only a fraction of the Turkish people had ever been able to master the old Ottoman Turkish with its heavy content of Persian and Arabic words, and with its difficult Arabic script. All Turks were now required to take surnames in the Western manner, and Kemal himself appropriately took that of Atatürk, "Father of the Turks." By the time of his death in 1938, Atatürk had indeed revolutionized his country, even though westernization was only just beginning to trickle down to the grass roots of Turkish society. And he had insured its independence of the West, as the neutrality of Turkey during World War II was soon to demonstrate.

The example of Turkey was followed, though less sweepingly and less effectively, by the other traditionally independent major state of the Middle East—Persia, or, as it has been officially styled since 1935, Iran ("Land of the Aryans"). The Iranian revolution began in 1905–1906 in response to the imperialist encroachments by Britain and Russia that were making Persia a kind of Middle Eastern China. The political structure inherited from the Middle Ages was altered in the direction of limited monarchy, with an elected parliament and with the shah as a constitutional ruler. The Iranian revolution proved to be abortive. The country, with its highly powerful class of wealthy landlords and its millions of poor peasants and restless tribesmen, did not adapt itself readily to modern Western political institutions. The shah was unwilling to give up his traditional powers, and the British and Russians were unwilling to give up the respective spheres of influence they had delimited for themselves in their agreement of 1907. During World War I they both stationed troops in an ostensibly neutral Persia.

The Russian revolution eased one threat to Persian sovereignty, and at the end of the war Persian nationalists were strong enough to force a supine government to reject a British attempt to negotiate a treaty that would have made the country a virtual British protectorate. The leader of the nationalists was Reza Khan, an able army officer and the closest Iranian counterpart of Atatürk. But he lacked Kemal's familiarity with the West and his sense of the possible, so that his erratic attempts to modernize his isolated and backward country often failed. He was chosen shah in the mid-1920's and ruled in increasingly arbitrary fashion until 1941, when his pro-Nazi sympathies led Britain and Russia to send in troops and force his abdication. The fate of Reza Shah served as a reminder that some of the seemingly sovereign states of the non-Western world were not yet strong enough to maintain their independence against the might of the great powers. By the time of World War II, imperial ties had been loosened, but they were by no means severed or dissolved; the revolution against imperialism was yet to come.

Reading Suggestions on the Democracies and the Non-Western World, 1919–1939

THE POLITICAL AND ECONOMIC CLIMATE

H. S. Hughes, *Contemporary Europe: A History*, rev. ed. (Prentice-Hall, 1966); A. J. P. Taylor, *From Sarajevo to Potsdam* (*Harcourt). Surveys stressing intellectual and military-diplomatic history, respectively.

New Cambridge Modern History. Vol. XII, rev. ed.: *The Shifting Balance of World Forces, 1898–1945* (Cambridge Univ. Press, 1968). Comprehensive review.

E. Fischer, *The Passing of the European Age* (Harvard Univ. Press, 1943); Felix Gilbert, *The End of the European Era, 1890 to the Present* (*Norton). Two reasoned defenses of the thesis that Europe has lost its old predominance.

J. K. Galbraith, *The Great Crash* (*Sentry). Wall Street in 1929 revisited.

Arthur W. Lewis, *Economic Survey, 1919–1939* (*Humanities Press); H. V. Hodson, *Slump and Recovery, 1919–1937* (Oxford Univ. Press, 1938); H. W. Arndt, *Economic Lessons of the Nineteen Thirties* (Oxford Univ. Press, 1944); I. Svennilson, *Growth and Stagnation in the European Economy* (United Nations, 1954). Very instructive studies of the depression and its implications.

J. M. Keynes, *The End of Laissez-Faire* (Woolf, 1926); J. Schumpeter, *Capitalism, Socialism, and Democracy* (*Torchbooks). Essays by distinguished economists.

GREAT BRITAIN

C. L. Mowat, *Britain between the Wars, 1918–1940* (Univ. of Chicago, 1955); A. Marwick, *Britain in the Century of Total War, 1900–1967* (Little, Brown, 1968); W. N. Medlicott, *Contemporary England, 1914–1964* (McKay, 1967); D. Thomson, *England in the Twentieth Century* (*Pelican). Valuable general surveys.

R. Graves and A. Hodge, *The Long Weekend* (*Norton). Lively history of British society between the wars.

G. E. Elton, *The Life of James Ramsay MacDonald* (Collins, 1939); K. Middlemas and J. Barnes, *The Life of Baldwin* (Macmillan, 1970); W. R. Rock, *Neville Chamberlain* (Twayne, 1969). Good biographies of important political leaders.

FRANCE

N. Greene, *From Versailles to Vichy* (*Crowell), and E. J. Knapton, *France since Versailles* (*Holt). Lucid brief surveys.

D. Brogan, *France under the Republic* (Harper, 1940). Informative but allusive.

R. Albrecht-Carrié, *France, Europe and the Two World Wars* (Harper, 1961). Illuminating study of French difficulties against their international background.

Stanley Hoffmann et al., *In Search of France* (*Torchbooks); J. Joll, ed., *The Decline of the Third Republic* (Chatto and Windus, 1959). Two very useful compilations.

A. Werth, *The Twilight of France, 1933–1940* (Harper, 1942). Condensation of several longer studies by a most perceptive correspondent.

M. Wolfe, *The French Franc between the Wars* (AMS Press, 1951). Indispensable study of the monetary difficulties that plagued France.

THE UNITED STATES

W. E. Leuchtenburg, *Perils of Prosperity, 1914–1932* (*Univ. of Chicago Press) and *Franklin D. Roosevelt and the New Deal, 1932–1940* (*Torchbooks). Well-balanced studies by a most competent historian.

F. L. Allen, *Only Yesterday* (*Perennial Library) and *Since Yesterday* (*Bantam). Evocative social histories of the 1920's and 1930's, respectively.

A. M. Schlesinger, Jr., *The Age of Roosevelt*, 3 vols. (*Sentry). A major study by a historian friendly to the New Deal but not uncritical.

Frances Perkins, *The Roosevelt I Knew* (*Colophon). By a close associate of F.D.R.

J. M. Burns, *Roosevelt: The Lion and the Fox* (*Harvest). F.D.R. as a politician.

THE NON-WESTERN WORLD

J. K. Fairbank, *The United States and China* (*Compass); E. O. Reischauer, *The United States and Japan* (*Compass); W. N. Brown, *The United States and India and Pakistan* (Harvard Univ. Press, 1963); W. R. Polk, *The United States and the Arab World* (Harvard Univ. Press, 1965); J. F. Gallagher, *The United States and North Africa* (Harvard Univ. Press, 1963). Basic information about the areas indicated.

L. Fischer, *Gandhi* (*Mentor), and E. Erikson, *Gandhi's Truth* (*Norton). Respectively, a sympathetic biography and a psychological study.

F. Hutchins, *The Illusion of Permanence* (Princeton Univ. Press, 1967). Perceptive study of British Imperialism in India.

Geoffrey Lewis, *Turkey,* 3rd ed. (Praeger), and Lord Kinross (Patrick Balfour), *Atatürk* (Weidenfeld and Nicolson, 1964). Respectively, a lively survey of the Turkish revolution and a careful biography of its principal architect.

G. Antonius, *The Arab Awakening* (*Capricorn). The classic account; may be supplemented by Sylvia Haim's anthology, *Arab Nationalism* (California, 1962).

J. and S. Lacouture, *Egypt in Transition* (Methuen, 1958); S. H. Longrigg, *Syria and Lebanon under French Mandate* (Oxford Univ. Press, 1958); and J. M. Upton, *The History of Modern Iran: An Interpretation* (*Harvard Univ. Press). Enlightening studies of important Middle Eastern states.

HISTORICAL FICTION

André Malraux, *Man's Fate* (*Vintage). Chinese communists in the 1920's.

Evelyn Waugh, *Decline and Fall* and *A Handful of Dust* (*Dell). A single volume incorporating two corrosive satires of English society in the interwar years.

John Steinbeck, *The Grapes of Wrath* (*Compass). On the Great Depression.

29

The Second World War

General or world wars in our state system are usually born of a previous war, or, perhaps better, of a previous peace settlement that fails to solve certain important problems. We have already been obliged in seeking the origins of the First World War to go back to 1870, to Bismarck, to the "rape of Alsace-Lorraine" and the consequent rise of the spirit of revenge among Frenchmen. We shall now have to go back to 1919 and the grave difficulties that arose in the attempt to carry out the settlement of Versailles. So troubled were international relations for the twenty years after 1919, so closely in time did the Second World War follow on the First, that the interval between the two has been christened the "twenty years' truce." And it is not impossible that historians in the future will actually consider the two wars really one war, as they now consider the wars of the French Revolution and Napoleon

Above: Hitler in Paris, 1940.
Above right: Fighting in the streets of
Stalingrad, October 1942. Right: Hiroshima
after the bomb.

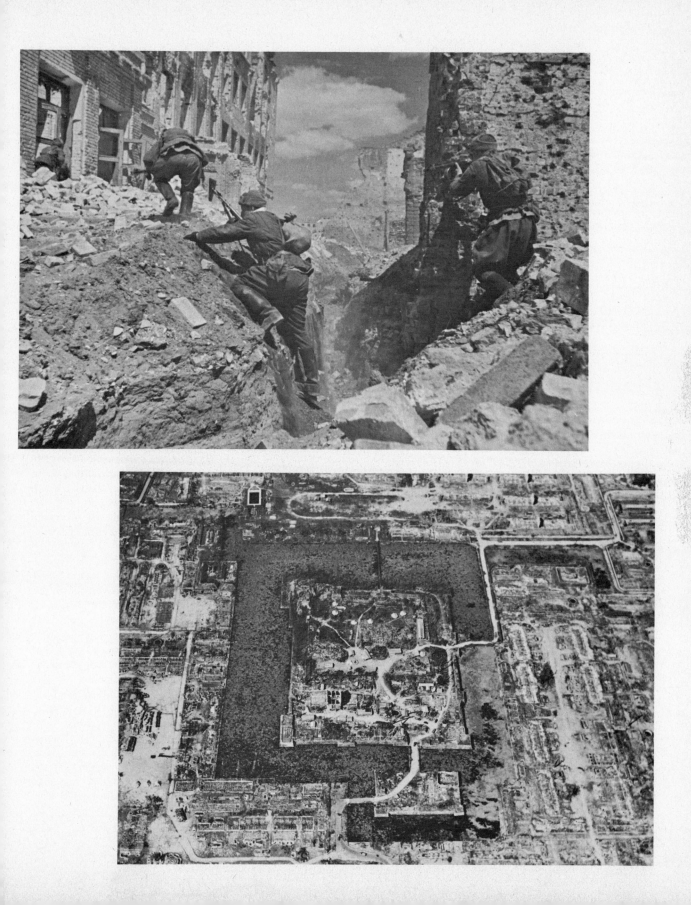

essentially one war. A historian might argue that the first world wars were perhaps those of Louis XIV, if not those of Charles V and Philip II, but for the present we use the accepted terms: World War I (1914–1918) and World War II (1939–1945). Such usage has at least the advantage of emphasizing by the use of roman numerals the close relationship between these two wars. In both of them Germany appears as the perturber.

I International Politics, 1919–1932

During the first part of the twenty years' truce, international leadership of the democratic world rested with Britain and France. Though supported in principle and often in practice by the United States, they were increasingly unable to stem the rise of powers hostile to liberal democracy—Italy, Germany, Spain, Russia, Japan. In the end, the beaten perturber of 1918, Germany, once more waged aggressive warfare against the major Allies of 1918. This time Germany allied with two of its former enemies, Italy and Japan, each disappointed with its share of the spoils of victory in 1918.

Why was the peace settlement of 1919 followed in a short space of twenty years by a second great war? Why was it so unlike the last great settlement, that of 1815 following the Napoleonic wars, which had inaugurated a long period of general peace, interrupted only by localized wars? Nazi Germany maintained that the second war was the direct and inevitable result of what her leaders called the *Diktat*, the "dictated peace" of Versailles that ended the first war. Supported by most Germans and many German sympathizers, the Nazis claimed that Germany was humiliated by the war-guilt clause, stripped of territories and colonies that were rightfully hers, saddled with an astronomical and unpayable reparations bill, denied the normal rights of a sovereign state in armaments—in short, so badly treated that simple human dignity made revolt against the Diktat and its makers a necessity. It is perfectly true that the settlement of Versailles did saddle the new German Republic with a heavy burden—a burden that was dictated in part by revenge and fear. A wiser Allied policy would perhaps have tried to start the new government off without too great a burden, as the Allies in 1815 had done with the France of Louis XVIII.

The "Era of Fulfillment"

But the Diktat thesis is very far from containing the whole truth. What breaks down the argument that the iniquities of Versailles alone explain the second war is the "era of fulfillment." In spite of the Treaty of Versailles, the Germans and their former enemies did manage to come together in the 1920's.

The great landmark of the "era of fulfillment" was a general treaty negotiated in October 1925 at Locarno in Switzerland. Germany there agreed with France and Belgium on a mutual guarantee of their common frontiers; Britain and Italy agreed to act as guarantors—that is, to provide military aid against the violator if a violation of the frontiers occurred. Germany affirmed her acceptance of the western frontier drawn for her at Versailles, and France, for her part, affirmed the new moderate direction that her German policy had taken since the failure of her occupation of the Ruhr.

The "Locarno spirit" of reconciliation endured for the next several years. It was nourished by the general prosperity of both the French and Germans and by the constructive policies of their respective foreign ministers, Briand and Stresemann. In 1926, Germany was admitted to the League of Nations, an event that seemed to signify not only the restoration of Germany to international respectability but also German acceptance of the peaceful purposes and duties of League membership. These hopeful impressions received confirmation when Germany signed the Kellogg-Briand Peace Pact of 1928. In 1929, the French consented to withdraw the last of their occupation troops from the Rhineland during the forthcoming year, thus ending the Allied occupation of Germany at a

date considerably in advance of the one stipulated in the Versailles Treaty.

Meantime, other international developments
were bolstering the "Locarno spirit." The great
worldwide organization planned by Wilson, the
League of Nations, began its operations in 1920.
We shall soon see that the League was never able
to impose its will on a determined and defiant
aggressor. Yet the record of the League during
the 1920's was by no means one of unmitigated
failure. In the first place, the League became a
going concern. Its Council, dominated by the
great powers, and its Assembly, representing all
its members, met regularly at the League's "capital," the Swiss city of Geneva. Second, the
League played a direct part in the peaceful resolution of two crises that, had they not been resolved, might well have led to little wars—in 1920
a dispute between Sweden and Finland over
some Baltic islands, and in 1925 a frontier incident involving Greece and Bulgaria.

Although the United States Senate had voted
down President Wilson's proposal that America
join the League, our government did take a leading part in furthering one of the League's chief
objectives—disarmament. Soon after the first
war, the United States invited the other principal
sea powers to consider the limitation of naval
armaments. Meeting in Washington during the
winter of 1921–1922, the naval conference
achieved an agreement establishing a ten-year
"holiday" in the construction of capital ships
(battleships and heavy cruisers). The agreement
also set the allowed tonnages of capital ships at
a ratio of 5 for the United States, 5 for Britain,
3 for Japan, and 1.67 each for France and Italy.

A conference at London in 1930, however,
had less success in limiting "noncapital" ships,
including submarines. The partial failure of the
London naval conference was a portent. Two
years later, after long preparation, the League
itself convoked a meeting to address the still
more pressing problem of limiting military
armaments. Not only the League members, but
also the United States and the Soviet Union,
sent representatives to Geneva. The Geneva
disarmament conference of 1932, however, accomplished nothing. It was wrecked above all
by a renewal of Franco-German antagonism, by
the German demand for equality in armaments
with France, and by the French refusal to grant
the demand.

The Failure of "Fulfillment"

In 1932, then, the "Locarno spirit" was dead,
and the "era of fulfillment" had ended. There is
one very obvious factor in any explanation for
the failure of the hopes aroused in the 1920's—
the world depression that began in 1929. In Germany itself, as we have seen, the depression was
a last straw, a decisive factor in putting Hitler
in power. In the democracies, too, it had heavy
consequences for the peace of the world, for the
depression sapped their morale and made them
less confident. But the great worldwide depression is no more in itself a sole explanation of
World War II than is the Diktat of Versailles.

Another factor that was unsettling to international politics was Soviet Russia. In the eyes
of the Western nations, Russia was a revolutionary power that could not be trusted, that
could not be fully integrated into the international state system. The Soviet Union was the
center of a revolutionary faith hated and distrusted by the politicians of the West, who
feared, by no means without justification, communist agitation among their own peoples.
Westerners simply could not trust a Marxist
government which was based on the belief that
all Western "capitalist" democracies were destined to collapse and become communist after
a violent class war.

Still another basic factor that led to the second war was the continuing failure of the three
great Western democracies, Britain, France, and
the United States, to present anything like a
united front. Americans of internationalist sympathies have probably exaggerated the results of
the sudden American withdrawal into isolationism in 1919. It is hard to believe, especially in
light of the rivalry and cross-purposes that
Britain and France displayed *within* the League
of Nations, that formal American membership in
the League would have helped the situation
greatly. Still, the isolation of the United States
undoubtedly exacerbated French fears and the
French sense of weakness, and pushed France
toward the sort of intransigence that was illustrated by her disastrous intervention in the Ruhr
in the mid-1920's.

More serious was the failure of France and Britain to work together effectively. France, exhausted and in this decade with a declining population, endeavoring to play the part of a first-rate power but supported only by second-rate resources, lived in perpetual fear of a revived Germany. She sought not only to carry out to the full the economic and political measures of the Versailles Treaty that aimed at weakening Germany and keeping Germany weak, but also to make up for Russia's defection as her Eastern ally against Germany. This she did by making alliances, beginning in 1921, with the smaller states to the east of Germany—Poland, Czechoslovakia, Romania, and Yugoslavia. All of them wanted French protection against the possible restoration of the Hapsburg Empire, whose former lands made up so much of their own territory (Czechoslovakia, of course, had been entirely formed out of Austria-Hungary). All of them except Poland were informally linked together as the "Little Entente."

To a Britain whose statesmen knew well the long story of Anglo-French conflicts from the Hundred Years' War to Napoleon, the France of the 1920's seemed once more aiming at European supremacy, seemed once more an active threat to the traditional British policy of preventing any such supremacy. Although it is now plain that the French were animated rather by fear than by ambition, and that they could never again be major aggressors, it is true enough that many of their statesmen seemed to be falling into old ways, or at least old words, of aggression. The mistaken British diagnosis was at least understandable.

Finally, something of the old British isolationism had survived the war, and made the British—and especially their dominions—unwilling to commit themselves firmly to guarantees to intervene with force in continental Europe. Britain did indeed accept Locarno, but in the previous year the dominions had played a large part in her rejection of the more sweeping Geneva protocol which had been urged upon her by France, and which would have committed its signatories to compulsory arbitration of international disputes.

The difficulties of the Anglo-French partnership also go far to explain the weakness of the League of Nations. The effectiveness of any piece of machinery is bound to hinge on the skill and coordination of the mechanics who operate it. The League lacked a means of enforcing its decisions. And it was somewhat top-heavy, since the fully representative Assembly counted for less than did the smaller Council, where Britain and France took a preponderant role. When these two mechanics disagreed, therefore, the machinery scarcely operated at all. One example of the way in which the grand purposes of the League suffered from Anglo-French friction is the rejection of the Geneva protocol. Another is the Corfu incident of 1923, when Mussolini for a time defied the League and set a sinister precedent for the later use of gangster tactics by the dictators. In the midst of the Corfu crisis, the League was crippled by Anglo-French discord over the Ruhr policy of France.

The Aggressors

The Corfu incident underlines the presence of one more element, the most important of all, in the rapid deterioration of the twenty years' truce. This, of course, was the fact of aggressions by Italy, Germany, and Japan. We have seen how the ruthlessly ambitious programs of fascism and Nazism steadily led Mussolini and Hitler to a foreign policy of adventure and aggression. We have seen, too, how the somewhat similar totalitarian policies of the Japanese militarists led them to begin the seizure of China by their occupation of Manchuria in 1931. Against this background of underlying tensions —the punitive features of the Versailles settlement, the disastrous effects of the depression on the Locarno spirit, the continuance of the revolutionary focus in Russia, the defensive attitude of the western democracies and their mutual mistrust, the new aggressive faiths of fascism and Nazism, and the rise of imperialist Japan— we may now consider the actual steps taken by the nations along the road to a second world war.

II   The Road to War, 1931-1939

The First Step: Manchuria, 1931

It is now clear that the first step along the road to World War II was the Japanese seizure of Manchuria in 1931. Stimson, President Hoover's secretary of state, responded to the seizure by announcing that the United States would recognize no gains made by armed force. Stimson hoped that Britain and the other democracies might follow this American lead, but his hopes were largely disappointed. The League of Nations did send out a commission headed by an Englishman, the earl of Lytton, and the subsequent Lytton Report condemned the Japanese act as aggression. Neither the United States nor the League, however, fortified verbal protests by effective action; force was not met by force. Japan, refusing to accept the Lytton Report, withdrew from the League of Nations in March 1933, making the first formal breach in the League's structure.

The Second Step: German Rearmament, 1935-1936

The next breach in the League's structure, and the next step toward war, was made by Germany. In October 1933 Hitler withdrew from the League, thereby virtually serving notice on the world of his aggressive intentions. On March 16, 1935, he denounced the clauses of the Treaty of Versailles that limited German armaments and set about the open rebuilding of the German armed forces.

The response to this illegal act set the pattern for the next few years. On April 17, 1935, the League of Nations formally condemned Germany's repudiation of treaty obligations—and Germany continued to rearm. In May 1935 France hastily concluded with the Soviet Union a treaty of alliance against German aggression—and Germany continued to rearm. In June 1935 the British, realistically but short-sightedly—for their action seemed like desertion to the French—signed with rearming Germany a naval agree-

ment limiting the German navy to one-third the size of the British, and German submarines to 60 percent of those of Britain.

It is hardly surprising that Hitler's next act drew no more than the customary protests from the signatories of Locarno. This was the "reoccupation" of the Rhineland in March 1936—that is, the sending of German troops into the western German zone that had been demilitarized by the Treaty of Versailles. Britain and France once more did nothing, although many military critics thought then—and still think—that united British-French military action in 1936 could have nipped Hitler's career of aggression in the bud. Such action would have been fully legal in terms of existing treaties and might well have succeeded, for German rearmament was far from complete. In retrospect, this moment in 1936 seems to have been the last opportunity to avert war in Europe.

The Third Step: Ethiopia, 1935

Meanwhile the Italians struck in Ethiopia. In that pocket of old Africa an independent state had precariously maintained itself, largely because its imperial neighbors, Britain, France, and Italy, would neither agree to divide it nor let any one of the three swallow it whole. The Italians, who wanted it most, had lost the disastrous battle of Adowa to the native Ethiopians in 1896. This humiliation rankled with the fascists, who felt they had to show the world that there was more than rhetoric in their talk about a revived Roman Empire.

In 1934, a frontier incident at Ualual, a desert post in Italian Somaliland—or in Ethiopia, for both sides claimed the place—put the matter before the international politicians. France and Britain were characteristically quite ready for appeasement of Italy, partly because they hoped to align Mussolini with them against Hitler. Over the protests of the Ethiopian ruler, the emperor Haile Selassie, they offered Mussolini rich economic concessions and virtually everything else in Ethiopia. But since Ethiopia was a member of the League, the French and the British had to insist that its formal independence be observed. This Mussolini would not accept, and in October 1935 his troops began the invasion of Ethiopia. Italian airplanes, artillery, and tanks make it impossible for the Ethiopians to repeat their victory of 1896. Mussolini's poison gas finished the task early in 1936, and the king of Italy acquired the coveted title of emperor of Ethiopia. Once more there was an emperor—of sorts—in Rome!

The League of Nations had already formally condemned the Japanese aggression in Manchuria and the German denunciation of the disarmament clauses of the Treaty of Versailles. In 1935, it at once declared that Italy, by invading Ethiopia, a League member, had violated her obligations under the Covenant of the League. Now the League made the momentous decision to test its power to move from words to deeds. This action had the accord of most of its members, and was urged on by the British, less vocally by the French, and strongly in a moving and dignified speech delivered to the League in Geneva by Haile Selassie, speaking in Amharic, the language of Ethiopia, while Italian fascists hissed and booed. On October 11, 1935, fifty-one member nations of the League voted to invoke against Italy the famous Article 16 of the League Covenant, which provided for economic sanctions against a member resorting to war in disregard of its covenants.

The sanctions thus invoked failed. There were loopholes; oil, for instance, was not included in the list of articles barred from commerce with Italy, which had only meager stockpiles of this vital war material. There was much mutual recrimination among members of the League over what articles should be placed on the prohibited list, and over the fact that Britain and France did nothing to check Italian movements of troops and munitions through the Suez Canal, which Britain then in fact controlled. Germany was no longer in the League, and was wholly unbound by its decision. No major power applied these sanctions rigorously. To that extent, it is true that the method of economic sanctions was not really tried.

The Ethiopian fiasco was a disastrous blow to the League, which from now on was helpless in high international politics. Its special services as a group of trained international civil servants, its "functional groups," dealing with labor problems, international police matters like the drug traffic and prostitution, and much else, persisted, however, to be absorbed after World War II by the United Nations. But for the rest of the 1930's, the League was hardly even a formal factor in the increasing tensions. No one was surprised or greatly concerned when Italy followed the example set by the other aggressors, Japan and Germany, and withdrew from the League in December 1937.

The Fourth Step: The Spanish Civil War, 1936-1939

The next step after Ethiopia on the road to war is of great psychological and moral interest. No doubt the later direct aggressions of Hitler in Czechoslovakia and Poland were the politically decisive steps. But the Spanish Civil War, which broke out in July 1936, was the emotional catalyst that divided millions of men and women all over the Western world.

As we know, the war was fought between the fascists, monarchists, and just plain conservatives of the Right against the socialists, communists, anarchists, and a few liberals or just plain democrats of the Left. As in most great civil wars, there was really no Center. It was a quasireligious war, waged with the great violence and with the consecrated devotion that mark wars of principle. No one can say for sure how the struggle would have ended if it had remained a purely Spanish one, as the American Civil War had remained a purely American one. Certainly the "Loyalists" of the Left would have been in a much stronger position if the democratic powers had followed the usual practice in international law of sending arms to the *de jure* government of Spain. Such speculation, however, is useless. Almost from the very start the Spanish Civil War engaged, not merely the vicarious emotional participation of the West, not merely individual foreign enlistments, but the active though never wholly open intervention of other nations. This intervention was decisive and effective on the part of the fascist powers, Italy and Germany; it was less determined and effective on the part of communist Russia; and feeblest of all on the part of Britain and France. Early in 1939, with the fall of Barcelona, the Civil War was in effect over. Once more a fascist group had won.

Pablo Picasso's "Guernica" (1937): the artist's protest to the Spanish Civil War.

Meantime, dizzy with success, Mussolini was going on to other adventures. In October 1936, he signed a pact with Hitler, thereby formally establishing the Rome-Berlin "Axis" and committing fascist Italy to alliance with Nazi Germany. Mussolini gave strong support to Franco's rebellion in Spain. And, late in 1938, he orchestrated a public outcry in Italy for the French to hand over certain territories. He wanted not only Nice and Savoy, which had been ceded to Napoleon III during Italian unification negotiations almost a century earlier, but also the Mediterranean island of Corsica, which had been French since the days of Louis XV in the eighteenth century, and Tunisia, which had never been under Italian rule and had been a French protectorate since 1881. These demands came to nothing, but they further impaired relations between France and Italy. Finally, on Good Friday (April 7), 1939, Mussolini attacked Albania, across the Adriatic Sea from Italy and so long coveted by the Italians, and quickly subjugated this backward little Balkan state. For a few years, Victor Emmanuel was to be king of Albania as well as emperor of Ethiopia.

The Fifth Step: Anschluss, 1938

The immediate origins of World War II lie, however, in the mounting series of German aggressions. Hitler had begun the open rebuilding of German armed forces in 1935. Three years later, he felt strong enough to undertake the first enterprise of expansion, an enterprise which, like all he undertook, he insisted was no more than a restoration to Germany of what the Diktat of Versailles had deprived her. Austria, German in language and tradition, had been left a mere fragment by the disruption of the Hapsburg Empire. Ever since 1918 there had been a strong movement among Austrians for union (*Anschluss*) with Germany proper. This movement had been strenuously opposed by the victors of the first war, and especially by France, but agitation for Anschluss kept on, nourished by Nazi propaganda and, in 1934, an attempted Putsch.

Hitler carefully laid the ground for the success of the next Nazi attempt. The pact with Italy that formally established the Rome-Berlin Axis (October 1936) disarmed Mussolini's opposition to Anschluss. Early in 1938 Hitler began what turned out to be his standard technique of softening his victims for the final blow. He unleashed a violent propaganda campaign by press, radio, and platform against the alleged misdeeds of the government of independent Austria. In February 1938 he summoned the Austrian chancellor Schuschnigg to his Bavarian retreat at Berchtesgaden. There he let loose a bullying tirade against the hapless Schuschnigg. In March, he moved his troops into Austria and made Anschluss a fact.

Hitler now had six million more German-speaking nationals in the fold; and in the union of Austria and Germany he had achieved something that no Hapsburg and no Hohenzollern had been able to do. But he showed no signs at all of being content with what he had gained. Almost at once he went to work on the acquisition of the Sudeten Germans of Czechoslovakia.

The Sixth Step: Czechoslovakia Dismembered, 1938-1939

The Czechoslovak republic was the only state in central or eastern Europe where parliamentary democracy had achieved a real success after World War I. The republic faced a difficult problem of national minorities, but it had the good fortune to inherit some of the most highly developed industrial regions of the old Hapsburg Empire. Its economy, consequently, was far better balanced between industry and agriculture than was that of the other states of eastern Europe. This healthy economy was mirrored in the social structure, where a working balance was maintained among peasants, middle classes, and industrial workers. The period immediately after the war, as well as the great depression of the 1930's, times of great suffering elsewhere, affected Czechoslovakia very lightly. Yet these advantages could hardly have preserved democracy in the republic had it not been for the enlightened policies of Thomas Masaryk, liberator and president of his country until his resignation at the age of 85 in 1935.

Even the enlightened Czech regime, however, could not keep the country from ultimately being smashed by outside pressures working on its sensitive minorities. The Sudeten German mi-

nority of 3¼ millions were the heirs of all those Germans who had so long opposed Czech aspirations within the Hapsburg Empire. As Germans, they looked down on the Slavic Czechs, and resisted the new republic at every turn, even when the Prague government made concessions to satisfy their just grievances. Sudeten extremists early turned to Hitler, but even moderates and socialists among the Sudetens were more or less pan-German in their views. From 1933 on, Nazi agitation, supported by Hitler with men and money, became increasingly serious in Czechoslovakia. Early in 1938, having secured Austria, Hitler decided to push the Czech affair next. Henlein, his Sudeten agent, made demands on the Prague government for what amounted to complete Sudeten autonomy. The summer of 1938 was spent in negotiations and in mutual propaganda blasts. The Czechs relied heavily on their French allies and on the friendly, though not formally allied, British. But by the spring of 1938, it seems clear now, Britain and France had agreed not to defend the territorial integrity of Czechoslovakia.

By the autumn of 1938, Hitler was ready for action. On September 12 he made a violent speech at Nuremberg, insisting on self-determination for the Sudeten Germans. This was the signal for widespread disorders in Czechoslovakia and for the proclamation of martial law by its government. The situation was now a full-fledged European crisis that called for the personal intervention of heads of state. The British prime minister, Neville Chamberlain, made two preliminary visits to Hitler in Germany in an effort to moderate German demands, and finally —with the help of Mussolini—persuaded Hitler to call a full conference of the four great Western powers. This conference—Hitler, Mussolini, Chamberlain, with Daladier for France—met in Munich on September 29, 1938. Russia was not invited; her exclusion was to complete her abandonment of the "Popular Front" policy.

Munich was a sweeping victory for Hitler. Czechoslovakia was partially dismembered; her Sudeten rimlands were turned over to Germany; the Czechs were obliged to hand over Teschen and certain other areas to the Poles; the whole economy and transportation system were lamed; the defense of the frontiers was made impossible by the loss of the border mountains and their fortifications; and Slovakia was given autonomy within a federal state, emphasized by the official

Members of the Henlein Party Labor Corps in Czechoslovakia, 1938.

change in spelling from Czechoslovakia to Czecho-Slovakia. The Czech leaders had felt it impossible to resist the Germans without the aid of the French and British; their people acquiesced bitterly in the settlement of Munich. The Germans had played fully on the differences between the more industrialized Czechs and the still largely agricultural Slovaks. But even had the country been strongly united, the laming blow of Munich would have ruined its morale. Hitler acted quickly. In the very next spring, before the final lines of demarcation set at Munich had actually been drawn, he summoned the Czech president, Hacha, to Germany for another of those ghastly interviews, in which he announced that the fate of the Czech people "must be placed trustingly in the hands of the Fuhrer." In March 1939, Hitler sent his army into Prague, and took over the remaining Czech lands, meeting no real resistance. Hungary, long anxious to reclaim some of its lost territory, with German consent occupied the easternmost provinces of Czechoslovakia, Ruthenia.

The most respectable defense that can be made of Munich and "appeasement" rests on the argument that the West was buying time to prepare for a war which it knew to be inevitable but for which it was not yet ready. Chamberlain may have thought so; but Winston Churchill and others have pointed out most cogently that the democracies were in a stronger military position relative to that of Germany in September 1938 than in September 1939. It also seems likely that Chamberlain and Daladier, as well as millions all over the world, believed or hoped that the acquisition of Sudeten Germans would

Neville Chamberlain's return from Munich, September 30, 1938. In his hand is the agreement that was to mean "peace with honor" for Europe.

satisfy Hitler, that after Munich he would behave as Bismarck had behaved after Sedan, and that he would settle down and try to preserve the balance of power. Some Westerners even hoped that Hitler would perhaps ally with them against communist Russia or obligingly get himself so entangled in eastern Europe that he would bring on a Russo-German war. Hitler's words and deeds, however, had given no real foundation for the belief that he would now "play ball" with the West. And we now know that he had as early as November 5, 1937, announced to his close advisers his unalterable intention of destroying Czechoslovakia and moving on into Poland and the Ukraine.

The actual destruction of old Czechoslovakia in March 1939 seems not to have surprised anyone. Indeed the curious mixture of resignation, condemnation, and resolution with which this action was greeted in the West marks a turning point. The days of appeasement were over. Munich had proved to be an epoch-making event, a catalyst for both professional Western diplomatists and statesmen and for Western opinion generally. Hitler's next aggression would not lead to a Munich. We can never be quite sure whether Hitler and his aides realized this, or thought they could take their next step without bringing on a general war. In public and semipublic, Hitler, Goering, and the other Nazi leaders made no secret of their feeling that the British and French were decadent, spineless, inefficient societies, quite unable to summon the courage needed to resist an inspired and rejuvenated Germany. Yet there is good evidence that Hitler now expected at least a local war with Poland, and that he was quite prepared to face involvement with the French and the British. "Whom the gods would destroy, they first make mad."

The Final Step: Poland, 1939

Poland was inexorably Hitler's next victim. The Polish corridor dividing East Prussia from the rest of Germany was an affront to great-power psychology. So, too, was the separation from Germany of the Free City of Danzig, on the edge of the Polish corridor. Danzig was thoroughly German in language and tradition. Germans, even quite enlightened Germans, thought of the Poles, as indeed of all Slavs, as inferior people who would benefit from capable German supervision. Hitler began his Baltic adventure in March 1939, when he took the port town of Memel from Poland's northern neighbor, Lithuania.

The critical issue in the tense half-year that led up to the outbreak of war on September 1, 1939, was not at all the possibility that Poland, unsupported by Britain and France, would undergo the same fate as Czechoslovakia. The British government publicly supported Poland by signing a pact of mutual assistance with her in April. Indeed, in the midst of the final week of crisis, Chamberlain's foreign minister, Lord Halifax, sent a telegram to Hitler himself in which he made a pathetic appeal to the lessons of history:

The Nazi motorized cavalry sweeps into Poland.

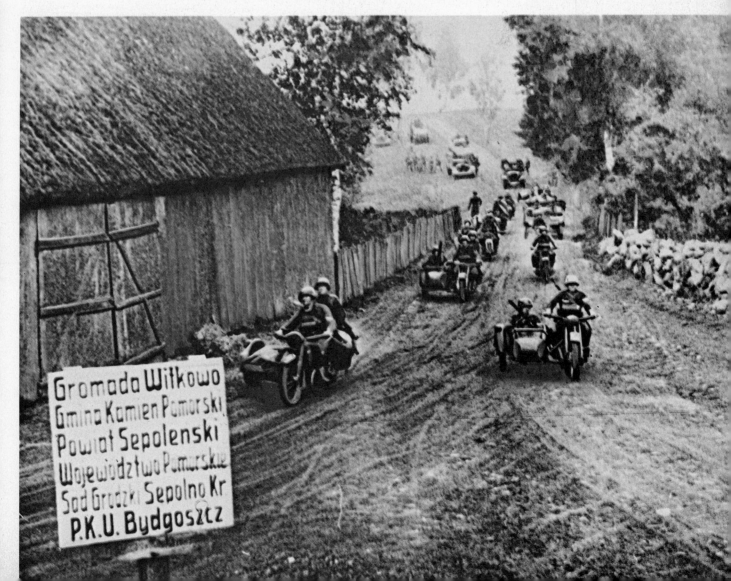

It has been alleged that if His Majesty's Government had made their position more clear in 1914 the great catastrophe would have been avoided. Whether or not there is any force in that allegation, His Majesty's Government are resolved that on this occasion there shall be no such tragic misunderstanding. If the need should arise, they are resolved and prepared to employ without delay all the forces at their command. . . . I trust that Your Excellency will weigh with the utmost deliberation the considerations which I have put before you.*

The real critical point at issue was the attitude of Russia. Hitler had an understandable fear of a war on two fronts, a war against major powers to the east and to the west, like the war on which Germany had embarked in 1914. He was in fact to be drawn within two years into just such a war. Even if he had been faced in 1939 by the united front of Britain, France, and Russia in support of Poland, it is perfectly possible that he could not have restrained himself and his followers. One is tempted to see the Nazi top command as driven on by some abnormal and obsessive motivation and quite oblivious to ordinary considerations of self-interest. Hitler perhaps could no more keep his hands off Poland than an alcoholic can keep his hands off liquor. But, as events developed, Hitler was able to seize Poland without fear of Russian intervention. Indeed, he was able to arrange with Stalin a partition of Poland that recalls the eighteenth-century partitions.

Why did the Russians make an agreement with Hitler? They resented their exclusion from the negotiations over the Czechoslovakian crisis of the year before, an exclusion that they blamed primarily on the British and the French. From the failure of the Western powers to stand up to German violations of the Versailles Treaty ever since 1934, the Russians had drawn conclusions at least as disparaging to the Western will to fight as those drawn by Hitler. In particular, they deeply distrusted the British Tories under Neville Chamberlain, for they believed that in many ways Tory Britain was more fundamentally hostile to communist Russia than even Nazi Germany was.

The Russians' mistrust of the West was not dispelled by the diplomatic mission that Britain

*Documents on British Foreign Policy, 1919–1939, ed. E. L. Woodward and R. Butler (London, 1954), 3rd series, Vol. II, No. 145.

and France sent, belatedly and grudgingly, to negotiate with Russia in this critical summer of 1939. The Western powers proposed a mutual assistance pact, but the efforts of their negotiators were inept and halfhearted. Moreover, Chamberlain's government made a tactless choice of negotiators. One of them, Ironside, had been involved in the British intervention against the Reds at Archangel in the early beleaguered days of the Bolshevik state—he had, indeed, been made a peer under the title "Baron of Archangel and of Ironside"; another was a mere professional functionary of the foreign office. The Russians like to deal with top people; they like to be made to feel important. Significantly, Hitler, who was also negotiating with Russia at the time, put Foreign Minister Ribbentrop himself on the job. So the Anglo-French overture to Moscow came to nothing. The Russian leaders had apparently reached the conclusion that if they themselves did not come to terms with Hitler he would attack them anyway. They possibly also calculated that the French armies would resist the Germans successfully for some time, and that the Western powers would thus reduce themselves to weakness and enable the U.S.S.R. to profit by the consequences, or at least gain valuable time to arm itself further.

Finally, the Russians were quite as distrustful of the Polish government as of anyone else. The Western, especially the French, policy of encouraging the smaller powers of eastern Europe to act as counterweights to *both* Germany and Russia now bore its natural fruit. The Polish government would not accept Russia as protector; it would not, in these hectic months of negotiations, consent to the passage through Polish territory of Russian troops in case of war with Germany. The Russians were tempted by the opportunity to recover lands in eastern Poland that they had lost in World War I and its aftermath.

So, to the horror of the West, the U.S.S.R. signed at Moscow on August 23, 1939, a non-aggression pact with Germany, the "Hitler-Stalin" or "Ribbentrop-Molotov pact," a cynical about-face of two supposedly irreconcilable ideological enemies. A week later, the German army marched into Poland. On September 3, Britain and France honored their obligations and declared war on Germany. The twenty years' truce was at an end.

Europe on the Eve, August 1939

Neutral countries

0 ___ 300
Miles

The Axis Powers
Areas annexed by Germany, 1935-39
Areas made "protectorates" of Germany, 1939
Annexed by Italy, 1939

Democratic Policy in Review

It is not really difficult to understand why the democracies behaved as they did in these years. Britain, France, and the United States were the victors of 1918, and by the very fact of their victory they were on the defensive. Wisdom and luck might have made their defense more effective than it was, but nothing could have altered the fact that they were on the defensive. In the long past of our state system, the defensive has always proved a difficult position, has always been—perhaps from the very nature of Western culture with its drives toward change —at a disadvantage against aggression. This disadvantage seems by no means associated with democracies as such. Absolute monarchies have suffered quite as much from the difficulties of the defensive, as the failure of Metternich shows.

In the years between the two world wars, the normal tendency of the victors to relax was no doubt increased by some of the facts of democratic life. The Western democracies were committed to an effort to secure for every citizen some minimum of material comforts; they were committed to the pursuit of happiness. Their normal tendency was to produce butter rather than guns. Their totalitarian opponents may well have been quite as "materialistic" as they, but for them the butter was to be attained in the future, and by means of the guns. In short, the German, Japanese, and Italian governments were able to get their societies to tighten their belts in order to make military preparation possible. Yet it was exceedingly difficult for democratic governments to get such sacrifices from their citizens until war actually broke out.

III   The Nature of the War

The first world war of our century had, in its main theater, the western front, been one long siege. Since the military experts tended to fight it over and over again in their planning, both France and Germany in the 1930's built two confronting lines of fortifications on their common frontier. The Maginot Line, on the French side, and the Siegfried Line, on the German, were far more formidable than the improvised trenches of the war of 1914-1918. So it is not surprising that on the outbreak of hostilities in September 1939, most people expected first, that the war would be decided primarily in the area between France and Germany, and second, that it would be a closely confined war of siege in the West, with at most diversional activity in other parts of the world.

But the war itself showed once more the perils of prediction in great human affairs. As Germany was joined by her Axis partners, Italy and Japan, and as the United States entered on the other side, this second world war became much more truly a world war than the first had been. It was decided in Russia, in the Pacific, even in the Mediterranean, quite as much as in the West. And it turned out to be one of the most extraordinarily open wars of movement in history. Indeed, the armies of the British Montgomery and the German Rommel in North Africa moved through the desert with the freedom of nomad hordes of old; but the gasoline engine had replaced the horse and camel.

It was also a war in which for the first time the airplane played a major role, a role foreshadowed in the fighting waged in Ethiopia and Spain during the 1930's. Over the water, the airplane, both land-based and carrier-based, soon established itself as a central factor in naval warfare; in the opinion of many experts, it had made the great warship obsolete. Over the land, the airplane soon established itself as an essential arm of the fire power of land armies, an arm that needed and in the end got careful integration with the ground forces. But even in this war the airplane did not live up to the advanced billing given it by its more imaginative proponents; it did not become the sole means of warfare, superseding all others. Air power by itself alone proved inadequate in the great test of 1940, when the Germans tried to reduce Britain from the air.

Aerial bombardment—toward the end of the war carried on by German pilotless aircraft and rocket missiles—did indeed bring the horrors of warfare back to the civilians of the cities. Military experts had been inclined to believe that civilians could not possibly stand aerial bombardment, and that any country whose cities were subject to a few such bombardments would be obliged to sue for peace. Yet European and Asian civilian populations proved able to stand up to months of bombardment. German civilian deaths from air bombardment have been estimated at about 500,000. Organized systems of shelter, partial dispersal of populations, the obvious but not previously noted fact that much of the space of modern cities is made up of streets, parks, gardens, churches, and other public buildings not used at night (when much of the bombing was done)—all combined to make it possible for the people of heavily bombed cities like London, Berlin, and Tokyo to endure what were in effect front-line conditions.

Yet at the very end of the war a technical innovation was introduced that may have altered radically the character of war, may indeed make any future war so unendurably destructive that it will at least be brief. This was the atomic bomb, developed in secrecy by American, Canadian, and British experts, with scientific support from German and Italian refugees from fascism, and first used on the Japanese city of Hiroshima on August 6, 1945. A single bomb destroyed something over half the city. Somewhat less material damage was done by a second and somewhat different bomb dropped on Nagasaki, a

hilly city, three days later. But over a hundred thousand people were killed in the two cities by the two bombs—then the only ones in existence—an incidence of death that seems to justify fully the fears that the atomic bomb and its still more powerful hydrogen bomb successors have aroused throughout the world in our own generation.

IV Early Successes of the Axis

Polish and Finnish Campaigns

The first campaign of World War II reached a by no means unexpected conclusion. No one had seriously supposed that isolated Poland could possibly stand up for long against the German and Soviet armed forces, or that Britain and France could possibly get into action rapidly enough to help their Polish ally decisively. Yet the speed of the German conquest surprised almost everyone. The German air force, the Luftwaffe, soon gained absolute command of the air, and used it to disrupt Polish communications and to spread terror with its dive bombers. Special German task forces, fully motorized, swept through and around the more primitively armed Poles. This was what the Germans called a Blitzkrieg, or lightening war. The German word was later simplified by the English into "blitz," and was used by them to apply to the German air bombardment of Britain in the years 1940-1941.

Anxious to get his share of Poland, Hitler's new collaborator, Stalin, hastened to push the Russian armies in from the east on the hapless Poles. He also established Russian military bases in the Baltic republics of Estonia, Latvia, and Lithuania, which had been created out of Russian provinces at the close of World War I. "Mutual assistance" pacts between giant Russia and the tiny Baltic states were to be the entering wedge for their full occupation by the U.S.S.R. in 1940 and their amalgamation, as constituent republics, into the Union of Soviet Socialist Republics.

Fear of Germany, or an imperialistic desire to expand, or both, also drove the Russian leaders into a war with neighboring Finland for bases in the Baltic (November 1939). The Russians,

who had perhaps miscalculated the strength of their little opponent, did rather badly at first. For a time, the British and French were even considering massive aid to the Finns. By March 1940, however, Soviet forces had worn down the Finns; they secured their bases and annexed Finnish lands very close to Leningrad. It seems quite possible that this "winter war" with Finland had a major effect in encouraging Hitler to his fateful decisions of 1941 to make war on Russia. The German military experts drew from Russian difficulties in this war conclusions extremely disparaging to Russian capabilities.

"Phoney War" and Blitzkrieg in the West

Meanwhile in the West what the British called the "phoney war" was pursuing its uneventful course. The French and the British duly mobilized as in 1914, and as in 1914 the British sent a few divisions to the Continent. But the Germans refused to repeat the pattern of 1914. Busy in Poland, they did nothing in the West. Occasionally, a French patrol from the Maginot Line would exchange shots with a German patrol, but for the most part the troops exercised, ate, slept, and went on leave as though they were merely in training.

The Germans, however, had no intention of sitting out a defensive war in the West. But the German general staff was not prepared to begin a decisive campaign in the West with the winter ahead. They waited until spring. In April 1940 they made sure of their northern flank, as they had not in 1914, by making without declaration of war a sea and air invasion of neutral Denmark and Norway. Denmark, totally unprepared, was occupied almost without resistance. Norway,

European and Mediterranean Theaters, 1939–1945

Miles
0   500

Sinking of the "Bismarck"

Axis Countries
Greatest military expansion by Axis
Allies
Heaviest Allied bombing

NORWAY
FINLAND
SWEDEN
Helsinki
Oslo
Stockholm
Leningrad 1943
Moscow

R U S S I A

Volga R.
Stalingrad 1942
Don R.

IRELAND
GREAT BRITAIN
Dublin
Coventry
London
Dunkirk
Dieppe

North Sea
Baltic Sea
DENMARK
Hamburg
NETH.
BELG.
Bastogne
Rheims
Paris
Trier
Cologne
RUHR
Elbe R.

ESTONIA
LATVIA
LITHUANIA
EAST PRUSSIA
Königsberg
Danzig
Berlin
Potsdam
Torgau
Frankfurt
Stuttgart
Munich
Berchtesgaden

POLAND
Warsaw
Vistula R.
Oder R.
Prague
CZECHOSLOVAKIA
Vienna
AUSTRIA
Budapest 1944
HUNGARY

Dnieper R.
Kiev
1944
1945
1944

ROMANIA
Bucharest
Danube R.
BULGARIA
Sofia
Belgrade
YUGOSLAVIA

Black Sea
Yalta
Sevastopol
Istanbul
Ankara
TURKEY
SYRIA
TRANS-JORDAN
CYPRUS
PALESTINE
Suez Canal
Nile R.
Cairo
EGYPT
El Alamein 1942

Atlantic Ocean
English Channel
NORMANDY
Loire R.
Bordeaux
FRANCE
Vichy
Border of Vichy France
Seine R.
Maginot Line
SWITZ.
Rhine R.
Nice
Marseilles

PORTUGAL
Lisbon
SPAIN
Madrid
Ebro R.
Gibraltar
Tangier
Casablanca
FRENCH MOROCCO
ALGERIA
Oran
Algiers
Bone
Bizerte
Tunis
TUNISIA
LIBYA
Tobruk

BALEARIC IS.
CORSICA
SARDINIA
Rome
Anzio
Monte Cassino
Florence
Po R.
ITALY
Trieste
Naples
Salerno
SICILY
Palermo
MALTA
Mediterranean Sea
Adriatic Sea
ALBANIA
GREECE
Athens
CRETE

1939
1942
1943
1944
1945

also unprepared, made a brave showing. But neither the British nor the French were able to help with more than token forces, and by the end of April important Norwegian resistance had been broken. The Germans now had admirable bases for air and submarine action against the British.

The great blow was struck, without warning, on May 10, 1940, when the German armies, brilliantly supported in the air, invaded the Low Countries and so went around the end of the Maginot Line. Holland, spared in 1914, was this time invaded so that the Germans might make doubly sure of their northern flank. A carefully planned attack on the key Belgian fort of Eben Emael, an attack that had been rehearsed on a dummy of the fort set up inside Germany, was at once successful, and opened the way into the Low Countries.

In the era of weakness among Western democracies in the 1930's, both the Belgians and the Dutch had been extremely anxious to avoid compromising themselves by planning for joint resistance with Britain and France against a possible German attack. They were now to suffer the full consequences of their own policy of attempting to appease Hitler. For the crucial failure to hold the Germans in actual battle came in the Low Countries. We cannot be sure that a carefully coordinated plan among French, British, Belgians, and Dutch would have stopped Hitler. But clearly the lack of such coordination was a major factor in the German success. Indeed, though much has since been written against the "Maginot mentality," it is a fact that the Germans did not take the French Maginot Line by frontal assault, but outflanked it at the critical point where it tapered off along the Franco-Belgian border in the hilly region of the Ardennes.

Through the Ardennes the Germans poured their best motorized troops into France. In a blitzkrieg that once more capitalized on the "lessons of 1914," the Germans resisted the temptation to drive at once for the prize of Paris, but instead pushed straight through northern France to the Channel, where the port of Boulogne fell on May 26, a little over two weeks after the start of the campaign. By this stroke the Germans separated the British, Belgian, and part of the French troops from the bulk of the French armies to the south. Shortly afterward the French replaced General Gamelin with General Weygand as commander-in-chief. Meanwhile in

Britain Neville Chamberlain had resigned after an adverse vote in the Commons on May 8 as a result of failure in Norway. He was succeeded as prime minister by Winston Churchill, whose advent was comparable to the replacing of Asquith by Lloyd George in World War I. Chamberlain was neither a man of action nor an appealing or heroic figure; Churchill was to prove himself all this and more.

The new leaders, in a desperate last moment, attempted to work out a plan for pinching off the adventurous German motorized thrust by a concerted attack from north and south. But the Belgians, badly disorganized, decided to capitulate, and neither the French nor the British could rally themselves to carry out the movement. In the last days of May and the first days of June the British did indeed achieve the miracle of the successful withdrawal to England of some 215,000 British and 120,000 French soldiers by sea from the beaches around Dunkirk at the northern tip of France. With protection from the Royal Air Force, an extraordinary flotilla of all sorts of vessels, including private yachts and motorboats, got the men off, though almost all their equipment had to be abandoned. Dunkirk was a courageous action, and one that did much to help British morale. But from German documents that fell to the Allies after the final defeat of Germany it is pretty clear (though the point is still controversial) that the miracle of Dunkirk was possibly largely because Hitler himself decided not to press home the destruction of the British forces penned on the coast, since he believed that Britain was no longer a real threat. At the last moment, moreover, Hitler did give in to the lure of Paris, and decided to push the attack on the French homeland at once. Here he was wholly and rapidly successful. The French under Weygand could not rally, and the Germans marched southward almost unopposed. The clear signal to the world that the rally of 1914 at the Marne would not be repeated was given on June 13, when the French declared Paris an "open city" and evacuated it without fighting.

"The Fall of France"

The battle of France was thus decided by mid-June 1940. But the French might yet have tried to defend the south, or, failing that, to use their navy and merchant marine to get as many men as possible across the Mediterranean into French North Africa. There, based on their great empire overseas, they might have continued with British aid the fight against the Germans. Some of the French leaders wished to do this, and to persuade them to do so Winston Churchill made France the extraordinary offer of a complete governmental union of the two countries to continue the struggle. But his offer was not accepted.

On June 16 the French premier, Reynaud, was supplanted by Marshal Pétain in what amounted to a kind of coup d'état. Pétain and his colleagues were determined on peace at any price, and this they got. On June 22, 1940, an armistice was signed at Compiègne at the spot where the armistice of November 11, 1918 had been signed. By this armistice, the French withdrew from the war, handed over three-fifths of France, including the whole Atlantic and Channel coasts, to German occupation, and retained under strict German supervision no more than the central and Mediterranean regions. This "unoccupied France" was ruled from the little resort city of Vichy, where Pétain—the hero of the World War I Battle of Verdun against the Germans, now aged and thoroughly defeatist—set up a French form of authoritarian, antidemocratic state of which he was "chief." History has labeled his government simply Vichy France. To most Frenchmen it was a German-imposed rule.

Some few of Pétain's collaborators were pro-German, convinced that totalitarianism was inevitable. But it is now clear that for most of them, even for men like the "collaborator" Laval, a dominant figure at Vichy, and indeed for Pétain himself, the important motive in those bewildering June days of 1940 was simply a desire to make terms with the inevitable. They were absolutely sure that Hitler had won the war. They did not believe that Britain had any chance of successfully resisting the German war machine that had crushed France. In this belief they were followed at first by the great majority of Frenchmen.

The new Vichy government attempted to remake France along conservative, indeed monarchist, lines that had not been practical politics since the Seize Mai of 1877. Symbolic of why the Vichy regime failed is its attempt to substitute for the great slogan "Liberty, Equality, Fraternity" a new trinity of "Labor, Family, Fatherland." Even an outsider can see that the new slogan lacked fire. More concretely, the Vichy regime from the start was compromised by its association with the hated Germans; born of defeat, it could do little in the few years it had to live before it died in the Allied victory.

Even in the dark days of June 1940, a few Frenchmen, led by General Charles de Gaulle, who was flown out to London at the last moment, refused to give up the fight. De Gaulle, a mere brigadier (one-star general) but a formidable intellectual and scientific student of war, now with British aid set up a French National Committee with headquarters in London. A nucleus of French soldiers taken off the beach at Dunkirk, and a stream of refugees who came out of France by all sorts of means in the next few years, made up the Free French or Fighting French. At home in France the Resistance movement gradually formed underground to prepare for eventual liberation. North Africa, strongest of the French colonies, remained under the control of Vichy. But some parts of the colonies rallied to the Free French from the start. Notably in Equatorial Africa, under the leadership of the black governor, Félix Eboué, a most useful base for Allied operations was secured from the first. Weak as these fighting French groups were in the early days, they were at least a rallying point. They were able to set up an effective radio center in England from which they conducted a skillful propaganda campaign against Vichy and the Germans, beamed across the Channel to the homeland, where, we now know, it achieved a large audience.

On June 10, Hitler's ally Mussolini had brought the Italians into the war against France and Britain, too late to affect the outcome of the battle of France. But this "stab in the back," as Franklin Roosevelt called it, further outraged American opinion, already alarmed by the Nazi successes. And Italy was now irrevocably engaged in the struggle, anxious to secure some kind of success that would offset the great gains of her German ally. The war, up to this time confined to northern and western Europe, now spread to the Mediterranean.

The Battle of Britain

The Germans, for all their miracles of planning and execution, had not really worked out a way to deal with Britain. Hitler seems to have believed that with France out of the war he could find groups in Britain who would see the light and with whom he could make a separate peace, a peace of compromise in which Germany would dominate the continent of Europe and Britain would continue satisfied with her overseas empire. This division of the spoils, Hitler reiterated in public and private, should be eminently satisfactory; he did not threaten the British Empire. Mixed with his hatred for England was a deep-rooted admiration, and an emotional and altogether misleading idea that Germany and England were natural allies—if only the English could be made to see it. Yet for over four centuries Britain had gone to war rather than accept the kind of one-power domination over western and central Europe that Hitler exercised after the fall of France. The British, therefore, paid no attention at all to his peace feelers.

Hitler was counting heavily on the possibility that German submarines could eventually cut off British supplies of food and raw materials from overseas, and thus starve her into submission. But at best this must take a long time. Hitler and his colleagues were impatient. The obvious thing to do was to attempt a landing in England ("Operation Sea-Lion"). But the Germans had made no real preparation for amphibious warfare; they had no specially designed landing craft. Moreover, the German air force and the German navy were at odds over the best way of combining for an invasion across the Channel. A hastily assembled flotilla of miscellaneous vessels was badly damaged by British aircraft, and early in August 1940 Hitler and Hermann Goering, his air marshal, made the fateful decision to try to do the job solely with air power.

The Battle of Britain that followed had two main phases. First, in August and September, the Luftwaffe attempted in daylight bombing attacks to wipe out British airports and fighter planes. The Royal Air Force, admirably organized and directed, and using the new detection apparatus called radar to spot the attackers early, proved just barely strong enough to check the Germans. In the critical actions of September 15–21, German official records now available show 120 planes lost (the British at the time claimed 268). This was, however, a rate of loss that Goering, head of the Luftwaffe, felt the Germans could not stand. This phase of the blitz was called off. In one of his imperishable phrases, Churchill said of the small group of British

fighter pilots who had saved Britain, "Never . . . was so much owed by so many to so few."

The second phase began in the autumn of 1940. The Germans sought by night bombing of major British industrial centers to destroy British production and to terrify the civilian population so that the government would be obliged to sue for peace. Neither aim was successful. Even at Coventry, an important center of the automotive industry, though grave damage was done, the industry was by no means knocked out. Indeed, more damage was done to the cathedral and other buildings in the center of the city than to the great factories on the outskirts. As for civilian morale, it is clear that these bombings strengthened the British will to resist. Civilian defense measures proved adequate to protect both persons and property from that extreme of destruction which might indeed have broken the will to resist. By winter, when the weather gave the British some respite, the Battle of Britain had been won.

Mediterranean and Balkan Campaigns

Hitler now faced the possibility of a long stalemate, something that conquerors like Napoleon in the past have rarely been able to face. Like Napoleon turning to Egypt in 1798, Hitler turned at first to the obvious strategy of getting at Britain through her Mediterranean lifeline to India and the East. His ally Mussolini, already itching to expand in the Mediterranean, invaded Greece from Albania in October 1940, without previously informing Hitler of his intention. The Greeks held on valiantly and even pushed the Italians back halfway across Albania. But, just as the Germans came in the first world war to the rescue of their Austrian ally, so they now came successfully to the rescue of Mussolini.

Just how far Hitler himself wanted to invest in action in this theater is not clear. Certainly he toyed with the idea of a campaign against the British fortress of Gibraltar through Spain, to be coordinated with Axis attacks in the eastern Mediterranean to clear that sea of the British. But the Spanish dictator Franco wanted too high a price from the French for his consent to a German march through Spain, and Hitler was unwilling to risk driving Vichy France, which still controlled French North Africa, too far. In the upshot, the Germans had to be content with backing up Mussolini in Greece and with an attack on Egypt from the Italian colony of Libya. Efforts to rouse native action against the British and French in the Near East were suppressed without grave difficulty by British and Free French action in Syria, and Turkey stood obstinately neutral.

Nevertheless, the German commitment to help the Italians in Greece took valuable German divisions away from another task in the spring of 1941. Though Hitler forced on a timid Yugoslav government a treaty allowing German forces free passage across Yugoslavia to Greece, a patriotic Serbian uprising overthrew the Yugoslav regime, and the Germans had thereafter to combat guerrilla resistance and to dismember Yugoslavia. In Greece the British did their best to back up their Greek allies, but once more they were not strong enough. German air power crippled British naval power in the Mediterranean and by June the Axis had conquered the Greek mainland. A spectacular attack on Crete followed, the German troops landing by glider. The British defeat appeared total, but in fact the Germans had invested far too much armament in the Balkan campaign.

The Invasion of Russia

The other task for which the German forces were to be used in the spring of 1941 was the conquest of Russia. Hitler had firmly resolved not to repeat what he thought was the fateful mistake of Germany in 1914; he would not engage in a war on two fronts. Yet by his invasion of Russia in June 1941—an invasion delayed for a perhaps decisive two months by the Balkan adventure—he committed himself to just such a war. Russia was indeed a tempting goal. The Nazi plan had always looked to the fertile areas of Poland and south Russia as the natural goal of German expansion, the Lebensraum of German destiny. With the precedents of successful blitzkrieg in Poland, western Europe, and now Greece, Hitler and his military experts believed that they could beat the Russians in a single campaign before winter set in. It was quite clear that neither Britain nor the United States—even though the latter should enter the war—could land armies in Europe in 1941. An attack on

Russia, then, Hitler seems to have told himself, would not *really* create two fronts. Indeed, once Russia was conquered, as in Hitler's mind it was sure to be, the Germans would have no trouble disposing of Britain, and, if necessary, the United States.

Russia was not conquered in 1941. But it was very close, closer perhaps than the Battle of Britain. Hitler's plan almost worked. There really was a successful blitzkrieg. Within two months the Germans were at the gates of Leningrad, and in the south they had conquered the Ukraine by the end of October. Hundreds of thousands of Russian troops had been killed or taken prisoner. In sheer distance, the German armies had pushed more than twice as far as they had in France.

Yet, as the Russian winter closed in, the Germans had taken neither Moscow nor Leningrad. Russian heavy industry had been in part transferred to the remote Urals, and existing plants there and in Siberia had been strengthened. The United States was beginning to send in supplies. The vast resources of Russian manpower were still adequate for Russian needs. The government had not collapsed, and national spirit was high. Moreover, the Germans had shown once more, as they had in the Battle of Britain, that their boasted planning was far from perfect. Their troops were not sufficiently equipped to stand the rigors of a Russian winter. Confident that one summer and autumn would be enough to finish the business, the German planners had left the winter to take care of itself. Indeed, in winter fighting between December 1941 and May 1942, the Russians regained much useful ground.

American Policy

Meanwhile, the Germans had fallen into a second fatal involvement. Impressed with what he thought were the disastrous failures of German policy in World War I, Hitler had sought to keep out of war with the United States. Although the United States had a strong isolationist element and even some vociferous Nazi sympathizers, American opinion had from the very beginning of the attack on Poland in 1939 been far more nearly unanimous against the Germans and Italians than it had been against the Central

Powers in 1914. With the fall of France in 1940, anti-Axis sentiment grew stronger, reinforced by a growing belief that if Hitler had his way in Europe the United States would be marked out as his next victim.

Between June 1940 and December 1941, the Roosevelt administration, with the consent of the Congress and with the general backing of American public opinion, took a series of steps "short of war" in aid of Britain and later Russia. By conventional standards of international relations, these steps were not in accord with America's technical status as a neutral; they would have given Hitler ample legal justification for declaring war against the United States. The American government transferred to the British fifty "overage" destroyers in exchange for Atlantic naval bases in British colonies, supplied the British with all sorts

of arms, and used the American navy to help get these supplies across the Atlantic. Above all, in March 1941, by the so-called Lend-Lease Act, the United States agreed to supply materials needed for defense, including footstuffs, to "any country whose defense the President deems vital to the defense of the United States." Supplies at once began rolling into England, and later to other anti-Axis powers without the unfortunate complications produced by the war-debt methods employed during World War I. This help went, as we have just noted, promptly to communist Russia. Churchill and Roosevelt recognized that, despite mutual hostility between the U.S.S.R. and the West, despite even the Stalin-Hitler alliance so rudely broken up only by Hitler, it was to the Allied interest to assist the U.S.S.R. vigorously. This clearly helped prevent

Winston Churchill and the American ambassador sign the Destroyers-Bases Agreement, March 27, 1941.

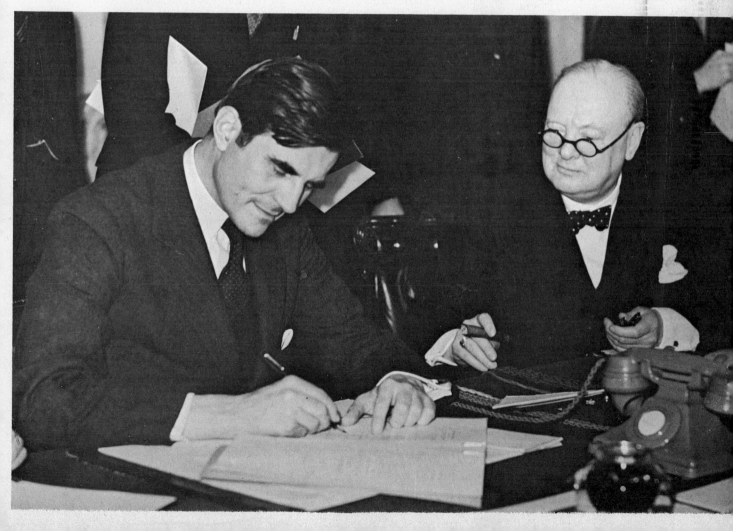

among Britain, the United States, Russia, and the Free French the kind of actual back-stabbing and desertion that characterized the failure of Europe to defeat, or even contain, the revolutionary French and Napoleon after 1792.

Yet Hitler still did not let himself get involved in war against the United States. He had, however, firm commitments to aid Japan. And Japan, controlled by a militarist group, had taken advantage of the fall of France and the Netherlands and the weakness of Britain to speed up vastly the policy of expansion in Asia that she had begun in Manchuria as far back as 1931. She early took advantage of the fall of France to penetrate into French Indo-China. She continued to press her campaign on the mainland of China. The American government, which had never in the days of technical peace in the 1930's been willing to accept Japanese conquests in China, did not now abandon its policy of opposition to what it considered Japanese aggression. It is indeed highly likely that had the American government been willing to allow Japan a free hand to do what she liked in the Far East there would have been no Pearl Harbor. But short of such complete abandonment of the previous American policy in the Far East, it is unlikely that the United States could have kept out of war with Japan.

Pearl Harbor and After

In the summer and autumn of 1941, the American government took steps to freeze Japanese credits in the United States, to close Japanese access to raw materials, and to get the Japanese to withdraw from China and Indo-China. Negotiations toward these ends were going on between the Japanese and the Americans when on December 7, 1941, the Japanese without warning struck with carrier-based airplanes at the American naval base at Pearl Harbor in Hawaii. Grave damage was done to ships and installations, but American power in the Pacific was by no means destroyed. Moreover, the psychological effect of the "day of infamy" on American public opinion was to produce in a nation of many millions an almost unanimous support for war against Japan. And the consequence was the immediate declaration of war against Japan by the United States. Germany and Italy honored their obligations to their Axis partner by declaring war against the United States on December 11. As the year 1942 began, the war was literally and fully a world war.

Although the United States was incomparably better prepared than she had been in 1917, she was still at a disadvantage. Against Germany she could for the moment do no more than continue, indeed increase, aid to Britain and Russia by Lend-Lease and take full part in the struggle against the German submarines. Against Japan she was almost as powerless. Her Pacific outposts of Guam, Wake Island, and the Philippines fell in rapid succession to Japanese arms. Nor could the British and the exiled Dutch governments protect their colonies in Southeast Asia. By the spring of 1942, the Japanese had taken Malaya from the British and Indonesia from the Dutch, and had virtual control of Siam (Thailand) and Burma. They seemed poised for an attack on Australia.

V   The Victory of the United Nations

The Turning Points

There were several turning points in the struggle. The earliest was a series of naval actions in which Japanese expansion was stopped. In these actions, carrier-based American airplanes played a decisive role. On May 7, 1942, in the battle of the Coral Sea in the southwest Pacific, Allied sea and air power halted a possible Japanese invasion of Australia and its protecting islands. In June, American sea and air power dispersed a Japanese fleet that was aiming at the conquest of Midway Island. Although the Japanese landed on American territory in the Aleutians, they never seriously threatened Hawaii or mainland Alaska.

In the West, the Americans and the British were as yet unwilling and unable to respond to Russian presure for a "second front" on the

European mainland. But in November 1942, they did effect a series of landings in French North Africa. Secret prior negotiations with anti-Axis elements among the French in North Africa were not completely successful, and the landings in Morocco were sharply though briefly resisted by the Vichy French. None the less, the Allies were rapidly established in force in Morocco and Algeria.

The Libyan segment of the long North African coast had been held by the Germans and their Italian allies since the beginning of the war in the Mediterranean, and there had been seesaw campaigns in these desert areas, campaigns that recaptured some of the adventure, even romance, of wars of old. At the time of the North African landings, the British under General Montgomery were holding a defensive line inside the Egyptian frontier; but on October 23, 1942, the British started on a westward offensive which was planned to coordinate with an eastward offensive by General Eisenhower, commander of the Allied forces in French North Africa, in the classic maneuver of catching the enemy in a vise. The Germans responded quickly to the threat, and succeeded in reinforcing their African armies through Tunis, which was delivered to them by the Vichy authorities. The planned expulsion of the Germans and Italians from North Africa was thus delayed, but the vise closely slowly. In May 1943, Free French, British, and American troops took the last Axis strongholds of Tunis and Bizerte, and accepted the surrender of some three hundred thousand Axis troops.

The North African campaign had clearly been a turning point. The Allies had successfully made large-scale amphibious landings, and they had annihilated one of the most renowned of Axis forces, commanded by one of the few German generals in this war to strike the imagination of the world, Rommel, the "desert fox." North Africa was by no means a great central operation, but it was never the less a major campaign in which the Allies gained confidence and prestige.

The great turning point on land was, however, the successful Russian defense of Stalingrad (now Volgograd), a defense that turned into an attack in the same month (November 1942) that saw the Allied landing in North Africa. After their check in the winter of 1941-1942, the Germans had turned their Russian summer offensive of 1942 away from Leningrad and Moscow and toward the oil-rich regions of southeastern European Russia. The Germans were already beginning to suffer oil shortages, partly because of Allied bombing, but even more because, though they held the oil fields of Romania, they simply did not have oil enough for the ravenous demands of mechanical warfare. This push toward the Russian oil fields carried the Germans a prodigious distance inside Russia, over a thousand miles from their original starting point. But again it failed, falling just short of the really rich oil fields of Grozny and Baku. Russian distance and Russian weather and Russian manpower, and the Russian ability to take punishment, were too much for these overextended Germans. Their armies were pinched off at Stalingrad, and early in 1943 the Russians started the long march westward that was to take them to Berlin two years later.

The Battle of Supply

A much less spectacular turning point than the engagements in the Coral Sea, in North Africa, and at Stalingrad was the Allied victory in the battle of supply. Yet this victory was of even greater importance, since naval and military successes ultimately depend on supplies. Even for Russia, an important source of supplies was the United States. But the United States was separated from its allies—and its enemies—by water, and all but the most precious and least bulky supplies, which could go by air, had to move across the seas. If the Germans could stop this movement, or even reduce it greatly, they might still be able to win in spite of the overwhelming resources of the Allies. They made important improvements in their submarines, notably the snorkel, a device that enabled submarines to travel submerged for great distances. Submarine crews and commanders were well trained and resourceful. But there were not enough submarines, and the countermeasures of the Allies—radar, coordination of naval vessels and aircraft, the convoy system, and others—slowly reduced the proportion of sinkings.

Early in 1942, after Pearl Harbor, the rate of sinkings had been really dangerous, and German submarines had operated close to the Atlantic coast of the United States. But by the end of

1942, the statistics showed a turn of the tide, and in the summer of 1943 the Allies were confident enough to announce publicly that the number of sinkings from U-boat action in the first half of 1943 was only a quarter of what it had been in the first half of 1942.

The Axis on the Defensive

In the last two years of the war, the Axis powers were on the defensive. Both in Europe and in Asia the Allies attacked with land forces along definite lines of march; these were "campaigns" of the traditional kind. But the way for these armies was made easier by two new factors in warfare, air power and modern propaganda, or "psychological warfare." These new methods did not "win" the war by themselves, but they were useful adjuncts, and they undoubtedly hastened the process. Air bombardment, at least until the atomic bomb at Hiroshima, was never quite the perfect annihilation that the prophets of air power had preached. The Germans put some of their key production underground. Allied "precision" bombing rarely reached perfection. But as the superior Allied air power grew, as it was used systematically to destroy enemy capabilities in critical materials like ball bearings, machine tools, locomotives, and oil, and as American airplanes dropped incendiary bombs on the relatively flimsy Japanese cities, it did much to destroy the Axis will and power to resist.

On Germany and Italy, the attack by land was pressed in three directions—by the Russians from the east, and by the British, French, Americans, and the other Allies from the south and from the west. In the south, the Allies moved from North Africa across to Sicily in a successful amphibious operation (July 1943) within two months of their final victory in Tunisia, and from Sicily they moved in another six weeks across the Straits of Messina to the mainland of Italy. German forces were able to keep the Italian campaign going for longer than the Allies hoped. The Allied victories of the summer of 1943 were, however, sufficient to put Italy itself for the most part out of the war. High officers of the Italian army and others close to the king, helped by dissident fascist leaders, engineered a coup in July which brought about the fall and imprisonment of Mussolini and the beginnings of negotiations between the Allies and the new government headed by Marshal Badoglio.

But the Germans were quite unwilling to abandon the peninsula, perhaps as much for reasons of prestige as for military reasons. A detachment of German troops rescued Mussolini from his Apennine prison (September 1943), and set him up as the head of a "fascist republic." The former duce continued in this post until he was executed by partisans in April 1945. Meantime, Italy had a civil as well as a foreign war on her hands. Many Italians, never really taken in by Mussolini's posturing as an imperial Roman, had never liked the war and were now heartily sick of it. Still, many were politically active in Italy in 1943–1945, and of these the pro-Axis group was far less strong than the pro-Allied group. Italy came naturally enough into the United Nations. The war in Italy went on. In June 1944 the Allies succeeded, after particularly severe fighting around Cassino, in breaking through to Rome, and by August they were in Florence. They could not effectively move further north until the final collapse of the Germans in the early months of 1945.

The Defeat of Germany

The great Allied push in the west, it was finally decided at the Teheran conference of Churchill, Roosevelt, and Stalin (December 1943), would be in France. After meticulous preparation, the long-awaited landings in France began on June 6, 1944. The Allies had chosen the Norman coast at the base of the Cotentin (Cherbourg) peninsula, and seem thereby to have gained some initial advantage of surprise, for the German high command believed the landings would come farther north and east along the Channel coast. The Germans had in their four years of occupancy fortified the French coastline with great thoroughness. But the Allies had also had those four years for study, invention, and planning. In the test, Allied landing craft, amphibious trucks called "ducks," naval and air support—by now the Luftwaffe had almost been driven from the skies—artificial harbors, and a well-organized supply system proved sufficient to gain a beachhead for the allied land forces. From this beachhead, a little over a month after D-Day, they were able to break out at

Avranches and sweep the Germans back across the Seine in a great flanking movement led by the American General Patton's Third Army.

A long-planned auxiliary landing on the French Mediterranean coast to be followed by a march north up the Rhone-Saône valleys was launched on August 15, 1944, and met very little resistance. Everywhere the French, by now well organized for resistance, welcomed the liberating forces, some of whom were French and French colonials fighting as heirs of the Free French of 1940. Paris, a symbol rather than a mere place, was liberated toward the end of August after its inhabitants had staged an uprising, barricades and all, in the style of 1848, against the German garrison.

The Germans were beaten, but not disorganized. In July 1944 an attempt to assassinate Hitler and to pave the way for negotiations was made by conservative elements, both military and civilian. But Hitler survived the bomb intended for him, and the Nazis retained their firm grip on the German state. The Allies were encouraged by their rapid successes in July and August to try to destroy the German armies before winter, or to cut them off from their homeland. Patton's mechanized troops, however, ran out of fuel; the new German pilotless planes and rocket-propelled missiles delayed the full use of Antwerp as a port of supply; and by late autumn it was clear that the Germans had retired in good order to their own Siegfried Line.

From the east, the Russians had been pushing on relentlessly ever since the turning of the tide at Stalingrad. In the campaign of 1943, while the Western Allies were busy in Italy, the Russians won back most of their own territories that had been lost in 1941 and 1942. They kept up the pressure during the winter and started an early spring campaign in the south. By the autumn of 1944, the Russians had been able to sweep across Romania and Bulgaria, only half-hearted allies of Hitler, to a juncture with the Yugoslav communist guerrillas under their leader Marshal Tito, and were ready for the attack on Hungary. In the center and north, they had recovered all their own territory and were ready to attack Germany itself from the east.

This year 1945 saw the rapid conclusion of the Battle of Germany. The Russians had not stopped for winter, but had pressed on through Poland to menace Berlin early in March. The Western Allies broke through the Siegfried Line

in February, crossed the Rhine, and entered the heart of Germany. Early in February 1945 the leaders of the three great Allied powers, Stalin, Churchill, and Roosevelt, met at Yalta in the Crimea and confirmed final plans for the conquest of Germany. It was plain that the Germans, whose key industries had been so riddled from the air that they no longer could support their armies adequately, and whose manpower had been reduced to the very bottom, could not hold out for long. But the Allied planners were anxious to prevent, or at least to check, the race to be the first to arrive in Berlin, and they wanted to arrange peacefully for demarcations between the parts of Germany that each ally was to occupy. The decision to give the Russians the honor of taking Berlin is one that, with many other decisions reached in the conference at Yalta, has since been severely criticized in the West. At the time, however, it seemed a natural decision, a legitimate recognition of the fact that during the two years of successful offensive against the Germans the Russians had worn down many more German divisions than had the Western Allies.

The Russians fought their way into a Berlin already pulverized by the air power of the Western Allies. Hitler went down to his death, as he had long promised, in a Germanic funeral pyre at his Berlin headquarters.

The Allied advance into Germany revealed for the first time the full ghastliness of Nazi treatment of slave laborers from conquered lands, of political opponents and of Jews, Poles, and other German-styled "inferior" peoples. One after another, the concentration camps were liberated—Auschwitz, Belsen, Buchenwald, Dachau, Nordhausen, and others. And the world was appalled at the gas ovens that had claimed so many victims, at the piles of emaciated corpses not yet cremated, and at the pitiful state of the prisoners who had survived. This was one of the horrors of war whose reality exceeded the grimmest expectations of Allied opinion.

By May 8, 1945, Churchill and Truman (who had become the American president on Roosevelt's death in April) were able to announce the end of German resistance, the day of victory in Europe, V-E Day. It was symbolic of difficulties to come that Stalin was offended because the Western Allies had accepted from some of the German army leaders a formal surrender at Reims in France. He chose to announce separately, on Russia's part, the final victory over Germany, and not until the next day.

The Defeat of Japan

V-J Day, the day of victory in Japan, was now the great goal of Allied effort. Russia had carefully refrained from adding Japan to its formal enemies as long as Germany was still a threat. Britain and the United States, on the other hand, were anxious to win Russia as a formal fighting ally against the Japanese. This natural desire—natural in the sense of historical precedent, for coalitions in the past have usually sought to rally as many allies as possible—was responsible for many of the concessions made to Russia in the last months of the German war.

The two years of Allied successes against Germany had also been two years of Allied successes against Japan. The attack on Japan had been pressed home in three main directions. First, in a process that the American press soon christened "island-hopping," the American navy drove straight toward Japan from the central Pacific. One after another, the small island bases that stood in the way were reduced by American naval forces, which used both air support and the amphibious methods that were being worked out simultaneously in Europe and North Africa. The names of these islands are now a part of the litany of American arms—Tarawa, Eniwetok, Kwajalein, Iwo Jima, Okinawa.

Second, in a series of operations calling for the close cooperation of air, sea, and land forces, the Americans and Australians, with help from other commonwealth elements, worked their way up the southwest Pacific through the much larger islands of the Solomons, New Guinea, and the Philippines. The base for this campaign, which was under the command of the American General MacArthur, was Australia and such outlying islands as New Caledonia and the New Hebrides. The start of the campaign goes back to the first major offensive step in the Far East, the dramatic and difficult seizure of Guadalcanal in the Solomons by the United States Marines on August 7, 1942. These campaigns involved jungle fighting of the hardest sort, slow and painful work. But by October 1944 the sea forces had won the great battle of the Philippine Sea and had made possible the successful landing of MacArthur's troops on Leyte and the reconquest of the Philippine Islands themselves from the Japanese.

The third attack on the Greater East Asia Co-Prosperity Sphere (as the Japanese, imitating the West, as propagandists, called their conquered land) came from the south, in the "CBI"—the China-Burma-India theater. No brief narrative can do justice to the complex interweaving of events in this theater, where the main effort of the Allies was to get material support to Chiang Kai-shek and the Chinese Nationalists at Chungking and, if possible, to damage the Japanese position in Burma, Thailand, and Indo-China. After Pearl Harbor, when the Japanese seized and shut the famous "Burma Road," the only way for the Allies to communicate with Chiang's Nationalists was by air. It is perhaps true that the Western Allies did not invest an overwhelming proportion of their resources in this CBI theater, but they did help keep the Chinese formally in the fight. And, as the final campaign of 1945 drew on, the British, with Chinese and American aid, were holding down three Japanese field armies in this CBI theater.

The end came in Japan with a suddenness that the Allied peoples, perhaps even the Allied governments, hardly expected. From Pacific island bases, American airplanes inflicted crippling damage on Japanese industry in the spring and summer of 1945; the Japanese fleet had been almost destroyed; submarine warfare had brought the Japanese economy near to strangulation; and there was impressive evidence of the declining morale of Japanese soldiers. None the less, American decision makers were convinced that only the use of their recently invented atomic bomb could bring a quick decision and avert the very heavy casualties likely in the proposed amphibious invasion of the Japanese home islands. The result was the dropping of the first atomic bomb, on Hiroshima, August 6, 1945. On August 8, the Russians, who had agreed to come into the war against Japan once Germany was beaten, began an invasion of Manchuria in full force. Faced, after the prompt dropping of the second atomic bomb, with what they felt was certain defeat, the Japanese government, unlike the German, decided not to make a last-ditch stand in their own country. On September 2, after brief negotiations, the Japanese made formal surrender at Tokyo. Japan gave up its conquests abroad and submitted to American military occupation. Contrary to the desires of part of Allied opinion, however, the emperor of Japan was not dethroned. Purged of most of its militarists, the Japanese government continued to rule under Allied—actually American—supervision.

The Allied Coalition

The Grand Alliance, as the historian Churchill liked to call it, but mostly known in its last years as the United Nations, had mustered overpowering strength against Germany, Japan, Italy, and such collaborators as the Axis powers could secure in the Balkans, Southeast Asia, and western Europe. Britain, Russia, and the United States were the heart of the Allied coalition. But Nationalist China, for all its inefficiencies, had occupied the attention of hundreds of thousands of Japanese soldiers, and the resources of the French Empire and the French resistance movements at home and abroad had been most useful. The United Nations had been able to count on the resources of Latin America, and Brazil had been an active member of the alliance. In this truly global war, Brazilian troops had fought in Italy, which at the end had been the most cosmopolitan of theaters. There American (including Japanese-American, or Nisei), French imperial, British imperial, pro-Allied Italian, Polish, and other troops had fought, in addition to the Brazilians. At the very end of the war, even Argentina was brought into the United Nations coalition, when she declared war on Germany and Japan on March 27, 1945.

The instruments of continuing Allied union were the conferences of the "Big Three"—Churchill, Roosevelt, and Stalin—with their political and military advisers and experts, and the more frequent Anglo-American conferences. Even before the United States entered the shooting war, Roosevelt and Churchill met off Newfoundland and issued the Atlantic Charter, on August 14, 1941, in which they declared for the freedom of the seas, equality of access to economic opportunity, abandonment of aggression, and the restoration of rights to conquered peoples. The Atlantic Charter had been attacked as no more than another empty assertion of impossible ideals, but the true realist sees in it an important step in rallying world opinion against the Axis. Later, formal conferences—between Roosevelt and Churchill at Casablanca (January

1943) and Quebec (August 1943), and among the "Big Three" at Teheran (December 1943) and Yalta (February 1945)—brought to a head consultations that had been steadily carried on at lower political and military levels. From July 17 to August 17, 1945, a final great conference at Potsdam near conquered Berlin brought Britain, Russia, and the United States, with two new figures, President Truman and Prime Minister Attlee, together to confirm in general the Yalta decisions.

There were always grave military and political matters to be ironed out. It was not easy to maintain even the Anglo-American collaboration, which was perhaps the closest military collaboration between two major sovereign powers ever achieved. For the actual direction of operations in the field, the British and Americans decided to set up, not just the sort of supreme command the Allies painfully achieved late in World War I under Foch, but a complete intermeshing of staffs. All down the line, an American in command always had a Britisher as his second, and a Britisher in command always had an American as his second. In the pinch, and in spite of normal national jealousies, the arrangement worked. An anecdote about General Eisenhower from North African days relates that he sent an American officer home, not because he called his immediate superior a so-and-so, but because he called him an *English* so-and-so. At the highest level, the Combined Chiefs of Staff, in close touch with top American and British government officials, did the overall planning. The Russians could never be brought into such close military cooperation, and in the field the Russians always fought on their own.

Political Issues

A political issue that bulked large at the time with liberals seems not to have seriously divided the Allies during the war itself. This was the issue of "unconditional surrender." Here recent history had an overpowering influence on the policy adopted. Hitler had simply followed widespread German opinion in insisting that in World War I Germany had not really been defeated in the field but had been betrayed by the false promises of Wilson's Fourteen Points into surrendering while still undefeated. This time the

Asian and Pacific Theaters, 1941–45

Area under Japanese domination, Aug. 1942 ("Greater East Asia Co-Prosperity Sphere")

Island hopping U.S. -- Australian joint drive

U. S. S. R.

MONGOLIA

CHINA

SZECHWAN

Yenan○

Peiping○

Kirin○

MANCHURIA

1945

Russian land army

1945

Russian land army

Vladivostok○

SAKHALIN

KURILE IS.

JAPAN

Tokyo○

KOREA

Hiroshima○

Nagasaki○

Shanghai○

Yangtze R.

Yellow R.

Chungking○

Kunming○

Lashio○

BURMA

Burma Road

Chinese land Army

YUNNAN

British land Army

TIBET

Hanoi○

FR. INDOCHINA

THAILAND (SIAM)

Saigon○

MALAYA

Singapore○

SUMATRA

Hong Kong○

HAINAN

Manila○

LUZON

PHILIPPINE IS. (U.S.)

CORREGIDOR

BR. N. BORNEO

SARAWAK

BORNEO

NETHERLANDS

JAVA

INDIES

CELEBES

MINDANAO

LEYTE

Philippine Sea

1944 Sea

PALAU

YAP

CAROLINE ISLANDS

TRUK

Darwin○

NEW GUINEA

Lae○

Hollandia○

ADMIRALTY IS.

BISMARCK ARCH.

SOLOMON IS.

GUADALCANAL

1942

Coral Sea

NEW HEBRIDES (Br. and Fr.)

FIJI IS.

NEW CALEDONIA (Fr.)

Nouméa○

SAMOA (U.S.)

AUSTRALIA

ATOM BOMB – Aug. 6, 1945

ATOM BOMB – Aug. 9, 1945

FORMOSA

OKINAWA

RYUKYU IS.

1945

BONIN IS.

IWO JIMA

1945

MARIANAS IS.

GUAM (U.S.)

ENIWETOK

KWAJALEIN

MARCUS I.

WAKE I. (U.S.)

BIKINI

MARSHALL IS.

GILBERT IS.

ELLICE IS.

1943

1943

Pacific Ocean

MIDWAY IS. (U.S.)

JOHNSTON I.

HOWLAND I. BAKER I.

PHOENIX IS.

LINE IS.

JARVIS I.

KINGMAN REEF PALMYRA I.

HAWAIIAN IS. (U.S.)

Pearl Harbor

ATTU I.

KISKA I.

ALEUTIAN IS. (U.S.)

Indian Ocean

45

30

15

0

15

105

165

180

165

15

Allied leaders were determined to give the Germans no excuse for a future rallying point of this sort. The Germans must be beaten unmistakably, and Allied troops must enter Berlin as conquerors. There must be no political negotiation at all, simply unconditional military surrender. There was some opposition to this policy during the war, at least in lands of free political expression like Britain and the United States. This opposition rested partly on humanitarian grounds, but also on the belief that the prospect of unconditional surrender would inevitably stiffen the German will to resist, and would unite the nation behind Hitler instead of allowing Allied psychological warfare its full effect by promising anti-Nazi elements some reward for deserting the Nazi cause. In retrospect, it does not seem that Hitler would ever have negotiated with the Allies; and after the failure of the attempt to kill him with a bomb in July 1944 there was little chance that the Germans themselves would overthrow the Nazi government.

Another political problem made a much clearer rift between the British and the Americans. The underlying issue was just how far anti-German elements in France, Italy, and other occupied lands must go in proving that they were good honest democrats in order to secure the backing of the democratic Western powers. Here the difference in the underlying tone of American and British policies was evident in the views of Roosevelt and Churchill. Roosevelt was convinced that if the Allies did not interfere to support scheming conservatives and reactionaries in the occupied lands, but instead allowed their peoples to choose their form of government freely, then they would choose democracy. Churchill was much less idealistic. He was eager to use any elements that were hostile to the Germans, even if their hostility was quite recent, and he had little faith in the capacity or desire of peoples like the Italians for Anglo-Saxon democracy. Therefore he was quite willing to back Badoglio and the monarchists in Italy; Roosevelt kept insisting that the Italians wanted and needed a republic. Yet the opposition between American support of democratic or Leftist elements and British support of conservative, monarchist, Rightist elements was not a clear one. We were hard on Badoglio and soft on Vichy; the British were hard on Vichy, soft on Badoglio.

In French politics the issue was further complicated by Roosevelt's suspicions of de Gaulle, whose firm resistance in June 1940 had made him the inevitable leader of the French movement for liberation. To Roosevelt, de Gaulle seemed a potential man on horseback, no better than Boulanger or Napoleon III. To Churchill, de Gaulle seemed indeed difficult, a man obsessed with the need to restore the greatness of France, but an indispensable ally. As it turned out, the Gaullists, in collaboration with the organized French resistance in the homeland, did take over the civilian administration of French territory as it was liberated, and France by free popular vote restored in the Fourth Republic a form of government essentially like that of the Third. In Italy, the liberated people voted the establishment of a republic. What had threatened at one time to be a serious difficulty between American policy and British policy was resolved by the action of the liberated people themselves.

The anger aroused in de Gaulle himself, and in many other French leaders, by Roosevelt's policy of refusing solid support to de Gaulle and the Fighting French has embittered Franco-American relations to this day. In particular, Roosevelt's intention to "occupy" France under AMGOT (Allied Military Government in Occupied Territory) wounded the French, who thought of themselves as allies, not enemies, of the democracies.

But the political issue that has bulked largest since World War II was by no means so clear an issue during the war itself. This is the problem of Russian domination in eastern and southeastern Europe. It is easy to say that at Yalta the Western powers took much too soft a line with the Russians, allowed them to push their armies much too far westward, and relied foolishly on Russian promises to permit free elections in Poland, Hungary, Czechoslovakia, and the Balkans. This criticism may be supplemented by the old British motif of the "soft underbelly," by maintaining that the Western powers should have struck as soon as possible, perhaps in 1943, from the Mediterranean into the Danube Valley in order to get there ahead of the Russians. Proponents of these criticisms present us with an Iron Curtain that would then have been drawn far to the east of where it now is, with an eastern and a southeastern Europe that would now be democratic and on the side of the West rather than on the side of the Russians.

The chief trouble with this argument is that it fails to take into account two basic facts. First, most of the small eastern European countries had no real tradition of Western-style democracy; most of them had moved toward fascist totalitarianism before World War II. Their transition to communist totalitarianism was easy. Second, during the war itself it was by no means clear to Western leaders, or to Western public opinion, that the Germans and the Japanese would be beaten so readily. Even leaders like Churchill, who seems never really to have trusted the Russians and who was to coin the phrase "the Iron Curtain" soon after the war, did not dare risk losing the aid of Russian manpower and material resources during the war itself. Even in 1945, at Yalta, with Japan still very much in the fight, appeasement of the Russians seemed absolutely essential, not only to Roosevelt, who hoped the Russians would collaborate with us in the postwar world, but also to Churchill, who seems to have had little if any hope of such collaboration from the Russians.

In the Far East, political problems seemed less serious—at least in wartime. There was general agreement that the Chinese Nationalists, however corrupt and inefficient their government was, had to be supported against the Japanese. Nor did the final decision to accept the continuance on the throne of the Japanese emperor arouse serious opposition in the West. The critical decisions on the Far East were rather the work of the troubled period after V-E and V-J days, when to the bitter disappointment of most Western peoples it became clear that the peace was likely for some time to be no more than a continuation of war. Indeed, there was no peace, and these years deserve a term that was soon coined, the years of "cold war." The once "colonial" peoples throughout the world were now roused against "imperialism."

In sum, as we all know now, and as we shall see in more detail in the next chapters, the great war of 1939–1945 ended indeed, but there was no peace. From our own Western point of view, and in plain language, the defeat of the perturbers, the aggressors, the villains, Germany and Japan, was almost immediately followed by the rise of a new perturber, a new villain, Russia, which had already given clear indications of its perturbing power. And indeed, it is easy to go on to the conclusion that just because the Germans and Japanese were beaten in the way they actually were, the present menace of Russia—pretty clearly a greater menace than the old German menace—was helped, was in fact made possible, by that defeat; from there it is a fatally easy step to the dangerous conclusion that Russia, not Germany, was our enemy all along.

Yet the wise student of history will not readily jump to the conclusion that any other Allied policy, and in particular a different American policy at Yalta and Potsdam, could have either prevented the rise of Russia or produced a virtuous, cooperative, democratic Russia. We are still far too close to World War II to understand its many ramifications. The historian who sticks to his last can do no more than conclude that in the perspective of modern Western history the sorely tried Western statesmen at Yalta in the midst of a hot war were using time-honored methods to win that war as quickly and as decisively as possible: and in particular, with the long record of failures of coalitions in the past before them, they were determined to hold together their extraordinary and by no means "natural" coalition, known hopefully as the United Nations, until *both* the mainstay powers of the Axis coalition had been beaten. This they did.

Reading Suggestions on the Second World War

GENERAL ACCOUNTS

W. S. Churchill, *The Second World War,* 6 vols. (Houghton, 1948–1953). Magisterial account by a chief architect of Allied victory.

E. H. Carr, *The Twenty Years' Crisis* (*Beacon). A stimulating review of interwar diplomacy by a capable and opinionated Englishman.

F. L. Snyder, *The War: A Concise History, 1939–1945* (Messner, 1960), and K. S. Davis, *Experience of War: The U.S. in World War II* (Doubleday, 1965). With full notes and bibliography.

J. F. C. Fuller, *The Second World War* (Duell, Sloane, and Pearce, 1949), and C. Falls, *The Second World War,* 2nd ed. (Methuen, 1948). Succinct military accounts.

D. Flower and J. Reeves, eds., *The Taste of Courage: The War, 1939–1945* (Harper, 1960). A good anthology of "war pieces."

F. Pratt, *War for the World: A Chronicle of Our Fighting Forces in World War II* (Yale Univ. Press, 1950). A good succinct American account.

United States Army in World War II (Dept. of the Army, 1947). The official history, in many detailed volumes, to be found in library catalogs under the general title above, or under "United States: Department of the Army."

S. E. Morison, *History of United States Naval Operations in World War II*, 15 vols. (Little, Brown, 1947–1962). Official but detached and professional history, with full attention to political and diplomatic problems.

C. Wilmot, *The Struggle for Europe* (Harper, 1952). Highly controversial study, critical of the American high command.

SPECIAL STUDIES   F. Gilbert and G. A. Craig, eds., *The Diplomats, 1919–1939* (Princeton Univ. Press, 1953). A helpful symposium.

A. Wolfers, *Britain and France between Two Wars* (Harcourt, Brace, 1940). A solid analysis of the foreign policies of the two powers.

S. R. Smith, *The Manchurian Crisis, 1931–1932* (Columbia Univ. Press, 1948). On the watershed between postwar and prewar periods.

J. W. Wheeler-Bennett, *Munich: Prologue to Tragedy* (Macmillan, 1948), and L. B. Namier, *Diplomatic Prelude, 1938–1939* (Macmillan, 1948). Good studies of the last international crises before World War II.

W. L. Langer and S. E. Gleason, *The Challenge to Isolation, 1937–1940* (Harper, 1952), and *The Undeclared War, 1940–1941* (Harper, 1953). Solid studies of America's role.

C. C. Tansill, *Back Door to War: The Roosevelt Foreign Policy* (Regnery, 1952). Alleging that Roosevelt pushed America into war.

H. F. Armstrong, *Chronology of Failure* (Macmillan, 1940); "Pertinax" (André Géraud), *The Gravediggers of France* (Doubleday, 1944); M. Bloch, *Strange Defeat* (Oxford Univ. Press, 1949). Three perceptive studies of the French defeat in 1940.

A. J. Liebling, ed., *The Republic of Silence* (Harcourt, Brace, 1947). Excellent collection of materials pertaining to the French resistance movement.

L. Collins and D. LaPierre, *Is Paris Burning?* (Simon and Schuster, 1965). Deservedly best-selling account of the liberation of Paris.

R. Wohlstetter, *Pearl Harbor: Warning and Decision* (Stanford Univ. Press, 1962). First-rate monograph.

A. Weber, *Farewell to European History; or, the Conquest of Nihilism* (Kegan Paul, Trench, Trubner, 1947). A German sociologist reviews—and regrets—his country's part in the crises of World War II.

D. L. Gordon and R. Dangerfield, *The Hidden Weapon: The Story of Economic Warfare* (Harper, 1947). A very good popular account by trained experts.

H. Feis, *Churchill, Roosevelt, Stalin* (Princeton Univ. Press, 1957). A fascinating and very fair-minded account of their wartime relationship.

There are many memoirs of actors in this great war. The following make a good beginning: D. D. Eisenhower, *Crusade in Europe* (Doubleday, 1948); H. Truman, *Memoirs*, 2 vols. (Doubleday, 1958); B. L. Montgomery, *Memoirs* (World, 1958); C. de Gaulle, *War Memories* (Simon and Schuster, 1964).

30

The Postwar World,
1945–1970

Part 1

The years between 1945 and 1970 were crowded years, too crowded to allow of even a full summary account in these pages. Moreover, the 1960's at least still were too close to us to make it possible to reach sound judgments on the meaning of events and their true historical relationships to each other. These were "current events," not history. Yet these events made up our lives, and it would be total abdication—we think—to have discoursed (as we cheerfully admit we have done) learnedly and at length about the more remote past and then to deny ourselves the duty and pleasure of selecting some of the obviously important occurrences and issues that had arisen even as late as the 1960's, and commenting upon them, even at the risk of having to eat our words in some later edition.

The two chapters that follow, then, try to meet this challenge. They come down to 1970.

Above: Unsettled conditions in postwar France: Policemen joining striking government workers in Paris, 1947. Above right: Police stopping passers through Berlin's famed Brandenburg Gate, postwar symbol of divided Germany. Right: National Guardsmen hurl tear gas at students of Kent State University, May 4, 1970.

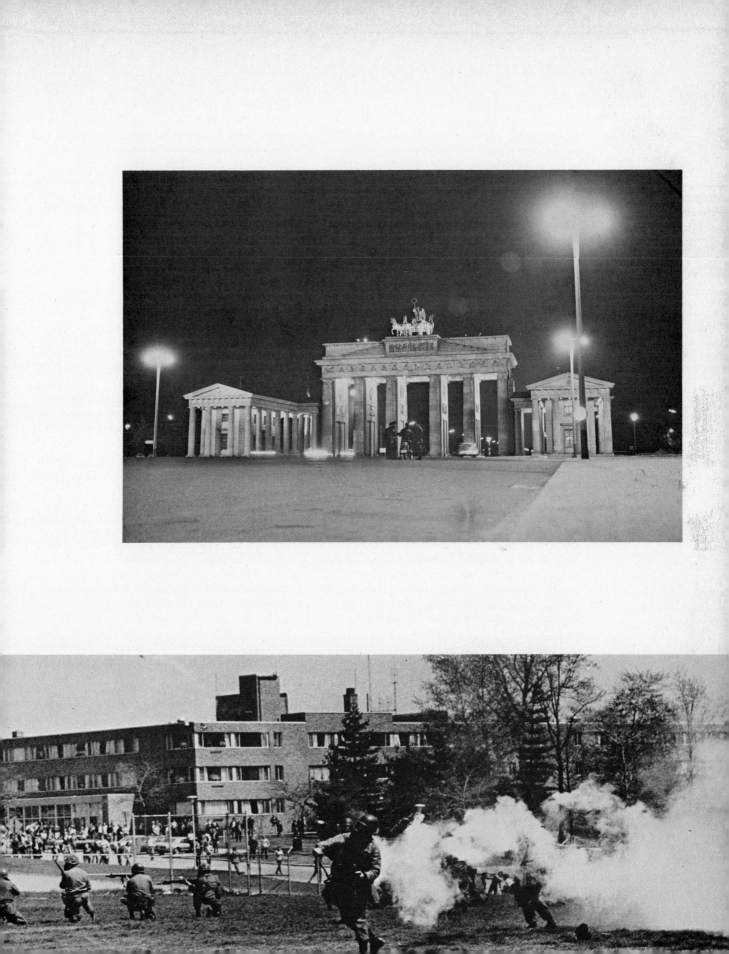

They belong together. In the first of the two, we discuss the phenomenon of the Cold War in general terms, and then turn to a brief account and estimate of the domestic affairs and prospects of the major Western nations and of the Soviet Union. In the second, we begin with Soviet foreign policy, and its relationship to international affairs in general, and then move on to the great international confrontation to which it made such a contribution: the U.S.S.R., China, and America in Asia, of which the Vietnam war was only the most recent manifestation. Finally we deal with the emerging nations of Africa, the Middle East, and Latin America, and try to view them both from within and from the point of view of great-power politics. The two chapters are divided for convenience only, and have been written as a unit.

I   The Cold War

By 1970 (the time of this writing) twenty-five years had elapsed since the end of World War II, four years more than the twenty-one years that separated the end of World War I in 1918 from the beginning of the Second World War in 1939. Already the world had exceeded, if only by a little, the time it allowed itself for peace and reconstruction after the first of its twentieth-century mass wars. It might seem ironical to take comfort in so negative and chilling a reflection, yet there were further ironies: The very existence of the new atomic weapons that would probably kill off much of the human race in another great war had acted as a deterrent. Man's worst fears had not been realized; Armageddon had not yet taken place, and this in itself was indeed a comfort. Nor did Armageddon in 1970 loom on the horizon, as several times during the tumultuous years since 1945 it had seemed to do. The years after 1945 were full of anxiety, of contention, of fighting in the various parts of the globe, but the worst had not happened, and perhaps it never would happen.

During World War II, most people expected that when the shooting stopped there would be a general peace conference, as there had been after all the major general wars of modern time. But as it turned out, basic differences in outlook between the Soviet Union and its Western allies, and the tensions that arose between them during the war itself made it impossible to plan for, much less convoke, a peace conference. So World War II bequeathed to mankind a legacy of problems to be solved one by one if at all.

The devastation wrought by the war greatly exceeded even that in World War I: 22 million dead, more than half of them civilians, and more than $2,000 billion in damage. Despite a sharply rising birth rate and vast programs of economic reconstruction, such losses could never be fully repaired. Moreover, new and terrifying problems faced the statesmen of the world. Atomic weapons, hydrogen bombs, the possibility—and soon the development—of guided missiles, made concrete and plausible the threat that a new general war might wipe out the human race or return what was left of mankind to something like another Stone Age. At the same time, the United States and the Soviet Union emerged initially as the only powers capable of initiating or pursuing the new warfare. Given the ideology of the U.S.S.R. and the suspicious and vengeful character of its supreme dictator Stalin, it was inevitable that the Russians would regard the Americans as their rivals for control of the world, and that the Americans should quickly have been forced to accept the same estimate of the situation. The postwar history of international politics thus became in large part a history of Soviet-American rivalry: the Cold War.

In 1945 enemy attack and occupation had caused incalculable devastation inside the Russian borders, and left millions of survivors destitute, while Russia's capitalist ally, the United States, had remained intact and had invented and used atomic weapons. Stalin, who liked nothing so much as the destruction of an enemy, and who regarded the whole capitalist world as his enemy, knew that if he had been the sole possessor of the atomic bomb, he would have used it. He attributed to his rival the strategy that he himself would have pursued. It seemed to him that all the technological advance of the Soviet period, undertaken precisely to bring the U.S.S.R. up to the industrialized West, had now been wiped out by the American development of the atomic bomb. It took Stalin four years (1945–1949) to catch up once again, by making his own atomic bomb. No doubt, scientific information given the Russians by agents and spies made some contribution to this achievement, but only the high level of Soviet science and technology and the Soviet capacity to concentrate their investments made it possible at all.

A Divided World: Germany and China

Even before the U.S.S.R. could join the United States as an atomic power in 1949, the two had engaged in a series of tests of will, in Europe and in Asia, that determined where the increasingly clear boundary between a Russian sphere of influence and an American sphere of influence would run. And the confrontation continued after 1949. In Iran, in Greece, in Berlin, in Korea the lines were drawn, tested, and redrawn, sometimes after bloodshed. Though the Soviet Union and its former Western allies were able to reach agreement on peace treaties with Italy and with three of the Axis powers' former European satellites—Hungary, Romania, and Bulgaria—no such treaty could be concluded with Germany itself or with Japan.

The United States occupied Japan alone. But defeated Germany was divided into four zones —American, British, French, and Russian. The U.S.S.R. obtained the eastern regions of Germany bordering on Poland and extending considerably west of Berlin, which, as the former capital, was also divided into four occupation zones, one for each of the Allies. This arrangement was designed for temporary military occupation, but continued in effect because no treaty could be reached. It proved extremely dangerous, for it left Berlin as an island surrounded by Soviet-dominated territory, yet an island including zones to which the Western allies were entitled to have access. The failure to reach any settlement over Germany left the most serious problem in Europe without a solution.

In 1949, the three Western powers allowed their respective zones to unite in the Federal Republic of Germany, called West Germany, with its capital at Bonn, and the Russians responded by creating the communist German Democratic Republic—East Germany—with its capital at Pankow outside Berlin. Many if not most West Germans were naturally eager for reunion with their fellow Germans in the Soviet

zone. Yet a reunion of Germany under Western capitalist auspices was precisely what the Russians feared most, believing that it would portend a revival of aggression. An all-communist Germany was equally intolerable to the Western powers. Indeed, few Frenchmen or Englishmen looked with enthusiasm upon the idea of any reunified Germany, and if there were more Americans who sympathized with reunion as an ultimate goal, there were no responsible men in high places who failed to understand the dangers of trying to bring it about unilaterally.

In Asia—with Japan under American occupation—the most grievous problem remained that of China. The communists, who had challenged Chiang Kai-shek's ruling Kuomintang (nationalist) party for power, kept their forces in being during the years of Japanese occupation. The United States tried in 1946-1947 to bring about an agreement between Chinese nationalists and communists that would end the civil war. The effort failed, and the civil war continued. By 1949, the communists had defeated Chiang Kai-shek, who took refuge on the offshore island of Formosa (Taiwan), where the communists could not follow because they had no fleet. In the last years of the struggle, Chiang had lost his hold over the Chinese people; the morale of his own forces was low, and an ever-mounting inflation ravaged the economy, already ruined by the long Japanese occupation. By 1950, mainland China had gone communist, and formed part of the Soviet bloc. Only Chiang's government in Taiwan remained a part of the American bloc. American foreign policy had suffered a major defeat. Some Americans blamed the failure on a conspiracy by a few evil men, but the magnitude of the change, the huge numbers of Chinese involved, rendered this explanation improbable.

Elsewhere too the Soviet Union pursued its goal of turning the whole world communist through the agencies of individual Communist parties. In virtually every country a Communist party existed, sometimes strong—as in France or Italy—sometimes weak—as in Britain or the United States—often varying in its precise degree of subservience to the Communist party of the Soviet Union (CPSU) and the Soviet government, but almost always prepared to act as the domestic agent for Soviet interests and policies. The United States, by contrast, had no such disciplined and reliable supporters in most of the world.

The Two Coalitions

The Soviet Union thus had a certain advantage in the Cold War, which consisted in part of a competition between the two superpowers for the allegiance and support of the rest of the world. Each became the leader of a great coalition, whose members were attached more or less tightly by bonds of self-interest to the senior partner.

The members of the loose American coalition in 1945 included the Western hemisphere, Great Britain, western Europe, Japan, the Philippines, Australia, and New Zealand. The Soviet coalition included the countries of eastern Europe and, by 1949, China. The border between the two coalitions in Europe—called the "Iron Curtain" by Winston Churchill in 1946—ran along a north-south line extending from Stettin on the Baltic to Trieste on the Adriatic. Yugoslavia lay in the Soviet sphere, and the frontier resumed again with the border between northern Greece and communist Albania, Yugoslavia, and Bulgaria. Turkey belonged to the Western coalition, and portions of the Middle East and of Southeast Asia were linked to it by a network of pacts. The

dividing line between North and South Korea, with the U.S.S.R. occupying the north and the United States the south, represented a kind of Asian extension of the long frontier between the two coalitions. Along the frontier came the aggressive Soviet probing operations that led to crises and in several cases to wars.

Repeatedly the United States sought in vain to ease the relationships between the two coalitions. In 1946, Stalin refused to join in a United Nations atomic energy commission, or to have anything to do with international control of atomic weapons. In 1947, the United States proposed an international plan of massive American economic aid to accelerate European recovery from the ruin of the war, the Marshall Plan, so called for George C. Marshall, then Secretary of State. The Soviet Union refused to accept the aid for itself, and would not let its satellites participate. The Marshall Plan nations subsequently formed the nucleus of the North Atlantic Treaty Organization (NATO: 1949). The Soviet coalition founded the Cominform (Communist Information Bureau) in 1947 as a successor to the former Comintern, "abolished" during the war, and created the Warsaw Pact (1955), binding eastern Europe together, as an answer to NATO. The United States and Britain sought in the 1950's and 1960's by a variety of means to pre-

Signing of the Warsaw Pact by the prime minister of Poland, 1955. The five figures at the right of the picture are Khrushchev, Zhukov, Malenkov, Bulganin, and Molotov.

vent the spread of atomic weapons: the chief device was to be a plan for a joint Multilateral (Nuclear) Force in which the Germans would participate. The French rejected MLF, and in 1966 their president, General de Gaulle, gave notice that at the expiration in 1969 of the treaty establishing NATO he would not renew it in its present form. At his insistence NATO headquarters were moved from France to Belgium.

In the Near East, the Baghdad Pact and its successor, the Central Treaty Organization (CENTO), proved no more than a series of agreements among the United States, Britain, Turkey, Iran, and Pakistan. With the withdrawal of Iraq from the Baghdad Pact in 1959, no direct alliances linked the Arab world with the West. In the Far East, on the other hand, the Southeast Asia Treaty Organization (SEATO) meant that the United States could count solidly on Australia, New Zealand, the Philippines, and Thailand.

Outside the coalitions remained the neutral nations. Some, like Switzerland or Sweden, were simply maintaining their traditional legal policies of not aligning themselves with any grouping of powers. But most belonged to the new nations that were now emerging as independent, having discarded their former colonial status. Of these India was the most influential, taking from both coalitions much-needed economic assistance. As economic aid became an instrument in the Cold War, neutral nations tried, often with success, to play the Americans off against the Russians, raising the not too subtle threat that if Washington saw fit to deprive them of something they wanted, they might regretfully have to go communist. It was not until the 1960's that the United States learned to regard neutrality as often positively helpful to its interests.

The United Nations

Through the years of cold war, and the occasional outbreaks of something hotter, the United Nations—formed during World War II from among the opponents of the Axis and chartered in 1945 at San Francisco—served as an international organization where members of both coalitions and neutrals alike could meet in peaceful discussion. As direct successor to the League of Nations, it inherited the League's duty of keeping the peace, but like the League it lacked independent sovereignty or authority over its members. To deal with threats to the peace its charter created a Security Council with eleven member states, five of which—the United States, the Soviet Union, Great Britain, France, and China—held permanent memberships. The other six were elected to rotating two-year terms by the General Assembly, to which all member states belonged. The Secretary General, elected by the Security Council, could exert great personal influence in international affairs. But each of the five permanent members of the Security Council had a veto over any substantive question. Decisions had to be unanimous before action could go forward. Both the U.S.S.R. and the United States insisted on this provision in the charter. As a result, the Security Council often found itself unable to act because of a veto: of the eighty vetoes cast between 1945 and 1955 the U.S.S.R. cast seventy-seven.

In the mid-Fifties new nations joined the UN: some pro-Western, like Austria and Italy (both former Axis states and so originally excluded), some pro-Soviet, like Romania, Bulgaria, and the other former Axis satellites in eastern Europe, and some neutral and mostly former colonies, like Ceylon or Libya. Japan joined in 1956. As former colonies obtained their independence during the late Fifties and early Sixties, each joined the United Nations, where the "Afro-Asian bloc" came to command a majority in the General Assembly. Germany remained outside the UN, but both East and West Germany had their observers there. The United States successfully opposed the seating of the Chinese communists, which left the permanent Chinese seat on the Security Council in the possession of Chiang Kai-shek's representative. The three successive secretaries general were the Norwegian Trygve Lie, the Swedish Dag Hammarskjöld, and the Burmese U Thant.

Though the UN could not "settle" the Cold War, or bring about the international control of atomic weapons, it did repeatedly manage to prevent small wars from becoming big ones. The League of Nations had never been able to put its own forces into the field, but the UN did so repeatedly: in Korea in 1950–1952 (where, because of the absence of the Soviet representative from the Security Council, the Russians failed to veto the Council's decision to intervene, and the American army fought under the sponsorship of the UN); on the Arab–Israeli frontiers (1956–1967); in the former Belgian Congo; and in Cyprus.

Through its functional councils and special agencies—the Economic and Social Council, the Educational, Scientific, and Cultural Organization (UNESCO), the World Health Organization, the Food and Agricultural Organization, and the World Bank—the UN advanced loans to governments to initiate new development plans, controlled epidemics, and provided experts on modern farming techniques. The UN's international civil servants deserved well of mankind. Occasional critics disliked the organization's striking buildings in New York, and wished that it had never left Switzerland because it might now be mistakenly taken for an instrument of American imperialism. Occasional isolationist Americans demanded that "the U.S. get out of the UN and the UN get out of the U.S.," while those who took the opposite view urged that the UN be given more "teeth," and that the nations abandon more of their sovereignty to it. Yet with its successes and its faults the UN reflected both the diversity and the elements of unity in the world of which it was the forum, and perhaps it would have been unreasonable to ask more of it than that.

II The Major Free-World States

The United States

Instead of reverting to isolationism, as it had in the years after 1918, the United States took the lead in organizing both the United Nations and the network of alliances that constituted its own coalition. Vigorously it put through various programs of economic aid to other countries, beginning with the Marshall Plan and continuing by assisting the newly emerging countries of the former colonial world. Some of the money went for military assistance, most for economic development. Grumblings at home were many, but both political parties generally espoused these programs, and it was not until the American government began to suffer from the special strains imposed by the Vietnam War in the years after 1965 that the sums appropriated for foreign aid were substantially cut.

The rough agreement between the Republicans and Democrats on foreign policy was actually shared on domestic policies as well, although this statement would be hotly challenged by professional politicians of either side. The stereotyped view continued to prevail that the Democrats were the more liberal and radical of the two parties and the Republicans the more conservative, yet when, in 1952, for the first time in twenty years, the Republicans elected a president, he was not really a politician at all, but General Dwight D. Eisenhower, a popular hero because of his performance as Supreme Allied Commander in World War II.

And during eight years (1953–1960) the Eisenhower administration not only did not repeal the New Deal enactments of the Roosevelt period, which had been continued and extended by Roosevelt's former vice-president Harry Truman in the years from 1945 to 1952, but left them intact and even expanded the system of social security. An occasional Republican politician might darkly threaten to sell the Tennessee Valley Authority to private companies, but no responsible Republican leader ever wasted his time trying to do so. Nor, despite the effort to tag the Democrats as the "war party," did the Republicans shift the bases of foreign policy: Eisenhower's secretary of state, John Foster Dulles, spoke of "rolling the Russians back" and "liberating" their satellites in eastern Europe, but when he was challenged by Soviet military intervention in Hungary in 1956 he did nothing—exactly what the Democrats would have done.

The early 1950's brought—as a kind of domestic response to the Cold War—an extraordinary episode, in which a single senator, the late Joseph McCarthy of Wisconsin, led an onslaught against American civil servants whom he called communists. The fact that some genuine American communists had actually obtained government posts and had in some cases passed valuable information to the Russians lent some credibility to McCarthy's performances. But he himself never located a single communist in high places, while he did attack many persons on the flimsiest evidence or none at all. Bad as it was, the McCarthy period was no reign of terror: no blood was shed, the prisons were not filled, brave men opposed him, and in 1954 he was condemned by his fellow senators 67 to 22 for abuse of his powers. The spectacle of McCarthy bullying witnesses on television—then a new device—helped arouse the public against him.

In 1946, the U.S. government "freed" the Philippine Islands, which became a sovereign state. Puerto Rico, a colonial dependency until 1952, in that year became a free associated state, or commonwealth, with its own constitution and its own government. In 1958 Alaska and in 1959 Hawaii became states of the Union.

The United States was generally extremely prosperous and productive during these postwar years, with only occasional recessions and readjustments. So remarkable was the steady growth of the gross national product, and so careful the attention given the economy by experts, that some came to feel that the Americans had learned how to avoid depression altogether. The general affluence, which made the United States, despite its very rich men, the most nearly classless country in the world, did not, however, by any means filter down satisfactorily to the poorest members of society. In the presidency of Lyndon Johnson (1963–1968), when a series of programs to assist the poor was proposed, much of the planned effort had to be abandoned because of the heavy expense of the war in Vietnam. The strains imposed by the war, accompanied by increasing domestic unrest and by inflation, and by rising unemployment continued to mount in the first two years of the presidency of Richard M. Nixon, a Republican and former vice-president under Eisenhower, elected in November 1968 by a narrow margin over the Democratic Hubert H. Humphrey. Humphrey, Johnson's vice-president, was nominated by his party after Johnson himself had refused to run again in recognition of the unpopularity of the Vietnam war.

The fact that so many of the poor in the United States were black exacerbated what was already the gravest American social problem. Though gifted blacks had won recognition in the arts, in sports, in the field of entertainment, and often in business and the professions, the race as a whole was none the less handicapped by the failure of American society to provide its members with equal opportunities for education and for jobs. This was true not only in the South, more agricultural than the North, with memories of slavery and the northern victory in the Civil War still fresh, where some whites retained bitter antiblack prejudice and refused to permit the black man to advance himself; but also in the cities of the North, where hundreds of thousands of blacks had flocked to live, and where their lot was often squalid and seemingly hopeless.

In 1954, the Supreme Court unanimously declared that the existence of separate compulsory public schools for blacks was unconstitutional. This major decision, of course, immediately affected chiefly the South, where "separate but equal" education for the two races had been the theoretical rule, but where the separate black schools had usually been markedly inferior. In any case, the Court declared, separate education could not be equal education. The years that followed saw varying degrees of compliance with the new requirement: most parts of the South were determined to disobey the Court by one means or another, or, if they obeyed, to admit only "token" numbers of black students to predominantly white schools. Many efforts were made to speed compliance. By 1970 there were some black students studying with whites in every state of the Union, and in the border states and in some cities of the Deep South, such as Atlanta, the number was large. Southern state universities were also desegregated, after some efforts at resistance. But of course the existence in the northern cities of the black "ghettos" and the prevalence of neighborhood schools everywhere meant that public education in New York or Boston was often as segregated as it was in Mississippi. Northern whites often opposed "bussing" children out of their home neighborhoods to school as a method of equalizing the numbers of black and white children just as vigorously as southern whites opposed desegregation in principle. Many predominantly white universities were striving to find and admit qualified black students, and institutions previously black had begun to worry about losing their most talented pupils. Southern white support for Nixon in the election of 1968 left him with a political debt to southern politicians, and many observers felt that the diminished efforts of the federal government to enforce desegregation reflected an effort to repay this debt. In 1970, the problem of equal education for the races remained a serious one. Moreover, Nixon was apparently trying to diminish the future political appeal of the outspoken segregationist George Wallace among southerners by "going easy" with further desegregation.

The drive to improve conditions for blacks extended far beyond education. In the late Fifties and early Sixties white and blacks worked to increase the registration of black voters in the South, and to liberalize real-estate practices to enable blacks to buy houses wherever they wished. Both drives made considerable headway. Some blacks, feeling that justice could never be gained by gradual means, turned away from the organizations—such as the National Association for the Advancement of Colored People (NAACP)—which had traditionally preferred to work by persuasion, toward more militant groups. Even the Reverend Martin Luther King, a nonviolent black minister from the South who had sponsored the successful black boycott of buses in Montgomery, Alabama, and forced the bus lines to end segregation, lost some of his large following to other groups advocating one form or another of "Black Power."

During the summers of 1965, 1966, and 1967, severe rioting broke out in the Watts district of Los Angeles and in Newark, Detroit, and other northern cities; blacks burned large portions of their own neighborhoods, looted shops, and engaged in gunfights with the police. The passage of a federal Civil Rights Bill in 1965 and the outlawing of discrimination in real-estate transactions did not calm the stormy situation. While black violence aroused bitter protest especially among whites who opposed any improvement in the Negro's status, even moderates who favored the black advance hated the riots, and grew more and more anxious about public order. This anxiety was surely a factor in Nixon's victory over Humphrey in the election of 1968.

Among black militant movements, by 1970 the Black Panther party had emerged as perhaps the most influential. Its founder, Eldridge Cleaver, had published a widely read autobiography, *Soul on Ice,* a fierce and shocking document that aroused both sympathy and horror among its many readers, white and black, perhaps replacing as the key book in the field the earlier *Autobiography of Malcolm X,* the Black Muslim leader assassinated by a rival faction. Cleaver, under a prison sentence, fled the United States, but continued from Algiers to command much influence over the movement. Panthers at home preached and engaged in violence, sometimes with the support of whites who believed in

one revolutionary doctrine or another, more often perhaps repudiating any white assistance whatever. Inevitably, the conflict often narrowed down in the cities to one between Panthers and the guardians of law and order, the police. In Chicago, on one such occasion, two Panthers were killed in a "shoot-out" with police that the Panthers claimed had been a deliberate police ambush. In New Haven, the scheduled trial of other Panthers, accused of murdering a former member of their own group, aroused tension not only local but national.

But the new wave of violence in American life derived not only from the race question. John F. Kennedy, the first Roman Catholic to be elected president, succeeding Eisenhower and defeating Nixon (1960), was a young man of intelligence, personal elegance, and charm. His successor movement to the New Deal, which he called the New Frontier, envisioned federal medical care for the aged, tax reform, civil rights, and anti-poverty measures. But Kennedy was assassinated in 1963 by a psychopathic killer with a rifle. Televised details of the crime came into every American home, as did the fantastic subsequent murder of the assassin by another psychopath.

The deaths and destruction in the summer riots of 1965, '66, and '67, the murder of Martin Luther King himself—also by rifle—in 1968, and the murder by pistol of President Kennedy's brother, Senator Robert F. Kennedy of New York, while he was campaigning to secure the Democratic nomination for the presidency in 1968, all combined with lesser crimes to produce a major public revulsion: but not one powerful enough to persuade the Congress to enact a drastic statute against the easy public procurement of guns. Crime continued to present a severe and growing problem.

Lyndon Johnson's administration successfully put through much of the social program that President Kennedy had not been able to achieve. But the gains were outweighed in the public mind by the cost in life and money of the war in Vietnam and the rising discontent with a society that could not better distribute its own affluence. City life, in particular, seemed to degenerate as rapidly as prosperity increased. Together with racial tension and crime, the pollution of the air and water, the intolerable pile-up of motor and truck traffic belching poisonous fumes, the multiplication of strikes by sanitation employees, teachers, air traffic control officers, and others made urban life hardly bearable. Your

Dr. Martin Luther King Jr. with James Foreman in Montgomery, Alabama.

garbage sometimes festered in the streets, your children failed to receive the public education for which you were paying, you were not safe if you walked home at night, and you could not even get out of town by car or plane, while the railroad system had apparently suffered a total breakdown. What you ate or drank was likely to be unsafe for human consumption, and your municipal government was probably both corrupt and bankrupt. Yet your taxes rose faster than your fast-increasing income. In the suburbs, neat lawns and good public schools concealed imperfectly what some felt to be a cultural desert, while others fought to preserve what they had so recently acquired from encroachments, aggressions, and looming threats.

Children of the well-to-do, pampered by any standard, were "opting out" of the society in large numbers. Some took drugs—the increasingly fashionable marijuana, or "pot," which they insisted (against much medical evidence) was no more harmful than the alcohol their parents had always indulged in; or more addictive and dangerous drugs such as heroin, or LSD, or even the deadly "speed." Many of these left home, congregated in special places (San Francisco's Haight-Ashbury district, New York's East Village), living from hand to mouth or handout to handout, eccentrically dressed in American Indian feathers or beads, affecting what they believed to be Buddhist ideas, speaking a special dialect, and protesting their love for everybody, which often looked uncommonly like hate. These were the "hippies." A multiple murder of incredible mindless violence in California allegedly committed by a roving group of hippies served to focus public attention on the number of young men and women self-outlawed from American society, who had apparently crossed the line into a new mad universe.

Other young people actively rebelled against the institutions of their immediate world, the university or the draft board. Some strongly supported the candidacy of Senator Eugene McCarthy of Minnesota for the Democratic nomination for president in 1968, and were bitterly disappointed when he lost out to Humphrey at the party convention in Chicago amid scenes of police and student violence in the streets. Some took Mao Tse-tung or the Cuban guerrilla leader Che Guevara, killed in Bolivia, as their heroes, and the difficult writings of Herbert Marcuse as their inspiration. Starting at the University of California in Berkeley and Columbia University in New York, and moving then to Harvard and Cornell and other institutions small and large, student radical violence in 1968 and 1969 usually took the form of sit-ins or building seizures, often accompanied by the disruption of classes, the theft of documents from files, and the intimidation of individual professors or administrators. The perpetrators of these acts generally argued that this was the sole means of obtaining favorable responses to one or another set of "demands," often local but usually including some that bore on the nation's problems (abolish ROTC because the Vietnam war is wicked, build more housing for the poor, grant open admission to blacks). Universities as such had as a rule no power to influence national policies; so the demands were often delivered to the wrong address.

The singling out of universities as the target clearly reflected radical student frustration with efforts to influence public life in other ways. From the beginning of the movement, however, one could observe among violent students some few who were eager to overthrow American society altogether, and were beginning with the institution closest to their own lives. "Tear it all down first, and then discuss what should be put in its place" was an argument that Bakunin would have recognized and welcomed. When university authorities summoned the police or the National Guard to quell violence, the usual effect was to turn moderate students into radicals. The universities were thus faced with a painful dilemma, as their radical enemies realized: either to submit to intimidation and violence from the Left, or, in fighting the Left, vastly to increase its numbers. When the National Guard fired into a student demonstration at Kent State University in Ohio, in 1970, killing four students, all white, and within a few days police in Mississippi killed two more, this time black, there was a national cry of outrage on the university campuses.

On the far Left fringe of the student radical movement were those who used bombs against university buildings, banks, or public buildings. Once at least they manufactured their explosives in the basement of a townhouse considerably provided by generous parents, which in this case the enthusiasts managed to blow up, presumably in error. And as student unrest swelled, outraged Americans of older generations and of all social classes grew more militant against it. The construction workers or "hard hats," the police in some communities, those everywhere who believed in seeking one's political and economic goals by traditional peaceful means, to some degree shared the sense of outrage. And the most unhappy among them found their spokesman in Nixon's vice-president, Spiro Agnew, who repeatedly flailed away at rebellious youth.

By no means exclusively an American phenomenon, the rebellion of the children of the rich reminded many observers of the Russian nihilists and anarchists of the nineteenth century. The Russian "establishment" of the nineteenth century had not understood how to isolate the extremists among the rebels by embracing the moderates. Perhaps twentieth-century Americans would ponder the lesson.

So it was that by 1970 America seemed to many to be trapped in full domestic crisis. Even the national prosperity was shaken, as the war continued, inflation grew worse, and the stock market fell. Race relations, public order, the crisis of the cities, the disaffection of the young: everywhere one turned one could read (interminably and not very helpfully) about all of them. The often strident voices of the "woman's liberation" movement added a new militant note to the chorus. Outraged by injustices such as the inability of talented women to obtain equal pay for equal work, the female militants sometimes sounded as if they were determined to end the human family as an institution.

Canada

After 1945, Canada enjoyed an economic growth and prosperity proportionately even greater than that of the United States. American capital poured in, and much was raised at home and in Britain. Though still producing vast amounts of raw materials from farm, mine, and forest, Canada came now to be a great industrial nation, exploiting her remarkable hydroelectric resources and her oil and mineral wealth. In the mid-Fifties Canada took the lead in carrying out a long-discussed plan for a canal from the Great Lakes to the lower St. Lawrence, deep enough to accommodate ocean-going ships, and producing in addition important hydroelectric power. In the United States, vested interests long succeeded in preventing American participation. But when Canada announced her intention of going ahead with the canal entirely on Canadian territory, the United States joined in a collaborative development; work began in 1954, and the canal was opened in 1959. Many Canadians had begun to worry over what they felt was undue cultural and economic dependence on the United States. But the three-thousand-mile frontier without a fort remained peaceful.

Until the late 1950's Canada was politically one of the stablest of Western nations. While other parties at times held power in the provinces, the federal government remained under the control of the Liberals, who depended for their support on an effective collaboration between the English-speaking provinces and the French-speaking province of Quebec. In 1957 the Conservatives won a close victory, and in 1959 a new election gave them a landslide majority. In 1963, the Liberals returned to power, but without a majority, which meant that they had to govern as the principal party in a coalition. Still another election in 1965 failed to give them a solid majority. In addition to Conservatives and Liberals there were minority parties— New Democrats, to the left; Social Credit, favoring unorthodox economic ideas but not socialist; and a French-Canadian variant of this last. It seemed possible that Canada was beginning to develop a splinter-party system like those of many European democracies.

One reason for this was the rise of French-Canadian nationalist feeling in the province of Quebec and French-speaking regions elsewhere. The few thousands of French left in Canada in 1763 had multiplied by the 1960's to some seven million. Since World War II they had for the first time enjoyed a vigorous economic growth and increasingly high standards of living, after lagging for decades, in this respect, behind the rest of Canada. Their unrest was in part a demand for a greater share in the Canadian managerial and financial worlds. It was also a demand for greater cultural participation in dominion life, and especially for true bilingualism after the Swiss pattern. Many people in the rest of Canada resisted their demands. By 1967, the French extremists who actually proposed to secede and set up an independent Quebec were probably no more than a noisy few. A federal commission on biculturalism was set up.

Into this somewhat tense situation the French president de Gaulle—with typical drama and concern for French *"grandeur"*—intruded in 1967, on a state visit to Canada. By shouting "Vive le Québec libre!" ("Long live free Quebec!") to an enthusiastic crowd he seemed to be sponsoring secession. When the Canadian federal government called his performance inadmissible he ended his visit, but made a strenuous attempt thereafter to open special official cultural and economic relations with Quebec. No doubt the episode reflected in part de Gaulle's eager wish to make trouble for all "Anglo-Saxons," and for all friends of the United States. The Canadians responded by producing a brand new political leader: when Prime Minister Lester Pearson resigned, a previously unknown Liberal, Pierre Elliott Trudeau, emerged as party leader, and won a smashing victory in 1968. Half-French, bilingual, handsome, and intelligent, he had a free hand to cope with separatism as with all other questions that might arise. By 1970, his new programs were beginning to emerge. But the kidnapping of a British diplomatic representative by one group of separatist terrorists, and of a Quebec government official by another, produced a major internal crisis. Proclaiming martial law, Trudeau's government captured one set of kidnappers, but only after their victim, the Quebec official, had been murdered; and obtained the release of the English diplomat, but only at the cost of letting his kidnappers go to Cuba. How Canada could weather this storm could not be foretold late in 1970.

Western Europe

The nations of western Europe preserved the form of the sovereign state, and many of the sentiments we call nationalism, but after 1945 they made real attempts to organize a "free Europe" on a level above and beyond that of the national state.

The first step was the successful establishment of the European Coal and Steel Community (1952), named for the man who did much to organize it as the "Schuman Plan." Schuman, appropriately enough, was a Frenchman with a German name. France, West Germany, and Italy joined Belgium, the Netherlands, and Luxembourg ("Benelux") in creating for their coal and iron industries a free market area of all six nations in which a joint administrative body could make certain final and binding decisions without the participation of any government officials. Each nation had given up some part of its sovereignty, and the plan was a success.

In 1957, these six countries set up, by the Treaty of Rome, the European Economic Community (EEC), better known as the Common Market, or sometimes "the Six." This was the beginning of true economic union under a central administration composed of delegates from each partner nation. Its administration had certain rights independent of any member government. The treaty also provided for increasing powers over trade, production, immigration, and other matters for the Common Market, according to a carefully worked-out schedule. By the 1970's, it was planned, there would be in effect one common trading and producing society, a single market free from internal tariffs, and a population of some 180 million or more, substantially equal to that of the United States and equipped with equal economic skills and experience, and with similar "mixed" economies—free enterprise under government regulation.

The years after 1957 saw substantial progress toward this goal. The tourist by car or rail, remembering prewar delays at the frontiers of the six countries, was astonished to be able to pass from one country to another almost as easily as he crossed state lines in the United States, and quite as easily as he crossed the Canadian-American frontier. Yet difficulties arose in the orderly carrying out of the schedule. Twice France vetoed Britain's proposed entry into the EEC, and insisted on specific provisions favoring French farmers in the Common Market. The difficulty about a British part in any European supranational arrangement was real, for many of the British regarded themselves as primarily part of the Commonwealth and not as Europeans.

The British set up in 1959 the European Free Trade Association, often called the "Outer Seven," with Britain, Sweden, Norway, Denmark, Austria, Switzerland, and Portugal as members. A much looser arrangement than the Common Market, it allowed each member to set its own external tariffs as it wished, thus protecting British "imperial preference" in favor of Commonwealth countries. Not until the disappearance of de Gaulle from French political life in 1969 did the possibility of British entry into the Common Market revive.

GREAT BRITAIN   In the United Kingdom of Great Britain and Northern Ireland (all of Ireland except six northern counties had gained complete independence), a general election held in July 1945, after the war had ended in Europe, ousted Churchill and his Conservative party, and for the first time returned the Labour party with an absolute majority in the House of Commons. The Liberal party was practically extinguished. The new prime minister was Clement Attlee, a middle-class social worker.

The new government—with a mandate for social change—proceeded to take over, with due compensation to the owners, the coal industry, the railroads, and some parts of commercial road transportation, and began to nationalize the steel industry. Britain already had a well-developed system of various social insurances; this was now capped by a system of socialized medical care for all who wished it. The educational system was partly reformed in an effort to make it more democratic, and to lengthen the required period of compulsory education. In accordance with Labour party philosophy, some parts of the old empire were given independence, and others were granted dominion status—that is, national independence within the extraordinary British multinational system, the Commonwealth.

What emerged was a British economy pushed a little more toward collectivism than before, but still a "mixed" economy. Coal and railroads, nationalized, did not become great state trusts run by bureaucrats on the Russian model, but rather public corporations with a structure not unlike that of impartial private industries in the West, run by boards not dominated by bureaucrats or politicians. Broad sectors of the economy remained in private hands, under no more than the kind of government regulation common in the United States.

Proof of the essential moderation of this British revolution was afforded by the conduct of the Conservatives, who with Churchill still at their head were returned to power once more in 1951 and remained there for twelve years. The nationalization of steel, which had begun, was stopped; but otherwise the Conservatives kept intact the "socialism" of their opponents, including the national health scheme. Churchill was succeeded by Anthony Eden (later Lord Avon) who fell from office after the débacle over Suez in 1956 (discussed below), and Eden in turn by Harold Macmillan, who governed until 1964.

In the postwar years the British were not resilient enough to keep up with the extraordinary pace of technological innovation. The British automobile industry, for example, which immediately after the war gained a big share of the world market, in the 1950's saw the Germans, with their inexpensive, standardized light car, the Volkswagen, take the lead. Although British production suffered by comparison with that of the United States or West Germany, the British were still a great industrial people, penalized ironically: because they had been the *first* to industrialize, their plant first tended toward obsolescence and inefficiency. Observers often found Britain's managers lacking in enterprise, unwilling to adopt new ways, and uninterested in research; while the workers were generally suspicious of any change in methods, regarded management as the perpetual enemy, and were more interested in the tea break than in the quality of the product.

And even in apparent prosperity, Britain remained in economic trouble. The pound, a currency still used as standard along with the dollar in the "free world," was always in danger. Its exchange value, already reduced in 1940 from $4.85 to $4.00, had after 1949 been pegged at $2.80. But continued pressure on the pound in the 1960's repeatedly required help from Britain's allies in the form of rather complex financial measures to maintain this value. This weakness of the pound signaled an unfavorable balance of trade: the British people were buying more from the rest of the world than they could sell to it.

In the Fifties and Sixties, in what came to be called the brain drain, some of Britain's distinguished scientists and engineers left home to migrate to the United States, Canada, or Australia. Having lost much of her nineteenth-century empire as well, Britain had to pay relatively more for necessary imports than she did in the nineteenth century, while at the same time facing even in her old "colonies" the competition of new and more efficient industries and new tariff barriers.

In the general election of 1964 the Conservatives gave way to the Labour party, which had won only a tiny majority of three in the House of Commons. The new Prime Minister, Harold Wilson, held on until a new election in 1966, when he emerged with a greatly increased majority. Thus strengthened, he proposed new measures to cope with the ever-present danger to the pound: a freeze of wages and prices in an effort to restore the balance between what British workmen—and managers—spent and what they produced. Wilson was asking the British to work harder for less cash return. His proposals threatened to split his own party; radical Labourites insisted that he was playing the capitalists' game, exploiting the poor to support the rich. At the critical Trades Union Congress of September 1966, he won a precarious victory. Yet in 1967 he had to devalue the pound once more, to $2.40, after heavy foreign pressure—largely French—against it. By 1968 he was personally unpopular and widely mistrusted.

Yet in 1968 and 1969, Labour's economic measures suddenly seemed to be solving the balance of payments problem. The deficits decreased, and even disappeared, but the general prosperity continued. Although taxes were high, and inflation was pushing prices up so fast that many of the gains from increased wages were proving somewhat illusory, more and more English workmen were able to buy cars and take their seaside holidays. The National Health scheme and education for working-class mothers had resulted in the virtual disappearance of the thin unhealthy infant from the British scene, as all classes seemed to produce an endless new supply of bouncing, rosy-cheeked, healthy specimens. But by and large doctors were underpaid, and their grievances not fully met.

An increasing number of new universities (often called "red-brick" to distinguish them from the older, originally medieval seats of learning with their Gothic or Jacobean or eighteenth-century stone buildings) sprang up to offer young people of all classes educational opportunities that had previously been available only to the upper and upper middle class. Even Oxford and Cambridge now included large numbers of working-class young men and women on

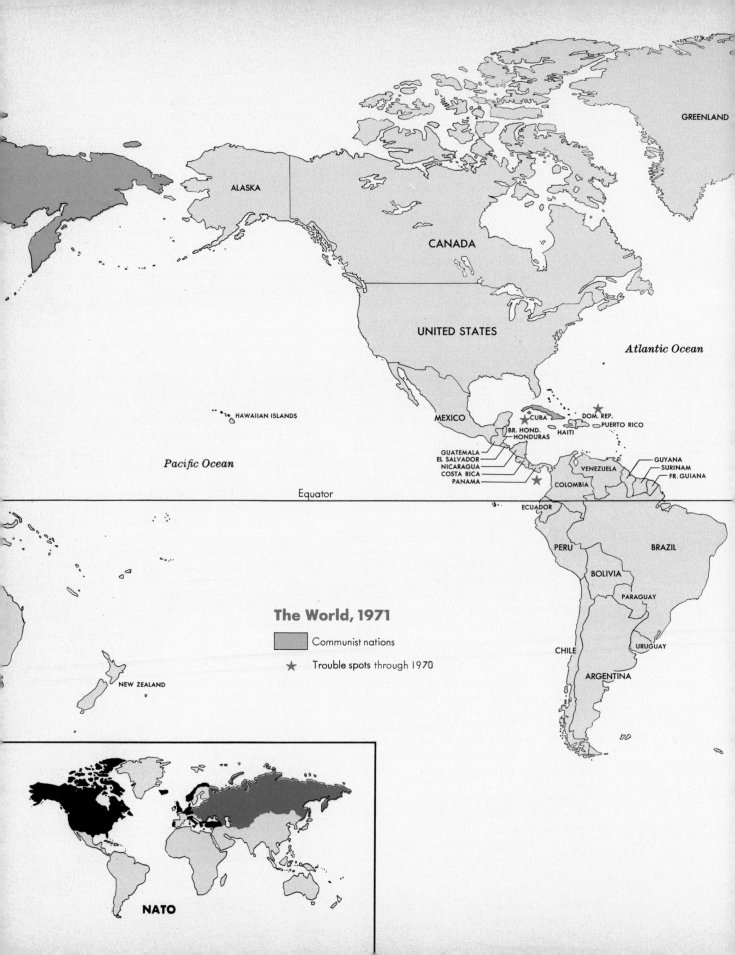

GREENLAND

ALASKA

CANADA

UNITED STATES

Atlantic Ocean

HAWAIIAN ISLANDS

MEXICO

CUBA

DOM. REP.

PUERTO RICO

BR. HOND.
HONDURAS

HAITI

GUATEMALA
EL SALVADOR
NICARAGUA
COSTA RICA
PANAMA

GUYANA
SURINAM
FR. GUIANA

VENEZUELA

Pacific Ocean

COLOMBIA

Equator

ECUADOR

PERU

BRAZIL

BOLIVIA

PARAGUAY

The World, 1971

Communist nations

★ Trouble spots through 1970

NEW ZEALAND

CHILE

URUGUAY

ARGENTINA

NATO

ICELAND

NORWAY
SWEDEN
FINLAND

UNITED
KINGDOM

EIRE

DEN.

NETH..
BEL.
L.
FRANCE
SW.

E.
GER.
W.
GER.
POLAND
CZECH.
AUST.
HUN.
YUG.
ALB.
ITALY

ROM.
BUL.

U.S.S.R.

MONGOLIA

CHINA

N. KOREA
S. KOREA
JAPAN

PORTUGAL
SPAIN

GREECE
TURKEY

MOROCCO
IFNI
SPANISH
SAHARA
MAURITANIA

ALGERIA
TUNISIA
LIBYA
U.A.R.

LEBANON
ISRAEL
SYRIA
JORDAN
IRAQ

IRAN
AFGHAN.
W. PAKISTAN

KASHMIR
TIBET
NEPAL
BHUTAN

SAUDI
ARABIA
OMAN
YEMEN
SOUTHERN YEMEN

INDIA

BURMA
E. PAK.

LAOS
THAI.
N. VIETNAM
S. VIETNAM
CAM.

TAIWAN

PHILIPPINE IS.

SENEGAL
GAMBIA
PORT.
GUINEA
GUINEA
SIERRA LEONE
LIBERIA
IVORY COAST
GHANA
TOGO
DAHOMEY

MALI
NIGER
UPPER
VOLTA
NIGERIA
CHAD
CAM.
EQ.
GUINEA
GABON
CABINDA
REP.
OF
CONGO

SUDAN

CENTRAL
AFRICAN
REPUBLIC
AFARS & ISSAS
TERRITORY
ETHIOPIA
SOMALI REPUBLIC

UGANDA
RWANDA
KENYA
CONGO
BURUNDI
TANZANIA
MALAWI
MOZAMBIQUE

CEYLON

BRUNEI
MALAYSIA

INDONESIA

NEW GUINEA
WEST IRIAN

PAPUA

Indian Ocean

ANGOLA
ZAMBIA
RHOD.
SOUTH-
WEST
AFRICA
BOTSWANA
SWAZILAND
REPUBLIC OF
SOUTH AFRICA
LESOTHO

MALAGASY
REPUBLIC
MAURITIUS

Atlantic Ocean

AUSTRALIA

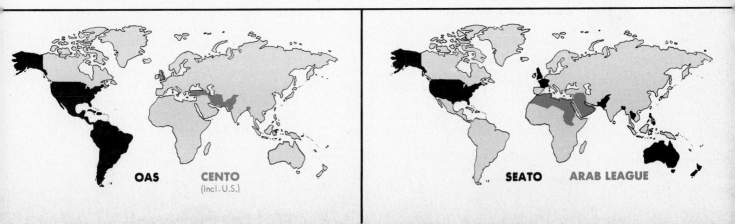

OAS   **CENTO**
(Incl. U.S.)

SEATO   **ARAB LEAGUE**

state scholarships. But not everything was harmonious in English education. Not only were radical students appearing in such predicatable places as the London School of Economics and some of the red-brick universities (a procession of naked men and women students caused some consternation at Keele in North Staffordshire in the spring of 1970), but there were sporadic incidents of violence even at Cambridge, producing the same responses of astonishment and confusion that had followed the early days of student unrest in the United States.

Perhaps more important politically was Labour's plan to modify the system of secondary education. Proclaiming the need to extend and democratize the school system, and to make it more egalitarian, Labour intended to institute a new program of "comprehensive" schools, which its opponents believed would do away with many of the existing opportunities for the ablest students to advance, and would reduce schooling to a low common denominator of mediocrity. The Conservatives opposed the Labour Party plan, and there was little doubt that a good many intellectuals within the Labour Party were less than enthusiastic about it.

Other severe problems plagued Britain. A new one was immigration and the resulting racial tensions, as Indians and Pakistanis, West Indian and African blacks entered the country in increasing numbers, to settle in London and in the industrial midlands, and to take jobs in factories, public transportation, and hospitals. Most of these, as Commonwealth citizens, had British passports and the right to come to England at any time without formalities. Many came as the result of unemployment or poor conditions at home. Dislike for blacks, almost unknown in England previously, rose markedly during the Sixties, and affected both political parties and their programs. Despite its liberal and antiracist protestations, the Wilson government was forced to curtail immigration sharply, even for those with British passports.

It was a Conservative member of the House of Commons, Enoch Powell, however, who voiced most sharply his fear of future troubles in England if black immigration should be allowed to continue and even if the blacks already in England were permitted to stay. Repeatedly predicting bloody race riots like those in the United States—a few of which on a far smaller scale had indeed already taken place in Britain—Powell seemed to some an unscrupulous demagogue, who was mentioning the unmentionable. Many members of the working class, however, life-long supporters of the Labour party, agreed with Powell on this issue, as his growing majority in a constituency including many antiblack white workmen demonstrated. Despite the efforts of the Conservative party to repudiate or at least soft-pedal "Powellism," and despite his official removal by his party leadership from a responsible position in the opposition, he himself continued to be a Conservative, and had the support of a considerable body of Conservative opinion. Appealing to those in both parties who shared his apprehensions about future racism in England, he loomed on the political horizon as a possible challenger to the established political order.

Closely related to the race issue at home was the question of official British relations abroad with South Africa (to which the Labour government had refused to sell arms because of the racial policies of the South African regime), and with the new white-dominated African state of Rhodesia (which the Labour government did not recognize and on which it had declared an economic boycott for similar reasons). Many Conservatives, Powell among them, deplored these policies, and charged that Labour had forgotten England's true interests and proper close bonds with countrymen overseas.

Prime Minister Wilson took advantage of the improving economic situation to call for new elections in June 1970. His former personal unpopularity seemed to have waned, and the polls all reported the likelihood of an easy Labour victory. But to the general surprise, even of the winners, the Conservative party won a majority of forty seats in Parliament, and its leader Edward Heath promptly took office as prime minister. In immediate retrospect it was clear that inflation—especially rising food prices—had irritated voters who usually voted Labour, probably housewives in particular, so that they either voted Conservative or stayed home, and thus cut the size of the Labour vote. No doubt Powell's insistent antiblack speeches also gained votes for the Conservatives, although they tried to repudiate him. On the South African and Rhodesian issues, the Labour party seemed to have taken a position less popular than they had hoped. Arms sales to South Africa would probably be resumed. And among members of the middle class at least, the Labour education program had obviously seemed to threaten much that they cherished in British schools. The first measure of the new Heath government was to withdraw Labour's overall "comprehensive" school scheme, and substitute one that solicited far more local initiative in proposals for change.

One ancient problem that had plagued Britain almost since the beginning of her history arose again in the late 1960's to trouble men of all political parties. This was the antagonism between Catholic and Protestant in Ulster, the five counties of Northern Ireland that were still part of the United Kingdom. Here in an industrial area, suffering from economic troubles, the Catholics by and large formed a depressed class. The first to lose their jobs in bad times in a Protestant-dominated land, and cherishing their traditional feelings as the oppressed, they were inflamed by the insistence of the Protestant extremists (the "Orangemen") on continuing to celebrate the anniversaries of those victories of William III in the 1690's that had ensured English domination over the region. Marching provocatively in parades through Catholic districts and crying out contemptuous slogans, the Orangemen in the summer of 1969 precipitated disorders that began in Derry (Londonderry), and spread to Belfast and other areas. The British army had to intervene to keep order, which was eventually reestablished.

But things in Ireland are never simple. The regular police in Ulster—the Royal Ulster Constabulary or R.U.C.—were accused by the Catholics of being mere tools of the Protestant oppressor, and had to be disarmed. The clearest voices of both sides in Ulster were those of extremists: for the Catholics Miss Bernadette Devlin, a young university student, who won a seat in Parliament in London and who participated actively in the demonstrations in Belfast; and for the Protestants the Reverend Ian Paisley, minister of a sect of his own, whose irreconcilable hostility to Catholics smacked more of the sixteenth century than of the twentieth, and who was also elected to Parliament in the election of 1970. Paisley had served a term in jail for incitement to riot, and Miss Devlin now was convicted and imprisoned for the same offense. Still further complicating the matter for the government of Northern Ireland and of Great Britain was the intense and embarrassing interest shown in the disorders by the government of independent Ireland to the south, which apparently felt compelled by the internal pressure of its own extremists (the Irish Republican Army, who had long claimed and illegally tried to secure the five northern counties for Ireland) to suggest that the United Nations be given responsibility for the problem, a suggestion quite unacceptable to the Northern Irish and British government, who regarded the matter as altogether an internal problem. When violence resumed in 1970, the British army was reinforced. The "orange" parades were held, but order was maintained. Not a party but a national matter, the troubles in Ireland continued to pose a serious threat to stability, order, and decency.

With both parties pledged to push the entry of Britain into the European Common Market, the Conservatives prepared—as Labour would also have done—for the early reopening of discussions with the Six. But among many Britons regardless of party, the long delay in consummating this marriage so often proposed, and Britain's double past rejection by the French, had brought second thoughts and a notable cooling of enthusiasm. Powell and many other Conservatives who might or might not share his views on other issues, openly opposed British entry. So did many Labourites, and so did many who were not primarily political but primarily English in their loyalty to the economic preference arrangements for the Commonwealth—which would have to disappear if the new economic union with western Europe should be achieved—or in their loyalty to their traditional insularity and dislike of Europeans generally, or even in their loyalty to their pocketbooks, since it seemed sure that food prices would rise sharply (by at least twenty percent) if England should accept the terms on which the French seemed likely to insist. In 1970 no observer could say with certainty how deep-seated these doubts about the Common Market were in Britain and how far they might delay or even prevent her entry. It was clear, however, that the discussions would involve far more than mere formality and that their eventual outcome was highly dubious.

No attempt to discuss Britain in the period since 1945 would be complete without mention of the phenomena that can be summed up in the public-relations-men's phrase "swinging London." Beginning with the enormous popularity of the four pop-singing Beatles in the late Fifties, England for a time set the international styles for young people in other countries, even if the young themselves often were not aware of it. The long hair for men, the "unisex" phenomenon in dress, the popularity of Edwardian, eighteenth-century, theatrical, and eccentric clothes, the whole "mod" fashion syndrome that spread across the Atlantic and across the Channel started in England. Carnaby Street, Twiggy, Mick Jagger and the Rolling Stones all had their counterparts elsewhere, but the originals were English.

Nor was this all an accident or trivial. It may not be too far-fetched to connect it with an extremely important cultural and social phenomenon, difficult to evaluate precisely: the slow eroding of class distinctions in England, the traditional bastion of political freedom but of social inequality. The Beatles were all working-class in origin, and all spoke (or sang) with a pure lower-class Liverpool accent. Lower class too, with variations, were all the leading English pacesetters of the new styles in song, dress, and behavior among the young of the 1960's. And these styles spread not only abroad but among the middle and upper classes of young people in England as well, marking perhaps a sign of an increasing impatient determination to have done with the class sentiment that had so long pervaded English life. Resistance and delay and examples of class prejudice up and down there would long continue to be, but the change seemed under way, and if it continued and increased, it would be perhaps the most important and epoch-making change in English social history at least since the Industrial Revolution, if not the Norman Conquest.

FRANCE   World War II inflicted on the French what psychologists call a trauma—a deep wound in the soul. Defeat by the Germans, a brutal German occupation and economic exploitation, the spectacle of much French collaboration with the enemy, all this was succeeded by liberation, which, in spite of the part played in it by the Fighting French and the French Resistance movement, was still clearly the work of American and British and, indirectly, of Russian arms. Nor had France since the early nineteenth century kept pace with the leading industrial nations in production, in finance, above all in population. Only one fact gave cause for optimism: while the "net reproduction rate" for 100 women had in 1942 sunk to 85

(that is, fifteen less than the figure needed to maintain without immigration the existing population), by 1949 it had risen to 133—that is, 33 above mere stability. The rate continued at 124 or higher through 1955. This meant that hundreds of thousands of French men and women deliberately decided to have children, a clear sign of the recovery that lay ahead.

The French government-in-exile, led by General de Gaulle, in 1944 easily reestablished in liberated France the old republican forms of government. Frenchmen called this state the Fourth Republic; but after de Gaulle, disappointed by his failure to attain real power in a state still ruled by unstable parliamentary coalitions of "splinter parties," retired from politics in 1946, the Fourth Republic began to look exactly like the Third. Cabinets lasted on an average only a few months; to the old splinter parties was added a Communist party of renewed strength, openly dedicated to revolutionary change. The problems of the old empire, now known as the French Union, seemed insoluble; its peoples were in ferment. After nine years of war, Indo-China (Vietnam) was lost in 1954 in a great defeat at Dienbienphu. In the same year an active rebellion against the French began in Algeria, which France regarded not as a colony but as an overseas portion of France itself. Morocco and Tunisia were both lost in 1956, and the crisis deepened.

In 1958 General de Gaulle took power again, as financial instability, inflation resulting from the war costs in Indo-China and Algeria, and a rising popular disgust with the "politicians" combined to bring about the fall of the Fourth Republic. A military and Rightist coup d'état in Algeria took place on May 13, 1958. De Gaulle then announced that he was willing to come out of retirement. The leaders of the coup wrongly assumed that he would carry out their policies for keeping Algeria French.

In France there was very little violence, as a plebiscite confirmed the change. The Constitution of the new Fifth Republic provided for a president of France, to be elected for a seven-year term by direct popular vote. An absolute majority was required, and, if not achieved in a first election, was to be obtained in a run-off between the two candidates with the greatest number of votes. Elected outright in 1958, de Gaulle was reelected to a second term in 1965 in a run-off. Under the constitution the French president appointed the premier, who could dissolve the legislature and order new elections at any time after the first year. Thus the new constitution gave the executive more power, the legislature much less. Those who disliked the new constitution complained that it made the legislature a mere rubber stamp.

De Gaulle's enemies called him a dictator. Cartoonists enjoyed drawing him as Louis XIV, the *roi soleil,* with wig and silk stockings, the personification of French haughtiness and superiority. He was certainly an obstinate, opinionated man, but though a general and personally authoritarian, he was no Napoleon III or Boulanger or Pétain. Frenchmen still enjoyed freedom of speech, of the press, of public assembly. French journalists could and did say as nasty things about their president as American journalists could and did say about theirs. Yet the regime did control radio and television. In the general election of 1965 it yielded to the pressure of public opinion, and consented to give de Gaulle's opposition candidates some time if not quite "equal time" on the air.

The French ruling classes believed that their colonial subjects, especially the Algerians, could be persuaded to want to become real Frenchmen. But most of the Muslim nine-tenths of the Algerian population disagreed. Against the wishes of those who had brought him to power, de Gaulle in 1962 worked out a settlement making Algeria independent, leaving France some "influence" and some rights over Saharan oil. The Right regarded this as treason. Most of the Leftists, on the other hand, never gave him even grudging credit for it.

Starting with the Marshall Plan aid in 1947, a great series of economic and social changes began in France. Unlike the United States and Britain and Germany, France had hitherto preserved much of the small-scale, individualistic methods of production and distribution characteristic of the period before the Industrial Revolution. Now there began a full-scale reorientation of the economy in accordance with the usual practices of modern industry. Helped by foreign investment, especially American, France began to experience a real boom. The growth rate in the Sixties was about a steady six percent per year, ahead even of West Germany; inflation, though a problem, had until 1966 or 1967 been held down to three percent. Prosperity meant that for the first time Frenchmen

by the hundreds of thousands got their first cars, television sets, and hi-fi record players; that they traveled in ever growing numbers; that they enjoyed fearful traffic jams and incredible highway accidents; and that many of those who found the new ways unsettling blamed all the changes, like Coca-Cola, *le drugstore,* and blue jeans, on the Americans.

In foreign policy, de Gaulle was a deeply committed old-fashioned nationalist Frenchman. His memoirs showed how much of a love affair with France his whole life had been, and how deeply he identified himself personally with his country. He never forgot a slight, and a slight to him was a slight to France, to be repaid in due course. The treatment accorded him by Churchill and Roosevelt during World War II he could never forget; and when he came to power he retained a healthy personal dislike of "les Anglo-Saxons." To him, the thought of the supranational bodies that would rob France of her sovereignty even to a small degree (the Common Market, NATO, and others) was uncomfortable, and talk of a United States of Europe, in which France would be submerged, anathema. He spoke instead of an *Europe des patries,* a "Europe of fatherlands," that would not stop at the Russian frontiers but would include Russia—at least the European part—with all its historic European associations. And within the *Europe des patries,* of course, France would take the lead.

To do this France must have her own atomic weapons. Therefore de Gaulle refused to join the U.S., U.K., and U.S.S.R. in a treaty barring atomic tests, and France continued, like Red China, to test nuclear weapons in the atmosphere, exploding her first hydrogen bomb in 1968 and continuing annually thereafter. She must also have her own *force de frappe,* the striking force capable of delivering atomic weapons to their targets, and so of deterring an enemy. Vigorously opposed to communism at home, de Gaulle none the less worked out a rapprochement with Russia. The U.S.S.R., he argued, in the 1960's no longer represented the threat to the general peace that it had represented in the '50's. Now—in balancing the scales against the industrial and military power of the United States and its special friend, Britain—France needed to be friends with Russia. To South America, to Canada, with appeals to French separatists in Quebec, to Poland, and to Romania, de Gaulle took his stately presence, and his mes-

French newspaper headlines announcing the rejection of President de Gaulle's referendum, April 28, 1969.

sage that France would be the leader of Europe.

In the spring of 1968, however, while de Gaulle was presenting his case in Romania, Paris erupted unexpectedly. The French universities, so overcrowded that there were no classrooms for students to use and no way of their listening to their lecturers, had been disregarded by the regime in a period when the young everywhere were full of resentment against the society their parents had brought them into. Led by anarchists and others, the students occupied their buildings, fought the police, and eventually drew a reluctant Communist party into the fray. In order not to lose the support of the French workers, who had already begun to strike in sympathy with the students, the Communist leadership had to support what looked for a few days as if it just might be the beginning of a new

French Revolution. De Gaulle returned to Paris, assured himself of army support, proposed a referendum, which he was obliged to abandon in favor of new elections, and won a great victory at the polls, obtaining a larger majority in the legislature than before.

Thereupon he dropped his prime minister, the chief organizer of victory, Pompidou, and embarked on a new phase of his regime. His economic and social program called for *participation* by the workers not only in the profits of industry but in its management. His new minister of education, acknowledging the justice of many of the grievances of the students, pushed through the legislature (November 1968) a major radical reform bill decentralizing the educational system. Having established his strength with the strong support of the Right—as in 1958—de Gaulle now appeared to be preparing at least to appease the Left—again, as in 1958. Perhaps the military and foreign programs would have to be slowed down; but nobody who had studied de Gaulle believed they would be abandoned.

Nobody could have predicted what actually happened. De Gaulle staked his political future on a comparatively unimportant political issue set before the public in a referendum, and lost. As he had done before, he withdrew into private life. His death in 1970 marked the disappearance of the last survivor of the great men of World War II, but had no political implications. In the 1969 elections, the Gaullists were returned to office with a substantial majority, and Pompidou became president of France. As in the remainder of the Western nations, inflation grew apace, but on the whole prosperity continued as well. Pompidou in general maintained de Gaulle's policies but pursued them far less flamboyantly. In 1970, Jacques Servan-Schreiber, a prominent anti-Gaullist editor and publicist turned politician, defeated his Gaullist opponent in a by-election, and was returned to the National Assembly. Energetic and far to the left of the regime, though not a leftist, Servan-Schreiber might possibly be the precursor to a more general disillusionment with Gaullism, but it was also probable that purely local issues had had a good deal to do with his election.

WEST GERMANY   In 1966 West Germany had a population of 59 million, some three times that of East Germany. The wartime destruction of much of Germany's industrial plant paradoxically soon proved beneficial: the new plant was built with the latest technological equipment. The Allied High Commission, never very severe, gradually abolished controls over German industry, save for atomic energy and a few other military restrictions. It advanced economic aid, and scaled down prewar German debts. By the early 1950's West Germany had a favorable balance of trade and was achieving industrial growth as high as 10 percent a year.

Gross national product rose from $23 billion in 1950 to $103 billion in 1964, with no serious monetary inflation. This prosperity was to a large degree spread through all classes of society. The workingman in West Germany had begun to enjoy the kind of affluence that his opposite number in the United States had had for some time. New buildings rose everywhere. The divided superhighways Hitler had built for largely military purposes grew overcrowded, and had to be widened and extended.

Politically, the Allies required "de-Nazification." At the Nuremberg trials in 1946, seventy-four top Nazi leaders were convicted of war crimes. Ten were hanged, after two had committed suicide; one was sentenced to life imprisonment, others to shorter terms; and three were acquitted. To have dismissed all civil servants who had held posts under the Nazi regime would have dismantled German administration altogether. A weeding-out of the most compromised Nazis was achieved, though not sufficiently to satisfy many Western anti-Nazis.

The independent West German state had a constitution that provided for a bicameral legislature, with a lower house representing the people directly and an upper house representing the states (Länder), together with a president elected by a special assembly for a five-year term, in practice largely a ceremonial figure. Real executive leadership was vested in the chancellor, a prime minister dependent on a parliamentary majority. The old splinter-party system did not return to plague the new republic. Under the leadership of Konrad Adenauer, the Christian Democrats, distant heirs of the old Centrist party, held power down to 1961.

A Rhineland Catholic, former Mayor of Cologne, conservative, pro-French, and thoroughly democratic, Adenauer was forced to retire only because of age, and continued to wield enough influence to weaken his successor, Ludwig Erhard, a Protestant, who remained in office for five more years. The twenty-year reign of the Christian Democrats was one supported by the voters, not the result of one-party totalitarian politics.

West Germany seemed to be approaching two-party democratic politics, with the Christian Democrats challenged chiefly by the Social Democrats, roughly similar to the British Labour party. The Social Democrats held power in some of the states and cities of the federal union, notably in West Berlin, whose popular mayor, Willy Brandt, ran unsuccessfully for the federal chancellorship against Erhard in 1964. A neo-Nazi minority existed in West Germany, but it achieved no very alarming successes at the polls. Militant organizations of war veterans and of refugees from the "lost" Eastern territories now included in Poland, the U.S.S.R., or Czechoslovakia perhaps posed more of a possible threat to stability.

The major political question remained that of an eventual reunion with Communist-dominated East Germany. Neither recognized the other. After long years during which East Germans, attracted by better West German living conditions, crossed the border by the tens of thousands, the East German government in August 1961 began building a wall between the two parts of the city. In 1970 this wall still stood, though on special holidays families in West Berlin were allowed to cross into East Berlin briefly to visit relatives and friends.

As part of the Cold War, the Americans, British, and French permitted the West Germans to rearm early in the 1950's and to join NATO. Military conscription was introduced in 1957, and by 1970 West Germany had a relatively large and very modern army, navy, and air force. Government and people supported the armed forces as a necessity, but the old Wilhelmine and Nazi militarism did not revive among the people at large. Access to the atom bomb was not included in this rearmament, but German public opinion apparently was not greatly exercised over the exclusion.

In the late autumn of 1966 there arose in West Germany a major political crisis. Neither the Christian Democrats nor the Social Democrats had a secure majority in the Reichstag. Chancellor Erhard was governing in coalition with a small right-wing party, the Free Democrats, basically non-Nazi conservatives opposed to "socialism." There was friction with some of the high command of the armed forces. It was hard to support American policies in Europe and yet not break with France. The slowing down of West German economic growth might, it was feared, presage a real recession. All this contributed to Erhard's downfall. In November 1966 the Free Democrats refused to support his proposals for higher taxes, and the government fell.

But the Christian Democrats came forward with Kurt George Kiesinger, a Catholic, who as premier succeeded in forming a "grand coalition" with his chief opponents, the Social Democrats. Willy Brandt became vice chancellor and foreign minister. Though some members of both parties disapproved, and though Kiesinger's past membership in the Nazi party aroused some alarm abroad, the grand coalition commanded popular support. It was designed to last until the elections scheduled for 1969. On the Right the neo-Nazis scored some provincial successes, and on the Left, uproariously rebellious students demonstrated in Berlin, largely against the newspaper and magazine empire of a rich and powerful publisher, Axel Springer, who began to reduce some of his holdings. A left-wing German refugee even played a considerable role in the 1968 French student uprisings.

In the elections of 1969 the Christian Democrats lost, and for the first time since its foundation, Western Germany was governed by a premier of another party. Willy Brandt, the Social Democrat, was able to take office by forming a coalition in his turn with the Free Democrats, who obtained the foreign ministry in his cabinet, much to the distaste of Brandt's more doctrinaire followers. In 1969 and 1970, Brandt moved slowly and cautiously toward the opening of discussions with the East Germans. There was an exchange of state visits, and a certain amount of rhetoric. But, as everybody knew, the chief stumbling block in the way of serious negotiations between the two Germanies lay in the Soviet fear of Western Germany. So it gradually became apparent that a treaty between West Germany and the U.S.S.R. in which both renounced the use of force for the future would be at least one of the necessary preliminaries. Keeping the Western nations fully apprised of his discussions, Brandt in the summer of 1970 succeeded in reaching agreement with the Russians on the text of such a treaty. It recognized all existing European frontiers, which Germans and Russians thus both agreed never to try to alter by force. Of course the Germans could still hope that perhaps a change in the frontiers of Poland might some day be negotiated. The next step was an agreement with Poland itself, and this too Brandt put through during 1970. The East Germans would be next. The U.S.S.R. stood to gain by the new accessibility of West German technical and industrial skills. And this prospect, together with the hardening of anti-American attitudes in Moscow in 1970, was creating doubts about Brandt's achievements in the very official American circles that had earlier encouraged his policies.

THE OTHER WESTERN COUNTRIES In Italy a plebiscite in 1946 showed 54.3 percent of the voters in favor of a republic, and in spite of the comparative narrowness of the margin, the republic, once it was established, proved viable. There were monarchists who regretted the forced departure of the House of Savoy, and there were even some who regretted the end of the fascist regime. But neither group was able to influence parliamentary politics to any great extent. A strong Christian Democratic party (a Catholic party with a relatively liberal reform program) under a succession of leaders, Alcide de Gasperi, Amintore Fanfani, Aldo Moro, and Mario Rumor, proved able to hold power thereafter with support from other groups. It took positive measures to break up the large landed estates in the south, with a view to redistributing the land. De Gasperi was challenged chiefly by a very strong Communist party, the largest in the West, with whom the larger faction of the Socialists—that led by Pietro Nenni—was allied. The firmly anticommunist socialist faction led by Guiseppe Saragat participated in the government.

In the Sixties a series of complicated negotiations began a process the Italians called the *apertura a sinistra,* the opening to the Left. In this process the Christian Democrats won over some Socialist support. A further weakening of the extreme Left was achieved in 1966, when the Socialists—long split between an anticommunist wing and a wing that often collaborated with the Communists—reunited as one party.

Italy's economic growth between 1953 and 1966 was so remarkable that the Italians themselves refer to it as their *"miracolo economico."* As in France, this was achieved with some government ownership and with much government regulation and planning. Italy was a mixed economy, but a free society. Milan, long a busy and active city, began to look like another Chicago. Rome had perhaps the most desperate traffic problem of any great city in the world. Membership in the Common Market and freedom from the troubles of imperial liquidation gave Italian enterprise opportunities that it had never had before.

The grave problems of the *mezzogiorno,* the southern part of the peninsula, and the islands of Sardinia and Sicily, were attacked by programs of investments, by providing jobs in the north or in Germany or Switzerland for the surplus workers of the south, and by old-age pensions. In the Italian balance of payments, an income of about $1 billion annually from tourists provided a useful item on the "export" side.

Yet in the late 1960's Italian political stability apparently began to crumble. In part this was due to the severe internal political strains and feuding within the Christian Democratic party. Cooperation among Christian Democratic politicians became more and more difficult, and their negotiations with each other tended to break down. In part it was due to the uncertainty of their relationship with their supposed partners, the Socialists, who, though anti-Communist on the national level, often cooperated with the Communists on the local political level, arousing bitter recriminations when such cooperation effectively blocked local Christian Democratic political success. In part it was due to the same sort of inflation that was plaguing the other Western countries, but that Italy, with its large poor population and its lack of any tradition of the welfare state, was perhaps less able to bear than any other advanced industrial nation. Strikes in 1969 and 1970 occurred sporadically and unpredictably but often. The government seemed frozen in bureaucratic incompetence. Personal vendettas were proving in many cases stronger than patriotism. Prosperity continued, and Italy might indeed weather a coming storm, but the storm clouds did look dark on the horizon. A prolonged political crisis ended at least temporarily with the success in 1970 of an experienced economist, Colombo, in forming a cabinet.

The smaller states of "free Europe" generally

shared the prosperity and problems of their larger brothers. In Belgium, which enjoyed great material well-being, the chronic difficulties between the minority of French-speaking Walloons and the majority of Dutch-speaking Flemings continued to worsen and to threaten the stability of the country. In the Iberian peninsula, which was part of anticommunist Europe without being "free," Spain—still in Franco's control more than thirty years after the end of the Civil War—had taken major steps toward modernization and a few mild measures to relax political tyranny. Low wages, especially to the depressed coal miners of the north, and bitter government opposition to the national sentiment of the Bas-

ques prevented full economic or political stability. It seemed probable that, on Franco's disappearance, the monarchy would be restored under Prince Juan Carlos, grandson of Alfonso XIII, and son of Alfonso's still-living kin Prince Juan, who, however, had not renounced the royal title. Portugal, under the rigidly conservative Salazar, dictator since 1932, lagged well behind Spain. The replacement of Salazar, because of illness, in 1968 promised to open a new chapter, though the expenditure of men and money involved in holding onto the Portuguese colonial empire made rapid changes unlikely.

All the "free world" nations had their troubles, but in 1970 they remained free.

III   The Communist Bloc: The U.S.S.R. at Home

Alone among the leaders of the Big Three of the war years, Stalin remained in power immediately after the war. His remaining years, 1945–1953, marked a continuation and even sharpening of the policies that he had made his own. Some four years of political uncertainty followed his death, but in 1957 Nikita Khrushchev emerged as supreme, and held onto power until 1964. He was succeeded by two co-chiefs, Brezhnev and Kosygin, who remained on top in 1970.

Stalin's Last Years

Facing the devastation caused by the war, and what he regarded as the immediate threat of American atomic weapons, Stalin felt obliged to decree a continuation of austerity into the postwar years, at just the moment when the Russian people most yearned for new housing and a few creature comforts. The party, still his docile instrument and experiencing regular purges to prevent any relaxation, dominated political life, with the constant assistance of the secret police; while the army, still mobilized at high strength and performing a variety of occupation duties abroad, remained the third Soviet institution with power of its own.

Not long before he died, Stalin in 1952 created a new Presidium, which he planned as a larger body than the Politburo, to include the

ten Politburo members and fifteen additional high-ranking Soviet officials. But he did not live to announce the membership of the new body or to summon a meeting of it. After his death, the new "Presidium" simply replaced the old Politburo, with the same ten members. Khrushchev later declared that, in enlarging the membership and changing the name of the Politburo, Stalin had been taking the first step toward the complete purge and liquidation of its ten existing members; so it is perhaps no wonder that, having survived this first step, they declined to take a second.

The fourth five-year plan (1946–1950) and its successor the fifth (1951–1955) continued to emphasize investment in heavy industry at the expense of consumer goods. Financial measures —the raising of prices, the wiping out of savings by the establishment of a new currency—kept the severest sort of economic pressure on the population. Reparations exacted from Germany and industrial loot from the eastern European countries gave massive stimulus to Soviet reconstruction. The fourth five-year plan saw the first Soviet atomic bomb completed; the fifth saw further advances in armaments and the building of the Volga–Don canal. In agriculture, the regime embarked on a policy of reducing the number and increasing the size of collective farms. In 1951, Nikita Khrushchev, now appearing as a leading party agricultural expert, proposed a plan to create great agricultural cities (*agrogoroda*), in order to concentrate farm labor and abolish rural backwardness.

The cultural policy of the regime was in keeping with the bleak austerity and terror of these years. The cultural boss, Andrei Zhdanov, decreed that literature had to take an active role in the "engineering" of human souls. The official school of "socialist realism" was the only permissible line for a writer to follow. Zhdanov denounced in particular Mikhail Zoshchenko, writer of witty and satirical short stories, whose "Adventures of a Monkey" accidentally set free by a bomb suggested strongly that life in a cage in a zoo was more agreeable than life at large among the Soviet people; and Anna Akhmatova, a sensitive lyric poet, who had had the unpatriotic ill-judgment to lament in verse her feeling of loneliness, which no proper Soviet citizen would do. Both were silenced. Though Zhdanov died suddenly in 1948, his principles continued to reign. Violent anti-Western propaganda filled Soviet books and resounded from the Soviet stage in such a play as *The Unfortunate Haberdasher*, in which President Truman was cast as Hitler.

With the attack on the Western nations went a constant drumbeat of new (and sometimes comic) claims for Soviet, or at least Russian, "firsts" in every field of intellectual and artistic endeavor. No scholar could safely investigate a topic without paying his respects to the supreme authorities on everything: Marx, Lenin, and, chiefly, Stalin. Archaeologists, historians, students of literature began their work with a compulsory quotation from Stalin, and genuflected before him as the great teacher, the "Choryphaeus of the sciences."

Stalin supported the geneticist Trofim Lysenko, who maintained—contrary to all accepted biological doctrine—that acquired characteristics were hereditary, strongly implying that "new Soviet man" would emerge as a biological phenomenon, and giving support to the political argument that communism would change the human species. In linguistics too, Stalin personally intervened in 1950 to denounce the prevailing theories originated by Nikolai Marr, then sixteen years dead, who had implied that the world's languages corresponded to the degree of social development reached by their speakers. Neither biologist nor linguist, Stalin laid down the law for both.

As Stalin grew older, the secrecy, censorship, and conspiratorial miasma at the top of the Soviet state and society all intensified. Catering to ancient prejudices and violating Leninist precepts, Stalin now moved against the Jews. Anti-Semitic propaganda reached its peak with the publicity given an alleged "doctors' plot," in which Jewish doctors were accused of plotting to poison Stalin. When Stalin died, the stage seemed set for a full-scale anti-Semitic drive reminiscent of Hitler. Fear of the West, and detestation of Zionism—many Soviet Jews wanted to live in Israel—did not alone explain Soviet anti-Semitism. Despite their long years of preaching cultural autonomy for nationalities, many Soviet leaders were personally anti-Semitic, and perhaps recognized that the population at large could be expected to welcome anti-Semitism at a moment when there was little else in the government policies that they could endorse. Official Soviet anti-Semitism would wax and wane in the Fifties and Sixties.

The Soviet Succession

By the early 1950's it had become a favorite occupation in the West to speculate on Stalin's succession. Would it be the Communist party, or the secret police, or the army that would emerge supreme? Would it be some combination of two of these against the third? Was this or that member of the Politburo identified with one or another of these three chief agencies? Would the world see a new bitter rivalry comparable to the struggle between Stalin and Trotsky for the succession to Lenin? If so, would the resulting instability go so far as to disrupt the machinery of Soviet government?

When the moment actually came, in March 1953, Georgi Malenkov, personally close to Stalin, succeeded him as premier, but surrendered his Communist party secretaryship to Nikita Khrushchev. It was thus clear that nobody would immediately inherit all of Stalin's power. Soon the regime began to denounce the "cult of personality" (i.e., Stalin's former one-man rule), and proclaimed a "collegial" system (i.e., government by committee). The dreaded chief of the secret police, Presidium-member Beria, was executed for treason.

But no free-for-all among the remaining members of the inner circle ensued. Malenkov vanished from the top post of premier, to be succeeded by the political general Bulganin; but Malenkov was at first simply demoted to a lower cabinet post, and remained in the Presidium. It was noteworthy that when Malenkov confessed error, he took responsibility for the failure of the agrogoroda, which were actually Khrushchev's idea. Khrushchev was certainly very powerful, but his fellow members on the Politburo had great influence, and showed no outward signs of fearing him as all had feared Stalin. On the whole, it appeared that the transfer of power had actually gone quite smoothly.

At a party congress held early in 1956, Khrushchev made a speech in which he denounced Stalin, emotionally detailing the ghastly acts of personal cruelty to which the psychopathically suspicious nature of the late dictator had given rise. Khrushchev thus echoed what Western observers of the U.S.S.R. had been saying for years. As the details of the speech were leaked out to the Soviet public, there was of course some distress at the smashing of the idol they had worshiped so long; but a good many of them no doubt had all along suspected that Stalin was something less than godlike. So the widespread disorders that some observers were predicting failed to materialize.

Abroad, however, the speech led to turmoil in the Soviet satellites in Europe, and so gave Khrushchev's opponents at home an opportunity to unite against his policies. Within the Presidium they had a majority. But Khrushchev was able to rally to his support the larger body of which the Presidium was the inner core, the Central Committee of the Communist party of the U.S.S.R. A veteran party worker, he had installed his own loyal supporters in all key party posts, repeating Stalin's performance after the death of Lenin, and he emerged from this greatest test with his powers immeasurably enhanced (June 1957). Now the Soviet press denounced the "antiparty group" of Malenkov, Molotov, and Kaganovich, three of the members of Stalin's own entourage. In Stalin's own day, this would have led them to the execution block. Khrushchev, however, acted differently. All three were expelled from the Presidium and removed from their high posts, but all three were given minor positions at a safe distance from Moscow. In 1958 Bulganin followed them into the discard: he too had sided against Khrushchev, whose succession to Stalin's position of undisputed power now seemed complete.

Domestic Policies under Khrushchev and His Successors

BUREAUCRATIC PROBLEMS. Yet there were certain differences. Already in his sixties, Khrushchev could hardly hope for a quarter-century of dictatorship such as Stalin had had. Moreover, in the very course of making himself supreme he had deprived himself of some of the instruments available to Stalin. After 1953 he had released millions of captives from prisons and slave-labor camps. Almost everybody in Russia had a relative or friend now freed. These men and women now took jobs, some of them even government jobs. Within a year or two Soviet society at every level except at the very top of the bureaucracy had absorbed these sufferers from tyranny. The secret police no longer enjoyed a power almost independent in the state, a power that might challenge the party or the army. Khrushchev himself had emotionally denounced its terror. It was still possible to prosecute and even persecute individuals by terrorist means, but Stalin's mass terror as a system of government had disappeared.

Instead of terror, Khrushchev embarked on a series of bureaucratic changes. He gave the Russian Republic, by far the largest and most populous of the republics, virtually a separate administration, and took complete control of its personnel. In 1963 he took parallel measures for central Asia and the Transcaucasus. Khrushchev was wrestling with the problems of efficiency, output, and morale. Under Stalin, centralization had reached an intolerable tightness. But how far could one decentralize so huge an operation as the Soviet economy and still retain control over local operations? How far could one centralize and still obtain local cooperation, loyalty, and, especially, production? Between 1953 and 1957, responsibility for many heavy industries was transferred from the ministries of the central government to those of the individual republics. In May 1957 a decree abolished many central ministries, and transferred their duties to 105 newly created regional economic councils (*sovnarkhoz*), in the hope of giving full play to informed, on-the-spot decisions, of improving the use of local resources, of consolidating overlapping services, and of reassigning experts from the central government to the grass roots. Regionalism—devotion to regional interests as against national ones—replaced what might be called devotion to one industry ahead of others. But patriots for Armenian industry (to the detriment of other regions) were no more helpful to the national economy than patriots for the cement industry (to the detriment of other industries).

By 1960 a process of recentralizing had begun. By the end of 1962, the sovnarkhozes were reduced from 105 to about 40, and new state committees appeared to oversee their work. These committees greatly resembled the old ministries, and in fact were before long reorganized as ministries. The pendulum had swung back almost the entire distance. Now all lower levels of the party were divided into agricultural and industrial wings, in an effort to make the political functionaries serve the economy more efficiently.

In mid-October, 1964, the world learned to its astonishment that Khrushchev had been removed from power and succeeded by two members of the Presidium. L. I. Brezhnev replaced him as first secretary of the Central Committee of the Communist party, and A. N. Kosygin as premier (chairman of the U.S.S.R. Council of Ministers). Both were "Khrushchev men": Brezhnev, aged 58, a metallurgist by training, had held posts in the Ukrainian, Moldavian, and Kazakhstan Communist parties, entering the Presidium in 1957; Kosygin, aged 50, an engineer, commissar of the textile industry in 1938, premier of the Russian Republic throughout World War II, member of the Politburo from 1949 to 1952, and minister for light industry, went into eclipse shortly before Stalin died and reemerged as a member of the Presidium only in 1957. The published communiqués spoke of Khrushchev's ill health and advanced age, but it was clear that he had not acquiesced in his own removal. How had Brezhnev and Kosygin managed it? And why? And what did they stand for?

Khrushchev did not practice the kind of constant vigilance over his associates that alone could have ensured him security in office. The plotters acted in his absence, and took careful steps to line up the members of the Central Committee in support of their action so that he could not appeal to the Committee over the head of the Presidium as he had done in 1957. Khrushchev continued to live in retirement in Moscow and in his country house. No large-scale purge followed his removal.

Khrushchev was responsible for major agricultural failures at home and much more serious Soviet setbacks abroad, as we shall see. Yet he might have continued in office had it not been for his personal rudeness. The communiqué that announced his replacement referred to his *prozhekterstvo* ("hare-brained scheming"), no doubt in reference to the virgin lands fiasco (see below), and to "half-baked conclusions and hasty decisions and actions, divorced from reality; bragging and bluster; attraction to rule by fiat [literally, "commandism"]." Caustic and crude, Khrushchev had apparently tried his former supporters too far.

INDUSTRY AND AGRICULTURE. Khrushchev had faced the same problem that had faced all Soviet leaders: how much emphasis could be put on consumer goods, and how much still must be devoted to heavy industry? Though temperamentally more interested in providing consumer goods than Stalin or Malenkov, Khrushchev made the same choice as they: continued emphasis on the means of production. The sixth five-year plan (1956–1960) set more ambitious goals than ever before, but the huge expenses involved in the Polish and Hungarian outbreaks forced the Soviet government to shelve the plan. By the end of 1958 it announced a new seven-year plan, to run until 1965. Starting from base figures of 500 million tons of coal, 55 million tons of steel, and 113 million tons of oil, output by 1964 had reached 554 million tons of coal, 85 million tons of steel, and 224 million tons of oil. In 1966, the regime returned to the system of five-year plans.

Most spectacular were the successes achieved in the field of rocketry and space. The U.S.S.R. successfully launched the first earth satellite (Sputnik, 1957) and first reached the moon with a rocket (1959). Heavy payloads soared aloft before American engineers could get their lighter ones off the ground. Spurred to some degree by the Soviet technical advance, the United States itself embarked in the late Fifties on an intensive program of research and development in space. Though the U.S.S.R. got the first man into space, and for some time held the lead in technical achievements, by the mid-Sixties the United States had logged more hours of flight by spaceships with one-man and two-man crews, and had virtually solved the problem of rendezvous in space, while the successful Mars-probe operation of 1965 overshadowed comparable So-

The Soviet Union, 1971

Arctic Ocean

Bering Sea

Pacific Ocean

NORWAY
SWEDEN
FINLAND

Barents Sea
Kara Sea
NOVAYA ZEMLYA

Murmansk
Archangel
Leningrad (Petrograd)
Moscow
Smolensk
Gerki
Vorkuta
Pechora R.
Dudinka
Igarka
Khatanga
Tiksi
Anadyr

S   I   B   E   R   I   A

U R A L   M T S.

Molotov (Perm)
Sverdlovsk
Kuibyshev
Volgograd
Don R.
Kharkov
Kiev
DONBAS
Dnipropetrovsk
Rostov
CRIMEA
Black Sea
Caspian Sea
Baku
Tiflis

KUZNETSK
Omsk
Novosibirsk
Novokuznetsk
Barnaul
Magnitogorsk
Karaganda
L. Balkhash
Aral Sea
Tashkent
Dushanbe
Frunze
Alma Ata
SINKIANG

Ob R.
Yenisei R.
Tunguska R.
Lena R.
Aldam R.
Angara R.
Krasnoyarsk
Irkutsk
L. Baikal
China
Yakutsk
Kolyma R.
Magadan
KAMCHATKA
Petropavlovsk

Sea of Okhotsk
SAKHALIN I.
KURILE IS.
Blagoveshchensk
Khabarovsk
Vladivostok
Amur R.
MANCHURIA
MONGOLIA

C H I N A

ALEUTIAN IS. (U.S.)

JAPAN
NORTH KOREA
SOUTH KOREA
TAIWAN (FORMOSA)
PHILIPPINE IS.

NORTH VIETNAM
SOUTH VIETNAM
THAILAND
CAMB.
LAOS
BURMA
E. PAK.
BHUTAN
NEPAL
INDIA
KASHMIR
W. PAKISTAN
AFGHANISTAN
IRAN
IRAQ
SAUDI ARABIA
JORDAN
SYRIA
LEBANON
ISRAEL
TURKEY
Mediterranean Sea
GREECE
ALB.
BULGARIA
YUGOSLAVIA
ITALY
AUST.
CZECH.
E. GER.
WEST GERMANY
POLAND
CARPATHO-UKRAINE

AFRICA

SOVIET SOCIALIST REPUBLICS

1. Russian Soviet Federated
   Socialist Republic
2. White Russia
3. Ukraine

4. Georgia
5. Armenia
6. Azerbaidjan
7. Turkmenistan

8. Uzbekistan
9. Tadjikistan
10. Kirghiz Republic
11. Kazakh Republic

12. Estonia
13. Latvia
14. Lithuania
15. Moldavia

Areas annexed since 1940
Other Communist countries
Industrial areas (in U.S.S.R.)

viet exploration of the solar system. The successful American landing of a manned space vehicle on the moon (1969) tended to overshadow Soviet efforts, despite an American failure to repeat the triumph and the landing of an unmanned Soviet vehicle in 1970.

Agriculture continued to present the Soviet planners with some of its seemingly most insoluble problems. In 1953 Khrushchev embarked on the "virgin lands" scheme, a crash program to plow under more than 100,000 acres of prairie in the Urals region, Kazakhstan, and Siberia. Drought and poor planning and performance led to a clear failure by 1963. By the following year, the number of collective farms was down to about 40,000 from an original 250,000 and the average size of the new units was far larger, perhaps about 5,000 acres. By 1965, the government recognized that many collectives were now too big.

To increase incentives, the regime in 1958 abolished compulsory deliveries of farm products, the most onerous of the peasants' burdens, and raised agricultural prices. Simultaneously, the government decreed the gradual abolition of the MTS (Machine Tractor Stations) and the sale of the tractors to the individual collectives, which the government undertook to subsidize in part. In 1964, the government for the first time extended its system of old-age and disability pensions to agricultural laborers; it removed the ceilings on the private allotment of land allowed to the individual peasant in a collective and on the number of cattle that he might own privately. Yet yields continued low; animal husbandry caused grave concern, and the regime's agencies thundered against inefficiency and "fascination with administration by fiat."

In the years after Khrushchev's fall from power in 1964, the Soviet authorities engaged in an open debate about the best way to revise the statutes governing the collective farm (artel) in view of the immense changes since 1936. The party and the government ordered the collective farms to guarantee the individual farmers a monthly sum in cash for their work, and to pay in addition for the produce actually received. The state bank would advance the farms the credit where necessary. Some economists were arguing for the introduction of a free market economy; others vigorously defended centralized planning (with improvements). Obviously the Soviet authorities were recognizing the impor-

tance of "capitalist" incentives in the field of agriculture as in many others.

Yet the problems of supply and production continued to be intractable, and the regime itself was often caustic in its denunciations of failures caused by stupidity and bad management. It was always difficult to decide how grave the problems really were, and how far the regime's shrillness was designed to frighten the Russians themselves into making further superhuman efforts.

EDUCATION AND THE ARTS. In 1958 Khrushchev introduced an important change in the Soviet educational system: "polytechnization," which emphasized vocational training and on-the-job experience. This represented a retreat from the goal of a ten-year general educational program for all. Khrushchev ordered the universities now to favor applicants who had had practical experience. By the mid-Sixties, almost all children in the U.S.S.R. finished the first four years of school (ages seven to eleven), and illiteracy had virtually disappeared. Almost as many finished the second four years (ages eleven to fifteen), which were now combined with "polytechnization." In 1964, the conventional next course of three years (ages fifteen to eighteen), usually taken by only about 40 percent of Soviet youth, was reduced to two years. Nationwide talent contests were held to discover the most promising candidates for university study in math and science.

Khrushchev extended to the field of arts and letters the same partial relaxation that accompanied de-Stalinization in other fields. It took Soviet writers some time to accustom themselves to the idea that it might now be possible to voice dissent: too many had vanished forever at Stalin's whim to make the risk an attractive one. Moreover, convinced Stalinists or party hacks who had grown up under Stalinism lay in wait to attack the innovator. Khrushchev was himself opinionated and autocratic, and kept artists and writers in constant uncertainty lest new purges break forth. The dangers of self-expression continued great indeed.

In a few individual books and authors we may find indices of the new policies. Ilya Ehrenburg, veteran propagandist for the regime, in *The Thaw* (1955) hailed the relaxation of coercive measures over artists. Vladimir Dudintsev's novel *Not By Bread Alone* (1956) had as its hero a competent and enthusiastic engineer whose invention of a new pipe-casting machine was thwarted at every turn by the entrenched bureaucrats. Government-controlled writers' agencies denounced Dudintsev, who retracted his views, and for six or seven years was forced to earn his living by translation only. Boris Pasternak's *Dr. Zhivago* (1958) became a *cause célèbre* throughout the world. Pasternak, a brilliant poet who had for years confined himself to translating Shakespeare, took advantage of the "thaw" to offer for publication his novel about a doctor who, through all the agonies of the First World War and the Russian Revolution, affirmed the freedom of the human soul. Accepted for publication in Russia, the novel was also sent to Italy to be published. Then the Soviet censors changed their minds, and forced Pasternak to ask that the manuscript in Italy be returned to him. The Italian publisher refused, and versions in Russian, Italian, English, and other languages appeared abroad, arousing great admiration. In 1958 the Nobel Prize Committee selected Pasternak as the winner of the prize for literature. He accepted. But then the Khrushchev regime reverted to Stalinism: Pasternak's fellow writers reviled him as a pig and a traitor, and the government threatened him with exile if he accepted the prize. As a patriotic Russian he then declined it.

In the same week that a Soviet physicist accepted the Nobel Prize for physics, the regime called the Nobel Prize for literature a capitalist invention. And a few years later, Mikhail Sholokhov, author of the famous Cossack trilogy *The Quiet Don* and a personal friend of Khrushchev, accepted the Nobel Prize for literature. Pasternak's persecution revealed the limits of the thaw as of 1958. His Jewish origins, his intellectualism, his proclamation of individualism touched hostile chords in Khrushchev himself and in other Soviet officials and writers, making it impossible to publish *Dr. Zhivago* in the U.S.S.R.

But the spirit of individualism, slow to express itself even when liberated in the older generation, found in the 1960's new and more vigorous expression among the younger poets and novelists who had grown up since the Second World War, and for whom the heroic age of the Revolution and the early Bolshevik struggles were ancient history. The young Ukrainian poet Yevtushenko denounced Soviet anti-Semitism in his *Babi Yar* (the name of the ravine near Kiev in which the Nazis had massacred thousands of Jews), and declared his identity with the murdered human beings. In another poem he begged the government to double and triple the guard over Stalin's tomb,

> *So that Stalin may not rise*
> *And, with Stalin the past.*

> *. . . the ignoring of the people's welfare*
> *The calumnies*
> *The arrests of the innocent.*

Former supporters of Stalin, he went on,

> *Do not like these times*
> *When the camps are empty*
> *And the halls where people listen to poetry*
> *Are crowded.* *

When Yevtushenko recited his verse, the halls were indeed always crowded with eager, excited, contentious young people, claiming the right to think for themselves. "We've found out," said another young poet, "what it leads to when somebody else does our thinking for us."

Yevtushenko's mention of "the camps" suggests another new phenomenon in the Soviet writing of the early Sixties, the deep interest in the terrible days of Stalin's labor camps and in the suffering of their inmates, reflected, for example, in Alexander Solzhenitsyn's novel *A Day in the Life of Ivan Denisovich*. Khrushchev viewed with some apprehension the flood of fiction about the camps that came pouring into the publishing houses, only a little of which was published. Khrushchev tried to remind the younger generation of the glorious revolutionary past through which their elders had triumphantly lived. He declared—as if in answer to their demands for full freedom—that even under full communism it would not be possible to give complete liberty to the individual, who would continue "like a bee in a hive" to make his contribution to society.

After Khrushchev's ouster in 1964, his successors denounced him for interfering in intellectual life, but here, as elsewhere, they did not depart very far from his policies. Indeed, they tightened the reigns of censorship and repression. In September 1965 two writers, Andrei Sinyavsky and Yuli Daniel, were arrested for writing under pseudonyms and sending abroad anti-Soviet fiction and essays. Writing as Abram

* *Pravda*, October 21, 1962.

Yevgeny Yevtushenko with the composer Dmitri Shosta-kovich, 1963.

allowed. In 1966, despite the protests of many young people, Sinyavsky and Daniel were tried and condemned to prison.

The defection in 1967 of Stalin's daughter, Svetlana Alliluyeva, to the United States and the publication in this country of her autobiography were treated vituperatively in the Soviet press as part of a plot arranged by American agents to spoil the celebrations planned for the fiftieth anniversary of the Revolution of 1917. At the Writers' Congress of 1967 old-line writers re-affirmed the theories of socialist realism, and attacked all who opposed them. In 1968 the authorities arrested three young men and one young woman and charged them with treasonable contact with a foreign agent, a spy of Russian origin who had allegedly paid them to circulate anti-Soviet materials from abroad. All were imprisoned after a trial against which some of the young writers protested, thereby bringing down upon themselves vigorous rebukes. At least one of the accused and one of the chief protestors were Jews.

Solzhenitsyn—whose somber and gripping novels *The First Circle* and *Cancer Ward* convinced Western readers that Russian humane values had found a spokesman of the stature of Tolstoy or Pasternak—found himself in 1970 expelled from the party's Union of Writers and silenced. When in his turn he was awarded the Nobel Prize in 1970, he accepted it, but explained that he could not come to Stockholm to receive it because he might not be permitted to return to Russia. He and others were denounced as "spiritual emigrants" from the U.S.S.R. The voices of the protesters were more clearly audible in the West than ever before, and this too infuriated the regime. Protesters in the arts and sciences were on the whole ruthlessly dealt with, and hackwork of the old Stalinist type was still rewarded. Early in 1971, it was plain that the regime continued to have severe problems in controlling its "intelligentsia," perhaps 20 percent of the Soviet working population, and equally plain that freedom of expression would continue to be curbed.

Tertz, Sinyavsky, in *The Trial Begins,* had given a candid and revolting picture of the life of the Soviet leaders under Stalin; his novel *Lyubimov* (translated into English as *The Makepeace Experiment*) dealt with a one-man revolt against communism in a small Russian town; and his essay *On Socialist Realism* damned what was still the official literary doctrine of the regime. Writing as Nikolai Arzhak, Daniel, in *Moscow Calling,* produced a fantasy in which the Soviet government set aside one day on which murder was

Reading Suggestions on the Postwar World

See the list at the end of Chapter 31.

31

The Postwar World,
1945–1970

Part 2

I Soviet Foreign Policy

The Last Years of Stalin, 1945–1953

EASTERN EUROPE, IRAN, GREECE, AND BERLIN
When the war ended, the Soviet Union did not
immediately terminate all forms of cooperation
with its allies. The joint plan for dividing and
ruling Germany went through. The four occupying powers together tried the chief surviving Nazi leaders at Nuremberg in 1946. In
February 1947 came the peace treaties with
Italy, Romania, Bulgaria, Hungary, and (for the
U.S.S.R.) Finland. These confirmed Soviet territorial gains: from Romania, Bessarabia and
northern Bukovina; from Finland, portions of
Karelia and a long lease on the naval base at
Porkkala. In addition, the U.S.S.R. annexed part
of former East Prussia and the extreme easternmost portion of Czechoslovakia.

In Poland, Romania, Hungary, and Bulgaria
the U.S.S.R., relying on the pressure of the Red

Above: May Day parade in Prague, 1960.
Above right: Third-world leaders Nasser, Nehru,
and Tito in 1956. Right: A cargo plane
leaves Tempelhof Air Base during the Berlin
blockade of 1948–1949.

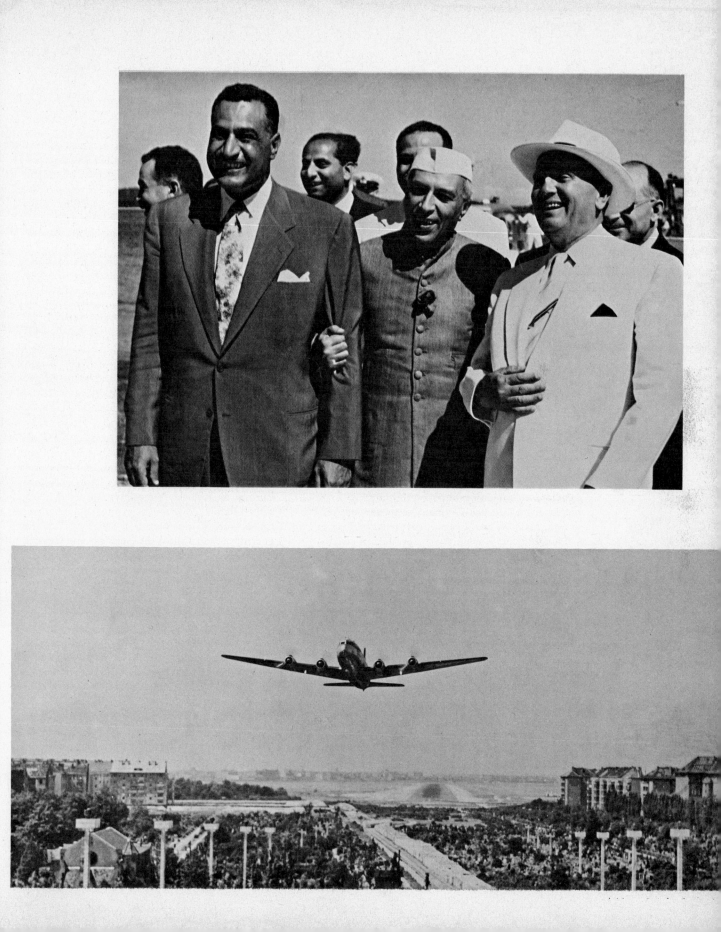

Armies, sponsored the creation of new "people's republics" under communist governments. In each country, the Russians eliminated all political groups that could be accused of collaboration with the Germans. Then they formed "progressive" coalitions of parties, and next destroyed all noncommunist elements in these coalitions: they split off from each party a small fragment that would collaborate unquestioningly with the communists, and then denounced and persecuted the remainder. Elections, despite the promises at Yalta, were accompanied by intimidation and atrocity. Western protest uniformly failed. These four states became true Soviet satellites.

Yugoslavia organized its own communist state, and had Albania as its own satellite. Soviet troops occupied about a third of Germany, roughly between the Elbe and the Oder rivers, where they organized the communist-ruled satellite of East Germany. The part of Germany lying east of the line formed by the Oder and Neisse rivers, save for the sections of East Prussia directly annexed to the U.S.S.R., the Russians handed over to their Polish satellite. Here a wholesale transfer of population removed the Germans, and replaced them with Poles. Finland became part of the Russian security system, but retained its prewar political institutions. The four Allied powers detached Austria from Germany, thus undoing Hitler's Anschluss of 1938; and divided it, like Germany, into four occupation zones. The presence of Soviet troops in Hungary and Romania was specifically guaranteed, in order to "protect" the communication lines between the Soviet Union and its occupying forces in Austria.

In 1948, the communists took over Czechoslovakia by a coup d'état, and ousted the government of Edward Beneš, brave enemy of Hitler in 1938, betrayed now for a second time. Within each satellite the communists aped Soviet policies, moving with all speed to collectivize agriculture, impose forced-draft industrialization, control cultural life, and govern by terror.

As early as 1946 the U.S.S.R. refused to withdraw its forces from northwest Iran, and yielded only to pressure from the United Nations. A more alarming probe of the Soviet perimeter came in Greece, where a communist-dominated guerrilla movement had already during World War II attempted to seize control, and had been thwarted only by British troops. In 1946, the Greek communists tried again, backed this time by the Soviet-dominated governments of Albania, Yugoslavia, and Bulgaria to the north. Simultaneously, Stalin exerted pressure on the Turks for concessions in the Straits area. In response President Truman proclaimed that countries facing the threat of communist aggression could count on help from the United States. Under this "Truman Doctrine," he sent American military aid to Greece and Turkey. The threat to the Turks evaporated, and by 1949, after severe fighting, the Greeks had put down the communist rebellion with the help of American advisers.

In Germany, the Russians began in 1948 one of the most bitter phases of the Cold War. By shutting off the land routes from the West into Berlin, they attempted to force the Western Allies to turn Berlin wholly over to them. The Allies stood firm, however, and in the next six months flew more than 2,300,000 tons of coal, food, and other necessities into West Berlin. Though the Russians gave up and reopened the land routes, Soviet determination to oust the Western powers from Berlin remained unaltered.

THE YUGOSLAV REBELLION   In 1948 the Russians found themselves faced with rebellion from a country that had hitherto seemed the most pro-Soviet of all the new communist states of eastern Europe: Yugoslavia. Yugoslavia had overthrown a pro-German government in 1941 and remained throughout World War II a theater of intense guerrilla action against the Germans and Italians. There were two main groups of guerrillas, the Chetniks, led by General Mikhailovich, representing the Serb royalist domination over the south Slav kingdom, and the Partisans, led by the Croatian-born communist Joseph Broz, better known by his underground name, Tito. As the war continued, the communist-dominated Partisans gained ground against the Chetniks, who preferred to compromise with the German and Italian occupying forces rather than continue a war in alliance with communists. By 1943, Prime Minister Churchill, with his eyes fixed on the paramount need to beat Hitler, decided to support Tito with supplies, and the United States followed suit. When the Russians entered Belgrade in October 1944, they helped put their fellow communist Tito in control.

Once in power, Tito installed his own communist government, abolished the Yugoslav monarchy, and for three years adopted all the standard Soviet policies. Yet in June 1948, the world learned with surprise that the U.S.S.R. had quarreled with Yugoslavia, and expelled Tito's regime from the Cominform. The Soviet satellites broke their economic agreements with Yugoslavia, unloosed great barrages of anti-Tito propaganda, and stirred up border incidents. We know now that Soviet arrogance and insistence on penetrating the Yugoslavia army and security organizations had aroused Yugoslav national feeling, never very far below the surface. Stalin believed that he could bully the Yugoslavs into submission. "I will shake my little finger," he said, "and there will be no more Tito."

But Tito remained in power, accepting the aid that was quickly offered him by the United States. Washington saw that a communist regime hostile to Stalin was a new phenomenon that could not but embarrass the Russians. Gradually Yugoslav communism evolved a modified ideology of its own, declaring that Stalin was a heretic, and Tito and his followers the only true Leninists. Tito decentralized the economy, beginning in the factories, where workers' committees now began to participate actively in the planning. From the economy, decentralization spread to the local government apparatus, then to the central government, and finally to the Yugoslav Communist party, now rechristened "League of Yugoslav Communists." Though the regime admitted its past outrageous excesses, the police continued to be a powerful force. Tito also gradually abandoned agricultural collectivization, which, as always, was most unpopular with the peasants. Yugoslavia remained communist, however, suspicious of the Western capitalists who were helping it.

In their fear of the spread of this new "national" communism to the other satellites, the Soviets directed the other eastern European regimes in a series of ferocious purges, executing leading communists for "Titoism," and thus terrorizing anyone who might hope to establish any sort of autonomy within the communist bloc. When Stalin died in 1953, his heirs gave high priority to healing the breach with Yugoslavia, and eliminating the weakness it had created in their European position.

ASIA: THE KOREAN WAR   When balked in Europe, czarist Russian governments had often turned to Asia. After the failures in Greece and Berlin, the Soviet Union similarly embarked on new Asian adventures. Here, communists had tried and failed to win power in Indonesia, Burma, Malaya, and the Philippines, and had succeeded in China. The Korean War, which broke out in June 1950, was in some measure a Soviet-sponsored operation, although the Russians themselves limited their contribution to support and sympathy, and allowed their Chinese ally to take the military lead.

Korea, a peninsula at the eastern extremity of Asia, bordering on Manchuria and Siberia and close to Japan, had been a target of Russian interest in the late nineteenth and early twentieth centuries, but the Japanese defeat of the Russians in 1905 had led instead to Japanese annexation of the country in 1910. In 1945, at the close of World War II, Russian troops occupied the northern part of Korea, and American troops occupied the southern part. The country was divided in the middle by a line along the 38th parallel of latitude. A communist-inspired People's Democratic Republic of Korea was set up on the north, and an American-inspired Republic of Korea on the south. When all American forces except for a few specialists were withdrawn from South Korea, the North Koreans marched south to unite the nation under communist control.

It is probable that the communists thought the operation was safe, since American pronouncements had seemed to refer to Korea as outside the American "defense perimeter." But when the invasion began, the United States—with UN approval, for the vote was taken in the absence of the Russians—at once moved troops into Korea. They halted the North Korean drive, and pushed the enemy back well north of the 38th parallel, almost to the Yalu River, the frontier of China. At this point, Communist China entered the war, and Chinese troops joined the North Koreans in pushing the Americans southward again. By 1951, the line of battle had been stabilized roughly along the old boundary between North and South Korea. After prolonged negotiations, an armistice was finally concluded in July 1953.

The Korean settlement by no means ended the tension between Communist China and the United States. Serious friction developed over Formosa (Taiwan) and the smaller offshore islands, Quemoy and Matsu, now in the hands of Chiang Kai-shek. Nor did the Korean settlement bring closer understanding between the U.S.S.R.

U.S. marines in North Korea, December 1950.

and the United States. It was at best a compromise: after all the fighting, the United States had managed to hang on to the devastated southern portion of the country, and the communists had been driven back to the north, which they governed undisturbed. Neither side could call it a victory. By the time it was reached, Stalin had been dead for more than three months.

Stalin's Heirs

Stalin's heirs realized that any attack that threatened the vital interests of the United States might well touch off the ultimate disaster. A policy of probing to see just which interests the United States considered vital had already led to the Korean War. Continued tension between the two superpowers required the U.S.S.R. to continue to devote its resources to guns rather than to butter. To relax the tension would theoretically have meant more butter, but would in turn raise the danger that the U.S.S.R. would lose its position as leader of the world communist movement. China, with its determination to seize Taiwan and to expand in Asia, might seize the leadership of revolutionary forces at least in Asia, and would represent the Russians as old and tired, no longer true Leninists. In the end it proved to be impossible for Khrushchev to hold all these threats in balance, and the choices he eventually felt forced to make led to a major split in the communist world.

EASTERN EUROPE   In eastern Europe, Khrushchev made a great effort to heal the breach with Tito. In May 1955 he went in person to Belgrade, and not only publicly apologized for the quarrel, taking the blame upon the U.S.S.R., but openly agreed that "differences in the concrete forms of developing socialism are exclusively matters for the people of the country concerned," which seemed to echo Tito's own views. Relations between Tito and Moscow were temporarily improved, although the Yugoslavs never abandoned their ties to the West. Khrushchev even went so far as to declare that many prominent victims of the "Titoist" purges had been executed wrongly, and he abolished the Cominform, the body that ostensibly had started the quarrel with Tito. But in making these admissions and healing the quarrel Stalin had started, Khrushchev had opened the door to new troubles.

Khrushchev's speech of 1956 denouncing Stalin and admitting so many past injustices proved far too strong a brew for the European satellites. Anticommunist riots by workers in Poznan, Poland, in June 1956, were followed by severe upheavals in the rest of that country. Though Polish national sentiment was declaring itself, the uprising remained within the grip of one wing of the Communist party, that led by Wladislaw Gomulka, who had been purged for alleged Titoism in 1951. Not even the presence in Warsaw of Khrushchev himself and other members of the Soviet Presidium prevented the rise of Gomulka to power, although at one moment the Russians seem to have contemplated using their army to impose their will by force. Yet because the new government in Poland was, after all, a communist government, they allowed it to remain in power.

In Hungary, however, the upheaval went farther. Starting, like the Polish uprising, as an anti-Stalinist movement within the Communist party, the Hungarian disturbance at first brought Imre Nagy, a communist like Gomulka, into office as premier. But popular hatred for communism and for the Russians got out of hand, and young men and women flew to arms in Budapest in the hope of ousting the communists and of taking Hungary altogether out of the Soviet sphere. They even denounced the Warsaw Pact, the Russian alliance of eastern European satellites set up by Moscow to oppose NATO. It was then that Khrushchev ordered full-fledged military action. In November 1956 Soviet tanks and troops, violating an armistice, swept back into Budapest and put down the revolution in blood and fire. A puppet government led by Janos Kadar was installed. More than 150,000 Hungarians refugees fled to Austria, to be resettled in various Western countries. Despite the Soviet charges that the uprising had

been trumped up by the Western "imperialists" and "fascists," the West in fact had played no part at all, not daring to help the Hungarians for fear of starting a world war.

Soviet military intervention in Hungary showed the world how limited was Khrushchev's willingness and ability to permit free choices to other communist states. Tito denounced the Soviet intervention against Nagy, though he was frightened by the wholly anticommunist character that the Hungarian revolt subsequently took on, and he failed to oppose the decisive Soviet military operations that put an end to the uprising.

For a second time, relations between Moscow and Tito were strained. They were patched up again in the summer of 1957, but Tito flatly refused to sign a declaration of twelve Communist parties denouncing "revisionism"—as Tito's own views had come to be known. Instead he published his own counterprogram declaring that each communist nation should make its own decisions freely. The old quarrel was renewed for the third time. Tito would not reenter a world communist union led by Russia. Khrushchev's efforts had failed.

Both the harshness of the onslaught against revisionism and Khrushchev's acceptance of defeat in his efforts to win the Yugoslavs by softness reflected Chinese influence. Eager to play a leading role in formulating world communist ideology, the Chinese displayed a strong preference for Stalinist orthodoxy and repression. By the spring of 1958, the Chinese and Khrushchev himself had declared that Stalin's original denunciation of the Yugoslavs back in 1948 had been correct after all. In June 1958 the Soviet government underlined this decision in grim fashion when it announced the executions of Imre Nagy and other leaders of the Hungarian uprising, in violation of solemn promises of safe-conduct.

All the eastern European satellites were bound together in the Council for Mutual Economic Aid (Comecon), established in 1949, which took measures to standardize machinery and coordinate economic policies, and issued blasts against western European efforts at cooperation like the Common Market. Yugoslavia never was a member, and after 1958 was not invited to send observers. In 1958–1959, Comecon called for a "specialization" plan, in accordance with which the more developed countries would concentrate on heavy industry, and Romania in particular on the production of raw materials (chiefly food and oil). The Romanian government, communist though it was, protested, pointing to its already considerable achievements in heavy industry; and in December 1961 Romania openly refused to accept the "principles" of the "international socialist division of labor," issued at the twenty-second congress of the CPSU. All through 1962 the disagreement persisted, with Khrushchev trying and failing to force the Romanians into line.

Thus the Romanians, like the Yugoslavs, were assuming an independent position within the communist bloc. They increased their trade with the noncommunist world, and they remained neutral in the growing Soviet–Chinese quarrel. In July 1963 the Russians gave in on the economic question, and sanctioned Romania's continued efforts to build a steel industry, while postponing the economic integration of the bloc until 1966, by which time Romania would be entitled to the same status as Czechoslovakia and Poland.

The Soviet–Romanian disagreement soon widened. Soviet propaganda called for integrating the lower Danube region—which would have meant taking territory from Romania—and denied that the Romanians had contributed to the Allied cause in World War II. The Romanians claimed full credit for their own "liberation from fascism," and—most important—even dared to demand the return to Romania of the provinces of Bessarabia and northern Bukovina, annexed by the U.S.S.R. in 1940. Yugoslav–Romanian cooperation became an important part of Romanian policy. Down to 1970, largely owing to the firmness and balancing skill of the Romanian Communist leader, Ceausescu, no doubt supported by the traditionally anti-Russian sentiments of Romanians generally, the Romanian effort to avoid being swallowed by the U.S.S.R. remained successful.

Elsewhere within the Soviet bloc in eastern Europe, there was a general liberalizing trend in Hungary. Increased tourism, wider trade with the West, better living conditions, even success with agricultural collectivization, a new agreement with the Vatican concerning the Hungarian church, and improved education all spoke of relaxed terror. In Poland, however, which had after Gomulka's success for some years enjoyed more freedom of discussion and contact with the West than any other communist country, the trend was reversed. In economic planning, in agriculture, in education, in religious policies, even in a return to anti-Semitism, a kind of neo-Stalinism emerged as standard. At the very end of 1970 a sudden rise of prices announced by the government just before Christmas precipitated serious riots, especially in the port cites of Gdansk (Danzig) and Szczecin (Stettin). Police and tanks put down the riots with heavy loss of life, and the Gomulka government fell. Edward Gierek, Gomulka's successor, seemed to have the situation under control, but once again the brittleness of communist control of the eastern European peoples had been demonstrated, although the cause of the disturbance had apparently been economic rather than ideological.

In Czechoslovakia, liberalization began in the middle Sixties, beginning before Khrushchev's ouster and continuing after it. Economic failure of the communist bureaucracy in a formerly prosperous industrial state and an entrenched and particularly brutal party leadership had aroused great discontent, which was to burst forth dramatically in 1968 and produce an international crisis (see below).

BERLIN AGAIN In East Germany (D.D.R., the Deutsche Demokratische Republik), the U.S.S.R. had created its most industrially productive European satellite, now fully geared into the Comecon. Except for a workers' riot in East Berlin in 1953, the German communist puppets had succeeded in repressing the population's aversion to Soviet and communist rule. Moreover, strategically the D.D.R. was of great importance to the U.S.S.R.: control over East Germany enabled the Russians to keep Poland surrounded, helpless to achieve more than a token autonomy. Yet the United States, Britain, and France each retained a zone of occupation in Berlin, deep in the heart of the D.D.R., and accessible by subway from East Berlin. Every year, thousands of East Germans showed how they felt about communism by escaping into West Berlin. The East German population actually declined by 2,000,000 between 1949 and 1961. For those who stayed behind in the D.D.R., West Berlin provided an example of prosperity and free democratic government that acted more effectively on their minds than any mere propaganda.

This situation accounted for Khrushchev's

determination to get the Western powers out of Berlin. The method he proposed in 1958 and later years was thoroughly Stalinist: he threatened to sign a peace treaty with the puppet government of East Germany, never recognized by the West; to turn over to it the communications to Berlin; and to support it in any effort it might then make to cut these communications and force the Western powers out. Western refusal to accept this abrogation of agreements concluded during World War II led to a prolonged diplomatic crisis during 1959.

The West could neither permit the U.S.S.R. to recreate the conditions it had fought during the airlift of 1948 nor accept the suggestion that, once Western troops were removed, Berlin would be a "free city." Defenseless and surrounded by communist territory, Berlin and its 2,000,000 "free" citizens, it feared, would soon be swallowed up. Moreover, the negotiations proposed by the U.S.S.R., whereby the D.D.R. would thereafter "confederate" with the West German Federal Republic, aroused the gravest doubts. How could a state that was a full member of the Western system of NATO federate with one that belonged to the Soviet system's Warsaw Pact? How could a state that stood for free capitalist development federate with one completely communized? How could a parliamentary state responsibly governed by a multi-party system with checks and balances federate with a communist totalitarian state? Khrushchev surely did not believe in the possibility of the confederation he was proposing, and hoped instead that any possible union of the Germanies would be discredited, and that the D.D.R., with full control over Berlin, would emerge as a permanent Soviet satellite. But even a Soviet success in Berlin short of this complete victory would have meant that the West had in some measure at least recognized East Germany, which in turn would have severely disturbed West German stability and disrupted NATO.

U-2, THE BERLIN WALL, TESTING, CUBA While the Berlin threat persisted, Vice-President Nixon visited the U.S.S.R., where he and Khrushchev had a famous confrontation in a model kitchen that was part of an American exhibit. President Eisenhower and Khrushchev agreed to exchange visits, and Khrushchev actually made a dramatic tour of the United States. When the leaders of the great powers met at the

summit in Paris (May 1960), tensions, however, were once again inflamed by the U-2 incident: a Soviet missile had brought down a lightweight, extremely fast American plane that had been taking high-altitude photographs of Soviet territory, and the Russians had captured the pilot unharmed. After an initial denial, President Eisenhower found himself obliged to acknowledge the truth of the charge; and the incident ended both the summit meeting and the plans for his own visit to the U.S.S.R.

When Eisenhower's successor, John F. Kennedy, met Khrushchev in Vienna (June 1961), Khrushchev insisted that the U.S.S.R. would sign the treaty with East Germany before the end of the year. Tension mounted, and the number of refugees fleeing East Berlin rose to a thousand a day. On August 13, East German forces cut the communications between East and West Berlin and began to build a barrier—the Berlin Wall—to prevent further departures. Taken by surprise, the United States realized that it could not resort to arms to prevent the closing of the East Germans' own border. The government protested, and sent Vice-President Lyndon Johnson to reassure the West Berliners of America's unshaken resolve. The wall itself became the symbol of a government that had to imprison its own people to keep them at home. Occasional hair-raising escapes and poignant recaptures or shootings continued to take place along the wall's length. But the crisis proved to be over. Khrushchev had backed away from unilateral abrogation of the Berlin treaties.

But Khrushchev announced on August 30, 1961, that the U.S.S.R. would resume atomic testing in the atmosphere, which had been stopped by both powers in 1958. In the two months that followed, the Russians exploded thirty huge bombs, whose total force considerably exceeded all previous American, British, and French explosions. President Kennedy now decided that, unless Khrushchev would agree to a treaty banning all tests, the United States would have to conduct its own new tests. Khrushchev refused, and the American tests began late in April 1962. All during the months that followed, conversations on disarmament, including of course arrangements for the banning of future tests, continued with the Russians at Geneva.

It was during the summer of 1962 that Khrushchev moved to place Soviet missiles with

Kennedy and Khrushchev at the Vienna summit meeting, 1961.

nuclear warheads in Cuba, where an American-sponsored landing directed against the pro-communist regime of Fidel Castro had failed dismally at the Bay of Pigs the year before. Castro may not have asked for the missiles, but he did accept them. Soviet officers were to retain control over their use. Their installation would effectively have doubled the Soviet capacity to strike directly at the United States, but the chief threat was political: when known, the mere presence of these weapons ninety miles from Florida would shake the confidence of all other nations in the American capacity to protect even the United States. It would enable Khrushchev to blackmail America on the question of Berlin. American military intelligence discovered the sites and photographed them from the air. Khrushchev announced that the Soviet purpose

was simply to help the Cubans resist a new invasion from the United States, which he professed to believe threatened.

But Kennedy could not allow the missiles to stay in Cuba. The only course of action at first seemed an air strike, which might well have touched off a new world war. Kennedy found a measure that would prevent the further delivery of missiles—a sea blockade ("quarantine") of the island—and combined it with the demand that the missiles already in Cuba be removed. He thus gave Khrushchev a way to avoid world war, and a chance to save face. After several days of almost unbearable tension, Khrushchev backed down, and agreed to halt work on the missile sites in Cuba and remove the offensive weapons there, while reaffirming the Soviet wish to continue discussions about disarmament. Soviet ships at sea on their way to Cuba with new missiles turned back to home ports.

The U.S.S.R. and U.S. since the Missile Crisis; Czechoslovakia

President Kennedy did not crow or allow American officials to crow. Khrushchev had moved aggressively in an area close to the United States, where Soviet national security was not threatened. By lying about the missiles, he had destroyed whatever case he might otherwise have had in world opinion. Kennedy did not misread the event by concluding that the U.S.S.R. would have backed down if Soviet vital interests had been affected. He exploited the American victory only to push for a further relaxation in tensions.

Months of often discouraging preparatory interchanges led in July 1963 to the signing by the United States, the U.S.S.R., and Great Britain of a treaty banning nuclear weapons tests in the atmosphere, in outer space, or under water. Ratified by the Senate in September, the treaty subsequently received the adherence of more than seventy nations, though France and China —a fledgling and a prospective nuclear power— would not sign it. The treaty was hailed as a first step toward reducing the likelihood of a new world war. The installation of the "hot line" communications system between the White House and the Kremlin so that the leaders of the two countries might talk to each other in case of need, and the sale of surplus American wheat to the Russians, marked the final few months of the Kennedy administration.

The administration of President Johnson saw no recurrence of a Soviet–American crisis as acute as that over the missiles. But relations between the two superpowers remained tense and suspicious, despite many American efforts to ease them. The war in Vietnam would alone have made a real relaxation of tension impossible, and the two powers found themselves on opposite sides in the Middle East as well. The visit of Kosygin to the United States in 1967, and the meeting with Johnson at Glassboro, New Jersey, accomplished little, but provided an opportunity for an exchange of views. Progress toward a mutual agreement to curb the increasingly expensive arms race was painfully slow, but the settlement in 1968 on the terms of a nonproliferation treaty, to prevent the spread of atomic arms beyond the nations that already possessed them, represented a step forward. The treaty awaited ratification by the Senate when Soviet intervention in Czechoslovakia in the summer of 1968 at least temporarily made any further rapprochement highly improbable.

Long the most Stalinist of the eastern European governments, the Czech regime aroused much discontent. But a major political upheaval was postponed until 1968, when, after ever-increasing public protest and something of a major literary renaissance, Alexander Dubcek, a Slovak communist trained in the U.S.S.R., took over the Communist party as first secretary, and ousted the repressive Antonin Novotny. The Dubcek government freed the press from censorship, and the pent-up protests of years now filled its columns. Soviet exploitation and the rigidity of communist dogma had crippled the Czech economy. It now seemed as though the Czechs and Slovaks might even allow opposition political parties to come into existence, and some of their military men apparently favored revision of the Warsaw Pact, which enabled the U.S.S.R. to hold military exercises in the territory of any member state. Both Yugoslavia and Romania, each of which in its own way had defied the Soviet Union earlier and gotten away with it, encouraged the Czechs in the liberal course they were pursuing, and something very like a revival of the old Little Entente between these three countries seemed to be in the making.

Occupying the westernmost European position in the Soviet sphere, and having long frontiers with both East and West Germany, Czechoslovakia—highly industrialized and with a strong Western cultural tradition—could not put through a radical liberalization without deeply worrying the Russians and the other eastern European communist states. East Germany in particular would be vulnerable to the spread of anti-Stalinist ideas and practices. By spring 1968 the Soviet press was denouncing the Czech leadership. The denunciations grew louder and more violent, and were followed by a summons to the whole Czech leadership to come to Moscow. Dubcek and his colleagues refused, and the entire Soviet Politburo then joined the Czechs for a conference on Czechoslovakian soil, at the border village of Cierna nad Tisou. It appeared that Dubcek had made the required concessions, at least with regard to the Warsaw Pact, and these were confirmed at a conference of all the Warsaw powers at Bratislava. It was expected that the Czechs might have to curb the freedom of the press to some extent, but it did appear as if they too had successfully defied the Russians. Both Yugoslavs and Romanians joined in the congratulations.

But the U.S.S.R. accused the Czechs of violating the agreements of Cierna and Bratislava. Soviet and satellite tank divisions, more than 500,000 strong, swept into the country, and met no active resistance. Unlike the Soviet attack on Hungary in 1956, that on Czechoslovakia in the summer of 1968 was not directed against a population already in armed rebellion against their communist masters. There was little bloodshed. But there was great shock. Those who had been arguing that the U.S.S.R. had outgrown the Stalinist repressive measures of earlier years—and they included many of the best-informed observers of international affairs—found themselves proved wrong. The French and Italian Communist parties joined the Yugoslav and Romanian in condemning the invasion. The Soviet government kidnapped the Czech leaders, and sought frantically but vainly for native communists who would govern as puppets, and so lend credence to the Soviet claim that their armies had only acted on an invitation from Czechs and Slovaks who feared "counterrevolution." In the end the Russians restored Dubcek and his colleagues, but apparently after extracting promises from them that the liberalization would be reversed. Soviet occupation of Czechoslovakia continued.

German cartoon commenting on the Russian invasion of Czechoslovakia. Mao is briefing his troops, saying ". . . and if the Russians complain, simply say that somebody called you." August 1968.

The Russians had been so alarmed by the Czech cultural, economic, and political ferment and its military and diplomatic implications that they had been willing to sacrifice much of the international goodwill that they had been able to accumulate. Within its eastern European sphere, the U.S.S.R. could obviously do with impunity just about anything it wished. Yugoslavs and Romanians were understandably alarmed. In the two years that followed, the return of Stalinism to Czechoslovakia was slow but inexorable. By 1970 Dubcek, a broken man, had been ousted from government and party; his followers were powerless; and the Czech government was once more a mere Soviet puppet. A grim purge of Czech intellectuals threatened the very existence of the country's cultural institutions.

Despite the original shock that swept the United States after the Czech affair, the setback to discussions with the U.S.S.R. proved only temporary. For the third time in thirty years—in 1938, 1948, and 1968—it had been demonstrated that disbelief and dismay at the sufferings of the Czechs at the hands of Nazis or Communists could sadden the prodemocratic nations but could not elicit action or even prevent continuation of discussions with the great power guilty of the offense. In 1969 and 1970 discussions between the United States and the U.S.S.R. with regard to limitations of armaments resumed, and were sufficiently successful to move from an inital tentative phase in Helsinki on to a more significant phase in Vienna and back to Helsinki for an inconclusive third round. These negotiations (SALT, Strategic Armaments Limitation Talks) would be long-drawn-out and difficult; but both powers had an interest in somehow reducing their expenditures on weapons and obtaining more resources to deal with the disorderly state of their internal economies. Like the United States the Soviet Union had plenty of worries at home, and was finding it impossible to deal with them adequately so long as the burdens of armaments remained crushing.

II   The U.S.S.R., China, and America in Asia, 1956-1970

The Soviet-Chinese Quarrel

During the years between Stalin's death in 1953 and Khrushchev's denunciation of Stalin in 1956, Chinese–Soviet relations were basically amicable, and Chinese influence rose in the communist world. The Russians returned Port Arthur and Dairen to China in 1955. But when Khrushchev denounced Stalin without consulting Mao, the Chinese disapproved. They continued to denounce Tito and the Yugoslavs as "revisionists," and to try to block Khrushchev's reconciliation with them. They also wanted far more economic aid than the U.S.S.R. had been able or willing to provide, especially aid in developing nuclear weapons. In 1957 Mao experimented briefly with a liberated public opinion ("Let one hundred flowers bloom"), but soon returned to, and remained on, a thoroughly Leftist militant course. At home he embarked on forced-draft industrialization, the "great leap forward," with its backyard blast furnaces and its mass collectivization of the "people's communes," with disastrous results to both industry and agriculture. The Russians disapproved, and the latent disagreement between the two communist giants now began to emerge.

In 1959 Khrushchev told Peking that the U.S.S.R. would not furnish China with atomic weapons, and launched what proved to be an unsuccessful intrigue against Mao. The Chinese bombardment of Quemoy and Matsu (1958), the savage conquest of Tibet, and—as a result—the first invasion of Indian territory in Ladakh (September 1959) were undertaken without consultation between China and the U.S.S.R.; and the Russians publicly declared themselves to be neutral as between the Chinese and the Indians. In 1960 Khrushchev withdrew all Soviet technicians from China.

The Chinese regularly tried to influence other Communist parties against the Russians, and did succeed in picking up a European satellite: Albania, smallest and poorest of the Balkan countries. The Albanian Communist party, trained and marshaled by emissaries of Tito during World War II into a guerrilla movement, had taken power, and had thrown off Yugoslav domination after Tito's rebellion from Stalin in 1948. More than anything else the Albanian communists feared a renewed subjection to the Yugoslavs. When Khrushchev made his repeated efforts to conciliate Tito, the Albanians found in the Chinese a counterweight to the U.S.S.R. Albania as a satellite was an economic liability, but the Chinese could rejoice in having subtracted a European communist state from the Russian bloc. As Tito continued to play the role, for the Chinese, of chief traitor to the communist cause, Khrushchev's own relations with Tito grew correspondingly warmer.

In the very midst of the 1962 crisis over Soviet missiles in Cuba, the Chinese chose to attack India, apparently intending chiefly to seize the border regions in Ladakh, including important road communications, which they had long claimed. The Chinese withdrew when they had what they wanted; but the U.S.S.R., though ostensibly neutral, was clearly, like the United States, pro-Indian.

The Chinese built up their own organizations in Africa and Asia, and began to make threatening remarks about their boundary with the U.S.S.R. When the test-ban treaty was signed, the Chinese called the Russians traitors to the international communist movement. Though Khrushchev tried to arrange for a general public excommunication of the Chinese by other Communist parties, he was unable to bring it off. During 1964, Mao not only called for Khrushchev's removal, but accused the Russians of illegally occupying eastern European and Japanese territory.

Implacably hostile to America, the Chinese did not seem to mind having the U.S.S.R. as an enemy at the same time. By the time of Khrushchev's ouster in October 1964, they had won the support of the North Korean and North Vietnamese Communist parties, and enjoyed a special position of strength in Indonesia and Algeria. In Africa the Chinese had established a predominant influence in two former French colonies, and they took the lead in sponsoring a major rebellion in the tormented former Belgian Congo. In South America they had supported Castroites within the pro-Soviet Latin American parties in the hope of starting active revolutionary movements. In the United States, Chinese propagandists won the support of some American blacks. They had defeated India. They had exploded an atomic bomb. They were actively supporting, as were the Russians, the communist efforts in South Vietnam. But 1965 saw major Chinese setbacks. A congress scheduled for Algiers, in which they had expected to condemn the Russians, had been cancelled, in part because the Algerians overthrew their pro-Chinese premier Ben Bella. The Congo revolt had been put down. An attempted communist coup in Indonesia had failed after the assassination of numerous leading army officers. The army had taken power and revenged itself heavily, with the help of the Muslim population, upon the Chinese minority and upon the native communists, of whom perhaps 500,000 were killed.

The Chinese threat to renew the attack on India during the Indian–Pakistani conflict of 1965 evaporated as the United States and the U.S.S.R. tacitly cooperated in the United Nations to force a temporary ceasefire. Early in 1966, Premier Kosygin at Tashkent acted as mediator between India and Pakistan, achieving an agreement to seek a peaceful solution, and thus depriving the Chinese of a pretext for intervention while reasserting Soviet influence in Asia.

Perhaps in part as the result of successive setbacks abroad, the Chinese in 1966 began to behave at home in ways suggesting that the regime was undergoing almost unbearable tensions. Denunciations and removals of important figures at the top of the government and party were accompanied by a new wave of adulation for Chairman Mao. Youngsters in their teens, the "Red Guard," erupted into the streets of the cities of China, beating and sometimes killing older people whose loyalty they professed to suspect, destroying works of art and other memorials of China's precommunist past, and rioting against foreigners and foreign influences. When in October 1966 the Chinese successfully fired a guided missile with a nuclear warhead—the third Chinese nuclear explosion in two years—it served notice that the political turmoil was not interfering with the development of military

hardware. Yet the turmoil continued, and all of China apparently became embroiled. The Chinese educational system was completely halted, and something like civil war raged in some of the provinces.

The artificially induced "cultural revolution" in China lasted about three years, and died down only gradually in 1969, when the ninth Chinese Communist party congress actually took place. In 1969 and 1970 the mystery that veiled China from the West only seemed to thicken. Obviously something like a fourth of the top party and government officials had been purged, leaving stagnation and disillusionment behind. Economic recovery brought production back only to about the 1965 level. Occasional executions still took place, but the crisis had eased for reasons as obscure as the reasons for its inception. Chairman Mao himself, now 77, disappeared from the news for months at a time, and when he showed himself it was not as the implacable foe of all heterodoxy but as a rather relaxed and even genial leader, with kind words for Queen Elizabeth II on her birthday, and amiable greetings for selected visitors from France and even India. Though Soviet–Chinese tension once or twice broke into open fighting on the frontiers, and though the hostile propaganda of both sides in 1969 reached a new pitch of shrillness if possible, the two countries did not stop engaging in talks. Nobody seemed qualified even to guess at the next turn that Chinese policies might take on the identity of Mao's putative successor, and—unlike the U.S.S.R.—there were in 1970 no new novels or other literary or artistic indicators to indicate what the Chinese might be thinking.

Behind the series of incidents that revealed the mounting Chinese–Soviet quarrel to the world there lay profound theoretical disagreements about the best way to impose communist control over the peoples of Africa, Asia, and Latin America. The Chinese favored direct sponsorship of local communist revolutionary movements, the Russians "peaceful" economic competition with the capitalist world for the loyalty and admiration of the emerging peoples. The Russians said the communists would win the competition without world war, while helping along local "wars of national liberation"—i.e., revolutions at least partly under communist control. The Chinese refused to grant that nuclear weapons had changed war or imperialism, and regarded world war as inevitable. "The bourgeoisie," they maintained, "will never step down from the stage of history of its own accord."

The Chinese insisted that communists alone must take charge of all revolutionary movements from the beginning, and claimed that aid to non-communist countries was a delusion. They particularly objected to Soviet aid to India, their own enemy. They opposed disarmament. They had expected Khrushchev to freeze Soviet living standards at a low level and to invest the savings in helping the Chinese catch up, but of course Khrushchev preferred to let his own people enjoy some of the fruits of their own labors. Remembering their own success as a guerrilla operation that first came to control the countryside and then moved in on the cities, Chinese theoreticians extended this lesson to the whole globe, regarding Asia, Africa, and Latin America—the underdeveloped areas—as the countryside, and Europe and North America as the cities. From the massed peoples of the backward continents the communists would mount an offensive against the peoples of the developed industrial world and conquer them. How seriously even the authors of this startling theory believed what they said we cannot know.

One additional factor, seldom mentioned but extremely important in the Chinese–Russian quarrel, was simply that of race. The Russians—though they would deny the charge—disliked and feared the Chinese, the yellow peril on their borders. The huge masses of Chinese—soon inexorably to number one billion people—who were crowded into territory adjacent to the vast, sparsely populated regions of the U.S.S.R. and already laying claim to some of them, would frighten any reasonable government. Because the threat came, not from fellow whites, but from yellow men, the fear increased. Despite their protestations to the contrary, the Russians were extremely race-conscious, as the experiences of many African students in Moscow testified, and they reserved for the Chinese the deepest dislike of all. The Chinese used race openly as a weapon in their efforts to win support among other Asians, Africans, and Latin Americans, lumping the Soviet Union with the United States as symbols of the evil white intention to continue dominating the colored world. Convinced of their own superiority to the rest of mankind, the Chinese were racists too.

Southeast Asia: Vietnam and Laos

A special problem for the Chinese, Russians, and Americans arose in Southeast Asia as the result of the revolt of the Viet Minh communist forces against France that broke out in French Indo-China with the end of World War II in 1945. During the Korean War, the United States, fearing that the Chinese communists would strike across the border into northern Indo-China, gave substantial assistance to the French. In 1954, with the French defeated after the fall of their stronghold of Dienbienphu, a conference of powers at Geneva gave independence to the Indochinese provinces of Cambodia and Laos.

Vietnam, the third and largest portion of the former French colony, was divided along the 17th parallel. The northern section, with its capital at Hanoi, was governed by the communist Viet Minh party, whose leader was the veteran communist Ho Chi Minh; the southern portion, with its capital at Saigon, was led by a Catholic nationalist leader, Ngo Dinh Diem. The Geneva agreements guaranteed free elections. Though the United States did not sign them, it endorsed their purport, and retained the hope that the area, in which it had already invested more than four billion dollars, might not fall to the communists.

Between 1954 and 1959 Ngo Dinh Diem created the bureaucratic machinery for a new regime, restored order in territory that had long been held by communist guerrillas and was now held by dissident sects, provided for almost a million refugees from the communist north, and resettled in the countryside millions of peasants who had fled to the cities. After the departure of the French in 1956, the Americans assumed the responsibility for assisting in the solution of these problems with financial aid and technical advice.

But Diem failed politically. He cancelled the scheduled elections and, together with his immediate family, governed despotically. In 1958 and 1959, communist-led guerrilla activity broke out again. Now known as the Viet Cong, the guerrillas set up a National Liberation Front. In September 1960 Ho Chi Minh endorsed the Viet Cong movement, which he was already supplying with arms and training. Using terror in the villages as a weapon, the guerrillas by 1961 were moving almost at will in South Vietnam, overrunning much of the countryside, murdering, looting, and burning.

Neighboring Laos, though strategically important, was no nation but rather a collection of unwarlike Buddhist tribes, where only a small clique of families traditionally indulged in politics. In 1953 a communist-oriented political faction, calling itself the Pathet Lao and supported by Ho Chi Minh, seized the northeastern portion of the country. The United States tried with massive financial and military aid to build a national Laotian army and establish a firm regime, but succeeded largely in creating corruption and factionalism. The head of the government, Souvanna Phouma, who was the brother-in-law of the head of the Pathet Lao, reached agreement with him in 1957 to set up a coalition government and neutralize the country, absorbing the Pathet Lao into the army. This the United States resisted, ousting Souvanna and introducing the right-wing Phoumi Nousavan. By 1960, Souvanna was working with the Russians, and a portion of the army under the neutralist Kong Le (not a communist) was working with the Pathet Lao. Soviet airlifts of supplies to their side enhanced the possibility that the country would fall to the communists, and that Thailand and Burma—to say nothing of South Vietnam—would be endangered also.

President Kennedy sought for ways to neutralize Laos, and to convince the U.S.S.R. that if his efforts failed, American military intervention would follow. In April 1961 the U.S.S.R. agreed to neutralization, but fighting in Laos itself between Soviet-backed and American-backed forces continued until mid-May, when Khrushchev apparently realized the full implications of American intentions to send marines from Okinawa to Laos. A conference at Geneva followed the ceasefire, but before an agreement was reached in July 1962 Kennedy had to send marines to Thailand in order to stop the Pathet Lao from continuing to violate the truce. And when the decision to neutralize the country was reached—many years too late—the Pathet Lao, now a strong force armed with Russian weapons and still supported by Ho Chi Minh, withdrew from the coalition and maintained control over its own portion of the country, which bordered on South Vietnam and included the "Ho Chi Minh trail," a road down which came supplies

from Hanoi for the Viet Cong guerrillas. But a form of stability had been created in Laos itself. Souvanna and Kong Le, who had all along been neutralist, were now no longer procommunist but anticommunist, since it now was the Pathet Lao (and not Phoumi—who fled the country—or the United States—which now helped Souvanna) that was keeping Laos divided and in turmoil.

Incomplete and unsatisfactory as the Laos solution was, it far surpassed any arrangement that could be reached for South Vietnam. There guerrilla warfare continued. Effective opposition required political reform, but American efforts to get Ngo Dinh Diem moving politically failed. All that emerged was the "strategic hamlet" plan: a program to create fortified villages and "relocate" peasants in them in the hope that this would provide protection against the guerrillas and thus make the enemy campaigns first expensive and then impossible. In May 1963, when Diem's troops fired on a crowd of Buddhists in the city of Hue, protesting against Diem's edict that they might not display flags in honor of Buddha's birthday, riots followed, and several Buddhists soaked themselves in gasoline and set themselves afire. Though the United States tried to persuade Diem to abandon his course, in August he staged a mass arrest of Buddhists, and in November he and his brother were ousted and murdered in a coup led by dissident generals.

Between the end of 1963 and the beginning of 1966, the South Vietnamese government changed hands several times, each time by military coup. The longest-lived regime, that of General Cao Ky, successfully conducted elections in September 1966, Ky emerging as vice-president under President Thieu. But the hamlet program was a failure; insurgency increased; North Vietnamese regular troops appeared in South Vietnam in support of the guerrillas; more than half a million peasant families were made refugees once more by floods and by terrorism.

Between 1965 and 1967, the United States stepped up the number of its troops from fewer than a single division to more than 500,000, and initiated a policy of bombing certain selected North Vietnamese installations. Massive American intervention made it impossible for the Viet Cong to conquer the entire country, and assured the United States of certain bases along the coast. Having increased the American commitment to such a level that none could doubt his earnestness, President Johnson, in the hope of bringing Ho Chi Minh to the conference table, then assured the enemy that the United States had no long-range intention of remaining in the country, and sought no military bases there. In 1966 he suspended the bombing for a time, but got no response. The enemy insisted that there could be no negotiations until all American troops had left the country. And the very act of offering to negotiate with the North aroused uneasiness in the South.

Much articulate public opinion in the United States itself disliked the war or professed not to understand it. Some voices called for American withdrawal. Opposing public opinion urged that it be intensified and "won." Its mounting costs endangered President Johnson's widely hailed domestic programs. On the one hand, continued intensification ("escalation," as it was lamentably called) threatened a land war in Asia of unprecedented difficulty and unpredictable length and severity. On the other hand, withdrawal threatened abandonment of the goals for which

the United States had fought the Asian portion of World War II: the Chinese communists of the 1970's, like the Japanese militarists of the 1940's, might dominate the Asian continent in a spirit of hostility to the United States.

There could be no doubt of the deep American unrest at the Vietnam War. In 1968, as the time for American elections approached, Senator Eugene McCarthy, Democrat of Minnesota, challenged the administration by announcing his own candidacy for the presidency on an antiwar platform. He scored impressive initial successes in early primaries, and stimulated another opponent of the war, Senator Robert F. Kennedy, Democrat of New York, to enter the race on his own. The visible strength of the antiwar candidates certainly influenced the withdrawal of President Johnson—who had been universally expected to run. Ho Chi Minh, who had always hoped that internal American politics would force the United States out of Vietnam, then consented to open peace talks, which began in

One of the impromptu factories that operated in Hanoi during the American bombing of the city. November 1967.

Paris, but dragged on inconclusively for more than a year. Early in November 1968 the North Vietnamese consented to permit the South Vietnamese government to join the discussions, and the United States agreed that the Viet Cong might send its representatives. The bombing of North Vietnam was halted. But the South Vietnamese refused to participate, and the deadlock continued.

The Nixon administration inherited both the increasingly unpopular war and the halting negotiations designed to end it. Nixon pledged the eventual withdrawal of American forces, and did indeed begin to reduce the number of troops there. The death of Ho Chi Minh in 1969 brought no crisis to the North Vietnamese government or change in its policies. On the whole, it seemed prepared to carry on with the war, obviously believing that the Americans had lost stomach for it, and that the communist cause would gain more by continuing the war than by ending it through negotiations. The military picture was further clouded for the United States by the increasing Viet Cong domination of Laos, where by 1970 the hard-won settlement of the early 60's was in jeopardy, and by the overflow of Viet Cong forces into those portions of Cambodia nearest to South Vietnam. In Cambodia the enemy was invulnerable to American and South Vietnamese pursuit: Cambodia furnished the kind of "privileged sanctuary" for the North Vietnamese and Viet Cong that Yugoslavia, Bulgaria, and Greece had afforded the Greek communist guerrillas in the late 1940's or that China had given the North Korean Communists in the early 1950's.

Cambodia had as its ruler a French-educated prince, of an old native ruling house, Norodom Sihanouk, personally shrewd and vain, who made some effort to maintain Cambodian neutrality as between the warring armies in Vietnam, and as between the larger forces of American ideology and communism contending for Southeast Asia. But Sihanouk did not conceal his basic view that in the end China would dominate his part of the world, and so must be appeased. These beliefs made him suspect in Washington, and unpopular at home with his own military and with many of his people, who, though peaceful, detested Vietnamese in general, and, for the moment, the intruding Vietcong and North Vietnamese in particular. In 1970, a coup d'état led by General Lon Nol overthrew Sihanouk, who

was at the time visiting Moscow and Peking. Not long afterward, American and South Vietnamese troops invaded Cambodia in response to an invitation from the new anti-Sihanouk government. Sihanouk himself, from Peking, soon announced the formation of a government in exile.

The invading forces captured some enemy troops and a great many supplies, but failed to wipe out the large numbers of enemy forces believed to be the chief target of the expedition. The public response in the United States to what seemed like an extension of hostilities (at precisely the moment when it was expected that they would be narrowed and diminished) was strident, more so, it is clear, than President Nixon had believed would be the case. He soon promised to withdraw American forces from Cambodia within a specific time, and he kept his promise. But there remained much doubt whether the Cambodian operation as a whole had been justifiable from a military point of view. Certainly there seemed to be more Vietnamese communists in the country than ever, and occupying more threatening military positions than before. During the Cambodian operations the U.S. briefly resumed the bombing of North Vietnam, but then abandoned it again. Bombing, indeed, and the threat of bombing were likely to be the most effective instruments left to the United States, as its land forces in Vietnam were reduced, and its "air presence" became again more important. At the end of 1970 even North Vietnam seemed to be showing signs of an impaired ability to carry on the war in the South.

The growing American opposition to the war in Vietnam, especially among students and other articulate groups, showed that many were discouraged with what now seemed like an interminable struggle, impossible to win. One thing was sure: if the United States did stop fighting the war, it would not win it; and so the calculations of Ho Chi Minh seemed to be working out as he had hoped. In South Vietnam, the government was surely both corrupt and cruel, but it also apparently represented the only defense against communist domination available to the thousands of South Vietnamese who had taken American pledges of help at their face value. How could we abandon them and face our consciences? And if we did, who would ever believe again in promises of American protection? At home, those who wanted the war won, and our commitments honored, grew correspondingly shrill, as those who wanted peace at any price raised the tones of their voices. And in Paris, though President Nixon appointed perhaps our most experienced senior diplomat to resume the interrupted peace negotiations, hope seemed slender indeed that a settlement could be reached. The Vietnam War had become the source of troubles that loomed far larger than the importance of the entire area it was being fought to protect.

III The Emerging Nations and World Politics

The Revolt Against Imperialism

Indo-China furnished only the most striking example of the problems involved in liquidating old colonial empires and endowing newly emerging nations with viable economic and political institutions. As in Indo-China, so elsewhere, this process of liquidation had been greatly accelerated and intensified by the Second World War. The use of colonial troops by the Western powers during the war increased the self-esteem of the peoples providing the troops. Wartime propaganda, designed to show the justice of the Allied cause, inevitably strengthened the native wish to possess the basic democratic rights of self-government and self-determination. Wartime inflation, shortages, conscription of labor, and the enjoyment of war profits by the few rather than the many added to the sense of grievance felt by colonial peoples.

Moreover, during the war Asians—Japanese—actually seized Western possessions in the Far East, putting an end to the myth of white Western invulnerability. Even though Japan was defeated in the end, Western prestige did not recover. Everybody knew that the French and Dutch had not really won, that British power had been seriously weakened, and that the defeat of Conservatives by the Labour party in 1945 promised new colonial policies. The only real victors in the war were the United States and the Soviet Union, each in its way anticolonial.

Deeper causes of anticolonialism lay in the 500-year record of Western expansion, and in the Western tradition itself. The West usually laid before educated natives the Bible, the American Declaration of Independence, the French Declaration of the Rights of Man, even the Communist Manifesto. It was hardly possible to keep on insisting that "all men are created equal" really meant "white men are created the superiors of colored men." In terms of ideals and ideology, Western imperialism carried within itself the seeds of its own transfiguration into self-determination for all peoples. The great instrument for the spread of Western ideas was the education provided by the West to a relatively small native minority among the non-Western peoples. Though some turned against this Western education and took refuge in a reaffirmation of the values of their traditional cultures, most of the educated came to feel that independence could be won only by learning the industrial, technological, and military skills of the West.

These educated natives wanted independence. Many were revolutionaries; some admired the Bolshevik revolution, and a few received training in Moscow. A great many Westerners made the mistake of assuming that these men were not representative of the native populations, and that the great colonial masses asked nothing better than to be ruled by the kindly whites. Instead, the urban masses and then, more gradually, the peasant masses began to share the feelings of nationalism and to demand that the foreigner must go. Often this demand was exacerbated by the rapid increases in population made possible by the dramatically lower death rates resulting from the sanitary engineering, the medical facilities, and the law and order introduced by the imperialist powers.

The two decades following World War II saw the liquidation of the British, French, Dutch, and Belgian empires. Portugal alone of the imperial powers in 1970 retained its major possessions overseas—chiefly Angola and Mozambique on the west and east coasts of Africa respectively—and this largely because the Portuguese government was a conservative dictatorship that would not yield to native pressures.

Britain, to be sure, continued to lead the Commonwealth of Nations, whose membership came to include some of the new nonwhite states. Although the Commonwealth continued to have great economic significance as an association of trading partners, its political importance diminished, in part because of the further loosening of the ties between the white dominions and the mother country. South Africa severed its bonds with the Commonwealth in 1961 and declared itself a wholly independent republic. Australia and New Zealand now looked more and more to the United States as the potential defender of their security.

The Far East

During the Second World War the Japanese had created a huge empire, the "Greater East Asia Co-Prosperity Sphere." To rule it they had relied chiefly on the time-honored Western device of setting up puppet native governments, and exploiting for their own benefit the economic resources of the conquered lands. Because the Japanese were an Asian people, a colored people, they might well have acted as the emancipators of Asians that their propaganda proclaimed them to be. Instead, their armies looted and committed atrocities; they behaved like a master race. They alienated the people they might have won. When the war ended they were stripped of their overseas possessions.

The occupation of Japan was wholly American. Despite some strong opposition in American opinion, the emperor was left on his throne, deprived of his divine status, and subjected to the close control of General MacArthur and the forces of occupation. Americans found that, on the surface, at least, the Japanese people did not take the occupation with hostility, but seemed anxious to learn what democracy meant. By the time of the peace treaty in 1952, they had made a promising start on a democracy of the Western type. Their economy—the only well-developed industrial economy in the non-Western world—grew so rapidly in the late 1950's and the 1960's that experts began to predict that it would soon overtake France and West Germany and rank third in the world after the U.S. and the U.S.S.R. Sales of Japanese goods in other quarters of the world continued to mount, and the domestic market underwent a phenomenal expansion.

Signs of change and of affluence multiplied.

Programs of birth-control education were successful, and the birth rate dropped, to become one of the lowest in the world. Peasants migrated to the cities, especially to Tokyo, which surpassed London and New York as the world's largest city. Tokyo and Osaka, Japan's second city, were linked by a new high-speed rail line, the fastest in the world, while weekend traffic jams resulted from the rush of Tokyo residents to the beaches in the summer and the ski slopes in winter. As of 1970, inflation appeared to be the main threat to Japan's continued prosperity and to her social and economic westernization.

Politically, the democratic parliamentary institutions so carefully fostered by the American occupation forces flourished under successive cabinets of the essentially conservative Liberal Democratic party. The left-wing opposition, including both socialists and communists, objected to the mutual security pact binding Japan and the United States after the official restoration of full Japanese sovereignty in 1952. The opposition staged demonstrations, causing the last-minute cancellation of President Eisenhower's planned visit to Japan in 1960. Anti-Americanism derived from resentment over the continued United States occupation of the island of Okinawa (to the south of the main Japanese islands), from a bitterness left by the atomic blasts over Hiroshima and Nagasaki, and from left-wing mistrust of American policy and aims in Vietnam. In addition, despite the claim of the Japanese to have the highest rate of literacy in the world, the extreme insularity of many Japanese and their ignorance of the world outside their islands combined to make Japan seem at times more nationalist and neutralist than pro-Western. To these factors in the late 1960's was added a particularly virulent case of that student extremism that plagued most other countries as well. The Japanese university system—always intensely competitive and full of emotional strain —was now halted for months at a time by armed conflicts between rival groups of students and between radical students and police.

South Korea also attempted constitutional government in the Western manner but ran into serious difficulties. After the disruptive Korean War of the early 1950's, the government of Syngman Rhee, the perennial South Korean president, came under mounting criticism for its corruption and its arbitrary actions. In 1960, massive protests by students forced the 85-year

Asia, 1971

Communist bloc nations

500   1000
Miles

Pacific Ocean

Indian Ocean

Arabian Sea

Bay of Bengal

South China Sea

Sea of Japan

U. S. S. R.

SAKHALIN

KURILE IS. (U.S.S.R.)

TRANS-SIBERIAN RAILROAD

Sverdlovsk
Omsk
Novosibirsk
Novokuznetsk
Barnaul
Semipalatinsk
Krasnoyarsk
Irkutsk
Chita
Khabarovsk
Vladivostok

Yenisei R.
Ob R.
Lena R.
Amur R.

L. Baikal

KUZNETSK BASIN

Karaganda
L. Balkhash
Alma Ata
Tashkent
Dushanbe

MONGOLIA
Ulan Bator

GOBI DESERT

Qomul
Urumchi

SINKIANG

MANCHURIA
Harbin
Mukden
Dairen

N. KOREA
38°
Seoul
S. KOREA

JAPAN
Tokyo
Osaka
Nagasaki

Yalu R.

CHINA

Peking
Nanking
Shanghai
Lanchow
Siking
Changsha
Chungking
Kunming
Canton
Hong Kong (Br.)

Yellow R.
Yangtze R.

TIBET
Lhasa
MT. EVEREST
HIMALAYAS

NEPAL
BHUTAN

Salween R.

BURMA
Mandalay
Rangoon
Irrawaddy R.
Tavoy

HAINAN
NORTH VIETNAM
Hanoi
LAOS
Vientiane
THAILAND
Bangkok
SOUTH VIETNAM
CAMBODIA
Pnom Penh
Saigon
Mekong R.

TAIWAN (FORMOSA)

PHILIPPINE IS.
Manila
Tacloban
Davao
Zamboanga

RYUKYU IS. (U.S. Administration)
OKINAWA

MARIANAS IS.
GUAM (U.S.)

CAROLINE IS.
(U.S. Trust Territory)

NEW GUINEA
WEST IRIAN

AUSTRALIA
Darwin

MALAYSIA
SABAH (N. BORNEO)
Jesselton
BRUNEI (Br.)
SARAWAK
Kuching
MALAYA
Kuala Lumpur
Singapore
Medan
Palembang

BORNEO
Balikpapan
Makassar

CELEBES
CERAM
AMBOINA

TIMOR (Port.)

REPUBLIC OF INDONESIA
SUMATRA
JAVA
Djakarta
Surabaja

INDIA
New Delhi
Lahore
Benares
Calcutta
Chittagong
Ahmedabad
Hyderabad
Bombay
Madras

KASHMIR
Srinagar

W. PAKISTAN
Karachi

E. PAK.

Indus R.
Ganges R.

AFGHANISTAN
Kabul
Herat
Kandahar

IRAN

CEYLON
Colombo

ANDAMAN IS. (India)
NICOBAR IS. (India)

LACCADIVE IS. (Br.)
MALDIVE IS.

CHINA

FRENCH INDO-CHINA

TONKIN

ANNAM

COCHIN CHINA
Saigon
Mekong R.

THAILAND

old Rhee out of office, and inaugurated a tumultuous period marked first by the political intervention of the army and then by another attempt at constitutional rule. The economy depended heavily on American assistance. The South Koreans sent troops to fight in Vietnam, and in the years after 1965 were deeply alarmed when the communist North Koreans stepped up their military pressure. The threat remained, as part of the pressure used by the communist states in the Vietnam war.

Once the Japanese occupation ended in Southeast Asia, the major Western colonial powers found that they could not revert to the prewar arrangements. In 1949, the Dutch had to recognize the independence of the Netherlands East Indies as the Republic of Indonesia, with a population of 100,000,000 people. The United States gave the Philippines independence in 1946. Britain gave Burma independence outside the Commonwealth (1948) and the Federation of Malaya independence within the Commonwealth (1957); the port of Singapore at the tip of Malaya, with its largely Chinese population, secured a special autonomous status (1958). When Malaya joined with the former British protectorates on the island of Borneo in the Federation of Malaysia (1963), Singapore at first participated, then withdrew (1965).

The Dutch in Indonesia had not prepared the people for independence by education. Nevertheless, the Indonesians attempted to run their government along the lines of a parliamentary democracy. Almost everything went wrong. The economy was crippled by inflation and shortages, by administrative corruption and the black market, and by the expulsion of experienced Dutch businessmen. The Muslims, who made up the bulk of the population, proved unable to form responsible political parties. The outlying islands of the archipelago, resentful of domination by the island of Java, which contained the capital (Djakarta, the former Batavia) and two-thirds of the population, rebelled against the central government. As the high expectations raised by the achievement of independence were disappointed, President Sukarno, the hero of the Indonesian struggle for independence, began to speak of the need for "guided democracy" and for the operation of indigenous rather than borrowed political institutions.

In 1959 and 1960, Sukarno suspended the ineffectual parliamentary regime, and vested authority in himself and in the army and an appointive council. But "guided democracy" created still more turmoil. Inflation ran wild, necessities vanished from the market, pretentious new government buildings were left unfinished for lack of funds, and all foreign enterprises were confiscated. In external policy, Sukarno initiated an alternating hot and cold war with the new Federation of Malaysia for control of the island of Borneo, where both states had territory. By threat and intimidation he managed to annex former Dutch New Guinea (called West Irian by the Indonesians). When the United Nations recognized Malaysia, Sukarno withdrew Indonesia from membership early in 1965; he also told the United States "to go to hell with their aid" and moved closer and closer to Red China.

But a coup planned by Indonesian communists misfired at the last moment in the autumn of 1965, and the result was a wholesale slaughter of local communists. The anticommunist forces came to power under military leaders, among whom General Suharto took the lead. For a time they allowed President Sukarno to remain in office, but they reduced his authority, brought some of his procommunist associates to trial, and reversed his policies by reaching a settlement with Malaysia and rejoining the United Nations. By the time of Sukarno's death in 1970, Indonesia was gradually reviving.

Communist efforts in Southeast Asia were not confined to Indonesia and Vietnam (Indo-China). In the Philippine Republic and Malaya too, the communists launched stubborn guerrilla campaigns, which were not checked until the late 1950's. Wherever there were large colonies of "overseas Chinese," some of these became sympathizers of Mao.

India and Pakistan

The Labour victory in Britain in 1945 made Indian emancipation a certainty. But the deep-seated tension between Muslims and Hindus now assumed critical importance. When the Hindus' Congress party and the All-India Muslim League faced the need to make a working constitution for the new India, they found themselves in complete disagreement. The Muslims had long been working for a partition into separate Hindu and Muslim states, and this was in the end reluctantly accepted by the Hindus. In 1947, Hindu India and Muslim Pakistan were set up as self-governing dominions within the British Commonwealth.

Pakistan ("land of the pure," a name coined by Muslim students in Britain in the 1930's) was a state divided into two parts, widely separated by intervening Indian territory—the larger, arid West Pakistan in the northwest, and the smaller, more fertile, and more densely populated East Pakistan in East Bengal. The rest of the former British Indian Empire and four-fifths of its inhabitants became the Republic of India by virtue of its constitution of 1950. Pakistan, with its smaller population (still well over 100,000,000 people) and its relatively poorly developed industry, was weaker than India, and at first kept closer political ties with the British Commonwealth.

Violence accompanied partition. It was not possible to draw a boundary that would leave all Hindus in one state and all Muslims in another. Bitter Hindu-Muslim fighting cost hundreds of thousands of lives, as Hindus moved from Pakistani territory into India and Muslims moved from Indian territory into Pakistan. A particular source of trouble was the beautiful mountainous province of Kashmir. Though mainly Muslim in population, it was at the time of partition ruled by a Hindu princely house which turned it over to India. India continued to occupy most of Kashmir, to the great economic disadvantage of Pakistan. The United Nations sought to determine the fate of Kashmir by arranging a plebiscite, but failed to secure the needed approval of both parties.

In domestic politics the two states went through sharply contrasting experiences. The chief architect of Pakistani independence, Mohammed Ali Jinnah (head of the Muslim League), died in 1948. Deprived of its leader, Pakistan floundered in its attempts to make parliamentary government work and to attack pressing economic difficulties. In 1958 the army commander, the British-educated Ayub Khan, took full power, attacked administrative corruption and the black market, and instituted a program of "basic democracies" to train the population in self-government at the local level and thence gradually upward through a pyramid of advisory councils. For a long period Ayub's "basic democracies" proved more workable than Su-

karno's "guided democracy," and led to the proclamation of a new constitution in 1962, which provided for a national assembly and also for a strengthened president, an office that Ayub continued to fill. But as Ayub grew older, charges of corruption were made against his family and his officials, and the teeming and depressed people of East Bengal insisted that their region was suffering from policies that discriminated in favor of West Pakistan. Disorder spread, and in 1969 a new military government ousted Ayub. The tension between West Pakistan, whose Punjabis had a disproportionately large role in the government, and the underrepresented and miserably poor Bengalis of East Pakistan was exacerbated by a dreadful tropical storm late in 1970 that wiped out many thousand Bengalis.

Newly emancipated India suffered a grievous loss when Gandhi was assassinated by an anti-Muslim Hindu fanatic in 1948. But Jawaharlal Nehru, already a seasoned politician, at once assumed leadership. India successfully inaugurated a genuine parliamentary democracy of the Western type, and conducted free and hotly fought elections, based on universal suffrage, among voters who were in the main illiterate and rural. Understandably, Indians were proud of their accomplishment. India faced in an acute form the problem of overpopulation: by 1960 there were over 500,000,000 people, with approximately 15,000,000 added annually. The threat of famine and actual death through starvation was always present. In 1950, the government launched the first in a series of five-year plans for economic development, permitting the expansion of private industry but stressing government projects: irrigation and flood control, transport and communications, and especially agricultural education. Low yields could be improved by more fertilizers, by small local irrigation projects to supplement the showy large ones, and by modern tools, equipment, and varieties of grain. Expert opinion held that India put too much stress on industrial growth and too little on the agricultural sector. The United States helped by furnishing technicians, money, and the surplus grain need to avert the repeated threat of famine. In the late 1960's a new strain of high-yielding Mexican wheat was planted experimentally; the initial results were promising. But the very success of the new foods (the "green revolution") threatened a new form of crisis, as farmers displaced from the countryside by new agricultural techniques flooded into the cities of India, where there was no employment for them. Starvation and political unrest always threatened in India. Meantime, the government sponsored a campaign for birth control, which was, however, repugnant to many Hindus.

Indeed, Hindu society found it difficult to adopt Western ways. The tradition of Hinduism, an immensely complex and ancient way of life, taught that each living man, indeed each living thing, was a soul alienated by the very fact of living from the ultimate, universal soul which is peace, absence of struggle and desire, ineffable nonbeing. By turning away entirely from the world, by living without desire, the holiest of men could perhaps attain this nonbeing in the end. But most human beings—and all animals— were now living out in this world the consequences of a sinful life as another personality in the past. That is why the most orthodox of Hindus would harm no living thing. This specifically included the millions of "sacred" cattle that competed with starving people for food. Proposals for curbing the cattle were anathema, and led to riots as late as 1966.

Hindus believed that man's sins in past incarnations were reflected by his status, his *caste*. The poor and humble were poor and humble because their sins had been greater; they could not improve their lot, for they could only slowly in subsequent incarnations redeem their wickedness by living as holy a life as possible. Below and outside the caste system were the "untouchables," so called because even their shadow would corrupt a caste-Hindu. The Indian Constitution of 1950 abolished the outcast status of the untouchables (Harijans) as undemocratic. The legal change, however, penetrated Indian custom only very slowly.

In 1964, when Nehru died, and again early in 1966, when his successor, Shastri, fell victim to a heart attack, India chose a new prime minister by due constitutional process. The choice in 1966 was Nehru's daughter, Mrs. Indira Gandhi, who remained in power in 1970. The Congress party, long the spearhead of Hindu nationalism, continued to dominate the Parliament, though torn increasingly by factionalism. Several times Mrs. Gandhi had to offer to resign in order to maneuver in such a way as not to have to do so.

Political controversy arose over the question of language. There were about a dozen major regions in India each with its own distinctive tongue. Believing that a common language was essential to a common sense of national identity, the government supported a new national language, Hindi, to which it gave official status in 1965. It also recognized English as an associate language, though ardent nationalists deplored this as an "ignoble concession" to colonialism. In fact, English was indispensable, both because of its modern scientific and technical vocabulary, which Hindi could not provide, and also because it was the only common language of educated Indians, who could not understand one another's native tongues. The elevation of Hindi to official status aroused especially strong opposition among the speakers of Tamil in the south, who viewed it as an instrument of the central government's hostility to regional or provincial pride in language and political home rule. The government met the problem by making some concessions but without abandoning its aim.

Relations with Pakistan also continued to be strained. Sporadic outbreaks of religious warfare took place, especially near the line dividing Bengal between India and East Pakistan. The Kashmir question continued open, since neither side would concede anything. In 1965 war broke out briefly over the issue, until the Soviet Union invited leaders of both countries to confer at Tashkent, where they agreed on a mutual withdrawal of troops from their common frontier but not to a permanent settlement. The Pakistanis, who tended to measure every country by its attitude toward India, remained suspicious of the United States because of American aid to India, despite U.S. eagerness to provide it for Pakistan as well; Pakistan was similarly suspicious of the U.S.S.R., because the Russians also helped the Indians; and so the Pakistanis began to develop a curiously unnatural friendship with Red China because it at least was anti-Indian.

The Middle East

The region formerly and properly called the Near East, but since World War II always called by the meaningless term "Middle East," possessed in Arabia, in the small states along the Persian Gulf, and in Iraq and Iran the greatest oil reserves in the world, a producing area second only to North America. Developed by European and American companies, which paid royalties to the local governments, these oil resources directly and indirectly influenced the policies of all the powers. Dissatisfaction over

The Middle East, 1971

Legend:
▲ Oil Fields
Pipelines
Arab League
Occupied by Israel, June, 1967

the amounts of royalties led to upheavals in Iran in 1951–1953. Western European dependence on Middle Eastern oil led to general alarm over the closing of the Suez Canal by Egypt in 1956 and 1967. No doubt General de Gaulle's abandonment in 1967 of Israel, an ally of the French in 1956, and the new pro-Arab policies of France had something to do with oil. But except for Iran no crisis depended upon oil alone; and unquestionably the greatest single issue in the area in the postwar years was that between the Arabs and Israel.

Since the 1890's Zionism had maintained its goal of creating a new Jewish state on the site of the ancient Jewish homeland. It received a great lift from the Balfour Declaration of 1917, after which the British admitted Jewish immigrants into Palestine. Nazi anti-Jewish policies before and during World War II left the remnant of European Jews more determined than ever to go to Palestine. But after the war Britain wished to protect its interests in the Middle East by cultivating the friendship of the Arabs, who had long been settled in Palestine and felt that this was their homeland.

Finding compromise impossible, the British turned the problem over to the General Assembly of the United Nations, which proposed to partition the country into an Arab state and a Jewish state. When the British withdrew their forces from Palestine in 1948, the Jews proclaimed their state of Israel and secured its recognition by the UN. The Arab nations declared the proclamation illegal and invaded the new state from all directions. Outnumbered but faced by an inefficient enemy, the Israelis won the war. A truce, but not a formal peace, was patched up under the auspices of the United Nations (1949).

Israel now secured more of Palestine than the UN had proposed, and took over the western part of Jerusalem, the spiritual capital of Judaism—but also of compelling religious importance to Christians and Muslims—a city which the UN had proposed to neutralize. The eastern part or "old city" of Jerusalem, however, including the site of Solomon's temple, the Wailing Wall, together with eastern Palestine, remained in the hands of the Arab state of Jordan. During the 1949 war almost 1,000,000 Palestinian Arabs fled from Israel to the surrounding Arab states. The United Nations organized a special agency that built camps and gave relief to the refugees, and tried to arrange for their permanent resettlement. The Arab states, however, did not wish to absorb them, and many refugees regarded resettlement as an abandonment of their belief that the Israelis would soon "be pushed into the sea," and that they themselves would return to their old homes. This acute problem made the truce of 1949 a most uneasy affair, frequently broken in frontier incidents by both sides.

The new state of Israel could not trust its Arab minority, numbering about 200,000. It continued to admit as many Jewish immigrants as possible, some of them from Europe, but others from North Africa and Yemen, still largely living in the Middle Ages. The welding of these disparate human elements into a single nationality was a formidable task. Much of Israel was mountainous, and some of it was desert. The Israelis applied talents and training derived from the West to make the best use of their limited resources, but they depended on outside aid, especially from their many sympathizers in the United States. To most Arabs Israel appeared to be a new outpost of Western imperialism, set up in their midst under the influence of Jewish financiers, Jewish journalists, and Jewish voters. Therefore it was difficult for the United States and other Western nations to retain cordial relations with the Arabs, who were in any case passing through a highly nationalistic phase.

In 1952, less than four years after the Arab defeat in Palestine, revolution broke out in Egypt, where a corrupt royal regime was overthrown by a group of army officers chiefly sparked by Gamal Abdel Nasser. They abolished the monarchy, established a republic, encouraged the emancipation of women, and pared down the role of the conservative courts of religious law. Only one party was tolerated, elections were closely supervised, and press campaigns were orchestrated by the Ministry of National Guidance. As an enemy of the West, which he associated not only with past colonialism but with support for Israel, Nasser turned for aid to the U.S.S.R. Czechoslovak and Russian arms flowed to Egypt, and Russian technicians followed. Nasser was determined to take the lead in uniting the disunited Arab world to destroy Israel.

Nasser's chief showpiece of revolutionary planning was to be a new high dam of the Nile at Aswan. He had expected the United States to contribute largely to its construction, but in June 1956 John Foster Dulles, Eisenhower's secretary of state, told Nasser that the United States had changed its mind. In retaliation Nasser nationalized the Suez Canal, hitherto operated by a Franco-British Company, and announced that he would use the revenues thus obtained to build the dam. For several months, contrary to expectation, the new Egyptian management kept canal traffic moving smoothly. The French and British governments, however, concealing their intentions from the United States, determined to teach Nasser a lesson, and secretly allied themselves with Israel.

In the fall of 1956, the Israeli forces invaded Egyptian territory, and French and British troops were also landed at Suez. The Israeli operations were skillful and successful; the British and French blundered badly. The Soviet

Union threatened to send "volunteers" to defend Egypt, despite the fact that Soviet troops were at the very moment of the Suez crisis engaged in putting down the Hungarian revolution. Nor did the United States, angry at its British and French friends for concealing their plans, give them support. With the United States and the Soviet Union on the same side of the issue, the United Nations condemned the British-French-Israel attack, and eventually a United Nations force was moved into the Egyptian-Israeli frontier areas, while the Canal, blocked by the Egyptians, was reopened, and finally bought from the company by Nasser. Nasser experienced some disillusion with Russia during the summer of 1958, when revolution broke out in Iraq, where Soviet-sponsored communists were opposing Nasser's own pan-Arab aims. Prompt American intervention in Lebanon and British intervention in Jordan may have temporarily countered the threat of the spread of Soviet

Nasser receiving the plaudits of fellow Egyptians after announcing the nationalization of the Suez Canal, 1956.

influence. The Russians provided the aid that eventually made possible the high dam at Aswan and much armament for the Egyptian armies, but Nasser remained unaligned with either major bloc.

In 1958, Nasser proclaimed the merger of Egypt and Syria into the United Arab Republic. The two components of the U.A.R. were separated by the territories of Israel, Lebanon, and Jordan; Nasser was trying to prevent a coup by Syrian communists or fellow travelers. When the almost ungovernable Syrians revolted in 1961, Nasser announced that he could never fire on "brother Arabs," and permitted them to regain their independence as the Syrian Arab Republic. Yet Egypt continued to style itself the U.A.R. The Arab League, a loose association of the Arabic-speaking states of the Middle East and North Africa, proved to be little more than a forum for expressing the conflicts of views and personalities that kept the Arab world disunited.

After the Suez crisis, Nasser tried one experiment after another to create a party and other institutions that would gain support for his regime at the grass roots. His economic policy was governed by the grim struggle to support a fast-growing population (the birth rate in Egypt was double that in the United States). He undertook programs to reclaim land from the desert by exploiting underground water, and to limit the size of an individual's landholdings so that the surplus might be redistributed to landless peasants. To provide more jobs and to bolster national pride he also accelerated the pace of industrialization, often at very high cost. Most foreign enterprises were nationalized.

But the temptations of foreign adventure proved irresistible to Nasser. In far-off Yemen, a primitive kingdom in southern Arabia where republican rebels overthrew the monarchy in 1962, Nasser sent Egyptian forces to assist the revolution. This was a blow to the largest state of Arabia proper, the Saudi Kingdom, generally aligned with the United States, since the activities of American oil companies on its soil provided much of its enormous revenues. Not even in tiny Yemen could Nasser's modern forces score a victory, though they freely used poison gas against their brother Arabs. By 1967 the Egyptian forces had suffered a defeat, though the Yemeni republican regime continued in power.

Needing a victory, Nasser in 1967 demanded

that the United Nations troops which had kept Egyptians and Israelis separated since 1956 be removed. Secretary General U Thant complied, and the Egyptians simultaneously began a severe propaganda barrage against Israel, and also closed the Strait of Tiran at the northeast corner of the Red Sea that provided the only water access to the newly developed Israeli port of Eilath. Expecting an attack at any moment, and with no likelihood that they could recover initiative or territory once it had begun, the Israelis struck the first blow, knocking out the Egyptian air force on the ground, and hitting also at Jordan, Syria, and Iraq. In six days, they overran the Sinai peninsula, all of Palestine west of the Jordan, including the Jordanian portion of Jerusalem, and the heights on their northern frontier with Syria, from which the Syrians had been launching dangerous and painful raids for several years. The third Arab–Israel war in nineteen years ended in an all-out Israeli victory.

It was a humiliation not only for Nasser but for the U.S.S.R., which had supplied so much of the equipment he had now lost. The Russians moved vigorously to support the Arab position, arguing their case in the United Nations, moving token naval forces into the Mediterranean, denouncing Israel, and ostentatiously beginning at once the rearmament of Egypt. Israeli armies remained in control of all the territory they had occupied. Had it been possible to begin negotiations soon after the war, much of this territory could perhaps have been recovered. As time passed, the Israeli attitude hardened, and it became difficult to imagine that any Israeli government could ever consent to give up any part of Jerusalem, now reunited in an emotional wave of Jewish religious sentiment, or the Syrian heights, whose possession insured Israeli territory against attack. Sinai, the Gaza strip, perhaps the west bank of the Jordan might be negotiable.

But the Arabs, led by Nasser, steadfastly refused to negotiate directly with the Israelis or to take any step that would admit the existence of the state of Israel. Rearmed and partly retrained by the Russians, the Egyptians repeatedly proclaimed their intention of trying again, while occasionally leaking a suggestion that a new United Nations force might be acceptable. Since the last one had been withdrawn by Nasser's unilateral request, this had little appeal for Israel. Blocked again, the Suez Canal was now being somewhat outmoded by the development of oil tankers that would have been too large to pass through the canal in any case, and that went around the Cape of Good Hope, transporting oil more cheaply because of their great capacity. Perhaps the most important result of the war of 1967, however, was not the Israeli victory but the fact that the U.S.S.R.—whose ally had lost— had gained naval bases at Alexandria and even in Algeria. The Russians had a firmer position in the Mediterranean area than ever before.

In 1969 and 1970, tension mounted dangerously in the Middle East. As before the 1967 war, Arab Palestinians organized guerrilla attacks on Israeli or Israeli-occupied territory, from Jordan, Syria, and Lebanon. The Lebanon government, balanced between Christians and Muslims, and hitherto the most moderating influence among the Arab regimes in the area, was threatened by the Palestinian guerrillas, and forced to concede to them for their operations the Lebanese territory nearest the Israeli frontier. In various European airports—Zurich, Athens—Arab terrorists attacked planes carrying or thought to be carrying Israelis, and Israel tried to avenge such murderous acts and prevent their recurrence by such measures as a parachutists' raid on the Beirut airport and the destruction of Arab-owned commercial airliners on the ground. At times the Palestinian Arab terrorist movement took on the aspects of an independent power, negotiating with the Chinese, compelling Nasser to modify his pronouncements. In the autumn of 1970, the guerrillas hijacked four large planes in a single day, holding the passengers as hostages in Jordan for the release of certain captives of their own. In the midst of the tense negotiations that followed, full-scale hostilities broke out between the Arab guerrillas and the Jordanian government. The Syrians intervened on the side of the guerillas, and the threat of American intervention on the side of Jordan, and of a Soviet response, was suddenly very real. Jordanian successes, Syrian withdrawal, and American and Soviet restraint helped the critical moment pass. But the danger had been incalculable.

Just as grave was the continual Arab-Israeli confrontation in Egypt. Here Egyptian raids across the Suez Canal into Israeli-occupied territory in Sinai were more than overborne by Israeli commando raids into Egyptian territory on the west side of the Canal, and especially by deep Israeli air raids into Egypt. Until 1970 it was apparently the Israeli belief that such raids would prevent the installation of Soviet missile sites near the canal, but the calculation proved erroneous, and missile sites were indeed installed, and rendered operative, forcing the Israelis at least to suspend their air raids into Egypt. Moreover, Soviet pilots allegedly had begun to fly fighter-plane sorties against Israeli bombers. In view of the traditional sympathy of all American governments for Israel, such active operational Russian involvement in the defense of Egypt threatened the kind of confrontation between the Soviet Union and the United States that had been avoided since the Cuban crisis of 1962. American policy sought to avoid this danger, and simultaneously to create a situation in which the Russian military could be withdrawn from Egypt without forcing the Russians to lose face.

To this end, the United States, Britain, and France held regular four-power discussions with the U.S.S.R. on the Arab–Israeli conflict. With the Russians totally committed to the Arab side, and the French, even after de Gaulle's departure from office, making no change in an essentially anti-Israeli policy, with Britain balancing between the two sides, and the United States trying hard to help Israel but determined to avoid even the possibility of another Vietnam—or worse, since the Middle East was far more sensitive than southeast Asia—it was perhaps little wonder that Israel regarded with skepticism the possibility of any favorable solution emerging from the big powers' discussions, and firmly insisted that only direct talks between them and the Arabs could lead to a satisfactory settlement. Arab insistence that a return of all occupied territory must precede discussions rendered discussions impossible. Irritating and contradictory American government pronouncements, domestic pressures on the Nixon government, Soviet intransigence, and renewed domestic anti-Semitism all helped to prolong the stalemate. In the summer of 1970, however, as the result largely of American initiative, both Egyptians and Israelis agreed to a cease-fire. But as hope renewed that discussions might at least begin, President Nasser died suddenly, to be replaced by Anwar el-Sadat, who pledged to regain all occupied territories. The ceasefire continued, but prospects for talks were uncertain at the end of 1970.

Among the other Arab states, Iraq, closely aligned with the British after the war, and using its share of profits from the Western-controlled Iraq Petroleum Company to build public works, in 1958 experienced a nationalist uprising which ousted the monarchy and proclaimed a republic. Pro- and anti-Nasser factions, pro- and anti-communists, thereafter subjected the country to a series of coups and abortive coups, and the rebellious Kurdish tribes in the northern mountains contributed to the disorder and to the abrupt slackening of economic development after 1958. By 1970 Iraq had the most paranoid regime of all the Arab states, publicly executing from time to time amid general celebration various of its resident Jews or members of earlier Iraqi governments on charges of working for Israel or the American CIA or both, and always surprised at the hostile response such authorized terrorism brought even from their own Arab allies. Nasser himself rebuked the Iraqis for their excesses of zeal. The Kurdish question, however, apparently moved toward a solution, as the Iraqis, after negotiations with the Kurds, publicly stated in a new 1970 draft constitution that the Kurds were an official people of Iraq, and proposed that a Kurdish leader be chosen vice-president of the country.

In Iran, where the Anglo-Iranian Oil Company had the oil concession, the government after the war demanded that the company follow the example set in Saudi Arabia by the Arabian American Oil Company, which paid fifty percent of its profits to King Saud. Supported by a wave of antiforeign nationalism, the demagogue Mossadeq in 1951 secured the nationalization of the oil company. But the Iranian economy was badly hurt by an international boycott of the oil, and Mossadeq himself was overthrown in 1953 by a coup d'état allegedly masterminded by the American CIA. The government reached an agreement to pay foreign oil companies to assist in exploiting and marketing the oil. A measure of land reform sponsored vigorously by the shah himself led to improved economic conditions. Iran maintained satisfactory relations with both the United States and the U.S.S.R., though rivalry with Iraq over the future of the small Persian Gulf oil sheikhdoms clouded the horizons in 1970.

In Turkey, Atatürk's Republican People's party, the only political formation allowed in

Atatürk's own day, after the war permitted the activities of an opposition, and in the election of 1950 went down to defeat at the hands of the young Democrat party. Western opinion saluted this peaceful shift of power as the coming of age of Turkish parliamentary democracy. The Democrat government of Prime Minister Menderes proceeded to promote both state and private industry, to build roads and schools, and in other ways to bring the spirit of modernization to the villages, which had been neglected in Atatürk's day but contained three-quarters of the population. To propitiate Muslim opinion, some of Atatürk's secularist policies were moderated, religious instruction was restored in the schools, and the call to prayer sounded once more in Arabic from the minarets (sometimes on amplified tape recordings made in Mecca).

But Menderes' regime became increasingly arbitrary, muzzling the press, persecuting the Republican opposition both in and out of the Grand National Assembly, and restricting more and more the free conduct of elections. In May 1960 student riots touched off a coup by the Turkish army, which overthrew the government, outlawed the Democrat party, and brought Menderes to trial and eventual execution. A new constitution, in 1961, sought to avert a repetition of the experience with Menderes by strengthening the legislature and judiciary against the executive. It was the army, however, that exercised the real power. Moreover, the new Justice party, to which followers of Menderes gravitated, won a majority of the seats in the parliamentary election of 1965. Thus tensions persisted between the urban champions of secularization and westernization, represented by army leaders and by Atatürk's old Republican People's party, and the defenders of the conservative Muslim way of life in Turkish towns and villages, who tended to support the Justice party.

Meantime, low wages and the lack of employment opportunities at home were impelling tens of thousands of Turks to take jobs abroad, especially in West Germany, and the marginal quality of much Anatolian farmland, with its thin soil and scanty rainfall, promoted an even greater exodus from the villages to the towns and cities. Turkey appeared to be suffering a sharp attack of social and economic growing pains. Its hopes for achieving a quick "take-off" were thwarted by the country's meager resources, by its chronic

difficulty in paying for needed imports, especially oil, and by the government's slowness in fashioning an effective organization for economic planning. Friendship for the United States, very warm down to the 1960's, and cemented especially by the brave Turkish fighting in the Korean War, dwindled because of the disenchantment of sensitive Turkish nationalists with NATO and with the American refusal to support Turkey wholly against Greece in the Cyprus question. Anti-American feeling ran high by 1970, and radical student groups and others had even begun to look to the U.S.S.R.—traditionally the bugbear of all Turks.

Africa

The revolution against imperialism reached Africa in the 1950's, although there had long been ominous rumblings, such as an uprising in 1947 on the large French island of Madagascar off the east coast, put down by the French in a bloody massacre. The independent Empire of Ethiopia was taken from its Italian conquerors after the war, and restored to the durable emperor Haile Selassie, who had been ousted in 1935. He still ruled in 1970. In 1952 he annexed the former Italian colony of Eritrea. He had embarked on various programs of internal modernization—though not liberalization—and he worked hard to assist in the development of African unity.

Among the northern tier of states bordering the Mediterranean, all Muslim and Arabic-speaking, the former Italian colony of Libya achieved independence in 1951, and the French-dominated areas of Morocco and Tunisia in 1956, Morocco as a somewhat autocratic monarchy, Tunisia as a republic under the moderate and intelligent presidency of Habib Bourguiba, a veteran nationalist leader, educated at the Sorbonne. The huge area of Algeria, between Morocco and Tunisia, followed, but only after a debilitating and severe war of independence against the French. Its first ruler after independence, Ahmed Ben Bella, was intimate with the Chinese communists. Colonel Houari Boumédienne, who ousted Ben Bella in 1965—perhaps in large part because of the slumping economy—seemed to favor the U.S.S.R. Algeria and Libya strongly supported the Arab cause against Israel,

Africa, 1971

Independent
French
Portuguese
Spanish

Member countries of the British Commonwealth

Member countries of the French Community

Dates indicate years of independence

Eritrea: united with Ethiopia in 1952

Atlantic Ocean

MOROCCO 1956
(Sp.) IFNI
TUNISIA 1956
Mediterranean Sea
ALGERIA 1962
LIBYA 1951
U.A.R. (EGYPT) 1958
SPANISH SAHARA
MAURITANIA 1960
MALI 1960
NIGER 1960
CHAD 1960
SUDAN 1956
Red Sea
ERITREA
AFARS & ISSAS TERRITORY (Fr.)
SENEGAL 1960
GAMBIA 1965
PORTUGUESE GUINEA
GUINEA 1958
UPPER VOLTA 1960
NIGERIA 1960
1960
CENTRAL AFRICAN REPUBLIC
ETHIOPIA
SIERRA LEONE 1961
IVORY COAST 1960
1957 GHANA
LIBERIA
CAMEROON 1960
SOMALI REPUBLIC 1960
TOGO 1960
DAHOMEY 1960
EQUATORIAL GUINEA 1968
1960 GABON
REP. OF CONGO 1960
UGANDA 1962
KENYA 1963
RWANDA 1962
CABINDA (Angola)
THE CONGO 1960
BURUNDI 1962
TANZANIA 1964
ZANZIBAR (Tanzania)
ANGOLA
ZAMBIA 1964
MALAWI 1964
MOZAMBIQUE
MALAGASY REPUBLIC 1960
MAURITIUS 1968
SOUTH-WEST AFRICA (South Africa)
BOTSWANA 1966
RHODESIA 1965
LESOTHO 1966
SWAZILAND 1968
REPUBLIC OF SOUTH AFRICA

distant Morocco more feebly, and Tunisia under Bourguiba not at all. Bourguiba's voice could occasionally be heard calling for a reasonable accommodation between Arabs and Israelis. In Libya, a colonels' coup d'état in 1969 brought to power a group of army officers who apparently modeled their movement on Nasser's. Moderate at first, they proceeded in 1970 to announce the confiscation of Italian and Jewish-owned property. American evacuation of a huge airbase in Libya and the purchase of French and Soviet arms by the Libyans added to the general apprehension in North Africa. But there might be

some economic hope, if little political validity, in a loose "union" of Egypt, Libya, and the Sudan announced in 1970.

South of the Muslim tier lay the colonies of the French, British, and Belgians, inhabited chiefly by blacks. West African climatic conditions had always discouraged large-scale white settlement except in portions of the Belgian Congo; but in East Africa—in the British colonies of Kenya and Uganda especially—whites had settled in the fertile highlands in large numbers, farmed the land, and regarded the country as their own, as of course did the large white population of the Union of South Africa—which seceded from the British Commonwealth in 1961 and became the Republic of South Africa—and the whites of some of the lands in between, such as Rhodesia.

In the areas of small white settlement, the revolution moved swiftly. Often regions whose names were barely familiar in the West took new and totally unfamiliar names as they became independent. The Gold Coast—a West African British colony with a good many well-educated natives and a start on economic development—became the nation of Ghana in 1957. Its leader, the American-educated Kwame Nkrumah, the pioneer of African emancipation, made what seemed like a hopeful start on economic planning within a political democracy. But he grew increasingly dictatorial, jailing and mistreating his political enemies, and insisting on being worshiped as a virtual god by his subjects. He also abandoned sound and gradual policies of development in favor of unrealistic and grandiose projects that enriched him and his followers personally. And he became fanatically anti-Western and determined to court Chinese communist favor in an effort to unite Africa into a kind of personal empire. He was ousted in 1966, and his successors embarked on a sober program of putting Ghana back on the track once more.

The French colonies—covering huge areas of territory often sparsely populated—achieved independence simultaneously in 1960, except for Guinea, a small West African state that broke away in 1958 under the leadership of a pro-Russian politician, Sekou Touré. With independence, some of the colonies retained close economic ties with France, as members of the French Community. Guinea did not; all Frenchmen had left in 1958, and the country had virtually come to a stop. The neighboring state of Mali (formerly French Sudan) and Mauritania also pursued a generally pro-Russian line. By the late 1960's Touré had apparently begun to regret his economic dependence on the U.S.S.R., and was seeking change.

Some of the newly independent French colonies—Upper Volta, Niger, Chad, Gabon—were hardly more than geographical expressions without national traditions or even tribal cohesion. Others proved stable and successful, such as Senegal—governed by Léopold Senghor, a celebrated poet who wrote in French of the beauties of négritude (being black); Ivory Coast—whose leader Houphouet-Boigny had long parliamentary experience as a deputy in Paris; and the Malagasy Republic (formerly Madagascar)—which had a flourishing economy based in large part on vanilla. In at least one case (Gabon), the French intervened with troops to save the government from a military coup d'état. In others—Togo, Dahomey, Cameroon—the coups took place unimpeded and sometimes repeatedly. In 1970, for instance, large numbers of French troops were fighting a little publicized war in Chad; while the regime in the former French Congo (captal, Brazzaville) was thoroughly pro-Communist.

In 1960, Nigeria, most important of the British colonies, achieved independence. With 60,000,000 people and large and varied economic resources, it represented a great hope for the future. The British had carefully educated and trained many thousands of Nigerians both in England and in excellent schools and universities established in the country itself. A land of many tribes, Nigeria was divided into four regions, each semiautonomous, to ease mutual tribal tensions, of which perhaps the most severe was that between the Muslim Hausa tribe of the northern region and the Ibo tribe of the eastern region. In the Hausa areas, the well-educated, aggressive, and competent Ibos ran the railroads, power stations, and other modern facilities, and formed an important element in the cities. When army plotters led by an Ibo officer murdered the Muslim prime minister of Nigeria, and seized power in 1966, the Hausas rose and massacred the Ibos living in the north, killing many thousands, while others escaped in disorder to their native east. By 1967, the Ibo east had seceded and called itself the Republic of Biafra, and the Nigerian central government embarked on full-scale war to force the Ibos and other eastern tribesmen to return to Nigerian rule. The general who headed the central government and the officer who headed Biafra were both graduates of British institutions. Misery and famine accompanied the operations, and the war dragged on until 1969. Both Britain and the Soviet Union had helped the Nigerian government. The Biafrans got much sympathy but no real help except from the French, who as usual were interested in future oil concessions. When the war finally ended, the mass slaughter that had been feared did not materialize, and efforts at recovery were under way by the end of 1970.

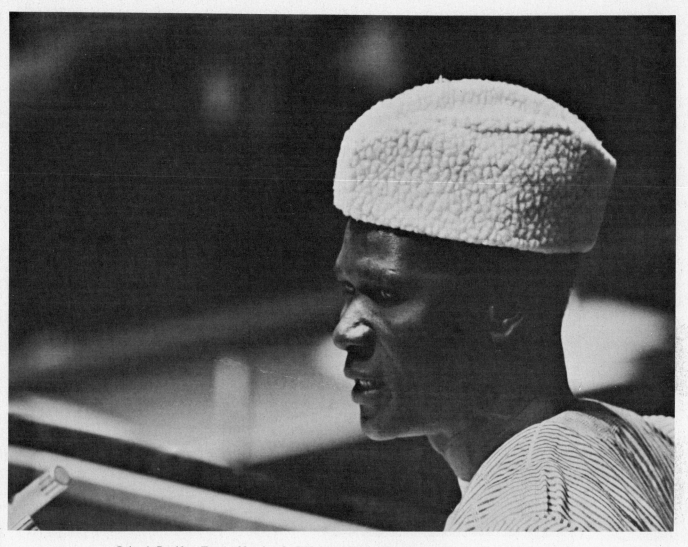

Guinea's President Touré addressing the UN General Assembly, 1960.

In East Africa, the British settlers in Kenya struggled for eight years (1952–1960) against a secret terrorist society formed within the Kikuyu tribe, the Mau Mau, whose aim was to drive all white men out of the country. The Mau Mau horribly murdered white settlers and their families, and also Kikuyus and other tribesmen who would not join them. Though the British imprisoned one of its founders, the educated Kikuyu Jomo Kenyatta, and eventually put down the movement, they did give Kenya independence in 1963, against the bitter protests of many

white settlers. Kenyatta became the first post-liberation chief of state. By 1962 neighboring Uganda attained independence, and in 1964, under the leadership of Julius Nyerere (educated at Edinburgh), so did Tanganyika—which had been German before World War I, and British since. A violent pro-Chinese communist coup d'état had taken place on the offshore spice island of Zanzibar, which merged with Tanganyika as the new country of Tanzania. Nyerere, who had been pro-Western, thereafter became more notably neutralist. In 1964, Nyasaland became

Malawi under Dr. Hastings Banda, who had formerly been a dentist in London, and Northern Rhodesia became Zambia under Kenneth Kaunda, a Western-educated moderate.

In contrast to the British, who had at least tried to prepare the way for African independence by providing education and administrative experience for Africans, and who could not be held responsible for the troubles in Ghana and Nigeria, the Belgians, who had since the late nineteenth century governed the huge Central African area known as the Congo, made no such effort. When the Belgian rulers suddenly pulled out in 1960, leaving a wholly artificial Western-style parliamentary structure, it was not long before tribal and regional rivalries between native leaders asserted themselves, and virtual chaos prevailed. A leftist leader, Patrice Lumumba, was assassinated (the Russians soon named their "university" for Africans in Moscow after him); the province of Katanga, site of rich copper mines with many European residents, seceded under its local leader, Moise Tshombe, who was strongly pro-Belgian. Other areas revolted. Africans in rebellion murdered whites, or took them prisoner and kept them as hostages; white mercenaries enlisted in the forces of Tshombe and others. The United Nations sent troops to restore order and force the end of the Katangese secession, while the Chinese supported certain rebel factions, and the South Africans and Belgians others. By 1968 (after an improbable interlude in which Tshombe had returned from exile to lead the country briefly, and had eventually wound up in an Algerian jail after the plane he was flying had been hijacked) the military regime of General Joseph Mobuto seemed relatively firmly in control, and by 1970 many Belgians were back in the country, and the Belgian king himself could be observed on a royal visit reviewing the new republican Congolese armies.

The Congolese troubles overflowed the borders of the Congo into Portuguese Angola to the south, where a local rebellion, at first supplied from the Congo, forced Portuguese military intervention. In 1970 Angola, which provided Portugal with much of its oil, together with Mozambique on the east coast and the tiny enclave of Portuguese Guinea on the west, remained under Lisbon's control. Portuguese political theory regarded these countries not as colonies but as overseas extensions of metropolitan Portugal, and it was Portuguese policy to grant the status of an "assimilated" Portuguese to every African who had had a certain minimum education. Nor did the Portuguese draw the color line as other colonial powers had generally done. Against the overwhelming trend toward setting former colonies free the Portuguese held fast. But the guerrilla warfare they had to fight was proving expensive and unpopular at home.

Most intransigent of all were the white-dominated Republic of South Africa and its northern neighbor, the state of Rhodesia (formerly Southern Rhodesia), which broke its political ties with Britain in 1965 rather than agree to any African participation in political life. In South Africa, the whites included not only descendants of the Dutch settlers, the Boers or farmers who in the nineteenth century had made the great trek northward from the Cape, settled in the countryside, and now called themselves Afrikaners, but also a minority of English descent. But altogether the whites were themselves a minority, of about one in five of the population. The nonwhites included blacks, "coloreds," as those of mixed European and African blood were called, and Asians, mostly Indians who were usually shopkeepers.

The Afrikaners, who had tried unsuccessfully to keep South Africa from fighting on Britain's side in World War II, and some of whom sympathized with Hitler, emerged after the war as a political majority. Imbued with an extremely narrow and reactionary form of Calvinist religion that taught that God had ordained the inferiority of the blacks, the ruling group moved steadily to impose on the black majority their policies of rigid segregation: *apartheid*. Separate townships to live in, separate facilities of all sorts, no political rights, no opportunity for higher education or advancement beyond manual labor, internment of black leaders including the Zulu chief Albert Luthulli, winner of the Nobel Peace Prize: these were the conditions that a succession of Afrikaner governments defended and extended. Supported by some of those of English descent, who were fearful that the black upheaval to the north would spread to South Africa, the Afrikaners also introduced emergency laws making it possible to arrest people on suspicion, to keep them incommunicado, and to punish them without trial. Severe censorship prevailed, and dissent was silenced. It was no doubt true that communist agents had been at work among the Africans, but the combination of policies known as apartheid was calculated not to thwart them but to make their message more credible.

The regime sought to disarm criticism by founding in Botswana and Lesotho (1966) two black states on South African territory. Lesotho was the former Basutoland, an enclave entirely surrounded by South African territory, and Botswana the former Bechuanaland, which had also previously had the status of an African reservation. Inhabited solely by blacks, but dominated by whites, these two states were not likely to produce much black enthusiasm. In 1949, defying the UN, South Africa annexed the former German colony and League mandate of South-West Africa. Here too the policies of apartheid held sway.

White South African writers who opposed apartheid, like Alan Paton or Nadine Gordimer, were heard and appreciated outside South Africa, and vilified and repressed at home. The Rhodesians who defied the British in 1965 rather than allow Africans to participate in politics were many of them originally emigrants from South Africa. Boycotted by the British Labour government and later by the UN, they managed to get supplies from South Africa and from Mozambique. With the 1970 victory of the Conservatives in England, both South Africa and Rhodesia could expect a considerable relaxation of British policies. To American observers, the whites at the southern end of the African continent seemed determined to defy what seemed to be the lessons of history elsewhere. Whenever the blacks of the remainder of the continent could put aside their own rivalries long enough to work out some practicable plan of unity—and that would no doubt take a long time—the whites of the south might expect short shrift.

Latin America

Although most of the Latin American republics had by 1945 enjoyed political independence for more than a century, they had much in common economically and socially with the emerging nations of Asia and Africa. Like the Asians and Africans, the Latin Americans had traditionally been suppliers of foods and raw materials to the rest of the world. Bananas, coffee, sugar, beef, oil, nitrates, and copper fluctuated widely in price on the world market, and before the Latin Americans could raise their standards of living they would have to build on a more stable economic base. Like the other emerging nations too, most of Latin America had a racially mixed population: some native-born whites (Creoles) or immigrants from Europe (like the Italians in Argentina), some descended from the indigenous Indians, and some blacks (chiefly in Brazil and Haiti). Nominally governed under a democratic system of elected officials and parliaments, they had all too often lived under military dictatorships that shifted whenever a new army officer felt strong enough to challenge the one in power.

Toward the United States, Latin Americans traditionally felt a mixture of envy, dislike, and suspicion. The United States was rich and powerful, the "Colossus of the North." Upper-class Latin Americans educated in Europe believed that North Americans lacked true culture. North Americans generally seemed to know little and care less about Latin America. Whenever the United States ceased to be indifferent and devoted some attention to Latin America, it did it by what seemed like intervention in Latin affairs. Upper-class Latin Americans, aware of the miserable poverty in which the majority of their people lived, often had a bad conscience. Usually they did not care whether the conditions of the poor improved or not: theirs was not the Anglo-American tradition of *richesse oblige*. By and large they cared only for their own comforts and hoped that nothing—least of all a social revolution—would disturb the system. So it made them uneasy to find the United States worrying more about the Bolivian or Peruvian peasant than the Bolivians or Peruvians themselves had ever done. Craving attention and admiration yet at the same time longing to be left alone, the Latin Americans made it very difficult for the United States to develop consistent satisfactory policies toward them. And by and large the Latin complaints about us were true: we were indifferent except when crises arose. When crises arose we tended to intervene. We were tactless, we were crude, we did not understand, our motives were often questionable.

President Franklin Roosevelt's "Good Neighbor" policy after 1932 was an attempt to overcome these difficulties. The Pan-American Conference that dated back to 1890 became a Pan-American Union in 1910; both of these were primarily cultural in emphasis. But after World

Caribbean Sea

PANAMA CANAL Cartagena

Caracas

VENEZUELA

TRINIDAD AND TOBAGO

GUYANA

SURINAM

Medellín

Bogotá

COLOMBIA

Orinoco R.

Georgetown

Paramaribo

DEVIL'S ISLAND

GUIANAS

Cayenne

FRENCH GUIANA

ECUADOR Quito

Guayaquil

Negro R.

Manaos

Amazon R.

Belem (Pará)

Iquitos

Amazon R.

Fortaleza

A N

Purus R.

Madeira R.

Tapajos R.

Natal

PERU

B R A Z I L

Recife (Pernambuco)

Callao

Lima

Cuzco

Araguaia R.

Tocantins R.

São Francisco R.

Salvador (Bahia)

Arequipa

L. Titicaca

La Paz

BOLIVIA

Paraguay R.

FEDERAL DISTRICT

Brasilia

Tacna

Arica

Sucré

GRAN CHACO

Belo Horizonte

Pacific Ocean

Antofagasta

Parana R.

São Paulo

Santos

Rio de Janeiro

PARAGUAY

Asunción

Tucuman

Parana R.

Pôrto Alegre

Atlantic Ocean

Cordoba

CHILE

URUGUAY

Valparaiso

Mendoza

Santiago

Buenos Aires

Montevideo

Rio de la Plata

ARGENTINA

Colorado R.

Bahia Blanca

0   500

Miles

Capital cities

South America, 1971

FALKLAND IS. (Br.)

Str. of Magellan

Punta Arenas (Magallanes)

CAPE HORN

War II the Pan-American Union became the Organization of American States (OAS). Somewhat looser than an alliance, the OAS provided a means for consultation among all the American nations, North, South, and Central, on all important matters of mutual concern. The United States was—quite naturally—accused by its enemies of having forged just another instrument of its imperialistic policies, yet OAS did in fact enable all the American states to reach genuine joint decisions. The Alliance for Progress, launched under President Kennedy's impulse and designed to enable the United States to help the Latin Americans to help themselves, proved a disappointment, in part because it was so difficult to allay Latin American suspicions of our intentions, in part because of the deeply entrenched oligarchies that dominated most Latin American countries.

Broad generalizations are of course subject to challenge: not every Latin American country was oligarchical or backward. Uruguay, for example, a small country with a population largely European in origin, had gone further toward creating an advanced welfare state than any other in the world, even the Scandinavian countries or Britain—so far, indeed, that the Uruguayan economy by 1970 was near collapse, largely because of the payment of state funds to individual citizens for the many types of benefits available. Venezuela, with rapidly developing oil resources, in 1959 ousted the last of its long line of military-oligarchic dictators, and eleven years later had apparently made the transition to moderate democratic rule, though still threatened by communists sponsored from outside.

Colombia experienced a lengthy terrorist campaign in the countryside—virtually a civil war—in which many thousands were killed, and even when this drew to an end was still experiencing extremes of wealth and poverty. Brazil, the enormous Portuguese-speaking land larger than any other Latin American country, suffered from recurrent economic crises and military coups. Its poverty-stricken northeast, where many thousands lived in virtual peonage on big plantations, contrasted sharply with the luxurious apartment-house and beach life of the big cities; but each of these too had its festering slums. In 1970 its government was a tight military dictatorship, and stood accused of torturing its political prisoners.

Chile, too, though plagued by a continual economic crisis and by occasional military intervention, maintained democratic government. Indeed, in the autumn of 1970, Chileans freely elected a Marxist, Salvador Allende, as president. Though Allende was a minority president, having won less than 40 percent of the votes, he took office in relative calm (only the army chief of staff was assassinated), and it was widely predicted that he might move gradually in expropriating foreign properties. In any case, Chile was the only country to move left by democratic processes.

Alone in Latin America, Mexico had passed through and recovered from a true social revolution. The overthrow of the emperor Maximilian in 1867 was followed only nine years later by the advent of the dictator Porfirio Diaz, who ruled in the interests of foreign investors and large landholders until 1910, when a peasant revolution broke out that lasted with interruptions for thirty years, marked by violence and insurrection, by revolutionary reformers who turned into wealthy dictators, and by radical social and economic experimentation. The Catholic church, long regarded by many Mexicans as opposed to economic and political reform and indifferent to the welfare of the masses, was the target of extreme anticlerical measures. The foreign oil companies, American and British, suffered expropriation. The revolutionary governments gave labor unions extensive privileges and power, expropriated great estates to emancipate the poor peasant, and began a vigorous program of educating the large and neglected population of native Indians. A remarkable cultural awakening took place, based on native traditions and crafts. Mexican revolutionary painters like Rivera and Orozco won international fame. The Mexican revolution, however, stopped short of installing a socialist system, and by 1945 had lost much of its radical dogmatism. The new leaders were more reconciled to the need for foreign capital, for patience in the long task of raising the standards of the masses. The Mexican regime was dominated by a single political party whose leaders in turn were elected president every seventh year, and each in turn stepped down peacefully to make way for his successor. Though suspicious of any imagined American attempt to influence its policies, each new Mexican government cemented further a relationship that was not only peaceful but friendly.

But the successful Mexican revolution was an exception in Latin America. By contrast, Argentina, peopled almost entirely by European immigrants and their descendants, and dependent on the export of beef and grain to Europe, continued to have a social system that gave power to a small landlord class. The beginnings of industrialization, and especially the growth by 1945 of the capital, Buenos Aires, into a great metropolis of nearly five million, increased the numbers of working-class and middle-class people and deepened popular dissatisfaction with the regime.

Brought to power in the national election of 1946, Colonel Juan Perón became a dictator on the model of Mussolini, Hitler, and Franco. In 1955 he went down before a characteristic Latin American military coup d'état. He had begun more and more to appeal to the poorer masses, the descamisados ("shirtless ones"), and thus lost much of his following in the conservative upper classes. Moreover he quarreled with the Roman Catholic church and put through anticlerical measures that cost him further support. Nor could he solve the grave economic and financial problems arising out of his country's essentially colonial position; indeed, his extravagant spending on public works and welfare projects virtually bankrupted Argentina.

During the years that followed, Perónist sentiment continued strong among workers and some other groups, and twice (1962 and 1966) a weak elected government was overthrown by a military coup. The army regime installed in 1966 promised to purge Argentina of corruption but aroused much opposition by its repression of academic freedom. In 1970 the old problems remained unsolved, almost untackled. And they remained unsolved as well in Peru, which had a relatively advanced urban life at the time of the latest military coup in 1968, and in Ecuador and Paraguay, which were still largely rural, as well as in Haiti, where a brutal dictatorship had brought economic and political desolation.

It was, of course, Cuba that in the postwar years provided the new revolution. Beginning in the late 1950's under the leadership of Fidel Castro as a guerrilla movement in the hills of the eastern province (Oriente), it succeeded in ousting the government of Fulgencio Batista in 1959. American attitudes toward Castro had been ambivalent: on the one hand, the Batista regime was singularly corrupt and unsavory; on the other, nobody really knew how deeply Castro was committed to communism or to Soviet domination. After his success, he made a series of increasingly pro-Soviet pronouncements, and quarreled bitterly with the United States, which boycotted Cuban goods. Since the Cuban economy was dependent upon the export of sugar and tobacco, Castro soon found himself exporting largely to the U.S.S.R. and its associated powers, and obtaining most of his imports from them. In 1961, the Kennedy administration backed an expedition of anti-Castro exiles, who landed at the Bay of Pigs and were thoroughly defeated.

In 1962, as we have seen, Castro opened Cuba to the installation of Soviet missiles, leading to the great crisis of October. Once the crisis was over and the missiles were withdrawn, Castro seemed to grow more and more impatient with what he felt to be the inadequate amount of Soviet assistance, and tried to take advantage of the Soviet–Chinese quarrel to extract more from the U.S.S.R. He also tried strenuously to export his revolution into the rest of Latin America: to

Prime Minister Fidel Castro signing a decree nationalizing American-owned banks in Cuba, 1960.

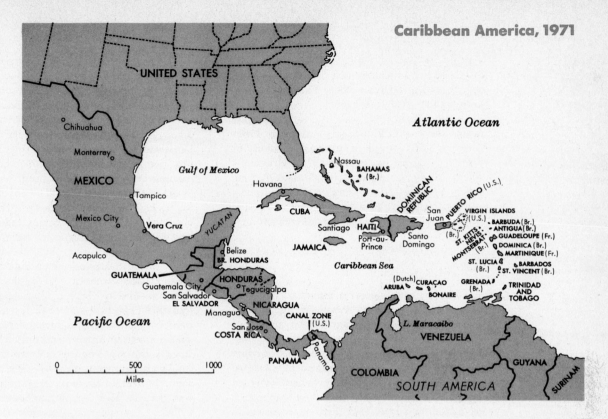

Venezuela, where there was a great deal of Castroite violence especially just before the presidential elections of 1963; to Guatemala, where communist terrorists dominated portions of the country and murdered the American ambassador in 1968; and to Bolivia, where a band of guerrillas operating under the Argentine revolutionary theorist Ernesto ("Che") Guevara, formerly a member of Castro's cabinet, was finally wiped out in 1967. Guevara was killed, and his diary captured and sold abroad by the Bolivian interior minister, Arguedes, in 1968. But a new leftist military coup took over Bolivia in 1970.

In 1965, the United States concluded, perhaps prematurely, that a revolution in the Dominican Republic, on the neighboring island to Cuba, was inspired by Castro. Between 1930 and 1961, the Dominican Republic had been ruled by General Trujillo, a ruthless, corrupt and bloodthirsty dictator. After his assassination, the first freely elected government in a generation took office under Juan Bosch, but increasing tension between the army and the new reformers led to military coups and finally to a civil war in 1965. Fearing that communists might soon take over, President Johnson sent in a division of marines, and then tried to internationalize the intervention by appealing to the Organization of American

States. By a narrow margin, the OAS responded, and five of its member states, all with conservative military regimes, sent troops to join the Americans. The Dominican Republic was pacified sufficiently for constitutional elections to be held in 1966; a moderate, Joaquin Balaguer, became president and retained his office in the elections of 1970.

It would have been political suicide in 1965 for any President of the United States to allow another Caribbean country to fall into pro-Soviet hands at a time when public opinion in this country had hardly reconciled itself to the existence of the Castro regime. But the entire episode aroused much opposition among Americans, despite the fact that the OAS had backed Johnson's actions. And in Latin America, where Mexico, for example, had opposed intervention, the reappearance of American marines served to heighten the suspicion that the United States was still up to its bad old tricks.

Physically located in Latin America, but with a population consisting chiefly of East Indians and Negroes, deeply at odds with each other, British Guiana also had a strong communist movement, led by an Indian, Cheddi Jagan. When it appeared that independence from Britain would be followed by Jagan's assuming power, the British postponed independence until an effective anticommunist coalition of Jagan's opponents was safely in office. The new state of Guyana was created in 1966.

In 1970, then, there was little cause for optimism about the immediate future in Latin America. The spread of terrorist methods to Brazil, to Argentina, and even to Uruguay—where the foreign diplomats or local politicians were kidnapped and sometimes murdered—added a frightening new development to a region whose problems were already grim enough.

Final Reflections

Not the least important aspect of the Cold War was the competition between the United States and the Soviet Union for the support of the emerging nations. In their programs of foreign aid, both countries made mistakes: as when American aid enabled a Ghanaian politician to buy himself a solid gold bed, or when Soviet aid supplied quantities of obsolete and inappropriate agricultural machinery that rusted uselessly on a Guinean dock. In the larger sense, it was a mistake for an American or a Russian to promise that his system would usher in the millennium promptly for those who imitated it. New nations would have to wait for most of the consumer goods they yearned for until they had educated enough of their own people to do the work of modernizing that would earn the money to buy them. Then political stability and economic growth might each contribute to the other. Perhaps the American experiment of the Peace Corps, launched by President Kennedy, provided the most hopeful model: education by example for the hard pull ahead.

As to the Cold War itself, many by the mid-Sixties had for some time thought the term was obsolete, that the United States and its partners had won without realizing it, that the U.S.S.R. was undergoing a fundamental change, and that a worldwide relaxation of tensions might be in prospect had America not—by its policies in Vietnam—forfeited such a large measure of international goodwill and weakened its ability to negotiate. These views vanished like a puff of smoke after the Soviet intervention in Czechoslovakia in 1968. The U.S.S.R. would still intervene with force in its own bailiwick; if it showed signs of wanting the Vietnam war to end, this was because such a solution would hurt the Chinese; it would negotiate only when it could further its own immediate interests. American intervention in Vietnam had perhaps helped save us from still worse agonies. In 1970, the Cold War was still very much with us, and in its next phases would require of us a clear understanding of its origins and development since 1945.

Reading Suggestions on the World Since 1945

GENERAL ACCOUNTS

N. A. Graebner, ed., *The Cold War: Ideological Conflict or Power Struggle?* (*Heath). Introduction to divergent interpretations.

D. Donnelly, *Struggle for the World* (St. Martin's, 1965). A history of the Cold War, tracing it back to 1917.

C. Quigley, *The World since 1939,* rev. ed. (*Collier). Thoughtful survey.

P. Calvocoressi, *International Politics since 1945* (*Praeger). Helpful factual survey.

C. E. Black, *Dynamics of Modernization* (*Torchbooks). Illuminating comparative study.

S. Kuznets, *Post-War Economic Growth* (Harvard Univ. Press, 1964). Very good analysis.

S. P. Huntington, *Political Order in Changing Societies* (Yale Univ. Press, 1968); L. L. Snyder, *The New Nationalism* (Cornell Univ. Press, 1968). Wide-ranging and provocative surveys.

THE FREE WORLD   J. Freymond, *Western Europe since the War* (Praeger, 1964). Good brief manual.

T. H. White, *Fire in the Ashes* (*Apollo). Postwar economic recovery and the role of the Marshall Plan.

M. M. Postan, *An Economic History of Western Europe, 1945–1964* (*Barnes & Noble). Comprehensive and most informative review.

W. O. Henderson, *The Genesis of the Common Market* (F. Cass, 1963); U. W. Kitzinger, *Politics and Economics of European Integration* (*Praeger); L. B. Krause, ed., *The Common Market: Progress and Controversy* (*Spectrum). Useful works on an important economic development.

A. Marwick, *Britain in the Century of Total War* (Little, Brown, 1968). Controversial assessment of the impact of war on society.

A. Sampson, *Anatomy of Britain Today,* rev. ed. (*Colophon). Lively analysis.

F. Boyd, *British Politics in Transition, 1945–1963* (Praeger, 1964). Solid account.

C. Cross, *The Fall of the British Empire, 1918–1968* (Hodder & Stoughton, 1968). Analysis of a central aspect of Britain's altered position.

S. Hoffmann et al., *In Search of France* (*Torchbooks). Essays on economics, politics, and society in twentieth-century France.

D. Pickles, *Fifth French Republic,* 3rd ed. (*Praeger). Good political handbook.

P. Williams, *Crisis and Compromise* (*Anchor). Analyzing the failures of the Fourth Republic.

D. Schoenbrun, *Three Lives of Charles de Gaulle* (*Atheneum). By an informed journalist.

C. Brinton, *The Americans and the French* (Harvard Univ. Press, 1968). Perceptive essay on the French in the postwar world.

H. S. Hughes, *The United States and Italy,* rev. ed. (*Norton). The intelligent American's guide to postwar Italian politics and society.

M. Salvadori, *Italy* (*Spectrum). Handy introduction.

K. P. Tauber, *Beyond Eagle and Swastika,* 2 vols. (Wesleyan, 1967). Detailed study of German nationalism since World War II.

A. Grosser, *The Federal Republic of Germany* (*Praeger). Good concise history.

G. M. Craig, *The United States and Canada* (Harvard Univ. Press, 1968). The intelligent American's guide to the problems of his northern neighbor.

T. H. White, *The Making of the President, 1960, The Making of the President, 1964,* and *The Making of the President, 1968* (*Signet). Highly informative political analyses.

Dean Acheson, *Present at the Creation* (Norton, 1969). Beautifully written memoirs of the 1950's by President Truman's secretary of state.

A. M. Schlesinger, Jr., *A Thousand Days* (Houghton, 1965), and T. C. Sorenson, *Kennedy* (*Bantam). Memoirs by aides of President Kennedy, particularly enlightening on foreign policy.

H. Sidey, *A Very Personal Presidency* (*Atheneum). Perceptive study of the Johnson presidency.

THE COMMUNIST BLOC   C. E. Black, *The Eastern World since 1945* (*Ginn). Instructive scholarly survey.

L. Schapiro, *The Government and Politics of the Soviet Union,* rev. ed. (*Vintage). Short treatment by a leading authority.

A. G. Meyer, *The Soviet Political System* (Random House, 1965). An interpretation by a capable political scientist.

Z. Brzezinski, *The Soviet Bloc,* rev. ed. (Harvard Univ. Press, 1967). Solid study of the elements of unity and conflict by a leading scientist.

Adam Ulam, *Expansion and Coexistence: The History of Soviet Foreign Policy, 1917–1967* (Praeger, 1968).

D. Zagoria, *The Sino-Soviet Conflict, 1956–1961* (*Atheneum); W. E. Griffth, *Albania and the Sino-Soviet Rift* and *The Sino-Soviet Rift* (*MIT). Useful studies of Russo-Chinese antagonism.

R. L. Wolff, *The Balkans in Our Time* (*Norton). Informed survey.

THE EMERGING NATIONS   S. C. Easton, *The Rise and Fall of Modern Colonialism* (Praeger, 1962). Sweeping survey.

V. M. Dean, *Nature of the Non-Western World* (*Mentor). Brief overview.

B. Ward, *Interplay of East and West* and *Rich Nations and Poor Nations* (*Norton). General study by an articulate economist.

F. W. Houn, *A Shirt History of Chinese Communism* (*Spectrum). Useful recent introduction.

J. K. Fairbank, *The United States and China,* rev. ed. (*Compass); E. O. Reischauer, *The United States and Japan,* rev. ed. (*Compass). Authoritative surveys.

D. J. Duncannon, *Government and Revolution in Vietnam* (Oxford Univ. Press, 1968). Authoritative political history.

B. B. Fall, *The Two Viet-Nams,* rev. ed. (Praeger, 1965), and R. Shaplen, *The Lost Revolution: The U. S. in Vietnam, 1946–1966* (*Colophon). Outstanding titles among the flood of works on the subject.

J. D. Legge, *Indonesia* (*Spectrum). Handy introduction.

W. N. Brown, *The United States and India and Pakistan,* rev. ed. (Harvard Univ. Press, 1963); S. Wolpert, *India* (*Spectrum); D. N. Wilber, *Pakistan Yesterday and Today* (*Holt). Useful introductory studies.

R. H. Davison, *Turkey* (*Spectrum); N. Safran, *The United States and Israel* (Harvard Univ. Press, 1963); W. R. Polk, *The United States and the Arab World* (Harvard Univ. Press, 1965); H. B. Sharabi, *Nationalism and Revolution in the Arab World* (*Van Nostrand); T. Prittie, *Israel: Miracle in the Desert,* rev. ed. (*Penguin); M. Harari, *Government and Politics in the Middle East* (*Spectrum); R. W. Cottam, *Nationalism in Iran* (*Pittsburgh). Recent studies of the Middle East.

J. Hatch, *A History of Postwar Africa* (*Praeger). Clear and helpful guide.

B. Ward, *Africa in the Making* (Norton, 1966). Stimulating general discussion.

L. G. Cowan, *The Dilemmas of African Independence,* rev. ed. (*Walker). A mine of information.

J. F. Gallagher, *The United States and North Africa* (Harvard Univ. Press, 1963); W. Schwarz, *Nigeria* (Praeger, 1968); J. Cope, *South Africa* (Praeger, 1965). Good studies of particularly important areas.

G. M. Carter, ed., *Politics in Africa: Seven Cases* (*Harcourt). Informative studies.

V. Alba, *Nationalists without Nations* (Praeger, 1968). Attack on the ruling oligarchies as barriers to progress in Latin America.

R. J. Alexander, *Today's Latin America,* 2nd ed. (*Anchor); T. Szulc, *Winds of Revolution: Latin America Today and Tomorrow,* rev. ed. (*Praeger). Suggestive introductions.

C. C. Cumberland, *Mexico: The Struggle for Modernity* (*Oxford Univ. Press); A. P. Whitaker, *Argentina* (*Spectrum); A. Marshall, *Brazil* (*Walker); K. Silvert, *Chile Yesterday and Today* (*Holt); J. E. Fagg, *Cuba, Haiti, and the Dominican Republic* (*Spectrum); H. Bernstein, *Venezuela and Colombia* (*Spectrum); M. Rodriguez, *Central America* (*Spectrum). Useful guides to particular areas.

LITERATURE DISCUSSED
IN THE CHAPTER

I. Ehrenburg, *The Thaw* (Harvil, 1955).

V. Dudinstev, *Not by Bread Alone* (Dutton, 1957).

B. Pasternak, *Dr. Zhivago* (*Signet).

M. Sholokhov, *And Quiet Flows the Don* (*Vintage); *The Don Flows Home to the Sea* (*Vintage); *Harvest on the Don* (*Signet).

A. I. Solzhenitsyn, *A Day in the Life of Ivan Denisovitch* (*several editions); *Cancer Ward,* trans. N. Bethell and D. Burg (Bodley Head, 1968); *The First Circle,* trans. T. P. Whitney (Harper, 1968).

A. Tertz, pseud., *The Makepeace Experiment* (*Vintage); *Socialist Realism: The Trial Begins* (*Vintage).

Y. Yevtushenko, *A Precocious Autobiography* (*Dutton); *Selected Poetry* (*Penguin); *Bratsk Station and Other New Poems* (*Anchor).

32

Man's Fate
in the Twentieth Century

I The Intellectual Revolution Speeds Up

Among the countless "ideas" that come to our attention through the printed or the spoken word, through symbols, diagrams, pictures, even through musical sounds, it is almost impossible to distinguish those ideas which are characteristic of our age, which give it its flavor or style, which establish its "climate of opinion." Indeed, it is tempting to conclude that this very *variety* of ideas, spread abroad among countless millions through all the channels of mass communication, is itself the distinguishing mark of our time. There is, moreover, a further difficulty confronting the historian of contemporary thought and feeling. As we shall note later in this chapter, the gap between the culture of the few, the "highbrows," and the culture of the many, who are not necessarily "lowbrows," just not highbrows—this gap seems nowadays especially wide and deep. The historian who relied wholly on

Above: Philip Johnson:
The Lehman Brothers Building, designed 1969–1970.
Right: Aristide Maillol's "The Mediterranean,"
1902–1905.

evidence from the work of "serious" modern poets or artists would come to quite different conclusions from one who rested on evidence from comic strips, popular music, conventional artists and illustrators, and what goes out over the air on television and radio.

Yet a historian writing in the twenty-first century and using only the evidence from "popular" culture would see and sense great differences from the popular culture of Victorian days. Our rock would not sound to him much like a Viennese waltz, the violent and sexy "whodunits" would not be to him much like the Sherlock Holmes stories, the picture magazines would not remind him of Currier and Ives prints, and even in the so-called comic strips the frustrations, the inferiority complexes, and pathetic illusions, even the horrors that fill many strips would seem worlds apart from the naïve buffoonery of the first such strips. Mutt and Jeff survive today, but they do not live.

Nor were such a twenty-first-century historian to concentrate on the high culture would he be any less struck with the great changes since 1890; perhaps in fact he would be more struck with the changes. It is true that he would readily see in the avant garde writers and artists and in the "antiintellectual" philosophers of the late nineteenth century precursors of twentieth-century philosophical and artistic movements. Yet he would surely be struck by the way the twentieth century has gone beyond its precursors. He would not confuse contemporary abstractionists with Monet or Cézanne, nor atonal music, let alone "concrete" music, with the music of Brahms, nor James Joyce's *Ulysses,* let alone some modern French "antinovels," with the novels of Henry James or even Sinclair Lewis.

We shall slowly return to some of these specific representatives of recent high culture. Here let us note that our hypothetical twenty-first century historian, though he would have to note the differences between the highbrow and the popular culture of our time, would not conclude that they were wholly separate and wholly different cultures. He would see that they have much in common, that both have strong elements of contrast with the culture of the nineteenth century. We cannot of course begin to guess how he would feel toward us and our culture, nor with what terms he would try and tell his readers about us. But he would surely have to call at-tention to the notes of violence and despair, the unprecedented frankness with which the Anglo-Saxon four letter words are printed as well as uttered, the repudiation of conventional representational art, the preoccupation with such psychological difficulties as are indicated by "alienation," "identity crisis," "commitment," the great premium set upon originality, novelty, youth against age, the rise of a popular slick urban cynicism, the doubts about even our basic institutions like the family, let alone the state, the prevalence of resentments and feelings of injustice. We shall in conclusion consider how far all this is in fact a repudiation of, a resistance to, our democratic inheritance from the eighteenth-century Enlightenment. Meanwhile, we must essay some more specific analysis of the attitudes, the tastes, the ideas of our confused and confusing age. We attempt by concentrating on representative figures to illustrate the characteristics of our high culture and how it differs from that of the nineteenth century.

Psychology: Freud

Following leads from the biological sciences, the nineteenth century came to put particular emphasis on *process,* on the dynamics of change in time. The twentieth-century, taking its cue from psychology, has come to put particular emphasis on the role of the unconscious in human thought and action, on the irrationality—or at least nonrationality—of much human behavior. Foremost among the thinkers responsible for this emphasis was Sigmund Freud (1856–1939). Freud was a physician, trained in Vienna in the rationalist medical tradition of the late nineteenth cetury. His interest was early drawn to mental illness, where he soon found cases in which patients exhibited symptoms of very real organic disturbances, for which no obvious organic causes could be found. Under analysis, as Freud's therapeutic treatment came to be called, the patient, relaxed on a couch, was urged to pour out what he could remember of his earliest childhood, or indeed infancy. After many such treatments the analyst, Freud argued, could find what was disturbing the patient, and by making him aware of what that was, hope to help him.

Had Freud merely contented himself with this kind of therapy, few of us would have heard

Sigmund Freud photographed with his fiancee, Martha Bernays, in September 1885.

of him. But from all this clinical experience he worked out a system of psychology that has had a very great influence, not only on psychiatry and psychology, but on some of our basic conceptions of human relations. Freud starts with the concept of a set of drives with which each person is born. These drives, which arise in the unconscious, are expressions of the id. Freud never

tried to locate the id physiologically; he used the term, which in Latin means "this [thing]," to avoid the moralistic overtones in words like "desires." These drives try to get satisfaction and pleasure, to express themselves in action. The infant, notably, is uninhibited—that is, his drives well up into action from the id without restraint from his conscious mind. But by no means without restraint from his parents or nurse—and there's the difficulty. The infant finds himself frustrated. As he grows, as his mind is formed, he comes to be conscious of the fact that some of the things he wants to do are objectionable to those closest to him, and on whom he is so dependent. He himself therefore begins to repress these drives from his id.

With his dawning consciousness of the world outside himself, the child has in fact developed another part of his psyche, which Freud at first called the censor, and later divided into two phases which he called the ego and the superego. The ego is the individual's private censor, his awareness that in accordance with what Freudians call the reality principle certain drives from his id—for example, the wish of the male child to become his mother's lover—simply cannot succeed. The superego in a way is what common language calls conscience; it is the individual's response as part of a social system in which certain actions are proper and certain actions improper. Now these drives of the id, and indeed in most of its phases the dictates of the superego, are for Freud a sort of great reservoir of which the individual is not normally aware—that is, they are part of his unconscious. In a mentally healthy individual, enough of the drives of the id succeed so that he feels contented. But even the healthiest of individuals has had to repress a great deal of his drives from the id. This successful repression the Freudians account for in part at least by a process they call sublimation. They think that the healthy individual somehow finds for a drive suppressed by ego or superego, or by both working together, a new and socially approved outlet or expression. Thus a drive toward sexual relations not approved in one's circle might be sublimated into the writing of poetry or music or even into athletics.

With the neurotic person, however, Freud held that drives, having been suppressed, driven back down into the unconscious, find no suitable other outlet or sublimation, and continue, so to speak, festering in the id, trying to find some outlet. They find all sorts of outlets of an abnormal sort, symptoms of illness in great variety. They display themselves in all sorts of neuroses and phobias, which have in common a failure to conform to the reality principle. The neurotic individual is maladjusted. And if the failure to meet the reality principle is really complete, the individual is insane, psychotic, and lives in an utterly unreal private world of his own.

Freud's therapy rested on the belief that if the individual neurotic could come to understand why he behaved as he did he could frequently make a proper adjustment and lead a normal life. But here Freud parted company with the rationalist tradition of the eighteenth century. He held that there was no use preaching at the individual, reasoning simply with him, pointing out what was unreasonable in his behavior. Reason could not get directly at the unconscious, where the source of his trouble lay. Only by the long slow process of psychoanalysis, in which the individual day after day sought in memories of his earliest childhood for concrete details, could the listening analyst pick from this stream of consciousness the significant details that pointed to the hidden repression, the blocking that came out in neurotic behavior. Freud gave special importance to the dreams of the patient, which he must patiently describe to the analyst; for in dreams, Freud thought, the unconscious wells up out of control, or but partly controlled, by the ego. Once the patient, however, got beneath the surface of his conscious life, and became aware of what had gone wrong with his hitherto unconscious life, he might then adjust to society.

The Implications of Freudianism

What is important for us in the wider implications of Freud's work, his part in the broad current of contemporary modifications of eighteenth-century rationalism, is first this concept of the very great role of the unconscious drives —that is, the unthinking, the nonrational, in our lives. Ordinary reflective thinking is for the Freudian a very small part of our existence. We are back at the metaphor of reason as simply the small part of the iceberg that shows above the water, while submerged down below is the great mass of the unconscious. Much even of our

conscious thinking is, according to the Freudian, what psychologists call rationalization, thinking dictated, not by an awareness of the reality principle, but by the desires of our id. One can get a good measure of the difference between eighteenth-century rationalism and Freudian psychology by contrasting the older belief in the innocence and natural goodness of the child, Wordsworth's "mighty prophet, seer blest," with the Freudian view of the child as a bundle of unsocial or antisocial drives, as in fact a little untamed savage.

But second, and most important, note that the Freudians do not wish to blow out the candle of human reason. They are moderate, not extreme, antirationalists; they are chastened rationalists. Their whole therapy is based on the concept, which has Christian as well as eighteenth-century roots, that "ye shall know the truth, and the truth shall make you free." Only, for the Freudian, truth is not easily found, cannot be distilled into a few simple rules of conduct which all men, being reasonable and good, can use as guides to individual and collective happiness. It is on the contrary very hard to establish, and can be reached only by a long and precarious struggle. Many will not reach it, and will have to put up with all sorts of maladjustments and frustations. The Freudian is at bottom a pessimist, in that he does not believe in the perfectibility of man. Indeed, there are those who see in the Freudian concept of human nature something like a return to the Christian concept of original sin. They continue the parallel, which many others find absurd or offensive, by maintaining that for the Freudian too there is, though difficult to find, a way out, a form of salvation, in the full self-knowledge that comes from successful psychoanalysis.

Freud, to whom religion was an "illusion," was himself a cult leader. His faithful disciples still form an orthodox nucleus of strict Freudian psychoanalysts. Other disciples parted with the master, notably the Swiss Jung (1875–1961), who did believe in religion, and whose great popular phrase was the "collective unconscious," and the Austrian Adler (1870–1937) who rejected the master's emphasis on the sexual, and coined the familiar phrase "inferiority complex."

Full psychoanalysis has usually remained an extremely expensive process limited to those who can afford it or can receive it through charity.

There are, however, modified forms of analytical therapy, such as group therapy and the like, which are much less expensive. The Freudian influence on imaginative writing, indeed on philosophy and the arts generally, was and remains very great indeed, though usually dispersed, vague, indirect, and very hard to summarize. Negatively, the life work of this nineteenth-century-trained scientist went in these "humanistic" fields to reinforce the reaction against nineteenth-century scientific and rationalistic materialism; positively, Freud's work helped all sorts of modernisms, strengthened the revival of intuition, "hunch," sensibility, and, perhaps paradoxically, a Stoic or existentialist rejection of bourgeois optimism. Anti-Freudians often charge that Freud himself was really more interested in research than in therapy: he wanted to find out all about the disturbances in the psyches of his patients, but, while the discovery added to his own knowledge, it did not necessarily cure them, as he maintained that it should. Others would add that he applied to the whole of the human race conclusions drawn from a practice among neurotic and psychotic Viennese of the late nineteenth and early twentieth centuries, and that other people in other cultures and at later times in different places differ greatly from Freud's patients. Yet these and other criticisms, however justified, only emphasize rather than diminish the depth of his influence on the attitudes of the generations that have followed him.

Psychology: Behaviorism

Of course the Freudians hold no monopoly of the field of psychology. Indeed, the eighteenth-century tendency to regard human nature, if not as wholly rational, at least as wholly malleable by those who could manipulate the human and nonhuman environment, still had representatives in the mid-twentieth century. The Russian psychologist Pavlov (1849–1936), Nobel prizewinner in 1904, has given us the now familiar term "conditioned reflex." Pavlov's laboratory dogs, after being fed at a given signal, came to water at the mouth at this signal, even when no food was within sight or smell. The "natural"—that is, inborn—response

of watering at the mouth would ordinarily come only when the dog's senses showed him actual food; Pavlov got the same response artificially by a signal that certainly did not smell or look like food to the dog. The upshot was clear evidence that training or conditioning can produce automatic responses in the animal that are essentially similar to the kind of automatic responses the animal is born with.

Pavlov's experiments had important implications for the social scientist. They confirmed eighteenth-century notions about the power of environment, of training and education, in the sense that environment can be manipulated to produce specific responses from organisms. But—and this was a bitter blow to eighteenth-century optimism—they suggested that once such training has taken hold, the organism has, so to speak, incorporated the results almost as if they had been the product of heredity, not environment, and further change becomes very difficult, in some instances impossible. Pavlov, after having trained some of his dogs, tried mixing his signals, frustrating and confusing the dogs by withholding food at the signal that had always produced food for them. He succeeded in producing symptoms of a kind close to what in human beings would be neurosis.

Still another lead, this time from biologists interested not in the most fashionable "microbiology" but rather in the behavior of individuals (the old-fashioned name for it was natural history), came from such scientists as the Austrian Konrad Lorenz (1903–   ) and the Dutchman Nikolaas Tinbergen (1907–   ), founders of what is called "ethology." Their key phrase is "species-specific behavior." This behavior does indeed depend on hereditary constitutional features of the organism, but especially at key moments when development of the organism must be triggered by specific normal features of the environment. Thus, for instance, newly hatched goslings normally see first and attach themselves to the mother goose; but if she is removed before they hatch, they will attach themselves to a foster mother, even to a human being. Modern ethology thus *reinforces* the notion that neither heredity nor environment alone "determine" behavior, including human behavior, but rather a complex and subtle interaction of the two. There is room for accident, and even for "will," if not quite free will.

such study, and gives full place to our contemporary awareness of the place of the subjective and nonrational in human life.

Pareto

Pareto (1848–1923), a scientifically trained engineer, was not the greatest or the most influential thinker, but his work well illustrated the difficulties of thinking about men as we think about things. Pareto tried hard to establish a genuine *science* of sociology. In his *The Mind and Society* (original Italian edition, 1916) he was concerned chiefly with the problem of separating in human actions the rational from the nonrational. What interested Pareto was the kind of action that is expressed in words, ritual, symbolism of some kind. Buying wool socks for cold weather is one such action. If they are bought deliberately to get the best socks at a price the buyer can afford, this is rational action in accord with the doer's interests; it is the kind of action the economist can study statistically. If, however, they are bought because the buyer thinks wool is "natural" (as compared with synthetic fibers) or because he finds snob value in improved English socks, or because he wants to help bring sheep-raising back to Vermont, we are in a field less "rational" than price. The practical economist will still study marketing and consumer demand, but he will have to cope with many complex psychological variables.

It is these that Pareto studied under the name of "derivations," which are close to what most of us know as rationalizations. These are the explanations and accompanying ritualistic acts associated with our religion, our patriotism, our feelings for groups of all kinds. Prayer, for instance, was for Pareto a derivation; he was, like so many of this period, a materialist, at bottom hostile to Christianity, though he approved of it as means of social concord, and was fascinated by its hold over men. It is irrational, or nonrational, to pray for rain, because we know as meteorologists that rain has purely material causes quite beyond the reach of prayer. These derivations are indeed a factor in human social life, but they do not really move men to social action.

What does move men in society, and keeps them together in society, says Pareto, are the *residues*. These are expressions of relatively per-

Sociopolitical Thought

We have in the foregoing already edged over naturally enough from psychology to the wider field of man's behavior as a political animal. In what are called the social or behavioral sciences, the twentieth century has continued to develop the critique of our eighteenth-century inheritance of belief in the basic reasonableness and goodness of human nature. In fact, the very term "human nature" seems to some social scientists to be so all-embracing as to make no sense. Of course, this "revolt against reason" is better described as a revolt against reason as exemplified in popular concepts of what science is and does. Moreover, many participants in this revolt did not attack scientific reason as such in its own fields of established sciences, but simply urged that there are other valuable ways of using the human mind. And furthermore, though many of these thinkers were antirationalists, and almost always "elitists," fascists, racists, reactionaries hostile to the democratic tradition, others were what we have called "chastened rationalists," thinkers who wished to salvage what they could of the eighteenth-century basis of the democratic tradition.

The specific programs, the emotional allegiances, the "values" of twentieth-century thinkers in this broad "sociological" field were varied indeed. And yet most of them had a sense of the subtlety, the complexities, the delicacy—and the toughness and durability—of the forces that bind human beings together—and hold them apart—in society. The Swiss writer Denis de Rougemont puts the same kind of challenge to our conventional notions of what makes sense, tensions between two terms that are *"true, contradictory, and essential."* * The distinguished American sociologist Talcott Parsons, in his *The Structure of Social Action* (1937) finds in the work of many different thinkers, such as the German Max Weber, the Frenchman Durkheim, the Englishman Alfred Marshal, the Italian Pareto, and others, a common aim to put the study of man in society on a basis that takes full account of the difficulties of "objectivity" in

---

*D. de Rougemont, *Man's Western Quest* (New York, 1957), p. 116.

manent, abiding sentiments in men, expressions that usually have to be separated from the part that is actually a derivation, which may change greatly and even quickly. Pagan Greek sailors sacrificed to Poseidon, god of the sea, before setting out on a voyage; a few centuries later, Christian Greek sailors prayed, lighted candles, and made vows to the Virgin Mary just before sailing. The derivations are the explanations of what Poseidon and the Virgin respectively do. They vary. The believer in the Virgin thinks his pagan predecessor was dead wrong. The residues are the needs to secure divine aid and comfort in a difficult undertaking, and to perform certain ritual acts that give the performer assurance of such aid and comfort. The residues are nearly the same for our two sets of sailors. Both the pagans and the Christians have the same social and psychological needs and satisfy them in much the same ways, though with very different "explanations" of what they are doing.

Two of the major classes of "residues" Pareto distinguished stand out, and help form his philosophy of history. These are first the "residues" of persistent aggregates, the sentiments that mark men who like regular ways, solid discipline, tradition and habit, men like the Spartans, the Prussians, or any rigorously disciplined military class. Second, there are the residues of the instinct for combinations, the sentiments that mark men who like novelty and adventure, who invent new ways of doing things, who like to cut loose from the old and the tried, men not easily shocked, men who hate discipline, men like most intellectuals and inventors—and many entrepreneurs and businessmen. In societies of many individual members, men influenced largely by one or the other of these major residues tend to predominate and to characterize that society. Like most philosophers of history, Pareto was far from clear on just how a conservative society where the residues of persistent aggregates predominate changes into another kind of society. But he did have this conception of a pendulum swing, even a struggle of thesis and antithesis.

The nineteenth century in the West was in Pareto's mind a society in which the residues of instinct for combinations played perhaps the greatest role of which they are capable in a human society. The nineteenth century was a century of competition among individuals full of new ideas, inventions, enterprises, convinced that the old ways were bad, that novelty was the great thing to strive for at the expense of every-

thing else. It was a society notably out of equilibrium. It had to run toward the other kind of residues, toward the persistent aggregates, toward a society with more security and less competition, more discipline and less freedom, more equality and less inequality, more uniformity and less variety. It had to go the way some writers hold that we are going in the twentieth century, toward the welfare state, even toward the totalitarian state.

The Planners and Persuaders

Yet the abiding influence of the newer psychological and sociological approach to the study of man in society has by no means been in the Paretan and conservative direction. Those who want to influence human behavior, all the way from the field of personal consumer choices to the field of international relations, have been willing to make use of the new psychological insights. From the latest piece of "motivational research" to show the cigarette manufacturer how to overcome the effects on his customers of medical research on the causes of lung cancer to the high-minded efforts of proponents of world government to devise some symbol, visual, musical, concrete, that will supplant nationalist symbols, such as patriotic hymns, flags, and the like, hard-working planners are busily engaged in trying, often successfully, to change our habits, even our prejudices. To use Pareto's now little-used terminology, they are seeking, not to change our behavior by appealing to our "reason" in the plain sense of that word; they are trying to "activate" certain of our sentiments, our residues, or to "deactivate" others, or both.

In the field of serious political and social thought, this characteristic twentieth-century emphasis on the psychology of motivation has been appealed to not only by conservatives or "reactionaries" like Pareto and others, including both Mussolini and Hitler, who had pretensions to philosophy, but also by many who were democrats, or at least "progressives," at heart. An early example of this latter type of political thinker is Graham Wallas, a British leftist, whose *Human Nature in Politics* (1908) was a most influential book. Wallas, campaigning as a Progressive for a seat in the London County Council, discovered by experience that the voters he canvassed were more pleased and influenced

Soren Kierkegaard: a caricature by Wilhelm Marstrand.

egy, even—indeed most of all—in a righteous cause. It still seems to these good children of the eighteenth-century Enlightenment that reason and high ethical principles must and will prevail together, and that to appeal to the "lower" elements in nature so emphasized by modern psychology is no way to rise above the evils of existing society. Such opinions are by no means commonly held, or, at any rate, not commonly put into practice, by active politicians, and one of the many gaps that seem in our society to widen rather than to narrow in these days is the old gap between the idealistic "theorist" and the "practical man" who wants to get things done.

Yet the intellectual leaders of mid-twentieth century progressive political thought are increasingly forced to the conclusion that more has to be done in the way of planning. Notably, they urge, we must plan in the whole sector of our economy which deals with such essentials as education, social service, housing, hospital care, scientific research, public transportation, and the means of preservation of fast-vanishing natural resources, especially our scenic wildernesses, as well as means for the prevention of air and water pollution. All these are expensive. The planners know that in a democracy plans cannot simply be imposed on those planned for, as to a great degree they can in a totalitarian state like Russia. They are paying great attention to the problems, on which modern thinking in the field of the social sciences does throw some light, of how to get the many to want and ask for—and pay for—what the planners think the people really need, and *ought* to want. A representative writer who is concerned with such matters is the persuasive American economist J. K. Galbraith (1908-   ), author of *The Affluent Society.*

by little tricks of baby-kissing, chitchat, and personal flattery than by appeals to reason or even to self-interest. Something of the same emphasis on the need to go beyond abstractions to practical psychology in politics appears in the earlier writings of the American Walter Lippmann, whose *Preface to Politics* appeared in 1913. It has, of course, always been known to politicians.

There remains, especially among American intellectuals, a strong current of thought-feeling that refuses to descend into Machiavellian strat-

Philosophy

In the field of formal (which nowadays tends to mean also university-supported) philosophy the mid-twentieth century displays once more its variety. It is safe to say that in the West at least there are today representatives of just about every philosophical system that has ever existed, from extreme idealism to extreme materialism and complete skepticism. Even in the communist countries, one suspects that there are lurking idealists ready to come out in the open if the regimes would ever allow any thought except official Marxist materialist metaphysics. The currents of voluntarism, pragmatism, and psychologism we noted earlier still flow, no doubt a bit diminished.

From such nineteenth-century sources as Nietzsche and the gravely disturbed and disturbing Danish theologian Kierkegaard (1813–1885), there has developed a philosophy known as existentialism. The existentialists find this existing reality of mid-twentieth century all there is, and pretty depressing, but are determined to face this reality as heroically as possible. They are sometimes divided into Christian existentialists, who retain a concept of God, and free-thinking or atheistic existentialists. The central theme of existentialism has been stated by the French writer Sartre (1905–   ) as "existence precedes essence." This cryptic pronouncement seems to mean that human awareness of living, of being, precedes in time, and is therefore somehow more important than our thinking, or our mental ticketing of "reality" by means of words. Clearly existentialism does at bottom belong in the current of antiintellectualism of our time.

Yet the existentialists are sensitive artists and intellectuals, by no means simple antiintellectuals who want us to "think with our blood"—or our hormones. They respect the instrument of thought, and use it themselves. But they do not quite trust it, and they do not trust its chief representatives in our time, the conventional scientists. Their noblest representative, though not formally one of the existentialist group, the French novelist and philosopher Albert Camus (1913–1960) is perhaps destined to be remembered as a classic of our age. Finally, formal philosophical idealism, which a generation ago seemed, save for Croce, to be languishing everywhere, has proved of recent years to have considerable vitality, perhaps basically in forms we may call Neo-Kantian, as with the late German philosopher Ernst Cassirer (1874–1945).

The most original, and in a sense most typical and vital, philosophic movement of our century bears clearly and paradoxically the stamp of the "revolt against reason." It looks to an outsider as if the movement called variously logical analysis, logical positivism, linguistic philosophy, and, in one of its phases, symbolic logic, accepted most of the strictures the new psychology made on old-fashioned rationalism and then went ahead to insist that, although only a tiny bit of human

experience could be brought under rubrics of rational thought, that tiny bit was indeed to be protected and explored carefully. This somewhat varied school can be considered as beginning early in the twentieth century in Vienna, the city of Freud. Such distiguished pioneers of the school as Ludwig Wittgenstein (1889–1951) and Rudolf Carnap (1891–1970) emigrated, the first to England, the second to the United States. Logical analysis could hardly flourish in Hitler's Germany or in Stalin's Russia. It is skeptical of too much to flourish in any but a very free and many-minded society.

The American physicist P. W. Bridgman put one of the school's basic positions clearly in various writings. When, on the pattern of scientific practice, a problem can be answered by the performance of an "operation" and the answer validated by logical and empirical tests or observations, knowledge can be achieved. But when no such "operation" is possible, as in such problems as whether democracy is the best form of government, whether a lie is ever justifiable, or whether a given poem is a good one or a bad one—in short, almost all the great questions of philosophy, art, literature, history—the problem is *for the logician* "meaningless."

Most of these logical positivists would admit that nonlogical or pseudological methods for getting at such problems, though they could not result in the kind of finally accepted answers the scientists expect to get, are none the less for normal human living useful and indeed necessary. Some of the popularizers of this philosophy, however, pretty explicitly held that all mental activity save logical analysis and empirical verification is at best inferior mental activity, or more likely, nonsense, a waste of time, or worse. A distinguished American popularizer, Stuart Chase, in his *Tyranny of Words* (1938) proposed to clarify our thinking by substituting "blah-blah" for terms that have no such good logical or "operational" clearance. Thus the famous French revolutionary slogan, "Liberty, equality, fraternity" would come out simply as "Blah-blah, blah-blah, blah-blah." Approaching their problems very differently from the way Freud and Pareto did, these logical analysts nevertheless came to a similar conclusion about the reasoning capacity of most human beings. Most human beings, they conclude, are at present incapable of thorough, persistent, successful logical thinking, and they cannot be taught to do this kind of thinking in any foreseeable future. Of course, just as there are radical Freudians who hold that if everybody could be psychoanalyzed all would be well, there are radical positivists, usually labeled semanticists, who hold that semantics, the study of meaning, if available to everyone would cure all our troubles. The leading expert of this rather naïve semantic therapy was the Polish-American scientist Alfred Korzybski (1879–1950), author of *Science and Sanity* (1933).

Once more we encounter the sharp tensions of modern intellectual life. Since these logical analysts seemed to set up the practices of science, as they understood them, as the sole right way of thinking, many of those devoted to the arts and the humanistic studies generally turned in revenge to the denunciation of science as a narrowing, dangerous use of the mind. Antiscientism is as characteristic of our age as scientism.

Probably the most widespread philosophical movement of our century developed outside of, or on the margin of, formal professional philosophy. This movement may be called *historicism*, the attempt to find in history an answer to those ultimate questions of the structure of the universe and of man's fate the philosopher has always asked. At bottom, the transfer of Darwinian concepts of organic evolution from biology to this great, sweeping field of philosophical questions contains the essence of twentieth-century historicism. Once the traditional Judeo-Christian concepts of a single creation in time, a God above nature, and the rest of the traditional world view were abandoned, men in search of answers to their questions about these ultimates had to fall back on the historical record. Man is not made by God, but by nature, which amounts to saying that *man makes himself* in the course of history. We get our only clues as to man's capacities here on earth, clues as to how he ought to behave, clues as to that future that so concerns him, from the record of the past.

But "clues" is a modest and misleading word here. Many of the thinkers who appealed to history found much more than indications of what *might* be, much more than the always tentative, never dogmatic or absolute "theories" the scientist produces in answer to the less-than-ultimate questions he asks. Many of these philosophers of history, to simplify a bit, found in what they held to be the course of history a substitute for the concepts of God or Providence. They found in

the record of the past substantially the equivalent of what Christians found in revelation—the explanation of man's nature and destiny, his *end* in the sense of a teleology or an eschatology. Paradoxically, they found in history something quite outside and beyond history, a substitute for a theology.

Of these historicisms, the most important and the most obviously a substitute for Christianity is of course Marxism. The theological parallels are plain, and have been frequently noted by non-Marxists: for God, absolute and omnipotent, the Marxist substitutes the absolutely determined course of dialectical materialism; for the Bible, he substitutes the canonical writings of Marx and Lenin; for the church, the party; for the Christian eschatology of divine judgment and heaven or hell, the revolution and the "classless society."

But Marxism, if the most rigorous, is only one of the historicisms of our time. The German Oswald Spengler (1880–1936) produced in his *Decline of the West,* published just at the end of World War I, a characteristic specimen. Spengler found from the historical record that societies or civilizations have, like human beings, an average life span, a thousand years or so for a civilization being the equivalent of seventy years or so for the individual human being. He traced several non-Western civilizations, but in the West he found three main ones, a Hellenic from 1000 B.C. to about the birth of Christ, a Levantine or Middle Eastern from the birth of Christ to about A.D. 1000, and our own modern Western, which began (according to him) about A.D. 1000 and was, therefore, due to end about A.D. 2000. We cannot here analyze his work at length. Spengler had real insights, but his work as a whole, most historians would say, is simply not history—it is metaphysics, or if you like a coined word, metahistory. There are critics who explain Spengler simply; he saw Germany was about to be defeated, and he therefore consoled himself by believing Western civilization was about to end.

Better known nowadays than Spengler's is the work of the English historian, Arnold Toynbee (1889–   ), whose many-volumed *Study of History* (1934–1954) has been neatly condensed by D. C. Somervell into two manageable volumes. Toynbee is worth studying as a symptom of the intellectual difficulties of historicism and of our age. He has a Christian background, a careful training in historical scholarship, and a strong family tradition of kindly humanitarian social service. World War I marked him with a great hatred for war, and a conviction that nationalism, which he once declared to be the real if unavowed religion of our Western society, is the villain of the piece. His great system is an attempt to trace the causes of the rise and fall of societies in the past, and owes a good deal to Spengler. But Toynbee is a gentle English Christian humanist, not a German romantic racist brought up on what is no doubt a perversion of Nietzsche. He does, like the majority of contemporary philosophers of history, conclude that our Western society is facing a very serious challenge, that in terms of the cyclical rise and fall of societies he has traced it looks as if we were about to give ourselves the "knockout blow." But he refuses to abandon hope. The facts of historical development may, he holds, indicate destruction for us; but we may transcend history, and under the influence of a revived, or new, or Buddhist-influenced Christianity of gentleness and love, pull ourselves out of the hole.

Historicism has, again quite characteristically in our culture, given rise to bitter protests and to its opposite. Almost all professional historians, in the West nowadays mostly conventionally democratic in their values, simply give these philosophers of history the cold shoulder. Independent existentialists like Camus (who did not consider himself an existentialist) are firm in their contention that, though we may not neglect history as a record of human experience, we must find in ourselves something—salvation, perhaps—quite beyond history. And as for the logical analysts, history is far too lacking in precise data to make it a subject worth their while.

The Sciences

No general history can readily deal substantively with the history of science and technology in the twentieth century. Each science, each branch of each science, has continued in this century its cumulative course. The cooperation (not without rivalry) among "pure" scientists, applied scientists, engineers, bankers, businessmen, and government officials has produced in all phases of human control over material things the kind of exponential increases that send the lines of our graphs quite off the paper. Man's

attained rate of travel is no doubt an extreme example, one not achieved in the same degree, for instance, in such fields as those of medicine and genetics. In 1820 the fastest rate was still 12 to 15 miles an hour; railroads made it 100 miles or so by 1880; piston-engined airplanes made it 300 miles or so by 1940; jet planes broke the sound barrier only yesterday in 1947, making speeds of close to 1,000 miles per hour possible; and in the 1960's rockets propelled living men in space free of our atmosphere at speeds of thousands of miles an hour.

Each science is of course highly specialized, and the active scientist usually is supreme master of only part of a given science. None the less at a broad, nonspecialist's level of understanding many educated men in the West have a good idea of what modern science is trying to do, and how it does it. No doubt scientific attitudes toward nature and natural laws, and scientific skepticism toward the supernatural, have added powerfully to the modern drive toward rationalism, positivism, materialism. Science continues to promote the world view we have seen arising in early modern times and culminating in the Enlightenment of the eighteenth century. Indeed, many scientists have managed to make of the pursuit of scientific knowledge itself a kind of religion.

More particularly, the great event of the twentieth century has been the revolution in physics symbolized for the public in the figure of Albert Einstein (1879-1955). The concepts of relativity, a space-time continuum, and quantum mechanics freed physics from the "Newtonian world-machine" and helped the very great modern innovations in the field, innovations that worked together with the late nineteenth-century discoveries of the phenomena of radiation (X rays, the researches of the Curies, Roentgen, and others) to make possible our contemporary developments in fields like electronics. Einstein's theories on the equivalence of mass and mechanical energy, his concept of time as a fourth dimension, and the representation of gravitation as a field (compare "magnetic field") rather than a force secured wide public attention, if not always comprehension. From all this a few laymen came to the conclusion that since the apparently rigid world of mechanical causation of classic physics had broken down, since there was associated with the name of the distinguished German physicist Werner Heisenberg an "indeterminacy principle" familiar to practicing scientists, the commonsense law of cause-and-effect had in fact been repealed, and the universe was once more a fine free space in which anything could happen. This of course is not true, and the work of Newton has not been so much contradicted by modern physics as supplemented. Heisenberg's principle resulted from close work on the particle called an electron. An *individual* electron observably can jump from one orbit to another without evident and predictable sequence. Yet *statistically* the behavior of many, many electrons together is predictable, as predictable as it was in Newton's day. It is quite likely that misunderstood doctrines of relativity in physics, misapplied to ethics and aesthetics, did have a part in the fashionable doctrines of moral and aesthetic relativism of only yesterday.

The development of astronomy has been largely influenced by that of physics. To the layman, such modern astronomical concepts as that of a finite but expanding universe, of curved space, and perhaps above all the almost inconceivable distances and quantities, light years, galaxies, and the like, have made astronomy the most romantic of sciences. And these distances and quantities *are* almost inconceivable. A light year is the distance traversed by light in one year, or roughly 5,880,000,000,000 miles; our own Milky Way galaxy has some thirty thousand million stars and nebulae, in the form of a disk with a diameter of about 100,000 light years. Recent developments in rocketry have made our moon attainable by actual human flight instead of merely by flight of the science-fiction imagination.

Chemistry has greatly affected our daily lives by its impact on our foods, our medicines, our clothing, almost all the material objects we use. Chemistry has also aided the very great gains that have been made in the twentieth century in the biological sciences and in their applications to medicine and public health as well. Not only in the United States and the rest of the West, but all over the world, infant mortality, many contagious diseases, even undernourishment, have been so far conquered that the average expectancy of life at birth has gone up as much as twenty years in advanced nations since 1900. In the economically backward areas of the globe, more children are born and more live, so that the population problem has become acute, and is still unsolved. Yet even in this matter of food supply, astonishing achievements by plant breeders, as with hybrid corn and wheat, the development of fertilizers, the use of irrigation, the possibilities of food from the sea opened up by marine biology and other scientific advances promise some considerable alleviation in a foreseeable future. It is significant, however, that the actual extreme limits of the human life span have not yet been significantly affected. It does not seem that a limit of something like 110 to 120 years for human life, historically known to have prevailed for centuries, has yet been exceeded.

There remains one more major problem which the progress of twentieth-century science has sharpened, a problem closely related to that of specialization in science and learning. There is in some senses a widening gap today between those who pursue what we call humanistic studies and those who pursue scientific studies. It is by no means difficult philosophically to reconcile these two pursuits; the poet and the physicist have, as creative human beings, more in common than we others usually can see. But the fact remains that from the point of view of the sociologist the two groups in our cultural life do clash, the scientists finding the humanists fuzzy-minded, sloppy intellectually, and clearly inferior, the humanists finding the scientists limited, pedestrian, cold, inhuman, and quite unable to manage the Frankenstein monster of modern technology they have created. Fortunately, there are good men who are at work mediating between these two sides, men who incline to the belief that the opposition is by no means one rooted in the facts of life and human nature, but merely in present-cultural fashion.

In sum, the very great achievements of modern science and technology have raised many problems for our Western democracy: the overriding problem presented by the fact that hydrogen bombs, missiles, and biological warfare have made the destruction of the human race no mere bit of rhetoric, nor a theological doctrine like that of Judgment Day, but a possible situation confronting even common sense; the problem of humanizing science; the problem of overpopulation; the problems of educating scientists and endowing scientific research; and many other problems. Yet the fact remains that science and technology seem to be the deciding factors that have raised the masses far enough beyond misery and near-starvation to make possible what we Americans call democracy. And perhaps even more important, the continuing very great vitality of Western civilization—a vitality as real in the arts as in the sciences—is at its clearest in the magnificent achievements of modern science. Modern science rightly worries the worriers, but it should also console them, for it shows man still in a light reflected long ago by the Greek Sophocles:

What a thing is man! Among all wonders
The wonder of the world is man himself
. . . . .
Man the Contriver! Man the Master-mind. *

Literature and the Arts

In the field of imaginative literature, music, painting, the fine arts, and the arts generally, we invent new styles and attitudes yet do not abandon what the past has left us. Here, as for all our culture, the contemporary historian has to note the great variety of tastes and standards that have piled up. But he must also note that there appears in the twentieth century with special sharpness another characteristic of our time on which we have already briefly touched, the wide and deep gap between the art—in the broad sense of "art" to include letters, music, architecture— of the few, or highbrow art, and the art of the many, or popular art. Bridges between the two there are, usually built on highbrow initiative from the highbrow side toward the lowbrow side. A good example is the fashion among the cultivated few for jazz. For many French intellectuals, as difficult, as refined, as remote from the masses as any intellectuals have ever been, "le jazz hot" is the only cultural achievement of the United States. Every now and then, if only briefly, some contributor to that most popular form of popular art, the American comic strip, gains a following among the highbrows.

High Art: Literature

In the twentieth century poetry and literary criticism remain, as they had begun to be in the

late nineteenth century, difficult, cerebral, and addressed to a very small audience. An occasional poet, like the American Robert Frost, broke from the privacy of the little magazines and the limited editions to wide popularity and a place enshrined in old-fashioned anthologies. But Frost was no more esoteric in form or substance than Wordsworth. More remarkable and more symptomatic, is the wide attention given to T. S. Eliot, born in St. Louis, but as an adult wholly Anglicized, an abstruse and allusive poet, an intellectual of intellectuals. The figure of speech with which he began "The Love Song of J. Alfred Prufrock" in 1917, which once seemed strange, "advanced," is now tame enough for any anthology:

Let us go then, you and I
When the evening is spread out against the sky
Like a patient etherised upon a table. *

The novel remains the most important form of contemporary imaginative writing. Critics have long bemoaned its exhaustion as an art form, and the French have even invented what they call the "antinovel," but the novel does not die. It is quite impossible here for us to give even a thumbnail sketch of the contemporary novel. It is not even wise of us to attempt to indicate writers likely to be read in the twenty-first century. It may be that a social novelist like the American J. P. Marquand (1893-1960), disliked by the pure highbrow because he wrote best sellers, will survive better than such a favorite of the pure as William Faulkner (1897-1962), who wrote existentialist novels about darkest Mississippi. The late Thomas Mann (1875-1955) seems already enshrined as a classic; but Mann, who began with a traditionally realistic novel of life in his birthplace, the old Hanseatic town of Lübeck, never really belonged to the avant garde. He is typical of the sensitive, worrying, class-conscious artist of the age of psychology.

More useful for us here, since it illustrates one of the problems of all contemporary art, is the career of the Irishman James Joyce (1882-1941). Joyce began with a subtle, outspoken, but formally conventional series of sketches of life in the Dublin of his youth, *Dubliners* (1914), and the novelist's inevitable, and with Joyce undis-

---

*Sophocles, *Antigone*, trans. John Jay Chapman (Boston, 1930), ll. 332-333, 340.

*T. S. Eliot, *Complete Poems and Plays* (New York, 1952), p. 3.

guised, autobiography, *Portrait of the Artist as a Young Man* (1916). Then, mostly in exile on the Continent, he wrote the classic experimental novel *Ulysses* (1922). This novel is an account of twenty-four hours in the life of Leopold Bloom, a Dublin Jew. It is full of difficult allusions, parallels with Homer, puns, rapidly shifting scenes and episodes, and is written without regard for the conventional notions of plot and orderly development. Above all, it makes full use of the then recently developed psychologies of the unconscious as displayed in an individual's "stream of consciousness." The last chapter, printed entirely without punctuation marks, is the record of what went on in the mind of Bloom's Irish wife as she lay in bed waiting for him to come home. What went on in her mind was in large part too shocking for contemporaries, and *Ulysses*, published in Paris, long had to be smuggled into English-speaking countries. It is now freely available everywhere.

Ulysses, though it took attentive reading, and even for those most fully abreast of the avant garde culture was often puzzling, is still a novel in English. Joyce's final big work, long known as simply *Work in Progress*, but finally published as *Finnegans Wake* (1939), is one of those works of radical experimentation about which, like many modern paintings, the ordinary educated layman simply has to say that it means nothing, or very little, to him. The continuities and conventions of narration and "plain English," not wholly flouted in *Ulysses*, are here quite abandoned. This is a dream novel, compounded of puns and free association. There are words, and even sentences; but *meaning* has to be quarried out by the reader and may when quarried turn out to be quite different from what Joyce intended. But there are keys to *Finnegans Wake*—we cite one in our reading list for this chapter—and the reader who wants to try to get at this interesting experiment in modern art can get his start there. Here are the beginning and ending of *Finnegans Wake*:

rivverrun, past Eve and Adam's, from swerve of shore to bend of bay, brings us by a commodius vicus of recirculation back to Howth Castle and Environs.

. . . A gull. Gulls. Far calls. Coming, far! End here. Us then. Finn, again! Take. Bussoftlhee, mememormee! Till thousendsthee. Lps. The keys to. Given! A way a lone a last a loved a long the*

Note once more: such writing may well be a blind alley, but the traditions of Western invention—we use that word in a very broad sense—insist that it may not be declared a blind alley until it has been well explored.

High Art: The Fine Arts

It is, however, the fine arts, painting perhaps in first rank, but with sculpture, architecture, and the minor decorative arts all included, that confront the ordinary cultivated Westerner with the problem of "modernism" in its most clear form. The process of getting beyond the camera eye and Renaissance ideas of perspective—in general, "realism"—has gone on right to this day. Indeed, painting done today can be almost —not quite—sharply divided into two groups: that done traditionally, academically, representational painting of the kind that surprises and puzzles no one though it still pleases many; and the many kinds of experimental or nonrepresentational, or simply "modern," painting. The variety of these experiments is great indeed. Most of them have been made by the great figure of contemporary painting, Pablo Picasso (1880–   ).

A native Spaniard, and an adopted Frenchman, Picasso has in his long life painted in many "styles" or "periods." The paintings of his "blue period," for instance, executed in the first years of our century, exemplify expressionism, the attempt to express in art such highly subjective emotional states as grief and despair. These pictures are said to have been influenced by the work of El Greco, the sixteenth-century master; certainly, both artists convey a sense of concentrated emotion by exaggerating human proportions. Around 1905, Picasso, stimulated in part by primitive art, turned to more daring innovations, striving, as Cézanne had striven, to transfer to the two dimensions of a picture the three dimensions of the real world but, so to speak, their dimensions *in motion*. Sometimes he used the techniques of abstractionism, the reduction of figures to a kind of plane geometry,

*J. Joyce, *Finnegans Wake* (New York, 1959), pp. 3, 628.

Picasso's "Dancer and Tambourine," 1938.

all angles and lines. Sometimes he used those of cubism, the reduction of figures to a kind of solid geometry, all cubes, spheres, and cones. Sometimes he even glued onto a picture bits of real objects—paper or the caning from a chair— in the process called *collage* ("paste-up"). In the range and inventiveness of his work Picasso calls to mind the masters of the Renaissance. On the one hand, he has done many portraits that are almost classical in style, as in the work of his "white period" following World War I. On the other hand, he has continued radical experimentation not only on canvas but also in sculpture, in ceramics, and in "constructions" of wood and other materials that might be called the sculptor's counterpart of collage. Most disturbing to the ordinary viewer, perhaps, are Picasso's recurrent

efforts, stemming from cubism, to show the human figure from two or more angles simultaneously—whence the apparently misplaced eyes and the anatomical distortions and rearrangements in many of Picasso's pictures.

Most remote from this world of sense experience as organized by common sense is the work of various kinds of abstract painters, paintings which are sometimes elaborate patterns of lines and colors, sometimes geometrical, sometimes apparently mere random daubs. It all means something, if only to the painter; but that meaning cannot be seized by the uninitiated.

The conservative worried by modern art can perhaps take some comfort in the fact that the most extreme manifestation of this art is now nearly fifty years past, and has never been quite equaled in its extraordinary defiance of all conventions, all rules, all forms. This extreme manifestation, perhaps more important sociologically than artistically, was the protest made by a very alienated group of intellectuals, the Dadaists, the "angry young men" of World War I and its aftermath. They reacted against a world so much sillier than their Dada that it could slaughter millions in warfare. Here are some characteristic passages from an account of Dada written by a sympathetic observer:

In Berlin as elsewhere we notice the persistent desire to destroy art, the deliberate intent to wipe out existing notions of beauty, the insistence upon the greatest possible obliteration of individuality. Heartfield works under the direction of Grosz while Max Ernst and Arp sign each other's paintings at random. . . .

In the first New York Independents' exhibition, 1917, he [Marcel Duchamp] entered a porcelain urinal with the title *Fontaine* and signed it R. Mutt to test the impartiality of the executive committee of which he himself was a member. By this symbol Duchamp wished to signify his disgust for art and his admiration for ready-made objects. . . .

At an exhibition in Paris among the most remarkable entries sent by the poets was a mirror of Soupault's entitled *Portrait of an unknown*. . . . Certain paintings by Duchamp supposed to be in this exhibition were replaced by sheets of paper marked with numbers which corresponded to the Duchamp entries in the catalog. Duchamp, who had been asked to take part in the exhibition, had just cabled from New York: "Nuts."*

*Georges Huguet in *Fantastic Art, Dada, Surrealism*, A. H. Barr, Jr., ed. (New York, 1936), pp. 23, 19, 33.

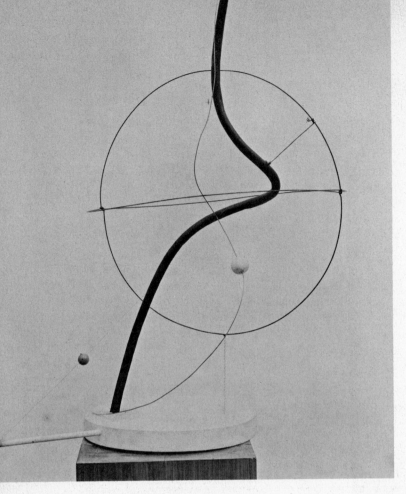

Alexander Calder's "A Universe," 1934.

Again we must repeat what we have said before: it is perfectly possible that in the long run of history the directions taken in the contemporary fine arts by those we now think of as leaders, pioneers, will prove stale and unprofitable. But no one who has not made an effort to understand these arts is justified in condemning them out of hand. And one hostile position the disgruntled conservatives in these fields often take seems quite untenable: this is the labeling of such modern art as pedantic or decadent, as a sign of exhaustion, death, lack of creative power. Quite the contrary, this art is alive, inventive, dynamic, an attempt to extend the confines of human experience, an attempt quite as remarkable, though in its results not so readily assessed, as that of modern science and technology. The historian must note that the extreme traditionalists, doing exactly what their forefathers have done, are much more vulnerable to the accusation that their work is a sign of exhaustion and decay.

This remark holds even more strikingly true in architecture. The twentieth century has seen the growth of the first truly original style in architecture since the end of the eighteenth century. "Modern" or "functional" architecture is no revival of a past style, no pastiche of elements of such past styles, no living museum of eclectic choice, like most of nineteenth-century architecture. It prides itself on its honest use of modern materials, its adaptation to modern living, its dislike of waste space and over-display. There is in modern architecture a certain touch of austerity, even puritanism, that should confound those who think that our age is sunk in lush sensuality. In the long run, mid-century modern architecture will probably seem to have carried its dislike for ornamentation, especially external ornamentation, rather too far. There are already signs that architects are beginning to tire of vast expanses of plain glass and steel.

"Modern" music, unlike "modern" painting or architecture, has never quite crystallized into a distinctive style. The twentieth century has produced a great many attempts to get beyond classical music and its rules of harmony—by using scales other than the conventional one, by stressing dissonance and discord, by borrowing the insistent rhythms of popular jazz, and, in extreme forms, by abolishing any formal notation and allowing the performer to bang away at will, even on pipes or tin pans. A generation ago, the general public came to identify musical innovation most closely with the Russian Igor Stravinsky (1882–   ), who on the eve of World War I composed two ballet scores, *Petrouchka* and *The Rite of Spring,* that were far removed from the polite and formalized ballet of tradition. Stravinsky may prove to be the musical counterpart of the successful artistic pioneer Picasso; significantly, however, although Stravinsky has continued experimental compositions, none of his later works has equaled his great ballets in impact or popularity, and in fact, one of his phases was a return to the modes of the eighteenth century.

In sum: all the "creative" modern arts are complex and difficult, and as of this moment far from being "understanded of the people." The very evident gulf between the tastes of the many and the tastes of the few may be an indication of a dangerous side of our democratic society. Certainly this is a subject on which no one is justified in taking an attitude of "holier than thou." But here the complete prevalence of the popular side,

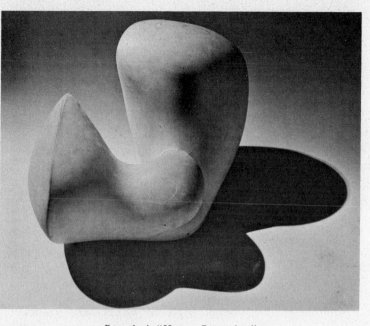

Jean Arp's "Human Concretion," 1935.

the elimination of the art of the few, seems most unlikely. It would seem that contrasting sets of standards and tastes, and the consequent great variety of works of art of all kinds, are one of the marks of our democratic society.

For it is fact that the two great attempts to put across a really totalitarian society in this century, that of Stalin in Russia and that of Hitler in Germany, were marked by very successful efforts to suppress highbrow culture, especially in art and in philosophy. Science, as we now know, flourished in Nazi Germany, and

continues to flourish in a Russia which bans Boris Pasternak's novel *Dr. Zhivago* and where Alexander Solzhenitsyn, author of *The Cancer Ward*, awarded the Nobel Prize for Literature in 1970 is afraid to go to Stockholm to receive it lest he not be allowed by his government to return home. Russia was in most ways the most extreme example. This great socioeconomic experiment, it may seem somewhat paradoxically, banned experiment in the arts and in the whole range of humanistic culture, at least after the accession of Stalin to power. Soviet architecture was even more atrociously monumental than the worst of nineteenth-century commercial architecture. Until Pasternak's novel, sent out of Russia in manuscript for translation into Italian under communist patronage, came in 1958 to widespread attention, no piece of Soviet writing really struck the imagination of the West. This failure cannot justly be laid to Western censorship or banning; it is simply that the crude propaganda literature of communist Russia did not greatly interest even fellow-traveling Western highbrows. Things got worse under Stalin, when such promising beginnings as Soviet movies—those of Eisenstein, for instance—and the more daring music of Russian composers like Shostakovich came under what one has to call censorship by bourgeois taste. For it is quite clear from the Russian experience that when the proletariat gets power, it wants, and in the arts at least gets, about what the conventional bourgeois of an earlier generation thought desirable and lovely. The Nazis, too, were all against any of the kinds of art and literature we have discussed in this chapter, all in favor of popular art in the taste of a century ago.

II   The Temper of Our Times

Modern Western man is acutely conscious of what may be called, a trifle imprecisely, the spirit of the age, the temper of the time, the climate of opinion. In the United States we incline to believe that each recent decade has had a character of its own, from the naughty Nineties to the fearful Fifties. For the present, and the immediate past, we have a number of popular phrases—the Age of Anxiety, the Aspirin Age, the Age of Longing, the Age of Conformity, the Age of Suspicion, the Age of Tranquilizers.

These phrases all have in common a tone of pessimism, mildly seasoned with the shrug-it-off, laugh-that-we-may-not-weep, not very profound cynicism which is a mark of our urban democratic culture. And it surely is also a mark of our age that its serious, its highbrow culture is to an extraordinary degree pessimistic about the present state of man, gloomy and fearsome about the future, though by no means in agreement either on diagnosis of what is wrong with our culture or in prognosis of its development. Here

Frank Lloyd Wright's "Fallingwater," 1936.

is a dignified and eloquent sample from the late Albert Camus's speech of acceptance of his Nobel Prize in 1958:

As the heir of a corrupt history that blends blighted revolutions, misguided techniques, dead gods, and worn out ideologies, in which second-rate powers can destroy everything today, but are unable to win anyone over; in which intelligence has stooped to becoming the servant of hatred and oppression, that generation [Casmus's own], starting from nothing but its own negations, has had to reestablish both within and without itself a little of what constitutes the dignity of life and death. Faced with a world threatened with disintegration, in which our grand inquisitors may set up once and for all the kingdoms of death, that generation knows that, in a sort of mad race against time, it ought to reestablish among nations a peace not based on slavery, to reconcile labor and culture again, and to reconstruct with all men an Ark of the Covenant. Perhaps it can never accomplish that vast undertaking, but most certainly throughout the world it has already accepted the double challenge of truth and liberty, and, on occasion, has shown that it can lay down its life without hatred. That generation deserves to be acclaimed wherever it happens to be, and especially wherever it is sacrificing itself.[*]

This is not, of course, sheer pessimism, but it is a kind of unhappy faith, a Stoic determination to fight against the way things are.

Let us note that, although from Plato, even from Ikhnaton on, our serious literary and artistic culture has always shown a strain of pessimism, our own intellectual leaders are, first, more than usually apprehensive and censorious and second, more than usually aware of the gulf between their way of living, their standards of value, and those of their fellow citizens. Just

[*] Reprinted with the permission of Alfred A. Knopf, Inc., from Albert Camus's Speech of Acceptance upon the award of the Nobel Prize for Literature, December 10th, 1957, translated by Justin O'Brien. Copyright © 1958 by Alfred A. Knopf, Inc.

one sample—here in a recent work is a well-known American writer complaining that most Americans confuse "normal" with "average," and suggesting that we need a genuine synonym for "average":

Fortunately, such a genuine and familiar synonym does exist. That which is "average" is also properly described as "mediocre." And if we were accustomed to call the average man, not "the common man" or still less "the normal man," but "the mediocre man" we should not be so easily hypnotized into believing that mediocrity is an ideal to be aimed at.*

This passage is hardly fair to American democratic beliefs; we Americans do not aim at mediocrity as an ideal, but on the contrary admire greatly the record breaker, the outstanding personality. But, unlike Mr. Krutch, we are not indignant over the failure of everybody to measure up to highbrow standards and we do not think "common" a synonym of "mediocre."

Now the historian, in attempting by comparative study of similar phenomena in different times and places to arrive at workable generalizations, has great difficulty with this problem of what is the "normal" or "usual" relation between intellectual classes—the writers, artists, scholars, teachers, preachers, and their followers—and other classes, even within our Western culture. Such study simply isn't well enough developed to permit measurement, graphs, quantitative generalization. Qualitatively, we may risk the assertion that the gravity and extent of the gap between the way American intellectuals, and to a degree Western intellectuals generally, think and feel and the way the rest of Western society thinks and feels—the phenomenon we may call in shorthand "the alienation of the intellectuals" —this phenomenon may well be a grave symptom of weakness in our society.

Yet the degree of alienation of the intellectuals is hard to measure, and we may have exaggerated it in the passage above. American intellectuals complain bitterly about the impossibility of the good life in the machine age, but they for the most part use the machines with apparent satisfaction. They find fault with our business civilization, but a great many of them do a very good business in it, and the rank-and-file are not

in terms of income as badly off as they think they are. They often regard themselves as a scorned and victimized minority in a hostile society of Babbitts, but a distinguished American sociologist has recently argued that they are in fact well regarded:

While he [the American intellectual] may feel himself neglected and scorned; his work poorly valued by the community, the community places him fairly high when polled on the relative status of occupations. In one such study of the ranks of ninety-six occupations, conducted in 1947 by the National Opinion Research Center of the University of Chicago, college professors ranked above every non-political position except that of physician; artists, musicians in a symphony orchestra, and authors ranked almost as high. . . . [In another poll in 1950] professors came out fourth among twenty-four categories, and thirty-eight percent of those polled placed them definitely in the "upper class."*

At any rate, it is clear that the great majority of Americans, and even the great majority of Europeans, are not as cosmically worried, not as pessimistic about man's fate, as are the intellectuals. Indeed, it seems likely that the many in Western society still adhere basically to the eighteenth-century belief in progress, moral as well as material. A recent candidate for the American presidency could say in a campaign speech, which by its very nature must be what hearers want to hear, "It is an article of the democratic faith that progress is a basic law of life."† In fact, one of the reproaches the intellectuals make to the many in the West is that the many appear on the whole quite contented with their material prosperity, their gadgets, their amusements, their American-style "classless society," a society where one man can be said to be as good as another, where all have a high level of consumption, but where there are inequalities, "status seekers," failures, tragedies, not the utopian, theoretical Marxist heaven of an unrealized "classless society."

Yet the pessimism of the intellectuals is understandable. The almost-utopia which many of the thinkers of the Enlightenment believed was just around the corner in the eighteenth

* J. W. Krutch, *Human Nature and the Human Condition* Random House (New York, 1959), p. 93.

* S. M. Lipset, *Political Man* (New York, 1960).

† Adlai Stevenson, quoted in C. A. Chambers, "Belief in Progress in Twentieth Century America," *Journal of the History of Ideas* (April 1958), p. 221.

century is not here yet. Let us, in conclusion, briefly review that eighteenth-century basis of our Western democratic faith, and see what our intellectual guides are making of that faith now, two hundred years later.

The Optimism of the Enlightenment

As we have seen, there grew up among Western men in the early modern centuries, and there came to full bloom in the eighteenth and nineteenth centuries, a view of man's fate here on earth which was essentially new. This is the view that all men may rightly expect to be happy here on earth. As Saint Just, the youthful colleague of Robespierre in the French Revolution, put it, "Happiness is a new idea in Europe"; or as Jefferson, with his gift for phrasing, put it, one of the unalienable rights of man is the "pursuit of happiness." Of course men have presumably always sought happiness here on earth. In historic Christianity, however, they did not really expect it here on earth, but only in an afterlife in heaven; indeed, Christianity had an overtone of belief that happiness in heaven was in part at least a reward for suffering here on earth.

The philosophes, the eighteenth-century thinkers who set the broad terms of this modern optimistic world view, meant by happiness a condition or state in which each man had at any given moment what he wanted, a state in which each man—each woman, and, incredibly, even each baby—was not aware of being thwarted, frustrated. To the inner state of this happiness there would conform an outer state of material plenty in which everyone would have what he wanted to eat, would be well housed, would have a satisfactory sex life, and would of course enjoy good health, both mental and physical. The matter may indeed be put in terms of modern psychology. Man can rightfully expect in this world, certainly before very long, a society in which everyone would have a life of perfect adjustment, a life without conflict, aggression, insecurity.

Broadly speaking, the philosophes held that such perfect happiness had not yet been attained on earth—an obvious fact—because there had grown up a whole set of institutions, habits, and beliefs that had brought evil into human life. Men in 1750, the philosophers believed, were not following the natural laws that would make them happy, but the unnatural laws that made them unhappy. The formulators of the new idea of happiness believed that the unhappy state of the world could be traced to a combination of the privileges unnaturally acquired over the centuries by the few rich and powerful (the leaders in church and state), together with the unnatural ignorance and prejudices these few had imposed on the many. They therefore concluded that the solution lay first in depriving the few of their unnatural privileges and, second, in disclosing to the many by a natural system of education and government the key to their own happiness. In short, they believed that men are *by nature* good not evil, reasonable not foolish, intelligent not stupid, certainly improvable. Though it is perhaps unfair to say that they believed in the "natural goodness of man," at a very minimum most of the philosophers held that men as they are now, but under the rule of "cultural engineers," "engineers of the soul," instead of under their present rulers, could all be happy, certainly again at a minimum, much much happier. Something close to utopia was to them just around the corner.

This, then, though put oversimply, is the essence of what may be called the democratic dream of the eighteenth-century philosophes, the dream of a heavenly city here on earth. But two hundred years later the dream has not come true. Some men still persist in it, holding that we have not yet conquered the privileged classes, not yet opened men's minds, not yet really tried full democracy or not yet allowed free play to the kindly cultural engineers. We must insist: many are now alive who think and feel about man's destiny in essentially eighteenth-century ways. Marxism, for example, in its simplest outline, is the eighteenth-century formula all over again: the bad institutional environment under which men cannot help being miserable is capitalism; the good institutional environment under which men cannot help being happy is socialism. In fact, it seems that Stalin invented that phrase "engineer of the soul." It is, however, quite unfair to limit these believers in what is essentially eighteenth-century rationalist empiricism to the Marxists. There are many respected and influential Americans—and a few such Europeans—who preserve intact a belief in the "principles of 1776 and 1789." They may concede that some men are irrational, but they hold that man is rational. Needless to say, the Soviet Russian experiment has not yet brought this kind of socialism to earth.

But the failure of the dream had caused many more men, at least in the free world, to question its very basis, the doctrine of the basic rationality of man, or at least to question man's complete pliability to the best-intentioned cultural engineering. Such men hold that something profoundly rooted in human nature, and not merely in man's institutions, or in his environment, makes a measure of unhappiness the natural lot of mankind. The modern Western world, in consequence, has witnessed a process of reaction and adjustment to the contrast between the high hopes of the Enlightenment and the continuing evils of the world. We may distinguish three broad classifications of these reactions and adjustments, which we may compare with the reactions and adjustments that faced early Christianity once the promise of an immediate Second Coming of Christ had to be abandoned.

Repudiation or Revision of the Enlightenment

First, there is the reaction of complete repudiation of all the Enlightenment stood for. This reaction takes many forms. One of them, limited largely to some emotional intellectuals, is the sense of doom we have just discussed, the feeling that in trying to make this earth a heaven man has in fact made it a hell. More commonly, this reaction takes the form of denying all the premises of democracy. It is maintained that most men are wicked or stupid or foolish, or at any rate not up to the burden a democratic society sets on them, that they need to be ruled by their betters, who are always few in number, and that therefore we must return to divine-right monarchy or to the feudal-clerical aristocracy of the Middle Ages, or follow the "new conservatism," or devise some new authoritarianism of the Right or Left. Such views are not commonly held, or at any rate not commonly expressed in the United States. Not even our extreme Rightists quite repudiate the language of Jefferson, however much at bottom they disagree with his democratic ideals.

Second, there is the Christian view that men must return to the basic Christian concept of an unavoidable mixture of good and evil in humanity. In this view, life on earth must always demonstrate the conflict between the divine and the animal in man, a conflict tragic and profound, not mean, vile, and hopeless as the mere pessimist sees it, and, above all, not for the individual a ceaseless existentialist conflict, but a conflict that has an end in heaven or hell, and that takes place in a universe dominated by purpose, not by accident or the merely natural. For some of these Christians, the desirable earthly society is indeed rather an aristocracy than a democracy. But many of them, like the American theologian and moralist Reinhold Niebuhr, may be described as moderate democrats. Though they believe that the democratic dream in its radical eighteenth-century form is impious nonsense, they none the less hold that a balanced democratic society is the best way of attaining justice on earth, that such a society is the best, or least bad, earthly reflection of man's dual nature.

Third, there are those who accept the aims of the philosophes and even in part the eighteenth-century estimate of human nature. But they find that the Enlightenment of the eighteenth century went wrong in its time sense, wrong in its hope that its claims could be attained in a generation or two. These thinkers are essentially chastened children of the Enlightenment. They share the view that men are made to be happy, but are convinced by the events of the last two generations that wickedness and unreason are not, as the philosophes believed, rooted shallowly in a few bad institutions. On the contrary, they believe that evil, prejudice, and stupidity are deeply rooted in very complex institutions, in tradition, and perhaps even in man as a biological organism.

These thinkers have been greatly influenced by the emphasis that modern psychology has put on the irrational character of the human personality, on the subconscious and the unconscious, and on the consequent difficulty of the actual task of "enlightenment." They now think the task of making the world better will be long and difficult. But it is a task they believe can and must be continued. And they differ basically from the Christians in that they refuse to accept the Christian tension between this world and the next one, or any other one. They do not subscribe necessarily to naïve scientific "reductionism" which holds that all productive thinking will end up by accepting simple scientific materialism—

or in the popular language of the cliché, that "it's all physics or chemistry." But they do hold that man is a product of nature, that the supernatural does not exist, and that individual immortality is impossible.

The important thing is for us to note at the end of this long historic record is that between the second and the third groups we have been discussing, between the Christians and the chastened children of the Enlightenment, a practical accord is possible, and necessary. It is indeed being worked out in the West. In this accord lies the possibility that the men of the first group, the enemies of democracy, may be defeated, and that democracy may live on to give the lie to the prophets of doom. In such an accord we may preserve the willingness to put up with restraints, with imperfections, with frustration, and with suffering without losing the hope, the dream, that is still alive for us in "liberty, equality, fraternity," in "life, liberty, and the pursuit of happiness," in the "principles of 1776 and 1789." Perhaps, above all, those of us called to intellectual pursuits can relearn the great Christian lesson of humility, can cease in our pride to berate our fellow men as mediocre men. We may thus avoid the illusions and retain the ideals of our historic heritage.

Reading Suggestions on Man's Fate in the Twentieth Century

SCIENCE AND TECHNOLOGY

I. Asimov, *The Intelligent Man's Guide to the Physical Sciences* and *The Intelligent Man's Guide to the Biological Sciences* (*Pocket). Informative surveys by a prolific popularizer of often difficult material.

C. T. Chase, *The Evolution of Modern Physics* (Van Nostrand, 1947), and L. Barnett, *The Universe and Dr. Einstein*, rev. ed. (*Bantam). Helpful popular accounts of key developments in twentieth-century science.

G. Gamow, *Mister Tompkins in Paperback* (*Cambridge). "Mr. Tompkins" explores the atom and other areas in a scientific wonderland; by an accomplished scientific popularizer.

LITERATURE
AND THE ARTS

C. Mauriac, *The New Literature* (Braziller, 1959). Essays translated from the French, and treating mainly French writers.

E. Wilson, *Axel's Castle* (*Scribner's). A study in imaginative literature from 1870 to 1930, extending down to Joyce and Gertrude Stein.

H. Slochower, *Literature and Philosophy between Two World Wars* (*Citadel). Originally called *No Voice Is Wholly Lost;* an informative study of the relations between intellectual and literary history.

F. J. Hoffman, *Freudianism and the Literary Mind,* 2nd ed. (Louisiana State Univ. Press, 1957). A suggestive exploration.

J. Campbell and H. M. Robinson, *A Skeleton Key to Finnegans Wake* (*Compass), and W. P. Jones, *James Joyce and the Common Reader* (Univ. of Oklahoma Press, 1955). Two guides to a baffling writer.

L. Mumford et al., *The Arts in Renewal* (Univ. of Pennsylvania Press, 1951), and B. Richman, *The Arts at Mid-Century* (Horizon, 1954). Two wide-ranging collections of essays.

A. H. Barr, Jr., *What Is Modern Painting?*, rev. ed. (*New York Graphic Society). Good short introduction.

J. Canaday, *Embattled Critic* (*Noonday). Modern art viewed by the knowledgeable critics of *The New York Times.*

Illustrations